W9-BBX-682

HMH

into Literature™

Front Cover Photo Credits: (outer ring): ©joyfull/Shutterstock, (inner ring): ©Vadim Georgiev/Shutterstock, (inset): ©Stockbyte/Getty Images, (c): ©Carrie Garcia/Houghton Mifflin Harcourt, (c overlay): ©Eyewire/Getty Images, (bc overlay): ©elenamiv/Shutterstock

Back Cover Photo Credits: (Units 1-6): ©Anthony Aneese Totah Jr./Dreamstime; ©Iryna Kuznetsova/Dreamstime; ©Dfikar/Dreamstime; ©StockTrek/Photodisc/Getty Images; ©Monkey Business Images/iStock/Getty Images; © Hemera Technologies/Ablestock/Getty Images

Printed in the U.S.A.

ISBN 978-1-328-47478-0

9 10 0868 27 26 25 24 23 22

4500848476 B C D E F G

into Literature™

GRADE 7

Program Consultants:
Kylene Beers
Martha Hougen
Elena Izquierdo
Carol Jago
Erik Palmer
Robert E. Probst

HMH

Into Literature

PROGRAM CONSULTANTS

Kylene Beers

Nationally known lecturer and author on reading and literacy; coauthor with Robert Probst of *Disrupting Thinking, Notice & Note: Strategies for Close Reading,* and *Reading Nonfiction;* former president of the National Council of Teachers of English. Dr. Beers is the author of *When Kids Can't Read: What Teachers Can Do* and coeditor of *Adolescent Literacy: Turning Promise into Practice,* as well as articles in the *Journal of Adolescent and Adult Literacy.* Former editor of *Voices from the Middle,* she is the 2001 recipient of NCTE's Richard W. Halle Award, given for outstanding contributions to middle school literacy. She recently served as Senior Reading Researcher at the Comer School Development Program at Yale University as well as Senior Reading Advisor to Secondary Schools for the Reading and Writing Project at Teachers College.

Martha Hougen

National consultant, presenter, researcher, and author. Areas of expertise include differentiating instruction for students with learning difficulties, including those with learning disabilities and dyslexia; and teacher and leader preparation improvement. Dr. Hougen has taught at the middle school through graduate levels. In addition to peer-reviewed articles, curricular documents, and presentations, Dr. Hougen has published two college textbooks: *The Fundamentals of Literacy Assessment and Instruction Pre-K–6* (2012) and *The Fundamentals of Literacy Assessment and Instruction 6–12* (2014). Dr. Hougen has supported Educator Preparation Program reforms while working at the Meadows Center for Preventing Educational Risk at The University of Texas at Austin and at the CEEDAR Center, University of Florida.

Elena Izquierdo

Nationally recognized teacher educator and advocate for English language learners. Dr. Izquierdo is a linguist by training, with a Ph.D. in Applied Linguistics and Bilingual Education from Georgetown University. She has served on various state and national boards working to close the achievement gaps for bilingual students and English language learners. Dr. Izquierdo is a member of the Hispanic Leadership Council, which supports Hispanic students and educators at both the state and federal levels. She served as Vice President on the Executive Board of the National Association of Bilingual Education and as Publications and Professional Development Chair.

Carol Jago

Teacher of English with 32 years of experience at Santa Monica High School in California; author and nationally known lecturer; former president of the National Council of Teachers of English. Ms. Jago currently serves as Associate Director of the California Reading and Literature Project at UCLA. With expertise in standards assessment and secondary education, Ms. Jago is the author of numerous books on education, including *With Rigor for All* and *Papers, Papers, Papers,* and is active with the California Association of Teachers of English, editing its scholarly journal *California English* since 1996. Ms. Jago also served on the planning committee for the 2009 Reading NAEP Framework and the 2011 NAEP Writing Framework.

Erik Palmer

Veteran teacher and education consultant based in Denver, Colorado. Author of *Well Spoken: Teaching Speaking to All Students* and *Digitally Speaking: How to Improve Student Presentations.* His areas of focus include improving oral communication, promoting technology in classroom presentations, and updating instruction through the use of digital tools. He holds a bachelor's degree from Oberlin College and a master's degree in curriculum and instruction from the University of Colorado.

Robert E. Probst

Nationally respected authority on the teaching of literature; Professor Emeritus of English Education at Georgia State University. Dr. Probst's publications include numerous articles in *English Journal* and *Voices from the Middle,* as well as professional texts including (as coeditor) *Adolescent Literacy: Turning Promise into Practice* and (as coauthor with Kylene Beers) *Disrupting Thinking, Notice & Note: Strategies for Close Reading,* and *Reading Nonfiction.* He regularly speaks at national and international conventions including those of the International Literacy Association, the National Council of Teachers of English, the Association of Supervisors and Curriculum Developers, and the National Association of Secondary School Principals. He has served NCTE in various leadership roles, including the Conference on English Leadership Board of Directors, the Commission on Reading, and column editor of the NCTE journal *Voices from the Middle.* He is also the 2004 recipient of the CEL Exemplary Leader Award.

UNIT 1

TAKING ACTION

? ESSENTIAL QUESTION

What helps people rise up to face difficulties?

ANALYZE & APPLY

COLLABORATE & COMPARE

Key Learning Objectives

- Analyze plot
- Make Inferences
- Analyze myths
- Analyze form in poetry
- Analyze tone
- Determine author's purpose
- Analyze character
- Analyze setting and conflict
- Analyze structure

Visit the Interactive Student Edition for:

- Unit and Selection Videos
- Media Selections
- Selection Audio Recordings
- Enhanced Digital Instruction

REALITY CHECK

PAGE 96

ESSENTIAL QUESTION

What can blur the lines between what's real and what's not?

ANALYZE & APPLY

COLLABORATE & COMPARE

Key Learning Objectives

- Analyze character
- Analyze conflict
- Determine author's purpose
- Analyze folk tales
- Analyze humor
- Analyze rhyme
- Analyze sound devices and mood
- Analyze drama

Visit the Interactive Student Edition for:

- Unit and Selection Videos
- Media Selections
- Selection Audio Recordings
- Enhanced Digital Instruction

UNIT 3

INSPIRED BY NATURE

PAGE 180

? ESSENTIAL QUESTION

What does it mean to be in harmony with nature?

ANALYZE AND APPLY

COLLABORATE & COMPARE

Key Learning Objectives

- Analyze argument
- Analyze point of view
- Analyze memoir
- Analyze figurative language
- Analyze sonnets
- Analyze rhyme scheme
- Analyze theme
- Analyze odes
- Analyze lyric poetry
- Analyze media

Visit the Interactive Student Edition for:

- Unit and Selection Videos
- Media Selections
- Selection Audio Recordings
- Enhanced Digital Instruction

UNIT 4

THE TERROR AND WONDER OF SPACE

PAGE 262

? ESSENTIAL QUESTION

Why is the idea of space exploration both inspiring and unnerving?

ANALYZE AND APPLY

COLLABORATE & COMPARE

Key Learning Objectives
- Analyze structural elements
- Analyze organizational patterns
- Analyze author's purpose
- Analyze repetition
- Analyze science fiction
- Analyze mood
- Analyze graphical elements
- Analyze theme
- Analyze media
- Analyze rhetorical devices

Visit the Interactive Student Edition for:
- Unit and Selection Videos
- Media Selections
- Selection Audio Recordings
- Enhanced Digital Instruction

UNIT 5

MORE THAN A GAME

PAGE 360

? ESSENTIAL QUESTION

How do sports bring together friends, families, and communities?

ANALYZE AND APPLY

COLLABORATE & COMPARE

Key Learning Objectives

- Analyze point of view
- Make predictions
- Analyze organizational patterns
- Analyze novels in verse
- Analyze metaphor and personification
- Analyze voice in poetry
- Make inferences

Online Ed

Visit the Interactive Student Edition for:

- Unit and Selection Videos
- Media Selections
- Selection Audio Recordings
- Enhanced Digital Instruction

UNIT 6

CHANGE AGENTS

PAGE 434

? ESSENTIAL QUESTION

What inspires you to make a difference?

ANALYZE AND APPLY

NOTICE & NOTE READING MODEL

COLLABORATE & COMPARE

COMPARE AUTHORS' PURPOSES AND MESSAGES

Key Learning Objectives

- Analyze author's point of view
- Analyze elements of documentary
- Analyze realistic fiction
- Analyze character qualities
- Analyze free verse in poetry
- Analyze theme
- Analyze history writing
- Determine key ideas
- Analyze text structure

Visit the Interactive Student Edition for:

- Unit and Selection Videos
- Media Selections
- Selection Audio Recordings
- Enhanced Digital Instruction

SELECTIONS BY GENRE

FICTION

SHORT STORY

ORAL TRADITION

NOVEL

NONFICTION

INFORMATIONAL TEXT

ARGUMENT TEXT

POETRY

DRAMA

MEDIA STUDY

HMH

Into Literature Dashboard

Easy to use and personalized for your learning.

Monitor your progress in the course.

Ed your friend in learning | Class 1 | Welcome, Oliver

Discover | Assignments | Data & Reports

Into Literature

View by CONTENT STANDARDS

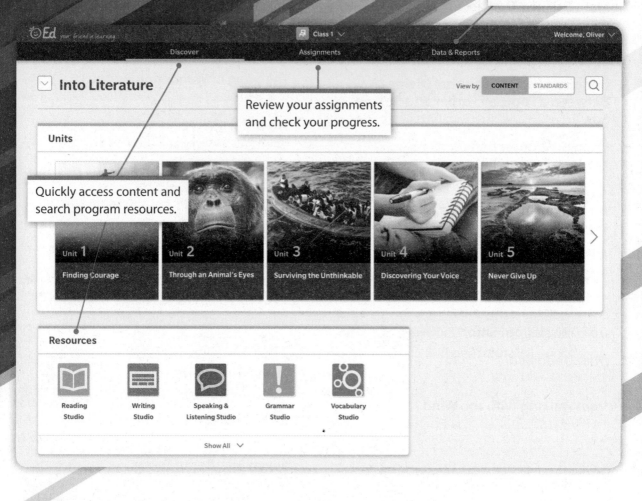

Review your assignments and check your progress.

Units

Quickly access content and search program resources.

Unit 1 Finding Courage

Unit 2 Through an Animal's Eyes

Unit 3 Surviving the Unthinkable

Unit 4 Discovering Your Voice

Unit 5 Never Give Up

Resources

Reading Studio | Writing Studio | Speaking & Listening Studio | Grammar Studio | Vocabulary Studio

Show All

Explore Online to Experience the Power of HMH Into Literature

All in One Place

Readings and assignments are supported by a variety of resources to bring literature to life and give you the tools you need to succeed.

Supporting 21st Century Skills

Whether you're working alone or collaborating with others, it takes effort to analyze the complex texts and competing ideas that bombard us in this fast-paced world. What will help you succeed? Staying engaged and organized. The digital tools in this program will help you take charge of your learning.

Ignite Your Investigation

You learn best when you're engaged. The **Stream to Start** videos at the beginning of every unit are designed to spark your interest before you read. Get curious and start reading!

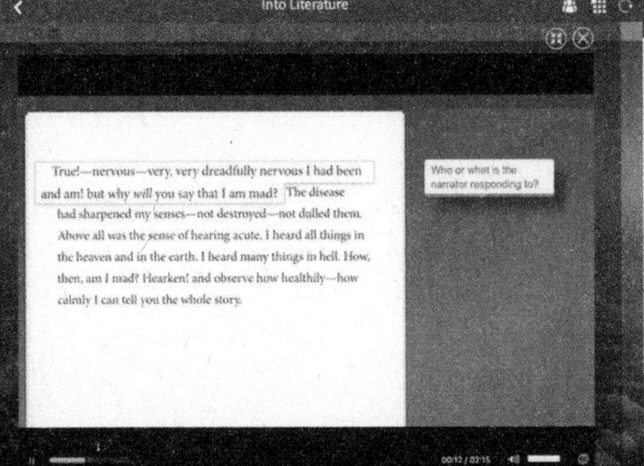

Learn How to Close Read

Close reading effectively is all about examining the details. See how it's done by watching the **Close Read Screencasts** in your eBook. Hear modeled conversations on targeted passages.

Bring the Meaning into Focus

Text in Focus videos dig deeper into complex texts by offering visual explanations for potential stumbling blocks.

Personalized Annotations

My Notes encourages you to take notes as you read and allows you to mark the text in your own customized way. You can easily access annotations to review later as you prepare for exams.

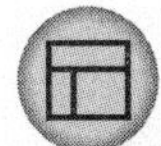

Interactive Graphic Organizers

Graphic organizers help you process, summarize, and keep track of your learning and prepare for end-of-unit writing tasks. **Word Networks** help you learn academic vocabulary, and **Response Logs** help you explore and deepen your understanding of the **Essential Question** in each unit.

No Wi-Fi? No problem!

With HMH *Into Literature,* you always have access: download when you're online and access what you need when you're offline. Work offline and then upload when you're back online.

Communicate "Raise a Hand" to ask or answer questions without having to be in the same room as your teacher.

Collaborate Collaborate with your teacher via chat and work with a classmate to improve your writing.

HMH

Into Literature STUDIOS

   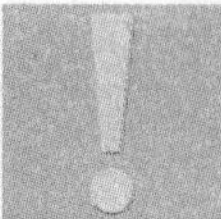 

All the help you need to be successful in your literature class is one click away with the Studios. These digital-only lessons are here to tap into the skills that you already use and help you sharpen those skills for the future.

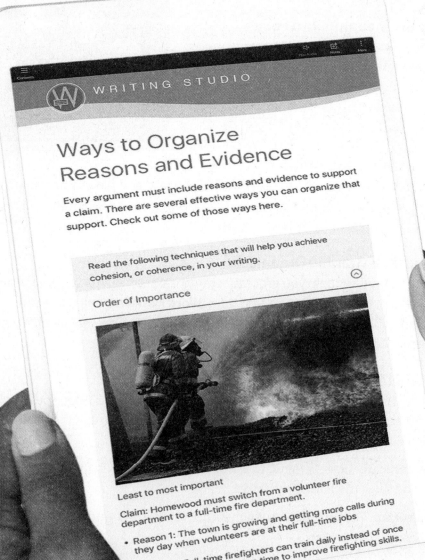

WRITING STUDIO
Ways to Organize Reasons and Evidence
Every argument must include reasons and evidence to support a claim. There are several effective ways you can organize that support. Check out some of those ways here.
Read the following techniques that will help you achieve cohesion, or coherence, in your writing.
Order of Importance
Least to most important
Claim: Homewood must switch from a volunteer fire department to a full-time fire department.
• Reason 1: The town is growing and getting more calls during they day when volunteers are at their full-time jobs
• Reason 2: Full-time firefighters can train daily instead of once a month, giving them more time to improve firefighting skills.

Easy-to-find resources, organized in five separate STUDIOS. On demand and on ED!

Look for links in each lesson to take you to the appropriate Studio.

READING STUDIO

Go beyond the book with the Reading Studio. With over 100 full-length downloadable titles to choose from, find the right story to continue your journey.

WRITING STUDIO

Being able to write clearly and effectively is a skill that will help you throughout life. The Writing Studio will help you become an expert communicator—in print or online.

SPEAKING & LISTENING STUDIO

Communication is more than just writing. The Speaking & Listening Studio will help you become an effective speaker and a focused listener.

GRAMMAR STUDIO

Go beyond traditional worksheets with the Grammar Studio. These engaging, interactive lessons will sharpen your grammar skills.

VOCABULARY STUDIO

Learn the skills you need to expand your vocabulary. The interactive lessons in the Vocabulary Studio will grow your vocabulary to improve your reading.

An ABSOLUTELY, POSITIVELY, MUST READ ESSAY in the FRONT of your Literature Book

YOUR
TEACHER
AGREES!

BY TWO PEOPLE YOU HAVE NEVER HEARD OF

Dr. Kylene Beers and Dr. Robert E. Probst

If you are reading this essay when we think you are, it's early in the school year. You have this big book in front of you and, for some reason, your teacher has asked you to read these pages by two people you've never met.

Let's begin by telling you something about us.

From Dr. Beers:

"I've been a teacher all my adult life. I've worked with students at all grades and now I spend most of my time working with teachers, maybe even your teacher! I live in Texas and when I'm not on an airplane flying off to work in a school, I'm on my ranch, plowing a field. I like to read, cook, read, garden, read, spend time with my family and friends, and (did I mention?) read!"

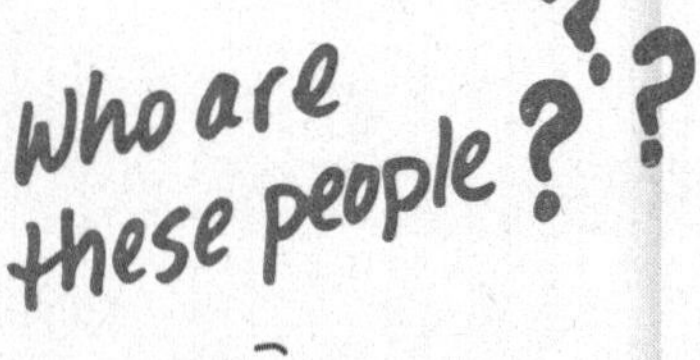
Who are
these people???

From Dr. Probst:

"I've also been a teacher all my adult life. When I first started teaching, I taught kids in middle school and high school, and then I spent most of my career teaching people how to be teachers. For many years now, Dr. Beers and I have written books together, books that are about teaching kids how to be better readers. I live in Florida and when I'm not in schools working with teachers and kids, I enjoy watching my grandkids play soccer and baseball and I love going out on my boat. And, like Dr. Beers, I love reading a great book, too."

So, we're teachers. And we're writers. Specifically, we write books for teachers, books teachers read so that they can help their students become better readers...

. . . and we're going to try to help you become a better reader this year.

We will because we both believe TWO things.

1st

First, we've never met a kid who didn't want to get better at reading. Reading is important for almost everything you do, so doing it well is important.

2nd

Second, we believe that reading can change you. Reading something can open up your mind, your thinking, your ideas, your understanding of the world and all the people in it, so that you might choose to change yourself. Reading can help you change yourself.

We think too often it's easy to forget why reading is important. You can come to believe that you need to read better just so your grades will go up, or you need to read better so that you do well on a big state test. Those things are important—you bet—but they aren't as important as reading better so that you can become better. Yes, reading can help you change.

How would that happen—how can reading help you change yourself? Sometimes it is obvious. You read something about the importance of exercise and you start walking a little more.

How can reading help me change myself?

Or, you read something about energy and the environment and you decide to make sure you always turn off the lights when you leave any room.

Other times, it might be less obvious. You might read *Wonder* and begin to think about what it really means to be a good friend. Maybe you walk over to that person sitting alone in the cafeteria and sit with him or her. Perhaps you'll read *Stella by Starlight* and that book helps you become someone who stands against racism. Or maybe it happens as you read *Mexican Whiteboy* and discover that who you are is more about what you are on the inside than what anyone ever sees on the outside. And when you realize that,

"Hello! I wanted to discuss the Important Message with you!"

perhaps it will give you the courage you need to be truer to yourself, to be the person you really want to be.

Reading gives us moments to think, and as we think we just might discover something about ourselves that we want to change. And that's why we say reading can help us change ourselves.

Finding Important Messages

It sure would be easy to find important messages in the things we read if the authors would just label them and then maybe give us a call.

The reality is, though, that would make the reading less interesting. And it would mean that every reader is supposed to find the same message. Not true! While the author has a message he or she wants to share, the reader—that's you!—has at least three jobs to do:

My Job

1→ **First**, enjoy what you are reading.

2→ **Second,** figure out the message the author wanted to share. Authors write for a reason (no, not to make a lot of money!), and part of that reason is to share something important. That's the author's message, and this year we'll be showing you some ways to really focus in on that.

3→ **Third,** you need to figure out the message that matters most to **YOU.** (YES, WE SAVED THE BEST FOR LAST!!!) Sometimes the author's message and what matters most to you will be the same; sometimes not. For instance, it's obvious that J.K. Rowling wrote the Harry Potter series to show us all the sustaining power of love.

From Dr. Beers:

"But when I read these books, what really touched my heart was the importance of standing up to our fears."

From Dr. Probst:

"And what mattered most to me was the idea that one person, one small person, can make a huge difference in the world. I think that's a critically important point."

Understanding the author's message requires you to do some work while you read, work that requires you to read the text closely. No. You don't need a magnifying glass. But you do need to learn how to notice some things in the text we call **SIGNPOSTS.**

How do I find the author's message?

A signpost is simply something the author says in the text that helps you understand how characters are changing, how conflicts are being resolved, and, ultimately, what theme—or lesson—the author is trying to convey.

So, as I read, I have to think about something called signposts?

You can also use signposts to help you figure out the author's purpose when you are reading nonfiction. If you can identify the author's purpose—why she or he wrote that particular piece of nonfiction—then you'll be better able to decide whether or not you agree, and whether you need more information.

We do want you thinking about signposts, but first, as you read, we want you to remember three letters: BHH.

B	Book	As you read, we want you to remember that you have to pay attention to what's in the book (or article).
H	Head	And, you need to think about what you are reading as you read—so you have to think about what's in your head.
H	Heart	And sometimes, maybe as you finish what you're reading, you'll ask yourself what you have taken to heart.

To think carefully about what's in the book and what's in your head, you need to become an alert reader, one who notices things. If you're reading fiction, for instance, you ought to pay attention to how characters act. When a character starts acting in a way you don't expect, something is up! That's as if the author has put up a blinking sign that says "Pay attention here!" Or, if you are reading nonfiction, and the author starts using a lot of numbers, that's the same as the author waving a huge flag that says "Slow down! Pay attention! I'm trying to show you something!"

Pay attention HERE!

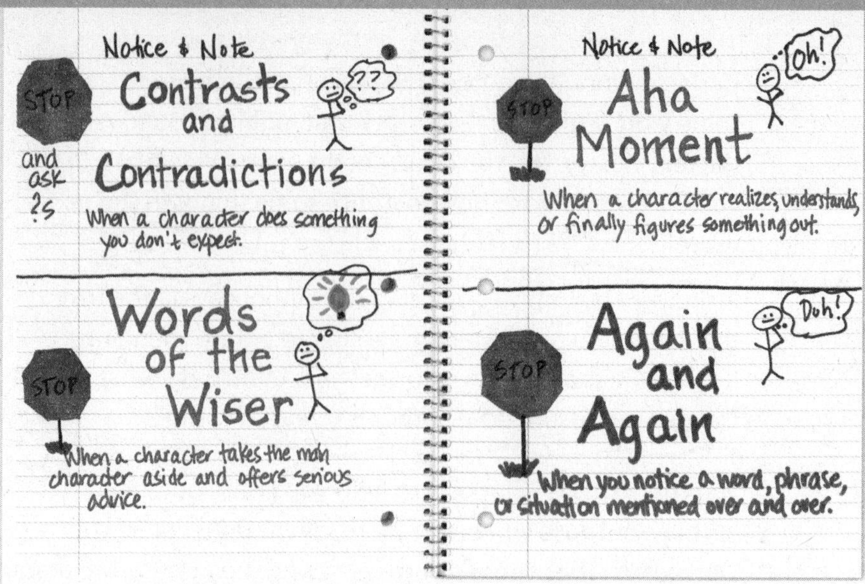

Notice & Note
STOP
Contrasts and Contradictions
and ask ?s
When a character does something you don't expect.
Notice & Note
Oh!
STOP
Aha Moment
When a character realizes, understands, or finally figures something out.
Words of the Wiser
STOP
When a character takes the main character aside and offers serious advice.
Doh!
STOP
Again and Again
When you notice a word, phrase, or situation mentioned over and over.

Don't worry about memorizing all the signposts. You'll learn them this year. Your teacher will probably have you make some notes—perhaps as the student above did.

Some of the things you'll read this year, you might not like. (OK—just being honest!) But most of the things we bet you will. What we hope you'll do, throughout this year, is keep reading.

» Read every day.
» Read something hard.
» Read something easy.
» Read something you choose.
» Read what your teachers ask you to read.
» Read something that makes you laugh.
» And it's OK if sometimes what you read makes you cry.

One of us LOVES to read scary books while the other much prefers survival books, so don't worry if you like something your best friend doesn't. Read joke books and how-to books and love stories and mysteries and absolutely be sure you read about people who aren't like you. That's the best way to learn about the world around you, about other people, about other ways of thinking. The best way to become a more open person is to live for a while, in the pages of a book, the life of someone you are not.

We hope you have a great year. Stay alert for signposts that you'll be learning throughout this book.

And remember . . .

. . . reading is something that can help you become the person you most want to be.

NOTICE & NOTE SIGNPOSTS		
Signpost	**Definition**	**Anchor Question(s)**
FICTION		
Contrasts and Contradictions	A sharp contrast between what we would expect and what we observe the character doing; behavior that contradicts previous behavior or well-established patterns	Why would the character act (feel) this way?
Aha Moment	A character's realization of something that shifts his actions or understanding of himself, others, or the world around him	How might this change things?
Tough Questions	Questions a character raises that reveal his or her inner struggles	What does this question make me wonder about?
Words of the Wiser	The advice or insight about life that a wiser character, who is usually older, offers to the main character	What is the life lesson, and how might this affect the character?
Again and Again	Events, images, or particular words that recur over a portion of the story	Why might the author bring this up again and again?
Memory Moment	A recollection by a character that interrupts the forward progress of the story	Why might this memory be important?
NONFICTION		
Contrasts and Contradictions	A sharp contrast between what we would expect and what we observe happening. A difference between two or more elements in the text.	What is the difference, and why does it matter?
Extreme or Absolute Language	Language that leaves no doubt about a situation or an event, allows no compromise, or seems to exaggerate or overstate a case.	Why did the author use this language?
Numbers and Stats	Specific quantities or comparisons to depict the amount, size, or scale. Or, the writer is vague and imprecise about numbers when we would expect more precision.	Why did the author use these numbers or amounts?
Quoted Words	Opinions or conclusions of someone who is an expert on the subject, or someone who might be a participant in or a witness to an event. Or, the author might cite other people to provide support for a point.	Why was this person quoted or cited, and what did this add?
Word Gaps	Vocabulary that is unfamiliar to the reader—for example, a word with multiple meanings, a rare or technical word, a discipline-specific word, or one with a far-removed antecedent.	Do I know this word from someplace else? Does it seem like technical talk for this topic? Can I find clues in the sentence to help me understand the word?

READING AND WRITING ACROSS GENRES

by Carol Jago

Reading is a first-class ticket around the world. Not only can you explore other lands and cultures, but you can also travel to the past and future. That journey is sometimes a wild ride. Other books can feel like comfort food, enveloping you in an imaginative landscape full of friends and good times. Making time for reading is making time for life.

Genre

One of the first things readers do when we pick up something to read is notice its genre. You might not think of it exactly in those terms, but consider how you approach a word problem in math class compared to how you read a science fiction story. Readers go to different kinds of text for different purposes. When you need to know how to do or make something, you want a reliable, trusted source of information. When you're in the mood to spend some time in a world of fantasy, you happily suspend your normal disbelief in dragons.

GENRE: INFORMATIONAL TEXT

FEARS AND PHOBIAS

GENRE: SHORT STORY

THE FIRST DAY OF SCHOOL

In every unit of *Into Literature,* you'll find a diverse mix of genres all connected by a common theme, allowing you to explore a topic from many different angles.

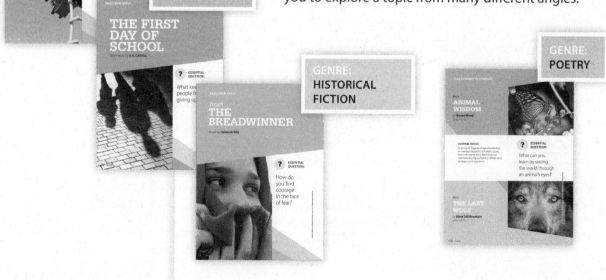

GENRE: HISTORICAL FICTION

from THE BREADWINNER

GENRE: POETRY

Writer's Craft

Learning how writers use genre to inform, to explain, to entertain, or to surprise readers will help you better understand—as well as enjoy—your reading. Imitating how professional writers employ the tools of their craft—descriptive language, repetition, sensory images, sentence structure, and a variety of other features—will give you many ideas for making your own writing more lively.

GENRE ELEMENTS: SHORT STORY
- is a work of short fiction that centers on a single idea and can be read in one sitting
- usually includes one main conflict that involves the characters and keeps moving
- includes the basic ele of fiction—plot, chara setting, and theme
- may be based on real and historical events

GENRE ELEMENTS: INFORMATIONAL TEXT
- provides factual information
- includes evidence to support ideas
- contains text features
- includes many forms, such as news articles and essays

GENRE ELEMENTS: HISTORICAL FICTION
- includes the basic elements of fiction: setting, character, plot, conflict, and theme
- is set in the past and includes real places and real events of historical importance
- is a type of realistic in which fictional c behave like real pe use human abilities with life's challenge

GENRE ELEMENTS: POETRY
- may use figurative language, including personification
- often includes imagery that appeals to the five senses
- expresses a theme, or a "big idea" message about life

Into Literature provides you with the tools you need to understand the elements of all the critical genres and advice on how to learn from professional texts to improve your own writing in those genres.

Reading with Independence

Finding a good book can sometimes be a challenge. Like every other reader, you have probably experienced "book desert" when nothing you pick up seems to have what you are looking for (not that it's easy to explain exactly what you are looking for, but whatever it is, "this" isn't it). If you find yourself in this kind of reading funk, bored by everything you pick up, give yourself permission to range more widely, exploring graphic novels, contemporary biographies, books of poetry, historical fiction. And remember that long doesn't necessarily mean boring. My favorite kind of book is one that I never want to end.

Take control over your own reading with *Into Literature's* Reader's Choice selections and the HMH Digital Library. And don't forget: your teacher, librarian, and friends can offer you many more suggestions.

SHORT STORY
Vanquishing the Hungry Chinese Zombie
Claudine Gueh
A girl faces terror to protect her parents and the family store.

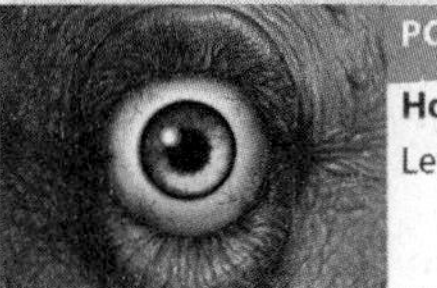

POEM
Horrors
Lewis Carroll
What are those terrible things that go bump in the night?

NARRATIVE NONFICTION
Running into Danger on an Alaskan Trail
Cinthia Ritchie
A long-distance runner has a terrifying encounter with a bear.

UNIT 1

TAKING ACTION

? **ESSENTIAL QUESTION:**

What helps people rise up to face difficulties?

> **The most effective way to do it, is to do it.**
>
> Amelia Earhart

ACADEMIC VOCABULARY

Academic Vocabulary words are words you use when you discuss and write about texts. In this unit you will practice and learn five words.

☑ **aspect** ☐ **cultural** ☐ **evaluate** ☐ **resource** ☐ **text**

Study the Word Network to learn more about the word **aspect.**

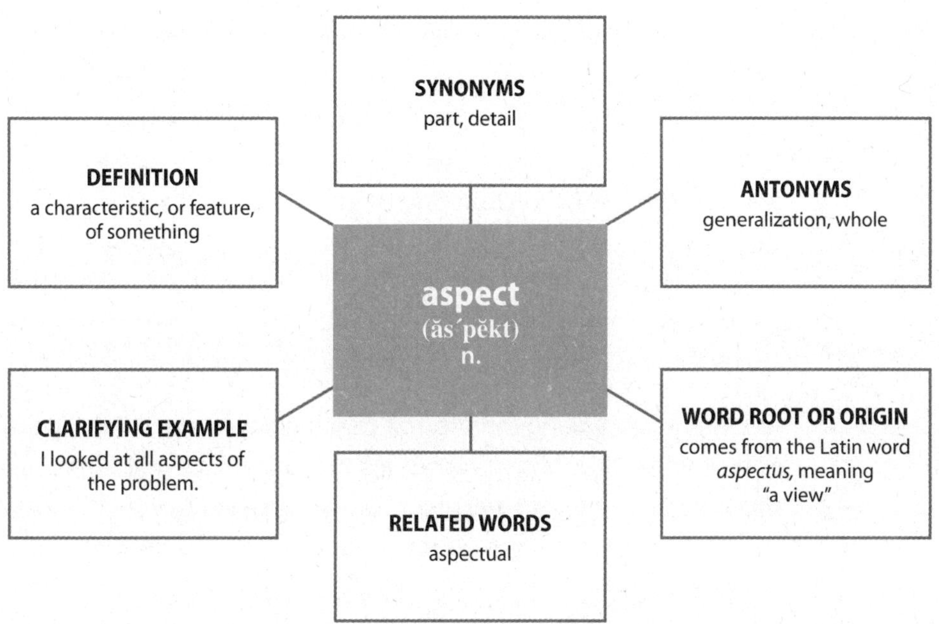

Write and Discuss Discuss the completed Word Network with a partner, making sure to talk through all of the boxes until you both understand the word, its synonyms, antonyms, and related forms. Then, fill out Word Networks for the remaining four words. Use a dictionary or online resource to help you complete the activity.

Go online to access the ***Word Networks.***

RESPOND TO THE ESSENTIAL QUESTION

In this unit, you will explore how different people take action to overcome difficulties. As you read, you will revisit the **Essential Question** and gather your ideas about it in the **Response Log** that appears on page R1. At the end of the unit, you will have the opportunity to write an **informational essay** about the qualities used by people to overcome obstacles. Filling out the Response Log will help you prepare for this writing task.

UNIT 1
RESPONSE LOG

Use this Response Log to record your ideas about how each of the texts in Unit 1 relates to or comments on the **Essential Question.**

Essential Question: What helps people rise up to face difficulties?

Rogue Wave	
The Flight of Icarus	
Icarus's Flight	
Women in Aviation	
Thank You, M'am	
A Police Stop Changed This Teenager's Life	

You can also go online to access the ***Response Log.***

READING MODEL

ROGUE WAVE

For more information on these and other signposts to Notice & Note, visit the **Reading Studio**.

You are about to read the short story "Rogue Wave." In it, you will notice and note signposts that will give you clues about the story's characters and themes. Here are three key signposts to look for as you read this short story and other works of fiction.

When you read and encounter phrases like these, pause to see if a phrase indicates a **Memory Moment** signpost:

"She remembered that . . ."

"He'd heard of . . ."

"It was just like when . . ."

"Earlier that week . . ."

"as a baby, she'd . . ."

Memory Moment You're sitting on the bench waiting for the coach to post the names of the kids who made the team. As you wait, your mind drifts back to when you started shooting hoops at the neighborhood courts. You were just eight. Others would laugh every time you missed. Not anymore. The coach comes out and you run over to read the list.

Our brains are linking the present to the past almost all of the time . Something—an image, a sound, a smell, an event—will trigger a memory of an earlier time. When an author introduces a memory, it's usually for a good reason. Paying attention to a **Memory Moment** can:

- provide background that relates to the current situation
- reveal details about characters' histories or relationships
- show what motivates or drives a character's actions
- show what leads a character to an "aha moment"

The paragraph below of "Rogue Wave" illustrates a student's annotation of a Memory Moment:

5 Below deck Scoot was listening to Big Sandy & His Fly-Rite Boys doing "Swingin' West," and singing along with them while slicing leftover steak from last night's meal. <u>They'd grilled it on a small charcoal ring that was mounted outboard on the starboard side at the stern, trailing sparks into the water.</u> The *Sea Dog* had every blessed thing, including a barbecue pit, she marveled.

Anchor Question When you notice this signpost, ask: Why might this memory be important?

What memory is introduced?	the memory of grilling steak the previous night
Why do you think this memory is important to the story?	The memory shows that Scoot is impressed by how well equipped the <u>Sea Dog</u> is. It also shows that she and her brother are enjoying this trip.

Again and Again Have you ever noticed how soft drink ads use certain words over and over—like *cool* and *refreshing*? They do this to create a certain image in your mind. When images, events, or words appear in a story **Again and Again**, they can also create or reinforce a certain image, idea, or feeling. Here a student marked an "Again and Again" example:

> 1 *A killer wave, known to mariners as a "rogue wave," was approaching a desolate area of Baja California below Ensenada. . . .*
>
> 4 Sullivan Atkins, Scoot's oldest brother, was steering the cutter-rigged boat on a northerly course about fifteen miles off desolate Cabo Colnett, south of Ensenada.

Anchor Question
When you notice this signpost, ask: Why might the author keep bringing this up?

What images or words appear again and again?	the word desolate; the location close to Ensenada
What effect does this have?	It makes clear that no other boats or people are around.

Aha Moment It's your birthday and you're mad because your mom has again put off getting you new running shoes. Then you open her present. Just the shoes you wanted! Now you have to reconsider what happened and why.

A character experiencing an **Aha Moment** may suddenly realize he or she faces a serious problem, discover the pathway to resolving the conflict or solving the problem, or reach a broader understanding about life. Here's an example of an Aha Moment a student discovered:

When you see phrases like these, pause to see if it's an **Aha Moment**:

"It took a little longer to realize . . ."

"That had to be the reason . . ."

"he sensed something . . ."

> 8 But a split second before it lifted the boat like a carpenter's chip, he sensed something behind him and glanced backward, toward the towering wall of shining water.

Anchor Question
When you notice this signpost, ask: How might this change things?

What does Sully suddenly realize in paragraph 8?	A huge wave is about to hit the boat.
How do we know Sully realizes this?	Sully glances backward and sees the wall of water.

ROGUE WAVE

Short Story by **Theodore Taylor**

ESSENTIAL QUESTION:

What helps people rise up to face difficulties?

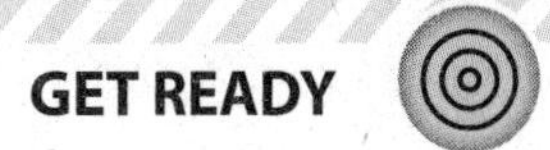

QUICK START

Do you panic or do you keep a clear head in a crisis? Make a list of the qualities needed to deal with a crisis. Discuss your ideas with a partner.

ANALYZE PLOT

The power of an adventure story, such as "Rogue Wave," comes from its action and events. Most stories recount a series of events, also known as a **plot**. An important part of the plot is the setting, or the time and place of the action. The setting influences the characters and the **conflict**, the struggle between opposing forces. As the characters try to resolve the conflict, the plot builds **suspense**, the growing tension felt by the reader. Writers also use **foreshadowing,** or hints that suggest future events, to create suspense and increase readers' interest in what will happen. Most plots have five stages:

- The **exposition** introduces characters, setting, and conflict.
- The **rising action** presents complications that intensify the conflict.
- The **climax** is the story's moment of greatest interest—and the point where the conflict is resolved.
- In the **falling action**, the story begins to draw to a close.
- The **resolution** reveals the final outcome of the conflict.

As you read "Rogue Wave," make notes about how the characters, setting, and plot work together to create suspense and excitement.

GENRE ELEMENTS: SHORT STORY

- includes one or more characters
- provides a setting
- develops a plot
- may be realistic or imaginary
- often conveys a theme or lesson about life
- characters in most realistic fiction stories face everyday problems; characters in adventure stories face extreme dangers

MAKE INFERENCES

Authors do not always describe every aspect of a story, character, or setting. Instead, they provide clues to help you make **inferences**, logical guesses based on story details and your own knowledge and experience. Making these connections helps you understand the plot.

To support inferences, you can **cite textual evidence** that provides specific information from the text. For example, you can identify story details that show how the setting influences the plot. As you read "Rogue Wave," notice details and use them to make inferences about the characters, events, and setting. Note them in a chart like this.

TEXT EVIDENCE	MY EXPERIENCE	INFERENCE
The title of the story is "Rogue Wave." The setting is a small sailboat.	Big waves can be dangerous.	The characters may be in danger on their small boat.

GET READY

CRITICAL VOCABULARY

swell **deck** **navigation** **submerge** **porthole**

To see how many Critical Vocabulary words you already know, use them to complete the sentences.

1. Our room on the ship had a small ____________ that let light in.
2. ____________, especially over long distances, was much more difficult before the invention of detailed maps and GPS.
3. I leapt from the dock and onto the ____________ of the boat.
4. Each ____________ gently rocked the boat.
5. Standing on the shore, we watched the submarine ____________ .

LANGUAGE CONVENTIONS

Sentence Structure In this lesson, you will learn about types of sentences and how to use punctuation between clauses. A **simple sentence** contains one main clause, as in "She was still inside." A **compound sentence** has two independent clauses. An example of this is, "The doors were jammed, and he returned to the surface for air." A **complex sentence** combines an independent clause with a subordinate clause. The sentence "In the blackness, water continued to lap at Scoot's chin." is an example of a complex sentence.

As you read "Rogue Wave," note the types of sentences the author uses to express ideas and how the punctuation makes the meanings clear.

ANNOTATION MODEL

NOTICE & NOTE 

As you read, notice and note signposts, including Memory Moments, Again and Again, and Aha Moments. Here is an example of how one reader responded to the opening of "Rogue Wave."

1 *A killer wave, known to mariners as a "rogue wave," was approaching a desolate area of Baja California below Ensenada. It had been born off the east coast of Australia during a violent storm; it had traveled about 7,000 miles at a speed of 20.83 miles an hour. Driven by an unusual pattern of easterly winds, it was a little over 800 feet in length and measured about 48 feet from the bottom of its trough to its crest. On its passage across the Pacific, it had already killed thirteen people, mostly fishermen in small boats, but also an entire French family of five aboard a 48-foot schooner . . .*

This sets a suspenseful tone and reminds me of reading a newspaper article about a dangerous situation in my city.

NOTICE & NOTE 

BACKGROUND

This adventure story features a cutter-rigged sailboat. Cutter-rigged boats are small sailing yachts, each with a single mast for the main sail and smaller sails up front. Cutters can be equipped with a cabin that usually includes a small kitchen, called a galley. Author **Theodore Taylor** *(1921–2006) wrote many stories about self-reliant characters who face great challenges. His best-known book,* The Cay, *depicts the struggles and revelations of a boy shipwrecked during World War II.*

ROGUE WAVE

Short Story by Theodore Taylor

SETTING A PURPOSE

Pay attention to the details and events that make this story an adventure. As you read, think about the setting and how the author builds excitement and anticipation throughout the short story.

1 *A killer wave, known to mariners as a "rogue wave," was approaching a desolate area of Baja California below Ensenada. It had been born off the east coast of Australia during a violent storm; it had traveled almost 7,000 miles at a speed of 20.83 miles an hour. Driven by an unusual pattern of easterly winds, it was a little over 800 feet in length and measured about 48 feet from the bottom of its trough to its crest. On its passage across the Pacific, it had already killed thirteen people, mostly fishermen in small boats, but also an entire French family of five aboard a 48-foot schooner . . .*

Notice & Note

Use the side margins to notice and note signposts in the text.

MAKE INFERENCES

Annotate: In paragraph 1, mark details that describe rogue waves.

Interpret: What do these details suggest about the conflict of this story?

NOTICE & NOTE

2 Melissa "Scoot" Atkins went below into the *Old Sea Dog's* tiny galley, moving down the three steps of the companionway, closing the two solid entry doors behind her, always a good idea in offshore sailing. The three horizontal hatch boards that were on top of the doors were also firmly in place, securing the thirty-foot Baba type against sudden invasion of seawater.

ANALYZE PLOT

Annotate In paragraphs 2 and 4, circle the names of the main characters. Underline details that describe where each is on the boat.

Predict: Why might it be important to the plot that these characters are in two different settings?

3 *Rogues and sneakers have been around since the beginning of the oceans, and the earliest sea literature makes note of "giant" waves. The U.S. Navy manual* Practical Methods for Observing and Forecasting Ocean Waves *says, "In any wave system, after a long enough time, an exceptional high one will occur. These monstrous out-sized waves are improbable but still possible and the exact time of occurrence can never be predicted." Naval hydrography*[1] *studies indicate that waves 15 to 25 feet high qualify for "sneaker" or "sleeper" status; the freak rogue is up to 100 feet or over. As waters slowly warm they seem to be occurring more frequently. In 1995 the* Queen Elizabeth 2 *(the* QE2*), the great British passenger liner, encountered a 95-foot rogue south of Newfoundland. More than 900 feet long, the* QE2 *rode over it, but her captain said it looked like they were sailing into the White Cliffs of Dover.*

4 Sullivan Atkins, Scoot's oldest brother, was steering the cutter-rigged boat on a northerly course about fifteen miles off desolate Cabo Colnett, south of Ensenada. Under a brilliant sun, the glittering blue Pacific rose and fell in long, slick **swells,** a cold light breeze holding steady.

swell
(swĕl) *n.* A *swell* is a long, unbroken wave.

deck
(dĕk) *n.* The *deck* is the platform on a ship or boat where people stand.

5 Below **deck** Scoot was listening to Big Sandy & His Fly-Rite Boys doing "Swingin' West," and singing along with them while slicing leftover steak from last night's meal. They'd grilled it on a small charcoal ring that was mounted outboard on the starboard side[2] at the stern, trailing sparks into the water. The *Sea Dog* had every blessed thing, including a barbecue pit, she marveled.

[1] **hydrography:** the scientific description and analysis of the earth's surface waters.
[2] **outboard on the starboard side:** positioned outside and on the right side of the boat.

6 Scoot was learning how to be a deep-water sailor. She was fourteen years old and pretty, with dark hair. Though small in size, not even five feet, she was strong. She'd started off with eight-foot Sabots. On this trip, her first aboard the *Sea Dog,* she'd manned the wheel for most of the three days they'd been under way. She'd stood four-hour watches at night. Sully was a good teacher.

7 It was one of those perfect days to be out, Sully thought: the three Dacron sails belayed and whispering, white bow waves singing pleasant songs as the fiberglass hull, tilting to starboard, sliced through the ocean. It was a day filled with goodness, peace, and beauty. They'd come south as far as Cabo Colnett, turning back north only an hour ago. They'd sailed from Catalina Island's Avalon Harbor, the *Sea Dog's* home port, out in the channel off Los Angeles. Sully had borrowed the boat from a family friend, Beau Tucker, a stockbroker with enough money to outfit it and maintain it properly. Built by Ta-Shing, of Taiwan, she was heavy and sturdy, with a teakwood deck and handsome teakwood interior, and the latest in **navigation** equipment. Sully had sailed her at least a dozen times. He'd been around boats, motor and sail, for many of his nineteen years. He thought the *Old Sea Dog* was the best, in her category, that he'd ever piloted.

navigation
(năv´ĭ-gā´shən) *n.* The *navigation* of a ship or boat is the act of guiding it along a planned course.

8 As he was about to complete a northeast tack, Sully's attention was drawn to a squadron of seagulls diving on small fish about a hundred yards off the port bow, and he did not see the giant wave that had crept up silently behind the *Sea Dog.* But a split second before it lifted the boat like a carpenter's chip, he sensed something behind him and glanced backward, toward the towering wall of shining water.

AGAIN AND AGAIN

Notice & Note: Mark words that are repeated in paragraph 9.

Predict: Why might the author have chosen to repeat these words? How do you think this repetition adds suspense to the rising action of this short story?

9 It was already too late to shout a warning to Scoot so she could escape from the cabin; too late to do anything except hang on to the wheel with both hands; too late even to pray. He did manage a yell as the *Sea Dog* became vertical. She rose up the surface of the wall stern first and then pitch-poled violently, end over end, the bow **submerging** and the boat going upside down, taking Sully and Scoot with it, the forty-foot mast, sails intact, now pointing toward the bottom.

submerge
(səb-mûrj´) *v.* To *submerge* is to descend beneath the surface of the water.

NOTICE & NOTE

ANALYZE PLOT

Annotate: In paragraphs 9–15, mark details that describe the conflict.

Predict: Based on other short stories you have read, how do you think the characters will respond to this conflict? Review the genre characteristics of short stories on page 5.

porthole
(pôrt´hōl´) *n.* A *porthole* is a circular window on a boat or ship.

10 Scoot was hurled upward, legs and arms flying, her head striking the after galley bulkhead and then the companionway steps and the interior deck, which was now the ceiling. She instantly blacked out.

11 Everything loose in the cabin was scattered around what had been the overhead. Water was pouring in and was soon lapping at Scoot's chin. It was coming from a four-inch **porthole** that had not been dogged securely and a few other smaller points of entry.

12 Sully's feet were caught under forestay sailcloth, plastered around his face, but then he managed to shove clear and swim upward, breaking water. He looked at the mound of upside-down hull, bottom to the sky, unable to believe that the fine, sturdy *Sea Dog* had been flipped like a cork, perhaps trapping Scoot inside. Treading water, trying to collect his thoughts, he yelled, "Scoot," but there was no answer. Heart pounding, unable to see over the mound of the hull, he circled it, thinking she might have been thrown clear. But there was no sign of her.

13 He swam back to the point of cabin entry, took several deep breaths, and dove. He felt along the hatch boards and then opened his eyes briefly to see that the doors were still closed. She *was* still inside. Maneuvering his body, he pulled on the handles. The doors were jammed, and he returned to the surface for air.

14 He knew by the way the boat had already settled that there was water inside her. Under usual circumstances, the hull being upright, there would be four feet, nine inches of hull below the waterline. There would be about the same to the cabin overhead, enabling a six-foot-person to walk about down there.

15 Panting, blowing, Sully figured there was at least a three-foot air pocket holding the *Sea Dog* on the surface, and if Scoot hadn't been knocked unconscious and drowned, she could live for quite a while in the dark chamber. How long, he didn't know.

16 In the blackness, water continued to lap at Scoot's chin. She had settled against what had been the deck of the galley alcove, her body in an upright position on debris. Everything not tied down or in a locker was now between the overhead ribs. Wooden hatch covers[3] from the bilges were floating in the water and the naked bilges were exposed. Just aft of her body, and now above it, was the small diesel engine as well as the batteries. Under the water were cans of oil, one of them leaking. Battery acid might leak, too. Few sailors could imagine the nightmare that existed inside the *Sea Dog*. Scoot's pretty face was splashed with engine oil.

17 Over the next five or six minutes, Sully dove repeatedly, using his feet as a fulcrum, and using all the strength that he had in his arms, legs, and back, in an effort to open the doors. The pressure of the water defeated him. Then he thought about

AGAIN AND AGAIN

Notice & Note: Mark the action that is repeated in paragraph 17 and explain why Sully does something over and over.

Infer: How does this add to the story's suspense?

[3] **Wooden hatch covers:** door-like coverings made of wood that fit over openings on the deck or hull of a boat.

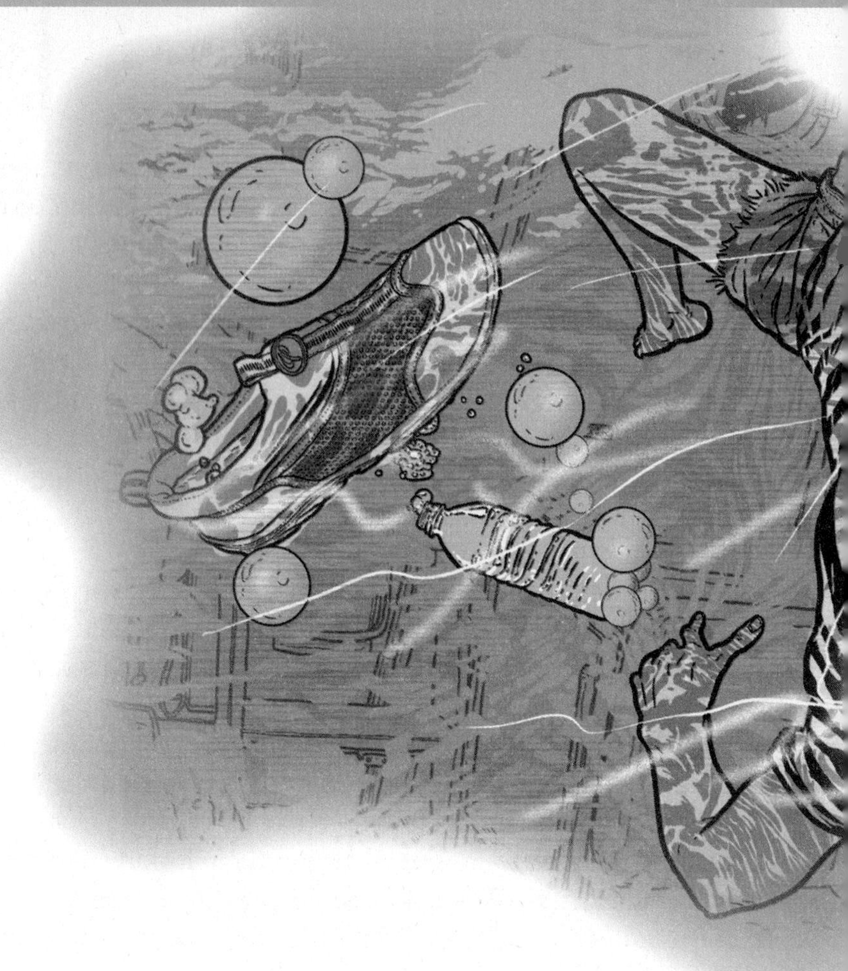

trying to pry the doors open with the wooden handle of the scrub brush. Too late for that, he immediately discovered. It had drifted away, along with Scoot's nylon jacket, her canvas boat shoes—anything that could float.

18 Finally he climbed on top of the keel, catching his breath, resting a moment, trying desperately to think of a way to enter the hull. Boats of the Baba class, built for deep-water sailing, quite capable of reaching Honolulu and beyond, were almost sea-tight unless the sailors made a mistake or unless the sea became angry. The side ports were supposed to be dogged securely in open ocean. Aside from the cabin doors, there was no entry into that cabin without tools. He couldn't very well claw a hole through the inch of tough fiberglass.

19 He thought about the hatch on the foredeck, but it could only be opened from inside the cabin. Then there was the skylight on the top of the seventeen-foot cabin, used for ventilation as well as a sun source; that butterfly window, hinged in the middle, could be opened only from the inside. Even with scuba gear, he couldn't open that skylight unless he had tools.

20 He fought back tears of frustration. There was no way to reach Scoot. And he knew what would happen down there. The water would slowly and inevitably rise until the air pocket was only six inches; her head would be trapped between the surface of the water and the dirty bilge. The water would torture her, then it would drown her. Seawater has no heart, no brain. The *Sea Dog* would then drop to the ocean floor, thousands of feet down, entombing her forever.

21 Maybe the best hope for poor Scoot was that she was already dead, but he had to determine whether she was still alive. He began pounding on the hull with the bottom of his fist, waiting for a return knock. At the same time, he shouted her name over and over. Nothing but silence from inside there. He wished he'd hung on to the silly scrub brush. The wooden handle would make more noise than the flesh of his fist.

22 Almost half an hour passed, and he finally broke down and sobbed. His right fist was bloody from the constant pounding. Why hadn't *he* gone below to make the stupid sandwiches? Scoot would have been at the wheel when the wave grasped the *Sea Dog*. His young sister, with all her life to live, would be alive now.

23 They'd had a good brother-sister relationship. He'd teased her a lot about being pint-sized and she'd teased back, holding her nose when he brought one girl or another home for display. She'd always been spunky. He'd taken her sailing locally, in the channel, but she'd wanted an offshore cruise for her fourteenth birthday. Now she'd had one, unfortunately.

24 Their father had nicknamed her Scoot because, as a baby, she'd crawled so fast. It was still a fitting name for her as a teenager. With a wiry body, she was fast in tennis and swimming and already the school's champion in the hundred-yard dash.

25 Eyes closed, teeth clenched, he kept pounding away with the bloody fist. Finally he went back into the ocean to try once more to open the doors. He sucked air, taking a half-dozen deep breaths, and then dove again. Bracing his feet against the companionway frames, he felt every muscle straining, but the doors remained jammed. He was also now aware that if they did open, more water would rush in and he might not have time to find Scoot in the blackness and pull her out. But he was willing to take the gamble.

26 Scoot awakened as water seeped into her mouth and nose. For a moment she could not understand where she was, how she got there, what had happened . . . Vaguely, she remembered the

LANGUAGE CONVENTIONS

Annotate: Writers use a mix of sentence types to convey ideas. Read the first two sentences in paragraph 22. Mark the simple sentence and circle the compound sentence.

Summarize: Explain how you were able to identify which sentence was simple and which was compound.

MEMORY MOMENT

Notice & Note: In paragraphs 23 and 24, underline memories Sully has about Scoot.

Infer: What do the memories suggest about how Sully is feeling about Scoot's chances of escape?

boat slanting steeply downward, as if it were suddenly diving, and she remembered feeling her body going up.

27 That's all she remembered, and all she knew at the moment was that she had a fierce headache and was in chill water in total darkness. It took a little longer to realize she was trapped in the *Sea Dog's* cabin, by the galley alcove. She began to feel around herself and to touch floating things. The air was thick with an oil smell. Then she ran her hand over the nearest solid thing—a bulkhead. *That's strange,* she thought—her feet were touching a pot. She lifted her right arm and felt above her—the galley range. The galley range above her? *The boat was upside down.* She felt for the companionway steps and found the entry doors and pushed on them; that was the way she'd come in. The doors didn't move.

MAKE INFERENCES

Annotate: In paragraph 28, mark details that describe the setting.

Interpret: How do these details add tension to the central conflict?

28 Sully crawled up on the wide hull again, clinging to a faint hope that a boat or ship would soon come by; but the sun was already in descent, and with night coming on, chances of rescue lessened with each long minute. It was maddening to have her a few feet away and be helpless to do anything. Meanwhile the hull swayed gently, in eerie silence.

29 Scoot said tentatively, "Sully?" Maybe he'd been drowned. Maybe she was alone and would die here in the foul water.

30 She repeated his name, but much more loudly. No answer. She was coming out of shock now and fear icier than the water was replacing her confusion. To die completely alone? It went that way for a few desperate moments, and then she said to herself, *Scoot, you've got to get out of here! There has to be some way to get out . . .*

31 Sully clung to the keel with one hand, his body flat against the smooth surface of the hull. There was ample room on either side of the keel before the dead-rise, the upward slope of the hull. The *Sea Dog* had a beam of ten feet. Unless a wind and waves came up, he was safe enough in his wet perch.

32 Scoot again wondered if her brother had survived and if he was still around the boat or on it. With her right foot she began to probe around the space beneath her. The pot had drifted away, but her toes felt what seemed to be flatware. That made sense. The drawer with the knives and forks and spoons had popped out, spilling its contents. She took a deep breath and ducked under to pick out a knife. Coming up, she held the knife blade, reaching skyward with the handle . . .

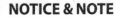

33 Eyes closed, brain mushy, exhausted, Sully heard a faint tapping and raised up on his elbows to make sure he wasn't dreaming. No, there was a tapping from below. He crawled back toward what he thought was the source area, the galley area, and put an ear to the hull. *She was tapping!* He pounded the fiberglass, yelling, "Scoot, Scooot, Scooot . . ."

34 Scoot heard the pounding and called out, "Sully, I'm here, I'm here!" Her voice seemed to thunder in the air pocket.

35 Sully yelled, "Can you hear me?"

36 Scoot could only hear the pounding.

37 "Help me out of here . . ."

38 Ear still to the hull, Sully shouted again, "Scoot, can you hear me?" No answer. He pounded again and repeated, "Scoot, can you hear me?" No answer. The hull was too thick and the slop of the sea, the moan of the afternoon breeze, didn't help.

39 Though she couldn't hear his voice, the mere fact that he was up there told her she'd escape. Sully had gotten her out of jams before. There was no one on earth that she'd rather have as a rescue man than her oldest brother. She absolutely knew she'd survive.

40 Though it might be fruitless, Sully yelled down to the galley alcove, "Listen to me, Scoot. You'll have to get out by yourself. I can't help you. I can't break in. Listen to me, I know you're in water, and the best way out is through the skylight. You've got to dive down and open it. You're small enough to go through it . . ." She could go through either section of the butterfly window. "Tap twice if you heard me!"

41 She did not respond, and he repeated what he'd just said, word for word.

42 No response. No taps from below.

43 Scoot couldn't understand why he didn't just swim down and open the doors to the cabin, release her. That's all he needed to do, and she'd be free.

44 Sully looked up at the sky. "Please, God, help me, help us." It was almost unbearable to know she was alive and he was unable to do anything for her. Then he made the decision to keep repeating: "Listen to me, Scoot. You'll have to get out by yourself. I can't break in. Listen to me, the best way out is through the skylight. You've got to dive down and open it. You're small enough to go through it . . ."

AHA MOMENT

Notice & Note: Mark what Sully realizes in paragraph 33.

Infer: What effect might this realization have on him?

AGAIN AND AGAIN

Notice & Note: In paragraphs 38–45, underline words and phrases that Sully repeats.

Infer: What does the repetition reveal about Sully?

NOTICE & NOTE

AHA MOMENT

Notice & Note: Mark two related realizations that Scoot has in paragraphs 47 and 48.

Connect: How do these realizations tie in with the words that Sully keeps repeating?

MEMORY MOMENT

Notice & Note: Underline what Scoot remembers in paragraph 50.

Infer: How do these memories help Scoot think through her situation?

45 He decided to keep saying it the rest of the day and into the night or for as long as it took to penetrate the hull with words. *Skylight! Skylight!* Over and over.

46 He'd heard of mental telepathy but had not thought much about it before. Now it was the only way to reach her.

47 Scoot finally thought that maybe Sully was hurt, maybe helpless up on that bottom, so that was why he couldn't open the doors and let her out. That had to be the reason—Sully up there with broken legs. *So I'll have to get out on my own,* she thought.

48 Over the last two days, when she wasn't on the wheel she had been exploring the *Sea Dog,* and she thought she knew all the exits. Besides the companionway doors, which she knew she couldn't open, there was the hatch on the foredeck for access to the sails; then there was the skylight, almost in the middle of the long cabin. Sully had opened it, she remembered, to air out the boat before they sailed. As she clung to a light fixture by the alcove, in water up to her shoulders, something kept telling her she should first try the butterfly windows of the skylight. The unheard message was compelling—*Try the skylight.*

49 Sully's voice was almost like a recording, a mantra, saying the same thing again and again, directed down to the position of the galley.

50 Scoot remembered that an emergency flashlight was bracketed on the bulkhead above the starboard settee, and she assumed it was waterproof. From what Sully had said, Beau Tucker took great care in selecting emergency equipment. It might help to actually see the dogs on the metal skylight frame. She knew she wouldn't have much time to spin them loose. Maybe thirty or forty seconds before she'd have to surface for breath. Trying to think of the exact position of the upside-down flashlight, she again tapped on the hull to let her brother know she was very much alive.

51 He pounded back.

52 Sully looked at his watch. Almost four-thirty. About three hours to sundown. Of course, it didn't make much difference to Scoot. She was already in dank night. But it might make a difference if she got out after nightfall. He didn't know what kind of shape she was in. Injured, she might surface and drift away.

53 The mantra kept on.

54 Scoot dove twice for the boxy flashlight, found it, and turned it on, suddenly splitting the darkness and immediately feeling

hopeful. But it was odd to see the *Sea Dog's* unusual overhead, the open hatchways into the bilge and the debris floating on the shining water, all streaked with lubricants; odd to see the toilet upside down. She held the light underwater and it continued to operate.

55 Every so often, Sully lifted his face to survey the horizon, looking for traffic. He knew they were still within sixteen or seventeen miles of the coast, though the drift was west. There was usually small-boat activity within twenty miles of the shore—fishermen or pleasure boats.

MAKE INFERENCES
Annotate: In paragraph 55, mark details that describe the setting.

Interpret: What effect do these details have on the plot?

56 Scoot worked herself forward a few feet, guessing where the skylight might be, and then went down to find the butterfly windows, the flashlight beam cutting through the murk. It took a few seconds to locate them and put a hand on one brass dog. She tried to turn it, but it was too tight for her muscles and she rose up to breathe again.

ANALYZE PLOT
Annotate: In paragraphs 56–61, mark the parts of the story that keep you anxious about what will happen.

Draw Conclusions: How does the action in these paragraphs help the plot advance?

57 Not knowing what was happening below or whether Scoot was trying to escape, Sully was getting more anxious by the moment. He didn't know whether or not the crazy telepathy was working. He wished she would tap again to let him know she was still alive. It had been more than twenty minutes since she'd last tapped.

58 Scoot had seen a toolbox under the companionway steps and went back to try to find it. She guessed there'd be wrenches inside it, unless they'd spilled out. Using the flashlight again, she found the metal box and opened it. Back to the surface to breathe again, and then back to the toolbox to extract a wrench. With each move she was becoming more and more confident.

59 A big sailboat, beating south, came into Sully's view; but it was more than two miles away and the occupants—unless he was very lucky—would not be able to spot the *Sea Dog's* mound and the man standing on it, waving frantically.

ANALYZE PLOT

Annotate: Mark and label the climax, the falling action, and the resolution.

Infer: Why are these three plot stages shorter than the rest of the story?

60 Four times Scoot needed to dive, once for each dog; and working underwater was at least five times as difficult as trying to turn them in usual circumstances. She'd aim the light and rest it to illuminate the windows. Finally, all the dogs were loose and she rose once again. This time, after filling her lungs to bursting, she went down and pushed on the starboard window. It cracked a little, but the outside sea pressure resisted and she had to surface again.

61 Sully sat down, almost giving up hope. How long the air pocket would hold up was anybody's guess. The boat had settled at least six inches in the last two hours. It might not last into the night.

62 On her sixth dive Scoot found a way to brace her feet against the ceiling ribs. She pushed with all her strength, and this time the window opened. Almost out of breath, she quickly pushed her body through and the *Old Sea Dog* released her. Treading water beside the hull, she sucked in fresh air and finally called out, "Sully . . ."

63 He looked her way, saw the grin of triumph on the oil-stained imp face, and dived in to help her aboard the derelict.

64 Shivering, holding each other for warmth all night, they rode and rocked, knowing that the boat was sinking lower each hour.

65 Just after dawn, the *Red Rooster,* a long-range sports fishing boat out of San Diego bound south to fish for wahoo and tuna off the Revilla Gigedo Islands, came within a hundred yards of the upside-down sailboat and stopped to pick up its two chattering survivors.

66 The *Red Rooster's* captain, Mark Stevens, asked, "What happened?"

67 "Rogue wave," said Sully. That's what he planned to say to Beau Tucker as well.

68 Stevens winced and nodded that he understood.

69 The *Old Sea Dog* stayed on the surface for a little while longer, having delivered her survivors to safety; then her air pocket breathed its last and she slipped beneath the water, headed for the bottom.

CHECK YOUR UNDERSTANDING

Answer these questions before moving on to the **Analyze the Text** section on the following page.

1 The setting is important to the story because —

A rogue waves are common south of Ensenada

B the characters wouldn't face as much danger anywhere else

C it is an essential part of the plot's central conflict

D Sully has never sailed so far off coast before

2 The details about Scoot's attempts to open the skylight serve to —

F slow the action down so that readers can relax

G show that Scoot isn't as experienced a sailor as Sully

H underscore how strong and well-built the boat is

J heighten suspense by emphasizing the difficulty of the task

3 Which of these is an important idea suggested by the story?

A People can solve problems with clear thinking and effort.

B Fear can cloud people's judgment and increase their danger.

C People who enjoy adventure are strong and resourceful.

D The ocean is the strongest force of nature.

ANALYZE THE TEXT

Support your responses with evidence from the text. NOTEBOOK

1. **Infer** Reread paragraphs 29–30. What inference can you make about Scoot's personality, based on those paragraphs?

2. **Connect** How does the information in paragraph 3 help foreshadow the conflict?

3. **Analyze** Identify two settings on the boat in this story. How does the shifting between these settings influence the plot and build suspense?

4. **Compare** What complications or conflicts do Scoot and Sully encounter in the story? Fill out a chart like this one to trace the conflicts or complications Scoot and Sully encounter in the story.

COMPLICATION	1	2	3	4	5
Scoot's					
Sully's					

5. **Notice & Note** Reread paragraphs 21–22 and 25. What words are repeated again and again to show how hard Sully tries to save Scoot?

RESEARCH

"Rogue Wave" is a fiction story that presents facts about rogue waves. How accurate are they? With a partner, research rogue waves. Begin by generating several questions to guide your research. Record your questions and the answers you learn in the chart.

QUESTION	ANSWER

RESEARCH TIP

Focused questions can help you research a topic more quickly and successfully. For example, to find a description of a rogue wave, you could ask, "How tall is a rogue wave?" To learn how dangerous a rogue wave is, you might ask, "Can a rogue wave sink a sailboat?"

Connect How accurately does the story depict the phenomenon of rogue waves? In a small group, share your research and discuss whether the author described rogue waves in a realistic and accurate way.

CREATE AND DISCUSS

Adapt as a Film How would you change "Rogue Wave" if you wanted to turn it into an action movie? Write a three-to-four-paragraph description of how this short story could be adapted as a film. Include each of the following:

- ❑ a clear controlling idea or thesis statement
- ❑ a description of the opening scene that establishes the characters, setting, and conflict
- ❑ a description of each important scene in the plot
- ❑ suggestions for how to shoot each scene to convey the suspense

Go to **Writing Informative Texts** in the **Writing Studio** to learn more.

Share and Discuss Plot Details In a small group, evaluate the plot of "Rogue Wave." Dissect the ways it builds tension and delivers suspenseful moments. Consider details about characters, setting, and events in each stage of the plot. Use text evidence to support your views. Remember to participate in the discussion using an appropriate tone and vocabulary in your responses. These are some of the things you might talk about:

- ❑ how story events build rising tension
- ❑ how characters' traits, thoughts, feelings, or actions affect the plot
- ❑ the role setting plays in heightening suspense

Go to **Participating in Collaborative Discussions** in the **Speaking and Listening Studio** for help.

RESPOND TO THE ESSENTIAL QUESTION

What helps people rise up to face difficulties?

Gather Information Review your annotations and notes on "Rogue Wave." Then, add relevant details to your Response Log. As you determine which information to include, think about:

- the kinds of difficulties the characters faced
- what happens to people when they face difficulties
- how people can overcome those difficulties

At the end of the collection, use your notes to write an informational essay.

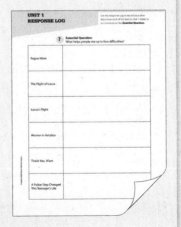

ACADEMIC VOCABULARY

As you write and discuss what you learned from the short story, be sure to use the Academic Vocabulary words. Check off each of the words that you use.

- ❑ **aspect**
- ❑ **cultural**
- ❑ **evaluate**
- ❑ **resource**
- ❑ **text**

CRITICAL VOCABULARY

swell **deck** **navigation** **submerge** **porthole**

Practice and Apply Complete each sentence to show that you understand the meaning of the boldfaced vocabulary word.

1. I can see the water's motion by watching how a **swell** . . .

   ____

2. One reason to be on the **deck** of a boat is . . .

   ____

3. **Navigation** becomes more difficult in bad weather because . . .

   ____

4. When the tide comes in on that beach, it could **submerge** . . .

   ____

5. There was a **porthole** in our room on the ship, so we . . .

   ____

VOCABULARY STRATEGY: Latin Roots

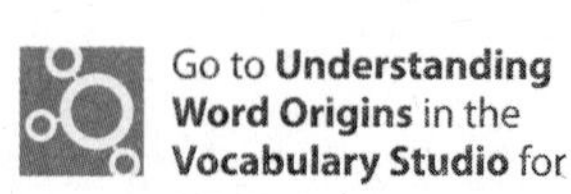
Go to **Understanding Word Origins** in the **Vocabulary Studio** for more.

A **root** is a word part—such as *nav* in the word *navigation*—that came into English from an older language. Roots from the ancient language of Latin appear in many English words. For example, the chart shows two words from "Rogue Wave" that have Latin roots.

WORD	LATIN ROOT	ROOT'S MEANING
navigation	nav	ship or sail
mariner	mar	sea

Often, by identifying Latin roots, you can figure out the meanings of words that seem unfamiliar. Using a resource such as a print or online dictionary can help you confirm your ideas.

Practice and Apply Identify the words in each sentence with the Latin roots *mar* and *nav*. Tell what each word means. Then use a print or online dictionary to check your ideas.

1. Sailors in the navy may spend time in submarines.

   ____

2. Mariners long ago navigated using the stars.

   ____

LANGUAGE CONVENTIONS: Sentence Structure

A **clause** is a group of words that includes a complete subject and a complete predicate. Every sentence includes at least one clause. A **complete subject** includes all the words that identify the person, place, thing, or idea that the clause is about. The **complete predicate** includes all the words that tell or ask something about the subject.

Go to **Sentence Structure** in the **Grammar Studio** to learn more.

COMPLETE SUBJECT	COMPLETE PREDICATE
"The *Sea Dog*	had every blessed thing. . . ."
"Sully	was a good teacher."

As in "Rogue Wave," authors use different types of sentences to convey meaning.

- A **simple sentence** contains only one clause, as in the sentence, "Sully looked at his watch."
- A **compound sentence** contains two or more clauses that are joined either by a comma and a **coordinating conjunction,** such as *and, but, or, for, so, yet,* and *nor;* or by a semicolon.

Independent Clauses	**She pushed with all her strength. This time the window opened.**
Compound Sentence	**"She pushed with all her strength, and this time the window opened."**

- A **complex sentence** is a combination of a subordinate clause an independent clause. A subordinate clause begins with a **subordinating conjunction,** such as *after, although, as, because, before, even though, if, since, so that, though, unless, until, when, where,* and *while.*

Complex Sentence	**Although sailing can be dangerous, Sully was an experienced sailor.**

Practice and Apply Write two pairs of related simple sentences. Then, for one set of sentences, use a comma and coordinating conjunction or semicolon to create a compound sentence. Use a subordinating conjunction to connect the other set of sentences to make a complex sentence. When you have finished, share your sentences with a partner and discuss the structure of each sentence.

THE FLIGHT OF ICARUS

Myth retold by **Sally Benson**

? ***ESSENTIAL QUESTION:***

What helps people rise up to face difficulties?

QUICK START

In a journal entry, describe an experience in which you wish you had acted differently. What should you have done instead? What did you learn from that experience?

ANALYZE GENRE: MYTH

"The Flight of Icarus" is a **myth**, an old and traditional story that tries to answer basic questions about the origins of the world, events in nature, human life, and social customs. Most myths share these elements:

- gods and other supernatural beings with special powers
- unrealistic or supernatural events and settings
- a lesson about life or human behavior

Myths can tell exciting, action-packed stories. Many myths also suggest values—for example, honesty, cleverness, or moderation (acting within reasonable limits)—that are important to a culture. In the past, in fact, myths often were used to encourage people to act in a way that reflected these values and helped society to function properly.

GENRE ELEMENTS: MYTH

- has characters who have special abilities or are gods
- is set in ancient times
- includes events that could not happen in real life
- often tells a story that teaches a lesson relating to a cultural value

DETERMINE THEMES

A **theme** is a message about life or human nature that a writer shares with the reader. An example of a theme might be "greed can lead to ruined lives" or "simple things in life are the most meaningful." Writers sometimes state a theme directly. More often, you must analyze story events and characters' actions to **infer**, or make logical guesses about, the theme of a story.

Myths often contain more than one theme. These themes reflect the cultural values of the society in which the myth was told. By analyzing the behavior of mythic characters in unusual situations, you can learn lessons about the traits that mattered to a culture. Think about these questions as you determine the life lessons or other big ideas—that is, the themes—in a myth.

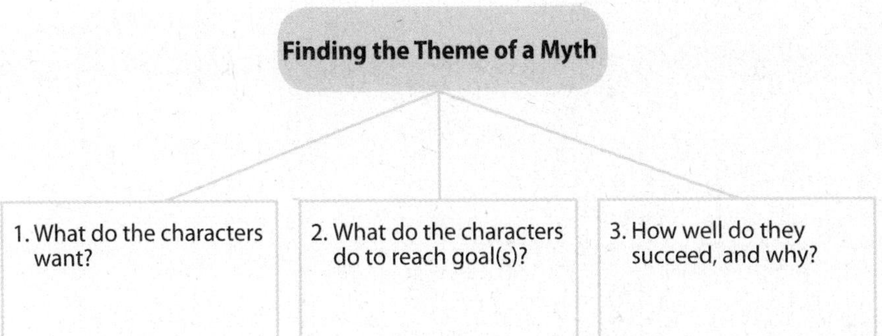
Finding the Theme of a Myth
1. What do the characters want?
2. What do the characters do to reach goal(s)?
3. How well do they succeed, and why?

GET READY

CRITICAL VOCABULARY

moderate **prowess** **frantic** **anxiety**

To see how many Critical Vocabulary words you already know, choose one to complete each sentence.

1. __________ politicians from both countries favored the treaty.

2. The young children became __________ and started crying when the earthquake began.

3. The __________ of the athletes during the tournament helped them win the championship.

4. The citizens' fear and __________ increased as food became scarce.

LANGUAGE CONVENTIONS

Commas and Coordinate Adjectives In this lesson, you will learn about the effective use of commas and coordinate adjectives in writing. Coordinate adjectives are describing words that equally modify the same noun:

Daedalus was a smart, purposeful man.

Notice that *smart* and *purposeful* appear before the noun *man* and are separated by a comma.

ANNOTATION MODEL

NOTICE & NOTE

As you read, note elements of myths that you can identify. You also can mark details that show aspects of the myth's theme. This model shows one reader's notes about "The Flight of Icarus."

2 Daedalus was an ingenious artist and was not discouraged by his failures. "Minos may control the land and sea," he said, "but he does not control the air. I will try that way."

Daedalus seems to have important values. Part of the theme, or not?

"control the air" = something special or even supernatural in a time before airplanes

BACKGROUND

Today we think of myths as stories that have been passed down through countless generations. In the ancient civilization of Greece, myths were the basis of an elaborate system of beliefs. Myths explained their mystifying world and offered wisdom on how to live in it. The myth of Daedalus and his son Icarus is one example.

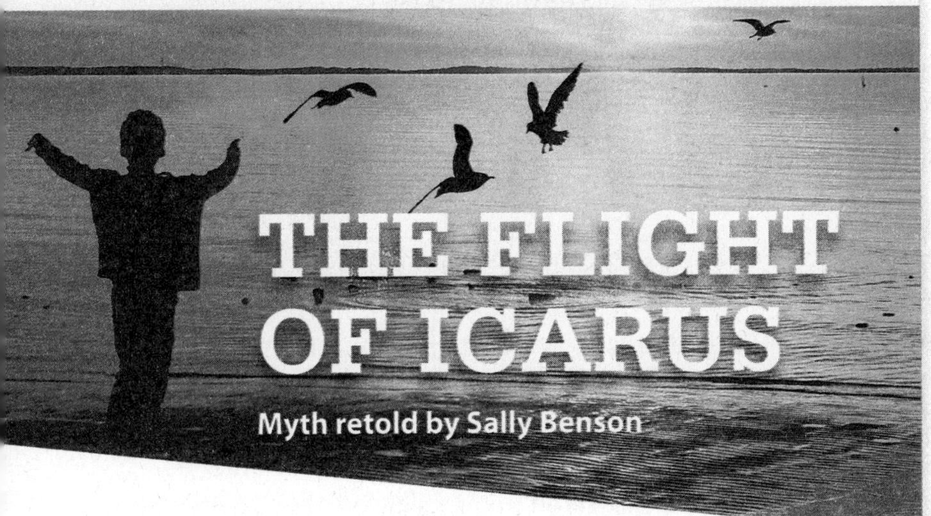

THE FLIGHT OF ICARUS

Myth retold by Sally Benson

SETTING A PURPOSE

As you read, pay close attention to the choices Icarus and his father make. What do these choices reveal? Write down any questions you may have while reading.

1 When Theseus escaped from the labyrinth, King Minos flew into a rage with its builder, Daedalus, and ordered him shut up in a high tower that faced the lonely sea. In time, with the help of his young son, Icarus, Daedalus managed to escape from the tower, only to find himself a prisoner on the island. Several times he tried by bribery to stow away on one of the vessels sailing from Crete, but King Minos kept strict watch over them, and no ships were allowed to sail without being carefully searched.

2 Daedalus was an ingenious artist and was not discouraged by his failures. "Minos may control the land and sea," he said, "but he does not control the air. I will try that way."

Notice & Note

Use the side margins to notice and note signposts in the text.

ANALYZE GENRE: MYTH

Annotate: Mark the detail in paragraphs 1–2 that states the problem Daedalus and Icarus face.

Draw Conclusions: How do you think Daedalus plans to solve the problem? Why do you think so?

NOTICE & NOTE

ANALYZE GENRE: MYTH

Annotate: Reread paragraphs 3 and 4. Mark words and phrases that show that Daedalus is happy about the work he and his son are doing.

Infer: What do these paragraphs suggest about the kind of family interactions that the Greek culture valued?

3 He called his son, Icarus, to him and told the boy to gather up all the feathers he could find on the rocky shore. As thousands of gulls soared over the island, Icarus soon collected a huge pile of feathers. Daedalus then melted some wax and made a skeleton in the shape of a bird's wing. The smallest feathers he pressed into the soft wax and the large ones he tied on with thread. Icarus played about on the beach happily while his father worked, chasing the feathers that blew away in the strong wind that swept the island and sometimes taking bits of the wax and working it into strange shapes with his fingers.

4 It was fun making the wings. The sun shone on the bright feathers; the breezes ruffled them. When they were finished, Daedalus fastened them to his shoulders and found himself lifted upwards, where he hung poised in the air. Filled with excitement, he made another pair for his son. They were smaller than his own, but strong and beautiful.

WORDS OF THE WISER

Notice & Note: In paragraph 5, mark the warning that Daedalus gives Icarus.

Connect: What might Daedalus's warning suggest about one theme of this myth?

5 Finally, one clear, wind-swept morning, the wings were finished, and Daedalus fastened them to Icarus's shoulders and taught him how to fly. He bade him watch the movements of the birds, how they soared and glided overhead. He pointed out the slow, graceful sweep of their wings as they beat the air steadily, without fluttering. Soon Icarus was sure that he, too, could fly and, raising his arms up and down, skirted over the white sand and even out over the waves, letting his feet touch the snowy foam as the water thundered and broke over the sharp rocks. Daedalus watched him proudly but with

NOTICE & NOTE

misgivings. He called Icarus to his side and, putting his arm round the boy's shoulders, said, "Icarus, my son, we are about to make our flight. No human being has ever traveled through the air before, and I want you to listen carefully to my instructions. Keep at a **moderate** height, for if you fly too low, the fog and spray will clog your wings, and if you fly too high, the heat will melt the wax that holds them together. Keep near me and you will be safe."

moderate
(mŏd´ər-ĭt) *adj.* When something is kept *moderate*, it is kept within a certain limit.

6 He kissed Icarus and fastened the wings more securely to his son's shoulders. Icarus, standing in the bright sun, the shining wings dropping gracefully from his shoulders, his golden hair wet with spray, and his eyes bright and dark with excitement, looked like a lovely bird. Daedalus's eyes filled with tears, and turning away, he soared into the sky, calling to Icarus to follow. From time to time, he looked back to see that the boy was safe and to note how he managed his wings in his flight. As they flew across the land to test their **prowess** before setting out across the dark wild sea, plowmen below stopped their work and shepherds gazed in wonder, thinking Daedalus and Icarus were gods.

prowess
(prou´ĭs) *n. Prowess* is the strength and courage someone has.

7 Father and son flew over Samos and Delos, which lay on their left, and Lebinthus,[1] which lay on their right. Icarus, beating his wings in joy, felt the thrill of the cool wind on his face and the clear air above and below him. He flew higher

LANGUAGE CONVENTIONS

Annotate: Mark the example of coordinate adjectives that appears in paragraph 7.

Interpret: What does the comma in that example tell you about those adjectives?

[1] **Samos . . . Delos . . . Lebinthus** (sā´mŏs´. . . dē´lŏs´. . . lu bĭn´thus´): small Greek islands in the eastern Aegean Sea.

NOTICE & NOTE

frantic
(frăn′tĭk) *adj.* If you do something in a *frantic* way, you do it quickly and nervously.

anxiety
(ăng-zī′ĭ-tē) *n. Anxiety* is an uneasy, worried feeling.

DETERMINE THEMES

Annotate: Mark the sentence in paragraph 9 that relates directly to the main theme of this myth.

Critique: Why is the placement of this sentence effective in emphasizing the theme?

and higher up into the blue sky until he reached the clouds. His father saw him and called out in alarm. He tried to follow him, but he was heavier and his wings would not carry him. Up and up Icarus soared, through the soft, moist clouds and out again toward the glorious sun. He was bewitched by a sense of freedom and beat his wings **frantically** so that they would carry him higher and higher to heaven itself. The blazing sun beat down on the wings and softened the wax. Small feathers fell from the wings and floated softly down, warning Icarus to stay his flight and glide to earth. But the enchanted boy did not notice them until the sun became so hot that the largest feathers dropped off and he began to sink. Frantically he fluttered his arms, but no feathers remained to hold the air. He cried out to his father, but his voice was submerged in the blue waters of the sea, which has forever after been called by his name.

8 Daedalus, crazed by **anxiety**, called back to him, "Icarus! Icarus, my son, where are you?" At last he saw the feathers floating from the sky, and soon his son plunged through the clouds into the sea. Daedalus hurried to save him, but it was too late. He gathered the boy in his arms and flew to land, the tips of his wings dragging in the water from the double burden they bore. Weeping bitterly, he buried his small son and called the land Icaria in his memory.

9 Then, with a flutter of wings, he once more took to the air, but the joy of his flight was gone and his victory over the air was bitter to him. He arrived safely in Sicily, where he built a temple to Apollo and hung up his wings as an offering to the god, and in the wings he pressed a few bright feathers he had found floating on the water where Icarus fell. And he mourned for the birdlike son who had thrown caution to the winds in the exaltation of his freedom from the earth.

NOTICE & NOTE 

CHECK YOUR UNDERSTANDING

Answer these questions before moving on to the **Analyze the Text** section on the following page.

1 The detail He bade him watch the movements of the birds, how they soared and glided overhead emphasizes that —

A birds were worshipped as gods in ancient Greece

B flying by your own power was possible but dangerous

C nature was highly respected by ancient Greeks

D Daedalus wanted to make wings from birds' feathers

2 Against his father's advice, Icarus flew higher and higher because he —

F was eager to prove that he was stronger than his father

G often disobeyed his father's commands

H became lost when the sun blinded him

J was overtaken by the thrill that came from flying freely

3 Which sentence states an important theme in this myth?

A Only true heroes can perform superhuman acts.

B People must know their place in the universe.

C Being able to live in freedom is worth any cost.

D Doing things with family members is always fun.

ANALYZE THE TEXT

Support your responses with evidence from the text. NOTEBOOK

1. **Summarize** Reread paragraphs 3–4. Summarize in a few sentences what Daedalus does to help himself and his son escape from the island.

2. **Cite Evidence** What specific evidence in paragraph 5 suggests that Daedalus's plan will not go well?

3. **Compare** How are the actions of Daedalus and Icarus related to the idea of moderation in this myth? Explain how their actions are based on similarities and differences in their personalities and experiences.

4. **Synthesize** Reread paragraph 9. Keeping in mind Daedalus's original goal, do you think that he succeeded, or failed? What does your answer suggest about the Greeks' beliefs concerning their place in the world in relation to their gods?

5. **Notice & Note** "The Flight of Icarus" includes some specific wise words from a father to his son. How does this myth, as a whole, illustrate the idea of "Words of the Wiser"?

RESEARCH

RESEARCH TIP
When you conduct online research, use several search terms that are specific. Include key words that reflect what you are looking for, such as a character's name, the setting of the story, a key event, and the genre of the selection.

The character of Daedalus appears in another famous Greek myth. In that story, he designed and constructed a labyrinth, or maze, in which a monster was kept as a prisoner. The monster would find and kill people who were sent into the labyrinth as a form of punishment. Use the questions below to analyze the themes of this myth.

QUESTION	ANSWER
Who are the characters in the myth about Daedalus and the labyrinth?	
What problem must the main character solve?	
How does the main character's solution reflect some of the same themes that appear in "The Flight of Icarus"?	

Extend Find out how the design of the labyrinth inspired actual maze-like structures or how it was used in other stories.

WRITE AND DISCUSS

Write an Explanation People today may refer to someone "who flew too close to the sun" as a cautionary tale. Write a two- to three-paragraph explanation of what this expression means and what it has to do with the myth of Icarus. Base your explanation on evidence from "The Flight of Icarus."

- ❑ Clearly state the topic in a strong thesis statement—a clear controlling idea.
- ❑ Support your thesis with evidence. Cite relevant examples from the myth.
- ❑ Use appropriate transitions to link ideas.
- ❑ Provide a conclusion that follows from and supports the information that you have presented.

Go to **Using Textual Evidence** in the **Writing Studio** for more.

Discuss with a Small Group Share your explanation with other students in a small group. Then discuss the following questions.

- ❑ How well does each explanation meet the criteria listed above?
- ❑ Which examples provide the strongest evidence? Why?
- ❑ What suggestions would improve the explanation?
- ❑ Have you listened closely and respectfully to all ideas?

Go to **Participating in Collaborative Discussions** in the **Speaking and Listening Studio** for help.

RESPOND TO THE ESSENTIAL QUESTION

? What helps people rise up to face difficulties?

Gather Information Review your annotations and notes on "The Flight of Icarus." Then, add relevant details to your Response Log. As you determine which information to include, think about:

- what kinds of difficulties people face
- what motivates people to want to rise above their difficulties
- what it means to overcome difficulties successfully

At the end of the unit, use your notes to write an informational essay.

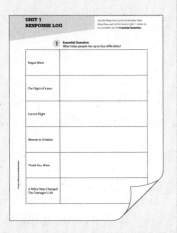

ACADEMIC VOCABULARY

As you write and discuss what you learned from the myth, be sure to use the Academic Vocabulary words. Check off each of the words that you use.

- ❑ **aspect**
- ❑ **cultural**
- ❑ **evaluate**
- ❑ **resource**
- ❑ **text**

RESPOND

CRITICAL VOCABULARY

WORD BANK
moderate
prowess
frantic
anxiety

Practice and Apply Circle the letter of the better answer to each question. Be prepared to explain your response.

1. Which of the following is an example of **moderate** behavior?
   a. yelling at a parent about a disagreement
   b. explaining the cause of a disagreement to a friend

2. Which of the following is more likely to cause **anxiety**?
   a. winning first prize in a contest or game
   b. not having a way to leave a bad situation

3. Which of the following involves **prowess**?
   a. the ability to accept failure when challenged
   b. the ability to solve a difficult problem successfully

4. Which of the following is an example of **frantic** behavior?
   a. a group of people running away from an out-of-control vehicle
   b. a crowd of sports fans cheering about a strong showing on the field

VOCABULARY STRATEGY: Latin Roots

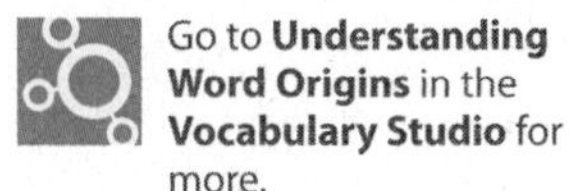

Go to **Understanding Word Origins** in the **Vocabulary Studio** for more.

A **root** is a word part that came into English from an older language such as ancient Latin. Roots can help you figure out the meanings of some unfamiliar words. In paragraph 5, Daedalus tells Icarus "to listen carefully to my *instructions*." The Latin root *struct* means "to build or create a pile." *Instructions* means "a set [pile] of directions telling someone what to do."

Practice and Apply In your own words, write the meaning of the boldface word in each sentence that uses the Latin root *struct*. You may use print or online resources to check your answers.

1. The astronomer's presentation was **instructive** to all of us.

   ____

2. The ocean waves caused widespread **destruction** in the area.

   ____

3. The new labyrinth, a magnificent **structure** made of wood and stone, cost a great deal to build.

   ____

4. The historic building had been damaged during a conflict, but it was **reconstructed** within a decade.

   ____

LANGUAGE CONVENTIONS: Commas and Coordinate Adjectives

Writers often include **coordinate adjectives** to make their descriptions more interesting and precise. In "The Flight of Icarus," the author occasionally includes coordinate adjectives.

In the two examples below, note that both adjectives appear before the noun that they describe. They have distinct meanings, but they have an equal effect in describing the noun.

one clear, wind-swept morning
the slow, graceful sweep of their wings

The fact that two adjectives appear just before a noun doesn't necessarily mean they are coordinate adjectives. In this example, dark modifies wild sea. The adjectives do not have an equal effect, so no comma is needed.

the dark wild sea

Do you need a comma? You can test by substituting the word *and* for the comma and by switching the order of the adjectives. If the new phrase makes sense, then the words are very likely coordinate adjectives, and a comma is needed.

the slow and graceful sweep of their wings
the graceful and slow sweep of their wings

Practice and Apply Write your own sentences using coordinate adjectives. Your sentences may be based on the selection or another myth you know. When you have finished, share your sentences with a partner and compare your use of coordinate adjectives.

Go to **Commas in Conventional Situations** in the **Grammar Studio** to learn more.

ICARUS'S FLIGHT

Poem by **Stephen Dobyns**

? ***ESSENTIAL QUESTION:***

What helps people rise up to face difficulties?

QUICK START

The poem you are about to read explores the myth of Icarus flying toward the sun and the thoughts that may have run through his head as he fell to earth. What is it about an unfortunate incident that causes people to want to review it in their minds and question what happened? List reasons why you think people review such events in this way. Is it better to think about these events, or to forget them?

ANALYZE FORM IN POETRY

Poetry is a type of literature in which words are carefully chosen to create certain effects. A poem's **form** is its structure, which includes the way its words and lines are arranged. This is linked to its meaning, which makes the poem's form important to its message. Here are some elements of form in poetry:

- The **line** is the main unit of all poems. The poet's thoughts can flow from one line to another. Poets also play with line length and words to establish meaning and to create rhythm.
- **Rhythm** is a pattern of stressed and unstressed syllables in a line of poetry, similar to the rhythmic beats in music. A repeated pattern of rhythm is called **meter.** The meter of a poem emphasizes the musical quality of a poem.
- Another element of poetry is the way the lines are presented in groups, called **stanzas**. It is important to pay attention to how lines are presented within a stanza and how punctuation may be used within and across stanzas.

Crafting a poem's form includes choices of words, rhythms, and sounds. Like songs, poems are meant to be heard. **Sound devices** are the use of certain words for their connection to the sense of hearing. Poets often choose different words for their sounds. **Alliteration** is a the repetition of consonant sounds at the beginning of words. It can establish rhythms in a poem that emphasize ideas and images.

Read aloud the following lines from "Icarus's Flight." Listen for the alliterative sounds. What do the repeated sounds suggest to you? How do they create rhythm and add emphasis to ideas or images in text?

> **from petal to petal within some garden**
> **forever? As a result, flight for him was not**
> **upward escape, but descent, with his wings**
> **disintegrating around him. Should it matter**

Notice how the alliterative words of *descent* and *disintegrating* emphasize similar sounds and create a sense of falling downward. As you read "Icarus's Flight," make notes about how the form, rhythm, and alliteration give you a better sense of the feeling the poet intended.

GENRE ELEMENTS: POETRY

- includes many forms, such as sonnets, haikus, and limericks
- conveys a poet's meaning through carefully selected words and structure (stanzas, line length, punctuation)
- uses imagery and a variety of sound devices and types of figurative language to express emotions and ideas

GET READY

ANALYZE PUNCTUATION AND TONE

Poets use structure and poetic elements to create mood and reinforce meaning. A key element of poetry is **tone**, or the writer's attitude toward his or her subject. Tone can convey emotions that suggest how readers should react to the poem. Poets also use certain kinds of **punctuation** to show tone. In "Icarus's Flight," the tone is shown through questions asked by the author to show his thoughts about Icarus's fall. The poet wonders if Icarus was aware of the consequences of his disobedience.

Read aloud the following lines from "Icarus's Flight." Notice how the punctuation helps you understand the tone.

> disintegrating around him. Should it matter
>
> that neither shepherd nor farmer with his plow
> watched him fall? He now had his answer,
> laws to uphold him in his downward plunge.

Pay attention to details as you dig deeper into the poem. Use text clues and punctuation to determine the poet's attitude and to analyze how the poet's meaning is developed.

ANNOTATION MODEL

NOTICE & NOTE

As you read, consider how the poem's punctuation helps to convey tone and emotion. You can also make notes about the poem's structure. This model shows one reader's notes about the first few lines of "Icarus's Flight."

> What else could the boy have done? Wasn't
> flight both an escape and a great uplifting?
> And so he flew. But how could he appreciate
> his freedom without knowing the exact point
> where freedom stopped? So he flew upward
> and the sun dissolved the wax and he fell.
> But at last in his anticipated plummeting
> he grasped the confines of what had been

The poem uses questions to justify Icarus's actions.

This question isn't answered here. Maybe I'll find the answer in a later stanza of the poem.

BACKGROUND

Writers have been fascinated by the characters of myths for centuries. They have featured famous mythic characters in such forms as dramas, stories, and poetry. "Icarus's Flight" reflects the poet's fascination with the myth of Icarus, the son of Daedalus, who flew too close to the sun. The author of "Icarus's Flight," **Stephen Dobyns** *(b. 1941), is the author of popular works of fiction, but he considers himself primarily a poet.*

ICARUS'S FLIGHT

Poem by Stephen Dobyns

SETTING A PURPOSE

As you read this poem, think about the way the poet portrays Icarus and his true intention.

What else could the boy have done? Wasn't
flight both an escape and a great uplifting?
And so he flew. But how could he appreciate
his freedom without knowing the exact point

Notice & Note

Use the side margins to notice and note signposts in the text.

ANALYZE PUNCTUATION AND TONE

Annotate: Underline the instances where the poet asks questions.

Infer: Based on the questions asked, what can you determine about the author's opinion of Icarus?

NOTICE & NOTE

ANALYZE FORM

Annotate: Mark where the sentences in lines 5–8 begin and end.

Infer: What does the poet achieve by allowing ideas in the form of questions and sentences to flow from one stanza to the next?

where freedom stopped? So he flew upward
and the sun dissolved the wax and he fell.
But at last in his anticipated plummeting
he grasped the confines of what had been

his liberty. You say he flew too far?
He flew just far enough. He flew precisely
to the point of wisdom. Would it
have been better to flutter ignorantly

from petal to petal within some garden
forever? As a result, flight for him was not
upward escape, but descent, with his wings
disintegrating around him. Should it matter

that neither shepherd nor farmer with his plow
watched him fall? He now had his answer,
laws to uphold him in his downward plunge.
Cushion enough for what he wanted.

CHECK YOUR UNDERSTANDING

Answer these questions before moving on to the **Analyze the Text** section on the following page.

1 Why does the author ask questions in "Icarus's Flight"?

- **A** To offer insight into his opinion of Icarus's actions
- **B** To express that he understands Icarus
- **C** To show that Icarus never acknowledged his mistake
- **D** To prove that Icarus was reckless in his actions

2 What does the author argue about Icarus?

- **F** His decision to fly toward the sun was ignorant.
- **G** He deserved to fall from the sky.
- **H** Daedalus should have kept a closer eye on him.
- **J** Icarus was aware of the consequences of his flight.

3 In the sentences He flew just far enough. He flew precisely to the point of wisdom., what tone does the poet express?

- **A** Irritation
- **B** Surprise
- **C** Disappointment
- **D** Admiration

ANALYZE THE TEXT

Support your responses with evidence from the text. NOTEBOOK

1. **Identify** Look closely at how certain sentences of "Icarus's Flight" extend from one stanza into the next one. What effect is created by extending a sentence into the next line or the next stanza?
2. **Analyze** Examine the questions in lines 1–2. What is the purpose of these questions in the poem? What do they show about Dobyns's beliefs about Icarus?
3. **Analyze** Look at the last stanza in "Icarus's Flight." What tone is conveyed here, and how does the poet achieve it?
4. **Interpret** In poems, the speaker is the voice that expresses feelings and emotions. The speaker in "Icarus's Flight" uses the poem to show opinions of Icarus. What do lines 10–11 show about the speaker's attitude towards Icarus?
5. **Compare** Consider what you already knew about the mythological character of Icarus before reading this poem. How does this poem cause your perception of Icarus to change? Explain.

RESEARCH

RESEARCH TIP
When you are looking for specific information about the works of an author or publisher, make sure that you check the resources at the author's or publisher's official website.

Research other poems about the myth of Daedalus and Icarus. Discover what themes or other details are common across these poems. Record what you learn in the chart.

POEMS	THEMES

Extend Find another poem by Stephen Dobyns. Compare the form of the poem with "Icarus's Flight" and the poems you researched. Discuss with your partner what effects the forms of the poems create and what emotions the poems make you feel.

CREATE AND CRITIQUE

Write a Poem Write a poem in which an observer comments on witnessing a compelling event.

- ❑ Decide whether you want your poem to be humorous or serious.
- ❑ Choose examples of situations that create the most vivid picture in your mind or evoke the strongest feelings.
- ❑ Focus on form, punctuation, and rhythm to emphasize the meaning of the poem and express a tone about the subject.

Go to **Writing as a Process** in the **Writing Studio** to learn more.

Critique a Poem Orally Review "Icarus's Flight" and think about its conversational tone. Then work with a partner to read the poem aloud and analyze the content.

- ❑ Take turns reading the poem aloud.
- ❑ As your partner reads, take notes on the questions the poet asks throughout the poem. What is the purpose of these questions? Can you relate to Icarus's struggle and goals?
- ❑ With your partner, review your notes and think about the questions and the views the poet presents. Be sure to come up with examples to support your views.
- ❑ Share your views with the class in an oral critique. Make sure your points are clear and convincing.

Go to **Analyzing and Evaluating Presentations** in the **Speaking and Listening Studio** for more help.

RESPOND TO THE ESSENTIAL QUESTION

What helps people rise up to face difficulties?

Gather Information Review your annotations and notes on "Icarus's Flight." Then, add relevant details to your Response Log. As you determine which information to include, think about:

- how poets use form and punctuation to create meaning and express tone
- the use of questions to show Stephen Dobyns's opinion of Icarus's actions

UNIT 1 RESPONSE LOG

Essential Question: What helps people rise up to face difficulties?

Rogue Wave	
The Flight of Icarus	
Icarus's Flight	
Women in Aviation	
Thank You, M'am	
A Police Stop Changed This Teenager's Life	

At the end of the unit, use your notes to help you write an informational essay.

ACADEMIC VOCABULARY

As you write and discuss what you learned from the poem, be sure to use the Academic Vocabulary words. Check off each of the words that you use.

- ❑ **aspect**
- ❑ **cultural**
- ❑ **evaluate**
- ❑ **resource**
- ❑ **text**

WOMEN IN AVIATION

History Writing by **Patricia and Fredrick McKissack**

? ***ESSENTIAL QUESTION:***

What helps people rise up to face difficulties?

QUICK START

Make a web of the traits that you think can help a person who is pursuing a dream. Discuss your choices with the class.

DETERMINE AUTHOR'S PURPOSE

An **author's purpose** is the reason the author wrote a work. Usually an author writes for one or more purposes, as shown in this chart.

AUTHOR'S PURPOSE	EXAMPLES OF WRITTEN WORKS
To inform or explain	encyclopedia entries, informational articles, how-to articles, biographies
To persuade	editorials, opinion essays and blogs, advertisements
To entertain	short stories, novels, plays, humorous essays
To express thoughts or feelings	poems, personal essays, journals

To determine an author's purpose, consider how the details and evidence in a text fit together to lead to a main idea or message for readers. Consider, too, how you feel about the topic (for example, informed, entertained, or challenged) after reading the text.

GENRE ELEMENTS: INFORMATIONAL TEXT

- provides factual information
- presents evidence to support ideas
- includes biographies, news articles, how-to instructions, and many other forms
- may focus on historical events or trends

CITE EVIDENCE AND EVALUATE DETAILS

After reading informational text, you will often be asked to **cite evidence** to support your own ideas. Before you can do that, you must first **evaluate details**—make judgments about the facts, quotations, examples, and other details in the text. In order to evaluate details, ask: How do these details support the author's purpose and main idea or message of the selection? Next, consider your own knowledge about or experience with the topic. Based on your evaluation of the details, cite the evidence that best supports your ideas.

If you were asked whether women were pioneers in aviation, you might evaluate details from paragraph 2 of the selection, which is about women who piloted hot-air balloons in the early 1800s. Even if you have never piloted a hot-air ballon yourself, you may know that it takes great skill and courage. Now, you could cite evidence to support the idea that women were pioneers in aviation in the early 1800s.

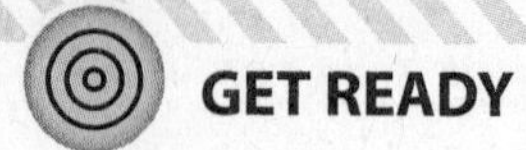

GET READY

CRITICAL VOCABULARY

inundate **restrictive** **exhibition** **precaution**

To see how many Critical Vocabulary words you already know, use them to complete the sentences.

1. The pilot's photographs appeared in a(n) __________ at the library.
2. A 20-pound weight limit for suitcases seems a little __________.
3. Airline passengers must take the __________ of wearing seatbelts.
4. The hurricane may __________ the coast with a heavy storm surge.

LANGUAGE CONVENTIONS

Consistent Verb Tenses In this lesson, you will learn about the importance of using the correct verb tense to clarify meaning and of using a single tense unless you have a good reason to switch:

[Coleman's] mother, who had been a slave, . . . encouraged all of her children to attend school in order to better themselves.

Encouraged is in the past tense; *had been* is in the past perfect tense. The switch shows that the mother's time as a slave came earlier. As you read "Women in Aviation," note how the authors consistently use the past tense and switch only when necessary to make the meaning clear.

ANNOTATION MODEL

NOTICE & NOTE

As you read, note clues about the authors' purpose in writing. You can also mark up evidence and note how you are evaluating it. In the model, you can see one reader's notes about "Women in Aviation."

2 The story of women in aviation actually goes back to the time of the hot-air balloons. A number of women in Europe and America gained fame for their skill and daring. Sophie Blanchard made her first solo balloon flight in 1805. She grew in fame and was eventually named official aeronaut of the empire by Napoleon. By 1834, at least twenty women in Europe were piloting their own balloons.

aviation came before airplanes

women aviators of the era

These details support the idea that women flew long before there were airplanes.

BACKGROUND

In the early 1900s, flying in "aeroplanes"—fixed-winged, self-propelled flying machines—was a bold undertaking. Male pilots were dashing heroes. However, female aviators—especially African American women—had to struggle for acceptance. **Patricia and Fredrick McKissack** *(1944–2017; 1939–2013) wrote more than 100 biographies and other nonfiction books, most focusing on the achievements of African Americans.*

WOMEN IN AVIATION

History Writing by Patricia and Fredrick McKissack

SETTING A PURPOSE

As you read, pay attention to the details that describe what it was like for a woman to become a pilot during the early 1900s. What obstacles did each pilot face? Write down any questions you have while reading.

1 American aviation was from its very beginnings marred with sexist and racist assumptions. It was taken for granted that women were generally inferior to men and that white men were superior to all others. Flying, it was said, required a level of skill and courage that women and blacks lacked. Yet despite these prevailing prejudices, the dream and the desire to fly stayed alive among women and African-Americans.

2 The story of women in aviation actually goes back to the time of the hot-air balloons. A number of women in Europe and America gained fame for their skill and daring. Sophie Blanchard made her first solo balloon flight in 1805. She grew in fame and was eventually named official aeronaut of the empire by Napoleon. By 1834, at least twenty women in Europe were piloting their own balloons.

Notice & Note

Use the side margins to notice and note signposts in the text.

DETERMINE AUTHORS' PURPOSE

Annotate: Mark groups of words in paragraph 1 that signal details about the topic—women in aviation.

Draw Conclusions: Based on these details, what seems to be the authors' purpose in writing "Women in Aviation"? Be specific.

NOTICE & NOTE

QUOTED WORDS

Notice & Note: In paragraph 3, mark the comment that Orville Wright made about Katherine, his sister.

Compare: How is his attitude different from the attitude described in paragraph 1?

3 Though she did not fly, Katherine Wright was a major supporter of her brothers' efforts. Orville so appreciated his sister's help that he said, "When the world speaks of the Wrights, it must include my sister. . . . She inspired much of our effort."

4 Although Raymonde de la Roche of France was the first woman in the world to earn her pilot's license, Harriet Quimby held the distinction of being the first American woman to become a licensed pilot.

5 On August 1, 1911, Quimby, who was described as a "real beauty" with "haunting blue-green eyes," strolled off the field after passing her pilot's test easily. To the male reporters who **inundated** her with questions, Quimby fired back answers with self-confidence. Walking past a group of women who had come to witness the historic event, Quimby was overheard to quip with a smile and a wink: "Flying is easier than voting." (The Woman's Suffrage Amendment wasn't passed until 1920.)

inundate
(ĭn´ŭn-dāt´) *v.* To *inundate* is to overpower with a huge amount of something.

6 As difficult as it was for women to become pilots in significant numbers, it was doubly hard for African-Americans, especially black women. That's why Bessie Coleman, the first African-American to earn her pilot's license, is such an exciting and important figure in aviation.

7 Bessie Coleman was born in 1893 in Atlanta, Texas, the twelfth of thirteen children. Her mother, who had been a slave, valued education and encouraged all of her children to attend school in order to better themselves. The encouragement paid off, because Coleman graduated from high school, a feat not too many black women were able to accomplish in the early 1900s.

CITE EVIDENCE AND EVALUATE DETAILS

Annotate: Mark the information in paragraphs 8 and 9 that reveal a major change in Coleman's thinking.

Evaluate: How effective are these text details in explaining why Bessie Coleman decided to become a pilot?

8 Bessie Coleman refused to accept the limitations others tried to place on her. She attended an Oklahoma college for one semester but ran out of money. Accepting the offer of one of her brothers to come live with him and his family in Chicago, Coleman found a job as a manicurist. She fully intended to return to school after saving enough money. But she never did. While in Chicago she learned about flying and made a new set of goals for herself. She wanted to be a pilot.

9 Coleman learned about flying from reading newspaper accounts of air battles during World War I. She tried to find a school that would accept her as a trainee. But no American instructor or flying school was willing to teach her.

10 When the war ended, a friend, Robert S. Abbott, the founder of the *Chicago Defender*, one of the most popular

The image above shows Bessie Coleman's pilot's license. Regarded as the world's first female African American aviator, Bessie receives a bouquet at an appearance at Curtiss Field in Garden City, Long Island.

black-owned and -operated newspapers in the country, suggested that Coleman go to France, where racial prejudice was not as **restrictive** as it was in America. Even though the United States was the birthplace of flight, it was slower than other countries to develop an organized aviation program. European leaders immediately saw the commercial and military advantages of a strong national aviation program. Bessie knew from her reading that both French and German aircraft were among the best in the world.

restrictive
(rĭ-strĭk´tĭv) *adj.* When something is *restrictive*, it is limiting in some way.

NOTICE & NOTE

CITE EVIDENCE AND EVALUATE DETAILS

Annotate: In paragraph 11, mark details that describe Coleman's dream at this point in her life. Then, in paragraph 12, mark her plans for making that dream a reality.

Draw Conclusions: Based on this evidence, what can you conclude about Coleman and her dream? Which text detail would you cite as being most important to your conclusion?

DETERMINE AUTHORS' PURPOSE

Annotate: Underline the problem that the authors introduce in paragraph 14. Then circle the way that Coleman tried to solve it.

Critique: Are these facts effective in supporting the authors' purpose? Explain.

exhibition
(ĕk´sə-bĭsh´ən) *n.* An *exhibition* is an organized presentation or show.

11 Coleman had also read about Eugene Jacques Bullard, the well-decorated[1] and highly honored native of Georgia who had become the first African-American to fly an airplane in combat as a member of the French Lafayette Flying Corps during World War I. Other blacks had gone to Europe to get their training, too. Coleman realized that if she were ever going to get a chance to fly, she, too, would have to go to France. But she didn't have any money to get there, and besides, she couldn't speak a word of French.

12 For almost two years, Coleman worked part-time as a manicurist and as a server in a Chicago chili parlor and saved every penny to finance her trip to France. Meanwhile she learned to speak French, so when the time came, she'd be able to understand her instructors.

13 In 1921, Coleman made it to France, where she found an instructor who was one of Tony Fokker's chief pilots. Fokker, the famous aircraft manufacturer, said Coleman was a "natural talent." On June 15, 1921, Coleman made history by becoming the first black woman to earn her wings, thus joining the ranks of the handful of American women fliers.

14 Returning to the United States determined to start a flying school where other African-American pilots could be trained, Coleman looked for ways to finance her dream. There were very few jobs in the aviation industry for women or blacks. She soon learned that there was little or no support for a black woman who wanted to start a flying school. To call attention to aviation and to encourage other women and African-Americans to take part in the new and growing field, Coleman gave flying **exhibitions** and lectured on aviation. She thrilled audiences with daredevil maneuvers, just as Quimby had done before her.

15 Along with racism, Coleman encountered the burden of sexism, but she made believers out of those who doubted her skill. "The color of my skin," she said, "[was] a drawback at first. . . . I was a curiosity, but soon the public discovered I could really fly. Then they came to see *Brave Bessie*, as they called me."

[1] **well-decorated:** term used to describe a person in the military who has received many awards.

16 The strict rules and regulations that govern aviation today didn't exist during the first three decades of flying. For example, it wasn't uncommon for aviators to ignore safety belts and fly without parachutes. One of these simple safety **precautions** might have saved the lives of both Harriet Quimby and Bessie Coleman.

precaution (prĭ-kô´shən) *n.* A *precaution* is an action taken to avoid possible danger.

In 1912, Harriet Quimby (shown holding the propeller to start the engine of her monoplane) became the first woman to fly across the English Channel.

17 On a July morning in 1912, Quimby, and a passenger named William P. Willard, set out to break an over-water speed record. When Quimby climbed to five thousand feet, the French-made Blériot monoplane[2] suddenly nosed down. Both Quimby and Willard were thrown from the plane and plunged to their deaths in the Boston Harbor.

18 The *New York Sun* used the opportunity to speak out against women fliers:

> Miss Quimby is the fifth woman in the world killed while operating an aeroplane (three were students) and their number thus far is five too many. The sport is not one for which women are physically qualified. As a rule they lack strength and presence of mind and the courage to excel as aviators. It is essentially a man's sport and pastime.

LANGUAGE CONVENTIONS

Annotate: Mark the present-tense verbs in this quotation from the *New York Sun*.

Critique: We usually use past-tense verbs to talk about past events. Why is the present tense appropriate here?

19 Fourteen years later, Bessie Coleman died in a similar accident. With almost enough savings to start her school, Coleman agreed to do an air show in Florida on May Day for the Negro Welfare League of Jacksonville. At 7:30 P.M. the night before, Coleman, accompanied by her publicity agent, William Wills, took her plane up for a test flight. When she reached an altitude of about five thousand feet, her plane flipped over. Coleman was thrown from the plane and plunged to her death April 30, 1926. Wills died seconds later when the plane crashed.

20 Once again critics used the tragedy to assert that neither women nor blacks were mentally or physically able to be good pilots. "Women are often penalized by publicity for their every mishap," said Amelia Earhart, the most famous female pilot in aviation history. "The result is that such emphasis sometimes directly affects [a woman's] chances for a flying job," Earhart continued. "I had one manufacturer tell me that he couldn't risk hiring women pilots because of the way accidents, even minor ones, became headlines in the newspapers."

DETERMINE AUTHORS' PURPOSE

Annotate: Mark the text that gives the name and description of the person whom the authors quote in paragraph 20.

Connect: What purpose does this quotation serve in the paragraph? How does it relate to the overall purpose of the selection?

21 Although Bessie Coleman died tragically, her plans to open a flight training school for blacks were continued by those she had inspired.

[2] **monoplane:** an airplane with only one pair of wings.

CHECK YOUR UNDERSTANDING

Answer these questions before moving on to the **Analyze the Text** section on the following page.

1 The authors include information about women hot-air balloonists in order to —

A prove that women tend to avoid careers in aviation

B give examples that help readers know what an "aeronaut" is

C explain that women have been interested in aviation for a long time

D entertain readers with amusing stories about women who inspired pilots

2 Which fact from the selection most clearly explains why Harriet Quimby and Bessie Coleman died?

F Both pilots performed daredevil maneuvers in the air.

G They did not take safety precautions that are standard today.

H Their planes suddenly malfunctioned during test flights.

J Both women were victims of racial and gender prejudice.

3 The authors' main purpose for ending the selection by mentioning Bessie Coleman's flight training school is to —

A show one effect of her inspiring example

B remind readers that she died doing something she loved

C explain how women today learn to become pilots

D persuade readers to consider a career in aviation

ANALYZE THE TEXT

Support your responses with evidence from the text. NOTEBOOK

1. **Interpret** Reread paragraph 5. What impression of Harriet Quimby do the authors create by using facts and quotations?
2. **Cite Evidence** Reread paragraphs 11 and 12. Based on your evaluation of the text details in these paragraphs, what conclusion can you draw about Bessie Coleman's personality? Fill out a chart like this one to show support for your conclusion.

TEXTUAL EVIDENCE	MY EXPERIENCE	CONCLUSION

3. **Compare** In what ways were Harriet Quimby and Bessie Coleman probably most alike? Explain.
4. **Evaluate** Do you think the authors presented Bessie Coleman's life in an overly positive way? Why or why not?
5. **Notice & Note** Think about Harriet Quimby's statement, "Flying is easier than voting." What situation does her comment highlight? How does the quote help the authors achieve their purpose?

RESEARCH

RESEARCH TIP
The best search terms are very specific. Along with the person's name, you will want to include a word such as *aviator* or *achievements* to make sure that you get the information you need.

Bessie Coleman is the main focus of "Women in Aviation," but other female aviators are mentioned in the text. Do some in-depth research into the achievements and importance of one of these aviators. Use question words such as *who, what, why,* and *how* to form questions. In the chart below, record what you learned in your research.

QUESTION	ANSWER

Connect Consider how the aviator you chose seems similar to Bessie Coleman. Compare your thoughts with those of a classmate who chose another aviator. What conclusions can you draw about these aviators?

CREATE AND DISCUSS

Write an Informational Essay Write a three- to four-paragraph essay in which you present research on a female aviator other than Bessie Coleman—either one mentioned in the selection or someone else.

- ❑ Review the information you gathered in the Research activity, or conduct research on another female aviator.
- ❑ Write an introduction in which you introduce the topic and express your controlling idea about the aviator you chose.
- ❑ Then, provide information about this aviator's life and work. Be specific with your facts, details, and examples. Arrange information in a way that makes sense (perhaps chronological order) and remember to use transitions to connect ideas.
- ❑ In your final paragraph, sum up the aviator's achievements.

Go to **Writing Informative Texts** in the **Writing Studio** to learn more.

Discuss with a Small Group Have a meaningful discussion about how information in "Women in Aviation" helps readers understand the challenges faced by women in the early 20th century as they struggled to gain acceptance in male-dominated fields.

- ❑ As a group, review the text and decide which information is relevant to the discussion topic.
- ❑ Have the group prepare ideas and details that relate to the topic.
- ❑ Review the ideas and decide which can help someone overcome obstacles. Listen closely and respectfully to all ideas. Provide constructive feedback and accept the feedback you receive.

Go to **Participating in Collaborative Discussions** in the **Speaking and Listening Studio** for more.

RESPOND TO THE ESSENTIAL QUESTION

What helps people rise up to face difficulties?

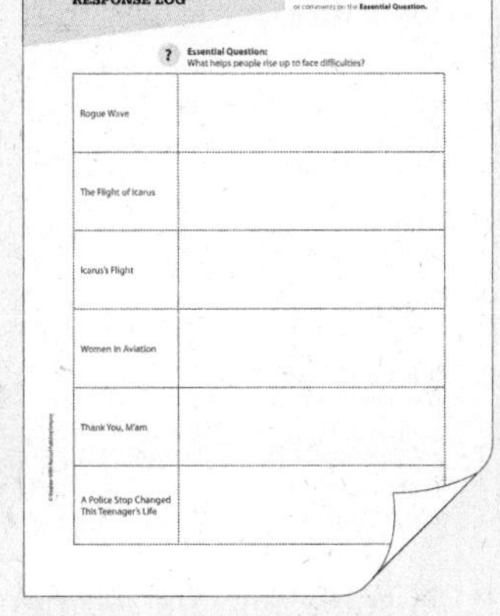

UNIT 1 RESPONSE LOG

Use this Response Log to record your ideas about how each of the texts in Unit 1 relates to or comments on the **Essential Question.**

? **Essential Question:** What helps people rise up to face difficulties?

Rogue Wave	
The Flight of Icarus	
Icarus's Flight	
Women in Aviation	
Thank You, M'am	
A Police Stop Changed This Teenager's Life	

Gather Information Review your annotations and notes on "Women in Aviation." Then, add relevant details to your Response Log. As you determine which information to include, think about:

- the attitudes that keep people from pursuing their dreams
- the traits that help people pursue a dream and overcome challenges

At the end of the unit, use your notes to write an informational essay.

ACADEMIC VOCABULARY

As you write and discuss what you learned from the informational text, be sure to use the Academic Vocabulary words. Check off each of the words that you use.

- ❑ **aspect**
- ❑ **cultural**
- ❑ **evaluate**
- ❑ **resource**
- ❑ **text**

RESPOND

CRITICAL VOCABULARY

WORD BANK
inundate
restrictive
exhibition
precaution

Practice and Apply Mark the letter of the situation that better shows the meaning of the Critical Vocabulary word. Explain your choice.

1. **inundate**
   a. More than 400 people came to the airshow.
   b. One or two visitors came to the museum.

2. **restrictive**
   a. The gate at the airport is locked at six o'clock.
   b. The gate at the airport has a rusty lock.

3. **exhibition**
   a. A crowd gathered at a school to hear an astronaut speak.
   b. The crowd watched a kite-making demonstration.

4. **precaution**
   a. The state lets people apply for licenses online.
   b. The government requires pilots to follow safety checks.

VOCABULARY STRATEGY: Connotations and Denotations

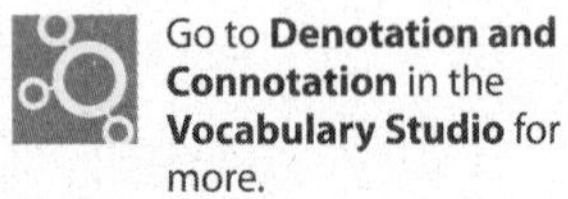

Go to **Denotation and Connotation** in the **Vocabulary Studio** for more.

A word's **denotation** is its literal, "dictionary" meaning. A word's **connotation** comes from the ideas and feelings, either positive or negative, associated with the word. For example, the authors of "Women in Aviation" state that Harriet Quimby "strolled off the field." The denotation of *strolled* is "took an unhurried walk," but the connotation suggests that Quimby was relaxed and assured.

Practice and Apply In each of the following sentences, the words in parentheses have similar denotations. Complete each sentence with the word that has the strongest positive or negative connotation.

1. Bessie Coleman refused to give up because she was (**serious, determined**) __________.
2. Early pilots sometimes performed (**foolhardy, risky**) __________ stunts—stunts that proved to be fatal.
3. Despite barriers, women pilots (**pursued, followed**) __________ their dreams.
4. Coleman died as a pioneer, but she has been a great (**help, inspiration**) __________ to the generations that came after her.

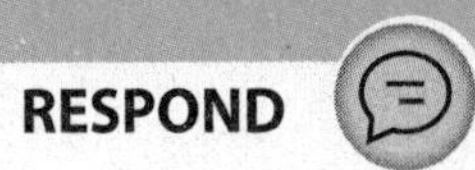

LANGUAGE CONVENTIONS: Consistent Verb Tenses

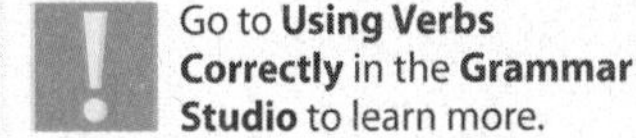
Go to **Using Verbs Correctly** in the **Grammar Studio** to learn more.

The **tense** of a verb indicates the time of an action or a state of being. An action or state of being can occur in the present, the past, or the future—or at times "in between" (the "perfect" tenses). Notice some of the ways that tenses are used in "Women in Aviation."

- **Present tense** is used to make general statements that are true now:

  The story of women in aviation actually goes back to the time of the hot-air balloons.

- **Past tense** is used to provide information about events in the past:

  . . . Coleman gave flying exhibitions and lectured on aviation.

- **Past perfect tense** is used to show that certain events happened before other events in the past.

  [Coleman] thrilled audiences with daredevil maneuvers, just as Quimby had done before her.

Usually, it's important to be consistent, but you sometimes need to change tenses to be clear, as you can see in the third example above.

INCORRECT: While in Chicago she **learned** about flying and **makes** a new set of goals for herself. [mix of past tense and present tense]

CORRECT: While in Chicago she **learned** about flying and **made** a new set of goals for herself. [consistent past tense]

Practice and Apply Rewrite these sentences so that the tenses are correct and consistent. Shift tenses only if necessary to make the meaning clear.

1. In the 1920s, stunt pilots called "barnstormers" attract crowds around the United States.

   ____

2. Their colorful name comes from the fact that barnstormers often perform their air shows at rural farms.

   ____

3. Some fliers were military pilots before they took up barnstorming.

   ____

4. People from small towns gasped in amazement as barnstormers dove, looped-the-loop, and even fly upside-down.

   ____

SHORT STORY

THANK YOU, M'AM

by **Langston Hughes**

pages 61–65

COMPARE ACROSS GENRES

As you read, notice how the ideas in both texts relate to your own experiences, as well as how they relate to the experiences of other teens. Then, look for ways that the ideas in the two texts relate to each other. After you read both selections, you will collaborate with a small group on a final project.

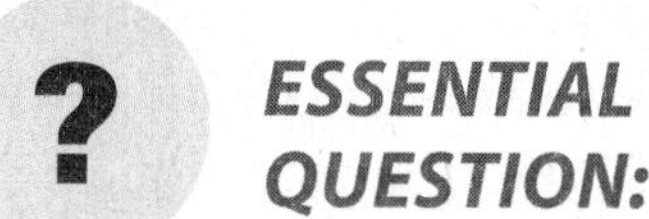

ESSENTIAL QUESTION:

What helps people rise up to face difficulties?

ARTICLE

A POLICE STOP CHANGED THIS TEENAGER'S LIFE

by **Amy B Wang**

pages 73–77

Thank You, M'am

QUICK START

Make a list of the people who have encouraged you in the past. Think about what you were able to do as a result of this support.

ANALYZE CHARACTERS' QUALITIES

The characters in a short story are the people, animals, or imaginary creatures that take part in the action. **Characterization** is the way that the author develops the characters by

- making comments about the character through the voice of the narrator
- describing the character's physical appearance
- presenting the character's speech, thoughts, and actions
- conveying ideas through the character's speech, thought, and actions

An author uses these methods of characterization to help readers identify **character traits,** which are the qualities of appearance and personality that make a character seem real. As you read "Thank You, M'am," analyze how the characters' traits influence events and affect the resolution of conflict by thinking about the characters' words, actions, thoughts, appearance, and interactions with other characters.

GENRE ELEMENTS: SHORT STORY

- short work of fiction
- centered around a single idea
- usually has one main conflict
- character interactions with the conflict keep the story moving

ANALYZE SETTING AND CONFLICT

The plot of a story centers on conflict, or the struggle between opposing forces. An **external conflict** is a character's struggle against an outside force, while an **internal conflict** takes place inside the character. Stories can have more than one type of conflict. Often the plot of a story is influenced by the setting, or the time and place of the action. As you read "Thank You, M'am," use a chart like this to analyze how setting and conflict affect the ending of the story.

<table>
<tr><td>Setting:</td><td>Where:</td><td>When:</td></tr>
<tr><td colspan="2">Major Characters:</td><td>Minor Characters:</td></tr>
<tr><td>Problem/Conflict:</td><td colspan="2">Events: (List important events in story.)</td></tr>
<tr><td colspan="3">Outcome/Resolution:</td></tr>
</table>

GET READY

CRITICAL VOCABULARY

suede **mistrust** **embarrass** **latch** **barren**

To preview the Critical Vocabulary words, complete each sentence with a word from the list.

1. Sometimes a person may feel self-conscious, or __________.
2. The shoes were __________, which is soft and fuzzy leather.
3. When someone __________ on to you, it's hard to free yourself.
4. It is easy to __________ a person who has done you harm.
5. An empty room looks uninteresting, or __________.

LANGUAGE CONVENTIONS

Capitalization In this lesson, you will learn about the use of capital letters for the first words of sentences and quotations. Proper nouns, such as names and titles, and time periods, such as days and months (but not seasons), are also capitalized. As you read the selection, note the author's use of capitalization and think about how you use correct capitalization in your own writing.

ANNOTATION MODEL

NOTICE & NOTE 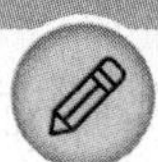

As you read, note the author's use of characterization to create realistic characters and move the plot along. You can also mark up details about the setting and conflict. In the model, you can see one reader's notes about "Thank You, M'am."

1 She was a large woman with a large purse that had everything in it but hammer and nails. It had a long strap and she carried it slung across her shoulder. It was about eleven o'clock at night, and she was walking alone, when a boy ran up behind her and tried to snatch her purse. . . . But the boy's weight, and the weight of the purse combined caused him to lose his balance so, instead of taking off full blast as he had hoped, the boy fell on his back on the sidewalk, and his legs flew up. The large woman simply turned around and kicked him. . . .

author gives details about the physical appearance of the woman

setting is in evening—it is dark-I wonder how the setting is part of the plot?

The details show the woman is strong and not intimidated.

BACKGROUND

Langston Hughes *(1902–1967) was raised by his grandmother in Lawrence, Kansas. As a child, he began a lifelong exploration of literature and blues music. He went to Columbia University in New York City and eventually was recognized for his talent for writing poems. He went on to write novels, short stories, and plays as well as poems. Hughes's work shows a special understanding of everyday people—people who may not be famous or rich but whose lives are inspiring and valuable nonetheless.*

THANK YOU, M'AM

Short Story by Langston Hughes

PREPARE TO COMPARE

As you read, pay attention to how characters' traits affect events and influence how conflicts are resolved. This will help you compare this short story with the news article "A Police Stop Changed This Teenager's Life."

1 She was a large woman with a large purse that had everything in it but hammer and nails. It had a long strap and she carried it slung across her shoulder. It was about eleven o'clock at night, and she was walking alone, when a boy ran up behind her and tried to snatch her purse. The strap broke with the single tug the boy gave it from behind. But the boy's weight, and the weight of the purse combined caused him to lose his balance so, instead of taking off full blast as he had hoped, the boy fell on his back on the sidewalk, and his legs flew up. The large woman simply turned around and kicked him right square in his blue-jeaned sitter. Then she reached down, picked the boy up by his shirt front, and shook him until his teeth rattled.

Notice & Note

Use the side margins to notice and note signposts in the text.

ANALYZE SETTING AND CONFLICT

Annotate: Review paragraph 1 and mark evidence of the setting of the story.

Analyze: How does the setting influence the woman's external conflict with the boy?

ANALYZE CHARACTER

Annotate: In paragraphs 1–11, mark text details that show that Mrs. Jones is a strong person.

Interpret: What character qualities do these text details tell readers about Mrs. Jones?

NOTICE & NOTE

2 After that the woman said, "Pick up my pocketbook, boy, and give it here."

3 She still held him. But she bent down enough to permit him to stoop and pick up her purse. Then she said, "Now ain't you ashamed of yourself?"

4 Firmly gripped by his shirt front, the boy said, "Yes'm."

5 The woman said, "What did you want to do it for?"

6 The boy said, "I didn't aim to."

7 She said, "You a lie!"

8 By that time two or three people passed, stopped, turned to look, and some stood watching.

9 "If I turn you loose, will you run?" asked the woman.

10 "Yes'm," said the boy.

11 "Then I won't turn you loose," said the woman. She did not release him.

12 "I'm very sorry, lady, I'm sorry," whispered the boy.

13 "Um-hum! And your face is dirty. I got a great mind to wash your face for you. Ain't you got nobody home to tell you to wash your face?"

14 "No'm," said the boy.

15 "Then it will get washed this evening," said the large woman starting up the street, dragging the frightened boy behind her.

16 He looked as if he were fourteen or fifteen, frail and willow-wild, in tennis shoes and blue jeans.

17 The woman said, "You ought to be my son. I would teach you right from wrong. Least I can do right now is to wash your face. Are you hungry?"

18 "No'm," said the being-dragged boy. "I just want you to turn me loose."

19 "Was I bothering *you* when I turned that corner?" asked the woman.

20 "No'm."

21 "But you put yourself in contact with me," said the woman. "If you think that that contact is not going to last awhile, you got another thought coming. When I get through with you, sir, you are going to remember Mrs. Luella Bates Washington Jones."

22 Sweat popped out on the boy's face and he began to struggle. Mrs. Jones stopped, jerked him around in front of her, put a half nelson about his neck, and continued to drag him up the street. When she got to her door, she dragged the boy inside, down a hall, and into a large kitchenette-furnished room at the rear of the house. She switched on the light and left the door open. The boy could hear other roomers laughing and talking in the large house. Some of their doors were open, too,

ANALYZE CHARACTER

Annotate: Review paragraphs 15–21 and mark evidence that Mrs. Jones is explaining how Roger should behave with people.

Analyze: How have the characters' words, actions, and interactions with each other so far affected the events in the story? Would the events be the same with other characters?

LANGUAGE CONVENTIONS

Capitalization is useful in distinguishing titles and people. It can also be used for emphasis. Circle the capital letters in the woman's name in paragraph 21.

Infer: What is the author emphasizing by having the character state her entire name?

so he knew he and the woman were not alone. The woman still had him by the neck in the middle of her room.

23 She said, "What is your name?"

24 "Roger," answered the boy.

25 "Then, Roger, you go to that sink and wash your face," said the woman, whereupon she turned him loose—at last. Roger looked at the door—looked at the woman—looked at the door—*and went to the sink.*

26 "Let the water run until it gets warm," she said. "Here's a clean towel."

27 "You gonna take me to jail?" asked the boy, bending over the sink.

28 "Not with that face, I would not take you nowhere," said the woman. "Here I am trying to get home to cook me a bite to eat and you snatch my pocketbook! Maybe you ain't been to your supper either, late as it be. Have you?"

29 "There's nobody home at my house," said the boy.

30 "Then we'll eat," said the woman. "I believe you're hungry—or been hungry—to try to snatch my pocketbook."

31 "I wanted a pair of blue **suede** shoes," said the boy.

32 "Well, you didn't have to snatch *my* pocketbook to get some suede shoes," said Mrs. Luella Bates Washington Jones, "You could of asked me."

33 "M'am?"

ANALYZE SETTING AND CONFLICT

Annotate: Review paragraph 25 and mark the text that shows that Roger is conflicted about how to behave with Mrs. Jones in this unfamiliar place.

Infer: What does Roger's decision tell you about his internal conflict and his relationship with adults?

suede
(swād) *n. Suede* is leather that is treated to be fuzzy and soft.

ANALYZE CHARACTER

Annotate: In paragraphs 32–35, mark the text that shows that Roger is unsure about what to do and confused by Mrs. Jones's behavior toward him.

Draw Conclusions: Do Mrs. Jones's statements and actions cause Roger to think about what he has done? Why?

NOTICE & NOTE

34 The water dripping from his face, the boy looked at her. There was a long pause. A very long pause. After he had dried his face and not knowing what else to do dried it again, the boy turned around, wondering what next. The door was open. He could make a dash for it down the hall. He could run, run, run, run, *run!*

MEMORY MOMENT

Notice & Note: What is the woman telling the boy about her past?

Analyze: How does this help you understand how the woman is treating the boy?

35 The woman was sitting on the day-bed.[1] After awhile she said, "I were young once and I wanted things I could not get."

36 There was another long pause. The boy's mouth opened. Then he frowned, but not knowing he frowned.

37 The woman said, "Um-hum! You thought I was going to say *but,* didn't you? You thought I was going to say, *but I didn't snatch people's pocketbooks.* Well, I wasn't going to say that." Pause. Silence. "I have done things, too, which I would not tell you, son —neither tell God, if he didn't already know. So you set down while I fix us something to eat. You might run that comb through your hair so you will look presentable."

38 In another corner of the room behind a screen was a gas plate and an icebox. Mrs. Jones got up and went behind the screen. The woman did not watch the boy to see if he was going to run now, nor did she watch her purse which she left behind her on the day-bed. But the boy took care to sit on the far side of the room where he thought she could easily see him out of the corner of her eye, if she wanted to. He did not trust the woman *not* to trust him. And he did not want to be **mistrusted** now.

mistrust
(mĭs-trŭst´) *v.* To *mistrust* is to be without confidence or trust.

39 "Do you need somebody to go to the store," asked the boy, "maybe to get some milk or something?"

40 "Don't believe I do," said the woman, "unless you just want sweet milk yourself. I was going to make cocoa out of this canned milk I got here."

41 "That will be fine," said the boy.

42 She heated some lima beans and ham she had in the icebox, made the cocoa, and set the table. The woman did not ask the boy anything about where he lived, or his folks, or anything else that would **embarrass** him. Instead, as they ate, she told him about her job in a hotel beauty-shop that stayed open late, what the work was like, and how all kinds of women came in and out, blondes, red-heads, and Spanish. Then she cut him a half of her ten-cent cake.

embarrass
(ĕm-băr´əs) *v.* To *embarrass* is to cause to feel uncomfortable or self-conscious.

43 "Eat some more, son," she said.

44 When they were finished eating she got up and said, "Now, here, take this ten dollars and buy yourself some blue suede

[1] **day-bed** (dā'´bĕd´): a sofa or couch that is used as a bed.

shoes. And next time, do not make the mistake of **latching** onto *my* pocketbook *nor nobody else's*—because shoes come by devilish like that will burn your feet. I got to get my rest now. But I wish you would behave yourself, son, from here on in."

45 She led him down the hall to the front door and opened it. "Goodnight! *Behave yourself, boy!*" she said, looking out into the street.

46 The boy wanted to say something else other than, "Thank you, m'am," to Mrs. Luella Bates Washington Jones, but he couldn't do so as he turned at the **barren** stoop and looked back at the large woman in the door. He barely managed to say, "Thank you," before she shut the door. And he never saw her again.

NOTICE & NOTE 

latch
(lăch) *v.* To *latch* means to hold on to or get hold of.

ANALYZE CHARACTER

Annotate: In paragraphs 44–45, mark instances where Mrs. Jones gives Roger advice.

Analyze: How do Mrs. Jones's advice and actions affect the resolution of the conflict?

barren
(băr´ən) *adj.* Something that is empty and lacking interest or charm is *barren*.

CHECK YOUR UNDERSTANDING

Answer these questions before moving on to the **Analyze the Text** section on the following page.

1 How does the author's use of setting advance the plot of the story?

A It causes the characters to be embarrassed.

B It allows the characters to witness an unusual event.

C It offers the characters a chance to learn about each other.

D It provides the solution to the characters' problems.

2 In paragraph 39, Roger wants to go to the store for Mrs. Jones in order to —

F get sweet milk to drink with dinner

G take the money for the milk and run away

H show Mrs. Jones he is trustworthy

J buy the blue suede shoes he wants

3 Based on the details in paragraphs 35–37, the reader can conclude that Mrs. Jones most likely —

A thinks that hunger has driven Roger to snatch her purse

B expects Roger to try to steal things from other people

C regrets things she has done in the past to get what she wanted

D knows that Roger's parents are looking for him in the neighborhood

ANALYZE THE TEXT

Support your responses with evidence from the text. NOTEBOOK

1. **Infer** What details does the author provide to show the relationship between how Roger behaves with Mrs. Jones and how he deals with his internal conflict?
2. **Interpret** What does the setting of the story tell you about Mrs. Jones's life? Cite details from the text that support your answer.
3. **Draw Conclusions** Reread the descriptions the author provides of Mrs. Jones and Roger in paragraphs 1 and 22. Explain why Roger isn't able to break free from Mrs. Jones.
4. **Predict** How is Roger's external conflict resolved and why might Mrs. Jones's involvement in the resolution affect Roger's actions in the future?
5. **Notice & Note** Review paragraph 42. What role do Mrs. Jones's memories of her beauty-shop job play in making Roger feel more comfortable?

RESEARCH

Investigate Harlem, an area of New York City that became a vibrant African American community in the early 1900s. Find out why people moved to Harlem and how its social and cultural environment nurtured writers and artists. Note what you learn in the chart.

RESEARCH TOPICS	DETAILS ABOUT LIFE IN HARLEM
Reasons people moved to the area	
Social organizations that helped create a community in Harlem	
Cultural organizations that supported artists	

Connect In paragraph 22, the writer describes the house where Mrs. Jones lives and mentions that Roger could hear "other roomers laughing and talking in the large house. Some of their doors were open, too, so he knew he and the woman were not alone." With a small group, discuss how the setting points to a vibrant and supportive community.

RESEARCH TIP

Research terms can be specific, but also general. Along with a topic such as *Harlem*, you will want to include a description of the dates that you are interested in learning about. For example, you might include *early 1900s* in your initial search to make sure you get listings for websites that have the information you seek.

CREATE AND DISCUSS

Write a Letter of Request Conduct research to find an organization that promotes intergenerational leadership or mentorship. Then write a letter of request asking for more information about the advantages such partnerships hold for young people.

- ❑ Start your letter with a heading that includes your school address, the date, and the inside address of the organization. Finally, give a salutation, or greeting, such as "Dear Sir/Madam."
- ❑ In the body of the letter, explain why you are writing, what you already know about the organization, and what information you are requesting about leadership or mentorship.
- ❑ Finish your letter with a closing such as "Sincerely, (your name)."

Discuss with a Small Group Now that you've read "Thank You, M'am," think about how Roger and Mrs. Jones both took action. Discuss the consequences of these actions and as a group decide whether the brief mentorship that Mrs. Jones offered could make a difference in Roger's life. To prepare for your discussion, review the text and think about the characters' actions at the beginning and end of the story.

- ❑ What clues does the text provide to support the idea that Roger has been positively influenced by Mrs. Jones's reaction to his attempt to steal from her?
- ❑ Could just a few minutes with a supportive person change someone's life? Support your ideas with details from the text and your general knowledge about how people react.

Go to **Participating in a Group Discussion** in the **Speaking and Listening Studio** for help.

RESPOND TO THE ESSENTIAL QUESTION

? What helps people rise up to face difficulties?

Gather Information Review your annotations and notes on "Thank You, M'am." Then, add relevant details to your Response Log. As you determine which information to include, think about:

- the differences in how people react to challenges
- how people can support each other in big and small ways
- the best way to take action to improve a challenging situation

At the end of the unit, use your notes to write an informational essay.

UNIT 1 RESPONSE LOG

? Essential Question: What helps people rise up to face difficulties?

Rogue Wave	
The Flight of Icarus	
Icarus's Flight	
Women in Aviation	
Thank You, M'am	
A Police Stop Changed This Teenager's Life	

ACADEMIC VOCABULARY

As you write and discuss what you learned from the short story, be sure to use the Academic Vocabulary words. Check off each of the words that you use.

- ❑ **aspect**
- ❑ **cultural**
- ❑ **evaluate**
- ❑ **resource**
- ❑ **text**

RESPOND

WORD BANK
suede
mistrust
embarrass
latch
barren

CRITICAL VOCABULARY

Practice and Apply Identify the vocabulary word that is tied in meaning to the italicized word in each question. Provide reasons for your choices.

1. Which word goes with *uncomfortable*? Why?
2. Which word goes with *empty*? Why?
3. Which word goes with *soft*? Why?
4. Which word goes with *suspicious*? Why?
5. Which word goes with *grip*? Why?

VOCABULARY STRATEGY: Suffixes *–able* and *–ible*

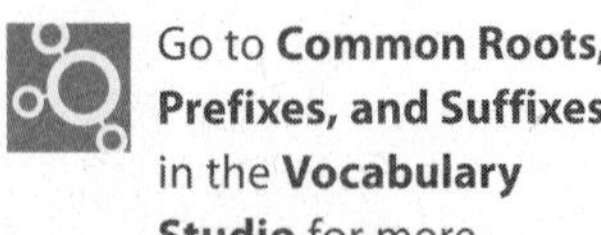
Go to **Common Roots, Prefixes, and Suffixes** in the **Vocabulary Studio** for more.

A **suffix** is a word part that appears at the end of a root or base word to form a new word. You can use your knowledge of suffixes to figure out word meanings. For example, look for a word with a suffix in this sentence from "Thank You, M'am."

> **You might run that comb through your hair so you will look presentable.**

Note that the word *presentable* is made of the base word *present* and the suffix *–able*. The suffixes *–able* and *–ible* mean "capable of or worthy of." Therefore, the meaning of *presentable* is "worthy of being introduced to others."

Practice and Apply Underline the suffix in each boldface word. Then, state the meaning of the boldface word in your own words.

1. People's behavior is often **changeable** because life experiences can influence thoughts, feelings, and actions.

   ____

2. It is **regrettable** when one friend lies to another friend.

   ____

3. The meal was **digestible**, but it was not very tasty.

   ____

4. The consequences of committing a crime are not easily **reversible**.

   ____

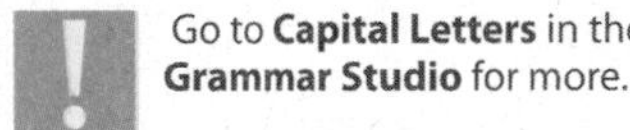

LANGUAGE CONVENTIONS: Capitalization

It is important for writers to capitalize words correctly so that readers do not get confused. Writers use capital letters to distinguish people and titles, geographical names, organizations or events, proper adjectives, first words in sentences or titles, and the pronoun *I*.

Here are some examples of capitalization in "Thank You, M'am."

- Starting sentences:

  Firmly gripped by his shirt front, the boy said, "Yes'm."

- Distinguishing the pronoun *I* and identifying a person:

  When I get through with you, sir, you are going to remember Mrs. Luella Bates Washington Jones.

Here are some other examples of capitalization.

CATEGORY	EXAMPLE
People and Titles	Langston Hughes, Professor Du Bois
Geographical Names	Brooklyn, Central Park
Organizations, Events, etc.	Thursday, March, Labor Day
Proper Adjectives	Hispanic restaurant, American colonies

Practice and Apply Using the examples above as a guide, rewrite each of the following sentences and correct the capitalization.

1. Tourists in new york City visit the empire state building.
2. The Boy in "Thank You, M'am" was named roger.
3. none of the other people in the House spoke to mrs. Jones.
4. The Story takes place in an urban area that could be harlem.
5. It is clear that the setting of the story is An american city.

Go to **Capital Letters** in the **Grammar Studio** for more.

ARTICLE

A POLICE STOP CHANGED THIS TEENAGER'S LIFE

by **Amy B Wang**

pages 73–77

COMPARE ACROSS GENRES

Now that you've read "Thank You, M'am," read "A Police Stop Changed This Teenager's Life." Explore how this news article connects to the ideas in "Thank You, M'am." As you read, think about the similarities and differences between the teenager in the news article and the boy in "Thank You, M'am." After you are finished, you will collaborate with a small group on a final project that involves an analysis of both texts.

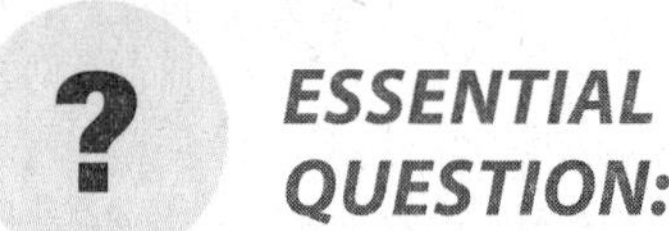

What helps people rise up to face difficulties?

SHORT STORY

THANK YOU, M'AM

by **Langston Hughes**

pages 61–65

A Police Stop Changed This Teenager's Life

QUICK START

Think about an everyday person in your school or community who reaches out to others in positive ways. Describe some examples of how this person helps others.

ANALYZE STRUCTURE

Every piece of writing has an organization, or a structure. An author will arrange ideas and information in ways that will help readers understand how they are related. Recognizing how a text is organized, or its **structural pattern,** makes the text easier to read and understand. One common structural pattern is chronological order.

Chronological order, or time order, is the arrangement of events in the order in which they occur. There are often clues to the order of events in a text. Look for:

- calendar dates, such as Wednesday, September 30, 2020
- clock time, such as *after 11 P.M.* and *around midnight*
- words and phrases that show time order, such as *at first, soon,* or *graveyard shift.*

You can use the sequence chain below to gather time order clues and track events in "A Police Stop Changed This Teenager's Life."

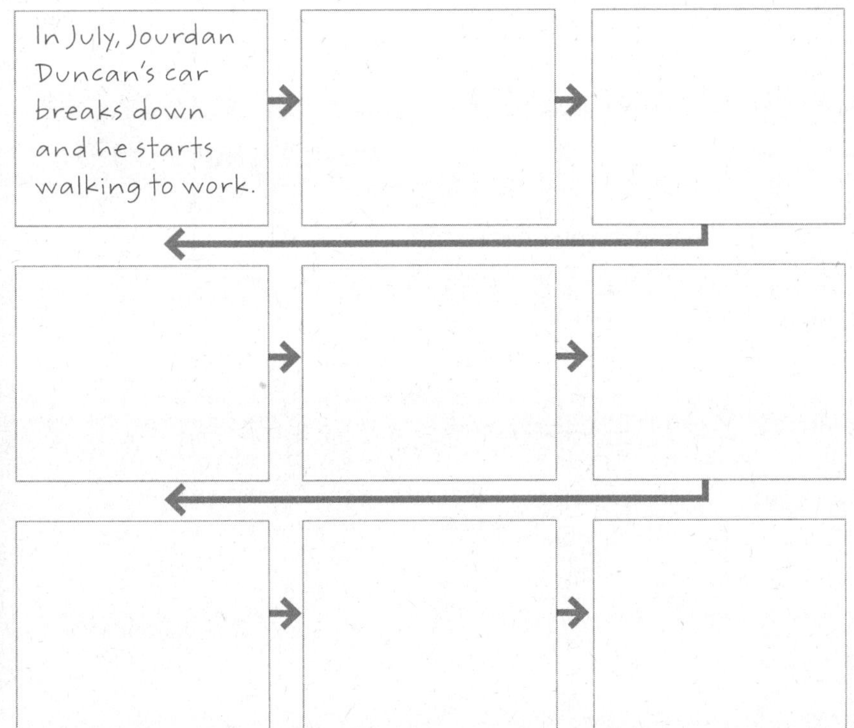

In July, Jourdan Duncan's car breaks down and he starts walking to work.

GENRE ELEMENTS: INFORMATIONAL TEXT

- reports on recent events
- presents the most important information first, followed by details
- remains brief and to the point

GET READY

CRITICAL VOCABULARY

absolute	**interaction**	**encounter**
burden	**reliable**	**token**
commute	**donate**	

To preview the Critical Vocabulary words, replace each boldface word with a different word or words that have the same meaning.

1. The **(encounter)** __________ between the walkers was a(n) **(absolute)** __________ surprise because it was early in the day.

2. The daily **(commute)** __________ to work or school requires **(reliable)** __________ and safe transportation.

3. An **(interaction)** __________ with another person can **(burden)** __________ you if that person is unfriendly.

4. Many families **(donate)** __________ their help in schools as a(n) **(token)** __________ of gratitude for educating their children.

LANGUAGE CONVENTIONS

Conjunctive Adverbs In this lesson, you will learn how to use conjunctive adverbs in writing. With conjunctive adverbs, two independent clauses can be connected to form a sentence. Notice how the clauses are connected in this sentence about a person featured in "A Police Stop Changed This Teenager's Life."

Jourdan estimated his walk to work would be long one; therefore, he prepared himself.

NOTICE & NOTE

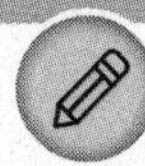

ANNOTATION MODEL

As you read, mark up words and phrases that help you understand how the text is organized. In the model, you can see one reader's notes about "A Police Stop Changed This Teenager's Life."

1 As its name might suggest, Industrial Way is <u>not known for being pedestrian-friendly</u>. . . . So when Corporal Kirk Keffer of the Benicia Police Department spotted a lone, lanky teenager walking on Industrial Way during the <u>graveyard shift</u> a few Saturdays ago, <u>he was curious</u>. It was <u>after 11 P.M.</u> and <u>dark outside</u>, and the boy was just nearing the highway overpass.

These first details show why the policeman was surprised to see a teenager there.

The author describes the setting early on; it is late at night and dark. Is it safe?

BACKGROUND

Amy B Wang *has been reporting the news since 2009. She is a general assignment reporter at* The Washington Post. *During her career, she has covered economic development, aviation, education, state politics, breaking news, and human-interest stories.*

A POLICE STOP CHANGED THIS TEENAGER'S LIFE

Article by Amy B Wang

PREPARE TO COMPARE

As you read, notice how the author indicates the sequence of events and highlights the actions of the people involved in these events.

1 As its name might suggest, Industrial Way is not known for being pedestrian-friendly. The road in the Northern California city of Benicia is lined with trucking companies, warehouses and metal-finishing factories. As it curves north, before it turns into Channel Road, the street cuts under busy Interstate 680. So when Corporal Kirk Keffer of the Benicia Police Department spotted a lone, lanky teenager walking on Industrial Way during the graveyard shift a few Saturdays ago, he was curious. It was after 11 P.M. and dark outside, and the boy was just nearing the highway overpass.

2 "Usually in the industrial area, there's no foot traffic, so it was kind of weird to see someone walking around on foot," Keffer told *The Washington Post*. He stopped his patrol car, got out and called out to the pedestrian. *Was he okay? What was he doing out there by himself?*

Notice & Note

Use the side margins to notice and note signposts in the text.

ANALYZE STRUCTURE

Annotate: Review the first paragraph and mark details that show when the events began.

Infer: What effect might the time of day have had on the actions of Corporal Kirk Keffer?

ANALYZE STRUCTURE

Annotate: In paragraph 2, mark how the author indicates what Keffer remembers seeing.

Analyze: How does including Keffer's memory help achieve the author's purpose? Why is it important to know what Keffer remembered?

NOTICE & NOTE

CONTRASTS AND CONTRADICTIONS

Notice & Note: How is Duncan getting to and from work?

Infer: What does Keffer's surprise about Duncan's actions indicate what most people would do instead in a similar situation?

absolute
(ăb´sə-lo͞ot´) *adj.* Something that is without qualifications or exceptions is *absolute*.

ANALYZE STRUCTURE

Annotate: Review paragraphs 5–6. Mark words and phrases that show the sequence of events.

Infer: Why is Duncan telling Keffer about the events that led up to his walking to and from work?

burden
(bûr´dn) *v.* If you *burden* someone, you create a situation that is difficult or stressful for him or her.

commute
(kə-myoot´) *n.* A *commute* is a person's travel to and from work or school.

3 The teenager, 18-year-old Jourdan Duncan, was equally startled at first. "I was **absolutely** nervous," he said. "I thought, okay, um, did I do anything wrong? Is he going to put me in cuffs? I didn't do anything bad." Duncan told Keffer he was walking back to his parents' home in Vallejo. He had just gotten off from his job, where the teen worked on the packaging line from 3 P.M. until around midnight.

4 "Vallejo? That's like seven miles away," Keffer said he remembered saying to Duncan. Soon, he had cleared out the passenger seat in his patrol car and offered Duncan a ride home. On the drive, Keffer asked the teen more questions. *Why Benicia? Why not drive to work?* He was agog[1] that anybody would walk more than two hours each way, every day.

5 Duncan explained that he had just graduated from Jesse Bethel High School the year before. He had gotten a job in May, and enjoyed being around his co-workers. He was saving money for college, he said—but really wanted to be an officer with the California Highway Patrol, to follow in the footsteps of some relatives who were in law enforcement.

6 When the timing belt and an engine valve on his 2001 Volvo broke in July, Duncan got a few rides from friends and co-workers, but soon decided he would try to walk to avoid **burdening** others. "I didn't want to always call somebody and be like, 'Hey, can you pick me up?'" he said. "That would have took a lot of people's time." Duncan never told his parents he started walking. ("They thought I was getting rides every day," he admits.) The first time he plotted out a walkable route on Google Maps, it spit out an estimated **commute** time of 2 hours and 15 minutes. "This is going to be a long walk," Duncan thought. On his first day going to work by foot, he didn't know

[1] **agog** (ə-gŏg'): full of surprise or astonishment.

NOTICE & NOTE

what to expect. "The whole way there I just had my earphones in, kept quiet and I just power-walked[2] the whole way." That was in July. Gradually, the foot commute grew easier for him. "The walk now, it's not a problem for me," he said.

7 By the time Keffer pulled up to Duncan's parents' house that night—all of 15 minutes later, by car—the police officer was impressed. Most people won't even walk down to the store, he joked. "I was just like, wow, Jourdan, that's really impressive, your dedication and your hard work," Keffer said. "At age 18, that's a good work ethic to have, and I said, you know, I admire that. Just keep doing what you're doing."

8 They parted ways and Keffer returned to the police department in Benicia. Still, he couldn't get Duncan's commute out of his head. He mentioned his **interaction** to his shift supervisor, who, like Keffer, happened to be a board member of the Benicia Police Officers' Association. "So I hit him up and say, 'I just had this contact with this young man,'" Keffer said. "'He's walking five hours a day, and I think it should be rewarded. What if we help him out?'"

9 They e-mailed the rest of the board to seek approval to buy a bicycle. It was, he said, one of the fastest votes they've ever taken: Within an hour, enough board members wrote back in agreement. And so, the following day, Keffer visited a local bike shop. He was looking for a good mountain bike, Keffer explained to the owner. Something with a **reliable** gearing system that could handle Benicia's steep hills. The longtime shop owner, Greg Andrade, helped him pick out a $500 bicycle—and loved the teen's story so much that he also **donated** a lighting system, brake light and helmet.

10 The only matter left was how to surprise Duncan. Keffer looked up and dialed Duncan's company, asking for Duncan's

[2] **power-walk:** to walk quickly with a definite purpose.

LANGUAGE CONVENTIONS
Annotate: Review paragraph 6 and mark *gradually,* which is acting as a conjunctive adverb.

Analyze: What does *gradually* show about how long it took for Jourdan's commute to get easier?

interaction
(ĭntər-ăk´shən) *n.* An *interaction* occurs when people speak or otherwise are in contact with one another.

reliable
(rĭ-lī´ə-bəl) *adj.* A person or object that can be trusted, or depended on, is *reliable.*

donate
(dō´nāt´) *v.* To *donate* is to give, or contribute, something to a person, cause, or fund.

NOTICE & NOTE

encounter
(ĕn-koun´tər) *n.* An *encounter* is a short meeting that is unplanned or unexpected.

ANALYZE STRUCTURE

Annotate: In paragraph 10, mark the words that Keffer says to Duncan's boss.

Analyze: What does the lack of quotation marks around Keffer's words indicate?

token
(tō´kən) *n.* A *token* serves as an expression or a sign of something else.

CONTRASTS AND CONTRADICTIONS

Notice & Note: What is Duncan's reaction to the attention of the police, and what philosophy does he have about his walking commute?

Infer: What do Keffer's actions show about how Duncan differs from other teenagers Keffer encounters?

boss. Then, he explained their **encounter** the night before. *Was Jourdan scheduled to work Monday? Would they mind if a few officers stopped by the warehouse to surprise him with something?*

11 That Monday night, September 19, Duncan's supervisor called him out and told him to go outside. Some policemen were waiting for him. Once again, Duncan was taken aback. His boss assured him he was not in trouble. Outside, he spotted Keffer, along with some other Benicia police officers. "We have something for you," he said they told him, pulling the bicycle out from behind a car. "'This is your bike' . . . I was like, wait, what? Is this some kind of trick?"

12 The bike was a **token** of their gratitude, the officers said. "We would like to acknowledge your hard work and dedication for what you do and setting the example for kids your age," Keffer said they told him. "Hopefully this'll make your trip easier."

13 Duncan said he was bowled over by the gift, but also stymied by the attention. Several local news stations wanted him on their shows. Normally reserved, he shyly agreed to talk to all of them—"I was so nervous; I've never been on TV"—but couldn't help but think: They want to interview me for *walking*? "The walk isn't hard," he said. "It's like a challenge. To me, it was like a challenge to see if I was willing to do whatever it takes to get to work."

14 Keffer said that was precisely what moved him to do something for Duncan. And Duncan said the bicycle has made him "feel more at ease" with his commute, which has now been cut down to an hour. Duncan said he and Keffer are keeping in

NOTICE & NOTE 

touch, and that Keffer has offered to take him on a ride-along[3] so he can get a better idea of what being a police officer is all about. "It's something I've been interested in since high school. A lot of my family members, they're in law enforcement," Duncan said. "It's like, what they do and, due to a lot of people thinking that there are bad cops out there, I want to prove that all cops aren't bad—which is true, due to what just happened to me."

ANALYZE STRUCTURE

Annotate: Review paragraphs 12–14. Mark words and phrases that express the actions of the police.

Infer: What does the quote from Duncan in the concluding paragraph indicate about the author's purpose in writing the article?

[3] **ride-along:** to accompany a professional, such as a police officer, on a ride in his or her vehicle to experience how the person works.

CHECK YOUR UNDERSTANDING

Answer these questions before moving on to the **Analyze the Text** section on the following page.

1 How does the author's organization of the news story contribute to the author's purpose?

A It entertains readers with details of events.

B It informs readers of the sequence of events.

C It persuades readers that Duncan needs a bike.

D It allows readers to draw conclusions about events.

2 In paragraph 3, Jourdan Duncan has just gotten off his job and is nervous about being stopped because —

F he knows there is a curfew for teenagers in Benicia

G his parents told him not to walk home from work

H he isn't sure what the policeman wants

J his friends didn't pick him up on time

3 Based on the details in paragraphs 7–8 and 12, which statement best expresses Corporal Keffer's opinion about Jourdan's situation?

A Corporal Keffer thinks that Jourdan should be getting rides.

B Corporal Keffer thinks that all teenagers should work at night.

C Corporal Keffer thinks the police should patrol the industrial area more often.

D Corporal Keffer thinks that keeping commitments and working hard can help someone succeed.

RESPOND

ANALYZE THE TEXT

Support your responses with evidence from the text. NOTEBOOK

1. **Identify** What details does the author provide to show that Jourdan Duncan and his parents have a caring relationship?
2. **Cite Evidence** How does the structure of the news story help inform the reader about the sequence of events? Cite details from the text that support your answer.
3. **Cause/Effect** What positive and negative effects resulted after the timing belt and engine valve broke on Jourdan's car?
4. **Connect** What parts of the news story point to Jourdan Duncan achieving his goal of working in law enforcement?
5. **Notice & Note** Review the many surprises that took place in this news story. Which one most surprised you, and why?

RESEARCH

Crowdfunding is an online fundraising method in which people seek contributions from a huge pool of donors. Crowdfunding sites typically allow people to propose ideas for new businesses or for social-service projects. Visitors to a crowdfunding site review the proposals and can support them by contributing money. Sometimes people seeking funds also promise to give goods or services to any donors. Search the Internet to find case studies, or examples, of people and organizations that have received support through crowdfunding. Record notes about two case studies in the chart.

RESEARCH TIP

Because the information on the Internet is not always verified for accuracy by website creators, a search on a general topic such as *crowdfunding* may produce results that are too broad or unreliable. Look for independent sites, not advertised ones, that list the top crowdfunding sites. These sites describe the major, legitimate crowdfunding sites and provide links to those sites for information about projects they funded and guidelines for seeking funding of new projects.

CROWDFUNDING	
Example 1	**Example 2**

Connect Paragraphs 8–9 of the news story describe how Corporal Keffer gets funding to buy Jourdan a new bike for his commute. With a small group, discuss how the process Keffer uses to raise money is similar to and different from crowdfunding a project.

CREATE AND DISCUSS

Write an Objective Summary A summary is a brief retelling, in your own words, of the main ideas and key supporting details of a text. When you summarize, you should be objective, or unbiased, and not include your own opinions or judgments about the text.

- ❑ Start by reviewing the news article. Mark main ideas and key supporting details in each paragraph.
- ❑ Summarize the news article by briefly restating in your own words the main ideas and key details you noted. Add a sentence to sum up the controlling idea of the news article.

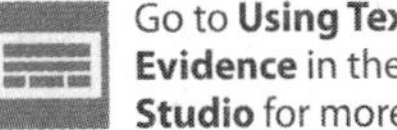

Go to **Using Textual Evidence** in the **Writing Studio** for more help.

Share and Discuss Opinions A human-interest story is a news article that focuses on a person or people. This type of article is intended to bring out an emotional response from readers. Review your notes and think about your response to "A Police Stop Changed This Teenager's Life."

- ❑ In a small group, share your opinions about the news article. What makes it an example of a human-interest story?
- ❑ Make sure to provide examples from the news article to support your opinions. In addition, listen to others' ideas and respond with appropriate register and tone to their opinions.

Go to **Participating in Collaborative Discussions** in the **Speaking and Listening Studio** to learn more.

RESPOND TO THE ESSENTIAL QUESTION

? What helps people rise up to face difficulties?

Gather Information Review your annotations and notes on "A Police Stop Changed This Teenager's Life." Then, add details to your Response Log. Think about:

- how people show determination
- why people are surprised by others' actions
- what people can do to help each other succeed

At the end of the unit, use your notes to write an informational essay.

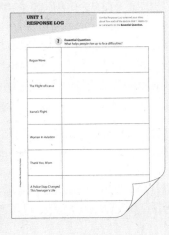

ACADEMIC VOCABULARY

As you write and discuss what you learned from the news article, be sure to use the Academic Vocabulary words. Check off each of the words that you use.

- ❑ **aspect**
- ❑ **cultural**
- ❑ **evaluate**
- ❑ **resource**
- ❑ **text**

RESPOND

CRITICAL VOCABULARY

WORD BANK
absolute
burden
commute
interaction
reliable
donate
encounter
token

Practice and Apply For each item, mark the letter of the word that differs most in meaning from the other words.

1. a. interaction b. discussion c. conversation d. quarrel

2. a. give b. contribute c. keep d. donate

3. a. ease b. burden c. encumber d. hamper

4. a. commute b. travel c. journey d. stop

5. a. meeting b. encounter c. evasion d. interview

6. a. reliable b. quality c. dependable d. untrustworthy

7. a. sign b. proof c. unimportant d. token

8. a. complete b. absolute c. limited d. pure

VOCABULARY STRATEGY: Context Clues

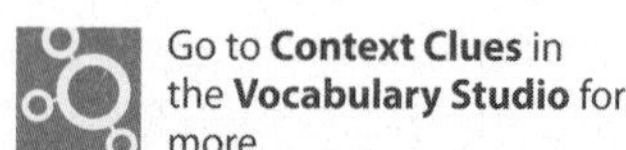
Go to **Context Clues** in the **Vocabulary Studio** for more.

When you encounter an unfamiliar word, examine its **context**—or the surrounding words, phrases, or sentences—for clues to its meaning. Look at the following example from the news article:

> **Industrial Way is not known for being *pedestrian-friendly.* The road . . . is lined with trucking companies, warehouses and metal-finishing factories. . . . So when Corporal Kirk Keffer of the Benicia Police Department spotted a lone, lanky teenager walking on Industrial Way . . . he was curious. . . .**

The writer has included **contrast clues** to help readers understand the term *pedestrian-friendly.* This type of context clue occurs when a term is contrasted with something familiar. In this case, "trucking companies, warehouses and metal-finishing factories" contrasts with something friendly. The context clue "walking" also helps readers understand that *pedestrian-friendly* means "welcoming for walkers."

Practice and Apply Use contrast clues in each sentence to figure out the boldfaced word's meaning. Write its definition below the sentence.

1. Unlike the calm officer, Jourdan was **anxious** when he was stopped.

____

2. Although Jourdan was uncertain how to get to work, he was able to **plot** out a walking route.

____

3. Instead of being overjoyed, Jourdan was **stymied** by the attention.

____

LANGUAGE CONVENTIONS: Conjunctive Adverbs

Go to **Conjunctions and Interjections** in the **Grammar Studio** for more.

Writers rely on conjunctions to link ideas smoothly. A **conjunctive adverb** can connect two independent clauses, in effect, to combine two sentences into one. It can also link ideas in two sentences.

Here is a list of some commonly used conjunctive adverbs by type. Notice that some consist of more than one word.

Comparison	similarly, besides, alternatively
Contrast	by contrast, nevertheless, instead, otherwise
Examples	for example, specifically, for instance, namely
Result	therefore, consequently, thus, so
Time	meanwhile, then, now, at last, gradually

When a conjunctive adverb joins two independent clauses, it functions as a coordinating conjunction. In this case, a semicolon must be used before the conjunction, as in this example about "A Police Stop Changed This Teenager's Life." A comma should follow the conjunctive adverb.

> **Corporal Keffer couldn't stop thinking of Jourdan's tough commute; consequently, he took action.**

A conjunctive adverb can also link ideas in two sentences. Again, a comma always follows the conjunctive adverb.

> **Jourdan's car had broken down. Nevertheless, he was determined to get to work.**

Practice and Apply Combine the two sentences in each item using a conjunctive adverb from the list.

1. Jourdan didn't want to burden others to give him rides. He walked to work.
2. Jourdan worked on a packaging line. He planned for a career in law enforcement.
3. Corporal Keffer was impressed with Jourdan's personal qualities. He liked his work ethic.
4. The officer phoned Jourdan's company. He learned details about Jourdan's work schedule.

Collaborate & Compare

THANK YOU, M'AM
Short Story by
Langston Hughes

A POLICE STOP CHANGED THIS TEENAGER'S LIFE
Article by Amy B Wang

COMPARE CHARACTERS AND PEOPLE

Comparing texts from different genres—such as an article and a short story—can lead to revelations about how characters and people are similar and different in what motivates them. The author may provide a direct motivation, or reason, for a character's actions, or the author may imply the character's motivation.

With a partner, complete the chart with information about the traits and motivations of the characters and people in the texts. Then use your notes to discuss similarities and differences in how Mrs. Jones supports Roger and how Corporal Keffer supports Jourdan.

Character/Person	Traits/Motivations	Textual Evidence
Mrs. Jones		
Roger		
Corporal Keffer		
Jourdan Duncan		

ANALYZE THE TEXTS

Discuss these questions in your group.

1. **Connect** What similarities do you see between the actions of Mrs. Jones in the short story and Corporal Keffer in the article?
2. **Compare** Consider how Roger and Jourdan each solve problems. How are they alike and how do they differ in solving problems?
3. **Infer** Based on what Jourdan said at the end of the article, what else might Roger have said at the end of the short story?
4. **Synthesize** What have you learned from these texts about how people can take positive action to make their own lives and the lives of others better?

RESEARCH AND SHARE

Now, your group can continue exploring the idea of taking positive action to help others presented in both texts by researching an organization that supports young people in your community and then writing a news bulletin about it. Follow these steps:

1. **Brainstorm Organizations** In your group, share ideas about local organizations that help young children or students. Some examples might be a public library, parks and recreation department, and teen or community center. Brainstorm and list these organizations and then choose several to research.

2. **Research the Organizations** Decide which group member will research each organization. Since these are community organizations, sources might include the organization's own **website** for information about its mission or goals and how it operates. Other sources may include local **newspapers.**

You can use a **5Ws and H Chart** to record information about each organization you research. Then use the chart as a framework for synthesizing your information into a news bulletin.

What is the organization's mission, or key goals?
Who is involved with the organization?
Why is the organization supporting young people?
When did the organization start its work with young people?
Where is the organization located?
How does the organization support young people?

3. **Share What You Learn** Everyone in your group is now an expert on an organization. Listen carefully as group members present their news bulletins. Ask questions to request and clarify information, and build on each other's ideas when you discuss how these organizations help young people in your community.

Go to **Conducting Research** in the **Writing Studio** to learn more.

RESEARCH TIP
To find reliable sources, begin by searching for specific organizations in your community. You may also learn more about these organizations by interviewing people at your school who know or are affiliated with the organization.

INDEPENDENT READING

? ESSENTIAL QUESTION:

What helps people rise up to face difficulties?

Reader's Choice

Setting a Purpose Select one or more of these options from your eBook to continue your exploration of the Essential Question.

- Read the descriptions to see which text grabs your interest.
- Think about which genres you enjoy reading.
- Remember to use what you already know, including any background information or personal experience with the topic, to connect with the text you select

Notice & Note

In this unit, you practiced noticing and noting three signposts: **Memory Moment, Again and Again,** and **Aha Moment.** As you read independently, these signposts will aid your understanding. Below are the anchor questions to ask when you read literature and nonfiction.

Reading Literature: Stories, Poems, and Plays		
Signpost	**Anchor Question**	**Lesson**
Contrasts and Contradictions	Why did the character act that way?	p. 99
Aha Moment	How might this change things?	p. 3
Tough Questions	What does this make me wonder about?	p. 362
Words of the Wiser	What's the lesson for the character?	p. 363
Again and Again	Why might the author keep bringing this up?	p. 3
Memory Moment	Why is this memory important?	p. 2

Reading Nonfiction: Essays, Articles, and Arguments		
Signpost	**Anchor Question(s)**	**Lesson**
Big Questions	What surprised me? What did the author think I already knew? What challenged, changed, or confirmed what I already knew?	p. 265 p. 183 p. 437
Contrasts and Contradictions	What is the difference, and why does it matter?	p. 183
Extreme or Absolute Language	Why did the author use this language?	p. 182
Numbers and Stats	Why did the author use these numbers or amounts?	p. 264
Quoted Words	Why was this person quoted or cited, and what did this add?	p. 437
Word Gaps	Do I know this word from someplace else? Does it seem like technical talk for this topic? Do clues in the sentence help me understand the word?	p. 265

You can preview these texts in Unit 1 of your eBook.

Then, check off the text or texts that you select to read on your own.

LEGEND

***from* Young Arthur**
Robert D. San Souci

Find out what obstacles King Arthur overcame in his youth to become king.

MYTH

Perseus and the Gorgon's Head
retold by Ann Turnbull

Perseus faces unimaginable and mysterious dangers as he embarks on a unique quest.

POEM

It Couldn't Be Done
Edgar Albert Guest

What would you do if someone said you couldn't do something?

POEM

Chemistry 101
Marilyn Nelson

Discover the wonders of learning through the eyes of a teacher.

Collaborate and Share With a partner, discuss what you learned from at least one of your independent readings.

- Give a brief synopsis or summary of the text.
- Describe any signposts that you noticed in the text and explain what they revealed to you.
- Describe any personal connections you may have discovered during your reading, as well as what you most enjoyed or found most challenging about the text. Give specific examples.
- Decide if you would recommend the text to others. Why or why not?

Go to the **Reading Studio** for more resources on **Notice & Note.**

WRITING TASK

Write an Informational Essay

Go to the **Writing Studio** for help writing your essay.

Either quite suddenly or with deliberate care, the characters and people in this unit take decisive action. For this writing task, you will write a short informational essay about the qualities needed for overcoming an obstacle and achieving a goal. For an example of a well-written informational text you can use as a mentor text, review "Women in Aviation."

As you write your essay, use the notes from your Response Log, which you filled out after reading the texts in this unit.

Writing Prompt

Read the information in the box below.

This is the topic or context for your essay.

> **Consider stories you have read or heard about people who worked hard to start a new business or who conquered their fears to climb mountains or soar into space. While the goals may differ, the qualities that help people overcome challenges and obstacles are often the same.**

Think carefully about the following question.

This is the Essential Question for the unit. How would you answer this question based on the texts in this unit?

> **What helps people rise up to face difficulties?**

Now mark the words that identify exactly what you are being asked to produce.

Write an essay explaining the qualities that are most important for overcoming obstacles and achieving a goal.

Review these points as you write and again when you finish. Make any needed changes or edits.

Be sure to—

- ❑ provide an introduction that grabs the reader's attention, clearly states the topic, and has a clear controlling idea or thesis statement
- ❑ develop the topic using facts, definitions, examples, and quotations
- ❑ organize information in a logical way
- ❑ use verb tenses consistently and switch tenses only if necessary
- ❑ use appropriate word choice and sentence variety
- ❑ end by summarizing ideas or drawing an overall conclusion

1 Plan

Planning the form and content of your informational essay is the first step in writing. When planning your draft, choose a genre that is appropriate for your topic, purpose, and audience. For this writing task, the topic is about overcoming obstacles, and the genre is an informational essay. On the previous page, you identified your purpose for writing. Now you must identify your audience. Is it an audience of your peers, or an audience of adults? Your audience helps determine word choice and tone. Additional strategies you can use in planning include brainstorming ideas with classmates, thinking about personal experiences and stories related to the topic, and listing questions about the topic. Use the table below to help you plan your draft.

Informational Essay Planning Table	
Genre	Informational essay
Topic	Qualities necessary for overcoming challenges and obstacles
Purpose	
Audience	
Ideas from brainstorming with classmates	
Experiences and stories related to the topic	
Questions about the topic	

Background Reading Review the notes you have taken in your Response Log after reading the texts in this unit. These texts provide background reading that will help you formulate the key ideas you will include in your essay.

Go to **Writing Informative Texts: Developing a Topic** for help in planning your essay.

Notice & Note

As you plan your essay, apply what you've learned about signposts to your own writing. Remember that writers use common features, called signposts, to help convey their message to readers.

Think about how you can incorporate evidence of **Quoted Words** into your essay.

Go to **Reading Studio** for more resources on **Notice & Note**.

Use the notes from your Response Log as you plan your essay.

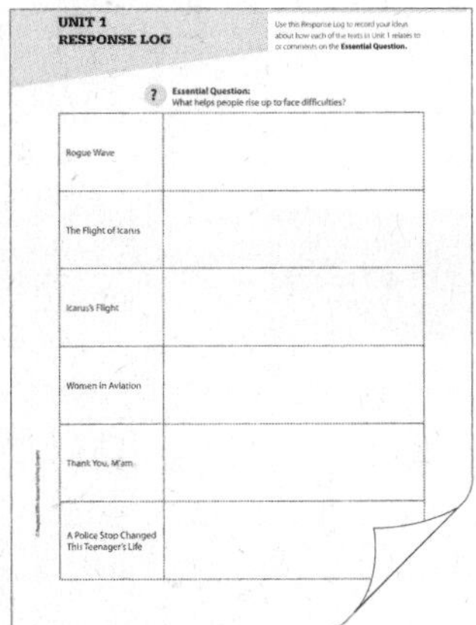

WRITING TASK

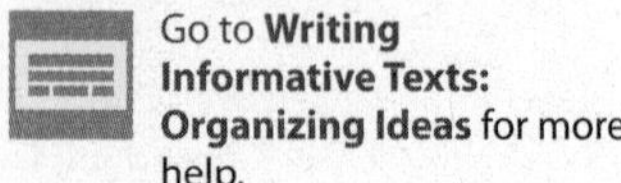

Go to **Writing Informative Texts: Organizing Ideas** for more help.

Organize Your Ideas The next step in planning your essay is to organize ideas and information in a way that will help you draft your essay. You can use the chart below to make a list of the topics you will cover. You can also use the chart to plan how you will support your ideas with supporting details and evidence.

Main Topic: Qualities for Overcoming Obstacles & Achieving a Goal

Kinds of difficulties that people face	Qualities that help people deal with difficulties	Ways that people rise up to face difficulties

2 Develop a Draft

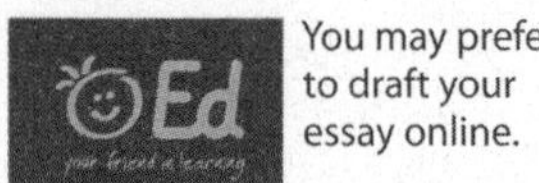

You may prefer to draft your essay online.

Once you have completed your planning activities, you will be ready to draft your informational essay. Refer to your Informational Essay Planning Table and the chart above, as well as any notes you took as you studied the texts in this unit. These will be like a road map for you to follow as you write. Using a computer program for writing or an online writing application can make it easier to rework sentences or move them around later when you are ready to revise your first draft.

Use the Mentor Text

Author's Craft

Your introduction is your first chance to grab the reader's attention. In addition to your controlling idea or thesis statement, your introduction should include something that makes readers want to keep reading your essay. Note how the writers of "Women in Aviation" introduce the topic and then transition to a concise thesis statement.

American aviation was from its very beginnings marred with sexist and racist assumptions. It was taken for granted that women were generally inferior to men and that white men were superior to all others. Flying, it was said, required a level of skill and courage that women and blacks lacked. Yet despite these prevailing prejudices, the dream and the desire to fly stayed alive among women and African-Americans.

The writers capture the reader's interest by making an assertion about prejudices in early aviation. They conclude the introductory paragraph with a thesis statement that is then supported throughout the text.

Apply What You've Learned Consider including a bold assertion or question, personal anecdote, or quotation that will interest your reader.

Genre Characteristics

Supporting details provide evidence to support a central idea and give readers more information about the topic. Note how this quotation from "Women in Aviation" supports a key idea about obstacles that women aviators faced.

Along with racism, Coleman encountered the burden of sexism, but she made believers out of those who doubted her skill. "The color of my skin," she said, "[was] a drawback at first. . . . I was a curiosity, but soon the public discovered I could really fly. Then they came to see *Brave Bessie*, as they called me."

The writers provide a quotation to help support the idea that black women aviators had to overcome discrimination to fly.

Apply What You've Learned The supporting details you include in your essay should relate directly to your key ideas. These details might be facts, examples, and quotations.

3 Revise

Go to **Writing Informative Texts: Introductions and Conclusions** for help in revising your essay.

On Your Own Once you've written a first draft of your essay, you'll want to go back and look for ways to improve it. As you reread and revise your essay, think about whether you have achieved your purpose. The Revision Guide will help you focus on specific elements to make your writing stronger.

Revision Guide

Ask Yourself	Tips	Revision Techniques
1. Does my introduction grab readers' attention?	**Highlight** the introduction.	**Add** an interesting fact, a question, an anecdote, or a famous quotation that illustrates the topic.
2. Does my introduction have a clear thesis statement?	**Underline** the thesis statement, or controlling idea.	**Add** a sentence that clearly states the idea you will develop in your essay.
3. Are ideas organized logically? Is there coherence within and across paragraphs? Do transitions connect ideas?	**Highlight** the main point or key idea in each paragraph that supports your thesis. **Underline** transitions that connect ideas.	**Rearrange** paragraphs to organize ideas logically and create coherence. **Add** transitions to connect ideas and clarify the organization.
4. Do I support each key idea with evidence?	**Underline** each supporting fact, definition, example, or quotation.	**Add** facts, specific details, examples, or quotations to support key ideas.
5. Do I use a variety of sentences?	**Underline** each compound and complex sentence.	**Combine** some simple sentences to form compound and complex sentences.
6. Does my conclusion support the topic?	**Highlight** the conclusion.	**Add** a statement that restates the thesis and summarizes the key ideas.

ACADEMIC VOCABULARY

As you conduct your **peer review,** be sure to use these words.

- ❑ **aspect**
- ❑ **cultural**
- ❑ **evaluate**
- ❑ **resource**
- ❑ **text**

With a Partner Once you have worked through the Revision Guide on your own, exchange essays with a partner and evaluate each other's draft in a **peer review**. Focus on suggesting revisions for at least three items mentioned in the Revision Guide. Explain why you think your partner's draft should be revised and what your suggestions are.

When receiving feedback from your partner, listen attentively and ask questions to make sure you fully understand the revision suggestions.

Edit

Once you have made necessary revisions to your essay, one important task remains. Don't let simple mistakes distract or confuse your readers. Edit your final draft for the proper use of standard English conventions and make sure to correct any misspellings, punctuation errors, and grammatical errors.

Language Conventions

Consistent Verb Tenses Shifting from one verb tense to another can be confusing for the reader. When writers shift verb tenses, it is usually because they want to show a change in the timing of events.

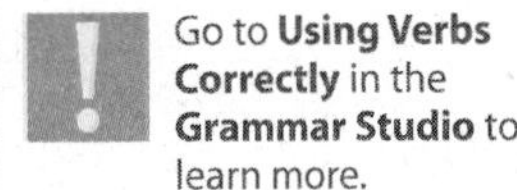

Go to **Using Verbs Correctly** in the **Grammar Studio** to learn more.

- Use a consistent verb tense within a **sentence**, unless there is a shift in the time frame.
- Use a consistent verb tense within a **paragraph**, unless it is necessary to refer to events that occurred in the past or to events that will occur in the future.

The chart below contains examples from "Women in Aviation." The first example is a sentence that consistently uses the past tense. The second is a paragraph that correctly shifts from the past tense to the present.

	Example
Consistent Verb Tense	But she didn't have any money to get there, and besides, she couldn't speak a word of French.
Correct Shift in Verb Tense	As difficult as it was for women to become pilots in significant numbers, it was doubly hard for African-Americans, especially black women. That's why Bessie Coleman, the first African-American to earn her pilot's license, is such an exciting and important figure in aviation.

5 Publish

Finalize your essay and choose a way to share it with your audience. Consider these options:

- Present your essay as a speech to a small group of students.
- Post your essay as a blog on a classroom or school website.

WRITING TASK

Use the scoring guide to evaluate your essay.

Writing Task Scoring Guide: Informational Essay			
	Organization/Progression	**Development of Ideas**	**Use of Language and Conventions**
4	• The organization is effective and appropriate to the purpose. • All ideas are focused on the topic specified in the prompt. • Transitions clearly show the relationship among ideas.	• The introduction catches the reader's attention and clearly identifies the topic. • The essay contains a clear, concise, and well-defined thesis statement. • The topic is well developed with clear key ideas that are supported by specific, well-chosen details, facts, examples, and quotations. • The conclusion effectively summarizes the information presented.	• Language and word choice is purposeful and precise. • A variety of simple, compound, and complex sentences is used; the sentences effectively show how ideas are related. • Spelling, capitalization, and punctuation are correct. • Grammar and usage are correct.
3	• The organization is, for the most part, effective and appropriate to the purpose. • Most ideas are focused on the topic specified in the prompt. • A few more transitions are needed to show the relationship among ideas.	• The introduction could be more engaging. The topic is identified. • The essay contains a clear thesis statement. • The development of ideas is clear because the writer uses specific and appropriate details, facts, examples, and quotations. • The conclusion summarizes the information presented.	• Language and word choice could be more purposeful and precise. • A greater variety of simple, compound, and complex sentences could be used; the sentences could more effectively show how ideas are related. • Spelling, capitalization, and punctuation are mostly correct. • Grammar and usage are mostly correct.
2	• The organization is evident but is not always appropriate to the purpose. • Only some ideas are focused on the topic specified in the prompt. • More transitions are needed to show the relationship among ideas.	• The introduction is not engaging; the topic is unclear. • The thesis statement does not express a clear idea. • The development of ideas is minimal. The writer uses details, facts, examples, and quotations that are inappropriate or ineffectively presented. • The conclusion is only partially effective.	• Language is often vague and general. • There is little sentence variety. • Spelling, capitalization, and punctuation are often incorrect but do not make reading difficult. • Grammar and usage are incorrect in many places.
1	• The organization is not appropriate to the purpose. • Ideas are not focused on the topic specified in the prompt. • No transitions are used, making the essay difficult to understand.	• The introduction is missing or confusing. • The thesis statement is missing. • The development of ideas is weak. Supporting details, facts, examples, and quotations are unreliable, vague, or missing. • The conclusion is missing.	• Language is vague, confusing, or inappropriate for the text. • There is no sentence variety. • Many spelling, capitalization, and punctuation errors are present. • Many grammatical and usage errors are present, making the writer's ideas difficult to understand.

Present a Film Critique

You have written an informational essay about people in the real world overcoming obstacles. Now think about movies that also tell stories of people overcoming obstacles. For example, consider movies from genres such as action, drama, and biography that portray strong characters and have event-filled plots—but are not rated beyond PG. Then choose a movie and watch it carefully, with a critical eye. Next you will plan and present a critique of the film, or movie review, to your classmates. You also will listen and respond to their presentations.

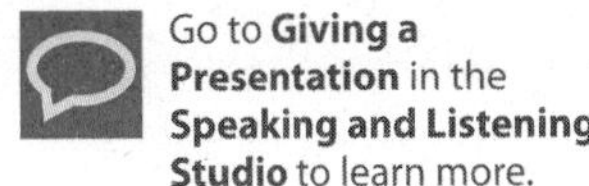
Go to **Giving a Presentation** in the **Speaking and Listening Studio** to learn more.

1 Plan Your Presentation

As you view the movie, take careful notes. Also think about the following questions to guide you in creating your film critique.

- How will you grab your audience's attention? Do you clearly state the central idea of your critique in the introduction to your presentation?
- Have any classmates already seen the movie? Will your review make them want to see it again? Will it make classmates who have not seen the movie want to see it for the first time?
- Do you clearly describe which obstacles the movie characters face, how they overcome the obstacles, and how they achieve their goals?
- Does your conclusion restate your central idea about the movie?

You can use this chart to take notes as you watch the movie and to record specific details for your presentation.

Main Character(s) and Goals	Obstacles and Challenges	How They Reach Their Goals

As you work to improve your presentations, be sure to follow discussion rules:

- ❑ **listen closely to each other**
- ❑ **don't interrupt**
- ❑ **stay on topic**
- ❑ **ask helpful, relevant, and thoughtful questions**
- ❑ **provide only clear, direct, and appropriate answers**

2 Practice with a Partner or Group

Once you've completed a draft of your film critique, practice presenting it with a partner or group.

Practice Effective Verbal Techniques

- ❑ **Enunciation** Replace words that you stumble over and rearrange sentences so that your words and ideas are clear.
- ❑ **Voice Modulation and Pitch** Use your voice to sound enthusiastic and to give emphasis to your key points.
- ❑ **Speaking Rate** Speak at a steady pace so that listeners can follow along. Pause now and then after making a key point.
- ❑ **Volume** Speak loudly enough so that everyone in the room can hear you clearly, but avoid shouting.
- ❑ **Tone** Use a formal tone and standard English grammar. Avoid using slang terms, such as *legit* instead of *legitimate*.

Practice Effective Nonverbal Techniques

- ❑ **Eye Contact** Try to let your eyes rest on each member of the audience at least once.
- ❑ **Facial Expressions** Use natural facial expressions—smiling, frowning, or raising an eyebrow—to emphasize key points.
- ❑ **Gestures** Stand tall and relaxed. Gesture with your hands to add meaning and interest to your presentation.

Provide and Consider Advice for Improvement

As a listener, pay close attention to the other presenters. Take notes about ways they can improve their presentations and more effectively use verbal and nonverbal techniques. Paraphrase and summarize each presenter's key ideas to confirm your understanding. Remember to ask questions to clarify any confusing ideas or details.

As a presenter, listen closely to the audience's questions and give thoughtful consideration to ideas for improving your presentation. Remember to ask for suggestions about how you could make your presentation clearer and more interesting.

3 Deliver Your Presentation

Use the advice you received during practice to make final changes to your presentation. Then, using effective verbal and nonverbal techniques, present your film critique to your classmates.

Reflect on the Unit

The informational essay you wrote enabled you to pull together and express some of your thoughts about the reading you have done in this unit. Now is a good time to reflect on what you have learned.

UNIT 1 SELECTIONS
- "Rogue Wave"
- "The Flight of Icarus"
- "Icarus's Flight"
- "Women in Aviation"
- "Thank You, M'am"
- "A Police Stop Changed This Teenager's Life"

Reflect on the Essential Question

- How do people rise up to face difficulties? How has your thinking about this question changed since the beginning of the unit?
- What are some examples from the texts you've read that show how people overcome obstacles and take decisive action? Explain.

Reflect on Your Reading

- Which selections were the most interesting or surprising to you? Why?
- From which selection did you learn the most about how people face challenges and take decisive action? Explain.

Reflect on the Writing Task

- What obstacles did you encounter while working on your informational essay? How might you avoid them next time?
- What parts of the essay were the easiest and the hardest to write? Why?

Reflect on the Speaking and Listening Task

- What aspects of verbal and nonverbal communication did you find most challenging as you delivered your presentation?
- What did you learn from the other presenters? How can this help you the next time you create and deliver a presentation?

UNIT 2

REALITY CHECK

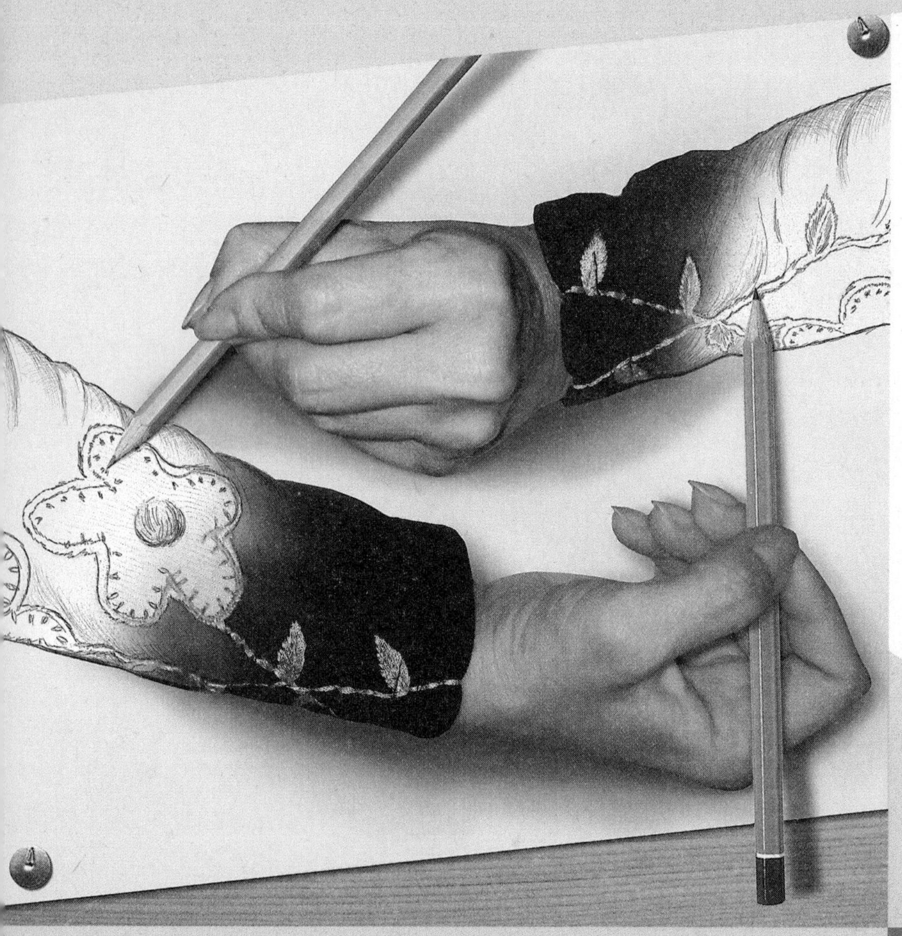

? **_ESSENTIAL QUESTION:_**

What can blur the lines between what's real and what's not?

> **"Always remember: Your focus determines your reality."**
>
> George Lucas

ACADEMIC VOCABULARY

Academic Vocabulary words are words you use when you discuss and write about texts. In this unit you will practice and learn five words.

☑ abnormal ☐ feature ☐ focus ☐ perceive ☐ task

Study the Word Network to learn more about the word **abnormal**.

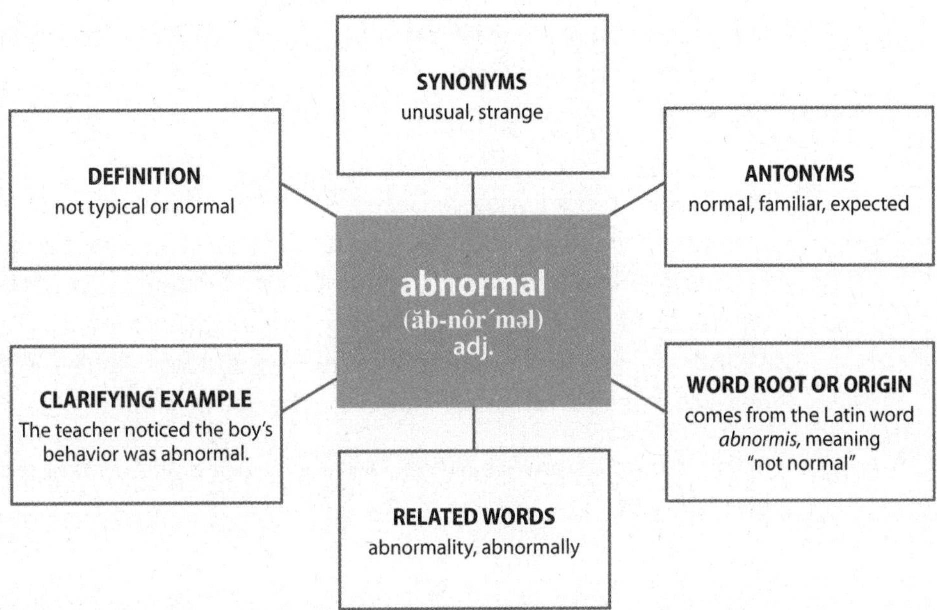

Write and Discuss Discuss the completed Word Network with a partner, making sure to talk through all of the boxes until you both understand the word, its synonyms, antonyms, and related forms. Then, fill out Word Networks for the remaining four words. Use a dictionary or online resource to help you complete the activity.

*Go online to access the **Word Networks**.*

RESPOND TO THE ESSENTIAL QUESTION

In this unit, you will explore how different people distinguish between reality and fiction. As you read, you will revisit the **Essential Question** and gather your ideas about it in the **Response Log** that appears on page R2. At the end of the unit, you will have the opportunity to create a **multimodal presentation** to demonstrate how things are not always as they seem. Filling out the Response Log will help you prepare for this writing task.

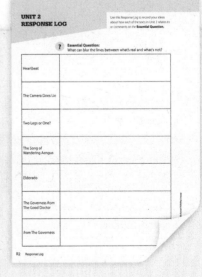

UNIT 2
RESPONSE LOG

Essential Question:
What can blur the lines between what's real and what's not?

Heartbeat	
The Camera Does Lie	
Two Legs or One?	
The Song of Wandering Aengus	
Eldorado	
The Governess *from* The Good Doctor	
from The Governess	

R2 Response Log

*You can also go online to access the **Response Log**.*

READING MODEL

HEARTBEAT

For more information on these and other signposts to Notice & Note, visit the **Reading Studio**.

You are about to read the short story "Heartbeat." In it, you will notice and note signposts that will give you clues about the story's characters and themes. Here are three key signposts to look for as you read this short story and other works of fiction.

When you see a phrase like one of these in a text, pause to see whether it may be an **Aha Moment** signpost:

"I finally realized . . ."

"That must be why . . ."

"and all of a sudden. . ."

"I decided to . . ."

Aha Moment Have you ever searched for something only to suddenly remember where you left it? A story character can also have an **Aha Moment**—a moment in which the character suddenly sees things differently or understands something. A character experiencing an Aha Moment may view something in a new way, suddenly solve a problem, or reach a deeper understanding about herself or himself.

In this example from "Heartbeat," a student found and underlined an Aha Moment:

3 . . . I was sitting in study hall two weeks ago when Sarah said the magic words: "Have you been working out, Dave? You look bigger." I couldn't tell if she was being sarcastic. I went home and inspected myself in the mirror. I did look bigger!

4 But then I realized the reason: I'd accidentally worn two T-shirts under my rugby shirt that day. It was just an illusion. I was futilely stuffing my face and religiously pumping iron and failing to alter my appearance, and now I'd stumbled on the simplest solution to looking bigger. I felt like I was reborn.

Anchor Question When you notice this signpost, ask: How might this change things?

What does Dave suddenly realize?	He realizes that wearing extra layers is the easiest way for him to look bigger.
What does this realization tell you about Dave?	He will go to any lengths—even "disguising" himself—to look bigger and less skinny.

Contrasts and Contradictions Have you ever ignored someone when you actually *liked* that person? People often act in contradictory ways. Just as in real life, **Contrasts and Contradictions** in stories can give you insight into a character. Here a student underlined an example in "Heartbeat" of Contrasts and Contradictions:

> 2 For the rest of fall, I did countless push-ups and curled free weights until I couldn't bend my arms. I got ridiculously strong and defined, but I wasn't gaining weight. I wanted to be *thicker*. I didn't care about getting stronger if nobody could tell. . . .

Anchor Question
When you notice this signpost, ask: Why did the character act that way?

What contradiction is expressed here?	The character wants to be thicker but doesn't care about being stronger.
Why do you think the character isn't gaining weight?	The character may be naturally thin.

Again and Again In a movie, you see a character having trouble writing. He scribbles words on paper and then wads it up and throws it into the trash. By showing balls of paper falling into the trash again and again, the director indicates that the character can't find the right words. When images, events, or words appear in a story **Again and Again**, they can create or emphasize a certain image, idea, or feeling. Here's an example of a student noting how Dave in "Heartbeat" does something Again and Again:

> 3 . . . I constantly weighed myself. At least once an hour, no matter where I was, I'd find a bathroom so I could take off my shirt and flex in the mirror for a couple of minutes. . . .

Anchor Question
When you notice this signpost, ask: Why might the author keep bringing this up?

What does Dave do again and again?	He weighs himself constantly, and he flexes his muscles in the mirror.
What do these repeated actions tell you about Dave?	Dave has become too concerned about getting bigger.

HEARTBEAT

Short Story by **David Yoo**

? ESSENTIAL QUESTION:

What can blur the lines between what's real and what's not?

QUICK START

Do you have friends who sometimes seem unsure of themselves? How do you think they could become more positive and brave? Make a list of some ways in which you think an individual can build confidence.

ANALYZE CHARACTER

Characters are the people who take part in a story. By analyzing a character's traits and motivations, you can understand the character—and the story—better.

Character traits are the qualities shown by characters or the expressions of their personality.	The writer may state the character's traits, or you may need to infer traits based on the character's words, thoughts, actions, appearance, or relationships.
Character motivations are the reasons why characters act the way they do.	To understand motivations, think about how the setting and other characters influence a character's actions.

As you read "Heartbeat," think about what the thoughts, words, and actions of Dave, the main character, reveal about him. Copy and complete this diagram to help you analyze his traits and motivations.

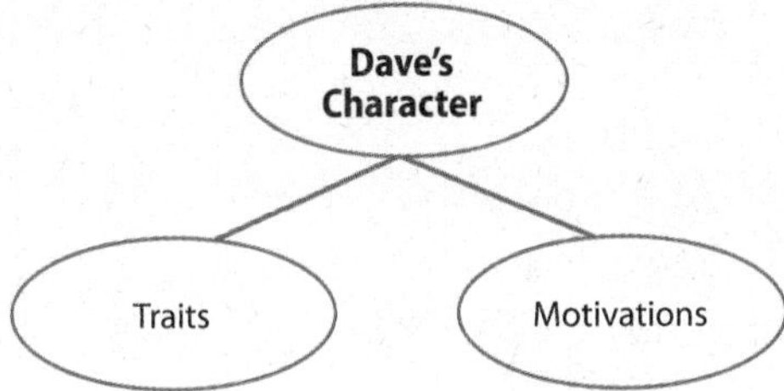

ANALYZE CONFLICT

Every story is built upon a **conflict**, a struggle between opposing forces. Two types of conflicts often appear in stories:

- An **external conflict** is a struggle against an outside force, such as nature, a physical obstacle, or another character.
- An **internal conflict** is a struggle that occurs in a character's mind, often due to a clash in feelings, thoughts, or values.

Authors may also use the **setting**—the time and place of the action—to shape the conflict and its **resolution** (how the conflict is resolved).

As you read "Heartbeat," look closely at the struggle that Dave faces. Infer whether it reveals a primarily external or internal conflict. Think, too, about why the conflict is important and how it is resolved.

GENRE ELEMENTS: SHORT STORY

- has a single idea and can be read in one sitting
- develops one or more characters
- presents a plot with one main conflict
- includes a setting
- may be realistic or imaginary
- often conveys a theme or lesson about life

GET READY

CRITICAL VOCABULARY

repulse **metabolism** **moot** **futile** **delirious**

Use the Critical Vocabulary words to complete each sentence.

1. The flu made her feel __________, so she knew it was __________ to try to go to work.

2. He was not a good cook and feared that he might __________his guests with his cooking.

3. Was it a __________ point to argue that his fast __________ prevented him from gaining weight?

LANGUAGE CONVENTIONS

Subject-Verb Agreement and Prepositional Phrases Verbs must agree (or match) their subjects in number. Look at this sentence:

The kids on the bus are waving.

Are waving (the verb) agrees with *kids* (the subject). Notice the prepositional phrase *on the bus* does not change the subject-verb agreement. As you read "Heartbeat," notice subject-verb agreement.

ANNOTATION MODEL

NOTICE & NOTE 

As you read, pay attention to signposts, including **Aha Moments**, **Contrasts and Contradictions**, and **Again and Again**. Here is an example of how one reader responded to the opening of "Heartbeat."

1 My nickname's "Heartbeat," because my friends swear that you can actually see the pulse on my bare chest. I've always been skinny. Everyone assumes I'm a weakling because I'm so thin (I prefer "lean and mean" or "wiry"), despite being a three-sport athlete. I decided to do something about it this fall when Sarah, the girl I have a crush on, said, "Oh my gosh . . . you are so skinny." She was visibly repulsed by my sunken chest as I stepped off the soccer bus after practice. I silently vowed to do everything within my power to become the "after" picture. I was sixteen years old, but looked like I was eleven.

This nickname explains the title of the story.

Aha! Sarah's words push him into a sudden decision.

I wonder if this story is going to show how he wins the girl?

BACKGROUND

Born in 1974, **David Yoo** *has often felt like an outsider. While attending an international school in Korea, he was the only Korean American student among German and Saudi Arabian classmates. When his family moved to Connecticut, he again encountered few Asian peers. He published his first book,* Girls for Breakfast, *when he was twenty-nine. The book is a humorous account of a Korean American teenage hero's efforts to fit in at a suburban American high school.*

HEARTBEAT

Short Story by David Yoo

SETTING A PURPOSE

As you read, pay attention to the way that the main character talks about himself and to the things that he decides to do. Note details that help you understand what he is like—his traits and motivations—and why he has a conflict.

1 My nickname's "Heartbeat," because my friends swear that you can actually see the pulse on my bare chest. I've always been skinny. Everyone assumes I'm a weakling because I'm so thin (I prefer "lean and mean" or "wiry"), despite being a three-sport athlete. I decided to do something about it this fall when Sarah, the girl I have a crush on, said, "Oh my gosh . . . you are so skinny." She was visibly **repulsed** by my sunken chest as I stepped off the soccer bus after practice. I silently vowed to do everything within my power to become the "after" picture. I was sixteen years old, but looked like I was eleven.

2 For the rest of fall, I did countless push-ups and curled free weights until I couldn't bend my arms. I got ridiculously strong and defined, but I wasn't gaining weight.

Notice & Note

Use the side margins to notice and note signposts in the text.

ANALYZE CHARACTER

Annotate: In paragraph 1, mark three things that Dave says other people say to him or think about him.

Infer: What does beginning the story with this information suggest about the kind of person Dave is?

repulse
(rĭ-pŭls´) *v.* Something that *repulses* you makes you want to reject it because you find it disgusting.

NOTICE & NOTE

I wanted to be *thicker*. I didn't care about getting stronger if nobody could tell. I did research, and started lifting heavier weights at lower reps and supplemented my meals with weight-gainer shakes, egg whites, boiled yams, and tubs of cottage cheese. I forced myself to swallow the daily caloric intake equivalent of three overweight men and still wasn't able to increase my mass. (I have a ridiculously fast **metabolism**.) Over Christmas break I cut out all useless movement, like Ping-Pong and staircases, because I'm like a sieve—the 83 calories in a mini-Snickers bar is **moot** because I waste 90 chewing it.

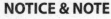

ANALYZE CONFLICT

Annotate: In paragraph 2, mark Dave's motivation for exercising.

Draw Conclusions: Does Dave struggle mostly with an external conflict or an internal conflict? Explain.

metabolism
(mĭ-tăb´ə-lĭz´əm) *n.* A living thing's *metabolism* is the chemical processes that give it energy and produce growth.

moot
(mo͞ot) *adj.* Something that is *moot* is unimportant or irrelevant.

3 I returned to school in January depressed, because I was still Heartbeat in everyone's eyes. I constantly weighed myself. At least once an hour, no matter where I was, I'd find a bathroom so I could take off my shirt and flex in the mirror for a couple of minutes. I was so frustrated that nothing was working—but the frustration didn't last. I was sitting in study hall two weeks ago when Sarah said the magic words: "Have you been working out, Dave? You look bigger." I couldn't tell if she was being sarcastic. I went home and inspected myself in the mirror. I did look bigger!

4 But then I realized the reason: I'd accidentally worn *two* T-shirts under my rugby shirt that day. It was just an illusion. I was **futilely** stuffing my face and religiously pumping iron and failing to alter my appearance, and now I'd stumbled on the simplest solution to looking bigger. I felt like I was reborn.

futile
(fyo͞ot´l) *adj.* When something is *futile*, it has no useful or meaningful result.

5 I went to school the next day wearing two T-shirts under my turtleneck. I felt solid. By the end of last week, I was wearing three T-shirts under my rugby shirt. This Monday I tucked four T-shirts under my plaid button-down. It gave me traps that didn't exist. My Q-tip-sized shoulders transformed

NOTICE & NOTE 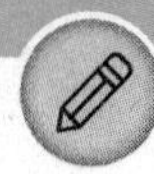

into NBA-grapefruit deltoids.[1] I could tell my classmates subtly regarded me differently. It was respect. Sarah gave me a look I'd never seen before, as if she felt . . . *safer* around me. I was walking down the hallway at the end of the day and must have twisted awkwardly because suddenly my zipper literally exploded, and all my T-shirts spilled out of my pants. Luckily, the hallway was empty and I was wearing a belt.

6 I realized I had artificially outgrown my clothes. My buttondowns were so tight that a few seconds after jamming the extra layers into my pants, the pressure would suddenly bunch the cloth up in random places so it looked like I had a goiter[2] on my shoulder or something. I complained to my parents over dinner last night. "I don't fit into anything anymore," I said. "It reflects poorly on you guys. You could get arrested."

7 "What are you talking about? You look the same as always. You're still my little boy," my dad replied, putting me in a headlock and giving me a noogie. I glared at him.

8 "I need a new ski jacket," I said. It was true. I could barely clap my hands with all the layers I was wearing. I was getting out of control at this point. The four T-shirts under my wool sweater were smushing my lungs together like a male girdle. It was a small price to pay; nobody called me Heartbeat anymore, I reminded myself.

9 After dinner I went to a party. Even though it was winter, I opted to hang out on the back porch as much as possible because it was so hot inside. Being indoors was like a sauna, but Sarah was in the basement so I headed that way. We were talking and she noticed that I was dripping with perspiration. "You're trembling," she said, touching my shoulder. She thought I was nervous talking to her and probably thought it was cute, but in reality I was on the verge of passing out because I was wearing four tight T-shirts and two long-sleeves under my wool sweater, not to mention the sweatpants tucked into my tube socks to add heft to my (formerly chicken-legs) quads. She squeezed my biceps.[3]

10 "Jeez, Dave, how many layers are you wearing?"

11 I couldn't even feel her squeezing them.

12 "I have to go," I said, excusing myself to another corner of the basement. Everyone was smushed together. It was so hot

AGAIN AND AGAIN

Notice & Note: In paragraph 5, mark each phrase that includes the word *T-shirts.*

Analyze: What does the growing number of T-shirts tell you about Dave's state of mind?

LANGUAGE CONVENTIONS

Annotate: In paragraph 8, mark the prepositional phrase that separates a subject and predicate in a sentence.

Analyze: How might the prepositional phrase in this sentence confuse subject-verb agreement?

CONTRASTS AND CONTRADICTIONS

Notice & Note: In paragraph 9, mark the sentence that shows a contrast between what Sarah believes and Dave knows to be true.

Interpret: How does the contrast add to your understanding of Dave?

---

[1] **traps . . . deltoids:** traps (short for trapezius) are large, flat upper-back muscles; deltoids are triangular muscles that connect the top of the shoulder to the arm.

[2] **goiter:** swollen thyroid gland often visible at the bottom of the neck.

[3] **quads . . . biceps:** quads (short for quadriceps) are long muscles in the front of the thigh; biceps are the large muscles in the front of the upper arm.

NOTICE & NOTE

delirious
(dĭ-lîr′ē-əs) *adj.* Someone who is *delirious* is temporarily confused, often because of fever or shock.

AHA MOMENT

Notice & Note: Mark what Dave suddenly realizes in paragraph 12.

Infer: What can you infer from that evidence, along with the question at the end of paragraph 12?

ANALYZE CONFLICT

Annotate: In paragraph 13, mark two reasons why Dave decides to stop wearing extra layers. Number them 1 and 2.

Interpret: Has Dave resolved his conflict? Explain.

everyone except me was hanging out in T-shirts and tank tops. I was sopping and **delirious** and felt claustrophobic. My chest was cold because I had four drenched T-shirts underneath my sweater. It looked like I was breaking out with Ebola[4] or something. When I coughed people turned away from me in fear. *Abandon ship, abandon ship!* I had no choice but to take some layers off. I lurched to the bathroom. My arms were ponderously heavy as I pulled off the sweater. Just lifting my arms exhausted me, and I had to stop midway and take a rest by sitting on the edge of the tub, gasping. I slowly peeled off the layers, one at a time. I took off my pants and peeled off my sweatpants, too, down to my undies. I dried myself off with a wash cloth. My red T-shirt had bled onto the three white Ts because of the sweat, so they now were faded pink tie-dyes. I hoisted the bundle of clothes and was shocked at the weight. I jammed them into the closet. I'd retrieve them later, before I left. I put my sweater back on without anything underneath. After two weeks of constricting my air supply and range of motion by wearing upwards of six layers, I was amazed at how much freedom I had with my arms. I felt like dancing for the first time in my life. I suddenly realized what I really looked like at this party: a padded, miserable, and frustrated puffball, burning up in all my layers. All this because I hated my nickname?

13 I got home and realized I'd left my bundle of wet clothes back at the party. I took this as a sign. My days of wearing extra layers was officially over. Had Sarah fallen for the padded me, she'd be falling for someone else. Besides, winter wasn't going to last forever, and I couldn't just revert back to wearing just one set of clothes like a normal human being come spring. The

[4] **Ebola:** deadly virus that causes high fever and bleeding.

change in my outward appearance would be the equivalent of a sheared sheep. From now on, I was going to just be me.

14 That was last night. *I'm not disgustingly thin*, I constantly remind myself. I am wiry. I'm lean and mean.

15 Outside it's snowing again. There's a party tonight, and my friends are on their way to pick me up. I don't know what to wear, so I lay out four different outfits on the floor as if they're chalk outlines of people. A car horn honks ten minutes later and I still haven't decided on an outfit. Maybe I'll just wear all of them.

ANALYZE CHARACTER

Annotate: Mark the sentences in paragraph 15 that show Dave's indecision.

Draw Conclusions: Has Dave's essential personality changed?

CHECK YOUR UNDERSTANDING

Answer these questions before moving on to the **Analyze the Text** section on the following page.

1 In paragraph 2, the details about Dave's attempts to gain body mass suggest that he —

A wants to get quick results without making an effort

B is disciplined and determined to reach his goal

C is strong and healthy but not very athletic

D cares about his health as much as his image

2 Why is the party scene important to the story's plot?

F At the party, Dave realizes that looking thicker isn't really important.

G Dave loses his extra clothing, and his deception is revealed.

H While dancing with Sarah, Dave is able to say how he feels about her.

J Dave's friends finally express their appreciation of him there.

3 Which of these best sums up the conflict in the story?

A Dave struggles to get the respect of his classmates.

B Dave struggles to gain control of his metabolism.

C Dave struggles to think correctly about his body image.

D Dave struggles to persuade Sarah to accept him as he is.

RESPOND

ANALYZE THE TEXT

Support your responses with evidence from the text. NOTEBOOK

1. **Cite Evidence** Reread paragraph 2. How can you tell that Dave is motivated by other people's feelings rather than by his own?
2. **Analyze** Dave thinks his friends view him with more respect now that he's wearing the layers. How does what Dave's father says in paragraph 7 bring that idea into question?
3. **Compare and Contrast** How does being at the party affect Dave's actions? Contrast how Dave feels before and after he takes off his extra layers of clothing at the party. Cite details from paragraph 12 to support your answer.
4. **Interpret** According to paragraph 13, how has Dave's thinking about Sarah changed? Explain.
5. **Notice & Note** As the story ends, what do Dave's thoughts suggest about how he has resolved his conflict?

RESEARCH

RESEARCH TIP
Focused questions can help you research a topic more quickly and successfully. For example, to get a better understanding of the term *self-esteem*, you might ask, "What is the definition of *self-esteem*?" or "What are the characteristics of *self-esteem*?"

Dave, the main character in "Heartbeat," thinks that he looks too skinny. Would he feel so self-conscious if he had healthy self-esteem? Research behaviors that can help boost self-esteem and self-confidence. Begin by generating several questions to guide your research. Record your questions and the answers you learn in the chart.

QUESTION	ANSWER

Connect Do you think it would have helped Dave to know some of the information that you gathered in your research? With a small group, discuss the information you uncovered and how it might have boosted Dave's self-confidence.

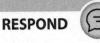

CREATE AND PRESENT

Write Text for an Infographic An **infographic** is a visual representation of information, such as a chart, that's made up of text and images. Using your research on boosting self-esteem, write several paragraphs about the benefits of rejecting negative thinking.

- ❑ Think about the members of your audience. What questions about this topic do you think they have? What message do you want your answers to convey to them?
- ❑ Draft several paragraphs that are brief and to the point. Make sure that each one has a clear, concise topic sentence that is supported by text evidence from your research.
- ❑ Think about how you might show this information visually for greatest effect.

Go to **Writing Informative Texts** in the **Writing Studio** to learn more.

Devise an Infographic Devise an infographic to illustrate the benefits of rejecting negative thinking. Then, prepare to present your infographic to the class.

- ❑ Sketch out visual elements you might include in the infographic.
- ❑ Create illustrations or other images to convey information visually.
- ❑ Incorporate the text that you wrote earlier into the infographic.

Go to **Using Media in a Presentation** in the **Speaking and Listening Studio** for help.

RESPOND TO THE ESSENTIAL QUESTION

What can blur the lines between what's real and what's not?

Gather Information Review your annotations and notes on "Heartbeat." Then, add relevant details to your Response Log. As you determine which information to include, think about:

- the difference between how we see ourselves and how others see us
- what affects how people see themselves and the world around them
- how people can lose a sense of what's "real" about themselves when trying to "fit in"

At the end of the unit, use your notes to help you create a multimodal presentation.

ACADEMIC VOCABULARY

As you write and discuss what you learned from the short story, be sure to use the Academic Vocabulary words. Check off each of the words that you use.

- ❑ **abnormal**
- ❑ **feature**
- ❑ **focus**
- ❑ **perceive**
- ❑ **task**

CRITICAL VOCABULARY

WORD BANK
repulse
metabolism
moot
delirious
futile

Practice and Apply Complete each sentence in a way that shows the meaning of the Critical Vocabulary words.

1. When we cleaned up after the party, we were **repulsed** when ____________.
2. He knows that he has a slow **metabolism** because ____________.
3. It would not be **moot** for a baseball team to practice because ____________.
4. I would probably be **delirious** if I ____________.
5. It is **futile** to try to be on time when you ____________.

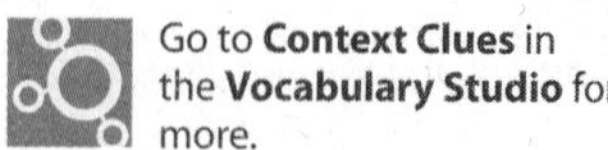

Go to **Context Clues** in the **Vocabulary Studio** for more.

VOCABULARY STRATEGY: Context Clues

The **context** of a word includes words, sentences, and paragraphs that surround the word. Context may provide clues to the meaning of an unfamiliar word. Look at the following example:

> **After two weeks of constricting my air supply and range of motion by wearing upwards of six layers, I was amazed at how much freedom I had with my arms.**

Context clues suggest that *constricting* is part of the effect of Dave's wearing many layers. Because Dave wore upwards of six layers of clothes, he limited his air supply and range of motion. Therefore, *constricting* probably means "limiting."

Practice and Apply Review "Heartbeat" to find the following words. Complete a chart like the one shown to determine their meaning.

WORD	CONTEXT CLUES	MY GUESSED DEFINITION	DICTIONARY DEFINITION
regarded (paragraph 5)			
lurched (paragraph 12)			
hoisted (paragraph 12)			

LANGUAGE CONVENTIONS: Subject-Verb Agreement and Prepositional Phrases

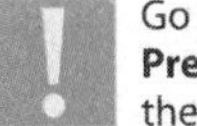

Go to **Intervening Prepositional Phrases** in the **Grammar Studio** for more.

The subject and verb in a clause must agree in number. (A **clause** is a group of words that includes a complete subject and predicate.) **Agreement** means if the subject is singular, the verb takes the singular form, and if the subject is plural, the verb takes the plural form.

SINGULAR: **David Yoo tells the story of "Heartbeat."**

PLURAL: **His characters seem very true to life.**

In the examples above, the subject and verb are right next to each other. Sometimes, however, a **prepositional phrase** comes between the subject and the verb. As a general rule, ignore the prepositional phrase or phrases. Focus only on the subject.

The opinion of his classmates is very important to Dave.

People at Dave's school call him "Heartbeat."

A few words from Sarah after soccer practice propel Dave into an important decision.

Exercise and shakes for gaining weight are not enough.

Occasionally, the prepositional phrase can influence subject-verb agreement. Note these rules for certain pronoun subjects.

- Pronouns such as *each*, *either*, *everyone*, *nobody*, *someone*, and *something* are always considered to be singular.

  Nobody in Dave's classes knows about Dave's plan.

- Pronouns such as *both*, *few*, *many*, and *several* are considered plural.

  Many of Dave's exercises make him stronger but not "thicker."

- For the pronouns *all*, *any*, *most*, *none*, and *some*, however, look at the object of the preposition.

  Most of his food metabolizes way too quickly.

  None of his meals gives Dave his desired "look."

Practice and Apply Choose and write the verb that agrees with the subject.

1. T-shirts under his rugby shirt (**transforms, transform**) __________ Dave's appearance.
2. The use of extra garments (**makes, make**) __________ a big difference.
3. Almost everyone around Dave (**senses, sense**) __________ a change in him.
4. All of his regular clothes (**were, was**) _______ too tight.

THE CAMERA DOES LIE

Article by **Meg Moss**

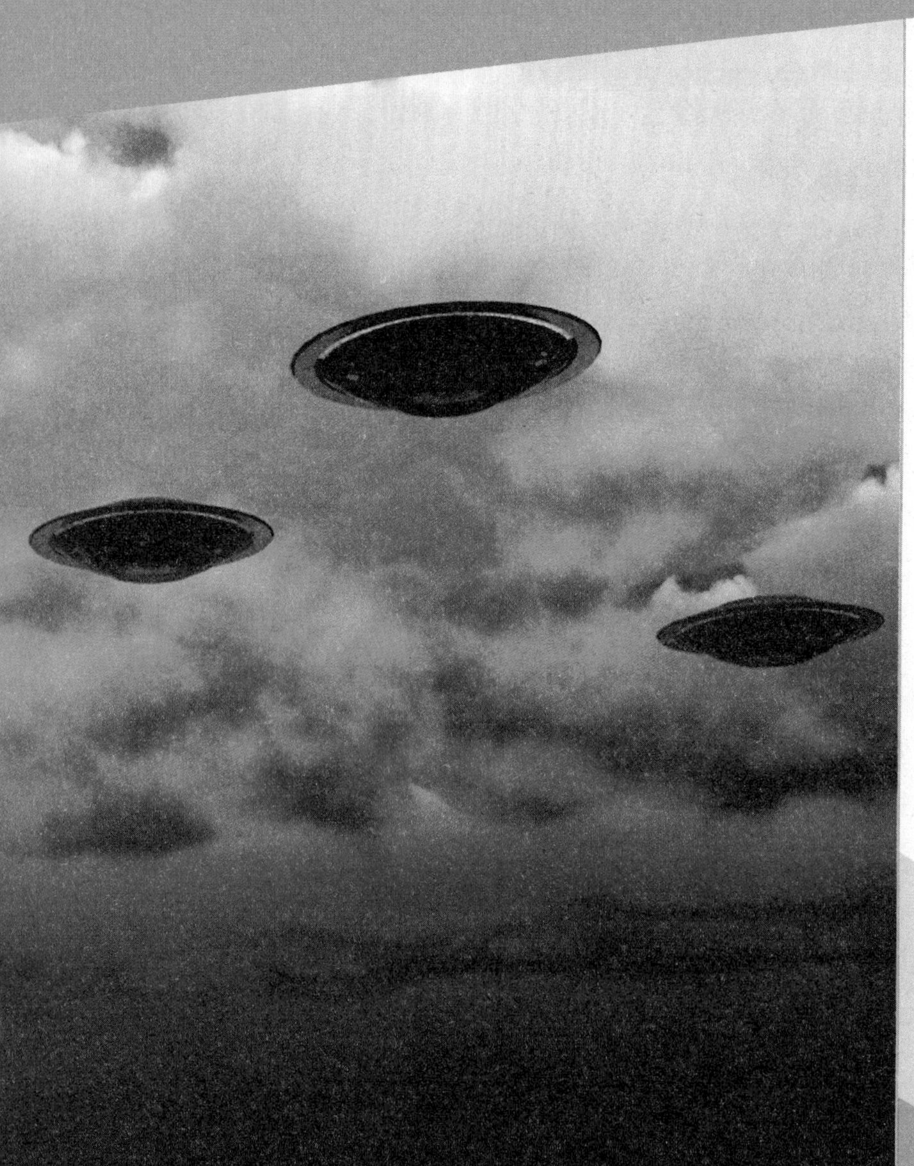

? ESSENTIAL QUESTION:

What can blur the lines between what's real and what's not?

QUICK START

Can you always trust what you see with your own eyes? Does seeing mean believing? Describe to a partner the last time you saw something that made you think that seeing *isn't* always believing.

GENRE ELEMENTS: INFORMATIONAL TEXT

- provides factual information
- includes evidence to support ideas
- includes many forms, such as magazine articles
- often contains text features such as headings, photographs, and captions

DETERMINE AUTHOR'S PURPOSE

An author's **purpose** is the reason the author wrote a particular work. In other words, it's what the author wants to do for you, the reader. This chart shows common purposes for writing different types of texts.

Author's Purpose			
Inform or Explain	Persuade	Entertain	Express Thoughts or Feelings
Examples			
• encyclopedia entries • informational articles • how-to articles • biographies	• editorials • opinion essays/blogs • advertisements	• stories • novels • some essays	• poems • personal essays • journals

To determine an author's purpose in an informational text, examine the kinds of facts and examples the author presents. Realize, too, that an author may have not only a main purpose for writing but also some additional purposes.

CITE EVIDENCE

When you **draw conclusions**, you make judgments or take a position. To reach a conclusion, you must evaluate details in a text to determine the key ideas. You can then combine this evidence with your own experience. Consider this example from "The Camera Does Lie."

> **While some people still debate whether the Bigfoot film is real, it looks plenty bogus compared to today's slick videos. The best modern fakers spare no expense or sleight of hand.**

The author makes a comparison to older, "bogus" videos, and she uses the terms *spare no expense* and *sleight of hand*. In addition, you probably have seen many recent videos—perhaps including some fake ones. You can conclude that today's fake videos are made to look so real that it is hard to tell that they are not real.

GET READY

CRITICAL VOCABULARY

bogus	**elaborate**	**accelerate**	**hoax**
obsess	**continuity**	**ruse**	

To see how many Critical Vocabulary words you already know, use them to complete the sentences.

1. At first, I trusted the "UFO expert," but he was totally __________. His UFO video wasn't real; it was a complete __________.
2. My family made up a(n) __________ plan to throw me a party. I saw through their __________, but I acted surprised anyway.
3. It's lucky that my sister likes to __________ over camera equipment.
4. The actor wore a different shirt in the second take, which caused __________ problems. Also, a falling object in the film did not __________ at a constant rate between the takes.

LANGUAGE CONVENTIONS

Correlative Conjunctions In this lesson, you will learn how to use correlative conjunctions in writing. A **correlative conjunction** is a pair of conjunctions that connects words used in the same way. Correlative conjunction word pairs must be used together. See how two subjects are connected in this sentence based on "The Camera Does Lie."

Both young **and** old have been fooled by fake videos.

ANNOTATION MODEL

NOTICE & NOTE 

As you read, note how the author expresses her purpose or purposes for writing. You can also mark up evidence that supports your conclusions. In the model, you can see one reader's notes about "The Camera Does Lie."

1 Let's face it: the Internet is a wonderful place. Where else can you read all the works of Shakespeare without leaving home? Or catch up on the news around the world with only a few clicks? <u>See eagles snatching children! Witness men flying with homemade bird wings! Cheer for pigs saving goats!</u>

2 Whoa. If you think those last three sound sketchy, you should. . . .

These examples are funny but untrue. I wonder if they help explain the title "The Camera Does Lie."

NOTICE & NOTE

BACKGROUND

"The camera doesn't lie" is an old saying from the time when photos were shot on film and were hard to alter. Digital technology has changed all that—and altered images can be posted online and go viral in a few hours! The author of this magazine article, **Meg Moss***, writes on a variety of topics, and she especially enjoys making complicated topics easy to understand. Here, she shares information to help readers understand why we can't always believe what we see.*

THE CAMERA DOES LIE

Article by Meg Moss

SETTING A PURPOSE

As you read, think about what the author means by the term video conartistry *(paragraph 2). Look for facts and examples that give you more information about that term.*

1 Let's face it: the Internet is a wonderful place. Where else can you read all the works of Shakespeare without leaving home? Or catch up on the news around the world with only a few clicks? See eagles snatching children! Witness men flying with homemade bird wings! Cheer for pigs saving goats!

2 Whoa. If you think those last three sound sketchy, you should. There's a whole world of video conartistry out there, and the Internet loves it. Besides ordinary pranksters and video artists, there are even corporations getting into the act, faking videos to sell products.

3 What's a trusting person to do? Learn to call out the fakes.

Notice & Note

Use the side margins to notice and note signposts in the text.

DETERMINE AUTHOR'S PURPOSE

Annotate: In paragraph 2, mark words and phrases that relate to the title of the article—that is, the idea of a "lying camera."

Predict: You already know that the author's main purpose is to inform or explain. What, specifically, do you think the author will provide information or explanations about?

NOTICE & NOTE

Ye Olde Fakeroo

4 There's nothing new about faking images. Falsified pictures of ghosts, unidentified flying objects (UFOs), and monsters have been around for years.

CONTRASTS AND CONTRADICTIONS

Notice & Note: In paragraphs 4–6, mark the examples of fake images the author provides.

Evaluate: What difference does it make if these images are fake? Does it really do any harm? Explain.

5 In the 19th century, "spirit photography" captured the public's imagination. Clever photographers created portraits of living people alongside ghostly versions of their deceased relatives or friends. (Fakers still love to record "paranormal activity" with cell phones and handheld video recorders.) "Photographing" UFOs became popular after World War II and remains so today.

6 Perhaps the most famous fake photograph ever was taken in 1934 at Loch Ness in Scotland. Gray and grainy, it supposedly shows the head and neck of Nessie, the dinosaur-like monster of the lake. And you can still view the first moving images of "Bigfoot," shot in 1967, on YouTube.

Fooled You Once

7 While some people still debate whether the Bigfoot film is real, it looks plenty **bogus** compared to today's slick videos. The best modern fakers spare no expense or sleight of hand.[1]

bogus
(bō´gəs) *adj.* Something that is *bogus* is fake or not genuine.

8 A few years back, you may have watched a video of a pig saving a drowning goat (all together now: awwww!). That 30-second scene took days to make. Legions of animal trainers participated (and were sworn to secrecy). An **elaborate** track was built for the pig to follow in the water. With millions of hits, the really good videos—like this one—go viral, spreading like wildfire and keeping the whole world guessing.

elaborate
(ĭ-lăb´ər-ĭt) *adj.* Something that is *elaborate* has been carefully planned and constructed with great attention to detail.

9 One person who'd rather not guess is Rhett Allain, an associate professor of physics at Southeastern Louisiana University and author of the Wired Science blog *Dot Physics.* Allain enjoys analyzing online videos. He smacks down those that don't live up to the rigors of physics and **obsesses** about those he suspects but can't pin down.

obsess
(əb-sĕs´) *v.* If you *obsess* over something, your mind is filled with thinking about a single topic, idea, or feeling.

10 Allain explains that when he looks at fishy videos, he asks, "Is this video physically possible?" Then he uses "known physics models to see if I could come up with a way to get the video to be real."

[1] **sleight of hand** (slīt ŭv hănd): a trick, such as a magic trick or card trick, performed so quickly and skillfully that no one notices it.

Fooled You Twice

11 A viral video in 2012 showed an eagle snatching a small child in its claws, then dropping the kid safely on the ground. Very convincing—until you do the math.

12 The best way to start your analysis is to ask questions like, "Could an eagle lift and carry a child that size?" The larger the bird is, the larger its wingspan must be to get it off the ground and keep it airborne. Doing a little research, Allain discovered that the golden eagle needs a 7.5-foot (2.3-meter) wingspan just to lift its own body weight of about 14 pounds (6.4 kilograms)—and perhaps some small prey. Estimating the size of the child in the video at about 28 pounds (13 kilograms) means the eagle is lifting almost twice its own weight. This would take a wingspan of about 33 feet (10 meters)!

13 In a video like this one, Allain also measures the way things move, **accelerate**, and fall to see if they obey natural laws. He asks more questions: At what angle does the child fall? How does the child move through the air as the eagle lifts him or her up? Does the child accelerate constantly through the fall like a falling object should? In the eagle video, none of these adds up.

CITE EVIDENCE
Annotate: In paragraph 12, mark the facts about golden eagles that Rhett Allain uncovered during his research.

Draw Conclusions: Could the video be real? Why or why not?

accelerate
(ăk-sĕl′ə-rāt′) *v.* When something *accelerates*, its speed increases.

Fake Shake

14 One of Allain's favorite techniques is to analyze camera shake—you know, that quaking picture people get from holding a camera in their hand instead of using a tripod.

15 Allain explains, "To make editing easier and the video more realistic, some people use a tripod for their camera to record the video. They then add fake shake to make it look like the camera was handheld." Voilà—the jerking and unsteady motion of a camera in the hands of someone walking. There's software that lets you graph camera shake by analyzing the movement of the background. If there's a pattern to the jumpiness, it's a fake. Real shake is random.

16 Of course, there are also some simple, common-sense ways to spot an imposter just by looking.

DETERMINE AUTHOR'S PURPOSE
Annotate: Mark the sentence in Allain's quotation that tells one way in which camera shake is analyzed.

Critique: How does this information help the author achieve her purpose for writing this article?

NOTICE & NOTE

continuity
(kŏn′tə-no͞o′ĭ-tē) *n.* In the movies, *continuity* refers to making sure that things that were filmed at different times or out of sequence look as if they were filmed at the same time or in the intended sequence.

hoax
(hōks) *n.* A *hoax* is something that is meant to trick or fool someone.

CITE EVIDENCE

Annotate: In paragraph 19, circle what happened when Allain used scientific analysis on the "birdman" film. Then underline how journalists proved the video to be a fake.

Draw Conclusions: What does this example suggest about the future of digital image analysis?

17 One factor to check is "**continuity**." Is everybody wearing the same thing throughout a video that is supposedly a single take? In a 2009 slip-and-slide video called "Megawoosh," a daredevil barrels down a giant water slide, off a launch pad, and into a tiny kiddie pool over 100 feet away. Amazing! . . . Until someone noticed that as he flies through the air, the jumper's helmet seems to be missing. The video was actually made in three segments and edited together; the middle section is an animation. The elaborate **hoax** turned out to be an ad for Microsoft Germany.

Faux Flight

18 As technology improves and fakers become more determined (with bigger budgets), it gets harder to weed out the hoaxes. Sometimes, a little old-fashioned research goes a long way.

19 When he watched the video of the Dutch "birdman" flying like a bird with gigantic artificial wings, Rhett Allain was on the fence. The fake was so good, even his scientific analysis couldn't

debunk it. But when journalists began looking into the résumé of the supposed birdman, nothing checked out. He didn't exist.

20 Finally, the person behind the hoax confessed. Dutch filmmaker Floris Kaayk admitted that it took eight months to achieve his near-perfect **ruse**.

21 People love to be entertained—and fooled. We are drawn to amazing feats and want to believe that they're real. With a willing audience, and social media making it easier all the time to reach us, there's no reason to think the fakers will quit anytime soon.

ruse
(ro͞oz) *n.* A *ruse* is a plan meant to deceive someone.

CHECK YOUR UNDERSTANDING

Answer these questions before moving on to the **Analyze the Text** section on the following page.

1 The author included the section Ye Olde Fakeroo in order to —

A entertain readers with stories of the Loch Ness monster

B explain that faking images is not a recent development

C persuade readers that images of Bigfoot and UFOs are fake

D share her opinion of people who create fake images

2 In paragraph 17, the writer describes the "Megawoosh" video in order to —

F provide a specific example of a continuity problem

G explain how different film segments can be edited together

H entertain readers with a funny story about a daredevil

J show how video continuity problems can be avoided

3 Which evidence most strongly supports the conclusion that the video of the eagle snatching the child was forged?

A A golden eagle weighs only about 14 pounds.

B A falling child would accelerate at a constant rate.

C The child probably weighs roughly 28 pounds.

D Lifting 28 pounds would require a 33-foot wingspan.

ANALYZE THE TEXT

Support your responses with evidence from the text. NOTEBOOK

1. **Infer** Reread each of the section headings. What do they suggest about one of the author's purposes for writing?
2. **Cite Evidence** How does graphing camera shake reveal fake videos? Cite evidence from the text in your answer.
3. **Synthesize** Review paragraphs 2 and 21. What reasons does the author provide for why fake videos are made and why some become viral?
4. **Interpret** Reread the last sentence of "The Camera Does Lie." Why might the author have spent time talking about ways to tell whether a video is real? Cite evidence to support your response.
5. **Notice & Note** In paragraph 2, how does the author highlight the contrast or contradiction between two examples of reliable information found on the Internet and three sketchy examples?

RESEARCH

Uncover another example or two of a photographic or video hoax. Also find an explanation of any techniques used to create such a deceptive image. In the following chart, record what you learn in your research.

RESEARCH TIP

When you are doing research, be sure to stay on topic. With a topic such as photographic or video hoaxes, it would be easy to get distracted and to spend your time looking at example after example. Remember that your topic is not just the hoax itself but also how it was made.

HOAX	DECEPTIVE TECHNIQUES

Connect In paragraphs 11–20, the author describes several ways that people analyze videos to determine whether they are authentic—that is, if the videos depict things that actually could happen. With a small group, take turns describing the video hoaxes you researched. Discuss ways that you could analyze those videos to expose them as hoaxes.

CREATE AND DISCUSS

Write an Opinion Essay Write a three- to four-paragraph essay in which you express your opinion about why fake images or videos fascinate people.

- ❑ Introduce the topic and state your opinion clearly.
- ❑ Provide reasons that support your opinion. Support each reason with facts, examples, and other details from the text and from additional research. Use transitions to connect ideas.
- ❑ In your final paragraph, state your conclusion about the topic.

Go to **Writing Arguments** in the **Writing Studio** to learn more.

Create a Multimodal Presentation A multimodal presentation is one that includes different modes of communication, such as writing, speech, and visuals (such as time lines, maps, or photos). With a partner or group, make a brief multimodal presentation about forged images and video.

- ❑ As a group, locate examples of images and video that seemed designed to be authentic but are not.
- ❑ Review the article for ways to detect fakery. Use those methods (and others, as appropriate) to analyze the images or video you located.
- ❑ Consider the information you discover and then work together to plan and organize your presentation.
- ❑ Present your findings to the class. Speak clearly and use eye contact and hand gestures to hold the audience's attention.

Go to **Using Media in a Presentation** in the **Speaking and Listening Studio** for tips.

RESPOND TO THE ESSENTIAL QUESTION

? What can blur the lines between what's real and what's not?

Gather Information Review your annotations and notes on "The Camera Does Lie." Then, add relevant details to your Response Log. As you determine which information to include, think about:

- the seeming "realness" of faked images
- how knowing about faked images might affect the way we think about all images, real or not

At the end of the unit, you can use your notes to help you create a multimodal presentation.

ACADEMIC VOCABULARY

As you write and discuss what you learned from the magazine article, be sure to use the Academic Vocabulary words. Check off each of the words that you use.

- ❑ **abnormal**
- ❑ **feature**
- ❑ **focus**
- ❑ **perceive**
- ❑ **task**

RESPOND

WORD BANK
bogus
elaborate
obsess
accelerate
continuity
hoax
ruse

CRITICAL VOCABULARY

Practice and Apply On separate paper, complete each sentence in a way that shows the meaning of the Critical Vocabulary word.

1. People who analyze fake videos **obsess** over . . .
2. I knew that the advertiser's claims were **bogus** because . . .
3. Filmed objects should **accelerate** . . .
4. There are many **hoaxes** on the Internet because . . .
5. They made an **elaborate** plan for the animal video; in fact, . . .
6. To create a funny video, I arranged a **ruse** in which . . .
7. To check the **continuity** of a film, you can . . .

VOCABULARY STRATEGY: Reference Resources

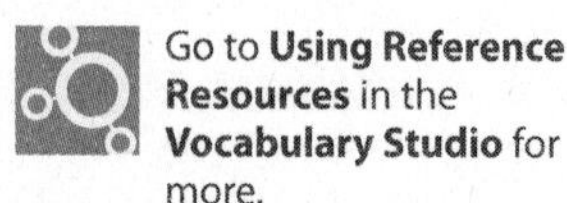

Go to **Using Reference Resources** in the **Vocabulary Studio** for more.

A **dictionary** is a valuable resource for those who want to check definitions and expand their vocabulary. The searching and browsing methods differ for print and digital dictionaries, but users can find the same basic information about each entry word.

- pronunciation
- one or more definitions
- part of speech label
- etymology (word origin or history)

a•nal•y•sis (ə-năl′ĭ-sĭs) *n.* **1.** The separation of an intellectual or material whole into its constituent parts for individual study. **2.** *Chemistry* The separation of a substance into its constituent elements to determine their nature. **3.** *Mathematics* A branch of mathematics principally involving differential and integral calculus, sequences, and series and concerned with limits and convergence.

[Medieval Latin, from Greek *analusis*, a dissolving < *analūein,* to undo]

Practice and Apply Review paragraph 9 of "The Camera Does Lie" and locate the sentence that contains the phrase *rigors of physics.* Look up the words *rigors* and *physics* in a print or digital dictionary. Note word meanings and parts of speech. Think about the origin of each word, too. Then, use your own words to tell what the sentence means.

LANGUAGE CONVENTIONS: Correlative Conjunctions

Writers rely on such single-word conjunctions as *and, but,* and *if* to link ideas. **Correlative conjunctions** are pairs of words that connect words, phrases, and clauses.

Go to **Using Conjunctions and Interjections** in the **Grammar Studio** to learn more.

Here is a list of commonly used correlative conjunctions:

either / or **neither / nor** **both / and**

no sooner / than **whether / or**

In using correlative conjunctions to construct sentences, be aware the two parts of the conjunction need to connect similar parts of speech, phrases, or clauses. The connected elements must be grammatically equal. For example, nouns must connect to nouns, a prepositional phrase must connect to a prepositional phrase, and so on. Using the word pairs in this way helps to maintain a **parallel structure**.

Notice how in the example below, two nouns are connected by the correlative conjunction *either . . . or.*

It was either a trick or a fake photograph.

It is also important to maintain pronoun-antecedent agreement when using correlative conjunctions, as shown in these examples.

INCORRECT: Neither Kenzo nor his friends understands how he was fooled.

CORRECT: Neither Kenzo nor his friends understand how he was fooled.

In the correct sentence, the verb *understand* agrees with the subject nearer to it—the word *friends.*

Practice and Apply Work with a partner to write sentences using correlative conjunctions. Use the examples above as models. Your sentences can be about funny videos or photographs you've seen, or they can be on another topic. When you have finished, share your sentences with another pair and review whether the sentences maintain pronoun-antecedent and subject-verb agreement. Apply what you have learned the next time you proofread your writing.

TWO LEGS OR ONE?

Folk Tale retold by **Josepha Sherman**

? ***ESSENTIAL QUESTION:***

What can blur the lines between what's real and what's not?

QUICK START

What can motivate someone to trick or fool someone else? Write down your thoughts in response to this question.

ANALYZE FOLK TALES

Folk tales are stories passed along by word of mouth from generation to generation. "Two Legs or One?" is a folk tale that would have been shared as an oral tradition for a long time before it was written down.

Folk tales vary among cultures, but many teach life lessons about values (such as honesty) or behaviors (such as helping the poor) that are central to the culture of origin (the culture in which the folk tale was first told). As you read, think about what life lessons this folk tale is trying to teach about values and behavior.

In a folk tale, the main character may be a **trickster**—a character who goes against acceptable behavior and fools someone. The trickster's motive may be selfish, or it may come from a desire to help others. The trickster may succeed or fail. The trickery may be discovered, or it may not. In any case, there is a life lesson to be learned. When you meet a trickster in a folk tale, ask yourself, "What can we learn from this trickster?"

GENRE ELEMENTS: FOLK TALES

- are usually set in the past and are based on an oral tradition
- often show the importance of a cultural value or behavior
- often focus on a problem that needs to be solved
- may feature supernatural characters or events
- sometimes feature a "trickster"

ANALYZE HUMOR

Like many folk tales, "Two Legs or One?" features humor. **Humor** is what causes us to laugh or be amused. Humor may come from plot events, characters' words, or the language a writer uses to tell a story.

These are some techniques writers use to add humor to a story:

- They include surprising characters or events.
- They use **exaggeration**, or extreme overstatements.
- They use **irony**, a contrast in which the reality is the opposite of what it seems to be.
- They choose words that create amusing mental images.
- They include clever and insightful dialogue.

Humor can influence the mood and tone of a story. **Mood** is the feeling or atmosphere that a writer creates through the use of descriptive words, imagery, and figurative language. The **tone** of a literary work expresses the writer's attitude toward his or her subject.

As you read "Two Legs or One?" look for humor in the folk tale. Analyze the techniques used to create that humor. Then think about how those techniques influence the mood and tone of the story.

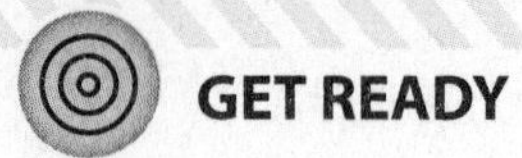

GET READY

CRITICAL VOCABULARY

scurry **procession** **dignified** **upright**

To preview the Critical Vocabulary words, replace each boldfaced word with a different word or words that have the same meaning.

1. When I returned home, I saw a mouse (**scurry**) __________ away.
2. The people marched proudly in a grand (**procession**) __________.
3. The judge was sworn in during a(n) (**dignified**) __________ ceremony.
4. After the lamp fell, she set it (**upright**) __________ on the table.

LANGUAGE CONVENTIONS

Commas Writers can use commas to control the **pace** of a story, or how fast it is read or told. A comma after introductory words or phrases lets readers pause, as in these examples from "Two Legs or One?":

- **Ah, but the meat was tender and perfectly cooked.**
  The pause after *Ah* helps you appreciate how good the meat must have been.
- **To his surprise, the dish his wife brought from the kitchen held one leg, and one leg alone.**
  The pause after *To his surprise* prepares you for a change in the plot.

As you read, think about how the author uses commas for pacing.

ANNOTATION MODEL

NOTICE & NOTE

As you read, note clues about characteristics of folk tales that you identify and mark examples of humor. In the model, you can see one reader's notes about "Two Legs or One?"

1 One day, a hungry man named Goha was walking in the marketplace, his mind on the dinner to come, when he chanced to pass a butcher's shop. There, hanging right in front of Goha's eyes, were two nice, meaty calf legs, every bit as tasty-looking to him as a good leg of lamb might be. He grew more hungry with every moment of looking, and at last bought them and scurried home.

The opening is like "Once upon a time."

Calf legs seem important—"legs" in title.

"Scurried" is funny to visualize.

BACKGROUND

Josepha Sherman *(1946–2012) wrote fantasy and science fiction tales as well as many biographies. Partly inspired by author J.R.R. Tolkien (who had a great love of folklore), Sherman studied folklore from cultures around the world, and she published several collections of her retellings of folk tales. In this story, Sherman shares one of the many Middle Eastern folk tales that feature a character named Goha.*

TWO LEGS OR ONE?

Folk Tale retold by Josepha Sherman

SETTING A PURPOSE

As you read, think about the characters in this story. Do they act as you might expect? Write down any "surprises" you encounter along the way. Also note what you think someone might learn from hearing or reading this tale.

1 One day, a hungry man named Goha was walking in the marketplace, his mind on the dinner to come, when he chanced to pass a butcher's shop. There, hanging right in front of Goha's eyes, were two nice, meaty calf legs, every bit as tasty-looking to him as a good leg of lamb might be. He grew more hungry with every moment of looking, and at last bought them and **scurried** home.

2 "Wife, come, cook these as quickly as you can, and I'll go back to the market and buy some rice to go with them."

3 The calf legs cooked quickly indeed, and when Goha's wife took the lid off the pot, she saw that they were done wonderfully well—so wonderfully well that the smell of them was sweeter to her than any rose.

Notice & Note

Use the side margins to notice and note signposts in the text.

scurry
(skûr´ē) *v.* To *scurry* means to hurry along with light footsteps.

ANALYZE HUMOR

Annotate: Mark the example of exaggeration that appears in paragraph 3.

Predict: What do you think will happen next? Explain.

NOTICE & NOTE

ANALYZE FOLK TALES

Annotate: Mark the detail in paragraph 5 that presents a problem to be solved.

Connect: Put yourself in the wife's situation. How would you solve the problem?

4 "I'd better taste one," she told herself. "Just to be sure they're done, of course. Just a taste."

5 Ah, but the meat was tender and perfectly cooked. She took a second taste, a third. And suddenly there was nothing more to taste. She had eaten the entire calf's leg! The wife worried, "I can't tell Goha how greedy I was! But what *am* I to tell him?"

6 Just then Goha returned. "I have the rice here, wife. Come, bring the calf's legs, and let us eat!"

7 To his surprise, the dish his wife brought from the kitchen held one leg, and one leg alone. "Where is the second leg?" Goha asked.

8 "What second leg?" his wife replied. "Here is the only one!"

9 "There were two legs!"

10 "There is only one!"

11 "There were two!"

12 "One!"

13 "Two!"

14 "One!"

LANGUAGE CONVENTIONS

Annotate: In paragraph 17, underline an introductory phrase that signals a sudden, surprising event, and circle the comma that follows it.

Interpret: How does this comma add to the storytelling "feel" of the selection?

15 So there they were, arguing so loudly it frightened the pigeons off the roof. "I will prove to you that there were two legs!" Goha shrieked. "I'll win this argument even if it means my very life!"

16 "There was one leg!" his wife shrieked back. "One leg!"

17 "There were two!" Goha shouted. But in the next moment, he clutched at his chest, gasping, "My heart, oh, my heart . . ."

18 With that, Goha fell to the floor and pretended to be dead. His wife at first thought this must surely be another of her husband's tricks. But when he remained so very still, she burst into tears and called the undertaker. Goha was carried from his house with great care. The funeral **procession** wound its slow, **dignified** way through the marketplace on its way to the cemetery, and everyone came running to see if the great and tricky Goha was, indeed, finally dead.

procession
(prə-sĕsh′ən) *n.* In a *procession,* people or things move along in an orderly and serious way.

dignified
(dĭg′nə-fīd′) *adj.* Someone or something that is *dignified* has or shows honor and respect.

NOTICE & NOTE

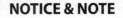

19 At last the procession passed the butcher shop. The butcher came out to see who had died, but by now such a crowd had gathered that he could see nothing.

20 "Who has died?" he asked loudly.

21 "Goha," came the answer from several mouths.

22 "Goha!" the butcher exclaimed. "But how can he be dead? He only just bought a pair of calf legs from me!"

23 On hearing this, Goha sat bolt **upright**. "You see?" he cried to his wife in triumph. "There *were* two legs. I win our argument!"

AHA MOMENT

Notice & Note: Mark the plot detail that could be called an "Aha Moment."

Infer: What does this moment help you understand about Goha's personality?

upright
(ŭp´rīt´) *adv.* Someone or something that sits or stands *upright* is in a strictly vertical position.

CHECK YOUR UNDERSTANDING

Answer these questions before moving on to the **Analyze the Text** section on the following page.

1 The author mentions that the calf legs were done wonderfully well in order to —

A introduce the problem that will shape the rest of the tale

B reveal that Goha appreciates his wife's good cooking

C explain why Goha needs to return to the marketplace

D show that this story could not happen in real life

2 The action that Goha takes after his wife brings one calf leg to the table indicates that he —

F cannot take the stress of arguing any longer

G does not understand why his wife seems so upset

H is tired of arguing and wants to make up with his wife

J is willing to take an extreme measure to be proven right

3 The butcher's words when the procession passes by his shop are important because they —

A show that Goha is loved by the townspeople

B summarize the lesson that the folk tale teaches

C prove that Goha's wife has been lying to Goha

D express the butcher's hope that Goha will come back to life

RESPOND

ANALYZE THE TEXT

Support your responses with evidence from the text. NOTEBOOK

1. **Interpret** In paragraphs 1–3, how does the author prepare readers for the conflict that will shape the rest of the folk tale?
2. **Analyze** Reread the couple's argument in paragraphs 6–17. What technique or techniques does the author use to make this a humorous moment in the story?
3. **Draw Conclusions** In paragraph 18, what description explains why people came running to see the procession? What can you conclude from that description?
4. **Evaluate** Identify two life lessons suggested by this folk tale. Explain which lesson is expressed more clearly and which lesson is expressed less clearly or directly.
5. **Notice & Note** What "Aha Moment" does Goha's wife have in paragraph 5 that causes her to lie to Goha about the calf's legs? Explain.

RESEARCH

Trickster tales appear in the oral traditions of many cultures. Research some trickster tales from around the world. Compare the central characters and humorous twists in the stories, as well as the cultural values that the tales reveal. Record your notes in this chart, and be prepared to share your results.

RESEARCH TIP

Whether you conduct a search online or at the library, the first source you locate may or may not contain exactly what you need. Be patient! Look at a few more sources before you decide which one or ones contain the most helpful information.

"TWO LEGS OR ONE?"	OTHER TALE: ___________
Character(s): *Goha, his wife*	**Character(s):**
Humorous twist(s):	**Humorous twist(s):**
Cultural value(s):	**Cultural value(s):**

Extend Explain why you think a "trickster" is often the main character in many cultures' folk tales. What is it about such characters that makes people want to hear about their adventures?

CREATE AND ADAPT

Write a Friendly Letter In a two-page letter to a friend, express your opinions about humorous writing or another form of entertainment that's designed to appeal to people's sense of humor.

- ❑ Begin by expressing a clear opinion about humor—such as what kind of humor you enjoy, or why you are writing about humor.
- ❑ Then, share specific facts and examples that support your opinion. You might mention the techniques in "Analyze Humor" (p. 125) or give examples from stories or shows you know.
- ❑ Keep the tone of your letter light. Aim for a friendly, conversational style and tone.
- ❑ In your conclusion, restate your opinion using other words. Leave your friend with something to think about.

Direct a Retelling With a partner, review "Two Legs or One?" or another trickster tale of your choice. Then prepare to take turns as director and reteller as you adapt the story for an oral retelling.

- ❑ As the director, listen carefully to your partner's retelling. Give constructive feedback and helpful tips for improvement.
- ❑ As the reteller, listen to your director about ways to convey the humorous or dramatic moments of the tale. If your director suggests different ways of speaking, give them a try. Work together to make the retelling the best it can be!

Go to in **Giving a Presentation** in the **Speaking and Listening Studio** for presentational style tips.

RESPOND TO THE ESSENTIAL QUESTION

? What can blur the lines between what's real and what's not?

Gather Information Review your annotations and notes on "Two Legs or One?" Then, add relevant details to your Response Log. As you determine which information to include, think about:

- the humor that can result when "surprises" happen in life
- the qualities that give folk tales their "staying power"

At the end of the unit, refer to your notes to help you create a multimodal presentation.

ACADEMIC VOCABULARY

As you write and discuss what you learned from the folk tale, be sure to use the Academic Vocabulary words. Check off each of the words that you use.

- ❑ **abnormal**
- ❑ **feature**
- ❑ **focus**
- ❑ **perceive**
- ❑ **task**

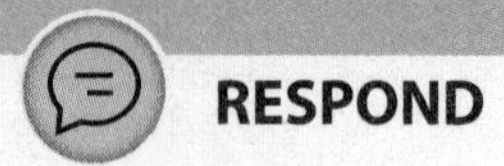

CRITICAL VOCABULARY

WORD BANK
scurry
procession
dignified
upright

Practice and Apply Answer each question using the Critical Vocabulary word in a complete sentence.

1. What kind of situation might cause you to *scurry*?
2. When have you seen (or been part of) a *procession*? What was the purpose of that *procession*?
3. How are you expected to react to a *dignified* person or event?
4. When might you need to remain *upright* for a long time?

VOCABULARY STRATEGY: Glossary

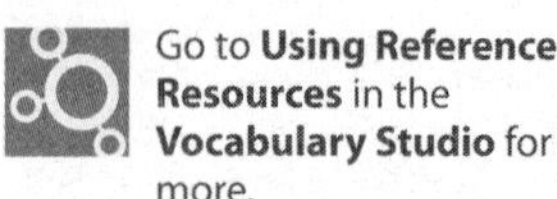

Go to **Using Reference Resources** in the **Vocabulary Studio** for more.

A **glossary** is a list of specialized terms and their definitions. A text may have more than one glossary if it refers to multiple types of specialized terms that a reader is not assumed to know.

- When a printed book contains a glossary, words are listed in the back of the book in alphabetical order.
- A digital, or electronic, glossary allows readers to click on a word in the text to see its definition and hear its pronunciation.

Notice the parts of this glossary entry for the word *procession*.

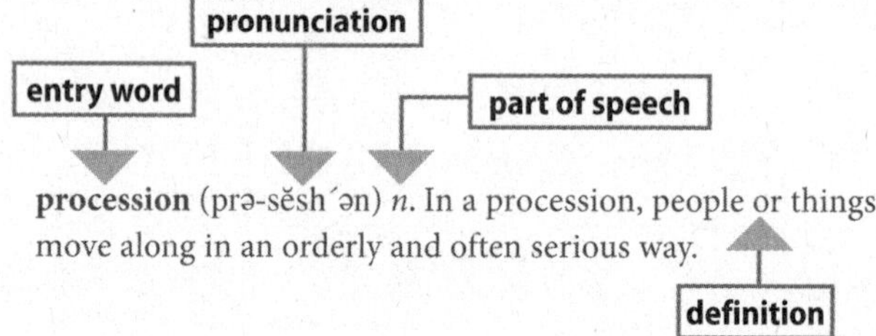

Practice and Apply This literature program contains multiple glossaries. Use the Resources table of contents and the glossaries at the back of this book to answer the following questions.

1. In which glossary would you expect to find a listing for the Critical Vocabulary words that are highlighted in each selection?
2. Use the Glossary of Academic Vocabulary to look up the words *feature* and *perceive*. What part of speech is given for each word? What is the glossary definition of *feature*?

LANGUAGE CONVENTIONS: Commas

Writers often use a **comma** when they want to indicate a very brief pause following an introductory word or phrase. By using a comma in this way, they can emphasize a plot event or signal a change in the plot. They can also help create the storytelling "feel" of a text.

The following examples from "Two Legs or One?" show how writers use commas after introductory words and phrases.

- Following an introductory noun of direct address:

  Wife, come, cook these as quickly as you can. . . .

- Following an introductory prepositional phrase (especially if there is more than one introductory prepositional phrase):

  With that, Goha fell to the floor and pretended to be dead.

  On hearing this, Goha sat bolt upright.

- Following an introductory interjection, adverb, or adverbial phrase that expresses time:

  One day, a hungry man named Goha was walking. . . .

Practice and Apply Write your own sentences with commas following introductory words and phrases. Use the examples above as models. Your sentences can be about an experience that you or someone you know had with a "trickster," or they can be about another topic related to folk tales or humor writing. When you have finished, share your sentences with a partner and compare your use of commas.

Go to **More Uses of the Comma** in the **Grammar Studio** for more.

COLLABORATE & COMPARE

POEM

THE SONG OF WANDERING AENGUS

by **W. B. Yeats**

pages 137–139

COMPARE MOODS

As you read, notice the words and sounds that help shape each poem's mood, or the feeling the poem creates for the reader. Then, think about what is similar about the mood of the two poems. After you read both poems, you will collaborate with a small group on a final project.

ESSENTIAL QUESTION:

What can blur the lines between what's real and what's not?

POEM

ELDORADO

by **Edgar Allan Poe**

pages 140–141

QUICK START

Has a friend ever told you a story about a strange or unexplained occurrence? Did it make you wonder what really happened? What reactions did the event stir in you? Discuss your reaction with the class.

ANALYZE RHYME

A poem's effect is created through sound and meaning. Poets choose their words carefully, since word choice, or **diction,** affects a poem's meaning and the way it sounds.

Rhyme is the repetition of sounds at the ends of words. Words rhyme when their accented vowels and the letters that follow them create identical or similar sounds.

dreary / weary   more / roar   chair / stare

Poets use rhyme for a number of purposes:

- to create a musical quality
- to emphasize sounds that suggest particular feelings, such as surprise or sadness
- to create rhythms, or patterns of stressed and unstressed syllables, that help convey sensory feelings, such as a sense of motion

GENRE ELEMENTS: POETRY

- includes imagery that appeals to the senses
- includes sound devices such as rhyme, alliteration, assonance, consonance, and repetition
- creates a mood
- expresses a theme, or message, about life

ANALYZE RHYME SCHEME

End rhyme refers to words that rhyme at the ends of lines of poetry. A **rhyme scheme** is a pattern of end rhymes in a poem. A rhyme scheme is noted by assigning a letter of the alphabet, starting with *a*, to each end rhyme.

FROM "ELDORADO"	RHYME SCHEME
Gaily bedight,	Gaily bedight, *a*
A gallant knight,	A gallant knight, *a*
In sunshine and in shadow,	In sunshine and in shadow, *b*
Had journeyed long,	Had journeyed long, *c*
Singing a song,	Singing a song, *c*
In search of Eldorado.	In search of Eldorado. *b*

As you read "The Song of Wandering Aengus" and "Eldorado," think about how each author's use of rhyme and rhyme scheme contributes to the poem's **mood**—the feeling the poem creates for the reader; its **voice**—the unique way the author uses language and expresses a human personality in the text; and its **tone**—the author's attitude toward the subject presented.

GET READY

ANALYZE SOUND DEVICES AND MOOD

Poets use **sound devices** to convey a poem's meaning and mood. **Rhythm** is the pattern of stressed and unstressed syllables in a line of poetry. Rhythm brings out a poem's musical qualities and helps create its mood, the feeling or atmosphere that the poet wishes to create.

Sound Device	Definition	Example
alliteration	repetition of beginning consonant sounds in words	"And when white moths…"
assonance	repetition of vowel sounds in non-rhyming words	"Though I am old…"
consonance	repetition of consonant sounds within and at ends of words	"When I had laid. . ."
repetition	restating the same words or phrases, or the same grammatical constructions	"apple blossom" "apples of the moon" "apples of the sun"

ANNOTATION MODEL

NOTICE & NOTE

As you read, note each poet's use of rhyme and sound devices. Explain how these sound devices help create the mood of the poem. In the model, you can see one reader's notes about "The Song of Wandering Aengus."

Though I am old with wandering
Through hollow lands and hilly lands
I will find out where she has gone,
And kiss her lips and take her hands;

First line: alliteration

Second line: alliteration and repetition

Second and fourth lines: end rhyme

The rhymes, the sound devices, and the rhythm remind me of a simple song.

BACKGROUND

"The Song of Wandering Aengus" was inspired by Aengus, the god of love and beauty in Irish mythology. In the original myth, Aengus falls in love with a girl he has dreamed about and has lost. **W. B. Yeats** *(1865–1939) was an Irish poet, a playwright, and a notable literary figure of the twentieth century. As a boy, Yeats visited a rural part of Ireland called Sligo where he heard stories about heroes, heroines, and magic. In Yeats's later life, this folklore influenced his poetry and drama. "The Song of Wandering Aengus" reflects this influence.*

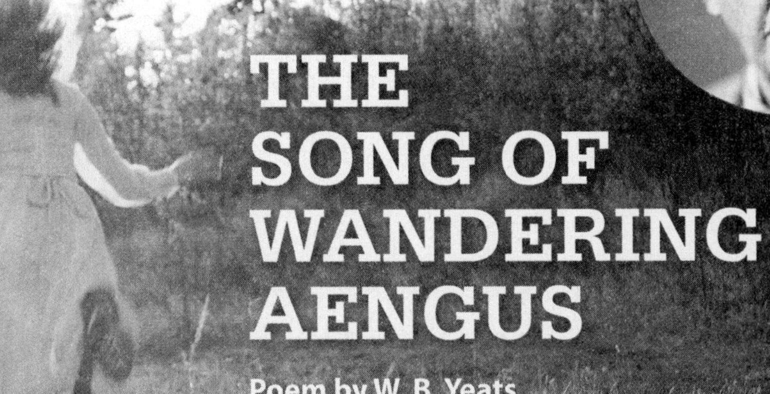

THE SONG OF WANDERING AENGUS

Poem by W. B. Yeats

PREPARE TO COMPARE

As you read, look for examples of rhyme, repetition, and other devices. Think about how the poet uses these devices to help create the poem's mood.

Notice & Note

Use the side margins to notice and note signposts in the text.

I went out to the hazel wood,
Because a fire was in my head,
And cut and peeled a hazel wand,
And hooked a berry to a thread;
And when white moths were on the wing,
And moth-like stars were flickering out,
I dropped the berry in a stream
And caught a little silver trout.

NOTICE & NOTE

ANALYZE RHYME SCHEME/ ANALYZE SOUND DEVICES AND MOOD

Annotate: Reread lines 9–16 aloud. Mark examples of end rhymes and alliteration.

Interpret: What effects do these rhymes and sound devices have in understanding the poet's intended meaning?

When I had laid it on the floor
I went to blow the fire aflame,
But something rustled on the floor,
And someone called me by my name:
It had become a glimmering girl
With apple blossom in her hair
Who called me by my name and ran
And faded through the brightening air.

Though I am old with wandering
Through hollow lands and hilly lands,
I will find out where she has gone,
And kiss her lips and take her hands;
And walk among long dappled[1] grass,
And pluck till time and times are done,
The silver apples of the moon,
The golden apples of the sun.

[1] **dappled:** marked with many spotted colors or light.

CHECK YOUR UNDERSTANDING

Answer these questions before moving on to the next selection.

1 Which word best describes the story told in the poem?

A Incident

B Quest

C Hallucination

D Mystery

2 Which event was most surprising to Aengus?

F He sleepwalked into the forest.

G Moths were all around him.

H The fish he caught became a girl.

J He found silver and golden apples.

3 In the line <u>I went out to the hazel wood</u>, the sound device used is called —

A rhyme

B alliteration

C assonance

D consonance

NOTICE & NOTE

BACKGROUND

Edgar Allan Poe *(1809–1849) was an American poet, short story writer, and literary critic. Orphaned at the age of three, he was raised by friends of his family. As a young man, Poe worked as a journalist while writing short stories and poems. Widely known for his short stories, Poe also was an influential poet. He focused a great deal on construction and style, using devices such as rhyme, alliteration, assonance, and repetition. He employs some of these devices in the poem "Eldorado."*

ELDORADO

Poem by Edgar Allan Poe

Notice & Note

Use the side margins to notice and note signposts in the text.

PREPARE TO COMPARE

As you read, think about the story the poem tells. Consider how the poet's use of rhyme and repetition affects the mood of the story and helps make it more enjoyable

Gaily bedight,
A gallant knight,
In sunshine and in shadow,
Had journeyed long,
Singing a song,
In search of Eldorado.

But he grew old—
This knight so bold—
And o'er his heart a shadow
Fell as he found
No spot of ground
That looked like Eldorado.

ANALYZE RHYME AND MOOD

Annotate: Reread lines 7–18 aloud. Mark examples of rhyme and lines that indicate the passage of time.

Interpret: What effect do these lines—and the rhyme within these lines—have on the mood of the poem?

And, as his strength
Failed him at length,
He met a pilgrim shadow—
"Shadow," said he,
"Where can it be—
This land of Eldorado?"

"Over the Mountains
Of the Moon,
Down the Valley of the Shadow,
Ride, boldly ride,"
The shade replied—
"If you seek for Eldorado!"

CHECK YOUR UNDERSTANDING

Answer these questions before moving on to the **Analyze the Text** section on the following page.

1 What is the knight's goal?

A To travel the world

B To please his love

C To find Eldorado

D To become famous

2 What sound device does the poet use in the last line of each stanza?

F Repetition

G Assonance

H Consonance

J Mood

3 What is the meaning of shadow as used in line 15?

A Traveler

B Knight

C Ghost

D Cloud

RESPOND

ANALYZE THE TEXT

Support your responses with evidence from the text. NOTEBOOK

1. **Summarize** What are the primary actions that take place in the three stanzas of "The Song of Wandering Aengus"?
2. **Infer** Who is the speaker—the person telling the story—in "The Song of Wandering Aengus"? How do you know?
3. **Interpret** Whom does the knight in "Eldorado" represent? What does Eldorado itself represent?
4. **Critique** Think about the words that appear at the end of each stanza of "Eldorado." How effectively do they connect to the changing mood of the poem?
5. **Analyze** The poet references a shadow in each of the four stanzas of "Eldorado." Why do you think the poet repeatedly refers to a shadow? How does the reference to the shadow change from the first stanza to the last?

RESEARCH

Over the centuries, the legend of El Dorado, the "city of gold," inspired adventurers, rulers, and others. Research where the legend of El Dorado comes from. Use what you learn to answer these questions.

QUESTION	ANSWER
Where was the lost "city of gold" supposedly located?	
Who was El Dorado, or "the golden one"?	
Why were the Spanish and other Europeans convinced that a city of gold actually existed?	
Did Europeans ever find El Dorado?	

Connect In the final stanza, the pilgrim shadow tells the knight that Eldorado is located "Over the Mountains/Of the Moon." With a small group, discuss how your research helps you understand the knight's quest and the pilgrim shadow's response.

RESEARCH TIP

The legend of El Dorado has long been featured in literature and popular entertainment. Because a search for "El Dorado" on the Internet will yield a range of results, look for sources that suggest content that deals with the history behind the legend. *National Geographic* and the BBC are both good sources, as are sites ending in *.org* and *.edu*.

CREATE AND PRESENT

Write a Poem Write a poem about a mysterious event and its effects. Think about the following questions.

- ❑ Who will be the speaker in your poem?
- ❑ What will be the theme of your poem?
- ❑ What structure will you use in your poem?
- ❑ Will your poem have rhyme and a rhyme scheme?
- ❑ What sound devices will you use?

Present Your Poem The way a poem is read aloud can help convey its meaning. Prepare a dramatic reading of your poem and present it to your group.

- ❑ Practice reading the poem, adjusting the rhythm of your reading according to different line lengths in the poem.
- ❑ Read in a strong, confident voice, but do not yell.
- ❑ Think about words that you want to emphasize and places where you might want to pause for effect.
- ❑ Use facial expressions and natural gestures to help convey the meaning of the poem.

Go to **Writing as a Process** in the **Writing Studio** for more.

RESPOND TO THE ESSENTIAL QUESTION

? What can blur the lines between what's real and what's not?

Gather Information Review your annotations and notes on "The Song of Wandering Aengus" and "Eldorado." Then, add relevant details to your Response Log. As you determine which information to include, think about how:

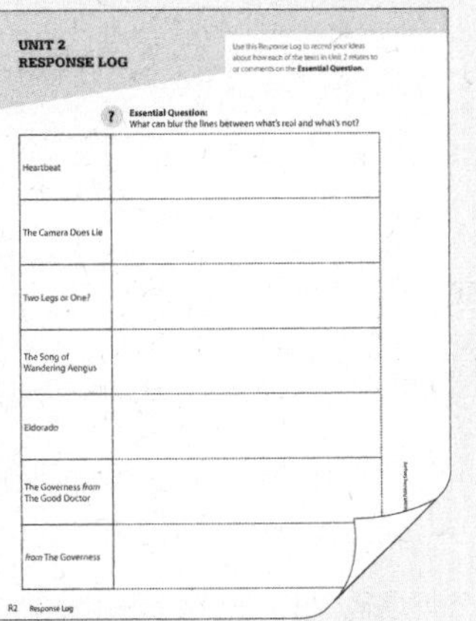

UNIT 2 RESPONSE LOG

Use this Response Log to record your ideas about how each of the texts in Unit 2 relates to or comments on the **Essential Question.**

? **Essential Question:** What can blur the lines between what's real and what's not?

Heartbeat	
The Camera Does Lie	
Two Legs or One?	
The Song of Wandering Aengus	
Eldorado	
The Governess *from* The Good Doctor	
from The Governess	

R2 Response Log

- people react to unexplainable events
- each person's experience of reality is unique
- people's reactions to events change over time

At the end of the unit, use your notes to help you create a multimodal presentation.

ACADEMIC VOCABULARY

As you write and discuss what you learned from the poems, be sure to use the Academic Vocabulary words. Check off each of the words that you use.

- ❑ **abnormal**
- ❑ **feature**
- ❑ **focus**
- ❑ **perceive**
- ❑ **task**

Collaborate & Compare

COMPARE MOODS

Both "The Song of Wandering Aengus" and "Eldorado" are poems that describe a quest, a journey in which someone searches for something desired. Although the poems share this idea, each poem creates a distinctly different mood. **Mood** is the general feeling, or emotional atmosphere, that a poem produces in readers. Mood in a poem is developed in several ways.

- **Setting/Events**—what happens and where
- **Speaker**—the person speaking the words to the reader
- **Diction**—the choice of words and images
- **Sound devices**—rhyme, rhythm, alliteration, assonance, consonance, and repetition

With your group, complete the chart with details from both poems.

	THE SONG OF WANDERING AENGUS	ELDORADO
Setting/Events		
Speaker		
Diction		
Sound Devices		

ANALYZE THE TEXTS

Discuss these questions in your group.

1. **Compare** With your group, discuss the goals of the quest in each poem. What do these goals symbolize?
2. **Interpret** In both poems, the speaker notes that the person on the quest has grown old. How does age affect the quest differently in the two poems? How does it affect the mood of each poem?
3. **Evaluate** Both poems use several sound devices to develop mood. Which poem do you think does this more effectively? Why?
4. **Critique** In "The Song of Wandering Aengus," Yeats uses the image of "apples" to develop mood. In "Eldorado," Poe uses "shadow." How do these words reflect the development of mood in each poem?

COLLABORATE AND PRESENT

Now, your group can continue exploring the ideas in these texts by identifying and comparing the mood of the poems. Follow these steps:

1. **Determine the Most Important Details** With your group, review the most important details about each poem. Identify points you agree on and resolve disagreements through collaborative discussion. Try to reach a consensus about how you would express the mood of each poem based on evidence from the texts.
2. **Create Mood Word Webs** Prepare a word web for each poem. In the center of each web, write a key word or phrase that describes the poem's basic mood. Then, add quotations from the poem or descriptive phrases that provide evidence about the poem's mood.

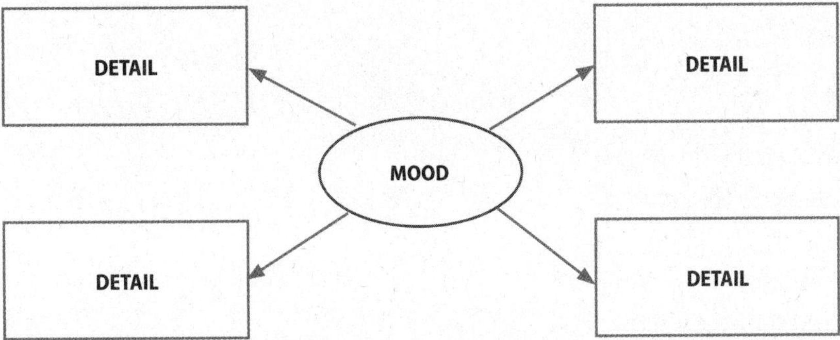

3. **Present to the Class** As a group, prepare a presentation of your ideas about the mood of each poem, using your word webs as visuals. For each poem, write a complete sentence stating your main idea about the poem's mood. Then, use your details to support your main idea, taking care that you cite specific evidence from both poems. Share your presentations with the class.
4. **Discuss Presentations** When all the groups have made presentations, discuss how the ideas presented were similar and different. Listen actively to the members of other groups and ask them to clarify any points you do not understand.

Go to **Giving a Presentation** in the **Speaking and Listening Studio** for help.

DRAMA

THE GOVERNESS

from The Good Doctor

by **Neil Simon**

pages 149–157

COMPARE VERSIONS

As you read the drama and view the production images, notice how each version conveys humor. Think about how the effect is different when you are reading the lines compared to viewing how one group staged the production. After going through both versions, you will collaborate with a small group on a final project.

ESSENTIAL QUESTION:

What can blur the lines between what's real and what's not?

PRODUCTION IMAGES

from THE GOVERNESS

presented by the
Theater Arts Department, Clackamas Community College

page 165

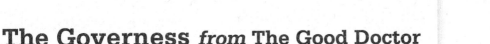

The Governess *from* The Good Doctor

QUICK START

We have all been in situations where we had to stand up for ourselves. With a group, discuss what it means to "stand up for yourself."

ANALYZE DRAMA

The play you are about to read is a **drama**, a form of literature intended to be performed. Like other literature, a drama presents events, called the **plot**, and conveys the time and place of those events, called the **setting**. The plot centers on a **conflict**, or a struggle between opposing forces, and unfolds through the characters' words and actions. Unlike other literature, a drama usually includes the following:

- **cast of characters**—a list of all the characters in the drama; the cast appears at the beginning of the drama.
- **dialogue**—the words that the characters say; the character's name precedes his or her lines of dialogue.
- **stage directions**—instructions for how the drama is to be performed; these instructions are often set in parentheses.

Because dramas are meant to be performed, reading the script requires you to focus on the dialogue and stage directions to picture the action and understand the drama's meaning.

GENRE ELEMENTS: DRAMA

- written by a playwright
- includes a cast of characters
- relies on dialogue and stage directions to tell a story

ANALYZE HUMOR

Playwrights create humor by using certain literary techniques. The **mood** of a play is the feeling that the playwright creates, such as happy or somber. **Voice** refers to the playwright's unique style of expression. **Tone** is the playwright's attitude toward the play, which might be playful or ironic. In this play, Neil Simon uses **irony**, in which characters say the opposite of what is expected, to create humor.

LINES FROM "THE GOVERNESS"	ANALYSIS
Julia. Only once since I've been here have I ever been given any money and that was by your husband. On my birthday he gave me three rubles. **Mistress.** Really? There's no note of it in my book. I'll put it down now. *(She writes in the book.)* Three rubles. Thank you for telling me. Sometimes I'm a little lax with my accounts . . .	Mistress's sharp voice helps to create a humorous mood. The difference between her point of view and that of the audience (and Julia) creates humor through irony.

As you read "The Governess," think about how the dialogue and stage directions help you understand the characters of Julia and Mistress.

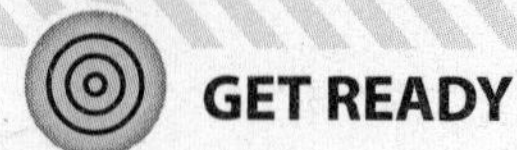

GET READY

CRITICAL VOCABULARY

madame **inferior** **discrepancy** **heirloom**

To see how many Critical Vocabulary words you already know, use them to complete the sentences.

1. Few trusted the young man because of the ________ between what he said in public and what he said in private.
2. Lena's employer had asked the young maid to call her ________, though the term was rarely used these days.
3. The vase that her grandmother gave her was an expensive family ________.
4. The staff at the newspaper treated the new hire as a(n) ________.

LANGUAGE CONVENTIONS

Complex Sentences: Subordinating Conjunctions In this lesson, you will learn about forming **complex sentences** by using **subordinating conjunctions** to connect ideas. Common subordinating conjunctions include *as, while, although, when, until, unless,* and *because.*

Example from "The Governess":

1st Idea		**2nd Idea**
I didn't bother making a note of it	because	I always do it.

As you read "The Governess," note the playwright's use of subordinating conjunctions to link ideas.

ANNOTATION MODEL

NOTICE & NOTE 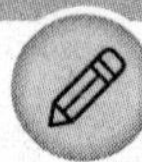

As you read, note dialogue and stage directions to help you understand how the playwright develops characters and creates humor through mood, tone, and voice. In the model, you can see one reader's notes about "The Governess."

17 **Mistress.** Head up . . . *(She lifts head up.)* That's it. Don't be afraid to look people in the eyes, my dear. If you think of yourself as inferior, that's exactly how people will treat you.

18 **Julia.** Yes, ma'am.

Why does Mistress keep saying this?

This is ironic, because Mistress treats Julia as inferior. But Mistress's words may reveal that she really is trying to help Julia.

BACKGROUND

Neil Simon *(1927–2018) has written many popular plays, movies, and television shows. Simon's collection of skits,* The Good Doctor, *which features "The Governess," was inspired by the Russian writer Anton Chekhov. Chekov, like Simon, uses humor to explore class and human nature. Simon acknowledges Chekhov's influence by including a Chekhov-inspired character, the Writer.*

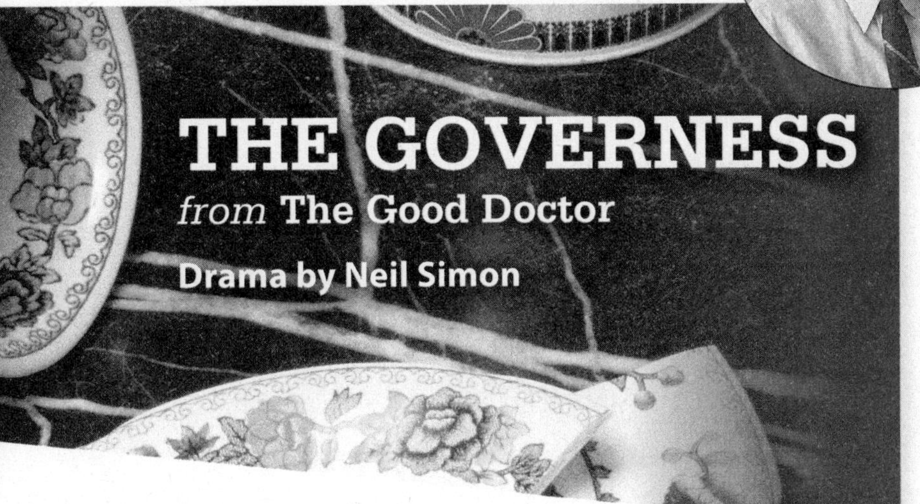

THE GOVERNESS

from The Good Doctor

Drama by Neil Simon

PREPARE TO COMPARE

As you read, make note of the dialogue and stage directions that help to shape the characters. This information will help you compare the drama with the production images that follow it.

Notice & Note

Use the side margins to notice and note signposts in the text.

1 **Writer.** *(Appears in a spot and addresses the audience).* Wait! For those who are offended by life's cruelty, there is an alternate ending . . . "Ivan Ilyitch Cherdyakov went home, took off his coat, lay down on the sofa . . . and inherited five million rubles." There's not much point to it, but it *is* uplifting. I assure you it is not my intention to paint life any harsher than it is. But some of us are, indeed, trapped. Witness the predicament of a young governess who cares for and educates the children of a well-to-do family.

2 *(Lights up on the* MISTRESS *of the house at her desk. She has an account book in front of her.)*

3 **Mistress.** Julia!

4 **Writer.** Trapped, indeed . . .

5 **Mistress** *(Calls again).* Julia!

ANALYZE DRAMA

Annotate: Mark the stage directions on this page.

Analyze: How do some of the stage directions help you understand the relationship between Mistress and Julia?

NOTICE & NOTE

6 *(A young governess,* JULIA, *comes rushing in. She stops before the desk and curtsies.)*

madame
(mə-dăm′) *n. Madame* is a form of polite address for a woman.

7 **Julia** *(Head down).* Yes, **madame?**

8 **Mistress.** Look at me, child. Pick your head up. I like to see your eyes when I speak to you.

9 **Julia** *(Lifts her head up).* Yes, madame.

10 *(But her head has a habit of slowly drifting down again.)*

ANALYZE DRAMA
Annotate: Mark the dialogue in which Mistress tells Julia to lift her head.

Infer: What do Mistress's constant reminders suggest about her?

11 **Mistress.** And how are the children coming along with their French lessons?

12 **Julia.** They're very bright children, madame.

13 **Mistress.** Eyes up . . . They're bright, you say. Well, why not? And mathematics? They're doing well in mathematics, I assume?

14 **Julia.** Yes, madame. Especially Vanya.

15 **Mistress.** Certainly. I knew it. I excelled in mathematics. He gets that from his mother, wouldn't you say?

16 **Julia.** Yes, madame.

inferior
(ĭn-fîr′ē-ər) *adj.* If something is *inferior*, it is lower in value and quality.

17 **Mistress.** Head up . . . *(She lifts head up.)* That's it. Don't be afraid to look people in the eyes, my dear. If you think of yourself as **inferior**, that's exactly how people will treat you.

18 **Julia.** Yes, ma'am.

LANGUAGE CONVENTIONS
Annotate: In paragraph 19, circle the subordinating conjunction *although*. Then underline the two ideas it connects.

Analyze: How are the two ideas you underlined related?

19 **Mistress.** A quiet girl, aren't you? . . . Now then, let's settle our accounts.[1] I imagine you must need money, although you never ask me for it yourself. Let's see now, we agreed on thirty rubles a month, did we not?

20 **Julia** *(Surprised).* Forty, ma'am.

21 **Mistress.** No, no, thirty. I made a note of it. *(Points to the book.)* I always pay my governesses thirty . . . Who told you forty?

22 **Julia.** You did, ma'am. I spoke to no one else concerning money . . .

ANALYZE HUMOR
Annotate: Mark Mistress's explanation in paragraph 23 for how Julia may have been confused about her salary.

Analyze: How would you describe Mistress's voice here?

23 **Mistress.** Impossible. Maybe you *thought* you heard forty when I said thirty. If you kept your head up, that would never happen. Look at me again and I'll say it clearly. *Thirty rubles a month.*

---

[1] **Settle our accounts:** pay a debt or receive payment for a debt.

24 **Julia.** If you say so, ma'am.

25 **Mistress.** Settled. Thirty a month it is . . . Now then, you've been here two months exactly.

26 **Julia.** Two months and five days.

27 **Mistress.** No, no. Exactly two months. I made a note of it. You should keep books the way I do so there wouldn't be these **discrepancies.** So—we have two months at thirty rubles a month . . . comes to sixty rubles. Correct?

discrepancy
(dĭ-skrĕp´ən-sē) *n.* When there is a *discrepancy* between two things, there is a difference or disagreement.

28 **Julia** *(Curtsies).* Yes, ma'am. Thank you, ma'am.

29 **Mistress.** Subtract nine Sundays . . . We did agree to subtract Sundays, didn't we?

30 **Julia.** No, ma'am.

31 **Mistress.** Eyes! Eyes! . . . Certainly we did. I've always subtracted Sundays. I didn't bother making a note of it because I always do it. Don't you recall when I said we will subtract Sundays?

ANALYZE DRAMA

Annotate: In paragraphs 31–38, mark Julia's response to Mistress as well as the stage directions that tell how Julia responds.

Draw Conclusions: Why do you think Julia changes her mind about remembering?

32 **Julia.** No, ma'am.

33 **Mistress.** Think.

34 **Julia** *(Thinks).* No, ma'am.

35 **Mistress.** You weren't thinking. Your eyes were wandering. Look straight at my face and look hard . . . Do you remember now?

36 **Julia** *(Softly).* Yes, ma'am.

37 **Mistress.** I didn't hear you, Julia.

38 **Julia** *(Louder).* Yes, ma'am.

ANALYZE HUMOR

Annotate: In paragraphs 39–43, mark the reasons Mistress is deducting from Julia's pay.

Infer: What tone does the playwright create with these reasons?

39 **Mistress.** Good. I was sure you'd remember . . . Plus three holidays. Correct?

40 **Julia.** Two, ma'am. Christmas and New Year's.

41 **Mistress.** And your birthday. That's three.

42 **Julia.** I worked on my birthday, ma'am.

43 **Mistress.** You did? There was no need to. My governesses never worked on their birthdays . . .

44 **Julia.** But I did work, ma'am.

45 **Mistress.** But that's not the question, Julia. We're discussing financial matters now. I will, however, only count two holidays if you insist . . . Do you insist?

46 **Julia.** I did work, ma'am.

47 **Mistress.** Then you *do* insist.

48 **Julia.** No, ma'am.

49 **Mistress.** Very well. That's three holidays, therefore we take off twelve rubles. Now then, four days little Kolya was sick, and there were no lessons.

50 **Julia.** But I gave lessons to Vanya.

51 **Mistress.** True. But I engaged you to teach two children, not one. Shall I pay you in full for doing only half the work?

52 **Julia.** No, ma'am.

53 **Mistress.** So we'll deduct it. . . Now, three days you had a toothache and my husband gave you permission not to work after lunch. Correct?

54 **Julia.** After four. I worked until four.

55 **Mistress** *(Looks in the book).* I have here: "Did not work after lunch." We have lunch at one and are finished at two, not at four, correct?

56 **Julia.** Yes, ma'am. But I—

57 **Mistress.** That's another seven rubles . . . Seven and twelve is nineteen . . . Subtract . . . that leaves . . . forty-one rubles . . . Correct?

58 **Julia.** Yes, ma'am. Thank you, ma'am.

59 **Mistress.** Now then, on January fourth you broke a teacup and saucer, is that true?

60 **Julia.** Just the saucer, ma'am.

61 **Mistress.** What good is a teacup without a saucer, eh? . . . That's two rubles. The saucer was an **heirloom**. It cost much more, but let it go. I'm used to taking losses.

62 **Julia.** Thank you, ma'am.

63 **Mistress.** Now then, January ninth, Kolya climbed a tree and tore his jacket.

64 **Julia.** I forbid him to do so, ma'am.

65 **Mistress.** But he didn't listen, did he? . . . Ten rubles . . . January fourteenth, Vanya's shoes were stolen . . .

66 **Julia.** By the maid, ma'am. You discharged her yourself.

67 **Mistress.** But you get paid good money to watch everything. I explained that in our first meeting. Perhaps you weren't listening. Were you listening that day, Julia, or was your head in the clouds?

68 **Julia.** Yes, ma'am.

69 **Mistress.** Yes, your head was in the clouds?

70 **Julia.** No, ma'am. I was listening.

71 **Mistress.** Good girl. So that means another five rubles off. *(Looks in the book.)* . . . Ah, yes . . . The sixteenth of January I gave you ten rubles.

72 **Julia.** You didn't.

73 **Mistress.** But I made a note of it. Why would I make a note of it if I didn't give it to you?

74 **Julia.** I don't know, ma'am.

ANALYZE DRAMA

Annotate: Review paragraphs 59–65 and mark the questions that Mistress asks Julia.

Analyze: What do you notice about these questions? Do you think Mistress really wants to know the answer?

heirloom
(âr´lo͞om´) *n.* An *heirloom* is a valued possession that was passed down in a family.

ANALYZE HUMOR

Annotate: Mark the questions Mistress asks Julia in paragraphs 67–73.

Infer: What is the tone in these paragraphs?

NOTICE & NOTE

ANALYZE HUMOR

Annotate: In paragraph 80, mark the character traits and flaws that Mistress admits to having.

Analyze: What is ironic about these admissions?

75 **Mistress.** That's not a satisfactory answer, Julia . . . Why would I make a note of giving you ten rubles if I did not in fact give it to you, eh? . . . No answer? . . . Then I must have given it to you, mustn't I?

76 **Julia.** Yes, ma'am. If you say so, ma'am.

77 **Mistress.** Well, certainly I say so. That's the point of this little talk. To clear these matters up . . . Take twenty-seven from forty-one, that leaves . . . fourteen, correct?

78 **Julia.** Yes, ma'am.

79 *(She turns away, softly crying.)*

80 **Mistress.** What's this? Tears? Are you crying? Has something made you unhappy, Julia? Please tell me. It pains me to see you like this. I'm so sensitive to tears. What is it?

81 **Julia.** Only once since I've been here have I ever been given any money and that was by your husband. On my birthday he gave me three rubles.

82 **Mistress.** Really? There's no note of it in my book. I'll put it down now. *(She writes in the book.)* Three rubles. Thank you for telling me. Sometimes I'm a little lax with my accounts . . . Always shortchanging[2] myself. So then, we take three more from fourteen . . . leaves eleven . . . Do you wish to check my figures?

83 **Julia.** There's no need to, ma'am.

84 **Mistress.** Then we're all settled. Here's your salary for two months, dear. Eleven rubles. *(She puts the pile of coins on the desk.)* Count it.

85 **Julia.** It's not necessary, ma'am.

86 **Mistress.** Come, come. Let's keep the records straight. Count it.

87 **Julia** *(Reluctantly counts it).* One, two, three, four, five, six, seven, eight, nine, ten . . . ? There's only ten, ma'am.

88 **Mistress.** Are you sure? Possibly you dropped one . . . Look on the floor, see if there's a coin there.

89 **Julia.** I didn't drop any, ma'am. I'm quite sure.

90 **Mistress.** Well, it's not here on my desk, and I *know* I gave you eleven rubles. Look on the floor.

91 **Julia.** It's all right, ma'am. Ten rubles will be fine.

92 **Mistress.** Well, keep the ten for now. And if we don't find it on the floor later, we'll discuss it again next month.

93 **Julia.** Yes, ma'am. Thank you, ma'am. You're very kind, ma'am.

94 *(She curtsies and then starts to leave.)*

95 **Mistress.** Julia! (JULIA *stops, turns.*) Come back here. (*She goes back to the desk and curtsies again.*) Why did you thank me?

96 **Julia.** For the money, ma'am.

97 **Mistress.** For the money? . . . But don't you realize what I've done? I've cheated you . . . *Robbed* you! I have no such notes in my book. I made up whatever came into my mind. Instead of the eighty rubles which I owe you, I gave you only ten. I have actually stolen from you and still you thank me . . . Why?

98 **Julia.** In the other places that I've worked, they didn't give me anything at all.

[2] **Shortchanging:** treating unfairly; cheating.

ANALYZE DRAMA

Annotate: In paragraph 97, mark the details that show that Mistress was playing a trick on Julia.

Analyze: What does this dialogue suggest about Mistress?

NOTICE & NOTE

ANALYZE DRAMA

Annotate: Mark the details in paragraph 99 that explain why Mistress cheated Julia.

Analyze: Are you surprised by Mistress's admission? Do you think she was right to try to teach Julia a lesson?

WORDS OF THE WISER

Notice & Note: In paragraph 102, mark where Mistress is asking how Julia can act the way she does.

Draw Conclusions: Read the stage directions and Julia's final response to Mistress. Is Mistress actually the wise one?

99 **Mistress.** Then they cheated you even worse than I did . . . I was playing a little joke on you, a cruel lesson just to teach you. You're much too trusting, and in this world that's very dangerous . . . I'm going to give you the entire eighty rubles. (*Hands her an envelope.*) It's all ready for you. The rest is in this envelope. Here, take it.

100 **Julia.** As you wish, ma'am.

101 (*She curtsies and starts to go again.*)

102 **Mistress.** Julia! (JULIA *stops.*) Is it possible to be so spineless? Why don't you protest? Why don't you speak up? Why don't you cry out against this cruel and unjust treatment? Is it really possible to be so guileless, so innocent, such a—pardon me for being so blunt—such a simpleton?

103 **Julia** *(The faintest trace of a smile on her lips).* Yes, ma'am . . . it's possible.

104 *(She curtsies again and runs off. The* MISTRESS *looks after her a moment, a look of complete bafflement on her face. The lights fade.)*

CHECK YOUR UNDERSTANDING

Answer these questions before moving on to the **Analyze the Text** section on the following page.

1 In Neil Simon's "The Governess," an upper-class woman tries to teach her children's nanny to —

A care for the children better

B speak up for herself

C listen to instructions

D curtsy like a servant

2 When Julia says to Mistress in paragraph 93, Yes, ma'am. Thank you, ma'am. You're very kind, ma'am, it reinforces the idea that Julia is —

F passive

G polite

H repetitive

J simple

3 At the end of the play, Julia is —

A fired for speaking out

B cheated by her employer

C paid what she deserves

D unhappy with her job

ANALYZE THE TEXT

Support your responses with evidence from the text. NOTEBOOK

1. **Draw Conclusions** Examine the Writer's lines at the beginning of the play. What conclusion can you draw about the meaning of the Writer's line "Trapped, indeed . . ."? Is Julia really trapped? Cite details from the play in your response.

2. **Infer** Reread paragraphs 45–49, when Mistress asks Julia if she insists that Mistress only count two holidays. Why is Mistress most likely asking Julia if she insists? What does this reveal about Mistress?

3. **Evaluate** Review paragraphs 59–61 when Mistress points out that the saucer was an heirloom but that she's used to taking losses. What makes this line funny?

4. **Analyze** Use Julia's actions and dialogue to analyze her character. In your own words, describe how her actions may be shaped as much by class as by her personality.

5. **Notice & Note** Reread the last few paragraphs of the play. What details suggest that Julia is not a simpleton?

RESEARCH

RESEARCH TIP
Use as many specific search terms as possible in locating information online. Then scan the descriptions of the results and note the source of the website (*.gov, .edu, .org, .com*) before choosing the results that can best answer your research question with reliable information.

"The Governess" is set in nineteenth-century Europe. Sociologists generally separate the society of that period into three distinct classes—upper, middle, and working (or lower) classes. Explore these distinctions as defined by sociologists and historians. Focus on the common characteristics and attitudes of each class.

CLASS	CHARACTERISTICS/ATTITUDES
Upper Class	
Middle Class	
Working Class	

Connect Does Mistress fit the description of someone from the upper or middle class? Explain.

CREATE AND ADAPT

Write a Personal Narrative Write about a situation in which someone was underestimating your efforts or bargaining unfairly with you. Describe what you said and did to change the situation in a positive way to improve your position.

- ❑ Introduce the topic with an engaging idea and include a conclusion that sums up the narrative in a satisfying way.
- ❑ Use details in your description of the situation and in explaining the actions you took to improve the situation for yourself.
- ❑ Use transitions to clarify the sequence of events and subordinating conjunctions to link ideas.

Go to **Writing Narratives** in the **Writing Studio** for more help.

Adapt Stage Directions Suppose you are staging the interaction between Mistress and Julia in the opening of the play. With your group, take turns as the play's director and giving instructions to the actors for performing the play's opening.

- ❑ Explain exactly how the actors should be positioned in relation to each other and to the audience.
- ❑ Guide the actors in how to convey emotion through their tone of voice and their gestures.

RESPOND TO THE ESSENTIAL QUESTION

? What can blur the lines between what's real and what's not?

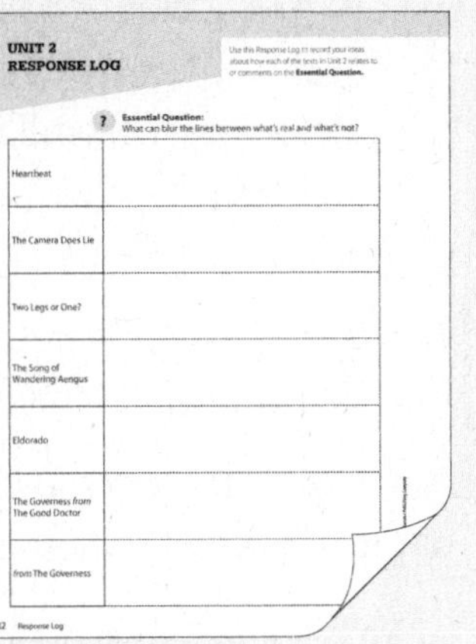
UNIT 2 RESPONSE LOG

Use this Response Log to record your ideas about how each of the texts in Unit 2 relates to or comments on the Essential Question.

? Essential Question: What can blur the lines between what's real and what's not?

Heartbeat	
The Camera Does Lie	
Two Legs or One?	
The Song of Wandering Aengus	
Eldorado	
The Governess from The Good Doctor	
from The Governess	

R2 Response Log

Gather Information Review your annotations and notes on "The Governess." Then, add relevant details to your Response Log. As you determine which information to include, think about:

- how your opinion of Mistress changed by the end of the play, and why
- how your opinion of Julia changed by the end of the play, and why

At the end of the unit, use your notes to create a multimodal presentation.

ACADEMIC VOCABULARY

As you write and discuss what you learned from the play, be sure to use the Academic Vocabulary words. Check off each of the words that you use.

- ❑ **abnormal**
- ❑ **feature**
- ❑ **focus**
- ❑ **perceive**
- ❑ **task**

RESPOND

WORD BANK
madame
inferior
discrepancy
heirloom

CRITICAL VOCABULARY

Practice and Apply With a partner, discuss and write an answer to each of the following questions. Then work together to write sentences using each Critical Vocabulary word.

1. Which vocabulary word goes with *difference* and *conflict*? Why?

2. Which vocabulary word goes with *inheritance*? Why?

3. Which vocabulary word goes with *lesser*? Why?

4. Which vocabulary word goes with *ma'am* and *Mrs.*? Why?

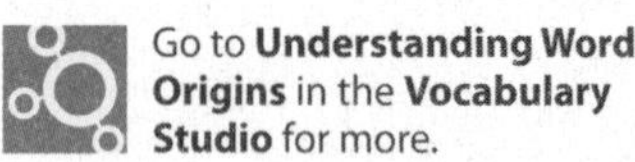

Go to **Understanding Word Origins** in the **Vocabulary Studio** for more.

VOCABULARY STRATEGY: Word Origins

An **etymology** shows the origin and historical development of a word. Studying a word's history and origin can help you clarify its precise meaning. Look at this example of an etymology for the Critical Vocabulary word *madame.*

> [French, from Old French *ma dame* : *ma,* my (from Latin *mea;* see **me-**[1] in the Appendix of Indo-European roots) + *dame,* lady (from Latin *domina,* feminine of *dominus,* lord, master of a household; see **dem-** in the Appendix of Indo-European roots).]

The etymology for *madame* shows that the word is French but has its roots in Latin words that mean "my lady."

Practice and Apply Use a dictionary to find the etymology or word origin of each of the other Critical Vocabulary words below.

WORD	ROOT LANGUAGE(S)	MEANING
inferior		
discrepancy		
heirloom		

LANGUAGE CONVENTIONS: Complex Sentences: Subordinating Conjunctions

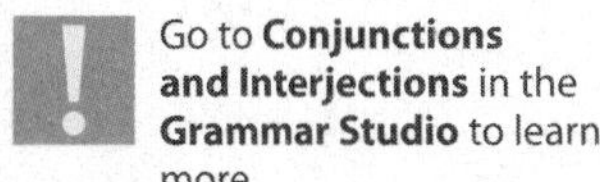

Go to **Conjunctions and Interjections** in the **Grammar Studio** to learn more.

A **complex sentence** consists of an independent clause and at least one subordinate clause. **Subordinate clauses** are clauses that contain subjects and verbs, but do not form complete sentences. **Subordinating conjunctions** are conjunctions that are used to introduce subordinate clauses.

Subordinating conjunctions provide links or transitions between ideas in a sentence. These conjunctions show place, time, or cause and effect relationships between ideas. A subordinate conjunction can also show that one idea in a sentence is more important than another idea.

In a line of dialogue from "The Governess," the playwright uses the complex sentence below to link two complete thoughts. The subordinating conjunction *when* is used at the beginning of a subordinate clause.

> I like to see your eyes **when** I speak to you.

The example sentence contains two complete thoughts:

1. *I like to see your eyes.*
2. *I speak to you.*

The playwright tells you how these two complete thoughts are related to each other by using the subordinating conjunction *when*. The word *when* indicates a time relationship between the ideas.

The chart below lists common subordinating conjunctions you can use when writing your own complex sentences:

after	before	since	until
although	even though	so that	when
as	if	though	where
because	once	unless	while

Practice and Apply Write three or four complex sentences summarizing what happens in "The Governess." Use a different subordinating conjunction in each sentence.

PRODUCTION IMAGES

from THE GOVERNESS

presented by the
Theater Arts Department, Clackamas Community College

page 165

COMPARE VERSIONS

Now that you've read "The Governess," examine some production images from a staging of the play. Think about how the sets and costuming reflect how the actors and director have interpreted the play and stage directions. Afterward, you will work with a small group on a final project that involves an analysis of both selections.

ESSENTIAL QUESTION:

What can blur the lines between what's real and what's not?

DRAMA

THE GOVERNESS

***from* The Good Doctor**

by **Neil Simon**

pages 149–157

from The Governess

QUICK START

Think about a scene in a play where a character is standing up for himself or herself. How was the drama (or the humor) of the situation shown? Describe the scene and discuss your reactions with a partner.

ANALYZE MEDIA

The production images of "The Governess" show the staging of a written work. Writers, directors, and theater technicians use various techniques to create humor, express irony, and tell a story.

- Writers of dramas create a cast of characters to add a dynamic element and use dialogue to drive the action forward.
- Directors instruct actors to use energetic facial expressions and movements to make things dramatic or humorous.

The technical aspects of producing a play are called **stagecraft.** Directors and other people involved in the staging may use scenery to convey the setting or costume design to highlight character traits and details. In the production images from "The Governess," look for these stagecraft techniques.

TECHNIQUE	WHAT IT IS	WHY IT IS USED
Scenery/ Sets	Two- and three-dimensional backgrounds or elements on stage	To show setting, time period, or mood
Costume Design	Clothes, masks, or headdresses worn by actors	To convey information about setting, character, and status
Props	Furniture and objects on the stage or handled by actors.	To illustrate the story and help actors show emotions and ideas
Makeup	Painting or changing the body of an actor	To allow actors' expressions and bodies to be seen

Stagecraft is all about the effect on the audience. Makeup can make a young person look old; scenery can transport the audience to another city or country. Other techniques that help convey meaning in a play are voice, sound, and music. Actors talk, laugh, or murmur. Sounds, such as city noises, support the setting, and music conveys emotions. All of these draw the audience into the story being told on stage.

GENRE ELEMENTS: MEDIA

- shared for a specific purpose, or reason
- combines visual and sound techniques
- play productions are a popular media format
- stagecraft includes scenery, lighting, costumes, makeup, props, music and sound effects

ANALYZE MEDIA (continued)

Directors may also use other techniques to convey mood, express humor, and focus viewers' attention on certain characters and events.

- **Lighting** is usually used to direct viewers' eyes to what is most important on the stage. Lighting can also be used to create a mood that is funny, confusing, or scary. Plays that express subtle humor might use a spotlight to highlight the expression on an actor's face.
- **Composition,** like a painting, can show the deliberate way characters or objects are arranged on stage. Viewers can learn much about how a scene is unfolding just by being aware of how the director is framing the characters and setting.
- **Motions and facial expressions** work together to convey meaning. These elements are often planned, or choreographed, as the play is rehearsed. Some directors also allow actors to improvise, or develop their own movements and expressions. For example, a director has to consider how close the actors stand to each other. In a play, actors needs to stand farther apart to allow the audience to see the action and to distinguish expressions. Another important "rule" is that actors shouldn't turn their back to other actors or the audience.

Use this chart to help you analyze the stagecraft techniques that are evident in the production images.

TECHNIQUE	EFFECT
1.	
2.	
3.	

When a director crafts a production of a drama, he or she has to make choices about how closely to follow the written work. Will the play:

- include all of the same characters?
- have the same setting?
- add or cut a scene?

As you examine these production images, think about how the director's choices are conveyed and how the images of the play production compare to your earlier reading of it.

BACKGROUND

These production images convey one interpretation of the dialogue and stage directions in the script. The images include a man talking to the audience. In the script for "The Governess," this man is the Writer. Look at his facial expression and the background scenery to analyze how the director and the actors are expressing the story and the mood of the play. Think about how the costumes convey class differences.

PREPARE TO COMPARE

As you view the production images, consider how the actors reflect the stage directions that you read in the script. Notice facial expressions that help you understand how the actors develop the characters of Julia and Mistress.

For more production images, log in online and select **"from The Governess"** from the unit menu.

As needed, pause and look carefully at the production images to make notes about what impresses you or to jot down ideas you might want to discuss later.

ANALYZE MEDIA

Support your responses with evidence from the production images.

NOTEBOOK

1. **Evaluate** Examine the photograph of the Writer. What do the scenery, props, costuming, and the Writer's expression convey about his attitude toward what he is telling the audience? Explain.
2. **Synthesize** How do the actors' costumes in the production images help to reinforce the idea of class?
3. **Interpret** Review the images of the Mistress and Julia together. How does Mistress's advice affect Julia? How can you tell?
4. **Analyze** Look at the image that shows Mistress holding Julia around her shoulders. What mood do the lighting and the actors' expressions convey? Explain.
5. **Critique** Think about the characters of Julia and Mistress in the production images. Do you think the actors who played them were chosen appropriately? How do these actors compare to how you imagined the characters as you read the play?

RESEARCH

RESEARCH TIP

Searching for the role of the governess in19th-century society might give you results for literature that features governesses. Look closely at the description and the source of the information as you scan your results. You want to make sure that you find historical information that comes from multiple reliable sites and is factually accurate.

The governess performed a specific role in 19th-century society. Research the role of the governess and record what you learn in the chart. Answer the two questions in the chart and add your own.

THE GOVERNESS	19TH-CENTURY ROLE
Who employed a governess?	
What duties did a governess have?	

Connect Given what you have learned about governesses in 19th-century society, do you think "The Governess" portrays the role of the governess accurately? Explain.

CREATE AND PRESENT

Write Dialogue Imagine that a year has passed since the scene portrayed in the production images. Julia and Mistress are now meeting to discuss a raise in pay. Create at least 15 lines of dialogue that portray this conversation.

- ❑ Determine who will bring up the topic: Julia, or Mistress.
- ❑ Maintain each character's traits through speaking style and gestures. Include stage directions with your lines.
- ❑ Make sure there is a clear ending to the conversation.

Stage the Scene Set up the scene in "The Governess" by using the front of the classroom as a stage.

- ❑ As a group, review the stage directions of the play and review the scenery, costuming, and props in the production images.
- ❑ Provide simple props. Then, using the front of the classroom as the stage, instruct two classmates representing the main characters to take positions facing the audience.
- ❑ Have the actors act out the first few lines of the play, using the script and stage directions to guide them. Then invite other students to take turns playing Julia or Mistress.

Go to **Writing Narratives** in the **Writing Studio** for more on point of view and characters.

RESPOND TO THE ESSENTIAL QUESTION

? What can blur the lines between what's real and what's not?

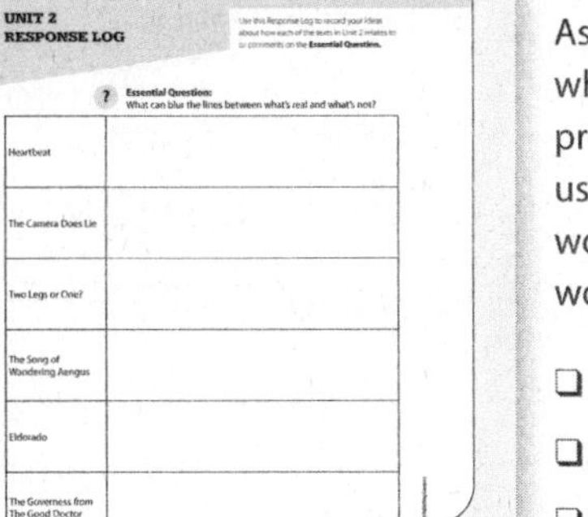

UNIT 2
RESPONSE LOG

Use this Response Log to record your ideas about how each of the texts in Unit 2 relates to or comments on the **Essential Question.**

Essential Question:
What can blur the lines between what's real and what's not?

Heartbeat	
The Camera Does Lie	
Two Legs or One?	
The Song of Wandering Aengus	
Eldorado	
The Governess *from* The Good Doctor	
from The Governess	

R2 Response Log

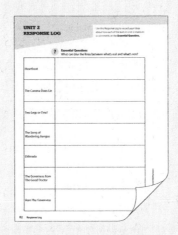

Gather Information Review your notes on the production images of "The Governess." Then, add relevant details to your Response Log. As you determine which information to include, think about:

- what you learned about each character from facial expressions, and gestures
- the staging used and how effective it was

At the end of the unit, use your notes to help create a multimodal presentation.

ACADEMIC VOCABULARY

As you write and discuss what you learned from the production images, be sure to use the Academic Vocabulary words. Check off each of the words that you use.

- ❑ **abnormal**
- ❑ **feature**
- ❑ **focus**
- ❑ **perceive**
- ❑ **task**

THE GOVERNESS
from The Good Doctor
Drama
by Neil Simon

from THE GOVERNESS
Production Images
Theater Dept., Clackamas Community College

Collaborate & Compare

COMPARE CHARACTERIZATION

Both the text of the play and the production images of "The Governess" feature characters: the Writer, the governess, Julia, and her employer, Mistress. While the scene is the same, how you imagined the characterization while reading the drama probably differs from the depiction in the production images.

A playwright develops characters through dialogue and stage directions, but directors and actors may interpret those directions differently. Work in a small group to review the text and production images. As you compare and contrast characterization in the two versions, consider:

- ❏ the stage directions in the drama versus the actors' gestures and facial expressions in the production images
- ❏ stage directions versus the costuming of the actors
- ❏ stage directions versus the sets in the production images

	Stage Directions	Production Images
Gestures/Facial Expressions		
Costuming		
Stage/Set Details		

ANALYZE THE VERSIONS

Discuss these questions in your group.

1. **Compare** With your group, review your chart. Which character depiction in the production images surprises you more: Julia, or Mistress? Explain.
2. **Analyze** In the text, Mistress calls Julia a simpleton. Where does Julia seem more gullible and awed by Mistress: in the text, or in the production images? Explain.
3. **Critique** Compare the lines of the Writer at the beginning of the script with the actor who plays the Writer in the production image. Is his depiction an effective interpretation of the stage directions and script? Why?
4. **Evaluate** Which version, the text or the production images, was more humorous? Why?

CRITIQUE AND SHARE

Now, your group can continue exploring the two versions of the play by taking turns presenting an oral critique of how the production images compare to the written play. Follow these steps:

1. **Develop Criteria** Brainstorm the criteria, or measures of what makes a drama and production of a drama interesting. Consider ideas such as how closely a production should follow the text of the script or play, how effectively the versions portray characters, and how stagecraft affects how a production conveys the story. Then, identify the four or five most important criteria.

2. **Record Your Thoughts** Use the criteria you developed to record your thoughts about the two versions, using this chart.

CRITERIA	MY THOUGHTS
1.	
2.	
3.	
4.	
5.	

3. **Write a Short Critique** Use your chart to write a brief critique about the script and production images. Begin with a clear controlling idea, or thesis, that states whether you think the production images compare favorably or unfavorably to the written version. You can support your thesis by noting how well the production images met the criteria you established in your chart. Remember to include specific details as evidence.

4. **Present the Critique** Now it is time to present your opinion to your group. As you speak, make eye contact with each group member and speak clearly, enunciating words carefully. Speak loudly enough so that everyone in the group can hear you. Use natural gestures and facial expressions.

RESEARCH TIP

To help you develop and write your critique, search online newspapers, journals, and magazines for examples of film and theater reviews.

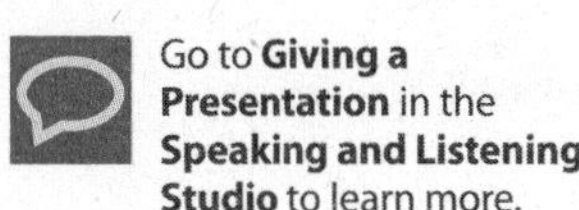
Go to **Giving a Presentation** in the **Speaking and Listening Studio** to learn more.

? ESSENTIAL QUESTION:

What can blur the lines between what's real and what's not?

Reader's Choice

Setting a Purpose Select one or more of these options from your eBook to continue your exploration of the Essential Question.

- Read the descriptions to see which text grabs your interest.
- Think about which genres you enjoy reading.

Notice & Note

In this unit, you practiced noticing and noting three signposts: **Aha Moment, Again and Again,** and **Contrasts and Contradictions.** As you read independently, these signposts and others will aid your understanding. Below are the anchor questions to ask when you read literature and nonfiction.

Reading Literature: Stories, Poems, and Plays

Signpost	Anchor Question	Lesson
Contrasts and Contradictions	Why did the character act that way?	p. 99
Aha Moment	How might this change things?	p. 3
Tough Questions	What does this make me wonder about?	p. 362
Words of the Wiser	What's the lesson for the character?	p. 363
Again and Again	Why might the author keep bringing this up?	p. 3
Memory Moment	Why is this memory important?	p. 2

Reading Nonfiction: Essays, Articles, and Arguments

Signpost	Anchor Question(s)	Lesson
Big Questions	What surprised me? What did the author think I already knew? What challenged, changed, or confirmed what I already knew?	p. 265 p. 183 p. 437
Contrasts and Contradictions	What is the difference, and why does it matter?	p. 183
Extreme or Absolute Language	Why did the author use this language?	p. 182
Numbers and Stats	Why did the author use these numbers or amounts?	p. 264
Quoted Words	Why was this person quoted or cited, and what did this add?	p. 437
Word Gaps	Do I know this word from someplace else? Does it seem like technical talk for this topic? Do clues in the sentence help me understand the word?	p. 265

INDEPENDENT READING

You can preview these texts in Unit 2 of your eBook.

Then, check off the text or texts that you select to read on your own.

SHORT STORY

Way Too Cool
Brenda Woods

A boy with asthma struggles to uphold his high social status at school.

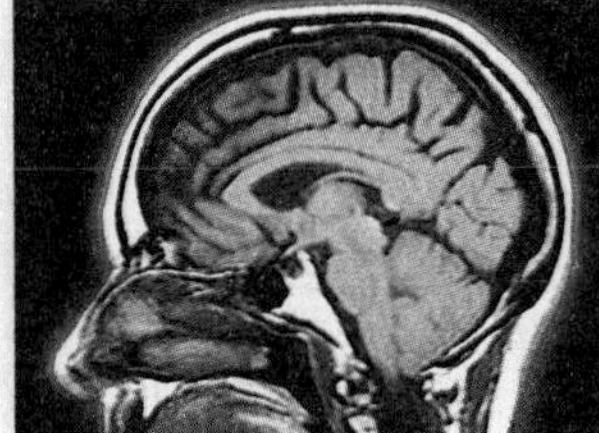

INFORMATIONAL TEXT

Forever New
Dan Risch

What is life like for those whose reality is affected by severe memory loss?

SHORT STORY

He–y, Come On Ou–t!
Shinichi Hoshi

A mysterious hole appears in a small fishing village.

PERSONAL ESSAY

A Priceless Lesson in Humility
Felipe Morales

Sometimes we have to be reminded of who we are and what we most value.

Collaborate and Share With a partner, discuss what you learned from at least one of your independent readings.

- Give a brief synopsis or summary of the text.
- Describe any signposts that you noticed in the text and explain what they revealed to you.
- Describe what you most enjoyed or found most challenging about the text. Give specific examples.
- Decide if you would recommend the text to others. Why or why not?

Go to the **Reading Studio** for more resources on **Notice & Note.**

Create a Multimodal Presentation

Go to the **Writing Studio** for help creating the script for your multimodal presentation.

This unit features many instances in which things are not as they seem. For this task, you will create a multimodal presentation that can include images, videos, music, and other elements of media. Review the article "The Camera Does Lie," which can help you think about how to create an interesting presentation. You might also refer to the notes from your Response Log, which you filled out after reading the texts in this unit.

Writing Prompt

Read the information in the box below.

This is the topic or context for your presentation.

> **We often take what we see at face value, believing that what we see is real and that our first impression is correct. A closer look, however, may change our mind.**

Think carefully about the following question.

This is the Essential Question for the unit. How would you answer this question based on the texts in this unit?

> **What can blur the lines between what's real and what's not?**

Now circle the word or words that identify exactly what you are being asked to produce.

Create and deliver a multimodal presentation to demonstrate and explain certain illusions and the techniques used to create them. Combine various media to illustrate your ideas. You may work alone or with a partner.

Be sure to—

Review these points as you develop your presentation and again when you finish. Make any needed changes.

- ❑ provide an intriguing opening that states your purpose
- ❑ include a thesis statement or controlling idea
- ❑ research examples of illusions
- ❑ devise an interactive activity for audience participation
- ❑ end with a summary and explain why illusions are interesting

1 Plan

The first step in planning your presentation is to do some research and gather materials. You can find examples of illusions online at various websites, including government and social media sites. You might also explore the methods of the artist M.C. Escher, whose mathematical prints and impossible constructions are compelling examples of the power of illusions.

Once you have gathered your materials, you can plan the elements of your presentation—both the script and the media components. If you are working with a partner, discuss ideas about how to structure your presentation. Use the table below to guide you as you create a script and identify various media that you will include.

Presentation Planning Table	
Introduction: How will you capture your audience's attention in the opening of your presentation? What is the main point you want to convey?	
Audience: What will your audience already know about illusions? How can you include the audience in your presentation?	
Visuals and other media: What images, videos, and music can you use in your presentation? What would add interest or help clarify ideas?	
Script: What information will you include in your script? How will you connect it to the media you will present?	

Background Reading Review the notes you have taken in your Response Log after reading the texts in this unit. These texts provide background reading that can support the key ideas you will include in your presentation.

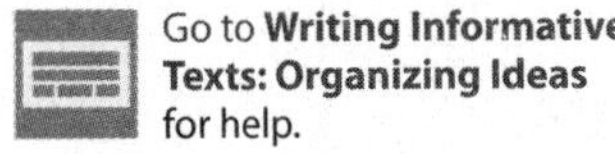
Go to **Writing Informative Texts: Organizing Ideas** for help.

Use the notes from your Response Log as you plan your presentation.

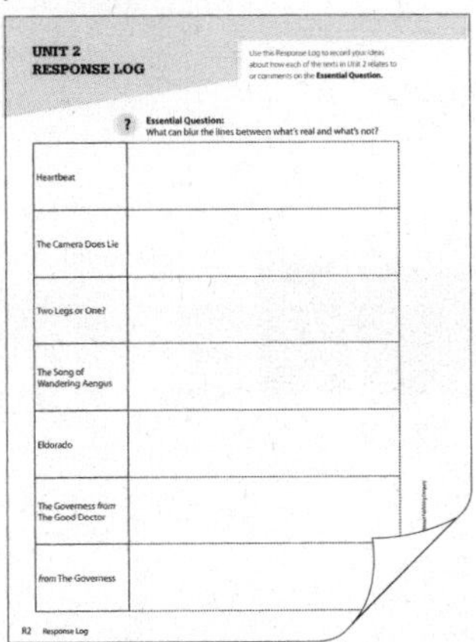
UNIT 2
RESPONSE LOG

Essential Question:
What can blur the lines between what's real and what's not?

Heartbeat	
The Camera Does Lie	
Two Legs or One?	
The Song of Wandering Aengus	
Eldorado	
The Governess from The Good Doctor	
from The Governess	

R2 Response Log

WRITING TASK

Go to **Writing Informative Texts: Using Graphics and Multimedia** for help in preparing your presentation.

Organize Your Ideas After you have gathered ideas and information from your planning activities, you need to organize the information in a way that will help you make your presentation effective. You can use the chart below to identify illusions you will display during the presentation. You can also use the chart to plan how you will demonstrate and explain how each illusion is created.

Main Topic: Illusions and How They Are Created		
Illusion: ______________	**Illusion:** ______________	**Illusion:** ______________
Description	Description	Description
How it is created	How it is created	How it is created

2 Develop a Draft

You might prefer to draft your script online.

Once you have completed your planning activities, you will be ready to begin drafting a script for your presentation. Refer to the chart above and the Presentation Planning Table you completed, as well as any notes you took as you studied the texts in the unit. These will provide a kind of map for you to follow as you develop your presentation. Using a word processor or online writing application makes it easier to make changes or move sentences around later when you are ready to revise the first draft of your script.

Use the Mentor Text

Author's Craft

Your introduction is your first chance to capture the audience's attention. In addition to your controlling idea or thesis statement, your introduction should include something that gets your audience interested in following your presentation. Note how the introduction to "The Camera Does Lie" captures your attention.

Let's face it: the Internet is a wonderful place. Where else can you read all the works of Shakespeare without leaving home? Or catch up on the news around the world with only a few clicks? See eagles snatching children! Witness men flying with homemade bird wings! Cheer for pigs saving goats!

The author begins with questions and some amazing "facts" that she will explore in the article.

Apply What You've Learned To capture your audience's attention, you have several options. You might open with a question that will make your audience curious. Or begin your presentation with a nonverbal demonstration of an illusion. Another option is to include a surprising fact, a famous quotation, or a personal anecdote related to the topic.

Genre Characteristics

Supporting details are words, phrases, or sentences that tell more about a central idea. Notice how the author of "The Camera Does Lie" uses details in the close analysis of a video.

. . . [T]he golden eagle needs a 7.5-foot (2.3-meter) wingspan just to lift its own body weight of about 14 pounds (6.4 kilograms). . . . Estimating the size of the child in the video at about 28 pounds (13 kilograms) means the eagle is lifting almost twice its own weight. This would take a wingspan of about 33 feet . . . !

The author provides details to explain why a video of an eagle snatching a child has to be fake.

Apply What You've Learned The details you include in your own presentation should clearly explain how the illusions work. Facts, examples, and quotations are some of the types of details you can use to support your ideas.

3 Revise

Go to **Writing Informative Texts: Introductions and Conclusions** in the **Writing Studio** for help.

Improving Your First Draft Once your draft is complete, you'll want to go back and look for ways to improve your script for the presentation. As you reread and revise, think about whether you have achieved your purpose. The Revision Guide will help you focus on specific elements to make the presentation stronger.

Revision Guide		
Ask Yourself	**Tips**	**Revision Techniques**
1. Does my introduction grab the audience's attention?	**Highlight** the introduction.	**Add** an interesting fact, example, or quotation about the topic.
2. Is my thesis statement clear?	**Underline** the thesis statement.	**Reword** the thesis statement using action verbs and specific nouns and adjectives.
3. Are ideas and examples organized logically? Do transitions connect ideas?	**Highlight** transitional words and phrases.	**Rearrange** sentences to organize ideas logically. **Add** transitions.
4. Do I support each main idea with evidence?	**Underline** each supporting fact, definition, example, or quotation.	**Add** more facts, details, examples, or quotations to support ideas.
5. Does my conclusion summarize the main ideas? Do I speculate about why illusions intrigue people?	**Underline** the summary. **Highlight** sentences that speculate about illusions.	**Add** a statement that summarizes the main ideas. **Insert** supporting sentences and speculations.

ACADEMIC VOCABULARY

As you conduct your **peer review,** be sure to use these words.

- ❑ **abnormal**
- ❑ **feature**
- ❑ **focus**
- ❑ **perceive**
- ❑ **task**

With a Partner If you have been working on your own, exchange scripts with another classmate and evaluate each other's drafts in a **peer review**. Provide revision suggestions for at least three of the items mentioned in the Revision Guide. When receiving feedback from your partner, listen attentively. If necessary, ask for clarification.

4 Edit

Once you have addressed the organization, development, and flow of ideas in your presentation, you can look to improve the finer points of your script. Edit for the proper use of standard English conventions and make sure to correct any misspellings or grammatical errors.

5 Practice Your Presentation

After completing your draft, practice with a partner or in a small group to improve both the presentation and your delivery.

Go to **Giving a Presentation** inthe **Speaking and Listening Studio** to learn more.

Practice Timing

Use notes or cues in your script to ensure that you incorporate video, images, and sound at the appropriate time.

Practice Effective Verbal Techniques

- ❑ **Enunciation** Replace words that you stumble over. Rearrange sentences so that your delivery is smooth.
- ❑ **Voice Modulation and Pitch** Use your voice to show enthusiasm and emphasis.
- ❑ **Speaking Rate** Speak a little slowly. Pause frequently to let the audience consider important points.
- ❑ **Volume** Speak so that everyone can hear you.

Practice Effective Nonverbal Techniques

- ❑ **Eye Contact** Look at each member of the audience at least once.
- ❑ **Facial Expression** Smile, frown, or raise an eyebrow to show your feelings or to emphasize points.
- ❑ **Gestures** Stand tall and relaxed, and use natural gestures (for example, shrugs, nods, or shakes of your head) to add meaning and interest to your presentation.

As you work to improve your presentations, be sure to follow discussion rules:

- ❑ **listen closely to each other**
- ❑ **don't interrupt**
- ❑ **ask helpful, relevant, and thoughtful questions**
- ❑ **provide only clear, direct, and appropriate answers**

Provide and Consider Advice for Improvement

As a listener, pay close attention. Take notes about how presenters can improve their presentations. Summarize each presenter's main points to check your understanding, and ask questions if you need clarification.

As a presenter, listen closely to questions. Consider how to make your presentation clearer or better organized. Ask for suggestions about changing onscreen text or images to improve your presentation.

6 Deliver Your Presentation

Use the advice you received to make final changes in your presentation. Then, using effective verbal and nonverbal techniques, present it to your classmates.

WRITING TASK

Use the scoring guide to evaluate your presentation.

Task Scoring Guide: Multimodal Presentation			
	Organization/Progression	**Development of Ideas**	**Use of Language and Conventions**
4	• The organization is effective and appropriate to the purpose. • All ideas are focused on the topic specified in the prompt. • Transitions clearly show the relationship between ideas.	• The introduction catches the audience's attention and clearly identifies the topic. • The script contains a clear, concise, and well-defined thesis statement. • The topic is well developed with clear main ideas supported by facts, details, examples, and appropriate media elements. • The conclusion effectively summarizes the information presented.	• Language and word choice are purposeful and precise. • There is a variety of simple, compound, and complex sentences; they show how ideas are related. • Spelling, capitalization, and punctuation are correct. • Grammar and usage are correct.
3	• The organization is, for the most part, effective and appropriate to the purpose. • Most ideas are focused on the topic specified in the prompt. • A few more transitions are needed to show the relationship between ideas.	• The introduction could be more engaging. The topic is identified. • The script contains a clear thesis statement. • The development of ideas is clear because the writer uses facts, details, examples, and mostly appropriate media elements. • The conclusion summarizes the information presented.	• Language is, for the most part, specific and clear. • Sentences vary somewhat in structure. • Some spelling, capitalization, and punctuation mistakes are present. • Some grammar and usage errors occur.
2	• The organization is evident but is not always appropriate to the purpose. • Only some ideas are focused on the topic specified in the prompt. • More transitions are needed to show the relationship between ideas.	• The introduction is not engaging; the topic is unclear. • The thesis statement does not express a clear point. • The development of ideas is minimal. The writer uses inappropriate facts, details, examples, as well as some ineffective media elements. • The conclusion is only partially effective.	• Language is often vague and general. • Compound and complex sentences are rarely used. • Spelling, capitalization, and punctuation are often incorrect but do not make reading difficult. • Grammar and usage are often incorrect, but the writer's ideas are still clear.
1	• The organization is not appropriate to the purpose. • Ideas are not focused on the topic specified in the prompt. • No transitions are used, making the relationship among ideas difficult to understand.	• The introduction is missing or confusing. • The thesis statement is missing. • The development of ideas is weak. Supporting facts, details, examples, and media elements are unreliable, vague, or missing. • The conclusion is missing.	• Language is vague, confusing, or inappropriate for the presentation. • There is no sentence variety. • Many spelling, capitalization, and punctuation errors are present. • Many grammatical and usage errors confuse the writer's ideas.

Reflect on the Unit

By completing your multimodal presentation, you have created a product that pulls together and expresses your thoughts about the reading you have done in this unit. Now is a good time to reflect on what you have learned.

Reflect on the Essential Question

- What can blur the lines between what's real and what's not? How has your answer to this question changed since you first considered it when you started this unit?
- What are some examples from the texts you've read that show how illusions are created?

Reflect on Your Reading

- Which selections were the most interesting or surprising to you?
- From which selection did you learn the most about how people respond to illusions?

Reflect on the Task

- What difficulties did you encounter while working on your multimodal presentation? How might you avoid them next time?
- What parts of the presentation were the easiest and hardest to complete? Why?
- What improvements did you make to your presentation as you were revising?

UNIT 2 SELECTIONS

- "Heartbeat"
- "The Camera Does Lie"
- "Two Legs or One?"
- "The Song of Wandering Aengus"
- "Eldorado"
- "The Governess" (drama)
- "The Governess" (production images)

UNIT 3

INSPIRED BY NATURE

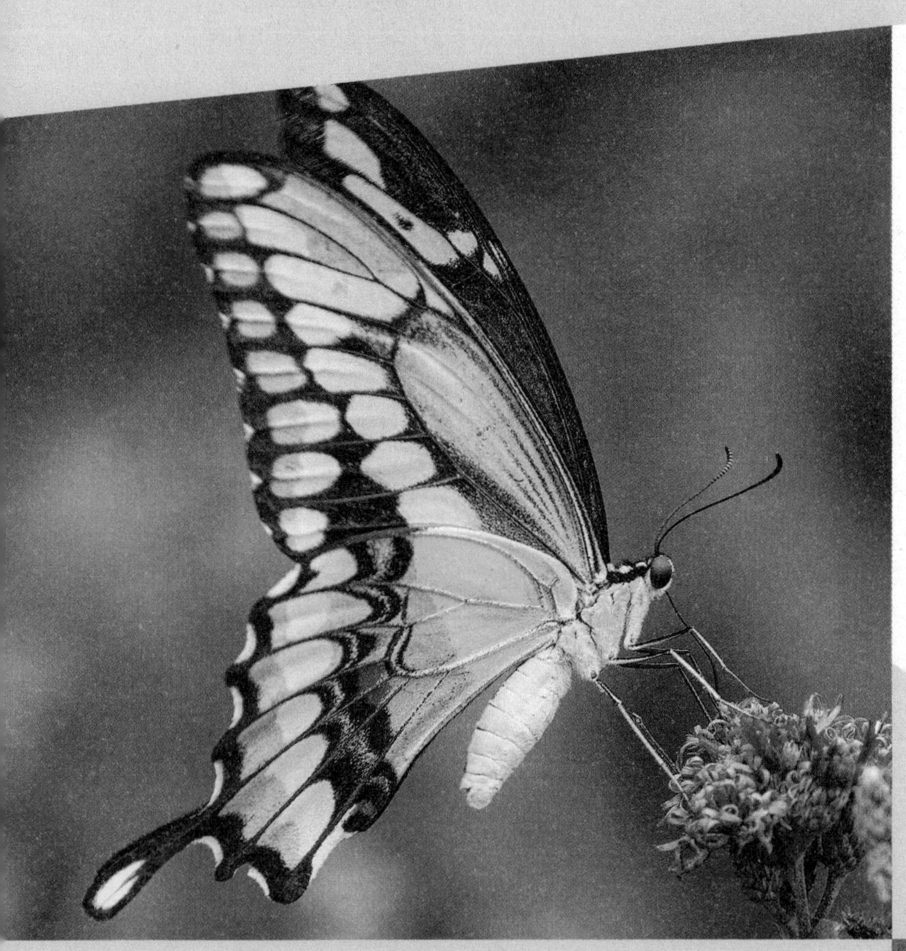

? **ESSENTIAL QUESTION:**

What does it mean to be in harmony with nature?

> **Here again we are reminded that in nature nothing exists alone.**
>
> Rachel Carson

ACADEMIC VOCABULARY

Academic Vocabulary words are words you use when you discuss and write about texts. In this unit you will practice and learn five words.

☑ **affect** ❑ **element** ❑ **ensure** ❑ **participate** ❑ **specify**

Study the Word Network to learn more about the word **affect.**

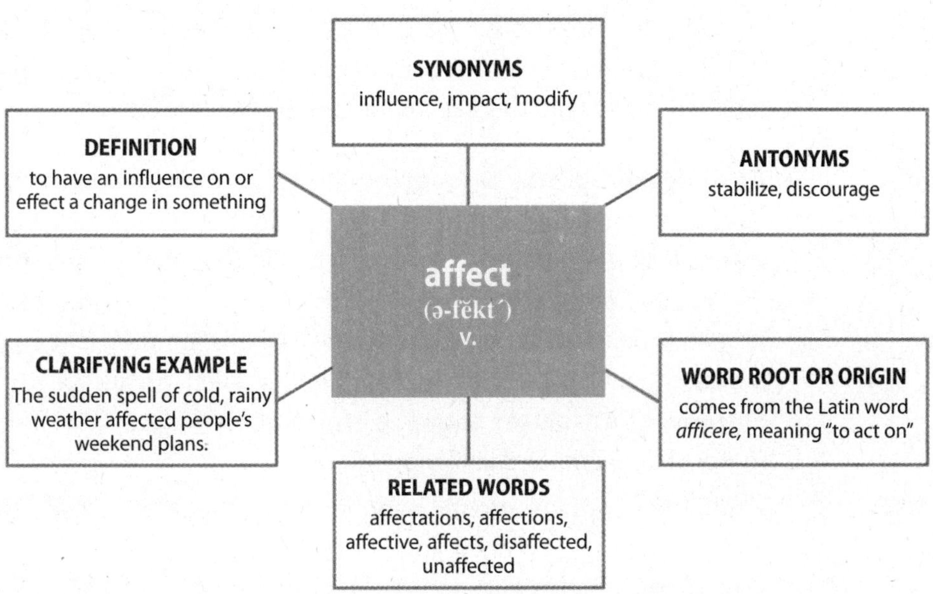

SYNONYMS
influence, impact, modify
DEFINITION
to have an influence on or effect a change in something
ANTONYMS
stabilize, discourage
affect
(ə-fĕkt´)
v.
CLARIFYING EXAMPLE
The sudden spell of cold, rainy weather affected people's weekend plans.
WORD ROOT OR ORIGIN
comes from the Latin word *afficere,* meaning "to act on"
RELATED WORDS
affectations, affections, affective, affects, disaffected, unaffected

Write and Discuss Discuss the completed Word Network with a partner, making sure to talk through all of the boxes until you both understand the word, its synonyms, antonyms, and related forms. Then, fill out Word Networks for the remaining four words. Use a dictionary or online resource to help you complete the activity.

*Go online to access the **Word Networks**.*

RESPOND TO THE ESSENTIAL QUESTION

In this unit, you will explore how different people find—or are challenged to find—harmony in nature. As you read, you will revisit the **Essential Question** and gather your ideas about it in the **Response Log** that appears on page R3. At the end of the unit, you will have the opportunity to write a **personal narrative** about an experience you had in nature or a lesson learned from nature. Filling out the Response Log will help you prepare for this writing task.

UNIT 3 RESPONSE LOG

Essential Question: What does it mean to be in harmony with nature?

Never Retreat *from* Eyes Wide Open	
from Mississippi Solo	
The Drought	
Allied with Green	
Ode to enchanted light	
Sleeping in the Forest	
from Trash Talk	
You're Part of the Solution	

*You can also go online to access the **Response Log**.*

READING MODEL

NEVER RETREAT

For more information on these and other signposts to Notice & Note, visit the **Reading Studio**.

You are about to read "Never Retreat," an argument presented in a book about environmental issues. In it, you will notice and note signposts for clues about the author's opinions and the techniques he uses to make his argument convincing. Here are three key signposts to look for as you read this argument and the other texts in this unit.

When you encounter words or phrases like these in a text, pause to see whether you have discovered an **Extreme or Absolute Language** signpost:

"It always happens that . . ."

"and the saddest part of all . . ."

"Of course, you have to realize that . . ."

"but few could doubt that . . ."

Extreme or Absolute Language While talking with a friend, you comment that your favorite basketball team lost because a key player was hurt. Your friend says, "Give me a break! That player is the worst in the league!" You reply, "No way! You couldn't tell a good player from a broken shoelace!" Both speakers have used exaggerated language to indicate that they are sure their opinion is correct. An author who uses **Extreme or Absolute Language** in an argument does so for a specific reason. For example, such language can:

- get other people's attention and force them to rethink their position
- introduce new and engaging details to support a claim
- emphasize the author's true feelings about a subject
- reveal an author's biases toward a subject

The paragraph below illustrates a student's annotation within "Never Retreat" and a response to a Notice and Note signpost.

Anchor Question When you notice this signpost, ask: Why did the author use this language?

3 With fossil fuels, new uses multiplied madly until we wove them into every corner of our lives. What used to be luxuries—garage-door openers, dishwashers, cell phones—came to feel like necessities. It's easy to go up the lifestyle ladder but painful climbing down. This is important.

What absolute or extreme language is used?	Extreme language: "multiplied madly" and "every corner" Absolute language: "This is important"
Why do you think this language is important to the argument?	The extreme language catches the reader's attention and emphasizes the author's feeling about the convenience items that grew from the expanded use of fossil fuels. "This is important" is an absolute statement that does not allow the reader to disagree.

Contrasts and Contradictions Have you ever had a situation turn out in an unexpected way? In nonfiction, **Contrasts and Contradictions** often point to a difference between what people generally think is true and what the author claims is actually true. That difference can surprise readers. It can cause them to wonder about their own views and be more willing to consider the author's argument and evidence. Here a student marked a Contrast and Contradiction.

6 When our standard of living is threatened by scarcity and side effects, you'd think we'd cut back. Instead, the common response is to maintain it at any cost. . . . We know our freshwater aquifers are limited, but we're draining them faster rather than slower. . . .

Anchor Question
When you notice this signpost, ask: What is the difference, and why does it matter?

Which statement does the underlined sentence contradict?	It contradicts the first sentence: "When our standard of living is threatened by scarcity and side effects, you'd think we'd cut back."
What effect does this have?	It makes the reader realize that people are not taking the problem as seriously as they may think they are.

Big Questions If a person assumes you know something when you actually don't—such as how to use an app or define a new term—you might feel a bit awkward or confused. If you feel a bit lost while reading a nonfiction text, ask yourself one of the **Big Questions**—"What did the author think I already knew?" The answer can help you better grasp the point the author is making. (Other Big Questions include "What surprised me?" and "What changed, challenged, or confirmed what I already knew?") In this example, a student underlined details that relate to a Big Question.

13 **Adaptability is one of humankind's hallmarks. We evolved during difficult climatic times . . . times so challenging that the twenty or so other strains of humans who weren't as flexible all died out. Is that ability to adapt still within us?**

Which words or details are confusing?	The detail "the twenty or so other strains of humans who weren't as flexible all died out" seems a little confusing.
What did the author think I already knew?	The author thought I already knew about the many different strains of humans.

NEVER RETREAT
from Eyes Wide Open

Argument by **Paul Fleischman**

? ESSENTIAL QUESTION:

What does it mean to be in harmony with nature?

QUICK START

Think about what it might mean to live a "simple" life. If you had to live more simply, what would you find easy—and difficult—to give up?

ANALYZE AN ARGUMENT

In an **argument,** the author expresses a position—an opinion—on an issue or a problem and provides supporting evidence for it. Strong arguments have the following key elements:

- a **claim,** which is the writer's position on the issue or problem
- **support,** which includes reasons and evidence the writer provides to back up the claim
- **counterarguments,** which are the writer's responses to opposing opinions—responses that show that the writer's position is stronger

Use a chart like the one below to help you analyze "Never Retreat."

ELEMENT	EXAMPLE FROM ARGUMENT
Claim	
Support	
Counterarguments	

GENRE ELEMENTS: ARGUMENT

- purpose is to share the author's claim and persuade readers to agree with it—and, sometimes, to take action because they agree
- presents reasons to support the author's claim
- supports reasons with statistics, examples, and other factual evidence
- may anticipate and respond to counterarguments, questions, and other points of view

ANALYZE SUBJECTIVE AND OBJECTIVE POINT OF VIEW

In arguments and other nonfiction texts, authors convey a **point of view,** or perspective, about their topic. How authors view a topic is often shaped by their ideas, feelings, and beliefs. In nonfiction writing, an author's point of view may be subjective, objective, or both.

- When writing from a **subjective point of view,** the author includes personal opinions, feelings, and beliefs.
- When writing from an **objective point of view,** the author leaves out personal opinions and instead presents information in a straightforward, unbiased way.

Many elements in an argument can suggest the author's point of view. Word choices such as *easy* or *threatened,* for example, can signal a subjective point of view—if not for the entire selection, at least for that part of it. In addition, an author sometimes will include a rhetorical question. A **rhetorical question** either has no answer or an answer that is so obvious that the author doesn't need to state it. In either case, a rhetorical question can emphasize a key point or just make readers think. As you read "Never Retreat," consider the author's point of view and the questions he asks. Consider why he asks each one.

CRITICAL VOCABULARY

combustion **scarcity** **aquifer** **adaptability**

To see how many Critical Vocabulary words you already know, answer these questions.

1. Why is the **combustion** of dried brush in a forest so dangerous?
2. If there were a **scarcity** of food, would people be eating well? Why?
3. Why would a city's government decide to tap into an **aquifer**?
4. Do people known for their **adaptability** react well to change? Why?

LANGUAGE CONVENTIONS

Conjunctions and Complex Sentences In sentences, conjunctions join words and word groups. **Correlative conjunctions** such as *either / or* or *neither / nor* are used as a pair to join words or word groups used in the same way. In a complex sentence, however, ideas may be connected in a way that shows which idea is stronger and which ideas are less important, or subordinate. Words such as *after, although, because, if,* and *when* signal the subordinate ideas. These words are called **subordinating conjunctions.** In the following complex sentences, the subordinate idea is underlined once and the subordinating conjunction twice.

> **With fossil fuels, new uses multiplied madly until we wove them into every corner of our lives.**
>
> **When a job is lost in the family, we cut budgets.**

As you read "Never Retreat," note the use of conjunctions. Decide what relationship it signals between ideas in the sentence.

ANNOTATION MODEL

NOTICE & NOTE 

As you read, notice and note signposts, including **Extreme or Absolute Language, Contrasts and Contradictions,** and **Big Questions.** Here is an example of how one reader responded to the opening of "Never Retreat."

1 Our dependence on fossil fuels didn't arise from an evil plot but through our curiosity and ingenuity. Coal was seen only as a heat source until we found it could power steam engines. Later we discovered that the gas it gave off when heated could light homes and streets. Gasoline was considered a useless by-product of petroleum—and then came the internal combustion engine.

Evil plot is extreme language. It's part of a sentence that contrasts two ideas about why we depend on fossil fuels.

I'll read on to learn why the author felt it was important to talk about engines.

BACKGROUND

Paul Fleischman *(b. 1952) grew up in Santa Monica, California, and lives in Santa Cruz today. He is the award-winning author of more than forty novels, short story and poetry collections, and nonfiction books for children and young adults. His* Joyful Noise: Poems for Two Voices, *which celebrates the insect world, received the Newbery Medal in 1989. Many of Fleischman's other books explore carefully researched historical settings and social issues.*

NEVER RETREAT

from Eyes Wide Open

Argument by Paul Fleischman

SETTING A PURPOSE

As you read, identify the author's opinions about modern environmental problems and about the way many people live today. In addition, pay attention to the historical and present-day evidence that he offers to support his argument.

1 Our dependence on fossil fuels didn't arise from an evil plot but through our curiosity and ingenuity. Coal was seen only as a heat source until we found it could power steam engines. Later we discovered that the gas it gave off when heated could light homes and streets. Gasoline was considered a useless by-product of petroleum—and then came the internal **combustion** engine.

2 Necessity is said to be the mother of invention, but the reverse is also true. We tinker and probe, then see if our discovery fills any need, including needs we didn't know we had.

3 With fossil fuels, new uses multiplied madly until we wove them into every corner of our lives. What used to be luxuries—garage-door openers, dishwashers, cell phones—

Notice & Note

Use the side margins to notice and note signposts in the text.

CONTRASTS AND CONTRADICTIONS

Notice & Note: In paragraph 1, mark the energy sources about which people's attitudes changed.

Cause/Effect: According to the author, why did people later contradict their original opinion of these sources?

combustion
(kəm-bŭs´chən) *n. Combustion* is the process of burning, which produces heat and light.

NOTICE & NOTE

ANALYZE ARGUMENT
Annotate: In paragraph 3, mark the author's claim about learning to live without the things we consider "necessary."

Connect: What would be an example of a change that would make this claim true in your life?

ANALYZE SUBJECTIVE AND OBJECTIVE POINT OF VIEW
Annotate: In paragraph 4, mark two details that show that the author is expressing a subjective point of view.

Critique: How do these details relate to the author's argument?

EXTREME OR ABSOLUTE LANGUAGE

Notice & Note: In paragraph 5, mark what the author says is the only time that Americans made a radical change in an energy source.

Analyze: What is it about his statement that makes it seem absolute? Explain.

scarcity
(skâr′sĭ-tē) *n.* When you experience a *scarcity*, you have a shortage or lack of something.

aquifer
(ăk′wə-fər) *n.* An *aquifer* is an underground layer of rock that contains water.

came to feel like necessities. It's easy to go up the lifestyle ladder but painful climbing down. This is important.

4 It's not hard to understand. The windfall of cheap fossil fuels that's fueled the West for two centuries got us used to ever-rising living standards. Energy buys convenience. And convenience is addictive—highly so. Each increased dosage quickly becomes our new minimum requirement. You see this whenever gas prices rise and endanger our freedom to drive as much as we want—causing politicians to leap into action on our behalf. They know that whatever level of comfort we're at feels like a must.

5 To escape from the environmental crunch, we don't need to throw out our entire lifestyle but simply to power it on something other than fossil fuels. We're on the way. Switching to renewables for electricity is probably the easy part. Harder will be getting oil out of transportation and agriculture and the military, as well as all the products it's currently in: the asphalt in your street, the carpet on your floor, the clothes in your closet, and all the plastic around you in furniture, appliances, cars, and packaging. Can we run this film in reverse? Only once have we replaced an energy source so central to our economy and lifestyle: when slave labor was abolished, a change so jarring that its threat brought on war.

6 When our standard of living is threatened by **scarcity** and side effects, you'd think we'd cut back. Instead, the common response is to maintain it at any cost. Bluefin tuna is in steep decline, but the tuna-loving Japanese are catching all they can. We know our freshwater **aquifers** are limited, but we're draining them faster rather than slower. Scarcity was humankind's enemy for so long that resistance to a downshift in lifestyle is

strong. At the first international climate summit in 1992, the U.S. delegation's attitude was that America's standard of living wasn't up for negotiation. Every U.S. administration since then has followed the same path.

7 Developing countries feel the same. People getting their first paved roads, safe water, electric lights, and refrigerators don't want to march backward any more than the West does.

8 Using less energy and consuming less—taking a step down the ladder—would make the West's transition to renewables that much easier. What would happen if we cut the amount of stuff we bought in half? We'd save hugely on resources as well as on the energy needed to make them into products. We'd also lose large numbers of jobs. To keep employment up, we need people to keep buying bacon-flavored dental floss and Elvis Presley mouse pads and other nonessentials. The call "Never retreat" comes from us both as consumers and breadwinners.

9 Many have sketched a sustainable economy that doesn't rest on unnecessary consumption. These proposals often favor decentralization—a more dispersed and rural society, with people growing more of their own food and generating more of their own power. This would give us an economy with greater resilience than our current highly connected one.

ANALYZE SUBJECTIVE AND OBJECTIVE POINT OF VIEW

Annotate: In paragraph 8, mark the two examples of "nonessentials" that the author mentions.

Analyze: Is the author presenting an objective point of view, or a subjective point of view? Why do you think so?

NOTICE & NOTE

ANALYZE ARGUMENT
Annotate: Mark the question that begins paragraph 10.

Infer: How does that question suggest a point of viewthat the author is going to challenge?

LANGUAGE CONVENTIONS
Annotate: Mark the two subordinating conjunctions in paragraph 10.

Interpret: What do the ideas introduced by these words add to the rest of each sentence?

BIG QUESTIONS

Notice & Note: In paragraph 12, mark two topics that the author thinks you may already know about.

Compare: What do these topics have in common?

adaptability
(ə-dăp′tə-bĭl′ĭ-tē) *n.* People who have *adaptability* can change to survive and fit in with new circumstances.

EXTREME OR ABSOLUTE LANGUAGE

Notice & Note: In the final paragraph, mark two word choices that recall some absolute/extreme language from earlier in the selection.

Interpret: What point does the author make by repeating this reference?

10 What's the problem with highly integrated systems? They're efficient and low cost, but brittle. Ours brings us fruit from South America and computer parts from China but leaves us in the lurch if anything interrupts trade. We're so connected that a single power outage or oil shortage affects millions. Sicknesses can more easily become epidemics. The American housing collapse of 2008 quickly brought on a worldwide recession.

11 Life used to be much more decentralized. The Transition movement, beginning in Britain, guides communities toward a lower energy, more self-sufficient future, with hundreds of branches active in the United States and elsewhere. The Slow Food movement, back-to-the-landers reviving rural skills, and those pursuing voluntary simplicity are pointed in the same direction.

12 What might a major lifestyle downshift feel like? Real-world Americans experienced a downshift during World War II. The U.S. auto industry stopped making cars and switched to building tanks and planes. Gasoline, milk, meat, coffee, cheese, sugar, heating oil, and shoes were strictly rationed. Could we do it again?

13 **Adaptability** is one of humankind's hallmarks. We evolved during difficult climatic times, when temperatures swung between ice ages and warmer interglacial periods, times so challenging that the twenty or so other strains of humans who weren't as flexible all died out. Is that ability to adapt still within us?

14 Consider a power outage's frustrations, then the gradual adaptation the longer it goes on until dining by lantern light feels almost normal. Use of mass transit goes up when gas prices rise. We adjust to water rationing. When a job is lost in the family, we cut budgets. People think they can't go backward, then find out that they can. We ended up succeeding in getting rid of slavery, after all. Stranger still to a time-traveling slave owner: we no longer even notice its absence.

CHECK YOUR UNDERSTANDING

Answer these questions before moving on to the **Analyze the Text** section on the following page.

1 In paragraphs 1–3, the author argues that —

A our dependence on coal is the result of a plot by energy companies

B we invent only those things that we know will be useful to everyone

C sometimes we unexpectedly find new uses for a discovery or invention

D fossil fuels have always been useful for powering machines

2 In paragraph 6, the author mentions the fishing of Bluefin tuna and the 1992 climate summit in order to support the idea that —

F the world's nations are interconnected in ways that eventually will harm their economies

G when facing a common problem, nations will work together to find a solution

H people want to maintain their current way of life, even when cutting back would be wise

J individuals, not governments, must lead the way in switching to renewable sources of energy

3 What evidence does the author offer to support the idea that we have become addicted to the convenience of fossil fuels?

A The greater amount of coal, the more nonessential products are manufactured.

B Developing countries require fewer roads and less electricity than industrialized nations.

C It's easier to go down the lifestyle ladder than up it.

D When gas prices rise, politicians take action to limit the increase.

ANALYZE THE TEXT

Support your responses with evidence from the text. NOTEBOOK

1. **Summarize** Reread paragraphs 1–2. Summarize the author's position on whether inventions are created to meet current needs.

2. **Cite Evidence** According to the author, what is the main difficulty in ending our dependence on fossil fuels? Cite text evidence in your response.

3. **Compare** In paragraph 4, to what does the author compare our dependence upon fossil fuels? How does this comparison relate to other instances of the author's use of extreme language?

4. **Analyze** In paragraph 10, do you think the author is presenting an objective point of view, a subjective one, or both? Explain.

5. **Notice & Note** Consider "Never Retreat" as a whole. What do you think the author feels his readers already know before they start reading? Why is that prior knowledge important to his argument?

RESEARCH

In paragraph 11, the author mentions the Transition movement, which began in Great Britain and spread to the United States. Use the chart to find out more about this movement and then share what you learn.

RESEARCH QUESTIONS	WHAT YOU LEARNED
What are the main goals of the Transition movement?	
What problems does the Transition movement try to address?	
What types of activities does the Transition movement engage in?	

RESEARCH TIP
When you conduct online research, be sure to evaluate the credibility of websites. Web addresses ending in *.gov*, *.edu*, or *.org* are often more reliable than other sites. Other reliable sources may include major news outlets. It's always a good idea to confirm information using multiple, reliable sites.

Extend Find out about another group concerned with the long-term sustainability of the environment. What is the major focus of the group? What activities does it engage in to promote its cause? Share your findings with some of your classmates.

WRITE AND DISCUSS

Go to **Writing as a Process** in the **Writing Studio** for more help.

Write a Letter Paul Fleischman began his writing career as a poet and then a novelist. Write a letter to the author requesting information about his decision to write about the environment.

- ❑ Start by explaining how you learned about his writing.
- ❑ Ask about event(s) in his life that inspired him to write *Eyes Wide Open*, especially the chapter entitled "Never Retreat."
- ❑ Discuss details from "Never Retreat" that you especially liked or that you had questions about. Mention issues about the environment that you have been involved in or that interest you.
- ❑ Write with a friendly, respectful tone, and follow the correct form for a friendly letter.

Go to **Participating in Collaborative Discussions** in the **Speaking and Listening Studio** for more help.

Group Discussion In a small group, discuss how your school or community promotes sustainability of the environment. How well do their approaches to sustainability seem to be working? What other ways to improve or expand those efforts would you suggest?

- ❑ Remember to stay focused on the discussion topic.
- ❑ Be prepared to share your thoughts with others in the group.
- ❑ Encourage all group members to participate in the discussion.
- ❑ Respect the ideas and feelings of other group members.
- ❑ Ask clarifying questions that build on others' ideas.

RESPOND TO THE ESSENTIAL QUESTION

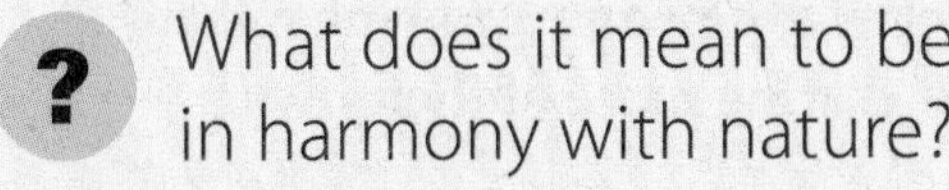

? What does it mean to be in harmony with nature?

Gather Information Review your annotations and notes on "Never Retreat." Then, add relevant details to your Response Log. As you determine which information to include, think about:

- how trying to rely on easy solutions can affect long-term problems
- how individual needs might conflict with social goals
- why people's behavior might not change when facing new problems

At the end of the unit, use your notes to write a personal narrative.

ACADEMIC VOCABULARY

As you write and discuss what you learned from the argument, be sure to use the Academic Vocabulary words. Check off each of the words that you use.

- ❑ **affect**
- ❑ **element**
- ❑ **ensure**
- ❑ **participate**
- ❑ **specify**

RESPOND

CRITICAL VOCABULARY

WORD BANK
combustion
scarcity
aquifer
adaptability

Practice and Apply Choose the letter of the best answer to each question. Then, explain your response.

1. Which of the following involves **combustion**?
   - **a.** squeezing into an over-crowded room
   - **b.** riding in a gasoline-powered vehicle
2. Which of the following is an example of **scarcity**?
   - **a.** store shelves filled with fruits and vegetables
   - **b.** store shelves empty of fruits and vegetables
3. Which of the following would be the most likely use of an **aquifer**?
   - **a.** irrigating crops
   - **b.** heating homes
4. Which of the following is an example of **adaptability**?
   - **a.** changing your decision after listening to a friend
   - **b.** sticking with your decision no matter what

VOCABULARY STRATEGY: Context Clues

Go to **Context Clues** in the **Vocabulary Studio** for more.

When you come across an unfamiliar word in your reading, look for **context clues.** These clues—found in surrounding words, phrases, or sentences—can help you figure out the word's meaning. In this example, the author provided a definition within the sentence itself.

> **These proposals often favor *decentralization*—a more dispersed and rural society, with people growing more of their own food and generating more of their own power.**

Practice and Apply Mark the word or phrase in each sentence that defines the boldfaced word. Then, use the boldfaced word in a sentence of your own.

1. The state set up a new website to **facilitate,** or make easy, the registration of first-time voters before Election Day.
2. The victims' names are inscribed on the wall so that they will be remembered by **posterity**—that is, by future generations.
3. At her new school, Riya was **reticent,** withdrawn, and silent even when classmates invited her to join in their activities.
4. The leaks from the gas tanks spread **noxious** fumes that caused residents to become nauseated and develop headaches.

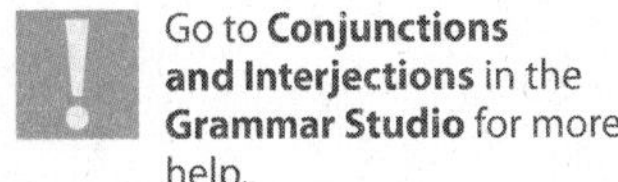

LANGUAGE CONVENTIONS: Conjunctions and Complex Sentences

Go to **Conjunctions and Interjections** in the **Grammar Studio** for more help.

A **conjunction** is a word that joins words or word groups. **Correlative conjunctions** are used as a pair to join words or word groups used the same way in a sentence. Common correlative conjunctions are *either / or, neither / nor,* and *both / and,* as in this example from the selection:

> **The call "Never retreat" comes from us both as consumers and [as] breadwinners.**

Subordinating conjunctions, such as *although, after,* and *because,* are used in complex sentences to introduce clauses that cannot stand by themselves as complete sentences. A **complex sentence** expresses two or more related ideas and shows that one idea is more important than the others. The more important idea in a complex sentence appears in an **independent clause,** which can stand alone as a sentence. The other clause (or clauses) in a complex sentence is the **subordinate clause.** It is less important and cannot stand alone as a sentence. This type of clause is a **sentence fragment,** or group of words that is only part of a sentence because it does not express a complete thought and may be confusing to a reader or listener. However, a subordinate clause still adds key information to a sentence.

Subordinate clauses often answer questions such as *How? When? Where? Why? To what degree? Under what condition?* In the example sentence below, the subordinating conjunction *because* joins the independent clause and the subordinate clause:

Question: *Why* did coal become a popular fuel?
Answer: Coal became popular **because** it was plentiful and cheap.
independent clause **subordinate clause**

In the following example, notice that because the subordinate clause comes before the independent clause, it is set off by a comma.

Question: *When* did gasoline become useful?
Answer: **After** the combustion engine was invented, gasoline became very useful.

Practice and Apply Write your own sentences using subordinating conjunctions to create complex sentences and correlative conjunctions to join words that are used the same way. Base your sentences on "Never Retreat" or another topic. Share your sentences with a partner. Make sure that you have avoided writing confusing sentence fragments that do not express complete thoughts. Discuss how different sentence constructions help readers and listeners understand your ideas and add interest to your writing.

from MISSISSIPPI SOLO

Memoir by **Eddy Harris**

? ***ESSENTIAL QUESTION:***

What does it mean to be in harmony with nature?

QUICK START

How connected to nature do you feel? Mark this scale with an X to indicate your connection. Compare your response with the response of at least one classmate.

ANALYZE MEMOIR

A **memoir** is a form of autobiographical writing in which the author shares his or her personal experiences and observations related to significant events and people. Memoirs are often written in the first person. Authors of memoirs often do the following:

- "talk" to readers, using informal language and sharing personal feelings
- recall actual events and emphasize their reactions to them
- show how the experiences affected their attitudes and lives

GENRE ELEMENTS: MEMOIR

- focuses on past events that are meaningful to the author
- reveals the author's thoughts and feelings about past events
- is told from the first-person point of view, with pronouns such as *I*, *me*, and *my*
- may address readers as "you," as if conversing with them

ANALYZE FIGURATIVE LANGUAGE

Figurative language is an imaginative use of words to express ideas that are not literally true but that convey meaningful and sometimes emotional ideas. Compare these common kinds of figurative language.

TYPE OF FIGURATIVE LANGUAGE	EXAMPLE	EFFECT
simile: a comparison of two unlike things using the words *like* or *as*	"Clouds rolled overhead in wild swirls like batter in a bowl." (paragraph 5)	vivid image of a changing sky
metaphor: a comparison of two unlike things that have qualities in common, without using *like* or *as*	". . . the far curtain of the insulated air, . . ." (paragraph 5)	warmth that is trapped inside a barrier
personification: the giving of human qualities to an animal, an object, or an idea	"The river was talking to me, . . ." (paragraph 2)	a feeling of connectedness

Analyzing figurative language can help you understand the author's experiences and feelings. This use of language can convey a mood or feeling, the author's voice and personality, and the tone, or the attitude that the author has about the events described in the memoir. Look for examples of figurative language as you read the excerpt from *Mississippi Solo.*

CRITICAL VOCABULARY

avalanche **insulate** **splinter** **ethereal**

To see how many Critical Vocabulary words you already know, use them to complete the sentences.

1. You can stay warm in cold weather if you ________ yourself.
2. She has a(n) ________ voice, but the song she sang was powerful.
3. A(n) ________ can bury people under many feet of snow.
4. The mirror will ________ into many pieces if you drop it on the floor.

LANGUAGE CONVENTIONS

Consistent Verb Tenses In this lesson, you will learn why it is important to maintain the consistency of verb tenses in your writing. When writing about events, be careful not to change needlessly from one tense to another. (Sometimes there is a need—but the change has to make sense.)

INCONSISTENT: Rains **come** [present tense] and **poured** [past tense] down bucketfuls.

CONSISTENT: Rains **came** [past tense] and **poured** [past tense] down bucketfuls.

As you read the excerpt from *Mississippi Solo,* note the author's use of consistent verb tenses.

ANNOTATION MODEL

NOTICE & NOTE 

As you read, note the author's use of figurative language. You also can mark up details that show characteristics of a memoir. In the model, you can see one reader's notes about the excerpt from *Mississippi Solo.*

3 . . . I didn't care about anything. The river kept me company and kept me satisfied. Nothing else mattered.

4 Then the river whispered, "Get ready. Get ready."

5 The day turned gray and strange. Clouds rolled overhead in wild swirls like batter in a bowl. I could see the rainstorm forming off in the distance but swirling rapidly to me like a dark gray avalanche.

The author is sharing his thoughts, not just facts about the event.

These comparisons are similes. They tell me that the storm probably will be fierce, powerful, and maybe even deadly.

BACKGROUND

Eddy Harris *(b. 1956) is a writer, adventurer, and seeker who spent his early years in New York City before moving to St. Louis. His first published book,* Mississippi Solo, *chronicles the canoe trip he took down the entire length of the Mississippi River in the 1980s—a risky trip for which this city dweller was unprepared. Harris also has written about adventurous journeys in other southern regions and in Africa.*

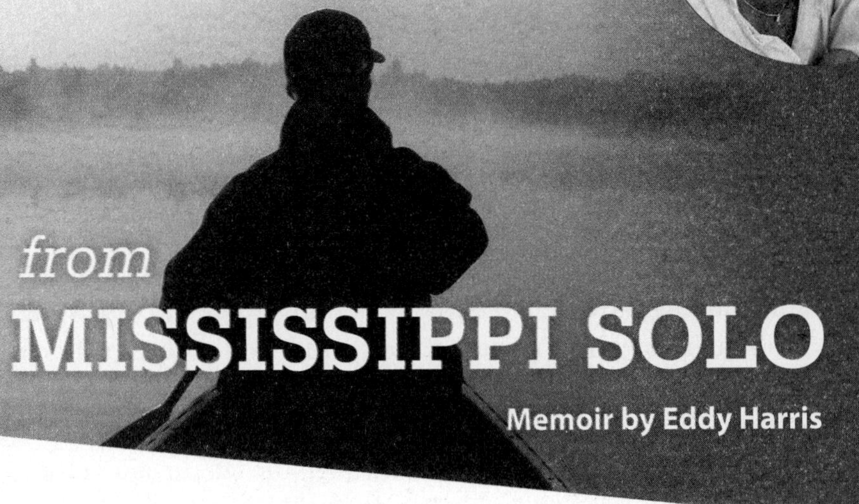

from MISSISSIPPI SOLO

Memoir by Eddy Harris

SETTING A PURPOSE

As you read, focus on how the author recounts a special moment from his life while he canoed by himself down the Mississippi River. What makes his experience so meaningful for him?

1 Too many marvelous days in a row and you begin to get used to it, to think that's the way it's supposed to be. Too many good days, too many bad days—you need some break in the monotony of one to appreciate the other. If you only get sunshine, someone said, you end up in a desert.

2 I guess I'd had enough hard days to last me for a while, enough scary times to be able to appreciate the peaceful, easy, glorious days. On the way to Natchez,[1] I had another one, and I took full advantage of it to do absolutely nothing. No singing, no thinking, no talking to myself. Just feeling. Watching the river, noticing the changes in color, seeing the way it rises and falls depending on the wind and on what lies on the river bed. Each change had something to say, and I listened to the river. The river was talking to me,

[1] **Natchez** (năch´ĭz): a city in southwest Mississippi on the Mississippi River.

Notice & Note

Use the side margins to notice and note signposts in the text.

ANALYZE MEMOIR

Annotate: Mark four places in paragraph 1 where the author seems to address readers.

Critique: How do you think this paragraph is meant to affect readers?

ANALYZE FIGURATIVE LANGUAGE

Annotate: Mark examples of personification in paragraph 2.

Analyze: What point does the author make by comparing the river to these particular human beings?

avalanche
(ăv´ə-lănch´) *n.* An *avalanche* is a large mass of snow, ice, dirt, or rocks falling quickly down the side of a mountain.

insulate
(ĭn´sə-lāt´) *v.* When you *insulate* something, you prevent the passage of heat through it.

changing colors from puce[2] to brown to thick, murky green. Saying nothing. The idle chatter you get when you walk with your favorite niece or nephew going no place in particular with nothing special on your minds and the little kid just jabbers away because it's comfortable and he feels like it. The river was like that to me. A comfortable buddy sharing a lazy day.

3 Nothing else mattered then. Going someplace or not. Arriving in New Orleans or shooting past and landing in Brazil. I didn't care about anything. The river kept me company and kept me satisfied. Nothing else mattered.

4 Then the river whispered, "Get ready. Get ready."

5 The day turned gray and strange. Clouds rolled overhead in wild swirls like batter in a bowl. I could see the rainstorm forming off in the distance but swirling rapidly toward me like a dark gray **avalanche.** I felt the river dip down and up—a shallow dale[3] in the water. I passed from the cool moisture surrounding me and into a pocket of thin air hot and dry. It was as though a gap had opened in the clouds and the sun streamed through to boil the water and heat up this isolated patch of river a scant[4] thirty yards long. My first thought was to shed a shirt and stay cool, but when I passed through the far curtain of the **insulated** air, I knew I had better do just the opposite. I drifted and donned my yellow rain suit and hood. The sky above grew serious and advanced in my direction with the speed of a hurricane. Looking for a place to land, I scanned the shore. There was no shore. Only trees. Because of the heavy rains and high water, the shore had disappeared, and the new shoreline of solid earth had been pushed back through the trees and beyond the woods. How far beyond, I couldn't tell. I looked across to the other side of the river half a mile away. No way could I have made it over there. Halfway across and the wind would have kicked up and trapped me in the middle.

6 The leading edge of the storm came, and the first sprinkles passed over like army scouts. The wooded area lasted only another hundred yards or so, and I thought I could easily get there before the rains arrived. I could then turn left and find ground to pull out and wait out the storm. But the voice of the river came out and spoke to me teasingly but with a chill of seriousness down my spine. I could have ignored it, but as if reading my thoughts and not wanting me to fight it, the river

[2] **puce** (pyo͞os): purplish brown.
[3] **dale:** valley.
[4] **scant:** just short of.

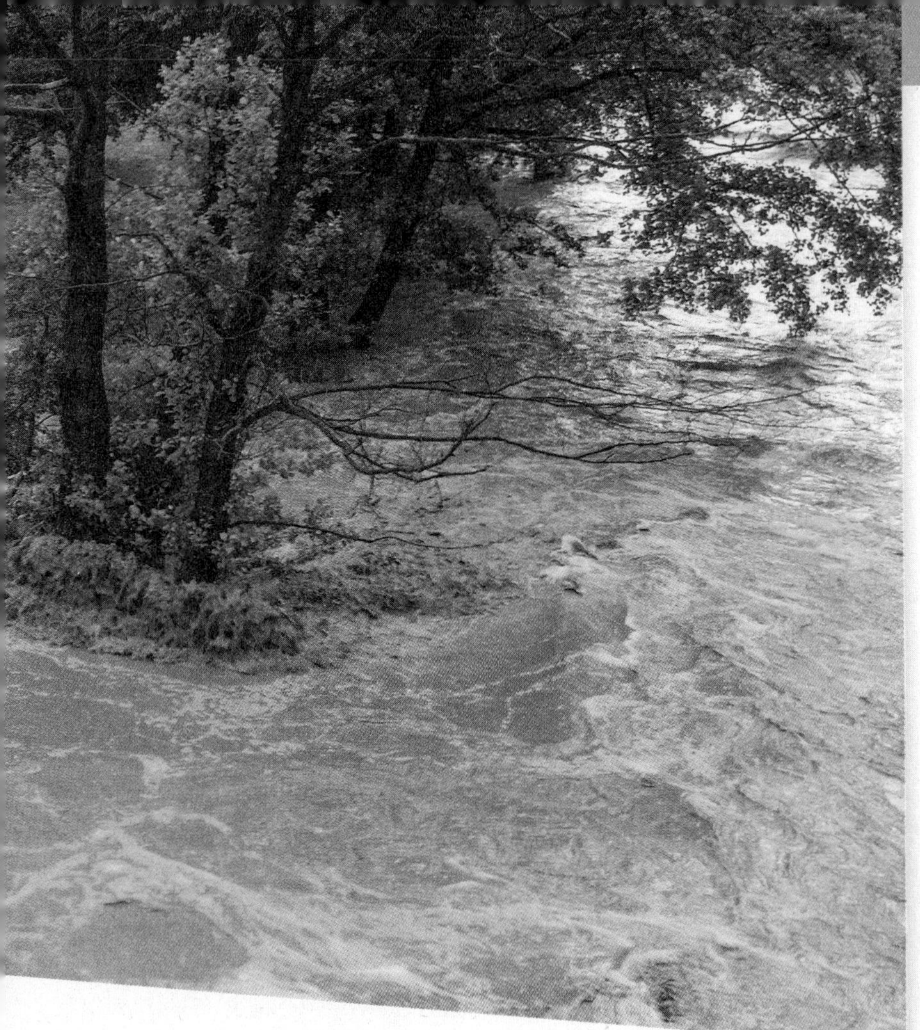

grabbed the end of the canoe and turned me toward the trees. I thought I was looking for land. I wasn't. I was looking for shelter.

7 The urge to get into the trees came on me quite suddenly and really without thought or effort on my part. Almost an instinct.

8 No sooner had I ducked into the trees than the sky split open with a loud crash and a **splintery** crackle of lightning. I was not going to make it through the trees. The wind came in at hurricane strength. The tips of the trees bent way over and aimed toward the ground, like fishing rods hooked on a big one. Water flooded like the tide rushing upstream. The trees swooshed loudly as the leaves and branches brushed hard together. Branches fell. Rains came and poured down bucketfuls.

9 The trees were tall and no more than three feet around. I maneuvered the canoe as best I could in the wind and rushing water, turned it to face upstream, and kept my back to the rain,

NOTICE & NOTE 

splinter
(splĭn´tər) *v.* To *splinter* means to break up into sharp, thin pieces.

LANGUAGE CONVENTIONS

Annotate: Mark the past-tense verbs in the final three sentences of paragraph 8.

Evaluate: Why is it important for all of these verbs to be in the past tense?

NOTICE & NOTE

which slanted in at a sharp angle. I reached out for the sturdiest tree I could get my arms around and I held on.

10 Water everywhere.[5] The river sloshed over the side and into the canoe. I tried to keep the stern pointed right into the flow so the canoe could ride the waves, but it didn't work. The canoe was twisted about, and water poured over the side. The rain was heavier than any I had ever been in or seen before. It really was more like a tropical storm. The heavy winds, the amount of water, the warmth of the air, and the cold rain. Only my neck was exposed to the rain. When the rain hit my neck, it ran under the rain suit and very cold down my back.

11 The wind shifted as the storm came directly overhead. Water streamed straight down. I was drenched, and the canoe was filling up quickly. Anything in the canoe that could float was floating. If the rain continued for long or if the wind kept up strong and the rain kept spilling into the canoe, I would sink. But I was not worried, hardly more than concerned. In fact I enjoyed the feeling of the water all around me and on me, enveloping me like a cocoon, and despite the drama I felt no real threat. I was more amazed than anything, trying to analyze the voice I had heard or whatever instinct or intuition it was that urged me to park in these trees. It had been something so very definite that I could feel it and yet so **ethereal** that I could not put my finger on it. So I stopped trying and just sat there patiently waiting and hugging my tree. I was one with this river, and nothing could happen to me.

12 The storm slid forward, and the rain slanted in on my face. Then it moved on farther up the river to drench someone else. It was gone as suddenly as it had arisen. Only the trailing edge was left, a light rain that lasted almost until I reached Natchez.

ANALYZE MEMOIR

Annotate: In paragraph 11, mark what the author says he enjoyed.

Compare: How is this information different from details about the storm itself?

CONTRASTS AND CONTRADICTIONS

Notice & Note: Mark the author's action at the end of paragraph 11. How does the author's action contrast with what he had planned to do?

Interpret: How does his action affect his feelings about the river?

ethereal
(ĭ-thîr´ē-əl) *adj.* If something is *ethereal*, it is light and airy.

[5] **Water everywhere:** The author is referring to the line "water, water, everywhere" from *The Rime of the Ancient Mariner*, a widely known poem about a sailor recounting supernatural events at sea.

NOTICE & NOTE

CHECK YOUR UNDERSTANDING

Answer these questions before moving on to the **Analyze the Text** section on the following page.

1 The simile used at the beginning of paragraph 6, which compares the first sprinkles of rain to army scouts, conveys the idea that —

A something powerful is about to happen

B the author will be safe during the storm

C the storm may be less severe than expected

D it is too late for the author to seek shelter

2 Which idea is supported most strongly by details throughout the selection?

F People who do not prepare for every situation are liable to get into trouble.

G Survival during natural disasters depends on having both experience and good equipment.

H A connection with nature can help someone make good decisions in a dangerous situation.

J Traveling alone is risky but rarely results in a bad outcome.

3 Why is the author no longer afraid as he hugs a tree during the most intense part of the storm?

A He feels sure that he will be rescued after the storm has passed.

B He has accepted that he probably will be stranded on the shore.

C He believes that his knowledge of the river has kept him safe.

D He trusts that listening to the river is always the right decision.

RESPOND

ANALYZE THE TEXT

Support your responses with evidence from the text. NOTEBOOK

1. **Cite Evidence** Reread paragraph 2. What is it about the author's way of writing that identifies the text as a memoir?
2. **Interpret** What does the author reveal about himself in paragraphs 1–3? What details support the ideas the author is trying to express?
3. **Interpret** Why could paragraph 4 be said to be a turning point in this selection?
4. **Evaluate** How effectively does the author use figures of speech to convey the mood of suspense connected to his experience during the storm? Explain.
5. **Notice & Note** Reread paragraphs 10–11. How do the author's thoughts and feelings during this experience contradict what you think most people would think and feel if they faced the same?

RESEARCH

RESEARCH TIP
The most effective search terms are very specific. Along with the river's name, you will want to include a word such as *history* or *characteristics* to make sure that you locate the most relevant information.

The Mississippi River has inspired many American writers and travelers, including Eddy Harris. With a partner, research why the river has been important to so many people. Use these questions and develop your own; then record what you learn in the chart.

QUESTION	ANSWER
Why is the Mississippi River important to people living along its banks?	
Why do people around the world depend on the Mississippi River?	

Extend How would you present the information you've learned about the Mississippi River in a video? With a partner, discuss ways you could use maps, other visuals, and perhaps filmed interviews to share what you have found most interesting during your research.

CREATE AND PRESENT

Write a Literary Analysis Look back through the excerpt from *Mississippi Solo* to list examples of how Eddy Harris uses similes and personifies the river. Focusing on examples from your list, write a two- to four-paragraph literary analysis that explains how Harris uses figurative language in this memoir.

- ❑ Introduce the topic and express a controlling idea about the use of figurative language in the memoir.
- ❑ Then, identify specific examples of each type of figurative language.
- ❑ Explain the meaning of each example and the way in which the example contributes to key ideas in the memoir.
- ❑ In your final paragraph, draw a general conclusion about the topic.

Go to **Writing Informative Texts** in the **Writing Studio** to learn more.

Produce a Podcast Work with a partner to create a podcast critique of this excerpt from *Mississippi Solo*.

- ❑ With your partner, review your literary analyses. Decide which parts you wish to record in the form of a conversation about the selection.
- ❑ Decide when each of you will speak and how you will connect your thoughts. Demonstrate that you understand the selection.
- ❑ Before you record your podcast, practice. You and your partner should consider your speaking rate, volume, and enunciation—but make it sound like a conversation, too.

Go to **Using Media in a Presentation** in the **Speaking and Listening Studio** for help.

RESPOND TO THE ESSENTIAL QUESTION

? What does it mean to be in harmony with nature?

Gather Information Review your annotations and notes on the excerpt from *Mississippi Solo*. Then, add relevant details to your Response Log. As you determine which information to include, think about:

- experiences—both good and bad—that can occur in nature
- how we can learn from experiences in nature
- how being connected to nature influences the way we live.

At the end of the unit, use your notes to write a personal narrative.

ACADEMIC VOCABULARY

As you write and discuss what you learned from the memoir, be sure to use the Academic Vocabulary words. Check off each of the words that you use.

- ❑ **affect**
- ❑ **element**
- ❑ **ensure**
- ❑ **participate**
- ❑ **specify**

CRITICAL VOCABULARY

WORD BANK
avalanche
insulate
splinter
ethereal

Practice and Apply Complete each sentence to show that you understand the meaning of the Critical Vocabulary word.

1. An **avalanche** was triggered when . . .
2. A layer of down helps **insulate** birds from . . .
3. A tree can **splinter** during a storm because . . .
4. A person's appearance can be called **ethereal** when . . .

VOCABULARY STRATEGY: Reference Resources

Go to **Context Clues** in the **Vocabulary Studio** for more.

A **dictionary** is a resource for those who are checking word meanings and expanding their vocabulary. The searching and browsing methods differ for print and digital dictionaries, but users can find the same basic information about each entry word.

- pronunciation and syllabication
- part of speech label
- one or more definitions
- word origins

Dictionary Entry

mo•not•o•ny (mə-nŏt'n-ē) *n.* **1.** Uniformity or lack of variation in pitch, intonation, or inflection. **2.** Tedious sameness or repetitiousness. [Greek *monotonos,* monotonous; see MONOTONOUS.]

Synonyms are words with similar meanings. The dictionary entry for *monotony* includes some synonyms within the definitions: *uniformity*, *sameness*, and *repetitiousness*. Some dictionaries provide a list of synonyms after an entry. A **thesaurus** is a reference aid that lists synonyms. Writers can use a print or digital thesaurus to help find the exact word they need.

Thesaurus Entry

monotony, *n.* boredom, tedium, uniformity, sameness, unchangeableness, dullness, repetitiveness

Practice and Apply Find the sentence with the word *maneuvered* in paragraph 9 of the excerpt from *Mississippi Solo*. Look up the word in a dictionary and a thesaurus. Check its meaning and look for synonyms and related forms of the word. Use your own words to tell what the sentence containing *maneuvered* means. Then revise the sentence using an appropriate synonym.

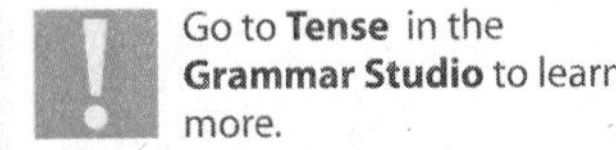

LANGUAGE CONVENTIONS: Consistent Verb Tenses

In your writing, use **consistent verb tenses** to express your meaning exactly. The tense of a verb indicates the time of an action or a state of being. In general, use the past tense to tell about events in the past and the present tense to tell about current events.

INCORRECT: The sky above me **grew** [past tense] serious and **advances** [present tense] in my direction with the speed of a hurricane.
CORRECT: The sky above me **grew** serious and **advanced** in my direction with the speed of a hurricane. [consistent past tense]

Note the exceptions in these examples from *Mississippi Solo*:

- You may use the present tense to set the scene for a "past" story as you talk to readers in the present.

  Too many good days, too many bad days—you <u>need</u> some break in the monotony. . . .

- You may use the present tense to state things that are always true.

  Watching the river, . . . seeing the way it <u>rises</u> and <u>falls</u> depending on the wind and on what <u>lies</u> on the river bed.

- You should use the past perfect tense (with *had* as the helping verb) to show that some events happened before other past-tense events.

  The rain was heavier than any I <u>had</u> ever <u>been</u> in or [<u>had</u>] <u>seen</u> before.

Practice and Apply Six of the boldfaced verbs in the following paragraph show errors in consistent verb tense. Think about what the writer probably means:

- Does the writer set a scene?
- Does the writer mention something that is always true?
- Does the writer refer to an event that happened before a past-tense event?

Also look for places where both verbs need to be in the past tense but are not. Then revise the paragraph, correcting the errors in verb tense.

If you **are** like me, you **knew** how hard it **is** to watch a movie when the person with you **kept** talking. Just last week, my cousin and I **watch** an exciting wilderness adventure movie together. I would like to say that I **enjoy** that movie, but my cousin's chatter **made** it impossible. He **kept** talking about what **happened** in an earlier scene. I **survived** the experience, but I **think** that it will be some time before I **invited** him to watch with me again.

Go to **Tense** in the **Grammar Studio** to learn more.

THE DROUGHT

Poem by **Amy Helfrich**

? ***ESSENTIAL QUESTION:***

What does it mean to be in harmony with nature?

QUICK START

The poem you are about to read explores a farmer's response to a drought—a long time without rain. Think about how a drought might affect a farmer. Jot down ideas and then discuss them with your group.

ANALYZE SONNETS

The **form** of a poem is the arrangement of its words and lines. One form of poetry is a 14-line poem called a **sonnet.** The sonnet originated in Italy but was altered by English poets, especially William Shakespeare. As a result, the following two traditional styles of sonnets emerged: Italian sonnets and English or Shakespearean sonnets. Here are some characteristics of each.

SHAKESPEAREAN SONNET	ITALIAN SONNET
• develops a single idea • idea is developed in three parts, each made up of four lines • final pair of lines, called a **couplet,** offers a sharp, insightful conclusion and shift in emotion	• develops a single idea or problem • idea or problem is laid out in the first eight lines • resolution appears in last six lines

The two kinds of sonnets also differ in their use of rhyme, as you will see on the next page.

A traditional sonnet has a specific **meter,** or pattern of stressed and unstressed syllables. Often, the pattern is this: da-DUM da-DUM da-DUM da-DUM da-DUM. The rhythm or pace of the poem is influenced by meter. Because meaning in poetry is expressed as much by sound and rhythm as by word choice, any variation in meter can impact meaning. Rhythm and meaning are also affected by **graphical elements,** such as punctuation and capitalization.

Notice the rhythm, word choice, and use of graphical elements in these lines from "The Drought." What idea is developed in these lines?

and see what he can salvage from the dust:
this season's bitterness has starved his grain
and left the soil with nothing but a trust
that time will make a friend out of the rain.

As you read "The Drought," note how the poet uses graphical elements, word choice, and rhythm to express emotions and develop ideas.

GENRE ELEMENTS: POETRY

- includes a core unit called a line that can be a complete sentence or part of a sentence
- uses carefully chosen words and sounds to express an idea and create a mood
- may include rhyme and meter

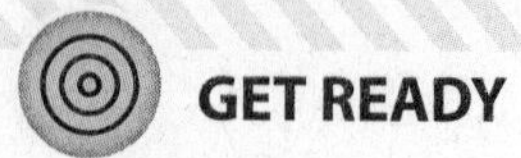

GET READY

ANALYZE RHYME SCHEME

Rhyme occurs when two or more words end with the same (or similar) sound. It is the sound, not the spelling, that matters; for example, *write, height,* and *megabyte* rhyme. In poems, rhyming words usually appear at the ends of lines, so they are called end rhymes.

A **rhyme scheme** is a pattern of end rhymes in a poem. You can keep a record of the rhyme scheme in a poem by assigning a letter of the alphabet (*a, b, c,* and so on) to each end rhyme. Lines with the same end rhyme get the same letter, as shown in this example of the first four lines of a sonnet:

At night I stand and watch the stars on high *a*
And think of how they twinkle, far away. *b*
I wonder if somewhere in that array *b*
There stands another watcher of the sky. . . . *a*

The rhyme scheme of these lines, then, is *abba*. That rhyme scheme helps identify it as an Italian sonnet, which has a rhyme scheme of *abbaabba* for the first eight lines and either *cdcdcd* or *cdecde* for the last six lines. A Shakespearean sonnet has a rhyme scheme of *abab cdcd efef gg.*

As you read "The Drought," determine the rhyme scheme. Also consider how rhyme may connect details and ideas.

ANNOTATION MODEL

NOTICE & NOTE

As you read, consider how the poet uses the sonnet form to develop an idea. You also can mark the rhyme scheme and other details that catch your attention. In the model, you can see one reader's notes about the beginning of "The Drought."

At dusk, he moves among the dying plains
of winter wheat and walks a sharpened pace
to stretch the life that's puddled in his veins,
muster up some color in his face, . . .

The idea seems to be about a farmer and his dying crop of wheat.

Veins rhymes with plains. Is there a connection—maybe that the farmer's life is tied up in his land?

BACKGROUND

The word drought *refers to a time of unusually dry weather. A drought is not merely a day or two without rain or snow. Instead, it is a dry time that lasts long enough to cause shortages in the water supply. Drought is a particular concern to farmers. In "The Drought," poet* **Amy Helfrich** *explores the impact of drought on one farmer and how he responds to the toll it takes on him and his land.*

THE DROUGHT

Poem by Amy Helfrich

SETTING A PURPOSE

Read "The Drought" several times. Start by reading it at least once to get a general idea of what it's about. Consider what the farmer thinks of his present situation and of the future. Next, reread the poem, focusing on its structure as a sonnet. How are the lines grouped? How does each group of lines add to the meaning of the sonnet as a whole? Be sure to read the sonnet aloud to appreciate its rhythm and rhyme scheme. Finally, think about the sonnet's overall effect on readers.

Notice & Note

Use the side margins to notice and note signposts in the text.

NOTICE & NOTE

ANALYZE RHYME SCHEME

Annotate: Use letters to mark the rhyme scheme.

Interpret: What kind of sonnet is this? What idea is expressed within each group of four lines?

ANALYZE SONNETS

Annotate: Mark the couplet.

Analyze: How does the mood, or feeling, expressed in the couplet differ from that in the lines above it?

At dusk, he moves among the dying plains
of winter wheat and walks a sharpened pace
to stretch the life that's puddled in his veins,
muster up some color in his face,
and see what he can salvage from the dust:
this season's bitterness has starved his grain
and left the soil with nothing but a trust
that time will make a friend out of the rain.
So now he wanders through the field he's turned
and tilled with care, a twenty acre grave
it seems. And, yet, because in years he's learned
that, often times, there's something left to save,
he stops to sift the dusty earth in hands
that look for breath inside the broken lands.

CHECK YOUR UNDERSTANDING

Answer these questions before moving on to the **Analyze the Text** section on the following page.

1 Why does the farmer walk quickly—at a sharpened pace—in line 2?

A He wants to feel more alive and hopeful.

B He is eager to get inside, out of the cold.

C He wants to escape from the dust quickly.

D He is hurrying to harvest his wheat crop.

2 The phrase this season's bitterness in line 6 is most likely a reference to —

F the soil

G the drought

H the wheat

J the farm

3 In lines 7 and 8, the use of personification, or giving human qualities to an animal, object, or idea, is intended to show that —

A the soil will be washed away in the first rain

B the farmer does not think that rain will come soon

C the soil will become healthy when the rain returns

D the farmer has waited too long for the rain

ANALYZE THE TEXT

Support your responses with evidence from the text. NOTEBOOK

1. **Infer** What does the poet mean by the phrase "a twenty acre grave" in line 10?
2. **Critique** Which word is meant to rhyme with *dust* at the end of line 5? How does the relationship between these two rhyming words help develop the idea of the poem?
3. **Connect** "The Drought" has an unusual graphical element—almost every line begins with a lowercase letter. What does this tell you about how the lines are structured? How does this structure help convey the poet's message or purpose?
4. **Analyze** How does the poet's use of commas in lines 11 and 12 change the rhythm of the poem? How does the use of commas affect the poem's meaning?
5. **Draw Conclusions** Is this ultimately a sad poem, or a hopeful one? Explain.

RESEARCH

RESEARCH TIP

To help narrow the focus of an Internet search, use quotes around a specific phrase—for example, "environmental effects of drought." To quickly find the online definition of a technical word or phrase you're not familiar with, try this tip: Search for "define [word]" (for example, "define drought").

In the Background note, you learned a little about droughts. With a partner, do research to find out the effects a drought can have on the environment and the economy. Use questions such as "How do droughts affect wheat crops?" to guide your research. Record your findings in the graphic organizer.

EFFECTS OF DROUGHT	
Environmental	**Economic**

Connect Based on your research, identify what kind of effect(s) a drought like the one in the poem would have on a farm. Compare your answers with those of a classmate. Do you agree? Why or why not?

CREATE AND PRESENT

Write a Sonnet Write a sonnet about some aspect of nature.

- ❑ Choose an aspect of nature that interests you—for example, something about plants, animals, rivers, oceans, or a weather event. Spend a few minutes making notes about your topic. Choose the idea that you want to develop and decide which sonnet form you will use: Italian, or Shakespearean.
- ❑ Think about a rhyme scheme. Try using a rhyming dictionary to list pairs of rhyming words that you might include. Think about the meter, too. See whether your lines make the pattern da-DUM da-DUM da-DUM da-DUM da-DUM or another meter.
- ❑ Don't be afraid to rewrite or replace lines to make the idea clearer or to make the poem fit the sonnet form more closely.

Listen to the Sonnet In pairs, take turns reading "The Drought" aloud and listening to it as it is read to you.

- ❑ As the reader, notice how the lines are structured. There are only three sentences in "The Drought." Read the sonnet as sentences instead of stopping at the end of each line.
- ❑ Plan how you will be expressive. Where should your voice be louder or softer? Where should you speed up, slow down, or pause? Which words should you emphasize or express with certain emotion?
- ❑ As the listener, pay attention to the speaker's words, pace, and tone. Listen closely to see whether you can interpret the sonnet's message. Does hearing the poem in addition to reading it make a difference to your understanding of its message?

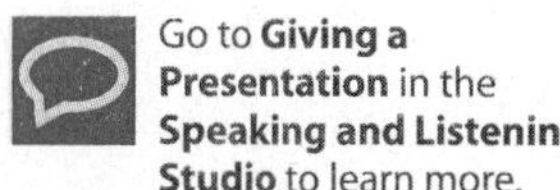

Go to **Giving a Presentation** in the **Speaking and Listening Studio** to learn more.

RESPOND TO THE ESSENTIAL QUESTION

? What does it mean to be in harmony with nature?

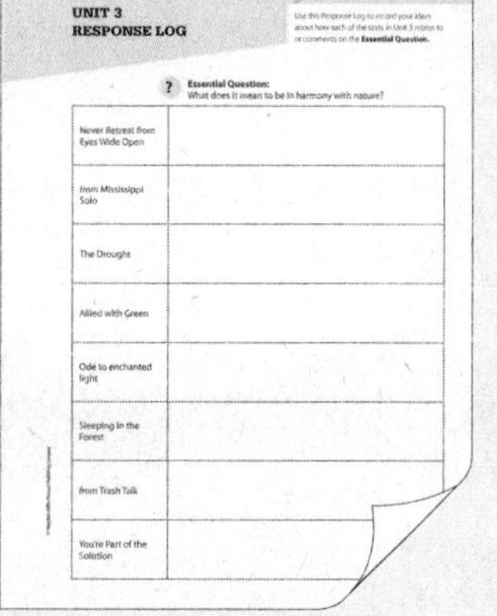

UNIT 3 RESPONSE LOG

Use this Response Log to record your ideas about how each of the texts in Unit 3 relates to or comments on the **Essential Question.**

? **Essential Question:** What does it mean to be in harmony with nature?

Never Retreat *from* Eyes Wide Open	
from Mississippi Solo	
The Drought	
Allied with Green	
Ode to enchanted light	
Sleeping in the Forest	
from Trash Talk	
You're Part of the Solution	

Gather Information Review your annotations and notes on "The Drought." Then, add relevant details to your Response Log. As you determine which information to include, think about:

- how nature challenges us and how we challenge nature
- how resilient or tough people and nature can be
- how we depend on nature and how nature depends on us

At the end of the unit, use your notes to write a personal narrative.

ACADEMIC VOCABULARY

As you write and discuss what you learned from the poem, be sure to use the Academic Vocabulary words. Check off each of the words that you use.

- ❑ **affect**
- ❑ **element**
- ❑ **ensure**
- ❑ **participate**
- ❑ **specify**

ANALYZE & APPLY

ALLIED WITH GREEN

Short Story by **Naomi Shihab Nye**

ESSENTIAL QUESTION:

What does it mean to be in harmony with nature?

QUICK START

Imagine that your community has announced an environmental program called "Changing Our Ways for Greener Days." Make a list of projects that you think might be part of such a program.

ANALYZE THEME

Authors often use the characters in short stories to share a theme with readers. A **theme** is a message about life or human nature. "Show kindness" and "We might not appreciate what we have until it's gone" are just two of the many themes that stories might convey.

The theme of a story is usually implied rather than stated directly. To infer a theme, it is helpful to do the following:

- Look at the title to see if it suggests a significant idea.
- Analyze the characters' words and actions.
- Consider whether the setting has special meaning to a character.
- Look for important statements by the narrator or a character.

As you read "Allied with Green," look for clues that suggest a theme.

GENRE ELEMENTS: SHORT STORY

- a fictional work that centers on a single idea and that can be read in one sitting
- has a limited number of characters and settings
- often presents a conflict, or challenge, that the main character or characters must try to overcome
- sometimes makes a point more through vivid language and powerful images than through a traditional plot

MONITOR COMPREHENSION

One way to be an effective reader, regardless of the kind of text you are reading, is to **monitor** your **comprehension**—that is, to check and adjust your understanding while you are reading. By monitoring your comprehension, you can clear up any confusion about the writer's intent and make sure that you understand the text.

Several strategies can help you monitor your comprehension. Each one has its benefits. The strategy or strategies you use will depend on the sentence or passage from the text that you are considering.

MONITORING STRATEGY	BENEFIT
Rereading	Reread text that you don't understand. You may need to reread slowly, aloud, or more than once—but repeated readings will help.
Connecting	Use what you already know, plus any background information provided with the text (such as an introduction or footnotes) to connect with the text.
Questioning	Develop and ask questions about the text as you read. Questions that start with *who, what, where, when, why,* and *how* will take you far!
Annotating	Mark words, phrases, and details that will help you understand the text. When reading a story, for example, mark details about characters, setting, and plot events.

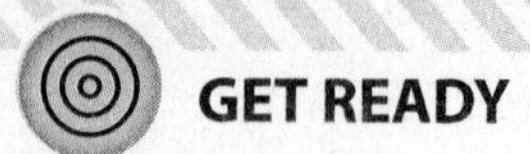

GET READY

CRITICAL VOCABULARY

addiction **remorseful** **median** **arboretum** **obituary**

To see how many Critical Vocabulary words you already know, answer each question with **yes** or **no.** In a small group, explain your answers.

1. Could someone have an **addiction** to chocolate?
2. Do **remorseful** people usually feel happy about their actions?
3. Would you expect to see a **median** on a single-lane road?
4. Is an **arboretum** like a garden?
5. Is an **obituary** like a biography?

LANGUAGE CONVENTIONS

Complex Sentences In this lesson, you will learn more about complex sentences. A **complex sentence** consists of one independent clause (which can stand on its own as a sentence) and one or more subordinate clauses (which need the independent clause to complete their meaning). In this example, the subordinate clause begins with *when*. It follows an independent clause, so it does not need a comma. (If the subordinate clause came first, a comma would need to follow it.)

The boulevard wakes up when a strip of green is planted down its center.

Notice that in each clause, the subject and its verb agree (*boulevard* + *wakes up*; *strip* + *is planted*). As you read "Allied with Green," note how the author uses correctly written complex sentences to express ideas.

ANNOTATION MODEL

NOTICE & NOTE

As you read, note clues about the theme of the story. You also can mark up anything that will help you monitor your comprehension. In the model, you can see one reader's notes about "Allied with Green."

1 For her paper on "What I Believe In," Lucy writes first "the color green."

2 That's how everything starts. A tiny shoot of phrase prickling the mind . . .

The theme may involve the word green.

Here's my question: Why is the author comparing language to a growing plant?

BACKGROUND

Naomi Shihab Nye *(b. 1952) was born to a Palestinian father and an American mother. During her adolescence, she lived in St. Louis, Missouri; Jerusalem, Israel; and San Antonio, Texas. She has traveled extensively as an adult, as well. Influenced by her heritage and the cultural diversity of the places she has known, Nye has written books of poetry as well as fiction for younger audiences.*

ALLIED WITH GREEN

Short Story by Naomi Shihab Nye

SETTING A PURPOSE

As you read, consider the author's use of the word green. *How is she using the term to describe something that Lucy, the story's main character, feels very strongly about?*

1 For her paper on "What I Believe In," Lucy writes first "the color green."

2 That's how everything starts. A tiny shoot of phrase prickling the mind . . .

3 Then she runs around for a few days doing other things but noticing the green poking up between buildings, on sides of roads, in front of even the poorest homes, how pots of green lined on rickety front porches, hanging baskets of green on light posts downtown, the new meticulous xeriscape[1] beds of puffy green grasses and plants alongside the river, are what seem to keep everything else going. If

[1] **xeriscape** (zîr´ĭ-skāp´): landscaping that is designed to save water and protect the environment.

Notice & Note

Use the side margins to notice and note signposts in the text.

MONITOR COMPREHENSION

Annotate: Mark the sentence that makes up most of paragraph 3.

Interpret: What does the author emphasize with the details in that sentence? Why might you need to reread that sentence before answering?

people could not see green from the windows of the hospital, the hospital might fall down. She believes this.

4 Once she starts making a list, it will not stop.

5 Green has had a terrible summer. Threatened by the longest drought and highest heat in recorded history, green has had many second thoughts.

6 Lucy's family could only water with a sprinkler on Wednesday evenings between eight and ten. When she and her mom wash lettuce, blueberries, peaches, they carry the plastic tubs of fruit water outside to pour onto a plant. It's ritual now. It's holy water. The city had a water waster hotline. It made the national news. You could turn people in for excessive watering.

7 Last semester, when asked to write a paper on **addictions,** Lucy wrote about trimming and got a C. Her teacher scrawled across the top of the paper, "What is this?" But Lucy often feels happiest with pruning shears in her hand, heading toward an overgrown jasmine vine.

8 It's a clear task, trimming. The longer you've done it, the more you know how it encourages green, in the long run. Also, you can have fine ideas while trimming. Queen's crown, germander, plumbago. *Snip, snip, snip.*

9 She knew it had been mentioned before, but thought she ought to include how cities assault their green for two reasons: money and greed. Later, feeling **remorseful,** or sickened by the new view, they name everything for green—Oak Meadows, Lone Pine. You could find it almost anywhere now.

10 Lucy's father demonstrated against developments when he was in college. She had a faded black and white picture of him holding a NO! sign, his hair bushy and wild. Highways slashing through green space—he now drives one of those highways almost every day, feeling guilty. He plants free trees in scrappy **medians,** as an apology. Sometimes people steal them. When he planted four little palms in pots as a gift to Freddy's Mexican Restaurant, they got plucked from the soil overnight. Obviously some people were desperate for green. And surely, with all the population issues now, some developments were necessary, but look at what happened before you knew it—hills sheared, meadows plucked, fields erased, the world turns into an endless series of strip centers—yo, Joni Mitchell! Joni sang about parking lots when the world had probably half the number it has now. Her dad told her that. She likes Joni Mitchell.

11 The boulevard wakes up when a strip of green is planted down its center.

NOTICE & NOTE

LANGUAGE CONVENTIONS

Annotate: Underline the complex sentence that appears in paragraph 6.

Analyze: In that sentence, what are the subjects and the verbs that agree with them? Where is a comma placed to set the subordinate clause apart from the independent clause?

addiction
(ə-dĭk´shən) *n.* An *addiction* is a habit upon which a person becomes physically or emotionally dependent.

ANALYZE THEME

Annotate: In paragraph 9, mark the new names that people create for places in cities.

Connect: How do these names relate to the message conveyed through Lucy's story?

remorseful
(rĭ-môrs´fəl) *adj.* If you are *remorseful*, you feel very sorry about something that you have done.

median
(mē´dē-ən) *n.* A *median* is a dividing area between opposing lanes of traffic on a highway or road.

MONITOR COMPREHENSION

Annotate: Mark the name of the singer mentioned in paragraph 10.

Identify: How would you find information about the singer so that you can clarify this reference?

NOTICE & NOTE 

12 The sad room smiles again when a pot of green is placed on a white tablecloth.

13 No one goes to Seattle to see the concrete.

14 An exhausted kid says, I'm going outside—sick of her mother's voice, she knows she will feel better with bamboo.

15 In Dallas people run around the lake or refresh themselves at the **arboretum.**

16 San Antonians send their kids to summer digging classes at the botanical gardens. The kids come home with broccoli. After a while.

17 Patience is deeply involved with green.

arboretum
(är´bə-rē´təm) *n.* An *arboretum* is a place where many trees are grown for educational or viewing purposes.

ANALYZE THEME

Annotate: Mark the two questions that appear in paragraphs 18 through 20.

Analyze: How do the different points of view in the questions help show a theme of the story?

AGAIN AND AGAIN

Notice & Note: In paragraphs 22–25, mark the things that Lucy loved.

Critique: How do you think the repetition of *loved* is meant to affect the reader?

obituary
(ō-bĭch′o͞o-ĕr′ē) *n.* An *obituary* is a public notice of a person's death.

ANALYZE THEME

Annotate: Reread paragraphs 26–28. Mark the verb that Lucy found especially important.

Interpret: Why do you think the story ends by focusing on this verb? What idea does it leave readers thinking about?

18 It's required.

19 So, why don't people respect green as much as they should?

20 This was the serious question growing small fronds and tendrils at the heart of Lucy's paper. She knew her teacher might turn a snide nose up at it. Oh, blah blah, isn't this rather a repeat of what you wrote last semester?

21 People took green for granted. They assumed it would always be skirting their ugly office buildings and residences and so they didn't give it the attention it deserved. Somewhat like air. Air and green, close cousins.

22 Lucy truly loved the words *pocket park.*[2]

23 She loved community gardeners with purple bandannas tied around their heads. She loved their wild projects—rosemary grown so big you could hide in it.

24 She loved roofs paved with grass.

25 She loved the man in New York City—Robert Isabell—who planted pink impatiens on the metal overhang of his building. He had started out as a florist, at seventeen, in Minnesota—green state in the summer, not so green in December. Then he moved to New York City and became a major party planner, incorporating flowers, lighting, tents, fabrics, to create magical worlds of festivity. He didn't attend his own parties. He disappeared once he got everything set up. Sometimes he hid behind a giant potted plant to see what people liked. Lucy found his **obituary** in the newspaper, clipped it out, and placed it on her desk. She wished she could have worked for him just to learn how he put flowers together on tables, how he clipped giant green stalks and placed them effectively around a tent to make Morocco, Italy, the French Riviera. Transporting. Green could take you away.

26 Save you. But you had to care for it, stroke it, devote yourself to it, pray to it, organize crews for it, bow down to it. You had to say the simple holy prayer, rearranging the words any way you liked best—"Dig, Grow, Deep, Roots, Light, Air, Water, Tend."

27 *Tend* was a more important verb than most people realized.

28 You had to carry a bucket.

[2] **pocket park:** a small park accessible to the general public.

NOTICE & NOTE 

CHECK YOUR UNDERSTANDING

Answer these questions before moving on to the **Analyze the Text** section on the following page.

1 Early in the story, the statement That's how everything starts is meant to show that —

A being "green" is essential to the character of Lucy

B belief in "the color green" should begin in childhood

C the world could not survive without its plant life

D talking about the environment leads to arguments

2 The author mentions Seattle, Dallas, and San Antonio to suggest that —

F only a few cities are taking steps to care for the environment

G cities are in great danger of having developers take over green spaces

H places have different ideas about how to care for the environment

J people in many places appreciate green spaces

3 Robert Isabell is important to Lucy because —

A he was a party planner known throughout New York

B his life represented a skill that she would like to have

C his beliefs about the environment are similar to her own

D he traveled the world in search of interesting plants

RESPOND

ANALYZE THE TEXT

Support your responses with evidence from the text. NOTEBOOK

1. **Infer** Once Lucy decides on the topic for her writing assignment, she can't help but notice the green around her. What does this tell you about her character and how she feels about her topic?
2. **Analyze** What is the theme of "Allied with Green"? Give examples of how the author develops the theme.
3. **Critique** What do you know about Lucy's father? Why does he matter to the story?
4. **Connect** Reread paragraphs 9 and 10. How might what you know about your own community, or other communities, help you connect with what the author is saying about Lucy?
5. **Notice & Note** Paragraph 6 mentions "holy water." At the end of the story, what else is called "holy"? How do those "holy" things help express the theme of "Allied with Green"?

RESEARCH

RESEARCH TIP
Before you start your research, make sure that you know just what kind of information you're looking for. To complete this activity, for example, you are asked to find out a little about the environmental movement in general, but you also are asked to learn about "green-focused" living. Make sure that you gather information about both topics.

As you have seen, the word *green* in "Allied with Green" means more than a color. It relates to the beliefs and goals of the environmental movement. Research the environmental movement and what it means to lead a green-focused lifestyle. Use what you learn to answer the questions in the chart.

QUESTION	ANSWER
What beliefs do many environmentalists share?	
What are some goals of the environmental movement?	
What does it mean to be "green"?	
What are some ways to lead a "green-focused lifestyle"?	

Connect Review your findings and share them with a small group. Then, think about how Lucy in "Allied with Green" is focused on "green" living. Which information from your research do you think Lucy would feel most strongly about? Why?

CREATE AND DISCUSS

Write a Poem Write a poem about the character Lucy in "Allied with Green" and what you think matters most to her.

- ❑ Use story details to make inferences about Lucy's character.
- ❑ Choose a poetic form. For example, you might follow a pattern of alternating end rhyme. Or you may prefer free verse, which does not contain regular patterns of rhythm or rhyme.
- ❑ Experiment with word choice and with figurative language.

Share and Discuss Opinions With a small group, discuss your opinions about Lucy in "Allied with Green." Is she an idealist, who dreams about a world that will never happen? Is she an activist, who has the will and the power to make changes in the world? How would you characterize her?

- ❑ Review the story with your group. Together, look for details about Lucy's actions, thoughts, and feelings.
- ❑ Then, discuss what the details in the story reveal about Lucy's character. Listen closely to each other. Ask each other questions to help clarify ideas.
- ❑ End your discussion by identifying each group member's characterization of Lucy. Then, work together to combine those responses into a sentence or two. Share your response with the class and see whether your classmates agree.

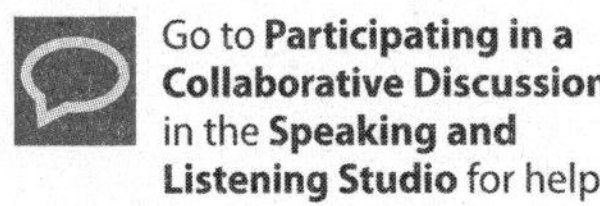

Go to **Participating in a Collaborative Discussion** in the **Speaking and Listening Studio** for help.

RESPOND TO THE ESSENTIAL QUESTION

? What does it mean to be in harmony with nature?

Gather Information Review your annotations and notes on "Allied with Green." Then, add relevant details to your Response Log. As you determine which information to include, think about:

- the ways that people sometimes ignore or even harm the natural world
- the things that Lucy does to show that she cares about the environment

At the end of the unit, use your notes to write a personal narrative.

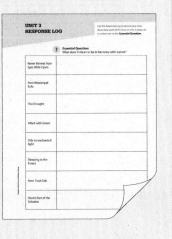

ACADEMIC VOCABULARY

As you write and discuss what you learned from the short story, be sure to use the Academic Vocabulary words. Check off each of the words that you use.

- ❑ **affect**
- ❑ **element**
- ❑ **ensure**
- ❑ **participate**
- ❑ **specify**

RESPOND

CRITICAL VOCABULARY

WORD BANK
addiction
remorseful
median
arboretum
obituary

Practice and Apply Answer each question using the Critical Vocabulary word in a complete sentence.

1. What help might people who have an **addiction** seek? Why?
2. What advice would you give to a **remorseful** person, and why?
3. Are **medians** more common in areas with light traffic, or with heavy traffic? Why?
4. Why would people visit an **arboretum**?
5. What information would you expect to see in an **obituary**?

VOCABULARY STRATEGY: Context Clues

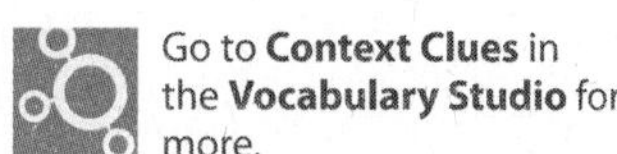

Go to **Context Clues** in the **Vocabulary Studio** for more.

When you encounter an unfamiliar word or phrase in your reading, one way to figure out the meaning is to use **context clues.** Context clues are hints about meaning that may appear in the words, phrases, sentences, and paragraphs that surround that unknown word or phrase.

In the example below from "Allied with Green," the word *sickened* provides a clue to the meaning of *remorseful.* Both words describe the negative feeling that Lucy thinks causes cities to "name everything for green" after the natural landscape has been destroyed.

> **She knew it had been mentioned before, but thought she ought to include how cities assault their green for two reasons: money and greed. Later, feeling remorseful, or sickened by the new view, they name everything for green—Oak Meadows, Lone Pine.**

Practice and Apply Use context clues in "Allied with Green" to help you define the meaning of the words in the chart. Then look up each word's precise meaning in a dictionary.

WORD	CONTEXT CLUES	MY GUESSED DEFINITION	DICTIONARY DEFINITION
sheared (paragraph 10)			
snide (paragraph 20)			
transporting (paragraph 25)			

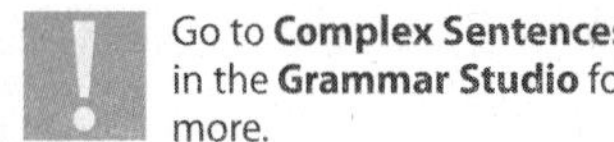

LANGUAGE CONVENTIONS: Complex Sentences

When you add a subordinate clause to an independent (main) clause, you create a **complex sentence,** as in this example:

> **Because I have told my friends about conservation, they care more about the environment.**

A clause is built on a subject and verb working together. Therefore, no matter how many clauses are in a sentence, the subject and verb in each clause must agree. In the example above, *I* agrees with *have told,* and *they* agrees with *care.*

Now, notice that the first clause in the example is a subordinate clause. It needs the rest of the sentence for it to make sense. If it were written with a period after *conservation,* it would be a sentence fragment. A **sentence fragment** is a group of words that is only part of a sentence. It does not express a complete thought. A sentence fragment may be lacking a subject, a predicate, or both. Be alert to errors like these and two other kinds of errors as you write:

Go to **Complex Sentences** in the **Grammar Studio** for more.

- In a **comma splice,** two independent clauses are joined with only a comma. You can correct a comma splice by making the clauses separate sentences, by changing the comma into a semicolon, by adding a coordinating conjunction, or by rephrasing the sentence as a complex sentence (as in the example above).

  INCORRECT: I have told my friends about conservation, they care more about the environment.

  REVISION: I have told my friends about conservation. They care more about the environment.

  REVISION: I have told my friends about conservation; they care more about the environment.

  REVISION: I have told my friends about conservation, so they care more about the environment.

- In a **run-on sentence,** there is no punctuation or conjunction between clauses: *I have told my friends about conservation they care more about the environment.* You can correct run-on sentences in the same ways that you correct comma splices.

Practice and Apply Write a paragraph about conservation and use complex sentences for most of your sentences. With a partner, make sure that all subjects and verbs agree and that you have avoided sentence fragments, comma splices, and run-on sentences.

COLLABORATE & COMPARE

POEM

ODE TO ENCHANTED LIGHT

by **Pablo Neruda**

pages 231–233

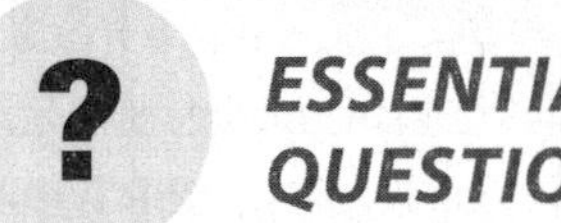

ESSENTIAL QUESTION:

What does it mean to be in harmony with nature?

COMPARE FORMS AND ELEMENTS

As you read, notice the form of each poem by focusing on the way words and lines are arranged on the page. Think about how each poem's structure—along with its use of rhythm, rhyme, and figurative language—deepens your understanding of its meaning and helps you make comparisons.

POEM

SLEEPING IN THE FOREST

by **Mary Oliver**

pages 236–237

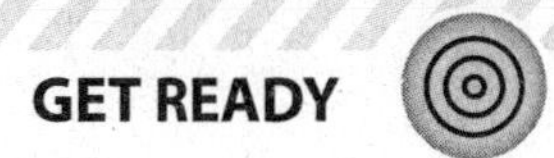

QUICK START

Think about a time when something in nature took you by surprise and caused you to pause and reflect for a moment. What did you experience in that moment—and what made it meaningful to you?

ANALYZE FORM: ODE

An **ode** is a type of lyric poetry (see next page) that deals with serious themes, such as justice, truth, or beauty. An ode celebrates or praises its subject, which is usually a person, event, thing, or element in nature.

The word *ode* comes from the Greek word *aeidein,* which means "sing" or "chant." A traditional ode is a long poem with a formal structure—often with patterns in its **meter,** or use of stressed and unstressed syllables, and its **rhyme,** its repetition of sounds at the end of words. Many modern poets experiment with the ode form to make it fresh and interesting for readers.

An ode and other types of poems reflect the poet's **style,** a manner of writing that involves *how* something is said rather than *what* is said. A poet can share ideas by using stylistic elements such as these:

GENRE ELEMENTS: POETRY

Form in poetry includes:

- how the poem's words and lines are presented on a page
- how the poem's sounds and rhythms are organized
- how the poem is structured with stanzas, line length, meter, and rhyme scheme

POETIC ELEMENT	WHAT IT DOES
Word choice poet's use of words	• A poet's word choice can be formal or informal, serious or humorous. • Well-chosen words and phrases help a poet express ideas precisely and creatively. They also help readers "see" what the poet is describing and better understand what she or he is feeling. • Through descriptive words, imagery, and **figurative language** (such as similes, metaphors, and personification), poets create a **mood,** or feeling or atmosphere.
Tone poet's attitude toward a subject	• Like word choice, a poet's tone can convey different feelings. • A feeling can often be described in one word—for example, playful, serious, or determined.
Voice poet's unique style of expression	• The poet's language lets a reader "hear" a personality in the poem. • The use of voice can reveal a poet's traits, beliefs, and attitudes.

As you read "Ode to enchanted light" and "Sleeping in the Forest," note how each poet uses these elements. Consider how they shape your experience of reading the poem.

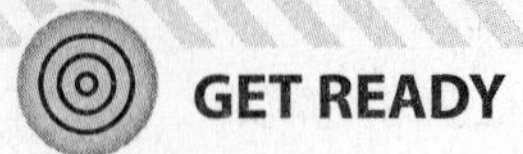

GET READY

ANALYZE LYRIC POETRY

A **lyric poem** is a short poem in which a single speaker expresses personal thoughts and feelings. Lyric poetry is a broad category that includes traditional forms such as odes and sonnets. Lyric poetry also includes **free verse,** a form that does not use a formal structure or rhyme scheme. In ancient times, lyric poems were meant to be sung and were often accompanied by a lyre, a simple stringed instrument like a harp.

- Lyric poems have some elements in common with songs, including the following:
  - rhythm and **melody,** a pleasing arrangement of sounds
  - the use of a **refrain,** one or more phrases or lines repeated in each stanza of a poem
  - imaginative word choice, or **diction**
  - the creation of a single, unified impression

As you analyze "Ode to enchanted light" and "Sleeping in the Forest," think about the images of nature presented in each poem. What do these images suggest about each speaker's relationship to nature? How does the poets' use of language affect the mood, voice, and tone that each poem conveys?

NOTICE & NOTE

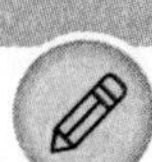

ANNOTATION MODEL

As you read, think about the poetic elements that each poet uses and how these create meaning for the reader. In the model, you can see one reader's notes about "Ode to enchanted light."

Under the trees light
has dropped from the top of the sky,
light
like a green
latticework of branches, . . .

It is interesting how the poet chooses to repeat the word light. I think this is done to show how important the effect of light is in nature.

I think these lines have a mood of playfulness even though this ode is about a more serious topic.

BACKGROUND

Nature has been a popular subject for poets throughout history. Two of the 20th century's most important poets, Pablo Neruda and Mary Oliver, continue this tradition. **Pablo Neruda** *(1904–1973) was the pen name of Ricardo Eliecer Neftalí Reyes Basoalto, who was born in Chile. Over his lifetime, he wrote hundreds of poems and was awarded the Nobel Prize for Literature in 1971 for his body of work. Neruda's poem "Ode to enchanted light" was written in Spanish. Its Spanish title is "Oda a la luz encantada."*

ODE TO ENCHANTED LIGHT

Poem by Pablo Neruda
translated by Ken Krabbenhoft

PREPARE TO COMPARE

As you read, note the different word choices and the structural and stylistic elements of an ode used in the poem.

Under the trees light
has dropped from the top of the sky,
light
like a green
latticework of branches,
shining
on every leaf,
drifting down like clean
white sand.

Notice & Note

Use the side margins to notice and note signposts in the text.

AGAIN AND AGAIN

Notice & Note: Mark instances where the poet is expressing how things look in the light.

Analyze: How does repeated use of similes (comparisons using *like* or *as*) create a mood or emotional effect?

NOTICE & NOTE

ANALYZE FORM: ODE

Annotate: Observe the difference in line lengths in the poem. Circle lines that stand out and underline shorter lines.

Interpret: How does the length and arrangement of lines in Neruda's poem impact its meaning?

A cicada sends
its sawing song
high into the empty air.

The world is
a glass overflowing
with water.

CHECK YOUR UNDERSTANDING

Answer these questions before moving on to the **Analyze the Text** section on the following page.

1 Which best expresses where the speaker in the poem is located?

- **A** In a meadow where cicadas sing
- **B** Near a river that is overflowing
- **C** Under the branches of some trees
- **D** In an airplane high in the air

2 Toward what does the poet express an appreciative tone, or attitude?

- **F** Cicadas
- **G** Natural light
- **H** Leaves
- **J** Empty air

3 Which word best describes the mood of the third stanza: A cicada sends / its sawing song / high into the empty air?

- **A** Happy
- **B** Ominous
- **C** Eager
- **D** Lonely

RESPOND

ANALYZE THE TEXT

Support your responses with evidence from the text. NOTEBOOK

1. **Interpret and Evaluate** What type of comparison does the poet make in lines 6–9 of "Ode to enchanted light"? Do you think this comparison is effective? Explain.
2. **Analyze** How do the comparisons made in lines 1–9 of "Ode to enchanted light" relate to the title of the poem? How is the light "enchanted"?
3. **Analyze** A cicada is an insect that makes a high-pitched, continual sound, usually in summer. Reread lines 10–12. What repeated first sounds, or **alliteration,** do you hear, and how are the sounds connected to the poem's meaning?
4. **Evaluate** Does this poem meet the requirements of an ode? Why or why not?
5. **Notice & Note** How is alliteration used in the final stanza of this poem? What does the repeated use of alliteration tell you about the author's style of writing?

RESEARCH

RESEARCH TIP
Once you select a poem for analysis, consider doing some further research about the historical, literary, social, or even geographical context in which the poet was writing.

Throughout history, poets have celebrated the beauty and power of nature. Research a few poets known for their nature poems—perhaps a poet you've read before and one you're curious about reading for the first time. Then select one poem that appeals to you and use the graphic organizer below to analyze its key elements.

QUESTION	ANSWER
What is the form of the poem?	
What is the mood of the poem?	
What memorable images does the poem contain?	
What tone, or attitude, does the poet have toward the subject?	
What is the theme of the poem?	

Connect With a small group, discuss whether nature poetry must always be about pleasant or positive experiences of nature. What other types of nature experience might be appropriate for a poem?

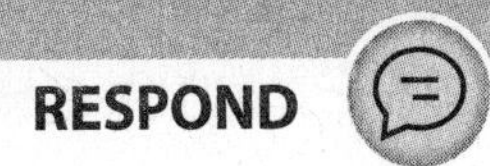

CREATE AND DISCUSS

Write an Ode Write an ode about a memorable experience that you have had in a natural setting, or perhaps something that you observed in nature and want to share. Think about the following questions.

- ❑ Who will be the speaker in your ode?
- ❑ How will you set up your lines and stanzas?
- ❑ How will you describe your experience or observation?
- ❑ What images or sound devices, such as alliteration, will you use?
- ❑ What will be the theme, or message, of your ode?

Listen for a Poem's Message In a group, take turns reading aloud and listening to your poems. Use the questions below to guide your listening and follow-up discussion.

- ❑ What is the poem about?
- ❑ What does the poem make me think about?
- ❑ How does the poem make me feel?
- ❑ What images and sounds in the poem do I like best?
- ❑ How can I state the message in the poem in a sentence?

Go to **Analyzing and Evaluating Presentations** in the **Speaking and Listening Studio** for help.

RESPOND TO THE ESSENTIAL QUESTION

What does it mean to be in harmony with nature?

Gather Information Review your annotations and notes on "Ode to enchanted light." Then, add relevant details to your Response Log. As you determine which information to include, think about how:

- people react to different types of experiences in nature
- your past experiences affect new ones
- your past experiences shape your views about yourself and the world around you

At the end of the unit, use your notes to write a personal narrative.

ACADEMIC VOCABULARY

As you write and discuss what you learned from the poem, be sure to use the Academic Vocabulary words. Check off each of the words that you use.

- ❑ **affect**
- ❑ **element**
- ❑ **ensure**
- ❑ **participate**
- ❑ **specify**

BACKGROUND

Mary Oliver *(b. 1935) is an American poet who was born in Maple Heights, Ohio. In her youth, she was an avid reader and writer. She also spent a lot of time walking through nearby woods and fields. Today, Oliver is regarded by many as a poetic guide to the natural world and an heir to the Romantic nature tradition in American poetry begun by Ralph Waldo Emerson and Henry David Thoreau. Oliver has published more than two dozen books and is the winner of many prestigious awards for her poetry.*

SLEEPING IN THE FOREST
Poem by Mary Oliver

PREPARE TO COMPARE

As you read, note the different structural and stylistic elements of a lyric poem that the author uses. How is the poem similar to or different from an ode?

Notice & Note

Use the side margins to notice and note signposts in the text.

MEMORY MOMENT

Notice & Note: Mark the place in the poem where the speaker mentions a memory.

Analyze: What does the memory mentioned in the poem say about the speaker's relationship to nature?

I thought the earth
remembered me, she
took me back so tenderly, arranging
her dark skirts, her pockets
full of lichens[1] and seeds. I slept
as never before, a stone
on the riverbed, nothing
between me and the white fire of the stars
but my thoughts, and they floated
light as moths among the branches
of the perfect trees. All night

[1] **lichens** (lī′kənz): fungi that grow together with algae and form a crust-like growth on rocks or tree trunks.

I heard the small kingdoms breathing
around me, the insects, and the birds
who do their work in the darkness. All night
I rose and fell, as if in water, grappling[2]
with a luminous doom. By morning
I had vanished at least a dozen times
into something better.

[2] **grappling:** struggling.

NOTICE & NOTE 

ANALYZE LYRIC POETRY

Annotate: Mark personal thoughts and feelings that the speaker expresses in lines 9–14.

Interpret: Is the speaker comfortable in the natural world? What text evidence supports your answer?

CHECK YOUR UNDERSTANDING

Answer these questions before moving on to the **Analyze the Text** section on the following page.

1 In lines 1–5, how does the speaker think of the forest?

A As an uncomfortable bed

B As a skirt with pockets

C As a comforting friend

D As a riverbed with rushing water

2 In lines 9–10, what is compared to light as moths among the branches?

F Thoughts

G Stones

H Lights

J Branches

3 How does the use of **personification**—the giving of human qualities to an animal, object, or idea—help achieve the poet's purpose?

A It downplays the importance of Earth.

B It downplays the importance of the speaker.

C It highlights the importance of Earth.

D It highlights the importance of the speaker.

ANALYZE THE TEXT

Support your responses with evidence from the text. NOTEBOOK

1. **Analyze** Reread lines 5–7. What is compared to "a stone / on the riverbed"? Where else does this image appear in the poem?
2. **Evaluate** Identify examples of each of the elements of a lyric poem that appear in "Sleeping in the Forest." Is Oliver's poem a good example of a lyric poem? Why or why not?
3. **Critique** In lines 9–11, how does the **simile,** or comparison of unlike things using *like* or *as*, affect the meaning of the poem?
4. **Interpret** In the last sentence, the speaker says, "By morning / I had vanished at least a dozen times / into something better." What might the speaker mean by the phrase "something better"?
5. **Notice & Note** What transitional phrases does the poet use in lines 11–18 to indicate the time during which the events are being remembered? How do these time-related transitional phrases help convey the theme of the poem?

RESEARCH

RESEARCH TIP
When you need to research a general topic to find examples, search first for the broadest category, such as "lyric poetry." Scan a few websites to find specific poems, poets, and topics that interest you and then jot down words that you can use to further pinpoint your search.

Look for more examples of lyric poetry. Choose two poems that you find interesting and then answer the questions below about the speaker in each poem. Remember, in a lyric poem, the speaker can be the poet but doesn't have to be. (Note: You need to write the title of each poem only once.)

Questions About Speakers	Answers
Is there just one speaker?	Title of Poem: Answer:
	Title of Poem: Answer:
What words and details suggest who the speaker is?	
What are the thoughts and feelings of the speaker?	
Is the speaker's experience similar to any that you have had? How?	

Connect With a small group, discuss the speakers in each of your poems. How does thinking about the speaker give you clues about the main message, or theme, of the poems? Read aloud the parts of the poems that support your ideas.

CREATE AND DISCUSS

Write a Lyric Poem Remember that a lyric poem has a sense of rhythm and melody, is imaginative in word use, and gives a unified impression. Think of a moment in which you have felt connected to nature. Then use the idea web to organize your ideas before you begin writing your poem.

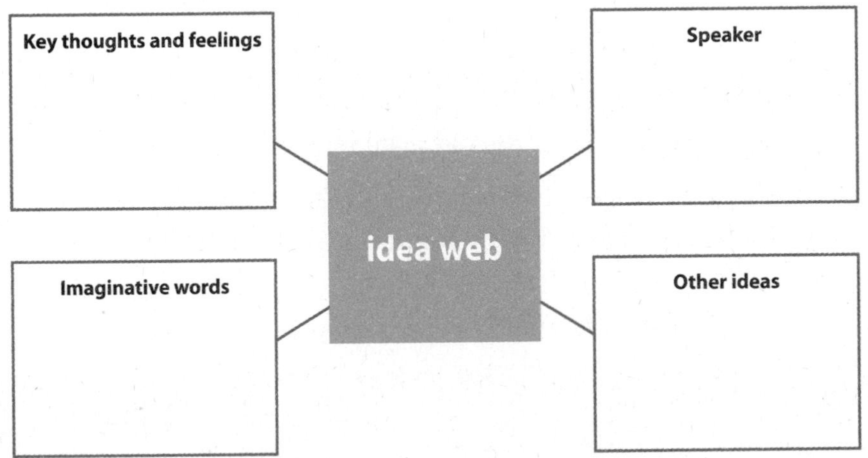

Listen for a Poem's Rhythm and Melody Find a partner and read your poems to each other. Do the following on your copy of the poem.

- ❑ Mark imaginative word choices.
- ❑ Write notes about how the arrangement of lines creates rhythm.
- ❑ Put an arrow at lines where the rhythm changes.
- ❑ Note the strongest impression the poem leaves in your mind.

Afterward, discuss ideas for revising word choice and other elements in each poem to strengthen the impression it conveys.

Go to **Giving a Presentation** in the **Speaking and Listening Studio** to learn more.

RESPOND TO THE ESSENTIAL QUESTION

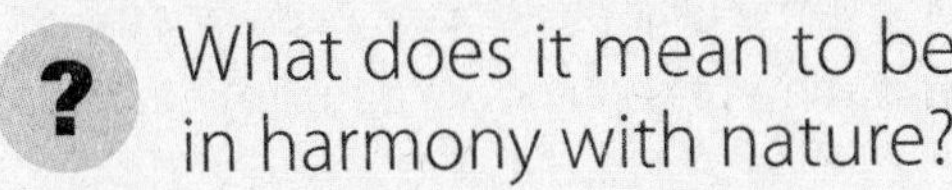

? What does it mean to be in harmony with nature?

Gather Information Review your annotations and notes on "Sleeping in the Forest." Then, add relevant details to your Response Log. As you determine which information to include, think about how:

- people make connections to nature
- rhythm can affect the mood of a poem

At the end of the unit, use your notes to write a personal narrative.

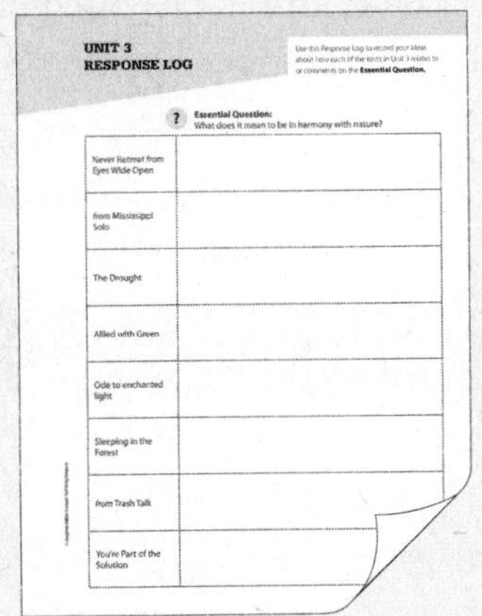

UNIT 3 RESPONSE LOG

Essential Question: What does it mean to be in harmony with nature?

Never Retreat from Eyes Wide Open	
from Mississippi Solo	
The Drought	
Allied with Green	
Ode to enchanted light	
Sleeping in the Forest	
from Trash Talk	
You're Part of the Solution	

ACADEMIC VOCABULARY

As you write and discuss what you learned from the poem, be sure to use the Academic Vocabulary words. Check off each of the words that you use.

- ❑ **affect**
- ❑ **element**
- ❑ **ensure**
- ❑ **participate**
- ❑ **specify**

Collaborate & Compare

COMPARE FORMS AND ELEMENTS

Both "Ode to enchanted light" and "Sleeping in the Forest" describe the speakers' responses to experiences they have had in nature. Despite the poems' thematic similarities, the poets use different poetic forms and styles to create unique visions. These include:

- **Organization**—length of lines, stanzas, punctuation
- **Sound Devices**—rhyme, rhythm, alliteration, repetition
- **Figurative Language**—such as the following:
  - metaphor: comparing two things that are unlike but have some qualities in common
  - simile: comparing two unlike things using the word *like* or *as*
  - personification: giving human qualities to an animal, object, or idea

With your group, complete the chart with details from both poems.

POETIC ELEMENTS	"ODE TO ENCHANTED LIGHT"	"SLEEPING IN THE FOREST"
Organization		
Sound Devices		
Figurative Language		

ODE TO
ENCHANTED LIGHT
Poem by Pablo Neruda
translated by Ken
Krabbenhoft

SLEEPING IN THE FOREST
Poem by Mary Oliver

ANALYZE THE TEXTS

Discuss these questions in your group.

1. **Evaluate** With your group, discuss the organization of each poem. How do they differ? Is the organization of each poem appropriate to its content? Explain.
2. **Compare** Reread lines 8–9 of "Ode to enchanted light" and lines 9–11 of "Sleeping in the Forest." What similarities do you observe in each poet's use of figurative language?
3. **Interpret** How would you describe the central image presented in each poem? How does the speaker's central image relate to each poem's theme?
4. **Critique** How effectively does each poem use figurative language to convey its theme? Explain.

EXPLORE AND PRESENT

Now, your group can continue exploring ideas about nature by comparing the different poetic forms and elements in these poems. Follow these steps:

1. **Choose a Focus for Your Comparison** As a group, review your completed charts. Identify the most important ways the poems are alike and different. Discuss the significance of these key points and how they relate to nature. Then, reach a consensus about what to focus on in your presentation. For example, think about comparing the figurative language in each poem and the way that it impacts the reader's thoughts and feelings about nature.

2. **Create a Venn Diagram** After selecting a focus for your comparison, use the Venn diagram below to organize the similarities and differences you identified. Then, add words and phrases from the poem as supporting evidence.

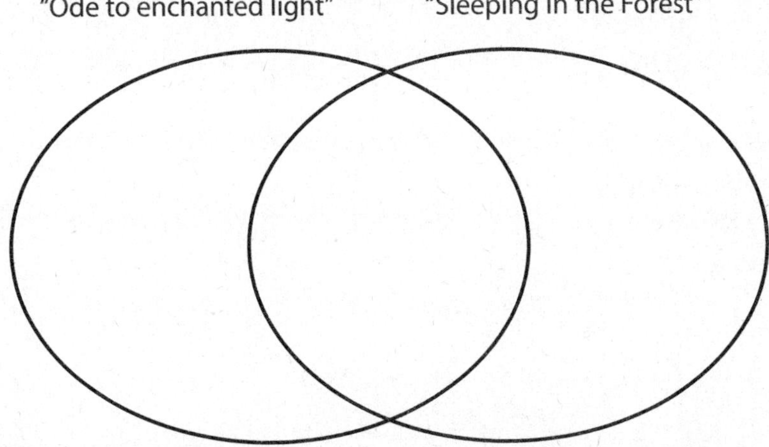

3. **Share What You Have Learned** As a group, prepare a presentation of your comparison. Consider using your Venn diagram, drawings, and other images as visual aids in your presentation. While other groups make their presentations, remember to listen actively and note any questions you have. After each group has presented, discuss what you learned about people's relationship to nature nature by analyzing and comparing the two poems.

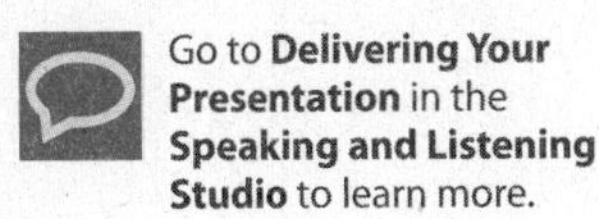

Go to **Delivering Your Presentation** in the **Speaking and Listening Studio** to learn more.

VIDEO

from TRASH TALK

by the **National Oceanic and Atmospheric Administration**

page 245

COMPARE PERSUASIVE MEDIA

As you view the video and poster, notice how each medium presents information. Consider the purpose and message of the video and the poster. Think, too, about how the purpose and message may have influenced the way each was designed. After you view both media, you will collaborate with a small group on a final project.

ESSENTIAL QUESTION:

What does it mean to be in harmony with nature?

POSTER

YOU'RE PART OF THE SOLUTION

pages 246–247

QUICK START

Think of a cause you care about. How could you persuade others to share your views about that cause? Write down your thoughts.

ANALYZE PERSUASIVE MEDIA

Creators of persuasive media use many techniques to communicate meaning and to influence you to adopt a position or take an action. Recognizing these techniques will help you analyze persuasive media.

TECHNIQUE	DESCRIPTION
Glittering generalization	Broad statement that includes words with a **positive connotation**—suggesting something pleasant—to influence an audience
Rhetorical question	Asks an obvious or unanswerable question to make a point or keep the audience thinking
Appeal to logic	Persuades through reason and evidence
Appeal to emotion	Persuades by appealing to strong feelings
Appeal by association	**Bandwagon** appeals urge you to do something because "everyone else" is doing it. **Testimonials** are endorsements or approvals from famous people or researchers.
Appeal to loyalty	Relies on people's connection to a particular group

Along with these techniques, look for signs of bias. **Bias** is an inclination for or against a particular opinion. A media piece may reveal bias by overlooking key facts, by stacking evidence on one side of an argument, by using unfairly weighted evidence, or by using loaded language (words with emotionally charged connotations). Asking questions like these will help you evaluate media pieces:

- Who is presenting the information? What motives or goals does that individual or organization have?
- Who is the intended audience?
- Is the evidence factual, accurate, relevant, current, and sufficient?

As you examine the media selections, analyze how ideas are presented. Decide whether each selection persuades you—and why or why not.

GENRE ELEMENTS: MEDIA

- created for a specific purpose
- convey a message
- target a specific audience
- come in many forms, including videos, posters, podcasts, and other digital texts

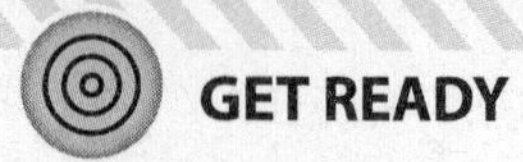
GET READY

ANALYZE DIGITAL TEXTS

When you view a video or a digital text such as a downloadable poster, think about the message and the intended purpose of the text. Is its goal to inform, to entertain, to persuade, or to express the feelings or thoughts of those who created it? Analyzing the elements of a digital text can help you understand and evaluate its message, purpose, reliability, and effectiveness.

Videos Producers of videos use words as well as visual and sound elements to convey information and encourage you to think or feel a certain way. Through effective use of these elements, a video can communicate a message, convince viewers that something is true and important, or persuade viewers to do something. These are some of the visual and sound elements that often appear in videos:

FILM FOOTAGE	Film shot with a video camera and then edited by cutting and pasting sections together
ANIMATION	Images created through drawings, computer graphics, or photographs that appear to move
COMPUTER-GENERATED IMAGERY (CGI)	Computer-created or manipulated images and animations; may combine elements of actual film footage with computer imagery
NARRATION	Words spoken by the narrator, which are carefully chosen to deliver facts and/or to persuade; quality of the narrator's voice and the way he or she expresses the words to convey a message
MUSIC	Singing, playing instruments, or using computer-generated tones; can create a mood or emphasize key moments in the video

As you watch *Trash Talk,* note how the producers use a variety of visual and sound elements to convey a message and persuade viewers.

Posters A poster combines text and visual elements to make a strong visual impact on viewers.

- **Text (print) elements** are the letters, words, and sentences on the poster. To analyze text elements, think about how language is used to communicate information and stir your emotions. Also think about the fonts (type styles) and sizes used to make text stand out.
- **Visual (graphic) elements** include all other visual information—images (photographs, designs, illustrations), colors, lines, and so on. To analyze visual elements, consider how the images and visual design help communicate information and express a message.

BACKGROUND

The video clip you're about to see was produced by the National Oceanic and Atmospheric Administration (NOAA) for World Ocean Day 2016. NOAA scientists and researchers monitor changes in the environment—from the very bottom of the ocean all the way to the surface of the sun. Then they communicate the information they gather to private citizens, emergency managers, and key government and business decision-makers. Marine debris—the topic of this video—is just one of the many areas that NOAA studies.

PREPARE TO COMPARE

As you view the video, make note of how the narrators define marine debris. *Also consider how the various visual and sound elements used to convey information in the video might or might not work in print.*

For more online resources, log in to your dashboard and click on "TRASH TALK" from the selection menu.

As needed, pause the video to make notes about what impresses you or about ideas you might want to talk about later. Replay or rewind so that you can clarify anything you do not understand.

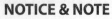

BACKGROUND

For more than 200 years, posters have been a popular way to convey information and share messages with the public. They have been used to proclaim laws, publicize events, advertise products, and communicate ideas. The earliest posters were simply words printed on paper in black ink. As printing and poster art techniques developed, posters became more sophisticated. Now, digital photography and computer applications have made it possible for almost anyone to combine text and graphics to make a poster.

PREPARE TO COMPARE

As you view the poster, consider the message that it conveys. Think of the responses the creator of the poster might be trying to inspire. Consider that as much deliberate design can go into the creation of a still image as in moving ones. Think about the ways in which persuasion is at work in the carefully chosen wording in the text and in how the visual elements have been deliberately chosen to catch the eye and capture attention. Be aware of the effectiveness of techniques that help to communicate messages in different types of media.

THIS PROBLEM SEEMS OVERWHELMING, BUT . . .
You're part of the solution!
Marine debris trashes all our coastlines and threatens ocean-dwelling creatures of every kind. It's a tough challenge to overcome, but young people like you have the desire and drive to tackle it.
Help save our precious oceans!
Take action now!
Get involved in ocean clean-up projects at government agencies and marine conservation groups.

ANALYZE MEDIA

Support your responses with evidence from the video and poster.

NOTEBOOK

1. **Draw Conclusions** According to the video, what items are found most often in marine cleanups? What can you conclude from that information?
2. **Evaluate** Describe the visuals used in the video. How do they work together to convey information?
3. **Analyze** Which persuasive techniques are used in the video? Provide examples to support your answer.
4. **Interpret** How do the visual elements in the poster help support the text elements?
5. **Critique** Look at how the text in the poster is presented. Why do you think the creators of the poster broke up the text and used different font styles and sizes?

RESEARCH

Choose two problems that you learned about in this lesson. Then do some research to find one or two possible solutions to each problem. Record what you learn in the chart.

PROBLEM	SOLUTION(S)

RESEARCH TIP

To research a problem and its possible solutions, try using phrases that you would expect to find in a piece of writing about the topic—for example, you could search for phrases such as *problems and solutions*, *solve the problem*, or *what you can do*, combined with a topic such as *trash in the ocean* or *plastic soda can rings*.

Extend If you wanted to share information about marine debris problems and solutions with a wider audience, would you use a poster, a video, or another type of media? Why?

CREATE AND PRESENT

Write a Letter to NOAA Write a letter to the National Oceanic and Atmospheric Administration to express your opinion about the effectiveness of their *Trash Talk* video.

- ❑ Introduce the topic and express your overall opinion about the video. Be truthful but tactful.
- ❑ Include details from the video to support your views. Describe particular visual or sound elements that you feel were very effective or that you think would be more effective if they were changed.
- ❑ In your final paragraph, state your conclusion about the video and your purpose for writing the letter—or whether you would like NOAA to take a particular action.

Go to **Writing Arguments: Persuasive Techniques** in the **Writing Studio** to build effective support for your opinions.

Present a Critique Examine the poster once more. Consider the effect created by the combination of text and visual elements. Write a critique that explains your ideas and then present it to your classmates.

- ❑ Identify which text and visual elements work well and why.
- ❑ Identify text or visual elements that do not work or that you think could be improved. Offer suggestions for improving the poster to make it more effective.
- ❑ Present your ideas clearly and persuasively. Include an opinion statement at the end of your presentation that summarizes your response to the poster.

Go to **Introduction: Using Media in a Presentation** in the **Speaking and Listening Studio** for help.

RESPOND TO THE ESSENTIAL QUESTION

? What does it mean to be in harmony with nature?

Gather Information Review your notes on the poster and the video. Then, add relevant details to your Response Log. As you determine which information to include, consider what these persuasive media suggest about how people can live in harmony with nature.

At the end of the unit, use your notes to write a personal narrative.

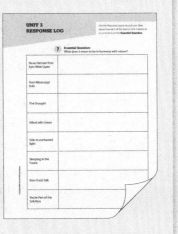

ACADEMIC VOCABULARY

As you write and discuss what you learned from the video and poster, be sure to use the Academic Vocabulary words. Check off each of the words that you use.

- ❑ **affect**
- ❑ **element**
- ❑ **ensure**
- ❑ **participate**
- ❑ **specify**

Collaborate & Compare

COMPARE PERSUASIVE MEDIA

The video clip from *Trash Talk* and the "You're Part of the Solution" poster both focus on the issue of marine debris. Their form and the way in which they present information is different, however. When you compare two or more media on the same topic, you analyze the information, making connections and expanding on key ideas in one medium by studying the other.

In a small group, complete the Venn diagram with similarities and differences in how you learned about marine debris in the two types of media you viewed.

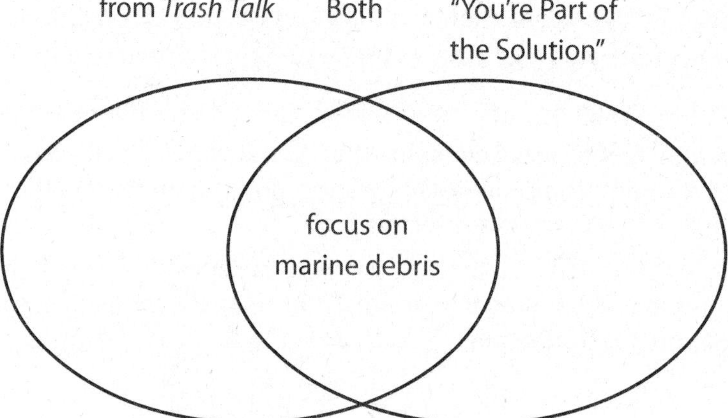

ANALYZE THE MEDIA

Discuss these questions in your group.

1. **Draw Conclusions** Are both the video and the poster targeted at the same audience? What evidence supports your conclusion?

2. **Compare** How does the purpose of the video differ slightly from the purpose of the poster?

3. **Connect** Examine the trash shown along the shore in the poster and think about what you learned in the video. What type of common debris is pictured in the poster, and what other type of marine debris is not pictured?

4. **Critique** Which is more effective at conveying its message: the video or the poster? Why do you think so?

RESEARCH AND SHARE

Imagine that the National Oceanic and Atmospheric Administration has asked you for help with its marine debris media campaign. A media campaign is a group of different media that work together to achieve a common purpose. As a team, collaborate to research, design, and pitch to NOAA a media campaign that builds on the ideas presented in the video and the poster. Follow these steps:

1. **Identify a Problem** In your group, brainstorm to choose a particular type of marine debris to focus on in your campaign. You may want to focus on one of the problems you already researched and expand that research. Come to an agreement about one problem to address.
2. **Gather Information** As you research the problem your group identified, make sure that your sources are reliable and credible.
3. **Synthesize Information** In your group, share the facts you learned about your problem and one or more possible solutions. Choose the most persuasive facts to include in your messaging.
4. **Develop a Message** As a group, decide who your target audience is. What message will you communicate to that audience?
5. **Plan a Video or Poster** Half the members of your group will plan a video and the other half will plan a poster. Talk about how the message will be conveyed in each form of media. Remember: The audience and message should remain the same; only the type of media will change. Each medium should include some of the persuasive techniques you learned about. Use an organizer like this one to capture your notes:

Problem:	**Possible Solutions:**
Target audience:	**Message:**
Type of media: **Description:** **Persuasive techniques:**	

Pitch Your Media Campaign With your group, present your ideas for a video and poster to a larger group. Include information about how and where the video and poster will be distributed. Be prepared to answer questions that your audience may have.

RESEARCH TIP

When searching for information online, a specific question can sometimes help you find information more quickly. For example, you might search for *How does plastic harm the environment?* or *How many plastic water bottles are saved each year by using reusable bottles?*

INDEPENDENT READING

Reader's Choice

? ESSENTIAL QUESTION:

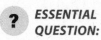

What does it mean to be in harmony with nature?

Setting a Purpose Select one or more of these options from your eBook to continue your exploration of the Essential Question.

- Read the descriptions to see which text grabs your interest.
- Think about which genres you enjoy reading.

Notice & Note

In this unit, you practiced asking **Big Questions** and noticing and noting two signposts: **Extreme or Absolute Language** and **Contrasts and Contradictions.** As you read independently, these signposts and others will aid your understanding. Below are the anchor questions to ask when you read literature and nonfiction.

Reading Literature: Stories, Poems, and Plays		
Signpost	**Anchor Question**	**Lesson**
Contrasts and Contradictions	Why did the character act that way?	p. 99
Aha Moment	How might this change things?	p. 3
Tough Questions	What does this make me wonder about?	p. 362
Words of the Wiser	What's the lesson for the character?	p. 363
Again and Again	Why might the author keep bringing this up?	p. 3
Memory Moment	Why is this memory important?	p. 2

Reading Nonfiction: Essays, Articles, and Arguments		
Signpost	**Anchor Question(s)**	**Lesson**
Big Questions	What surprised me? What did the author think I already knew? What challenged, changed, or confirmed what I already knew?	p. 265 p. 183 p. 437
Contrasts and Contradictions	What is the difference, and why does it matter?	p. 183
Extreme or Absolute Language	Why did the author use this language?	p. 182
Numbers and Stats	Why did the author use these numbers or amounts?	p. 264
Quoted Words	Why was this person quoted or cited, and what did this add?	p. 437
Word Gaps	Do I know this word from someplace else? Does it seem like technical talk for this topic? Do clues in the sentence help me understand the word?	p. 265

INDEPENDENT READING

You can preview these texts in Unit 3 of your eBook.

Then, check off the text or texts that you select to read on your own.

MEMOIR

***from* Unbowed**
Wangari Muta Maathai

A woman reflects on her childhood impressions of the natural world around her home.

POEM

Problems with Hurricanes
Victor Hernández Cruz

This poem asks and answers the question: What is the greatest danger for people during a hurricane?

ARTICLE

Living Large Off the Grid
Kristen Mascia

Discover how one family lives sustainably in a house that was built from straw in 2009.

POETRY

Haiku
Issa, Basho, and Buson, translated by Richard Haas

This selection of haiku poetry describes observations of people and nature.

Collaborate and Share With a partner, discuss what you learned from at least one of your independent readings.

- Give a brief synopsis or summary of the text.
- Describe any signposts that you noticed in the text and explain what they revealed to you.
- Describe what you most enjoyed or found most challenging about the text. Give specific examples.
- Decide if you would recommend the text to others. Why or why not?

Go to the **Reading Studio** for more resources on **Notice & Note.**

Write a Personal Narrative

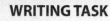

Go to the **Writing Studio** for help writing a personal narrative.

This unit focuses on ways in which people interact with nature. For this writing task, you will write a short personal narrative about an experience you had in nature or a lesson you learned from observing the natural world. For an example of a well-written personal narrative you can use as a mentor text, review the excerpt from the memoir *Mississippi Solo*.

As you write your personal narrative, you can use the notes from your Response Log, which you filled out after reading the texts in this unit.

Writing Prompt

Read the information in the box below.

This is the topic or context for your personal narrative.

> We all can remember experiences that changed our thinking or even our life. Events that took place in natural settings—in places either close to home or more remote—often create such memories. Some experiences were simple; others were dramatic. Because they were important to us, however, most of us enjoy remembering them and telling others about them.

Think carefully about the following question.

This is the Essential Question for the unit. How would you answer this question, based on the texts in this unit?

> What does it mean to be in harmony with nature?

Now mark the words that identify exactly what you are being asked to produce.

Write a personal narrative in which you share an experience in nature or a lesson you learned by observing some part of the natural world.

Be sure to—

Review these points as you write and again when you finish. Make any needed changes.

- ❑ provide an introduction that catches the reader's attention, indicates the topic, and sets the scene
- ❑ focus on a single experience
- ❑ describe events (parts of the experience) in chronological order, with transitions that make the sequence of events clear
- ❑ include vivid, specific, and sensory details that make people, places, and events seem real
- ❑ include your thoughts and feelings
- ❑ conclude by explaining why the experience was meaningful to you

1 Plan

Before you start writing, you need to plan your narrative. When you plan a draft, you often start by selecting a genre that is appropriate for a particular topic, purpose, and audience. For this writing task, you already know that the topic is related to experiences in nature, and you know that the genre is a personal narrative. Next, you should consider your purpose and audience. What key idea and details do you want to convey? Who might enjoy hearing about your experience? Try using a range of strategies in planning your draft. These might include discussing the topic with your classmates, doing some background reading, and thinking about personal interests you have that relate to the topic. Use the table below to assist you in planning your draft.

Personal Narrative Planning Table	
Genre	Personal narrative
Topic	An experience in nature
Purpose	
Audience	
Ideas from discussion with classmates	
Ideas from background reading	
Personal interests related to topic	

Background Reading Review the notes you have taken in your Response Log after reading the texts in this unit. These texts provide background reading that will help you formulate the key ideas you will include in your narrative.

Notice & Note

From Reading to Writing

As you plan your personal narrative, apply what you've learned about signposts to your own writing. Remember that writers use common features, called signposts, to help convey their message to readers.

Think about how you can incorporate **Aha Moment** into your essay.

Go to the **Reading Studio** for more resources on Notice & Note.

Use the notes from your Response Log as you plan your narrative.

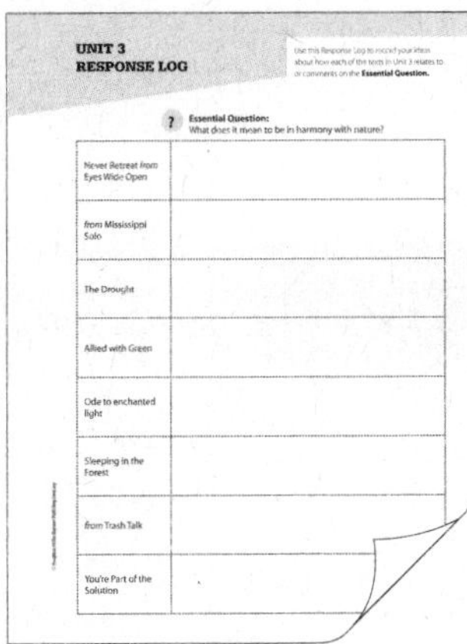

WRITING TASK

Go to **Writing Narratives: Narrative Structure** for help organizing your ideas.

Organize Your Ideas After you have gathered ideas and information from your planning activities, you need to organize your material in a way that will help you draft your narrative. You can use the chart below to record each part of the experience in chronological order. You also can use the chart to record how you thought and felt about the events then or how you think and feel about them now.

Main Topic: An Experience in Nature		
First Event	Second Event	Third Event
Key Details	Key Details	Key Details
Thoughts and Feelings	Thoughts and Feelings	Thoughts and Feelings

3 Develop a Draft

You may prefer to draft your narrative online.

Once you have completed your planning activities, you will be ready to begin drafting your personal narrative. Refer to your planning table and the completed chart above, as well as any notes you took as you studied the texts in the unit. These will provide a kind of map for you to follow as you write. Using a word processor or online writing application makes it easier to make changes or move sentences around later when you are ready to revise your first draft.

Use the Mentor Text

from
MISSISSIPPI SOLO

? ESSENTIAL QUESTION:
What does it mean to be in harmony with nature?

Author's Craft

Your introduction is your first chance to capture the reader's attention. Note how the author of *Mississippi Solo* does so.

Too many marvelous days in a row and you begin to get used to it, to think that's the way it's supposed to be. Too many good days, too many bad days—you need some break in the monotony of one to appreciate the other. If you only get sunshine, someone said, you end up in a desert.

By suggesting that bad days are as important as good ones, the author hints that he will share his memories of a difficult experience.

Apply What You've Learned To capture your reader's attention in your personal narrative, you might include a compelling hint of upcoming events or a thought-provoking question related to the topic.

Genre Characteristics

In a personal narrative, sensory details—details that appeal to our senses of sight, hearing, touch, smell, and taste—can help the reader picture the events. Notice how the author of *Mississippi Solo* uses vivid sensory details to help his readers picture the events and understand his feelings.

No sooner had I ducked into the trees than the sky split open with a loud crash and a splintery crackle of lightning. I was not going to make it through the trees. The wind came in at hurricane strength. The tips of the trees bent way over and aimed toward the ground, like fishing rods hooked on a big one. Water flooded like the tide rushing upstream. . . .

The author provides vivid details that appeal to the senses of sight and hearing. They help the reader understand how frightened he was when the storm began.

Apply What You've Learned The details you include in your personal narrative should be clearly related to your experience in nature and the lesson you learned from the experience. They should help readers imagine themselves in your place and understand why you think and feel the way you do about what you experienced.

3 Revise

Go to the **Writing as a Process** for help revising your narrative.

On Your Own Once you have written the draft of your personal narrative, you'll want to go back and look for ways to improve your writing. As you reread and revise, think about whether you have achieved your purpose. The Revision Guide will help you focus on specific elements to make your writing stronger.

Revision Guide		
Ask Yourself	**Tips**	**Revision Techniques**
1. Does my introduction grab readers' attention and set the scene?	**Underline** interesting or surprising statements. **Circle** details that show when and where the experience happened.	**Add** an attention-getting statement. **Add** details about where and when the event took place.
2. Are events in chronological order?	**Number** the events in the narrative. **Check** to make sure that they are in the correct order.	**Rearrange** events in the order in which they occurred, if necessary. **Add** transitions to link events.
3. Do vivid and specific sensory details make people, places, and events seem real?	**Highlight** vivid, specific, and sensory details.	**Add** more sensory details. **Delete** irrelevant details.
4. Have I included my thoughts and feelings?	**Put a check mark** next to statements of feelings or thoughts.	**Add** specific details about feelings and thoughts, if necessary.
5. Does my conclusion reveal why the experience was meaningful to me and/or what lesson I learned?	**Underline** the statement about why the experience is meaningful to you or what lesson you learned from it.	**Add** a statement that explains why the experience is important.

ACADEMIC VOCABULARY

As you conduct your **peer review,** be sure to use these words.

- ❑ **affect**
- ❑ **element**
- ❑ **ensure**
- ❑ **participate**
- ❑ **specify**

With a Partner Once you and your partner have worked through the Revision Guide on your own, exchange papers and evaluate each other's draft in a **peer review.** Focus on providing suggestions for at least three of the items mentioned in the Revision Guide. Explain why you think your partner's draft should be revised and what specific suggestions you have.

When receiving feedback from your partner, listen attentively and ask questions to make sure you fully understand the revision suggestions.

4 Edit

Once you have addressed the organization, development, and flow of ideas in your narrative, you can look to improve the finer points of your draft. Edit for the proper use of standard English conventions and be sure to correct any misspellings or grammatical errors.

Language Conventions

Commonly Confused Words Words that sound alike are often confused in writing. Some of these words are *its/it's*, *your/you're*, *two/too/to*, and *there/they're/their*.

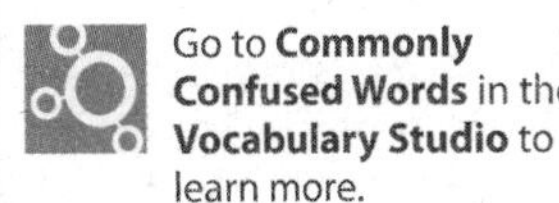

Go to **Commonly Confused Words** in the **Vocabulary Studio** to learn more.

To make sure that you are using the right word and spelling it correctly, ask yourself what it means and how you are using it in the sentence. Note the examples that appear in the excerpt from *Mississippi Solo*.

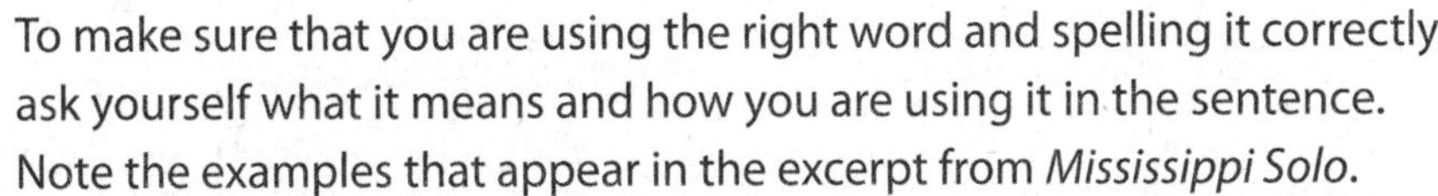

Commonly Confused Words	Example of Correct Spelling
two: one plus one **too:** excess, also **to:** part of a verb, preposition of direction	Too many marvelous days in a row and you begin to get used to it, to think that's the way it's supposed to be.
your: belonging to you **you're:** "you are"	The idle chatter you get when you walk with your favorite niece or nephew going no place in particular with nothing special on your minds . . .
its: belonging to something **it's:** "it is"	. . . the little kid just jabbers away because it's comfortable and he feels like it.
their: belonging to them **they're:** "they are" **there:** a place	The wooded area lasted only another hundred yards or so, and I thought I could easily get there before the rains arrived.

5 Publish

Finalize your personal narrative and choose a way to share it with your audience. Consider these options:

- Present your narrative as a speech to the class.
- Post your narrative as a blog on a classroom or school website.

WRITING TASK

Use the scoring guide to evaluate your personal narrative.

Writing Task Scoring Guide: Personal Narrative			
	Organization/Progression	Development of Ideas	Use of Language and Conventions
4	• The narrative is clearly focused on the events related to a single experience. • All events are presented in a clear and logical order. • Transitions clearly show the sequence of events.	• The introduction catches the reader's attention and sets the scene. • The narrative is well developed with key details and the writer's thoughts and feelings. • The conclusion of the narrative makes clear the significance of the experience to the writer.	• Precise words and vivid, sensory language are used throughout to bring people, places, and events to life. • Commonly confused words are used correctly. • Spelling, capitalization, and punctuation are correct. • Grammar and usage are correct.
3	• The narrative focuses primarily on events relating to a single experience but may include one or two unrelated events. • Most events are presented in chronological order, but some are not. • A few more transitions are needed to clarify the sequence of events and other details.	• The introduction could be more engaging. The scene is set adequately. • The narrative is somewhat well developed with key details and the writer's thoughts and feelings. • The conclusion of the narrative suggests but doesn't make clear the significance of the event to the writer.	• Precise words and vivid, sensory details are often used to describe people, places, and events. • Commonly confused words are generally used correctly. • Spelling, capitalization, and punctuation are mostly correct, with only a few errors. • Grammar and usage are mostly correct, with only a few errors.
2	• The narrative explores a number of events, with only a vague focus on one main experience. • The sequence of events is confusing. • More transitions are needed to show the sequence of events.	• The introduction is not very engaging or clear. • The narrative is missing key details or doesn't include enough of the writer's thoughts and feelings. • The conclusion of the narrative offers conflicting interpretations of the significance of the event to the writer.	• Precise words and vivid details are used only occasionally; descriptions are often vague and general. • There are several errors in the use of commonly confused words. • Spelling, capitalization, and punctuation are often incorrect but do not make reading difficult. • Grammar and usage are often incorrect, but the writer's ideas are still clear.
1	• The narrative wanders from event to event, with little or no focus. • Events are presented in random order, with no logical connections. • No transitions are used, making the narrative difficult to follow.	• The introduction is missing or very confusing. • The narrative is not well developed. There are no key details and the writer's thoughts and feelings are unclear. • The conclusion is missing or fails to convey the significance of the experience to the writer.	• Language is vague and confusing. • There are enough errors in the use of commonly confused words to cause confusion. • Many spelling, capitalization, and punctuation errors are present. • Many grammatical and usage errors confuse the writer's ideas.

Reflect on the Unit

By completing your personal narrative, you have created a writing product that helps pull together and express your thoughts about the reading you have done in this unit. Now is a good time to reflect on what you have learned.

Reflect on the Essential Question

- What does it mean to be in harmony with nature? How has your answer to this question changed since you first considered it when you started this unit?
- What are some examples from the texts you've read that show how people experience being in harmony with nature?

Reflect on Your Reading

- Which selections were the most interesting or surprising to you?
- From which selection did you learn the most about what it means to be in harmony with nature?

Reflect on the Writing Task

- What difficulties did you encounter while working on your personal narrative? How might you avoid them next time?
- What parts of the narrative were the easiest and hardest to write? Why?
- What improvements did you make to your narrative as you were revising?

UNIT 3 SELECTIONS

- **"Never Retreat"** ***from*** **Eyes Wide Open**
- **Mississippi Solo**
- **"The Drought"**
- **"Allied with Green"**
- **"Ode to enchanted light"**
- **"Sleeping in the Forest"**
- *from* **Trash Talk (video)**
- **"You're Part of the Solution" (poster)**

UNIT 4

THE TERROR AND WONDER OF SPACE

? **ESSENTIAL QUESTION:**

Why is the idea of space exploration both inspiring and unnerving?

"All adventures, especially into new territory, are scary."

Sally Ride

ACADEMIC VOCABULARY

Academic Vocabulary words are words you use when you discuss and write about texts. In this unit you will practice and learn five words.

☑ **complex** ☐ **potential** ☐ **rely** ☐ **stress** ☐ **valid**

Study the Word Network to learn more about the word **complex**.

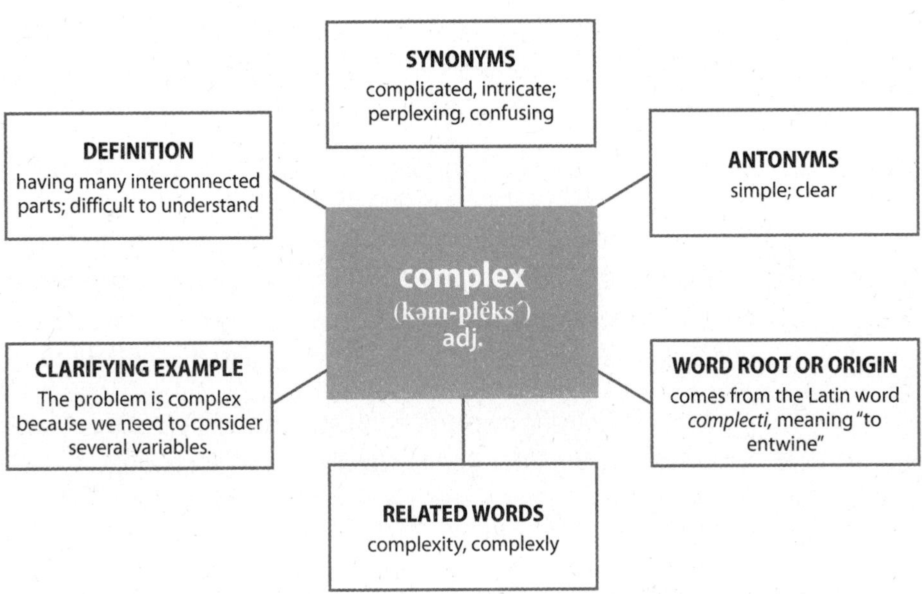

SYNONYMS
complicated, intricate; perplexing, confusing
DEFINITION
having many interconnected parts; difficult to understand
ANTONYMS
simple; clear
complex
(kəm-plĕks´)
adj.
CLARIFYING EXAMPLE
The problem is complex because we need to consider several variables.
WORD ROOT OR ORIGIN
comes from the Latin word *complecti*, meaning "to entwine"
RELATED WORDS
complexity, complexly

Write and Discuss Discuss the completed Word Network with a partner, making sure to talk through all of the boxes until you both understand the word, its synonyms, antonyms, and related words. Then, fill out Word Networks for the remaining four words. Use a dictionary or online resource to help you complete the activity.

 *Go online to access the **Word Networks**.*

RESPOND TO THE ESSENTIAL QUESTION

In this unit, you will explore how space exploration has affected our world. As you read, you will revisit the **Essential Question** and gather your ideas about it in the **Response Log** that appears on page R4. At the end of the unit, you will have the opportunity to write an **argument** in which you present and support your opinion about the necessity of human space travel. Filling out the Response Log will help you prepare for this writing task.

UNIT 4 RESPONSE LOG

Use this Response Log to record your ideas about how each of the texts in Unit 4 relates to or comments on the **Essential Question.**

Essential Question: Why is the idea of space exploration both inspiring and unnerving?

Martian Metropolis	
Dark They Were, and Golden-Eyed	
Challenges for Space Exploration	
What If We Were Alone?	
Seven Minutes of Terror	
Space Exploration Should Be More Science Than Fiction	
Humans Should Stay Home and Let Robots Take to the Stars	

R4 Response Log

 *You can also go online to access the **Response Log**.*

MARTIAN METROPOLIS

For more information on these and other signposts to Notice & Note, visit the **Reading Studio**.

You are about to read the informational text "Martian Metropolis." In it, you will notice and note signposts that will help you identify important details and make inferences about the text. Here are three key signposts to look for as you read this article and other works of nonfiction.

When you read and encounter quantities or a comparison with numbers, pause to see if it's a **Numbers and Stats** signpost:

Numerals such as eight, 98%, and 1,001

Numerals and stats used in a comparison: three out of ten, five times as many

Indefinite quantities, such as *most, some, many, bigger than, younger than*

Numbers and Stats Have you ever seen a commercial that promised that a product was 99% fat free? Or maybe you heard a sportscaster fire off a series of statistics about a basketball game. How did the use of numbers and statistics help you understand the information?

Authors use specific quantities and statistics to help support an idea or argument. Paying attention to **Numbers and Stats** can:

- help reveal the key points the author is making
- hint at the author's bias or purpose for writing
- show comparisons between two things

Here, a student underlined evidence of a Numbers and Stats instance in "Martian Metropolis":

15 But people on Mars will communicate with Earth pretty often. Because Earth and Mars are so far apart, signals are delayed by up to 24 minutes. Communication will mostly resemble email. Jay Dickson, a planetary geologist at Brown University, has lived at Antarctica's isolated McMurdo Station. "Just being able to send pictures back and forth is great for morale," Dickson explains.

Anchor Question
When you notice this signpost, ask: Why did the author use these numbers or amounts?

What statistic is used?	... signals [between Earth and Mars] are delayed by up to 24 minutes.
Why do you think the author included this statistic?	It supports the author's point that people on Mars will communicate often with Earth because there is only a 24-minute delay. It also helps show how far away Mars is.

Word Gaps Have you ever come across a word or phrase in a textbook that you didn't recognize? What did you do? Did you read on, or did you go back to look for clues in the text?

Noting **Word Gaps**, or unfamiliar words and phrases, can guide you to use context clues and a dictionary or other resources to determine meanings. Doing this can then help you understand important details and ideas in the text. Here's how a student marked the text to indicate an example of Word Gaps:

When you see the following, pause to see if it's a **Word Gaps** signpost:

- a boldfaced or highlighted word
- an unfamiliar word, phrase, or concept
- an unclear or confusing word, phrase, or concept

> 8 Settlers will need to grow food. Mars has dirt, but it doesn't have soil. Soil contains microbes that help plants grow. Fortunately, humans will take those organisms along with them! Poop makes excellent fertilizer, so the sewage treatment plant will be near the greenhouses. . . .

Anchor Question
When you notice this signpost, ask, "Do I know this word from someplace else?

What context clues helped you determine the meaning of *microbes*?	"that help plants grow," "those organisms"
How does understanding the word *microbes* help clarify how settlers can overcome the challenges of living on Mars?	Knowing the meaning of the word helps me understand that even though settling Mars will be difficult, there are solutions to problems.

Big Questions As you read nonfiction texts, you will likely encounter information that is new to you. It's time to think about this **Big Question**: **What surprised you?** Doing this can help you think more critically about the author's claims. A student marked what appeared to be a surprising detail in this way:

> 6 . . . On Mars, cosmic radiation is much higher than it is on Earth. This can cause serious damage to DNA, which increases the risk of cancer. The danger decreases if you burrow 16 feet (5 meters) under the surface of the Red Planet. The soil overhead would provide about the same amount of protection as Earth's atmosphere.

What surprised you in this passage?	The danger of cosmic radiation decreases if you burrow 16 feet under the surface of Mars.
Why might the author have included this information?	The author probably included the information to show that even though cosmic radiation is dangerous, there is a way to protect settlers.

MARTIAN METROPOLIS

Science Writing by **Meg Thacher**

ESSENTIAL QUESTION:

Why is the idea of space exploration both inspiring and unnerving?

QUICK START

Maybe you've seen amazing photographs of Mars. But have you ever thought about what it would be like to live there? Discuss with your class the likely challenges of humans living on Mars.

ANALYZE STRUCTURAL ELEMENTS

Text features are elements of a text that help organize and call attention to important information. Science writing—such as "Martian Metropolis"—and other informational texts often contain multiple text features, including **references** and **acknowledgments.**

- **References** include footnotes and endnotes. Footnotes appear at the bottom of the page and provide additional information about terms or ideas in the text, including sources. Endnotes appear at the end of the text and include the same information as footnotes.
- The **acknowledgments** is a list of statements that recognize the contributions made by people or organizations to the creation of the text. This might include research or image contributions, or other help that was given to the author.

GENRE ELEMENTS: INFORMATIONAL TEXT

- provides factual information
- includes evidence to support ideas
- contains text features to convey information
- can be presented in many forms, such as science writing, news articles, and essays

ANALYZE ORGANIZATIONAL PATTERNS

To ensure that informational texts are clear to readers, writers choose a **pattern of organization,** or a particular arrangement of ideas and information. Facts and details can be organized in a variety of ways. This chart shows a few common patterns of organization. As you read "Martian Metropolis," note the organizational patterns the author uses.

PATTERN	EXAMPLE FROM THE SELECTION
A **classification** pattern presents objects, ideas, and information in groups, or classes, based on common characteristics.	The city will need energy for heat and electricity. The best sources will be solar, geothermal, and wind, as there's no oil or gas on Mars. Settlers will also want to make fuel for trips back home. They'll likely use carbon dioxide from the Martian atmosphere to make methane gas. . . .
A **cause and effect** pattern shows the relationship between events and their causes.	Because it has to produce its own air, the Martian city will be small.
An **advantages and disadvantages** pattern divides ideas about a topic into the positive and negative points, or advantages and disadvantages.	Of all the planets in the solar system, Mars is the most Earth-like. It's made of rock and has a thin atmosphere. . . . The biggest danger on Mars, though, is radiation.

GET READY

CRITICAL VOCABULARY

atmosphere **radiation** **colonize** **geothermal**

To see how many Critical Vocabulary words you already know, use them to complete the sentences.

1. The large volcanic island got much of its energy from __________ resources.

2. __________ from the sun and other sources in space can pose a danger to humans.

3. Earth's __________ is thicker and more protective than that of Mars.

4. In order to __________ Antarctica, people would have to cope with the cold temperatures and lack of resources.

LANGUAGE CONVENTIONS

Capitalization In this lesson, you will learn about capitalization. Proper nouns—the names of specific people, places, and things—are always capitalized, as in this example from "Martian Metropolis":

"This could be our life raft," says Darby Dyar, an astronomy professor at Mount Holyoke College and a member of the Mars Curiosity rover team.

As you read, note the capitalization of proper nouns.

ANNOTATION MODEL

NOTICE & NOTE

As you read, notice and note signposts, including **Numbers and Stats, Word Gaps,** and **Big Questions.** Here is an example of how one reader responded to this paragraph from "Martian Metropolis."

5 It's farther from the sun than Earth, so Mars is much colder. On average, it's a bone-chilling -80° F / -62° C. The Martian day (called a "sol") is about 40 minutes longer than an Earth day; a Martian year is 668.6 sols. Its atmosphere is about 100 times thinner than Earth's,[1] and it's 95 percent carbon dioxide. Even if Mars' atmosphere were thicker, we wouldn't be able to breathe it. Earth's atmosphere is mostly nitrogen and oxygen, with 0.04 percent carbon dioxide—a combination that's friendlier to our planet's life forms.

The statistics in this paragraph help me see how different Mars is from Earth.

There is a footnote. It will tell me more about what I'm reading.

Stats about Earth and Mars show that life there won't be easy.

NOTICE & NOTE

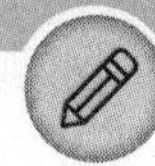

BACKGROUND

Meg Thacher *is an astronomy instructor at Smith College in western Massachusetts. In addition, she serves as the academic director for the college's Summer Science and Engineering Program, offered to high school girls who are interested in science, engineering, and medicine. Thacher explains her passion for science writing by saying, "I love all things science, and I love explaining it in terms that kids can understand."*

MARTIAN METROPOLIS

Science Writing by Meg Thacher

SETTING A PURPOSE

As you read, pay attention to the information about the Red Planet that surprised you. What do you think would be most challenging about living on Mars?

1 NASA plans to send humans to Mars in the 2030s, and several private entities aim to send settlers to live on Mars permanently.

2 There are several reasons to create an off-planet colony. One is survival of our species. "We never know what will happen to threaten the habitat. This could be our life raft," says Darby Dyar, an astronomy professor at Mount Holyoke College and a member of the Mars Curiosity rover team. "There's also the cool factor," she says. "Who would *not* want to live on Mars?"

3 Scientists living on Mars can study the planet up close better than rovers can. They can compare it to Earth and other planets. They can study its **atmosphere**—and humans'

Notice & Note

Use the side margins to notice and note signposts in the text.

WORD GAPS

Notice & Note: Mark the clues in paragraph 2 that help you understand the word *colony*.

Infer: Why did the author introduce this term so early in the text?

atmosphere
(ăt′mə-sfîr′) *n.* An *atmosphere* is the gaseous mass or envelope that surrounds a planet.

NOTICE & NOTE

effect on that atmosphere. If they find evidence for life on Mars, whether past or present, that will tell humans we're not alone in the universe.

Fourth Rock from the Sun

4 Of all the planets in the solar system, Mars is the most Earth-like. It's made of rock and has a thin atmosphere. The scenery is beautiful but also strange, with craters and sand dunes, dust and scattered rocks. It has massive landforms—the tallest mountains and deepest canyons in the solar system—all under a pink sky.

5 It's farther from the sun than Earth, so Mars is much colder. On average, it's a bone-chilling -80° F/-62° C. The Martian day (called a "sol") is about 40 minutes longer than an Earth day; a Martian year is 668.6 sols. Its atmosphere is about 100 times thinner than Earth's,[1] and it's 95 percent carbon dioxide. Even if Mars' atmosphere were thicker, we wouldn't be able to breathe it. Earth's atmosphere is mostly nitrogen and oxygen, with 0.04 percent carbon dioxide—a combination that's friendlier to our planet's life forms.

6 The biggest danger on Mars, though, is **radiation.** Mars has no magnetic field to protect humans from high-energy particles from the sun and other sources, called cosmic rays. On Mars, cosmic radiation is much higher than it is on Earth. This can cause serious damage to DNA, which increases the risk of cancer. The danger decreases if you burrow 16 feet (5 meters) under the surface of the Red Planet.[2] The soil overhead would provide about the same amount of protection as Earth's atmosphere.

Living Off the Land

7 Sending stuff to Mars is very expensive. The cheapest way to **colonize** will be to make everything there. "It's really all about the resources," says Dyar. "If we find things there that allow us to sustain human life, then we can settle there." Mars has plenty of metals and rock, and probably lots of water, but no wood or petroleum (which is used to make gasoline, plastic, and many other useful products). The settlers could make bricks from local dirt. Mars has plenty of silicon and iron, elements that will allow people to produce glass and steel.[3] And of course,

NUMBERS AND STATS

Notice & Note: In paragraph 5, mark the statistics the author provides about Mars.

Analyze: What does this information help you understand about what it would be like to live on Mars?

radiation
(rā′dē-ā′shən) *n. Radiation* is energy transmitted in the form of waves or particles.

ANALYZE STRUCTURAL ELEMENTS

Annotate: Circle the footnote number in paragraph 6 and underline its footnote at the bottom of the page.

Analyze: What information does this footnote provide?

colonize
(kŏl′ə-nīz′) *v.* When you *colonize* a place, you send a group of people to a new place to establish a colony or settlement.

ANALYZE ORGANIZATIONAL PATTERNS

Annotate: Mark the subheads on these pages.

Analyze: Which main organizational pattern is the author using? How can you tell?

[1] "The Terrestrial Planets," National Oceanic and Atmospheric Administration, https://www.esrl.noaa.gov/gmd/outreach/info_activities/pdfs/TBI_terrestrial_planets.pdf

[2] "Mission to Mars Would Double Astronauts' Cancer Risk," U.S. National Library of Medicine, https://medlineplus.gov/news/fullstory_166629.html

[3] "Oxygen in the Martian Atmosphere: Regulation of PO2 by the deposition of iron formations on Mars", NASA Technical Reports Server, Nov 7, 1995, https://ntrs.nasa.gov/search.jsp?R=19920019239

everything sent to Mars will stay on Mars. Martian citizens will be really good at recycling.

8 Settlers will need to grow food. Mars has dirt, but it doesn't have soil. Soil contains microbes that help plants grow. Fortunately, humans will take those organisms along with them! Poop makes excellent fertilizer, so the sewage treatment plant will be near the greenhouses. Martians will most likely eat a vegan diet. Animals are hard to transport, and it takes much less energy to grow plants than to raise animals. Plants also use up carbon dioxide and produce oxygen, which people need to breathe.

9 The city will need energy for heat and electricity. The best sources will be solar, **geothermal,** and wind, as there's no oil or gas on Mars. Settlers will also want to make fuel for trips back home. They'll likely use carbon dioxide from the Martian atmosphere to make methane gas. To do this, they'll need hydrogen. They could bring it from Earth, or get it from water found on Mars.

Smaller Is Better

10 Because it has to produce its own air, the Martian city will be small. At first, residents will probably live underground to protect against cosmic radiation. They'll work to develop radiation-blocking glass or plastic. Once that's in place, settlers can live above ground in brick buildings with windows, or even under a dome or tent.

11 To limit exposure to radiation, scientists will send rovers and drones out exploring and will use the information to decide where to send human explorers. Temporary shelters and labs will pop up all over the planet for short-term science projects.

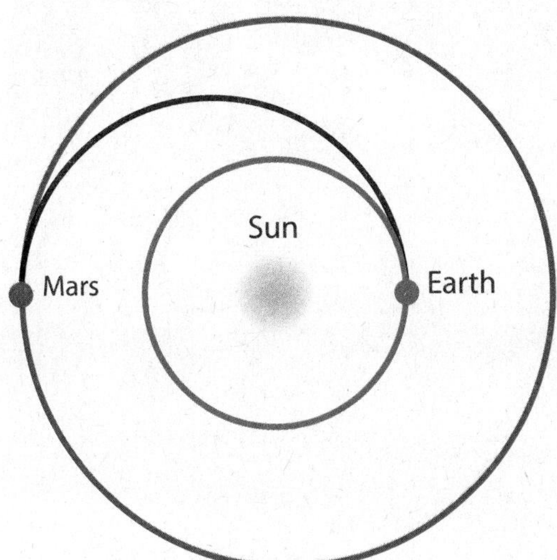

The black line traces the most efficient path from Earth to Mars. Space travelers will need to wait as long as two years for the planets' orbits to align.

NOTICE & NOTE 

BIG QUESTIONS

Notice & Note: Mark the information in paragraph 8 that most surprised you.

Infer: Why do you think the author included this information?

geothermal
(jē´ō-thûr´məl) *adj. Geothermal* relates to the internal heat of the earth.

WORD GAPS

Notice & Note: Mark the word *cosmic* in paragraph 10 and then use a dictionary or context clues in the article to determine its meaning.

Infer: Why might the author have used this term to describe the radiation?

NOTICE & NOTE

LANGUAGE CONVENTIONS

Annotate: In paragraph 13, mark the proper nouns.

Analyze: Why are these words capitalized, but nouns such as *television*, *radio*, and *movies* are not?

12 Wealthy tourists might visit the Red Planet, but you won't have to be rich or a scientist to live on Mars. The city will need farmers to grow crops, cooks, people to run the spaceport and sewage plant, trash collectors, doctors and nurses—the list goes on. Some jobs can be done by machines, which use fewer resources than human workers. So add robot mechanic to that list of careers!

All Work and No Play?

13 Colonists will keep busy with work, but they'll want entertainment too. They can venture outside for short sightseeing trips. They'll have television, radio, and movies—some transmitted from Earth, some made right on Mars. They can read and do crafts. Colonists will probably make up new sports that take advantage of Mars' low gravity. Zip lines, rock climbing, and trampolines will be popular.

14 But travel will be hard. The most fuel-efficient trip back to Earth (using gravity to do most of the work) will take around six to eight months. Earth and Mars are properly aligned for this trip for about 20 days every 26 months. Travelers in a spaceship will experience more radiation than people get

Artists at NASA's Jet Propulsion Laboratory collaborated with space scientists to create this poster. It imagines a time when human visitors celebrate the robot pioneers of Mars.

on Earth. Our muscles will weaken unless engineers create "artificial gravity" by spinning the ships. It adds up to a lot of wear and tear; humans will keep trips to a minimum.

15 But people on Mars will communicate with Earth pretty often. Because Earth and Mars are so far apart, signals are delayed by up to 24 minutes. Communication will mostly resemble email. Jay Dickson, a planetary geologist at Brown University, has lived at Antarctica's isolated McMurdo Station. "Just being able to send pictures back and forth is great for morale," Dickson explains.

16 A colony on Mars will be humankind's first steps in expanding our reach within the solar system and beyond.

The author wishes to acknowledge the factual contributions of the space exploration experts consulted for this article.

ANALYZE STRUCTURAL ELEMENTS

Annotate: Mark the acknowledgments.

Analyze: What experts is the author likely referring to?

CHECK YOUR UNDERSTANDING

Answer these questions before moving on to the **Analyze the Text** section on the following page.

1 The author mainly supports her ideas by —

A citing opinions of multiple experts

B providing amusing anecdotes

C using scientific evidence

D providing diagrams

2 Why does the author include the section Living Off the Land?

F To prove that colonizing another planet is possible

G To show that it will be expensive to live on Mars

H To convince readers that people should not farm on Mars

J To explain that colonists will need to make what they need

3 In paragraph 12, the author includes a list of jobs that will be available in a Mars colony to show that —

A there will be a need for people with many different skills

B running the colony will require too many people and resources

C there will be many opportunities for science and tourism

D many jobs in the colony will be done by machines

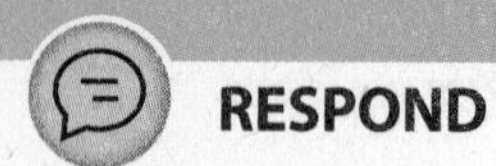

RESPOND

RESEARCH TIP

Remember that information about Mars research may change over time. One reliable source for updates is www.nasa.gov. However, always check to make sure the information you have is dated within the last year or so, whether it comes from a *.gov* site, an *.edu* site, or a news site.

ANALYZE THE TEXT

Support your responses with evidence from the text. NOTEBOOK

1. **Explain** Why does the author propose that humans colonize Mars rather than another planet?
2. **Cite Evidence** What natural resources does Mars have? Use evidence from the text to explain how settlers could use the natural resources of Mars to build a colony.
3. **Infer** Review paragraph 7. How does the use of a footnote help the author explain why colonists will have to make things?
4. **Compare** How does the organization of the text help you understand Earth and Mars? Review the text and explain how the atmosphere and soil of Mars differ from those of Earth.
5. **Notice & Note** Why did the author use numbers and stats?

RESEARCH

Although people have thought for decades about sending humans to Mars, we still need to learn much more before we could carry out such a complex mission. What questions do you have about colonizing Mars after reading "Martian Metropolis"? Brainstorm three specific questions about challenges or dangers that Meg Thacher mentions in the article. Then go online to find out what scientists already know about each of the questions you have raised.

QUESTIONS	WHAT SCIENTISTS KNOW

Connect In paragraph 11, the writer states that "scientists will send rovers and drones out exploring and will use the information to decide where to send human explorers." How could your Mars research help you decide where—and what—humans should explore there?

WRITE AND PRESENT

Write an Informative Report Use your research to write a two- to three-page report about the current status of Mars exploration.

- ❑ Introduce the topic and state your controlling idea, or thesis statement, about the current Mars missions you researched.
- ❑ In the body of your report, briefly describe each mission you researched and what we've learned about Mars from it. Remember to include references for the sources you used.
- ❑ In your final paragraph, restate your controlling idea and summarize the current status of Mars exploration.

Go to **Writing Informative Texts** in the **Writing Studio** to learn more.

Create a Timeline With a partner, use your combined research to create an annotated timeline for Mars missions.

- ❑ Review the research you both conducted on Mars explorations. Work together to determine key events that are most important to include in your timeline.
- ❑ Create your timeline on a computer or poster board. List the key dates for each event along with a brief description. To enhance your timeline, consider including diagrams and other visuals that you create or download from the NASA website.
- ❑ Share your timeline with a small group. Discuss the similarities and differences in the timelines—and what most surprised you.

Go to **Participating in Collaborative Discussions** in the **Speaking and Listening Studio** for help.

RESPOND TO THE ESSENTIAL QUESTION

? Why is the idea of space exploration both inspiring and unnerving?

UNIT 4 RESPONSE LOG

? Essential Question: Why is the idea of space exploration both inspiring and unnerving?

Martian Metropolis	
Dark They Were, and Golden-Eyed	
Challenges for Space Exploration	
What If We Were Alone?	
Seven Minutes of Terror	
Space Exploration Should Be More Science Than Fiction	
Humans Should Stay Home and Let Robots Take to the Stars	

Gather Information Review your annotations and notes on "Martian Metropolis." Then, add relevant details to your Response Log. As you determine what information to include, think about:

- the reasons for colonizing Mars
- the challenges of living on Mars
- the benefits of Mars exploration

At the end of the unit, use your notes to write an argument.

ACADEMIC VOCABULARY

As you write and discuss what you learned from the article, be sure to use the Academic Vocabulary words. Check off each of the words that you use.

- ❑ **complex**
- ❑ **potential**
- ❑ **rely**
- ❑ **stress**
- ❑ **valid**

RESPOND

CRITICAL VOCABULARY

WORD BANK
atmosphere
radiation
colonize
geothermal

Practice and Apply Mark the letter of the answer to each question. Then, explain your response.

1. Which of the following is a source of **geothermal** energy?
   a. fluids and rock found deep in the earth
   b. rushing rivers, streams, and ocean waves

2. Which place could people still **colonize**?
   a. Antarctica
   b. Australia

3. Which of the following would you find in Earth's **atmosphere**?
   a. a mixture of rock, fluids, and minerals
   b. a mixture of nitrogen, oxygen, and other gases

4. Where would you more likely be exposed to intense **radiation**?
   a. in outer space
   b. in a desert

VOCABULARY STRATEGY: Greek Roots *atmos* and *sphere*

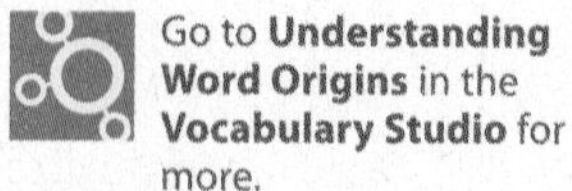

Go to **Understanding Word Origins** in the **Vocabulary Studio** for more.

A **root** is a word part that came into English from an older language, such as ancient Latin or Greek. The word *atmosphere* in "Martian Metropolis" comes from two Greek roots: *atmos* (Greek for "steam or vapor") and *sphaira* (Greek for "globe or ball"). The root *sphere* also appears in other English words related to the earth. One example is *troposphere,* which is a layer of Earth's atmosphere.

Practice and Apply Use context clues and your knowledge of the root *sphere* to write a likely meaning for each bold word. Use a print or online dictionary to confirm your word meanings.

1. For people in the southern **hemisphere,** winter falls in the months of June, July, and August.

   ____

2. To avoid turbulence, jets often fly in the lower part of the **stratosphere.**

   ____

3. The **hydrosphere** is made up of ocean waters, rivers, lakes, and streams.

   ____

4. Life on Earth can exist only in the **biosphere.**

   ____

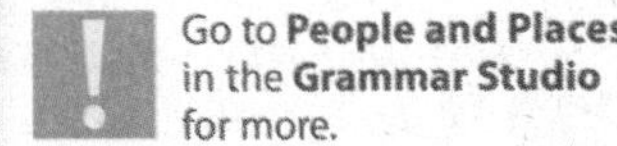

LANGUAGE CONVENTIONS: Capitalization

In your writing, you need to apply the rules of capitalization to proper nouns—the names of specific people, places, and things—including organizations and places for specialized research. In this example from "Martian Metropolis," note which proper nouns are capitalized.

> **But people on Mars will communicate with Earth pretty often. Because Earth and Mars are so far apart, signals are delayed by up to 24 minutes. Communication will mostly resemble email. Jay Dickson, a planetary geologist at Brown University, has lived at Antarctica's isolated McMurdo Station. "Just being able to send pictures back and forth is great for morale," Dickson explains.**

Go to **People and Places** in the **Grammar Studio** for more.

The chart below shows four types of proper nouns that require capitalization. When organizations are abbreviated, their abbreviations are also capitalized.

CAPITALIZATION OF PROPER NOUNS		ABBREVIATIONS
Organizations	National Aeronautics and Space Administration Jet Propulsion Laboratory	NASA JPL
Places	McMurdo Station Antarctica	
Planets	Venus Earth Mars	
Spacecraft	Mars rovers Spirit and Opportunity	

Practice and Apply The following sentences include proper nouns that lack correct capitalization. In each sentence, indicate which proper nouns should be capitalized. Consult reference materials for terms or titles that are unfamiliar to you.

1. The united nations (un) headquarters is in new york city.
2. In January 2006, NASA launched the spacecraft new horizons on a mission to explore pluto.
3. The space shuttle was launched from the kennedy space center at cape canaveral, florida.
4. Astronauts routinely conduct spacewalks from the international space station.

DARK THEY WERE, AND GOLDEN-EYED

Science Fiction by **Ray Bradbury**

? ESSENTIAL QUESTION:

Why is the idea of space exploration both inspiring and unnerving?

QUICK START

Films and TV shows often focus on characters who find themselves in predicaments—that is, difficult situations. What types of predicaments fascinate you? What is it about them that draws you in and holds your attention? Record your thoughts in your journal.

ANALYZE SCIENCE FICTION

Writers of science fiction often present readers with fantastical settings, characters, and events set in the future. At the same time, they often tell stories that in some way comment upon new and emerging science and technology, contemporary society, and human nature in general. As you read Ray Bradbury's story, use the chart to note characteristics of science fiction.

CHARACTERISTICS OF SCIENCE FICTION	EXAMPLES IN THE STORY
Scientific/Technological Information	
Familiar Elements of Life Today	
Imaginary Locations and Situations	

GENRE ELEMENTS: SCIENCE FICTION

- explores unexpected possibilities of the past, present, or future
- mixes scientific facts and theories with imaginative settings and plots
- usually includes familiar elements and conflicts found in real life

ANALYZE MOOD

Mood is the feeling or atmosphere that a writer creates for a reader. A writer creates mood by

- carefully choosing words to describe the plot, setting, and characters
- revealing what characters think and how they speak

Identifying mood helps you understand a story. As you read, think about how the story makes you feel and the effect that particular words have on you. Use the graphic organizer below to record your notes.

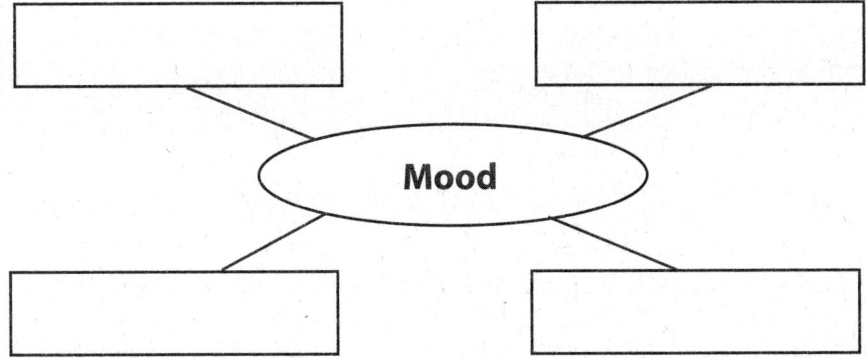

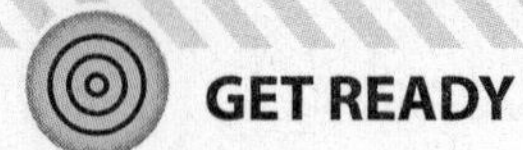

GET READY

CRITICAL VOCABULARY

convivial subtly idle forlorn recede pendulum muse

To see how many Critical Vocabulary words you already know, use them to complete the sentences.

1. As we drove away, the city's skyline began to __________.
2. Visitors could hear the regular swish of the old __________ clock.
3. I just want to __________ about the strange things I saw today.
4. People's opinions have shifted __________ during the past year.
5. The __________ host moved with ease from guest to guest.
6. The abandoned garden seems __________, sad, and empty.
7. It's too hot to work today; let's just __________ here in the shade.

LANGUAGE CONVENTIONS

Consistent Verb Tenses The **tense** of a verb tells the time of the action or the state of being. In writing, it is important to use the same tense to describe actions that take place at the same time. Unnecessarily shifting, or inconsistent, verb tenses can confuse the reader.

INCORRECT: Ms. Sherman **coaches** us as we **practiced** our songs.
CORRECT: Ms. Sherman **coached** us as we **practiced** our songs.

ANNOTATION MODEL

NOTICE & NOTE

As you read, note the author's use of the elements of science fiction and the choice of words to create mood. In the model, you can see one reader's notes about "Dark They Were, and Golden-Eyed."

2 The man felt his hair flutter and the tissues of his body draw tight as if he were standing at the center of a vacuum. His wife, before him, seemed almost to whirl away in smoke. The children, small seeds, might at any instant be sown to all the Martian climes.

This description makes me feel scared for the man.

The man's family is with him.

The setting is Mars.

BACKGROUND

Ray Bradbury *(1920–2012) grew up in Los Angeles, California, and began writing stories as a young teenager. Over the course of his adult life, he wrote science fiction, mysteries, and screenplays, including more than two dozen novels and hundreds of short stories. Several of his works, such as* The Illustrated Man *and* Fahrenheit 451, *became major motion pictures. Bradbury received dozens of awards, including a special Pulitzer Prize in 2007 for his distinguished literary career.*

DARK THEY WERE, AND GOLDEN-EYED

Science Fiction by Ray Bradbury

SETTING A PURPOSE

Pay attention to the elements of science fiction that appear in the story and the references to personal and social issues. Notice the author's choice of words and consider how they contribute to the mood of the story.

1 The rocket metal cooled in the meadow winds. Its lid gave a bulging *pop.* From its clock interior stepped a man, a woman, and three children. The other passengers whispered away across the Martian meadow, leaving the man alone among his family.

2 The man felt his hair flutter and the tissues of his body draw tight as if he were standing at the center of a vacuum. His wife, before him, seemed almost to whirl away in smoke. The children, small seeds, might at any instant be sown to all the Martian climes.

3 The children looked up at him, as people look to the sun to tell what time of their life it is. His face was cold.

4 "What's wrong?" asked his wife.

5 "Let's get back on the rocket."

6 "Go back to Earth?"

Notice & Note

Use the side margins to notice and note signposts in the text.

ANALYZE MOOD

Annotate: In paragraphs 1–6, mark details that reveal the man's first response to Mars.

Interpret: How would you describe the man's first impression of Mars? How might his feelings affect the mood of the story?

ANALYZE MOOD

Annotate: Mark details in paragraphs 8–13 that the author uses to create a feeling about the setting of the story.

Analyze: Does the author create a positive feeling or a negative feeling about the setting? What words help create this feeling?

7 "Yes! Listen!"

8 The wind blew as if to flake away their identities. At any moment the Martian air might draw his soul from him, as marrow comes from a white bone. He felt submerged in a chemical that could dissolve his intellect and burn away his past.

9 They looked at Martian hills that time had worn with a crushing pressure of years. They saw the old cities, lost in their meadows, lying like children's delicate bones among the blowing lakes of grass.

10 "Chin up, Harry," said his wife. "It's too late. We've come over sixty million miles."

11 The children with their yellow hair hollered at the deep dome of Martian sky. There was no answer but the racing hiss of wind through the stiff grass.

12 He picked up the luggage in his cold hands. "Here we go," he said—a man standing on the edge of a sea, ready to wade in and be drowned.

13 They walked into town.

14 Their name was Bittering. Harry and his wife Cora; Dan, Laura, and David. They built a small white cottage and ate good breakfasts there, but the fear was never gone. It lay with Mr. Bittering and Mrs. Bittering, a third unbidden partner at every midnight talk, at every dawn awakening.

15 "I feel like a salt crystal," he said, "in a mountain stream, being washed away. We don't belong here. We're Earth people. This is Mars. It was meant for Martians. For heaven's sake, Cora, let's buy tickets for home!"

ANALYZE SCIENCE FICTION

Annotate: Mark details that the author uses in paragraphs 18–19 to refer to familiar elements of life on Earth.

Interpret: Why do you think the author includes these details in the story?

16 But she only shook her head. "One day the atom bomb[1] will fix Earth. Then we'll be safe here."

17 "Safe and insane!"

18 *Tick-tock, seven o'clock* sang the voice-clock; *time to get up.* And they did.

19 Something made him check everything each morning—warm hearth, potted blood-geraniums—precisely as if he expected something to be amiss. The morning paper was toast-warm from the 6 A.M. Earth rocket. He broke its seal and tilted it at his breakfast place. He forced himself to be **convivial.**

convivial
(kən-vĭv´ē-əl) *adj.* A person who is *convivial* enjoys the company of others in a sociable manner.

[1] **atom bomb:** In 1945, in an attempt to end World War II, the United States dropped atomic bombs over the Japanese cities of Hiroshima and Nagasaki. The bombs killed more than 100,000 people and injured many thousands more.

20 "Colonial days all over again," he declared. "Why, in ten years there'll be a million Earthmen on Mars. Big cities, everything! They said we'd fail. Said the Martians would resent our invasion. But did we find any Martians? Not a living soul! Oh, we found their empty cities, but no one in them. Right?"

21 A river of wind submerged the house. When the windows ceased rattling Mr. Bittering swallowed and looked at the children.

22 "I don't know," said David. "Maybe there're Martians around we don't see. Sometimes nights I think I hear 'em. I hear the wind. The sand hits my window. I get scared. And I see those towns way up in the mountains where the Martians lived a long time ago. And I think I see things moving around those towns, Papa. And I wonder if those Martians *mind* us living here. I wonder if they won't do something to us for coming here."

23 "Nonsense!" Mr. Bittering looked out the windows. "We're clean, decent people." He looked at his children. "All dead cities have some kind of ghosts in them. Memories, I mean." He stared at the hills. "You see a staircase and you wonder what Martians looked like climbing it. You see Martian paintings and you wonder what the painter was like. You make a little ghost in your mind, a memory. It's quite natural. Imagination." He stopped. "You haven't been prowling up in those ruins, have you?"

24 "No, Papa." David looked at his shoes.

25 "See that you stay away from them. Pass the jam."

26 "Just the same," said little David, "I bet something happens."

27 Something happened that afternoon. Laura stumbled through the settlement, crying. She dashed blindly onto the porch.

28 "Mother, Father—the war, Earth!" she sobbed. "A radio flash just came. Atom bombs hit New York! All the space rockets blown up. No more rockets to Mars, ever!"

29 "Oh, Harry!" The mother held onto her husband and daughter.

30 "Are you sure, Laura?" asked the father quietly.

31 Laura wept. "We're stranded on Mars, forever and ever!"

32 For a long time there was only the sound of the wind in the late afternoon.

NOTICE & NOTE

ANALYZE MOOD

Annotate: Mark examples of sentence fragments in paragraph 33.

Interpret: What do these sentence fragments reveal about Bittering's state of mind? How do they help create a mood?

33 Alone, thought Bittering. Only a thousand of us here. No way back. No way. No way. Sweat poured from his face and his hands and his body; he was drenched in the hotness of his fear. He wanted to strike Laura, cry, "No, you're lying! The rockets will come back!" Instead, he stroked Laura's head against him and said, "The rockets will get through someday."

34 "Father, what will we do?"

35 "Go about our business, of course. Raise crops and children. Wait. Keep things going until the war ends and the rockets come again."

36 The two boys stepped out onto the porch.

37 "Children," he said, sitting there, looking beyond them, "I've something to tell you."

38 "We know," they said.

39 In the following days, Bittering wandered often through the garden to stand alone in his fear. As long as the rockets had spun a silver web across space, he had been able to accept Mars. For he had always told himself: Tomorrow, if I want, I can buy a ticket and go back to Earth.

40 But now: The web gone, the rockets lying in jigsaw heaps of molten girder and unsnaked wire. Earth people left to the strangeness of Mars, the cinnamon dusts and wine airs, to be baked like gingerbread shapes in Martian summers, put into harvested storage by Martian winters. What would happen to him, the others? This was the moment Mars had waited for. Now it would eat them.

41 He got down on his knees in the flower bed, a spade in his nervous hands. Work, he thought, work and forget.

CONTRASTS AND CONTRADICTIONS

Notice & Note: In paragraph 42, mark text that comments on the similarities between Martian and human civilizations.

Infer: What comment about present-day human civilization might Bradbury be making by having Bittering think about Martian civilizations?

42 He glanced up from the garden to the Martian mountains. He thought of the proud old Martian names that had once been on those peaks. Earthmen, dropping from the sky, had gazed upon hills, rivers, Martian seats left nameless in spite of names. Once Martians had built cities, named cities; climbed mountains, named mountains; sailed seas, named seas. Mountains melted, seas drained, cities tumbled. In spite of this, the Earthmen had felt a silent guilt at putting new names to these ancient hills and valleys.

43 Nevertheless, man lives by symbol and label. The names were given.

44 Mr. Bittering felt very alone in his garden under the Martian sun, anachronism[2] bent here, planting Earth flowers in a wild soil.

45 Think. Keep thinking. Different things. Keep your mind free of Earth, the atom war, the lost rockets.

46 He perspired. He glanced about. No one watching. He removed his tie. Pretty bold, he thought. First your coat off, now your tie. He hung it neatly on a peach tree he had imported as a sapling from Massachusetts.

47 He returned to his philosophy of names and mountains. The Earthmen had changed names. Now there were Hormel Valleys, Roosevelt[3] Seas, Ford Hills, Vanderbilt Plateaus, Rockefeller[4] Rivers, on Mars. It wasn't right. The American settlers had shown wisdom, using old Indian prairie names: Wisconsin, Minnesota, Idaho, Ohio, Utah, Milwaukee, Waukegan, Osseo. The old names, the old meanings.

48 Staring at the mountains wildly, he thought: Are you up there? All the dead ones, you Martians? Well, here we are, alone, cut off! Come down, move us out! We're helpless!

49 The wind blew a shower of peach blossoms.

50 He put out his sun-browned hand and gave a small cry. He touched the blossoms and picked them up. He turned them, he touched them again and again. Then he shouted for his wife.

51 "Cora!"

52 She appeared at a window. He ran to her.

53 "Cora, these blossoms!"

54 She handled them.

55 "Do you see? They're different. They've changed! They're not peach blossoms any more!"

56 "Look all right to me," she said.

57 "They're not. They're wrong! I can't tell how. An extra petal, a leaf, something, the color, the smell!"

58 The children ran out in time to see their father hurrying about the garden, pulling up radishes, onions, and carrots from their beds.

59 "Cora, come look!"

60 They handled the onions, the radishes, the carrots among them.

ANALYZE SCIENCE FICTION

Annotate: In paragraphs 53–63, mark the text that describes how the plants are changing.

Analyze: Is Bittering's concern about the changing plants realistic? Why do you think the author introduces this detail?

---

[2] **anachronism** (ə-năk′rə-nĭz′əm): something placed outside of its proper time period.

[3] **Roosevelt:** most likely refers to Franklin Delano Roosevelt, the 32nd president of the United States.

[4] **Hormel . . . Ford . . . Vanderbilt . . . Rockefeller:** names of industrial and financial "giants" in American history.

61 "Do they look like carrots?"

62 "Yes . . . no." She hesitated. "I don't know."

63 "They're changed."

64 "Perhaps."

65 "You know they have! Onions but not onions, carrots but not carrots. Taste: the same but different. Smell: not like it used to be." He felt his heart pounding, and he was afraid. He dug his fingers into the earth. "Cora, what's happening? What is it? We've got to get away from this." He ran across the garden. Each tree felt his touch. "The roses. The roses. They're turning green!"

66 And they stood looking at the green roses.

67 And two days later Dan came running. "Come see the cow. I was milking her and I saw it. Come on!"

68 They stood in the shed and looked at their one cow.

69 It was growing a third horn.

70 And the lawn in front of their house very quietly and slowly was coloring itself like spring violets. Seed from Earth but growing up a soft purple.

71 "We must get away," said Bittering. "We'll eat this stuff and then we'll change—who knows to what? I can't let it happen. There's only one thing to do. Burn this food!"

72 "It's not poisoned."

73 "But it is. **Subtly,** very subtly. A little bit. A very little bit. We mustn't touch it."

74 He looked with dismay at their house. "Even the house. The wind's done something to it. The air's burned it. The fog at night. The boards, all warped out of shape. It's not an Earthman's house any more."

ANALYZE MOOD

Annotate: In paragraphs 70–73, mark the sentence that identifies Bittering's latest fear.

Infer: What impact does this new plot turn have on the mood of the story?

subtly
(sŭt´lē) *adv.* To do something *subtly* means to do it in a manner hard to notice or perceive—that is, not obviously.

75 "Oh, your imagination!"

76 He put on his coat and tie. "I'm going into town. We've got to do something now. I'll be back."

77 "Wait, Harry!" his wife cried. But he was gone.

78 In town, on the shadowy step of the grocery store, the men sat with their hands on their knees, conversing with great leisure and ease.

79 Mr. Bittering wanted to fire a pistol in the air.

80 What are you doing, you fools! he thought. Sitting here! You've heard the news—we're stranded on this planet. Well, move! Aren't you frightened? Aren't you afraid? What are you going to do?

81 "Hello, Harry," said everyone.

82 "Look," he said to them. "You did hear the news, the other day, didn't you?"

83 They nodded and laughed. "Sure. Sure, Harry."

84 "What are you going to do about it?"

85 "Do, Harry, do? What *can* we do?"

86 "Build a rocket, that's what!"

87 "A rocket, Harry? To go back to all that trouble? Oh, Harry!"

88 "But you *must* want to go back. Have you noticed the peach blossoms, the onions, the grass?"

89 "Why, yes, Harry, seems we did," said one of the men.

90 "Doesn't it scare you?"

91 "Can't recall that it did much, Harry."

92 "Idiots!"

93 "Now, Harry."

94 Bittering wanted to cry. "You've got to work with me. If we stay here, we'll all change. The air. Don't you smell it? Something in the air. A Martian virus, maybe; some seed, or a pollen. Listen to me!"

95 They stared at him.

96 "Sam," he said to one of them.

97 "Yes, Harry?"

98 "Will you help me build a rocket?"

99 "Harry, I got a whole load of metal and some blueprints. You want to work in my metal shop on a rocket, you're welcome. I'll sell you that metal for five hundred dollars. You should be able to construct a right pretty rocket, if you work alone, in about thirty years."

ANALYZE MOOD

Annotate: In paragraphs 78–93, mark words that describe how the other men respond to Bittering's observation about changes in the plants.

Interpret: What feeling do the characters' reactions to Bittering suggest?

NOTICE & NOTE

ANALYZE SCIENCE FICTION

Annotate: In paragraphs 102–113, mark the sentences that describe changes in Sam's appearance, according to Bittering.

Analyze: Do you think the changes in Sam's appearance are real, or is Bittering imagining them?

100 Everyone laughed.

101 "Don't laugh."

102 Sam looked at him with quiet good humor.

103 "Sam," Bittering said. "Your eyes—"

104 "What about them, Harry?"

105 "Didn't they used to be gray?"

106 "Well now, I don't remember."

107 "They were, weren't they?"

108 "Why do you ask, Harry?"

109 "Because now they're kind of yellow-colored."

110 "Is that so, Harry?" Sam said, casually.

111 "And you're taller and thinner—"

112 "You might be right, Harry."

113 "Sam, you shouldn't have yellow eyes."

114 "Harry, what color eyes have *you* got?" Sam said.

115 "My eyes? They're blue, of course."

116 "Here you are, Harry." Sam handed him a pocket mirror. "Take a look at yourself."

117 Mr. Bittering hesitated, and then raised the mirror to his face. There were little, very dim flecks of new gold captured in the blue of his eyes.

118 "Now look what you've done," said Sam a moment later. "You've broken my mirror."

119 Harry Bittering moved into the metal shop and began to build the rocket. Men stood in the open door and talked and joked without raising their voices. Once in a while they gave him a hand on lifting something. But mostly they just **idled** and watched him with their yellowing eyes.

idle
(īd′l) *v.* When you *idle*, you pass time without doing anything purposeful.

120 "It's suppertime, Harry," they said.

121 His wife appeared with his supper in a wicker basket.

122 "I won't touch it," he said. "I'll eat only food from our Deepfreeze. Food that came from Earth. Nothing from our garden."

123 His wife stood watching him. "You can't build a rocket."

124 "I worked in a shop once, when I was twenty. I know metal. Once I get it started, the others will help," he said, not looking at her, laying out the blueprints.

125 "Harry, Harry," she said, helplessly.

126 "We've *got* to get away, Cora. We've got to!"

127 The nights were full of wind that blew down the empty moonlit sea meadows past the little white chess cities lying for their twelve-thousandth year in the shallows. In the Earthmen's settlement, the Bittering house shook with a feeling of change.

ANALYZE MOOD

Annotate: In paragraph 129, mark two examples of unusual sentence structure or word choice.

Interpret: What word would you use to describe the feeling this paragraph conveys?

128 Lying abed, Mr. Bittering felt his bones shifted, shaped, melted like gold.

129 His wife, lying beside him, was dark from many sunny afternoons. Dark she was, and golden-eyed, burnt almost black by the sun, sleeping, and the children metallic in their beds, and the wind roaring **forlorn** and changing through the old peach trees, the violet grass, shaking out green rose petals.

forlorn
(fər-lôrn′) *adj.* Something that is *forlorn* appears lonely or sad.

130 The fear would not be stopped. It had his throat and heart. It dripped in a wetness of the arm and the temple and the trembling palm.

NOTICE & NOTE

AHA MOMENT

Notice & Note: Mark the place in paragraphs 132–137 where Mr. Bittering is surprised.

Infer: What does Mr. Bittering suddenly realize?

131 A green star rose in the east.

132 A strange word emerged from Mr. Bittering's lips.

133 *"Iorrt. Iorrt."* He repeated it.

134 It was a Martian word. He knew no Martian.

135 In the middle of the night he arose and dialed a call through to Simpson, the archaeologist.

136 "Simpson, what does the word *Iorrt* mean?"

137 "Why that's the old Martian word for our planet Earth. Why?"

138 "No special reason."

139 The telephone slipped from his hand.

140 "Hello, hello, hello, hello," it kept saying while he sat gazing out at the green star. "Bittering? Harry, are you there?"

141 The days were full of metal sound. He laid the frame of the rocket with the reluctant help of three indifferent men. He grew very tired in an hour or so and had to sit down.

142 "The altitude," laughed a man.

143 "Are you *eating,* Harry?" asked another.

144 "I'm eating," he said, angrily.

145 "From your Deepfreeze?"

146 "Yes!"

147 "You're getting thinner, Harry."

148 "I'm not!"

149 "And taller."

150 "Liar!"

151 His wife took him aside a few days later. "Harry, I've used up all the food in the Deepfreeze. There's nothing left. I'll have to make sandwiches using food grown on Mars."

152 He sat down heavily.

153 "You must eat," she said. "You're weak."

154 "Yes," he said.

LANGUAGE CONVENTIONS

Annotate: Mark the past-tense verbs in paragraph 155.

Analyze: Why aren't all of the verbs in the paragraph in the past tense?

155 He took a sandwich, opened it, looked at it, and began to nibble at it. "And take the rest of the day off," she said. "It's hot. The children want to swim in the canals and hike. Please come along."

156 "I can't waste time. This is a crisis!"

157 "Just for an hour," she urged. "A swim'll do you good."

158 He rose, sweating. "All right, all right. Leave me alone. I'll come."

159 "Good for you, Harry."

160 The sun was hot, the day quiet. There was only an immense staring burn upon the land. They moved along the canal, the father, the mother, the racing children in their swimsuits. They stopped and ate meat sandwiches. He saw their skin baking brown. And he saw the yellow eyes of his wife and his children, their eyes that were never yellow before. A few tremblings shook him, but were carried off in waves of pleasant heat as he lay in the sun. He was too tired to be afraid.

161 "Cora, how long have your eyes been yellow?"

162 She was bewildered. "Always, I guess."

163 "They didn't change from brown in the last three months?"

164 She bit her lips. "No. Why do you ask?"

165 "Never mind."

ANALYZE MOOD

Annotate: In paragraph 160, mark the sentences that suggest a change in Bittering's thinking.

Draw Conclusions: How does this change affect the mood of the story and suggest what may happen next?

166 They sat there.

167 "The children's eyes," he said. "They're yellow, too."

168 "Sometimes growing children's eyes change color."

169 "Maybe *we're* children, too. At least to Mars. That's a thought." He laughed. "Think I'll swim."

170 They leaped into the canal water, and he let himself sink down and down to the bottom like a golden statue and lie there in green silence. All was water-quiet and deep, all was peace. He felt the steady, slow current drift him easily.

171 If I lie here long enough, he thought, the water will work and eat away my flesh until the bones show like coral. Just my skeleton left. And then the water can build on that skeleton—green things, deep water things, red things, yellow things. Change. Change. Slow, deep, silent change. And isn't that what it is up *there?*

172 He saw the sky submerged above him, the sun made Martian by atmosphere and time and space.

173 Up there, a big river, he thought, a Martian river; all of us lying deep in it, in our pebble houses, in our sunken boulder houses, like crayfish hidden, and the water washing away our old bodies and lengthening the bones and—

174 He let himself drift up through the soft light.

175 Dan sat on the edge of the canal, regarding his father seriously.

176 "*Utha*" he said.

177 "What?" asked his father.

178 The boy smiled. "You know. *Utha's* the Martian word for 'father.'"

179 "Where did you learn it?"

180 "I don't know. Around. *Utha!*"

181 "What do you want?"

182 The boy hesitated. "I—I want to change my name."

183 "Change it?"

184 "Yes."

185 His mother swam over. "What's wrong with Dan for a name?"

186 Dan fidgeted. "The other day you called Dan, Dan, Dan. I didn't even hear. I said to myself, That's not my name. I've a new name I want to use."

187 Mr. Bittering held to the side of the canal, his body cold and his heart pounding slowly. "What is this new name?"

188 "Linnl. Isn't that a good name? Can I use it? Can't I, please?"

189 Mr. Bittering put his hand to his head. He thought of the silly rocket, himself working alone, himself alone even among his family, so alone.

190 He heard his wife say, "Why not?"

191 He heard himself say, "Yes, you can use it."

192 "Yaaa!" screamed the boy. "I'm Linnl, Linnl!"

193 Racing down the meadowlands, he danced and shouted.

194 Mr. Bittering looked at his wife. "Why did we do that?"

195 "I don't know," she said. "It just seemed like a good idea." They walked into the hills. They strolled on old mosaic paths, beside still pumping fountains. The paths were covered with a thin film of cool water all summer long. You kept your bare feet cool all the day, splashing as in a creek, wading.

196 They came to a small deserted Martian villa with a good view of the valley. It was on top of a hill. Blue marble halls, large murals, a swimming pool. It was refreshing in this hot summertime. The Martians hadn't believed in large cities.

197 "How nice," said Mrs. Bittering, "if we could move up here to this villa for the summer."

198 "Come on," he said. "We're going back to town. There's work to be done on the rocket."

ANALYZE MOOD

Annotate: Reread paragraphs 175–194. Mark the words that express Dan's request.

Infer: Why do you think Dan wants to make this change? How does his father's reaction show a change in the story's mood?

AGAIN AND AGAIN

Notice & Note: Mark the details in paragraphs 189–200 that describe Bittering's changing attitude toward the rocket he is building.

Infer: Why does the author keep bringing up the rocket and Bittering's attitude toward the work?

recede
(rĭ-sēd´) *v.* To *recede* means to become fainter or more distant.

199 But as he worked that night, the thought of the cool blue marble villa entered his mind. As the hours passed, the rocket seemed less important.

200 In the flow of days and weeks, the rocket **receded** and dwindled. The old fever was gone. It frightened him to think he had let it slip this way. But somehow the heat, the air, the working conditions—

201 He heard the men murmuring on the porch of his metal shop.

202 "Everyone's going. You heard?"

203 "All going. That's right."

204 Bittering came out. "Going where?" He saw a couple of trucks, loaded with children and furniture, drive down the dusty street.

205 "Up to the villas," said the man.

206 "Yeah, Harry. I'm going. So is Sam. Aren't you Sam?"

207 "That's right, Harry. What about you?"

208 "I've got work to do here."

209 "Work! You can finish that rocket in the autumn, when it's cooler."

210 He took a breath. "I got the frame all set up."

211 "In the autumn is better." Their voices were lazy in the heat.

212 "Got to work," he said.

213 "Autumn," they reasoned. And they sounded so sensible, so right.

214 "Autumn would be best," he thought. "Plenty of time, then."

215 No! cried part of himself, deep down, put away, locked tight, suffocating. No! No!

216 "In the autumn," he said.

217 "Come on, Harry," they all said.

218 "Yes," he said, feeling his flesh melt in the hot liquid air. "Yes, in the autumn. I'll begin work again then."

219 "I got a villa near the Tirra Canal," said someone.

220 "You mean the Roosevelt Canal, don't you?"

221 "Tirra. The old Martian name."

222 "But on the map—"

223 "Forget the map. It's Tirra now. Now I found a place in the Pillan Mountains—"

224 "You mean the Rockefeller Range," said Bittering.

225 "I mean the Pillan Mountains," said Sam.

226 "Yes," said Bittering, buried in the hot, swarming air. "The Pillan Mountains."

227 Everyone worked at loading the truck in the hot, still afternoon of the next day.

228 Laura, Dan, and David carried packages. Or, as they preferred to be known, Ttil, Linnl, and Werr carried packages.

229 The furniture was abandoned in the little white cottage.

230 "It looked just fine in Boston," said the mother. "And here in the cottage. But up at the villa? No. We'll get it when we come back in the autumn."

231 Bittering himself was quiet.

232 "I've some ideas on furniture for the villa," he said after a time. "Big, lazy furniture."

233 "What about your encyclopedia? You're taking it along, surely?"

234 Mr. Bittering glanced away. "I'll come and get it next week."

235 They turned to their daughter. "What about your New York dresses?"

236 The bewildered girl stared. "Why, I don't want them any more."

237 They shut off the gas, the water, they locked the doors and walked away. Father peered into the truck.

238 "Gosh, we're not taking much," he said. "Considering all we brought to Mars, this is only a handful!"

239 He started the truck.

240 Looking at the small white cottage for a long moment, he was filled with a desire to rush to it, touch it, say good-bye to it, for he felt as if he were going away on a long journey, leaving something to which he could never quite return, never understand again.

241 Just then Sam and his family drove by in another truck.

242 "Hi, Bittering! Here we go!"

243 The truck swung down the ancient highway out of town. There were sixty others traveling in the same direction. The town filled with a silent, heavy dust from their passage. The canal waters lay blue in the sun, and a quiet wind moved in the strange trees.

244 "Good-bye, town!" said Mr. Bittering.

245 "Good-bye, good-bye," said the family, waving to it.

246 They did not look back again.

ANALYZE MOOD

Annotate: In paragraphs 227–239, mark the text that shows Bittering's feelings about what the family is taking to the villa.

Analyze: What effect does Bittering's response have on the overall mood of the story?

247 Summer burned the canals dry. Summer moved like flame upon the meadows. In the empty Earth settlement, the painted houses flaked and peeled. Rubber tires upon which children had swung in back yards hung suspended like stopped clock **pendulums** in the blazing air.

pendulum
(pĕn´jə-ləm) *n.* A *pendulum* is a weight that is hung so that it can swing freely. Sometimes it is used in timing the workings of certain clocks.

248 At the metal shop, the rocket frame began to rust.

249 In the quiet autumn Mr. Bittering stood, very dark now, very golden-eyed, upon the slope above his villa, looking at the valley.

250 "It's time to go back," said Cora.

251 "Yes, but we're not going," he said quietly. "There's nothing there any more."

252 "Your books," she said. "Your fine clothes."

253 "Your *Illes* and your fine *ior uele rre*" she said.

254 "The town's empty. No one's going back," he said. "There's no reason to, none at all."

255 The daughter wove tapestries and the sons played songs on ancient flutes and pipes, their laughter echoing in the marble villa.

256 Mr. Bittering gazed at the Earth settlement far away in the low valley. "Such odd, such ridiculous houses the Earth people built."

ANALYZE SCIENCE FICTION

Annotate: Mark details in paragraphs 249–259 that describe how the Bitterings have physically changed since their arrival on Mars.

Analyze: Do you think the Bitterings are still human? Explain.

257 "They didn't know any better," his wife **mused.** "Such ugly people. I'm glad they've gone."

muse
(myo͞oz) *v.* When you *muse*, you say something thoughtfully.

258 They both looked at each other, startled by all they had just finished saying. They laughed.

259 "Where did they go?" he wondered. He glanced at his wife. She was golden and slender as his daughter. She looked at him, and he seemed almost as young as their eldest son.

260 "I don't know," she said.

261 "We'll go back to town maybe next year, or the year after, or the year after that," he said, calmly. "Now—I'm warm. How about taking a swim?"

262 They turned their backs to the valley. Arm in arm they walked silently down a path of clear-running spring water.

263 Five years later a rocket fell out of the sky. It lay steaming in the valley. Men leaped out of it, shouting.

"We won the war on Earth! We're here to rescue you! Hey!"

264 But the American-built town of cottages, peach trees, and theaters was silent. They found a flimsy rocket frame rusting in an empty shop.

265 The rocket men searched the hills. The captain established headquarters in an abandoned bar. His lieutenant came back to report.

266 "The town's empty, but we found native life in the hills, sir. Dark people. Yellow eyes. Martians. Very friendly. We talked a bit, not much. They learn English fast. I'm sure our relations will be most friendly with them, sir."

267 "Dark, eh?" mused the captain. "How many?"

268 "Six, eight hundred, I'd say, living in those marble ruins in the hills, sir. Tall, healthy. Beautiful women."

269 "Did they tell you what became of the men and women who built this Earth settlement, Lieutenant?"

270 "They hadn't the foggiest notion of what happened to this town or its people."

271 "Strange. You think those Martians killed them?"

272 "They look surprisingly peaceful. Chances are a plague did this town in, sir."

273 "Perhaps. I suppose this is one of those mysteries we'll never solve. One of those mysteries you read about."

ANALYZE SCIENCE FICTION

Annotate: Reread paragraphs 263–274. Mark the sentences that describe what the rocket men found.

Predict: Based on what you know about science fiction, what do think will happen to the captain and the lieutenant? Remember science fiction often contains fantastical events and comments on human nature.

274 The captain looked at the room, the dusty windows, the blue mountains rising beyond, the canals moving in the light, and he heard the soft wind in the air. He shivered. Then, recovering, he tapped a large fresh map he had thumbtacked to the top of an empty table.

275 "Lots to be done, Lieutenant." His voice droned on and quietly on as the sun sank behind the blue hills. "New settlements. Mining sites, minerals to be looked for. Bacteriological specimens[5] taken. The work, all the work. And the old records were lost. We'll have a job of remapping to do, renaming the mountains and rivers and such. Calls for a little imagination.

276 "What do you think of naming those mountains the Lincoln Mountains, this canal the Washington Canal, those hills—we can name those hills for you, Lieutenant. Diplomacy. And you, for a favor, might name a town for me. Polishing the apple.[6] And why not make this the Einstein Valley, and farther over . . . are you *listening,* Lieutenant?"

277 The lieutenant snapped his gaze from the blue color and the quiet mist of the hills far beyond the town.

278 "What? Oh, *yes,* sir!"

---

[5] **bacteriological specimens:** samples of different kinds of single-celled living things.

[6] **Polishing the apple:** acting in a way to get on the good side of another person.

NOTICE & NOTE 

CHECK YOUR UNDERSTANDING

Answer these questions before moving on to the **Analyze the Text** section on the following page.

1 Why is paragraph 8 important to the story?

A It introduces a familiar setting.

B It helps establish a foreboding mood.

C It describes realistically what will happen.

D It describes the most important characters.

2 Rockets stopped coming to Mars because —

F fuel to power them had run out

G everyone was dying of a strange illness

H war had broken out on Earth

J people no longer wanted to live there

3 Based on the details provided in the selection about the lieutenant's reaction to Mars, he will most likely —

A leave Mars and forget about what he has seen

B try to continue building the old rocket

C move into a cottage in the American-built town

D continue visiting the Martians in the hills

RESPOND

ANALYZE THE TEXT

Support your responses with evidence from the text. NOTEBOOK

1. **Analyze** What words would you use to describe the overall mood of the story? Cite examples of Bradbury's use of language.
2. **Interpret** Why is it significant that the settlers are using the old Martian names of local landmarks and changing their own names?
3. **Compare** Why might Cora be more accepting of life on Mars than her husband Harry? What practical matters might affect her behavior?
4. **Predict** Who do you think will resist change more: the captain, or the lieutenant? Which details from the story best support your prediction?
5. **Notice & Note** How does the author's contrasting the eye color among the settlers connect to a main theme of the story? Explain how this connection relates to the title of the story.

RESEARCH

RESEARCH TIP
When researching to find examples of a particular genre, you can look for information using the genre name and/or particular author names. You can also narrow your search by looking for books recommended for a particular age group.

What is science fiction? Are science fiction stories always about space travel or colonization of other worlds? Find out more about science fiction. On your own, select two examples of science fiction to read and compare. You can either look for short stories or consider reading chapters in longer works. As you read, ask yourself why each text is an example of science fiction. What makes each one unique? Record what you learn about the characters, setting, and plot of each text in the chart below. Then discuss your impressions of science fiction with a partner.

SELECTION 1	SELECTION 2

Extend With a small group, discuss science fiction and how it expresses ideas about people, cultures, and the social and political challenges that societies face. During your discussion, share any personal connections you made to the characters and ideas expressed in the texts you selected.

CREATE AND DISCUSS

Go to **Writing as a Process** in the **Writing Studio** for help.

Write a Letter Write a letter to a friend in which you express your opinions about the possibility of alien life forms in space.

- ❑ Be sure to use correct letter form, including the date, greeting, body of the letter, and signature.
- ❑ In your introductory paragraph, state your opinion.
- ❑ In the paragraphs that follow, offer support for your opinion.
- ❑ In your final paragraph, restate your opinion. Encourage your friend to write back with his or her thoughts on the subject.

Go to **Participating in Collaborative Discussions** in the **Speaking and Listening Studio** to learn more.

Make a Graphic Track the gradual but important ways that Harry Bittering's attitude changes as the story unfolds.

- ❑ Review the text of "Dark They Were, and Golden-Eyed." Look for details about the changes in Bittering's thoughts about Mars.
- ❑ Record your findings, including quotations from the story, in a graphic organizer like the one shown.

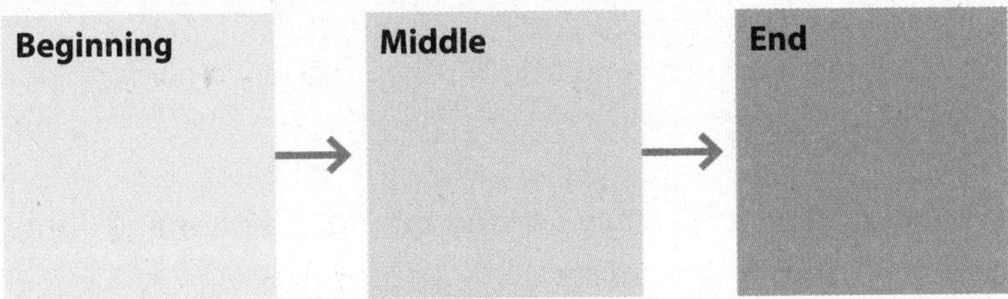

- ❑ Use your graphic organizer as the basis for discussion with other members of a small group.

RESPOND TO THE ESSENTIAL QUESTION

Why is the idea of space exploration both inspiring and unnerving?

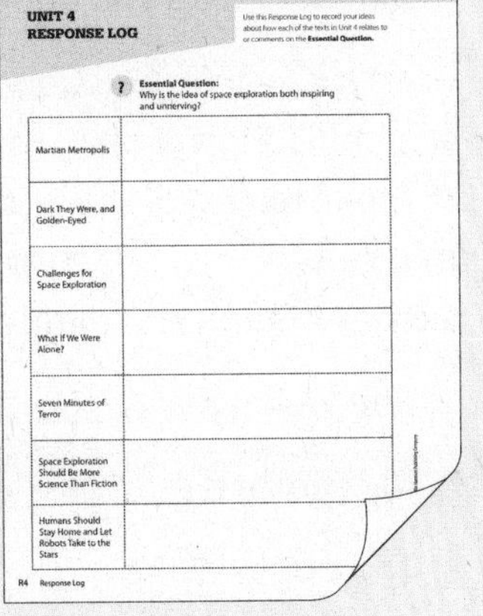

UNIT 4 RESPONSE LOG

Use this Response Log to record your ideas about how each of the texts in Unit 4 relates to or comments on the **Essential Question.**

? **Essential Question:** Why is the idea of space exploration both inspiring and unnerving?

Martian Metropolis	
Dark They Were, and Golden-Eyed	
Challenges for Space Exploration	
What If We Were Alone?	
Seven Minutes of Terror	
Space Exploration Should Be More Science Than Fiction	
Humans Should Stay Home and Let Robots Take to the Stars	

R4 Response Log

Gather Information Review your annotations on "Dark They Were, and Golden-Eyed." Then, add details to your Response Log. As you determine which information to include, think about:

- why people might want to settle on another planet
- how people might respond to having limited contact with Earth

At the end of the unit, use your notes to help you write an argument.

ACADEMIC VOCABULARY

As you write and discuss what you learned from the story, be sure to use the Academic Vocabulary words. Check off each of the words that you use.

- ❑ **complex**
- ❑ **potential**
- ❑ **rely**
- ❑ **stress**
- ❑ **valid**

CRITICAL VOCABULARY

WORD BANK
convivial
subtly
idle
forlorn
recede
pendulum
muse

Practice and Apply In each item, mark the phrase that has a connection to each Critical Vocabulary word.

1. **pendulum:** a writing instrument / a grandfather clock / a racing motorcycle
2. **recede:** a plane flying off into the distance / a plane landing on a runway / a plane parked at the gate
3. **forlorn:** a bitter quarrel / a heavy snowfall / a lonely child
4. **idle:** singers in a contest / striking workers with nothing to do / a parking lot filling with cars
5. **muse:** a person considering choices / a windy, rainy afternoon / a noisy rock band
6. **convivial:** a dog chasing a squirrel / a friendly crowd of people / a curving staircase
7. **subtly:** a fireworks show / a long bus ride / a dimming light

VOCABULARY STRATEGY: Latin Root *pend*

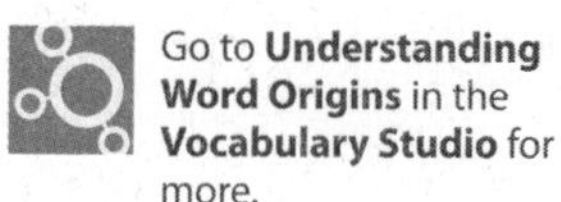
Go to **Understanding Word Origins** in the **Vocabulary Studio** for more.

The vocabulary word *pendulum* contains the Latin root *pend*, which means "hang." This root, sometimes spelled *pens*, is found in many English words. Use context clues and your knowledge of the root's meaning to help you understand unfamiliar words with *pend* or *pens*.

Practice and Apply Choose the word that best completes each sentence. Then explain to a partner how the root *pend* or *pens* relates to the meaning of the word.

pendulum	**suspenseful**	**dependent**
suspenders	**impending**	**pendant**

1. She wears that ____________ around her neck every day.
2. My choice is ____________ on what you decide to do.
3. The book was so ____________ that he could not put it down.
4. To hold up his pants, Dad prefers ____________ to belts.
5. They could not shake off their feeling of ____________ trouble.

LANGUAGE CONVENTIONS: Consistent Verb Tenses

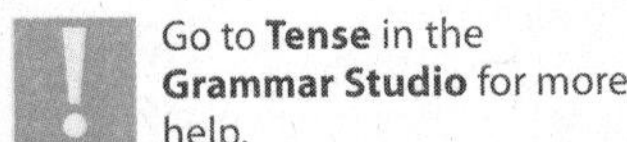

Go to **Tense** in the **Grammar Studio** for more help.

English verbs express the time of an action or state of being—past, present, or future—through verb tense. To keep the time of the verb clear in the readers' minds, writers usually are consistent. In these examples from "Dark They Were, and Golden-Eyed," Ray Bradbury uses consistent verb tenses:

- To express actions that happened in the past

    Mr. Bittering *hesitated*, and then *raised* the mirror to his face. (*Both verbs end in* -ed *and are in the past tense.*)

- To express actions that happen in the present

    Sometimes nights I *think* I *hear* 'em. I *hear* the wind. The sand *hits* my window. (*All three verbs—*think, hear, *and* hits*—are in the present tense. Notice how* hits *ends in* -s *because the subject—*sand*—is singular.*)

- To express actions that will happen in the future

    One day the atom bomb *will fix* Earth. Then *we'll be* safe here. (*Both verbs use the helping verb* will *to show the future tense.* We'll be *means "we will be."*)

Unexpected or inconsistent use of verb tenses can lead to confusion. On the other hand, sometimes tenses need to shift to show changes in time. What's important is to use the same tense to describe actions that take place at the same time. Change tenses only when you intend to shift from one time period to another.

Practice and Apply Write your own sentences based on the models from the story. You may write sentences about the story or about a topic of your own choosing. When you have finished, share your sentences with a partner and compare your use of verb tenses.

CHALLENGES FOR SPACE EXPLORATION

Argument by **Ann Leckie**

? ***ESSENTIAL QUESTION:***

Why is the idea of space exploration both inspiring and unnerving?

QUICK START

The possibility of humans exploring space is exciting—but dangerous, too. What do you think are the main challenges of space exploration? Make a list; then compare lists with two or three classmates.

ANALYZE AUTHOR'S PURPOSE

Purpose is an author's reason for writing a text. In an argument, the purpose is to persuade. The author presents a **claim**—a viewpoint or position on an issue—and then supports it with reasons and evidence.

Some arguments begin with a clear statement of the author's claim. Others imply a claim through the presentation of information and through **rhetoric,** the art of using language effectively to appeal to an audience. One aspect of rhetoric is **word choice.** Word choice helps to shape both tone and voice in a text.

GENRE ELEMENTS: ARGUMENT

- presents and defends a claim
- provides reasons to support the claim and factual evidence to support the reasons
- uses persuasive language
- can be formal or informal

SHAPED BY WORD CHOICE	EXAMPLE FROM SELECTION
Tone is the author's attitude toward a subject—for example, serious, lighthearted, or (as in this example) inspirational.	**It's a huge, dangerous, maybe impossible project. But that's never stopped humans from trying anyway.**
Voice is an author's unique use of language that allows a reader to "hear" a human personality in the author's work.	**. . . one good meteor strike and we all join the non-avian dinosaurs. And have you noticed the weather lately?**

ANALYZE REPETITION

One way to make a point in an argument is through **repetition.** Repetition is the use of the same word, phrase, clause, or sentence more than once for emphasis. Repetition is one of the **rhetorical devices**—specific ways of using language—authors use to emphasize key ideas, convey tone, and sometimes to encourage an emotional response in readers. In this example from "Challenges for Space Exploration," repetition of the word *there* emphasizes the idea of going into space. It also captures the curiosity and excitement that people have felt about exploring space:

What's up there? Could we go there? Maybe we could go there.

As you read "Challenges for Space Exploration," look for other examples of repetition that the author uses as she develops her argument.

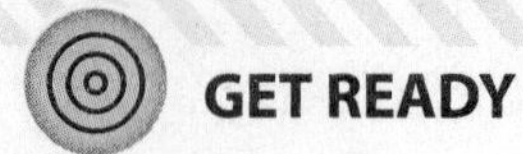

GET READY

CRITICAL VOCABULARY

infinitely **entail** **crucial** **habitat**

To see how many Critical Vocabulary words you already know, use them to complete these sentences.

1. Exploring another solar system would __________ many years of research and preparation.
2. If the __________ of a species is destroyed, the species must find a new environment that's suitable.
3. Protection from radiation is __________ if humans are to survive travel in space.
4. There are __________ more places to explore in space than people can imagine.

LANGUAGE CONVENTIONS

Commas After Introductory Phrases In "Challenges for Space Exploration," you will learn to use a comma after an introductory phrase. The comma gives the reader a moment to pause before moving on to the main part of the sentence. Note these examples:

> **Without a doubt, human beings have long had a thirst for exploring the unknown.**
>
> **Centuries before the first telescope, people studied the night sky and wondered what might be "out there."**

Look for comma usage as you read and write about the text.

ANNOTATION MODEL

NOTICE & NOTE

As you read, note how the author reveals her purpose for writing. You can also mark up examples of repetition and other rhetorical devices that make her argument effective. In the model, you can see one reader's notes about one paragraph in "Challenges for Space Exploration."

6 I could tell you that it might be good for us to unite behind a project that doesn't involve killing one another, that does involve understanding our home planet and the ways we survive on it and what things are crucial to our continuing to survive on it.

Author addresses readers directly to persuade them to accept her claim.

Repetition and contrast make the statement memorable.

I need to keep reading to figure out the point of this repetition.

BACKGROUND

Ann Leckie *(b. 1966) is an award-winning science fiction author. She has published many short stories but perhaps is best known for her novel* Ancillary Justice*, the first volume in the highly praised* Imperial Radch *series. The selection you are about to read, however, is persuasive nonfiction—an argument. It is Leckie's introduction to a feature in* Wired *magazine that explains problems humans face when they leave the relative safety of Earth.*

CHALLENGES FOR SPACE EXPLORATION

Argument by Ann Leckie

SETTING A PURPOSE

As you read, remember that this selection is an introduction to a longer piece, filled with specific challenges. Think about what Leckie says here about the challenges of space exploration in general and how she feels about facing those challenges.

1 Thousands of years ago, when our ancestors came to the sea, they built boats and sailed tremendous distances to islands they could not have known were there. Why?

2 Probably for the same reason we look up at the moon and the stars and say, "What's up there? Could we go there? Maybe we could go there." Because it's something human beings do.

3 Space is, of course, **infinitely** more hostile to human life than the surface of the sea; escaping Earth's gravity **entails** a good deal more work and expense than shoving off from the shore. But those boats were the cutting-edge technology of their time. Voyagers carefully planned their expensive, dangerous journeys, and many of them died trying to find out what was beyond the horizon. So why keep doing it?

Notice & Note

Use the side margins to notice and note signposts in the text.

LANGUAGE CONVENTIONS

Annotate: In paragraph 1, mark the introductory phrase that is set off by a comma.

Analyze: Why is it helpful to have a comma there?

infinitely
(ĭn′fə-nĭt-lē) *adv. Infinitely* means to a great extent, or with no limits.

entail
(ĕn-tāl′) *v.* To *entail* means to have or require.

NOTICE & NOTE

ANALYZE REPETITION

Annotate: Mark the clause that is repeated in paragraphs 4–8.

Analyze: How does the author's use of repetition help her support her claim?

crucial
(kro͞o′shəl) *adj.* Something that is *crucial* is extremely important or significant.

habitat
(hăb′ĭ-tăt′) *n.* In this instance, a *habitat* is a structure that provides a controlled environment for living in very hostile or even deadly locations.

ANALYZE AUTHOR'S PURPOSE

Annotate: Mark the words and phrases in paragraph 8 that help shape the tone of the paragraph.

Interpret: What tone, or attitude toward the subject, does the writing convey?

4 I could tell you about spinoff technologies, ranging from small products of convenience to discoveries that might feed millions or prevent deadly accidents or save the lives of the sick and injured.

5 I could tell you that we shouldn't keep all our eggs in this increasingly fragile basket—one good meteor strike and we all join the non-avian dinosaurs. And have you noticed the weather lately?

6 I could tell you that it might be good for us to unite behind a project that doesn't involve killing one another, that does involve understanding our home planet and the ways we survive on it and what things are **crucial** to our continuing to survive on it.

7 I could tell you that moving farther out into the solar system might be a good plan, if humanity is lucky enough to survive the next 5.5 billion years and the sun expands enough to fry the Earth.

8 I could tell you all those things: all the reasons we should find some way to live away from this planet, to build space stations and moon bases and cities on Mars and **habitats** on the moons of Jupiter. All the reasons we should, if we manage that, look out at the stars beyond our sun and say, "Could we go there? Maybe we could go there."

9 It's a huge, dangerous, maybe impossible project. But that's never stopped humans from trying anyway.

10 Humanity was born on Earth. Are we going to stay here? I suspect—I hope—the answer is no.

Inset image: An interplanetary vehicle orbits Mars.
Background image: a supernova

NOTICE & NOTE 

CHECK YOUR UNDERSTANDING

Answer these questions before moving on to the **Analyze the Text** section on the following page.

1 The author points out that our ancestors sailed great distances to unknown places in order to —

A express that it is important to go to new places

B suggest that it is human nature to be explorers

C warn about the risks of going to unknown places

D describe what might have happened to our ancestors

2 In paragraph 5, the author states that we shouldn't keep our eggs in this increasingly fragile basket. What does she mean?

F We need to create a safer environment on Earth.

G We must focus on the threat of meteor strikes.

H We must increase food production on Earth.

J We need to find other suitable planets to live on.

3 Which of the following is an example of repetition?

A *And have you noticed the weather lately?* (paragraph 5)

B *"Could we go there? Maybe we could go there."* (paragraph 8)

C *But that's never stopped humans from trying anyway.* (paragraph 9)

D *Humanity was born on Earth. Are we going to stay here?* (paragraph 10)

ANALYZE THE TEXT

Support your responses with evidence from the text. NOTEBOOK

1. **Analyze** What is the claim of the author's argument? Where is that claim stated most clearly?
2. **Summarize** Describe some of the reasons the author gives in support of her claim.
3. **Compare** According to the author, how were boats that set sail thousands of years ago like modern spaceships?
4. **Infer** How does the author's use of repetition convey tone, or her attitude toward space exploration? How does it help her achieve her purpose?
5. **Evaluate** Does the author's voice, or unique use of language, make her argument more or less effective? Explain.

RESEARCH

RESEARCH TIP
Remember to evaluate the websites to determine if they provide up-to-date and reliable information. Comparing information from several sites can be helpful.

Humans have been traveling into space for decades. They have orbited Earth and landed on the moon. Some have even lived for months at a time in space. However, space exploration is not without risk. Research some of the risks involved with going into space. Use several sources and record the information you find in the chart below.

RISK	PROBLEMS ASSOCIATED WITH RISK
Take-off	
Radiation	
Zero Gravity	

Extend Work with a partner to research and explain what scientists and engineers do to reduce one particular risk. Share your information with another pair of students.

CREATE AND DISCUSS

Write a Poem Write a poem in which an astronaut speaker considers the risks and sacrifices that she or he would face on a space mission.

- ❑ Make a list of feelings and ideas you have about the topic.
- ❑ Think about the main idea or message you want your speaker to express, even if she or he does not state it directly.
- ❑ Choose concrete words and phrases related to the topic that create strong images and appeal to the five senses.
- ❑ Include repetition, which is an effective rhetorical device in poetry as well as in nonfiction writing.

Go to **Writing as a Process** in the **Writing Studio** for more on planning and drafting text.

Listen for a Poem's Message Read your astronaut poem to a partner and listen to your partner's poem. Compare and discuss the poems.

- ❑ Take turns reading your poems aloud. Read with expression.
- ❑ As your partner reads, listen carefully to interpret the poem's message. Pay particular attention to specific words and phrases that stand out to you. (You may want to write them down or ask your partner to read the poem a second time.)
- ❑ Discuss which words and phrases convey each poem's message and what makes those words so powerful.

Go to **Participating in Collaborative Discussions** in the **Speaking and Listening Studio** for help having a partner discussion.

RESPOND TO THE ESSENTIAL QUESTION

? Why is the idea of space exploration both inspiring and unnerving?

UNIT 4 RESPONSE LOG

? Essential Question: Why is the idea of space exploration both inspiring and unnerving?

Martian Metropolis	
Dark They Were, and Golden-Eyed	
Challenges for Space Exploration	
What If We Were Alone?	
Seven Minutes of Terror	
Space Exploration Should Be More Science Than Fiction	
Humans Should Stay Home and Let Robots Take to the Stars	

Gather Information Review your annotations and notes on "Challenges for Space Exploration." Then, add relevant details to your Response Log. As you determine which information to include, think about:

- why space exploration is important
- the risks involved in space exploration

At the end of the unit, you may want to refer to your notes when you write an argument.

ACADEMIC VOCABULARY

As you write and discuss what you learned from the argument, be sure to use the Academic Vocabulary words. Check off each of the words that you use.

- ❑ **complex**
- ❑ **potential**
- ❑ **rely**
- ❑ **stress**
- ❑ **valid**

RESPOND

CRITICAL VOCABULARY

WORD BANK
infinitely
entail
crucial
habitat

Practice and Apply Write the Critical Vocabulary word asked for in each question. Be prepared to explain your response.

1. Which word goes with *environment*? ________________

2. Which word goes with *limitless*? ________________

3. Which word goes with *require* and *involve*? ________________

4. Which word goes with *important*? ________________

VOCABULARY STRATEGY: Etymology

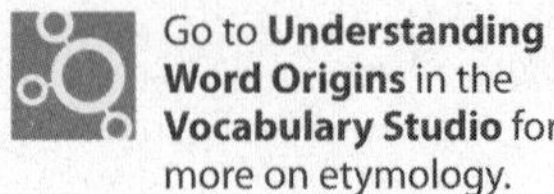

Go to **Understanding Word Origins** in the **Vocabulary Studio** for more on etymology.

Etymology is the origin and historical development of a word. When you study a word's history and origin, you can find out when, where, and how the word came to be used. For example, a dictionary entry for *solar* will tell you that the word comes from Middle English but that it can be traced back to the Latin word *sōlāris*, from *sōl*, which means "sun." *Solar* means "of or relating to the sun."

Practice and Apply Follow these steps to record the etymology of each Critical Vocabulary word in the chart below.

- Look up the word in a print or digital dictionary.
- Find the etymology of the word after the definition(s). If you are not sure about how to read the etymology, you can check the front or the back of a print dictionary. There should be a section that explains how the etymology is noted and what the abbreviations mean.
- Write the origin of the word and its original meaning in the chart below. Is the word's current meaning related to its original meaning? If so, explain how.

WORD	ETYMOLOGY/MEANING
infinitely	
entail	
crucial	
habitat	

LANGUAGE CONVENTIONS: Commas After Introductory Phrases

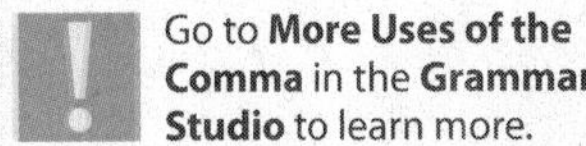
Go to **More Uses of the Comma** in the **Grammar Studio** to learn more.

Writers place a comma after most introductory phrases to signal the reader to pause and to avoid confusion. (Sometimes you will see a very short introductory phrase without a comma, but a comma there is not incorrect.) When you write, read your sentences aloud, noticing where you pause in the early part of a sentence. The places where you pause probably need to be punctuated by a comma. Study these examples based on "Challenges for Space Exploration":

> **Without a doubt, the long-term effects of zero gravity are a health risk for astronauts.**
>
> **Working in space, robots and other machines can perform tasks that are too dangerous for humans.**

Read the two sentences aloud, noticing where you pause. The comma after *doubt* in the first sentence signals the reader to pause. The comma after *space* in the second sentence signals the reader to pause and also avoids confusion. Without the comma, the reader might think at first that the writer is referring to space robots. Additional examples are shown in the following chart.

PURPOSE OF COMMA	EXAMPLE
To signal the reader to pause	To understand the health risks of living in space, scientists have studied astronauts living on the International Space Station.
To avoid confusion	Under the rules of NASA, astronauts must meet certain health requirements.

Practice and Apply These sentences include introductory phrases that need to be punctuated with commas. Read each sentence and insert the comma where necessary.

1. Having performed the experiments Anita recorded her findings.
2. Without better protection from radiation people could not possibly live on Mars.
3. Outside the laboratory five rockets blasted off and flew for about a mile.
4. On the other hand there is no reason to doubt that humans will eventually land on the moons of Jupiter.
5. To travel to other planets all I need to do is read my favorite science fiction stories.

WHAT IF WE WERE ALONE?

Poem by **William Stafford**

? ESSENTIAL QUESTION:

Why is the idea of space exploration both inspiring and unnerving?

QUICK START

The poem you are about to read challenges the reader to consider the idea of Earth's being alone in the universe. Think about your feelings when you are lonely and what makes you feel connected to the world around you. With a partner, create a web like this one, describing activities or people that help you feel connected. An example is given.

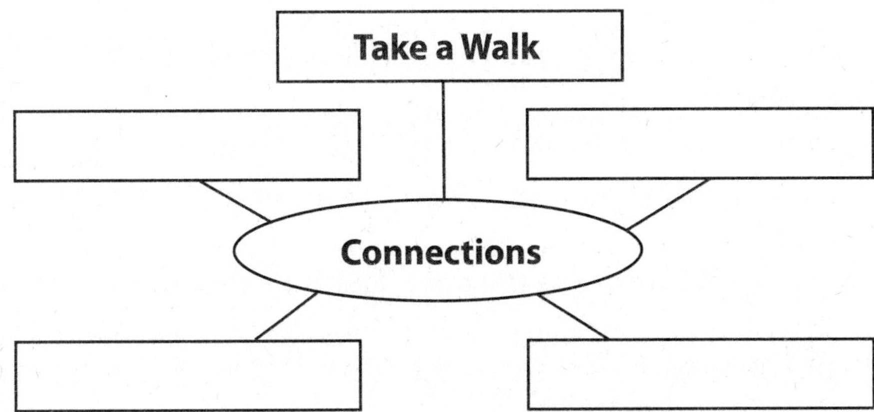

ANALYZE GRAPHICAL ELEMENTS

"What If We Were Alone?" is an example of **free verse,** a poem without regular rhyme or rhythm. The lines in the poem don't rhyme and it has strong rhythm in only a few places. Even without rhyme or rhythm, the poem has ways to affect the reader. Among these are **graphical elements**—the visual ways the poem is represented on the page. Here are a few common graphical elements:

CAPITALIZATION	We expect each line of a poem to start with a capital letter. When that doesn't happen, a thought probably runs from one line to the next.
PUNCTUATION	A dash signals a break in thought. Periods, question marks, and exclamation points in the middle of lines indicate pauses and changes in ideas. A comma signals a shorter pause, especially in the middle of a line. When you find these kinds of pauses, stop and think carefully about what you are reading.
LINE LENGTH	If you see lines in a poem that are much longer or shorter than usual, consider what effects they have on the poem's meaning.

All three kinds of graphical elements appear in "What If We Were Alone?" When you encounter one of them, stop and think about what the poet wants you to remember at that moment.

GENRE ELEMENTS: POETRY

- a form of literature structured into relatively short lines, often arranged into groups (stanzas)
- often focuses on feelings and impressions, and presented in ways that create images in the reader's mind
- often features sound devices that help create meaning
- includes graphical elements, such as capitalization, punctuation, and line length to help express ideas and themes

GET READY

ANALYZE THEME

Poems like "What If We Were Alone?" often have a **theme,** or a lesson about life or human nature that the poet shares with the reader. Examples of themes include statements such as "We must face challenges with courage" or "Friends are a positive part of life."

A theme is rarely stated directly at the beginning or end of a poem. Instead, the poet usually develops the message over the course of a poem. It is up to you, the reader, to read closely (several times, if possible, and maybe aloud as well as silently) and think carefully about questions such as these:

- Does the title of the poem hint at an important idea?
- What seems to be the main subject of the poem?
- If the poem has several **stanzas** (groups of lines), how does the main idea of each stanza relate to the main idea of the other stanzas?
- Is there a change of setting or focus in the poem? If so, why does the change happen?
- Are there words or phrases that are repeated or that stand out in other ways?
- What images come to mind as you read the poem?
- What do you know about the speaker of the poem? What seems to be important to the speaker?

As you think about answers to these questions, ask yourself, "What big message about life, or about human nature, is the poem trying to tell me?" Your response probably will be a theme—and possibly the main theme—of the poem.

ANNOTATION MODEL

NOTICE & NOTE

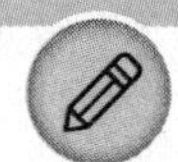

As you read, consider how the poet develops a theme. You also can mark graphical elements and other details that stand out to you. This model shows one reader's notes about the first stanza of "What If We Were Alone?"

What if there weren't any stars?
What if only the sun and the earth
circled alone in the sky? What if
no one ever found anything outside
this world right here?—no Galileo
could say, "Look—it is out there,
a hint of whether we are everything."

Three question marks = three questions. Why does the poet want me to think about these questions?

The poet includes a made-up quotation about space. The theme may have something to do with a lesson we can learn from space.

NOTICE & NOTE 

BACKGROUND

William Stafford *(1914–1993) was born in Hutchinson, Kansas. He attended the University of Kansas and earned a BA and MA. He later earned a PhD from the University of Iowa.* Traveling Through the Dark, *his first major collection of poems, was published in 1962 and won the National Book Award in 1963. Many of Stafford's poems have roots in the nature that he experienced in the West, and they focus on the lessons that nature can teach.*

WHAT IF WE WERE ALONE?

Poem by William Stafford

SETTING A PURPOSE

As you read, pay attention to the effect of graphical elements and to the words and phrases that catch your attention. How do these aspects of the poem work together to suggest one or more themes for the poem?

What if there weren't any stars?
What if only the sun and the earth
circled alone in the sky? What if
no one ever found anything outside
this world right here?—no Galileo
could say, "Look—it is out there,
a hint of whether we are everything."

Notice & Note

Use the side margins to notice and note signposts in the text.

WORDS OF THE WISER

Notice & Note: Mark the words that the speaker imagines Galileo saying.

Interpret: How are Galileo's words a response to the title of the poem?

NOTICE & NOTE

ANALYZE GRAPHICAL ELEMENTS

Annotate: Mark the dashes in lines 5–8.

Compare: Are the dashes used the same way in each line? Explain.

ANALYZE THEME

Annotate: In line 15, mark something found in space and something found on Earth.

Draw Conclusions: Does the poem's theme only relate to space? Explain.

Look out at the stars. Yes—cold
space. Yes, we are so distant that
the mind goes hollow to think it.
But something is out there. Whatever
our limits, we are led outward. We glimpse
company. Each glittering point of light
beckons: "There is something beyond."

The moon rolls through the trees, rises
from them, and waits. In the river all
night a voice floats from rock
to sandbar, to log. What kind of listening
can follow quietly enough? We bow, and
the voice that falls through the rapids
calls all the rocks by their secret names.

NOTICE & NOTE 

CHECK YOUR UNDERSTANDING

Answer these questions before moving on to the **Analyze the Text** section on the following page.

1 The poet uses questions in the first stanza in order to —

- **A** prove that everyone thinks about these questions
- **B** emphasize the seriousness of the question in the title
- **C** suggest that the universe really is an empty place
- **D** indicate that people think about space too much

2 According to the poem's speaker, what is the main purpose of the stars?

- **F** They encourage us to seek answers by looking beyond what we find familiar.
- **G** They urge us not to think about space because the universe is impossible to understand.
- **H** They remind us that we are limited and that human life is short.
- **J** They give us hope for a future in which we will travel among them.

3 In the third stanza, the voice that the speaker describes is a —

- **A** message from Galileo
- **B** message from the moon
- **C** power that exists throughout nature
- **D** listener that unites all human beings

RESPOND

ANALYZE THE TEXT

Support your responses with evidence from the text. NOTEBOOK

1. **Infer** What phrase is repeated in the title and the questions in the first stanza? What does this repetition indicate about the poem's speaker?
2. **Interpret** In line 5, why do you think a dash appears at the end of the third question?
3. **Compare** How does the poet suggest that both space and the earth itself are mysterious?
4. **Draw Conclusions** What do you think is the theme of "What If We Were Alone?" Why do you think so?
5. **Notice & Note** In the first stanza, you read some "words of the wiser" as spoken by Galileo. Whose "words" are described in the final stanza? What makes these "wise" words, too?

RESEARCH

RESEARCH TIP
When a topic is broad, such as astronomy, create a list of subtopics to use as key words in Internet searches. In this activity, you are given the subtopics. At other times, however, you will need to choose them. In that case, it can be helpful to start by reading an encyclopedia entry about the topic. Doing this can help you identify interesting subtopics.

People have been wondering about space for thousands of years. Astronomy is the scientific study of things that exist beyond Earth's atmosphere. With a partner, research these aspects of astronomy. You can use this graphic organizer to record your findings.

METHODS USED TO STUDY THE UNIVERSE	
In ancient times:	**Today:**

THREE TOPICS THAT ASTRONOMERS STUDY

TWO QUESTIONS THAT ASTRONOMERS TRY TO ANSWER

Connect In a small group, compare your findings. Discuss how you think astronomers view their work. How do you see that view addressed in "What If We Were Alone?"

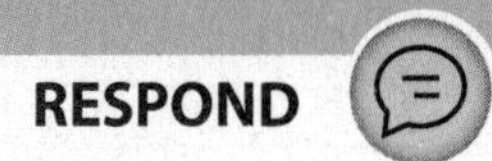

CREATE AND LISTEN

Write a Poem Imagine that an intelligent life form witnesses the arrival of a group of human space explorers who plan to start a colony. Create a poem written from the life form's point of view about the newcomers' arrival. The poem may use rhyme and rhythm, or it may be in free verse (like "What If We Were Alone?").

- ❑ Decide whether the life form is curious, frightened, or angry about the newcomers. Brainstorm words that express emotions.
- ❑ Consider how to include descriptions of what the life form is observing about the humans.
- ❑ Write a draft of your poem. Use graphical elements to help you express the message, or theme, that you want to convey.
- ❑ Revise your poem. Consider the specific effects the words, phrases, and graphical elements have.

Go to **Writing as a Process** in the **Writing Studio** to learn more.

Listen for the Theme Now share your poem with a partner. Take turns reading your poems aloud to each other with expression.

- ❑ Listen carefully as the poem is read. If you would like to hear it again, ask your partner to read it a second time.
- ❑ After the poems have been read, discuss your interpretation of each one's message, or theme.
- ❑ Give each other positive feedback about what works best in the poem or about how to revise the poem to strengthen its theme.

Go to **Analyzing and Evaluating Presentations** in the **Speaking and Listening Studio** for more details.

RESPOND TO THE ESSENTIAL QUESTION

? Why is the idea of space exploration both inspiring and unnerving?

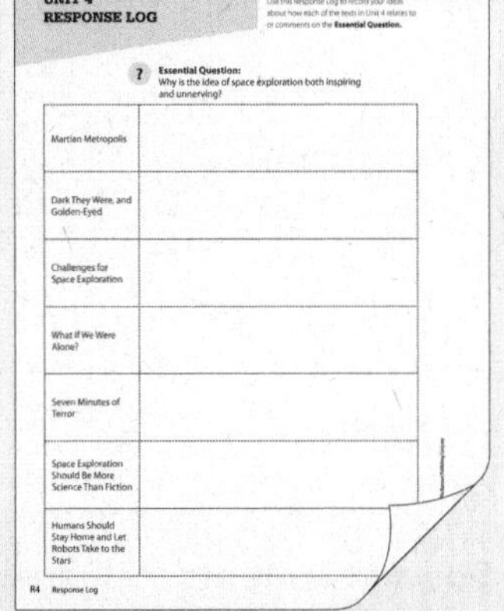

UNIT 4 RESPONSE LOG

Use this Response Log to record your ideas about how each of the texts in Unit 4 relates to or comments on the **Essential Question.**

? **Essential Question:** Why is the idea of space exploration both inspiring and unnerving?

Martian Metropolis	
Dark They Were, and Golden-Eyed	
Challenges for Space Exploration	
What If We Were Alone?	
Seven Minutes of Terror	
Space Exploration Should Be More Science Than Fiction	
Humans Should Stay Home and Let Robots Take to the Stars	

R4 Response Log

Gather Information Review your annotations and notes on "What If We Were Alone?" Then, add relevant details to your Response Log. As you determine which information to include, think about:

- why people are fascinated by the stars
- whether exploring space would be wonderful or terrible
- how interactions with nature inform our interest in space

At the end of the unit, you can use your notes when you write an argument.

ACADEMIC VOCABULARY

As you write and discuss what you learned from the poem, be sure to use the Academic Vocabulary words. Check off each of the words that you use.

- ❑ **complex**
- ❑ **potential**
- ❑ **rely**
- ❑ **stress**
- ❑ **valid**

MEDIA

SEVEN MINUTES OF TERROR

Video by the
National Aeronautics and Space Administration

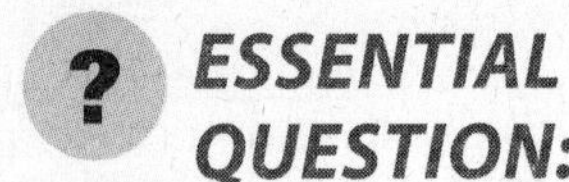

Why is the idea of space exploration both inspiring and unnerving?

QUICK START

As NASA scientists and engineers plan missions, what challenges might they face? Talk about your ideas with a partner or a small group.

ANALYZE VIDEO

GENRE ELEMENTS: MEDIA
- often conveys information
- may target a general or specific audience
- frequently includes experts or eyewitnesses who provide explanations and key insights
- examples include television broadcasts, newspapers, videos, magazines, and the Internet

The **purpose,** or intent, of an informational video is to explain a topic. The video's creator combines visual and sound elements to meet this purpose. An informational video may also use these elements to express the feelings and thoughts of the creator.

Visual elements include the images, the style of the images, and the ways in which the elements work together.

ANIMATION	images that appear to move; created through drawings, computer graphics, or photographs
FILM FOOTAGE	visual images captured on film or digitally; edited to deliver information clearly
GRAPHICS	drawings (maps, charts, diagrams, and so on) used to represent ideas or data

Sound elements include what you hear in a video.

MUSIC	instrumental and/or singing; emphasizes the emotional mood; may signal shifts in topic
NARRATION	words spoken over the images; carefully worded to present key facts

BACKGROUND

The people of the National Aeronautics and Space Administration (NASA) have always felt pressure, including the pressure of time. NASA had to detemine whether humans could survive in space before it sent anyone to the moon. It took NASA about a decade; but in 1969, American astronauts Neil Armstrong and Buzz Aldrin became the first humans to set foot on the moon. NASA went on to establish the space shuttle program, partner with space agencies from multiple countries on the International Space Station, and explore our solar system with orbital spacecraft telescopes. NASA's technological innovations continue to lead the world in space exploration and to improve life on Earth, especially in air travel and weather forecasting.

SETTING A PURPOSE

As you view the informational video, consider how it communicates a sense of time pressure. Pay attention to how experts explain a difficult process and the time pressures they feel as they try to ensure its success. NOTEBOOK

To view the video, log in online and select **"Seven Minutes of Terror"** from the unit menu.

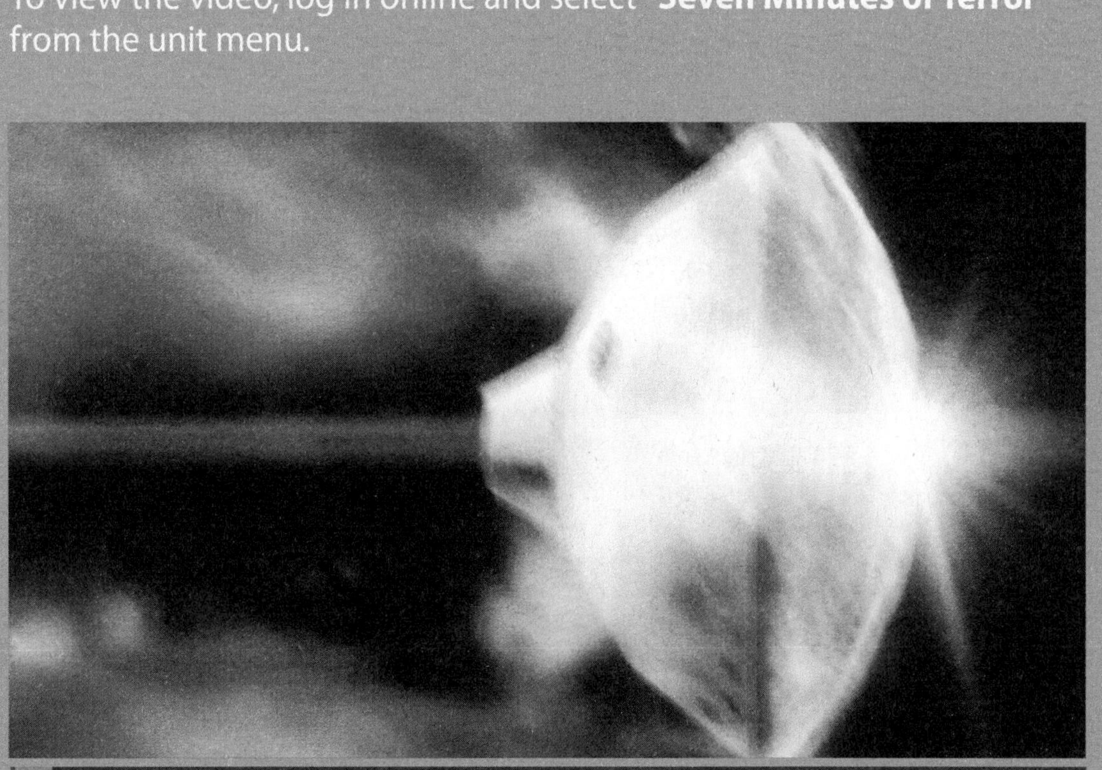

As needed, pause the video to make notes about what impresses you or about ideas you might want to talk about later. Replay or rewind so that you can clarify anything you do not understand.

RESPOND

ANALYZE MEDIA

Support your responses with evidence from the video. NOTEBOOK

1. **Interpret** Explain the title of *Seven Minutes of Terror.* How do the music, pacing of the video, and the experts' tone of voice suggest a sense of danger or even terror?
2. **Cause/Effect** Review the animation and the experts' narration about the parachute used in this mission. What problems did the NASA engineers identify that the parachute could solve?
3. **Evaluate** How effective was the video in explaining NASA's plan to prevent a dust cloud when Curiosity landed? Explain which visual and sound elements support your evaluation, and why.
4. **Draw Conclusions** Review the graphics and animation that show the EDL (entry, descent, and landing) sequence for Curiosity. What do they tell you about the complexity of landing safely on Mars?
5. **Critique** Think about the purpose of the video. Consider the techniques that are used to support the information presented. Do you think *Seven Minutes of Terror* is an effective informational video? Why or why not?

RESEARCH

RESEARCH TIP
Understanding complex technical information found on the Internet can be a challenge. It's often helpful to search specific technical terms using a reputable online encyclopedia, such as *Encyclopædia Britannica,* or dictionary, such as the *American Heritage Dictionary.*

As you've learned from the video, NASA engineers had to figure out how to meet several significant challenges in planning how to land Curiosity safely on Mars. With a partner, do some research to learn more about Curiosity beyond the account in the video.

QUESTION	ANSWER
What did Curiosity discover about water on Mars?	
What did Curiosity discover about the atmospheric conditions on Mars?	
How does Curiosity generate the power it needs to explore Mars?	

Connect How would you present your information about Curiosity in a video? With your partner, sketch out the sound and visual elements you would include to convey this information.

CREATE AND PRESENT

Write a Personal Narrative Write a personal narrative to tell what it might be like for you to encounter a being from another planet.

- ❏ Choose a setting (Earth? Another planet? In space?) and outline the beginning, middle, and end of the narrative.
- ❏ Decide whether your narrative will have a "lesson"—and, if so, how you will show it through events in the plot.
- ❏ Tell the events in a logical order, using a first-person point of view.
- ❏ Choose words and details that appeal to the senses.

Go to **Writing Narratives** in the **Writing Studio** to learn more.

Present the Techniques With a small group, talk about the visual and sound elements of the video. Which elements most effectively communicate the "terror" suggested by the video's title? Discuss how each element delivers a particular emotional effect.

- ❏ Make notes about visual and sound elements in the video that particularly impressed you, both positively and negatively.
- ❏ Using examples from the video, explain how each element you have chosen delivers an emotional effect. Present ideas for ways to improve the video, or note elements that you might use in a video of your own.
- ❏ Take notes on your group's discussion. Use your notes to present a summary of the discussion for a larger group.

Go to **Participating in Collaborative Discussions** in the **Speaking and Listening Studio** for help.

RESPOND TO THE ESSENTIAL QUESTION

? Why is the idea of space exploration both inspiring and unnerving?

UNIT 4
RESPONSE LOG

Essential Question: Why is the idea of space exploration both inspiring and unnerving?

Martian Metropolis	
Dark They Were, and Golden-Eyed	
Challenges for Space Exploration	
What If We Were Alone?	
Seven Minutes of Terror	
Space Exploration Should Be More Science Than Fiction	
Humans Should Stay Home and Let Robots Take to the Stars	

Gather Information Review your annotations and notes on *Seven Minutes of Terror*. Then, add relevant details to your Response Log. As you determine which information to include, think about:

- the planning that went into the Curiosity mission
- the unique features of Mars that made landing Curiosity a challenge

At the end of the unit, use your notes to help you write an argument.

ACADEMIC VOCABULARY

As you write and discuss what you learned from the video, be sure to use the Academic Vocabulary words. Check off each of the words that you use.

- ❏ **complex**
- ❏ **potential**
- ❏ **rely**
- ❏ **stress**
- ❏ **valid**

COLLABORATE & COMPARE

ARGUMENT

SPACE EXPLORATION SHOULD BE MORE SCIENCE THAN FICTION

by **Claudia Alarcón**

pages 329–333

COMPARE ARGUMENTS

As you read, notice the persuasive techniques and main points contained in each argument. Then think about each argument's central claim. After you read both arguments, you will collaborate with a small group on a project.

ESSENTIAL QUESTION:

Why is the idea of space exploration both inspiring and unnerving?

ARGUMENT

HUMANS SHOULD STAY HOME AND LET ROBOTS TAKE TO THE STARS

by **Eiren Caffall**

pages 338–341

QUICK START

An important debate has been taking place about the costs and risks of space exploration. How important is space exploration for our future? Is space travel too risky for humans? Discuss your ideas with the class.

ANALYZE ARGUMENT

In an **argument,** a speaker states a claim and supports it with reasons and evidence. A **claim** is the speaker's position on a problem or issue. The strength of an argument relies not on the claim itself but on the support. **Support** consists of reasons and evidence used to prove the claim. **Reasons** are declarations made to explain an action or belief. **Evidence** includes specific facts, statistics, or examples. To **trace,** or follow the reasoning of, an argument:

- Identify the claim, which may be stated directly or implied.
- Look for reasons and evidence that support the claim.
- Note how author connects the claim, reasons, and evidence.
- Identify **counterarguments,** statements that address opposing viewpoints. A good argument anticipates opposing viewpoints and provides counterarguments to disprove the opposing views.

GENRE ELEMENTS: ARGUMENT

- includes a claim and counterarguments
- includes reasons and evidence to support the claim
- may contain rhetorical devices
- may be formal or informal

ANALYZE RHETORICAL DEVICES

Rhetorical devices are techniques that writers use to enhance their arguments and communicate more effectively. A few rhetorical devices are described below, along with examples of each from the selections.

RHETORICAL DEVICE	EXAMPLE
Addressing readers using the pronouns *you* or *yourself* is a device called **direct address.** Direct address gets readers' attention and connects them to the topic.	Imagine yourself as an astronaut, a part of the first manned mission to Mars.
Rhetorical questions are those that do not need a reply. Writers use them to engage the reader or to suggest that their arguments make the answer obvious.	Would you want to trust a scientific mission to the people who run reality TV?
Sweeping generalizations are those that are too broad. Sweeping generalizations often include words such as *all, everyone, every time, anything, no one,* and *none.*	Obviously, no single government would want to take on that kind of funding.
Loaded language consists of words with strongly positive or negative connotations intended to influence a reader or listener.	This form of mining, therefore, would be incredibly beneficial for our survival and advancement.

GET READY

CRITICAL VOCABULARY

administration **beneficial** **plague** **erupt**
prominent **advancement** **dubious**

To see how many Critical Vocabulary words you already know, use them to complete the sentences.

1. One _________ official in the presidential _________ voiced concern about the expense of the Mars mission.
2. The crowd will _________ in cheers when the astronauts land.
3. Although problems continue to _________ the project, the results will be _________.
4. Some officials claim that the technology will lead to a(n) _________ for society, but most are _________ about such claims.

LANGUAGE CONVENTIONS

Subordinating Conjunctions A subordinate clause begins with a **subordinating conjunction,** such as *after, although, as, because, before, even though, if, since, so that, though, unless, until, when, where,* and *while.* A subordinate clause may also begin with a **relative pronoun,** such as *which, that, who,* and *whose.* As you read, watch for subordinating conjunctions and relative pronouns that are used to form **complex sentences,** those with one main clause and one or more subordinate clauses.

NOTICE & NOTE

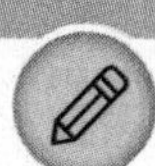

ANNOTATION MODEL

As you read, note the author's use of rhetorical devices. You can also mark reasons and evidence that support the argument. In the model, you can see one reader's notes about "Humans Should Stay Home and Let Robots Take to the Stars."

4 The risks of space exploration could be grave for a planet already plagued by pollution. There is an extra result of space travel: black carbon from rocket exhaust that's deposited in the outer atmosphere. . . . With no weather to wash it into the oceans, black carbon can stay put for up to ten years.

The negative connotation of these words suggests that the author is against space exploration.

The author is using this statistic to support her argument.

BACKGROUND

Exploring the outer reaches of our solar system and sending humans to Mars is no longer the stuff of science fiction. NASA has sent orbiters and rovers to the Red Planet for decades. But now the goal is to send humans to orbit Mars by the 2030s. Many scientists and politicians are rallying around this goal, as well as around other missions that will allow humans to probe the mysteries of space.

SPACE EXPLORATION SHOULD BE MORE SCIENCE THAN FICTION

Argument by Claudia Alarcón

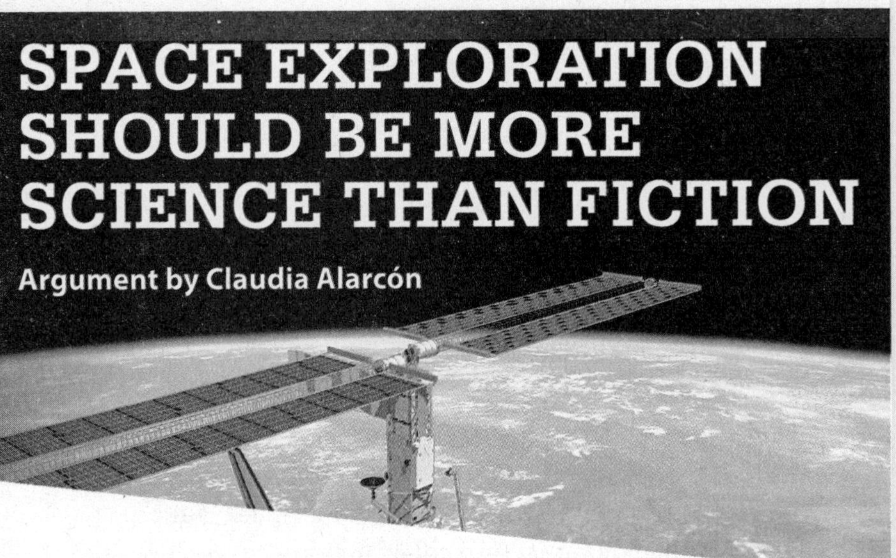

PREPARE TO COMPARE

As you read, pay attention to the persuasive language and to the reasons and evidence this author uses to support her argument. Consider how forms of persuasion can differ.

1 What is out there? Are we alone in the universe? Are there inhabitable planets in our galaxy and beyond? For decades, science-fiction novels, movies, and TV shows fired our curiosity. After the real-life *Apollo 11's* moon mission in 1969, enthusiasm for new discoveries soared. Now, well into the twenty-first century, we must face the fact that these same questions are still unanswered. With so much human investment made, we must go forward, fully embracing space exploration as an important priority. Our future in space depends on science.

2 Space exploration in the 1960s was fueled by the Cold War space race between the United States and Russia. The twenty-first century has brought a universal spirit of collaboration among scientists from around the globe.

Notice & Note

Use the side margins to notice and note signposts in the text.

ANALYZE ARGUMENT

Annotate: Underline the author's central claim in paragraph 1.

Interpret: What does the author think we should do?

NOTICE & NOTE

This section of the immense Carina Nebula was captured by the *Hubble Space Telescope*. Inset at right: a view of *Hubble*

An excellent example is the International Space Station. This orbiting laboratory and construction site combines the scientific expertise of 16 nations. It allows for a permanent human outpost in space. The hope is that the station can serve as a launching platform for further space exploration.

3 But space travel is not without risk. NASA's Space Shuttle Program, which was the main connection to the International Space Station, suffered two terrible losses. After the explosions of the *Challenger* in 1986 and *Columbia* in 2003, the program was shut down in 2011. Recent presidential **administrations** supported putting priority on the commercial space flight industry. A program was put into place to help private companies pursue work on human space flight. There are dozens of private companies in the industry known informally as "New Space." These companies have set their sights on what seem to be impossible goals. These range from tourist trips to the moon to the colonization of Mars. Space travel has its documented dangers; however, direct human involvement, aided by technological innovation, could likely boost the potential for discovery.

4 Technological innovations are developing to allow us to venture even farther into space. Such advances are opening windows into worlds we previously could not have imagined.

administration
(ăd-mĭn´ĭ-strā´shən) *n.* A president's *administration* is his or her term of office.

ANALYZE RHETORICAL DEVICES

Annotate: Mark examples of loaded language in paragraph 4.

Analyze: Why do you think the author chose these words? How do they enhance her argument?

Robotic spacecraft have conducted some of NASA's most exciting and productive missions. A **prominent** example is the *Hubble Space Telescope*, which has made more than 1.3 million observations since its mission began in 1990. It has traveled more than 4 billion miles, sending back stunning photos of faraway stars and galaxies.

prominent
(prŏm′ə-nənt) *adj.* If something is *prominent*, it stands out.

5 NASA has also conducted robotic missions within our solar system. The *Cassini*'s mission to Saturn was one of the most ambitious efforts in planetary space exploration. This robotic spacecraft carried the *Huygens* probe, which parachuted to the surface of Titan, Saturn's largest moon. The Juno spacecraft orbited around Jupiter, sending observations that can help scientists understand the beginnings of the solar system. The New Horizons spacecraft flew by Pluto in 2015 after an almost ten-year flight. According to the National Academy of Sciences, the exploration of Pluto and the Kuiper belt is the highest priority for solar system exploration. The asteroids in the Kuiper belt offer a great opportunity for mining. Space mining presents an important step for finding resources necessary for interstellar travel and exploration. In addition, icy asteroids may provide a cost-effective solution to space travel. Space entrepreneurs are looking into using hydrogen and oxygen from asteroid ice to

LANGUAGE CONVENTIONS

Annotate: Underline the two complex sentences in paragraph 5 and circle the relative pronouns.

Interpret: What two ideas do the relative pronouns connect in each sentence?

NOTICE & NOTE

manufacture rocket fuel. This space-made fuel can be used to launch expeditions farther out into space at considerably less cost.

6 Our moon contains helium-3, an element that could be useful on Earth for energy developments such as nuclear fusion research. Mining there can also yield rare-earth metals (REMs) that are used in electronics and in the construction of solar panels. This form of mining, therefore, would be incredibly **beneficial** for our survival and **advancement.** In recent years, geological surveys have indicated the presence of water on the moon, which can serve to sustain a human-inhabited lunar base.

beneficial
(bĕn´ə-fĭsh´əl) *adj.* When something is *beneficial*, it is good or favorable.

advancement
(ăd-văns´mənt) *n.* Something that is an *advancement* is an improvement or step forward.

ANALYZE ARGUMENT
Annotate: In paragraph 7, mark a reason that the author uses to support her claim that we must continue to explore space.

Evaluate: Is the reason relevant? Does it make sense? Explain.

7 Scientists are also looking toward Mars as a potential new home for humankind. New discoveries keep emerging that raise more questions. It is imperative that we use all our available resources to continue research on Mars.

8 Early missions to Mars such as Mars *Odyssey* were designed to make discoveries under the theme of "Follow the Water." These missions showed the possibility of liquid water below the surface of Mars. With the *Curiosity* rover, the Mars Exploration Program is following a next-step strategy known as "Seek Signs of Life." This exploration phase aims to discover the possibilities for past or present life on the Red Planet. *Curiosity* is seeking evidence of organic materials, the chemical building blocks of life. Future Mars missions would likely be designed to search for life itself in places identified as potential past or present habitats.

ANALYZE RHETORICAL DEVICES
Annotate: Mark the rhetorical question in paragraph 9.

Analyze: What purpose does the rhetorical question serve?

9 With all these advances and technologies in place and in development, will we see a human colony on the moon or on Mars in our lifetime? The best-case scenario will involve a partnership between NASA and international space travel companies.

10 Some New Space pioneers have tested supersonic retropropulsion technology, landing rocket boosters on floating platforms and on land. This technique could be important for future Mars landings. NASA's rovers, weighing up to a ton, have successfully landed on Mars. However, they have dropped to the planet's surface in air bags, using rockets, and with the assistance of cables extended from a "sky crane." A human mission would weigh much more, making landing more problematic. The previous solutions would not work for spacecraft carrying humans.

EXTREME OR ABSOLUTE LANGUAGE

Notice & Note: Mark the words in paragraph 11 that seem to exaggerate or overstate a case.

Analyze: How does the use of these words help the author's argument?

11 On the other hand, the future of the human race and Earth itself is at stake. We are close to surpassing our planet's carrying capacity and exhausting our natural resources. Yet scientists and space entrepreneurs remain hopeful. Private companies seeking

to colonize Mars believe the risk of space flight is similar to that of climbing Mount Everest. As we all know, this is a risky, but not impossible, proposition.

12 The final frontier is a vast and dangerous place, difficult and expensive to explore. But it offers infinite possibilities for expanding our scientific knowledge of our planet and its origins. Exploring outer space can yield new sources for precious natural resources and perhaps even find a home for future generations. We live in times where space travel and exploration should be more science than fiction. Let's keep pursuing the compelling questions that have driven us to these times. Space exploration may very well hold the key to humanity's future.

CHECK YOUR UNDERSTANDING

Answer these questions before moving on to the **Analyze the Text** section on the following page.

1 The author opens the text with questions most likely to —

A introduce the topics that she will cover in the selection

B suggest that her essay will attempt to answer the questions

C note that science fiction fuels our interest in science

D remind readers that there is much we still don't know

2 In paragraph 2, the author brings up the example of the International Space Station to make the point that space exploration —

F has come a long way since the 1960s

G encourages cooperation among scientists

H has led to a permanent human outpost

J requires a great deal of human investment

3 The author mostly supports her ideas with —

A expert opinions

B interesting anecdotes

C scientific evidence

D references to other texts

RESPOND

ANALYZE THE TEXT

Support your responses with evidence from the text. NOTEBOOK

1. **Infer** Why might the government have shifted from supporting space travel through NASA to prioritizing commercial travel?
2. **Cite Evidence** How could space mining aid in scientific research? Cite evidence from the text that explains the importance of space mining.
3. **Draw Conclusions** Review paragraph 8. What can you conclude from the support provided by the author about the connection between water and the possibility of life on Mars? Explain.
4. **Explain** Why does the fact that New Space pioneers are testing supersonic retropropulsion technology support the author's claim? How does it add to your understanding of the argument?
5. **Notice & Note** Explain the overall effect that the author's use of extreme or absolute language has on the reader. Does it make you more persuaded by the argument, or less so? Why?

RESEARCH

RESEARCH TIP
Remember that the *Cassini* mission has been in the news since its launch. To get an overview of its findings, scan search results that are dated 2017 and later.

The *Cassini* orbiter ended its journey in 2017. Research the details of its contributions. Record what you learn in the chart.

QUESTION	ANSWER
What were the goals of the *Cassini* orbiter mission?	
What important discoveries did *Cassini* make?	
What discoveries did *Cassini*'s probe Huygens make?	

Connect In paragraph 5, the author states, "The *Cassini*'s mission to Saturn was one of the most ambitious efforts in planetary space exploration." With a small group, discuss what made the *Cassini* mission so ambitious.

CREATE AND DISCUSS

Write a Letter Write to your representative in Congress to find out his or her views on space exploration.

- ❑ Determine who your representative is by going online to the U.S. House of Representatives website.
- ❑ Include a heading and a formal greeting. Then, begin the body of the letter by introducing the topic. Be clear in stating your reasons for writing.
- ❑ Close your letter by thanking your representative. Provide contact information so that he or she can send you the information you are seeking. Remember to end with a signature.

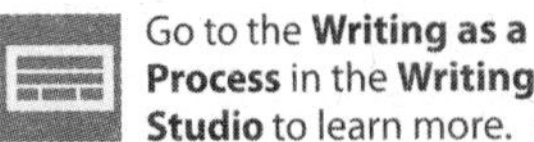

Go to the **Writing as a Process** in the **Writing Studio** to learn more.

Create a Loaded Language Chart Create a chart of the loaded language used in the text.

- ❑ As a group, review the selection and make a list of the loaded language that you find.
- ❑ Categorize the words in your chart according to whether each word has a positive connotation or a negative connotation.
- ❑ Review the words with positive connotations and those with negative ones. Discuss the author's purpose for using them.

Go to **Participating in Collaborative Discussions** in the **Speaking and Listening Studio** for help.

RESPOND TO THE ESSENTIAL QUESTION

? Why is the idea of space exploration both inspiring and unnerving?

Gather Information Review your annotations and notes on "Space Exploration Should Be More Science Than Fiction." Then, add relevant details to your Response Log. As you determine which information to include, think about the:

- reasons for sending humans into space
- risks associated with space travel
- benefits of robotic missions for space exploration

At the end of the unit, use your notes to help you write an argument.

ACADEMIC VOCABULARY

As you write and discuss what you learned from the argument, be sure to use the Academic Vocabulary words. Check off each of the words that you use.

- ❑ **complex**
- ❑ **potential**
- ❑ **rely**
- ❑ **stress**
- ❑ **valid**

RESPOND

CRITICAL VOCABULARY

WORD BANK
administration
prominent
beneficial
advancement

Practice and Apply Answer each question using the Critical Vocabulary word in a complete sentence.

1. Which presidential **administration** is in the White House?
2. Who is a **prominent** person in your school?
3. What is one thing that would be **beneficial** for your grades?
4. Why would someone work toward **advancements** in science?

VOCABULARY STRATEGY: Connotations and Denotations

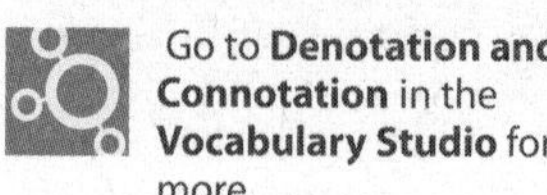

Go to **Denotation and Connotation** in the **Vocabulary Studio** for more.

A word's **denotation** is its literal dictionary definition. A word's **connotation** comes from the ideas and feelings associated with the word. Words can have positive or negative connotations. The author of "Space Exploration Should Be More Science Than Fiction" chose many words based on their connotation as well as their denotation.

> **Technological innovations are developing to allow us to venture even farther into space.**

Notice how the specific word choice of *venture*, rather than *go*, suggests daring. The word *venture* conjures up an adventure that requires courage. The context of a phrase, sentence, or paragraph can help you determine the connotation of a word.

Practice and Apply For each item, mark the word that better fits the meaning of the sentence. Use a print or online dictionary to help you with unfamiliar words. Then write the reason for your choice.

1. NASA scientists want to find out more about Mars. The scientists are (**inquisitive, prying**).

   ____

2. Astronauts on the International Space Station must work with each other for months at a time. The work requires them to (**conspire, cooperate**).

   ____

3. Radiation is a serious risk for astronauts working in space. It can be (**hazardous, menacing**) to their health.

   ____

4. The space program has enabled us to learn about our solar system and universe. It has provided (**interesting, useful**) information.

   ____

LANGUAGE CONVENTIONS: Subordinating Conjunctions to Form Complex Sentences

! Go to **Conjunctions and Interjections** in the **Grammar Studio** for more.

A **clause** is a group of related words that contains a subject and a verb. A **subordinate clause** cannot stand alone as a sentence because it does not express a complete thought. It is subordinate to—that is, it depends on—an **independent clause** (the main clause that can stand alone as a sentence). A sentence that contains at least one subordinate clause and an independent clause is called a **complex sentence.**

Consider these examples of complex sentences from "Space Exploration Should Be More Science Than Fiction."

> **As we all know, this is a risky, but not impossible, proposition.**

> **NASA's Space Shuttle Program, which was the main connection to the International Space Station, suffered two terrible losses.**

In the first example, the subordinate clause begins with a **subordinating conjunction** (*as*). The conjunction reveals a relationship between the two clauses. In fact, the subordinate clause introduces the independent clause. In the second example, the subordinate clause begins with a **relative pronoun** (*which*). Relative pronouns introduce a relative clause, a type of subordinate clause.

This chart shows some common subordinating conjunctions and relative pronouns.

SUBORDINATING CONJUNCTIONS	RELATIVE PRONOUNS
as, although, as much as, after, as long as, as soon as, before, since, until, when, whenever, while, because, so	who, whom, whomever, whoever, whose, that, which,

Practice and Apply Write your own complex sentences using a subordinating conjunction or a relative pronoun.

NOTICE & NOTE

BACKGROUND

While space travel and exploration have been widely celebrated since the first humans walked on the moon, not everyone is in favor of space travel. A short search on the Internet reveals blogs, editorials, and opinion essays expressing an opposing view. For these writers, there are other ways to find out about our solar system.

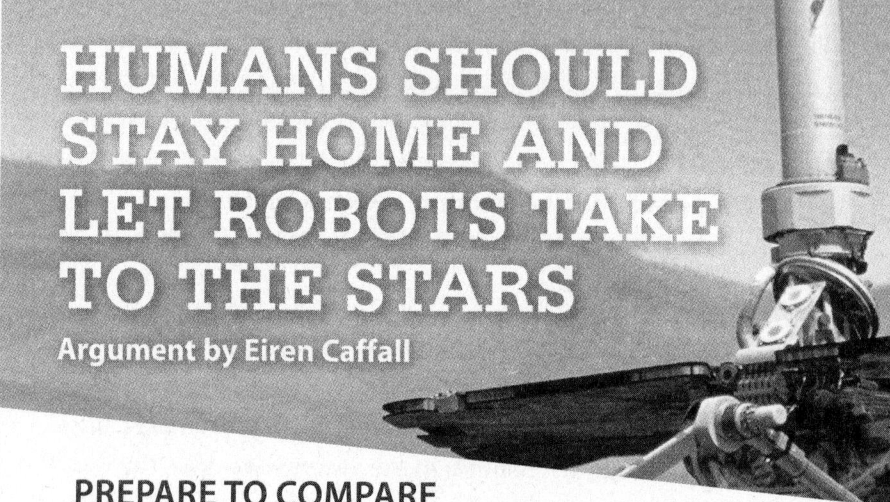

HUMANS SHOULD STAY HOME AND LET ROBOTS TAKE TO THE STARS

Argument by Eiren Caffall

PREPARE TO COMPARE

As you read, notice the way this author outlines her argument. Think about how she uses evidence to support her argument and whether that evidence makes the argument effective.

1 The lure of human space travel is undeniable. We've all grown up on endless types of entertainment set in the future that portray adventures on distant planets. Imagine yourself as an astronaut, a part of the first manned mission to Mars. Beyond that, there are generations of people who have been working to make space and space travel look cool, even inevitable. But high aspirations and romance aside, we need to face the harsh realities. Our notions about the inevitability and wonder of human space travel need to be checked, and any plans need to be reconsidered. Some of the best reasons to curtail space exploration come down to economics, human cost, and technology.

Space Travel Is Expensive

2 Space travel is extremely expensive. To get humans to Mars, it would take $1 trillion over a 25-year period. Obviously, no single government would want to take on that kind

Notice & Note

Use the side margins to notice and note signposts in the text.

ANALYZE ARGUMENT

Annotate: In paragraph 1, underline the author's central claim and circle the reasons the author will use to support the claim.

Interpret: What will the author's argument be? How does the title of the selection help clarify the author's argument?

of funding. A Mars mission would require international cooperation at a significant cost to each partner nation. A Mars mission might foster international cooperation, but it would consume funds that could be used for other things.

3 Some people suggest that the only way to get to Mars would be with the help of private companies. Because of this, the space exploration industry is made up not only of government agencies but also private companies headed by dreamers and people interested in profits over practicality. But these organizations are often badly managed. They don't work for the government, so accountability could be a problem. Even well-run companies are unlikely to have enough money to launch a Mars mission on their own. There are some experts who say that it wouldn't be possible to launch a mission to Mars without funding from commercials that would run during coverage of the project. That would turn a scientific mission into a reality television show. Would you want to trust a scientific mission to the people who run reality TV?

LANGUAGE CONVENTIONS

Annotate: In paragraph 3, circle the relative pronoun in the first sentence and underline the two ideas it connects.

Analyze: How are the two ideas related?

Space Travel Could Harm Our Polluted World

4 The risks of space exploration could be grave for a planet already **plagued** by pollution. There is an extra result of space travel: black carbon from rocket exhaust that's deposited in the outer atmosphere. The launch of a suborbital tourist craft is said to produce less carbon emissions than a standard flight from New York to London. However, once the rocket is above the atmosphere, the black carbon it releases can be pretty damaging. Try to imagine the black smoke from a diesel truck sitting above the sky. With no weather to wash it into the oceans, black carbon can stay put for up to ten years.

plague
(plāg) *v.* To *plague* something is to cause hardship or suffering for it.

5 Many space boosters are suggesting that being able to leave our planet once it's exhausted of resources is a priority. They seem to be proposing that we have some sort of Planet B. Somehow they think that a colony on Mars or the moon could take the pressure off our world. Many of these people planning to profit from two things at once are also fans of the **dubious** technology of geoengineering.

ANALYZE ARGUMENT

Annotate: In paragraph 5, mark an opposing viewpoint.

Analyze: What are the author's counterarguments to this viewpoint, as explained in paragraphs 5 and 6?

dubious
(do͞o′bē-əs) *adj.* If something is *dubious*, it is questionable or not to be relied upon.

6 As covered earlier, the essential ingredients for space exploration are international cooperation, vast investments of money, technological advances, global regulations, and the buy-in of the general population. Yet those ingredients may well be what's needed to tackle the problem of Earth's pollution.

NOTICE & NOTE

NUMBERS AND STATS

Notice & Note: In paragraph 7, mark specific numbers that identify amounts.

Analyze: What purpose does the use of specific numbers serve?

Space Travel Is More Suited to Robots

7 NASA recently collected data from the Mars Curiosity rover. The data were used to estimate the radiation impact on an astronaut traveling to and from Mars for 365 days and spending 500 days on the surface. It was determined that during that trip an astronaut would get a radiation dose that was about five percent of what he or she would get over a lifetime on Earth. That significantly increases the risk of cancer.

8 There is also the danger of running low on supplies. Once on the Red Planet, humans would eventually run out of food and materials. A Massachusetts Institute of Technology study guessed that agriculture would make too much oxygen for the small colony to support inside its dome. Without enough carbon dioxide, the colony would not be able to grow what it needed. Earth would constantly be sending supplies to the colonists. It's obvious that without that resupply, there would be no hope of agriculture supporting a manned station on Mars.

ANALYZE RHETORICAL DEVICES

Annotate: Mark an example of a sweeping generalization in paragraph 9.

Evaluate: How effective is this statement in convincing readers of the benefit of robots over astronauts?

9 Considering the extreme risks for humans, some scientists assert space exploration should be strictly robotic. Think about the achievements of the Hubble Space Telescope and the Mars Pathfinder and Opportunity. Their exploratory missions have captured the public imagination, and all of us love to see images from those robot explorers. When Opportunity landed safely on the surface of Mars, NASA's Mission Control Center **erupted** in as loud a cheer as greeted any human mission.

erupt
(ĭ-rŭpt´) *v.* When something *erupts,* it develops suddenly.

ANALYZE RHETORICAL DEVICES

Annotate: Mark an example of direct address in paragraph 10.

Infer: Why does the author use direct address here?

10 There are scientists who say that robots can't accomplish space travel as cheaply or efficiently as humans. But, as is often the case, those ideas are based on data from the distant history of space travel. As you might guess, the future of space exploration presents a very different picture, one where robots will replace humans as the better pilots and researchers.

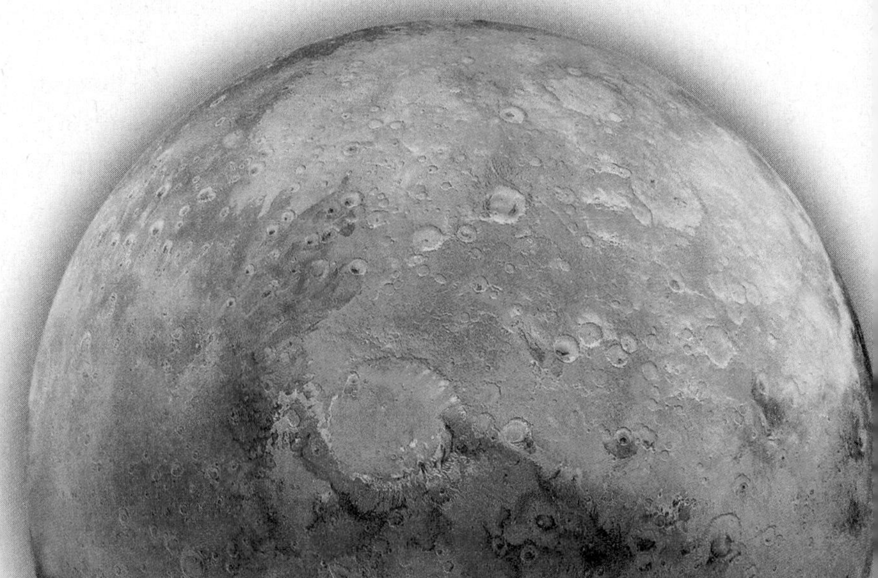

Space Travel Isn't Inevitable or Even Necessary

11 There are many solid arguments against spending money, time, and energy on manned space exploration. There is no solid reason to think of space as the only hope of our bright technological future. There are as many ways to innovate as there are human ideas. Just because the idea of space travel has been with us for decades doesn't mean that it's the best way to direct our dreams. Let's plot a course that doesn't involve humans. Without space travel as the default idea for our future, what new ideas might lead to amazing discoveries and inventions?

CHECK YOUR UNDERSTANDING

Answer these questions before moving on to the **Analyze the Text** section on the following page.

1 The author included the section Space Travel Is Expensive to —

A offer an opposing argument for sending robots

B support the claim that space travel should be reduced

C convince readers that space travel could be cheaper

D suggest that space travel requires international cooperation

2 The author refers to a Massachusetts Institute of Technology study in paragraph 8 to support the idea that —

F humans are not suited to live on Mars

G the Mars Curiosity rover has had great success

H agriculture on Mars would be possible

J a colony on Mars would require a lot of food

3 In paragraph 10, the author offers the counterargument that —

A robotic missions are as exciting as any human missions

B the future of space travel is dependent on scientific data

C data for space travel is often out of date or not trustworthy

D robotic missions are at least as efficient as human missions

ANALYZE THE TEXT

Support your responses with evidence from the text. NOTEBOOK

1. **Interpret and Analyze** Review paragraph 3. What is the author's position on using private companies for Mars missions? What rhetorical devices does the author use to support her position, and why?
2. **Evaluate** Review paragraphs 4–6. Does the author present an effective argument about why space travel could end up harming Earth? Explain.
3. **Critique** In paragraph 10, the author predicts robots will replace humans for space travel. Do you agree with the author? Why? Be sure to use reasons and supporting evidence in your response.
4. **Summarize and Analyze** Examine the headings and then summarize the reasons the author provides to support her claim. Explain why you think she put the reasons in the order that she did. Which reason is last? Why do you think she saved it for last?
5. **Notice & Note** How does the author use specific numbers and statistics to support her claim? Would her argument be as effective without specific numbers—for example, dollar amounts? Explain.

RESEARCH

RESEARCH TIP
You may need to follow several leads for your research, but you likely may find much of it on the NASA website. Begin with a specific search for International Space Station crew members. Then look for research information and updates that involve the crew members you have identified.

Explore the International Space Station (ISS). Find out about three crew members—past or present—including their length of time on the ISS and their research efforts. Record your findings in a chart like this one.

CREW MEMBER	TIME ON ISS/RESEARCH

Extend The International Space Station is exactly that—international. Find out which countries collaborate to support the International Space Station and how they work together.

WRITE AND PRESENT

Write a Short Story Write about an astronaut who is about to embark on a space mission but suddenly changes his or her mind.

- ❑ Introduce your characters and setting, and establish a point of view through your narrator.
- ❑ Then, establish and develop the conflict and sequence of events. Remember to use dialogue, pacing, and descriptive details.
- ❑ To conclude your story, resolve the conflict and leave readers with a message to consider.

Go to **Writing Narratives** in the **Writing Studio** to help develop a point of view.

Describe a Process Become familiar with the resources on NASA's website. Then, with a partner, demonstrate how to use the resources.

- ❑ With your partner, go to NASA.gov and explore the website. Notice the specific mission and project links on the home page, as well as recent NASA news.
- ❑ Note the pathways you must take to access various kinds of information (for example, to find recent crew members on the International Space Station or to view images).
- ❑ With your partner, demonstrate how to navigate the NASA site to access the site's resources. Walk your audience through the steps, noting the range of information and how to find specific items.

Go to **Giving a Presentation** in the **Speaking and Listening Studio** to learn more.

RESPOND TO THE ESSENTIAL QUESTION

? Why is the idea of space exploration both inspiring and unnerving?

Gather Information Review your annotations and notes on "Humans Should Stay Home and Let Robots Take to the Stars." Then, add relevant details to your Response Log. As you determine which information to include, think about:

- the roles humans and robots each play in space research
- the risks and benefits of space exploration
- your own position on space exploration

At the end of the unit, use your notes to help you write an argument.

ACADEMIC VOCABULARY

As you write and discuss what you learned from the argument, be sure to use the Academic Vocabulary words. Check off each of the words that you use.

- ❑ **complex**
- ❑ **potential**
- ❑ **rely**
- ❑ **stress**
- ❑ **valid**

CRITICAL VOCABULARY

WORD BANK
plague
dubious
erupt

Practice and Apply Mark the letter of the better answer to each question. Be prepared to explain your responses.

1. Which of these Internet articles is more likely to be **dubious**?
a. a report on a heat wave in California **b.** a report on an alien spaceship in Central Park

2. Which pair of factors is more likely to **plague** a city?
a. traffic jams and litter **b.** warm weather and sunshine

3. Which situation is more likely to make an audience **erupt** in applause?
a. a guitarist playing a solo **b.** a lecture on hygiene

VOCABULARY STRATEGY: Dictionary/Glossary Entries

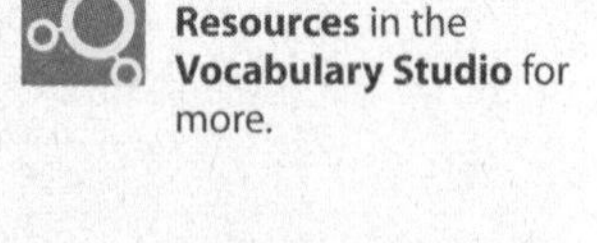

Go to **Using Reference Resources** in the **Vocabulary Studio** for more.

Print or digital dictionaries and glossaries are a great first step for checking the correct **spelling** and **definition** of a word. They can also give you information about the **syllabication, pronunciation, part of speech, alternate meanings,** and **word history** of entries.

Here is an example of a dictionary entry for the Critical Vocabulary word *erupt*:

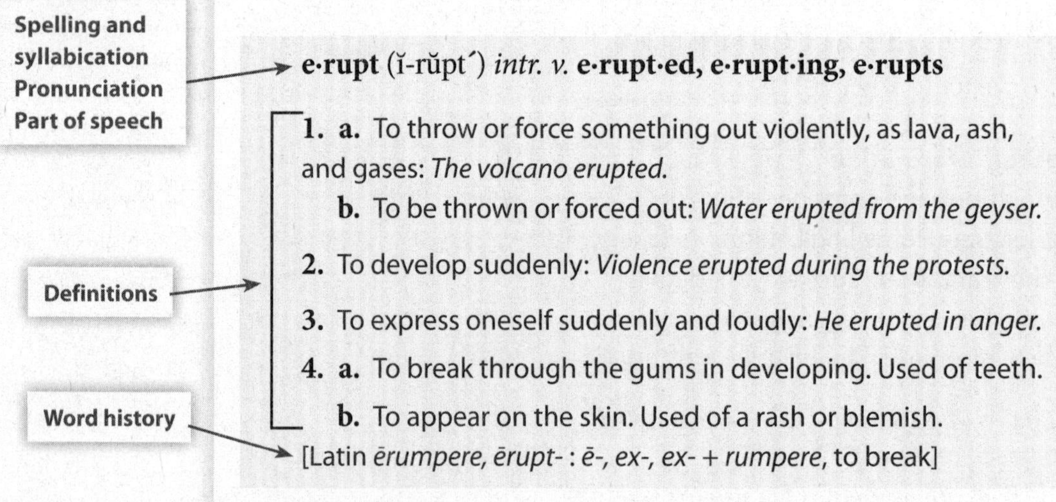

Spelling and syllabication
Pronunciation
Part of speech
e·rupt (ĭ-rŭpt′) *intr. v.* **e·rupt·ed, e·rupt·ing, e·rupts**
Definitions
1. a. To throw or force something out violently, as lava, ash, and gases: *The volcano erupted.*
b. To be thrown or forced out: *Water erupted from the geyser.*
2. To develop suddenly: *Violence erupted during the protests.*
3. To express oneself suddenly and loudly: *He erupted in anger.*
4. a. To break through the gums in developing. Used of teeth.
b. To appear on the skin. Used of a rash or blemish.
Word history
[Latin *ērumpere, ērupt-* : *ē-, ex-, ex-* + *rumpere*, to break]

Practice and Apply Use a print or digital dictionary to look up the Critical Vocabulary words *plague* and *dubious*. On a separate sheet of paper, write the syllabication, pronunciation, word history, and definition of each word as it is used in the selection. Then write a complete sentence using a Critical Vocabulary word of your choice.

LANGUAGE CONVENTIONS: Complete Complex Sentences

Go to **Sentence Structure** and **Run-on Sentences** in the **Grammar Studio** to learn more.

In this lesson, you learned that a **complex sentence** contains an independent, or main, clause and at least one subordinate clause. You also learned that a clause is a group of related words that includes both a subject and a verb.

In complex sentences, the subject and verb must agree in number in both kinds of clauses. **Subject-verb agreement** means that if the subject is singular, the verb must also be singular; if the subject is plural, the verb must also be plural. Study this example from "Humans Should Stay Home and Let Robots Take to the Stars."

> **As you might guess, the future of space exploration presents a very different picture, one where robots will replace humans as the better pilots and researchers.**

Note that there are two subordinate clauses in the sentence. In the first one, the subject *you* agrees with the verb *might guess*. In the second one, the subject *robots* agrees with the verb *will replace*. The subject and verb of the independent clause (*future* and *presents*) also agree.

A complex sentence that is **complete** must contain a subject and a verb in each clause. A **sentence fragment,** or a sentence that is not complete, lacks either a subject or a verb. To avoid sentence fragments, make sure that each clause contains both a subject and a verb.

Other types of errors to avoid as you create complete complex sentences include run-on sentences and comma splices. A **run-on sentence** is made up of two or more sentences written as though they were one. Sometimes a run-on sentence will have no punctuation. Other times, a comma will be used instead of a conjunction or a semicolon. You can often fix a run-on by adding a semicolon or conjunction.

A **comma splice** occurs when two independent clauses are joined with only a comma. One way to avoid a comma splice is to split the clauses into separate sentences, but you can also replace the comma with a semicolon, add a coordinating conjunction, or rephrase the sentence as a complex sentence with the use of a subordinating conjunction or relative pronoun.

Practice and Apply Draft a short paragraph about space travel or about the arguments you just read. Edit your draft to avoid including sentence fragments, run-on sentences, or comma splices. Then, check that every sentence is complete and uses correct subject-verb agreement.

Collaborate & Compare

SPACE EXPLORATION SHOULD BE MORE SCIENCE THAN FICTION
Argument by Claudia Alarcón

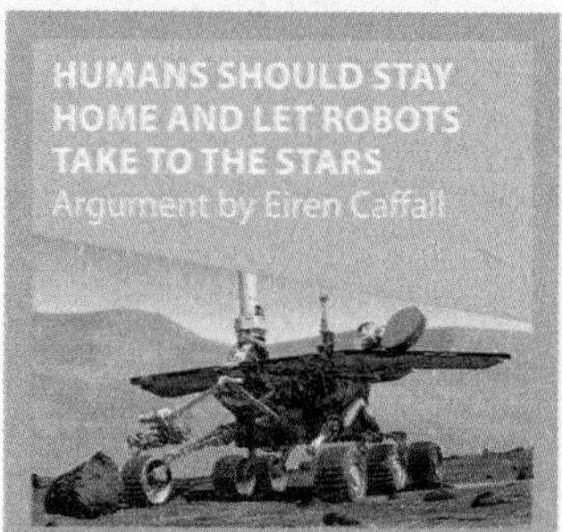

COMPARE ARGUMENTS

When you compare two or more texts on the same topic, you synthesize the information, making connections and expanding upon key ideas.

In a small group, complete the Venn diagram with similarities and differences in the two arguments you read. Consider the subjects being compared, claims made, reasons and evidence given, and rhetorical devices and persuasive techniques used by each author.

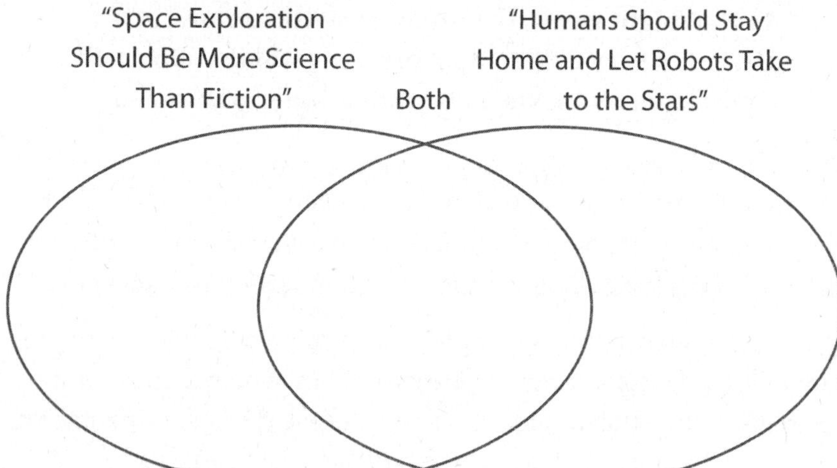

ANALYZE THE TEXTS

Discuss these questions in your group.

1. **Compare** With your group, study your Venn diagram. How do the claims in the two arguments differ? How are the ways each author presents their reasons and supporting evidence similar? How do they differ?
2. **Analyze** What similarities do you see between the authors' ideas about space exploration? Explain.
3. **Evaluate** What rhetorical devices and persuasive techniques does each author use? How effective is each author's use of these devices and techniques? Why?
4. **Critique** Which argument is more convincing? Why?

RESEARCH AND SHARE

Your group can continue exploring the ideas in these texts by working together to research and write a job description for being an astronaut. Then you will research specific astronauts and determine how well these candidates meet your job description. Follow these steps:

1. **Choose a Focus** In your group, decide who will research the requirements for becoming an astronaut and who will research specific astronaut candidates.

2. **Gather Information** As you research your specific focus, check that your sources are **reliable** (reputable and up to date) and **credible** (presenting ideas fairly and accurately). Take notes from at least one source, paraphrasing and summarizing key information. You can use this framework to record your findings.

Focus:
Source(s):
Information:

3. **Write a Job Description or Profile** Use your research notes to write either a job description for being an astronaut or a profile of the astronaut candidate you researched. Your profile should include information about the astronaut's education, work experiences, and training.

4. **Share What You Learn** Each person in your group now has a general idea of what it takes to become an astronaut. Listen as each group member presents a job description or profile. Then, discuss how well each astronaut candidate meets the job description. As a group, discuss what most surprised you about the astronauts' backgrounds and about specific job requirements. Talk about whether the research made you more or less interested in becoming an astronaut.

RESEARCH TIP

For help in writing a job description, look at the "help wanted" section in newspapers or the "careers" or "jobs" page on company or employment websites.

Go to **Evaluating Sources for Reliability** in the **Writing Studio** for help.

INDEPENDENT READING

Reader's Choice

ESSENTIAL QUESTION:

Why is the idea of space exploration both inspiring and unnerving?

Setting a Purpose Select one or more of these options from your eBook to continue your exploration of the Essential Question.

- Read the descriptions to see which text grabs your interest.
- Think about which genres you enjoy reading.

Notice & Note

In this unit, you practiced asking **Big Questions** and noticing and noting two signposts: **Numbers and Stats** and **Word Gaps.** As you read independently, these signposts and others will aid your understanding. Below are the anchor questions to ask when you read literature and nonfiction.

Reading Literature: Stories, Poems, and Plays		
Signpost	**Anchor Question**	**Lesson**
Contrasts and Contradictions	Why did the character act that way?	p. 99
Aha Moment	How might this change things?	p. 3
Tough Questions	What does this make me wonder about?	p. 362
Words of the Wiser	What's the lesson for the character?	p. 363
Again and Again	Why might the author keep bringing this up?	p. 3
Memory Moment	Why is this memory important?	p. 2

Reading Nonfiction: Essays, Articles, and Arguments		
Signpost	**Anchor Question(s)**	**Lesson**
Big Questions	What surprised me? What did the author think I already knew? What challenged, changed, or confirmed what I already knew?	p. 265 p. 183 p. 437
Contrasts and Contradictions	What is the difference, and why does it matter?	p. 183
Extreme or Absolute Language	Why did the author use this language?	p. 182
Numbers and Stats	Why did the author use these numbers or amounts?	p. 264
Quoted Words	Why was this person quoted or cited, and what did this add?	p. 437
Word Gaps	Do I know this word from someplace else? Does it seem like technical talk for this topic? Do clues in the sentence help me understand the word?	p. 265

INDEPENDENT READING

You can preview these texts in Unit 4 of your eBook.

Then, check off the text or texts that you select to read on your own.

☐ 

ARGUMENT

Let's Aim for Mars
Buzz Aldrin

A former astronaut proposes "opening space to the average person," by exploring and colonizing Mars.

☐ 

PERSONAL ESSAY

An Optimistic View of the World
Dan Tani

Based on his experiences in space, Dan Tani provides us with a uniquely optimistic perspective on life.

☐ 

POEM

Your World
Georgia Douglas Johnson

Discover inspiration in these well-crafted words about the importance of taking risks.

☐ 

BIOGRAPHY

Sally Ride *from* Headstrong
Rachel Swaby

Learn how America's first female astronaut launched into space and changed our approach to its exploration.

Collaborate and Share With a partner discuss what you learned from at least one of your independent readings.

- Give a brief synopsis or summary of the text.
- Describe any signposts that you noticed in the text and explain what they revealed to you.
- Describe what you most enjoyed or found most challenging about the text. Give specific examples.
- Decide if you would recommend the text to others. Why or why not?

Go to the **Reading Studio** for more resources on **Notice & Note.**

Write an Argument

Go to the **Writing Studio** for help writing your argument.

What are the short- and long-term consequences of space exploration? Are the risks worth the effort and the cost? For this writing task, you will write an argument about whether human space travel is necessary. For an example of a well-written argument you can use as a mentor text, review "Challenges for Space Exploration."

As you write your argument, you can use the notes from your Response Log, which you filled out after reading the texts in this unit.

Writing Prompt

Read the information in the box below.

This is the topic or context for your argument.

> **For more than half a century, we humans have reached farther and farther into space—not only walking on the moon, but exploring deep into our solar system. What more might we find out in space, if we keep exploring?**

Think carefully about the following question.

This is the Essential Question for the unit. How would you answer this question, based on the texts in this unit?

> **Why is the idea of space exploration both inspiring and unnerving?**

Write an argument in which you support a claim, or position, about whether or not human space travel is necessary.

Now mark the words that identify exactly what you are being asked to produce.

Be sure to—

Review these points as you write and again when you finish. Make any needed changes.

- ❑ provide an introduction with a claim that clearly states your position on the issue and reflects your depth of thought
- ❑ present at least two strong reasons to support your position
- ❑ support each reason with logical arguments and with various types of evidence from several reliable sources
- ❑ arrange reasons from least to most important
- ❑ group related ideas and organize ideas logically to create coherence within and across paragraphs
- ❑ use transitions to make the relationship between ideas clear
- ❑ use appropriate word choices and pronoun-antecedent agreement
- ❑ conclude by restating your position and summarizing your reasons

1 Plan

Before you start writing, you need to plan your argument. When you plan a draft, you begin by selecting a genre that is appropriate for the topic, purpose, and audience. For this writing task, you know that the topic is related to human space travel and that the genre is an argument. Next, consider your purpose and audience. Will you write to an audience of classmates, or to an audience of adults? Your audience helps determine the focus of your argument. In addition, you can use other helpful strategies to plan your draft. These might include discussing the topic with your classmates, doing some background reading, or thinking about personal interests related to the topic. Use the table below to assist you in planning your draft.

Argument Essay Planning Table	
Genre	Argument
Topic	The necessity for human space travel
Purpose	
Audience	
Ideas from discussions with classmates	
Ideas from background reading	
Personal interests related to topic	

Background Reading Review the notes you have taken in your Response Log after reading the texts in this unit. These texts provide background reading that can help you formulate the key ideas to include in your argument.

Go to **Writing Arguments: Introduction** for help planning your argument.

Notice & Note

From Reading to Writing

As you plan your argument, apply what you've learned about signposts to your own writing. Remember that writers use common features, called signposts, to help convey their message to readers.

Think about how you can incorporate evidence of **Contrasts and Contradictions** into your argument.

Go to the **Reading Studio** for more resources on Notice & Note.

Use the notes from your Response Log as you plan your argument.

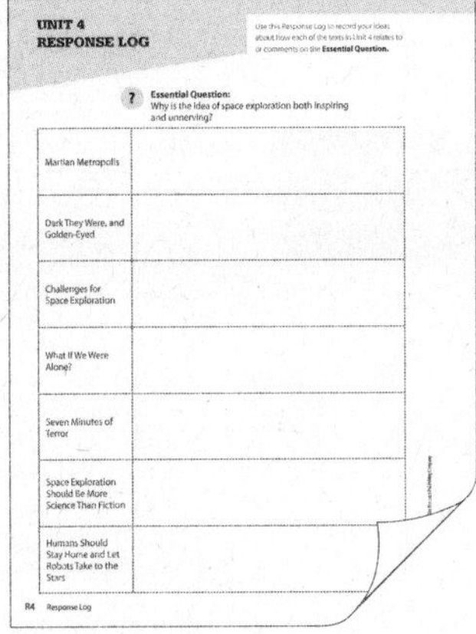

WRITING TASK

Go to **Writing Arguments: Support: Reasons and Evidence** for help organizing your ideas.

Organize Your Ideas After you have gathered ideas from your planning activities, organize your material in a way that will help you draft your argument. You can use the chart below to outline the reasons you will use to support your position and to choose the order of importance in which you will present them. You can also use the chart to gather relevant information and to plan how you will support your reasons with specific facts, details, and examples.

Main Topic: Human Space Travel		
IS HUMAN SPACE TRAVEL NECESSARY?		
First reason to support your position	**Second reason to support your position**	**Third reason to support your position**
Evidence	Evidence	Evidence

You may prefer to draft your argument online.

② Develop a Draft

Once you have completed your planning activities, you will be ready to begin drafting your argument. Refer to your planning table and the completed chart above, as well as any notes you took as you studied the texts in this unit. These will provide a kind of road map for you to follow as you write. Using a computer program for writing or an online writing application makes it easier to rework sentences or move them around later when you are ready to revise your first draft.

Use the Mentor Text

Author's Craft

The introduction to your argument should grab the reader's attention and introduce your claim, or position. In her multi-paragraph introduction to "Challenges for Space Exploration," the author engages readers by presenting an interesting fact and asking a question about it. Her answer suggests the claim she will support.

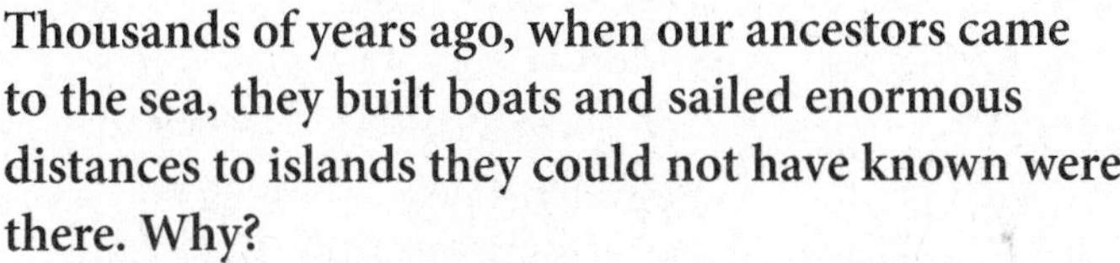

Thousands of years ago, when our ancestors came to the sea, they built boats and sailed enormous distances to islands they could not have known were there. Why?

Probably for the same reason we look up at the moon and the stars and say, "What's up there? Could we go there? Maybe we could go there." Because it's something human beings do.

The author grabs the reader's attention with an interesting fact followed by a question. Her answer allows her to introduce the topic of space exploration and suggest her claim: humans should continue exploring space.

Apply What You've Learned To introduce your argument, you might provide an interesting detail or example to capture your reader's attention and provide context for your claim, or position.

Genre Characteristics

Writers of argumentative texts use reasons to support their position. Notice how the author of "Challenges for Space Exploration" gives a reason to support her opinion about humans' exploration of space.

I could tell you that it might be good for us to unite behind a project that doesn't involve killing one another, that does involve understanding our home planet and the ways we survive on it and what things are crucial to our continuing to survive on it.

One reason the author gives to support her claim is that space exploration will help people be more successful living on Earth and surviving as a species.

Apply What You've Learned The reasons you give should clearly support the position you stated in the introduction. Remember, too, to supply facts, examples, and other evidence to support your reasons.

3 Revise

Go to the **Writing Studio: Concluding Your Argument** for revision help.

On Your Own Once you have written the draft of your argument, you'll want to go back and look for ways to improve your writing. As you reread and revise it, think about whether you have achieved your purpose. The Revision Guide will help you focus on specific elements to make your writing stronger.

Revision Guide		
Ask Yourself	**Tips**	**Revision Techniques**
1. Does my introduction contain a clear claim?	**Highlight** the introduction. **Underline** the claim.	**Add** a claim—the point your argument makes—or **revise** the claim to clarify or strengthen your position on the issue.
2. Are paragraphs arranged in order of importance?	**Number** the paragraphs and identify whether they are presented so that the most important reason comes last.	**Rearrange** paragraphs in order of importance.
3. Do I include at least two reasons to support my argument? Do I support my reasons with evidence?	**Put a star** next to each reason. **Highlight** the supporting evidence for each reason.	**Add** reasons, and/or **include** another specific fact, example, or comparison to further support each reason.
4. Do transitions connect ideas?	**Circle** transitions that connect ideas.	**Add** transitions to connect ideas and clarify the organization.
5. Does my conclusion restate my position and summarize my reasons?	**Underline** the restatement of the claim. **Highlight** the summary of reasons.	**Add** or **revise** a restatement of the claim and a summary of the reasons.

ACADEMIC VOCABULARY

As you conduct your **peer review**, be sure to use these words.

- ❑ **complex**
- ❑ **potential**
- ❑ **rely**
- ❑ **stress**
- ❑ **valid**

With a Partner Once you and your partner have each worked through the Revision Guide on your own, exchange papers and evaluate each other's draft in a **peer review.** Focus on suggesting revisions for at least three of the items mentioned in the chart. Explain why you think your partner's draft should be revised and what specific suggestions you have.

When receiving feedback from your partner, listen attentively and ask questions to make sure you fully understand the revision suggestions.

4 Edit

Once you have addressed the organization, development, and flow of ideas in your argument, look to improve the finer points of your draft. Edit your final draft to check for proper use of standard English conventions and to correct any misspellings or grammatical errors.

CHECK YOUR TONE

A **formal tone** works best for an argument. As you edit your draft, be on the lookout for informal language that might weaken your argument. For example, you wouldn't write, "Space exploration is stupid." Your audience is more likely to be convinced if your tone is more formal, serious, and respectful.

Language Conventions

Pronoun-Antecedent Agreement Effective writers make sure that pronouns agree with their antecedents in number, gender, and person. A **pronoun** (such as *I, you, he, she, we,* and *they*) usually refers to a noun or another pronoun, called its **antecedent.** An **indefinite pronoun** refers to a person, place, or thing that is not specifically named. Examples include *all, both, many, each, none, several,* and *any.* Both kinds of pronouns agree in number—singular or plural—with their antecedents. Some indefinite pronouns, like *each,* are always singular. Others, like *both,* are always plural. And some, like *all* and *none,* can be either singular or plural, depending on the noun they refer to.

Go to **Pronoun-Antecedent Agreement** in the **Grammar Studio** to learn more.

- The astronaut put on **her** spacesuit. [singular antecedent; **singular pronoun**]
- The astronauts put on **their** spacesuits. [plural antecedent; **plural pronoun**]
- All of them put on **their** spacesuits. [indefinite pronoun antecedent, in this case plural because of "them"; plural pronoun; **plural pronoun**]

Consider these examples based on "Challenges for Space Exploration."

Pronoun-Antecedent Agreement	Example
Agreement with an antecedent that is a noun	Voyagers [plural antecedent] to the stars will face dangers unimaginable to their [plural pronoun] ancestors.
Agreement with an antecedent that is an indefinite pronoun	Few [plural indefinite pronoun antecedent], however, would give up their [plural pronoun] chance to explore the universe.

5 Publish

Finalize your argument and choose a way to share it with your audience. Consider these options:

- Present your argument as a speech to the class.
- Post your argument as a blog on a classroom or school website.

WRITING TASK

Use the scoring guide to evaluate your argument.

Writing Task Scoring Guide: Argument			
	Organization/Progression	**Development of Ideas**	**Use of Language and Conventions**
4	• The organization is effective and appropriate to the purpose. • All ideas are focused on the topic specified in the prompt. • Reasons are clearly ordered from least to most important. • Transitions clearly show the relationship among ideas.	• The introduction catches the reader's attention. • The argument contains a clear, concise, and well-defined claim, or position. • The argument is very well developed, with reasons supported by convincing evidence. • The conclusion effectively restates the position and summarizes all the supporting reasons.	• Language and word choice are purposeful and precise. • Pronoun-antecedent agreement is correct. • Spelling, capitalization, and punctuation are correct. • Grammar and usage are correct.
3	• The organization is mostly effective and appropriate to the purpose. • Most ideas are focused on the topic specified in the prompt. • Reasons are ordered from least to most important. • A few more transitions are needed to show the relationship among ideas.	• The introduction could be more engaging. • The argument contains a clear claim, or position. • The argument is well developed, but not every reason is supported by convincing evidence. • The conclusion restates the position but may not summarize all the supporting reasons.	• Language and word choice show some thought but sometimes are ineffective. • Pronoun-antecedent agreement is mostly correct. • Spelling, capitalization, and punctuation are mostly correct, with only a few errors. • Grammar and usage are mostly correct, with only a few errors.
2	• The organization is evident but is not always appropriate to the purpose. • Only some ideas are focused on the topic specified in the prompt. • The order of importance of the reasons is not clear. • More transitions are needed to show the relationship among ideas.	• The introduction is not compelling. • The claim does not express a clear position. • The argument is not well developed and contains only one or two reasons, with evidence that is often unconvincing. • The conclusion does not restate the claim or summarize all the reasons.	• Language and word choice are often vague and general. • There are multiple errors in pronoun-antecedent agreement. • Spelling, capitalization, and punctuation are often incorrect but do not make reading difficult. • Grammar and usage are often incorrect, but the writer's ideas are still clear.
1	• The organization is not appropriate to the purpose. • Ideas are not focused on the topic specified in the prompt. • Reasons do not appear in order of importance. • No transitions are used, making the argument difficult to understand.	• The introduction is missing or confusing. • The claim is missing. • The argument is not well developed, lacking sufficient reasons and evidence. • The conclusion is missing or incomplete.	• Language and word choice are vague and confusing. • There are many errors in pronoun-antecedent agreement. • Many spelling, capitalization, and punctuation errors are present. • Many grammatical and usage errors are present, making the writer's ideas confusing.

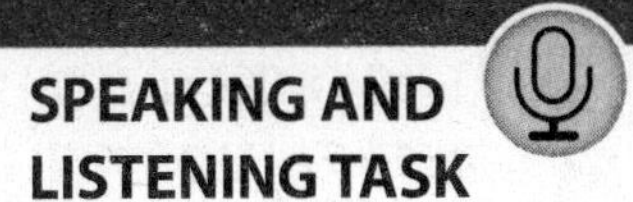

Prepare a Podcast

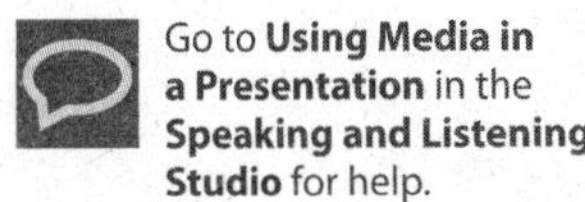

Go to **Using Media in a Presentation** in the **Speaking and Listening Studio** for help.

You have written an argument about the necessity of human space travel. Now you will consider one aspect of space travel: the spacewalk. With a group of your classmates, you will plan and present a 10-minute podcast explaining how this challenging task is accomplished. Each of you will research one aspect of the topic. Then, together, you will create a script for the podcast, practice it with your group, and record it so that you will have a permanent account of your work.

1 Plan Your Podcast Presentation

With your group, divide up the different aspects of a spacewalk that you will research for the podcast. Each group member should choose one of the following topics and become an "expert" in that topic:

- Purposes of spacewalks
- Training that prepares astronauts for a spacewalk
- Spacesuits and other equipment astronauts use on a spacewalk
- The procedure, or steps, for a safe, successful spacewalk

To research spacewalks, you can consult NASA's website and other reliable sources for information. In the chart below, you can answer the questions and take notes on the most important information you find. Then use the completed chart to create a draft of a script for your part of the podcast.

Questions	Answers and Notes
What is the best way to introduce my part of the podcast? How can I grab the audience's attention?	
What information will my audience already know? What information should I leave out or add?	
Which parts of my presentation should I simplify? Where can I add transitions such as *first, second, in addition,* and *finally*? Is my pronoun-antecedent agreement correct?	
What are ways to keep listeners' attention throughout the podcast? How can pacing help to make the discussion among group members more lively? How can participants show a grasp of the topic without becoming bogged down with details?	

As you work to improve your podcast presentation, be sure to follow discussion rules:

- ❑ **Listen closely to one another.**
- ❑ **Don't interrupt.**
- ❑ **Stay on topic.**
- ❑ **Ask only helpful, relevant questions.**
- ❑ **Provide only clear, thoughtful, and direct answers.**

2 Practice with a Partner or Group

Once you've completed the draft of your script, practice with the other "experts" in your group. Work collaboratively to improve one another's section of the podcast and delivery. Make note cards or an outline to guide you as you speak.

Practice Effective Verbal Techniques

- ❑ **Enunciation** Practice words that you stumble over and rearrange sentences so that your delivery is smooth.
- ❑ **Voice Modulation and Pitch** Use your voice to display enthusiasm and to emphasize key details and points.
- ❑ **Speaking Rate** Speak at a pace that allows listeners to understand you. Pause now and then after making a key point.
- ❑ **Volume** Speak loudly enough so that everyone can hear you, but avoid shouting.

Practice Effective Nonverbal Techniques

- ❑ **Eye Contact** Even for a podcast, letting your eyes rest briefly on audience members helps make the delivery feel more natural.
- ❑ **Facial Expressions** Use natural facial expressions, such as smiling, frowning, or nodding, to add emphasis to key points.
- ❑ **Gestures** Stand tall and relaxed. Gesture with your hands to add interest to your delivery and keep it feeling more natural.

Provide and Consider Advice for Improvement

As a presenter, listen closely to questions. Consider ways to revise your section of the podcast so that your key points are clear and logically sequenced. Remember to ask for suggestions about how you might make your presentation more interesting.

As a listener, pay close attention to each presenter. Take notes about ways that presenters can improve their delivery and more effectively use verbal and nonverbal techniques. Paraphrase and summarize each presenter's key points to confirm your understanding, and ask questions to clarify any confusing parts.

3 Record Your Podcast

With your teacher, plan how to record your presentation and share it as a podcast. After everyone in your group has practiced, record your podcast presentation. Then, as a group, review the recording and edit as needed. Share the final version—or just enjoy listening to it on your own!

Reflect on the Unit

By completing your argument, you have created a writing product that helps pull together and express your thoughts about the reading you have done in this unit. Now is a good time to reflect on all that you have learned.

Reflect on the Essential Question

- Why is the idea of space exploration both inspiring and unnerving? How has your response to this question changed since you first considered it when you started this unit?
- What are some examples from the texts you've read that show how people are inspired or unnerved by the idea of space exploration?

Reflect on Your Reading

- Which selections were the most interesting or surprising to you?
- From which selection did you learn the most about the challenges of space exploration, and from which one did you learn the most about its benefits?

Reflect on the Writing Task

- What challenges did you encounter while working on your argument? How might you avoid or overcome them next time?
- What parts of the argument were the easiest and hardest to write? Why?
- As you were revising, how did you decide what improvements to make to strengthen your argument?

Reflect on the Speaking and Listening Task

- What did you find most interesting about preparing the podcast on spacewalking?
- What aspects of verbal and nonverbal communication did you find most challenging as you delivered your presentation—first to your group, and then when you recorded your podcast?
- What did you learn from planning and presenting this podcast that you can use when developing your next presentation?

UNIT 4 SELECTIONS

- **"Martian Metropolis"**
- **"Dark They Were, and Golden-Eyed"**
- **"Challenges for Space Exploration"**
- **"What If We Were Alone?"**
- ***Seven Minutes of Terror* (video)**
- **"Space Exploration Should Be More Science Than Fiction"**
- **"Humans Should Stay Home and Let Robots Take to the Stars"**

UNIT 5

MORE THAN A GAME

ESSENTIAL QUESTION:

How do sports bring together friends, families, and communities?

> "I watched them play the game and get happy . . . and I wanted a chance to be that happy."
>
> Phiona Mutesi

ACADEMIC VOCABULARY

Academic Vocabulary words are words you use when you discuss and write about texts. In this unit you will practice and learn five words.

☑ **attitude** ☐ **consume** ☐ **goal** ☐ **purchase** ☐ **style**

Study the Word Network to learn more about the word **attitude**.

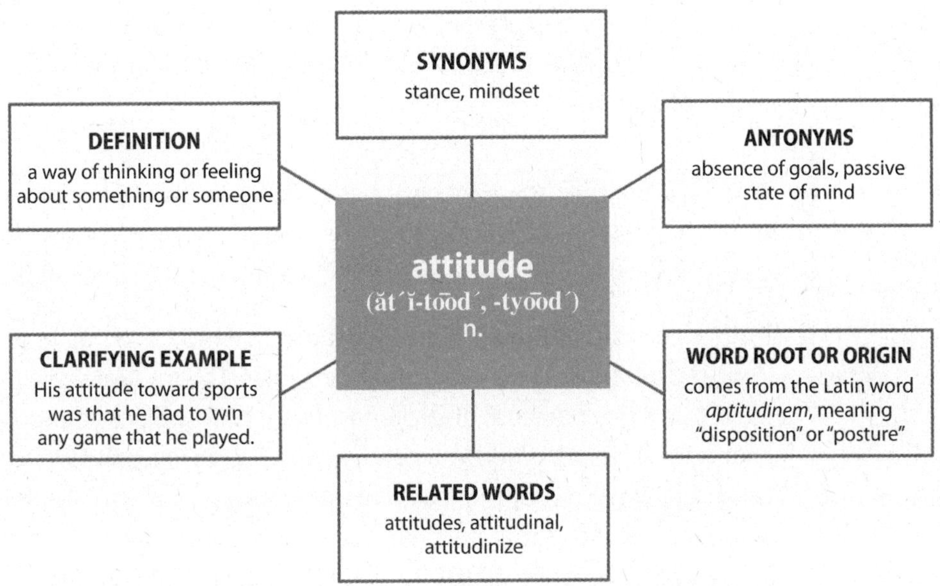

Write and Discuss Discuss the completed Word Network with a partner, making sure to talk through all of the boxes until you both understand the word, its synonyms, antonyms, and related forms. Then, fill out Word Networks for the remaining four words. Use a dictionary or online resource to help you complete the activity.

*Go online to access the **Word Networks**.*

RESPOND TO THE ESSENTIAL QUESTION

In this unit, you will explore how people participate in and respond to games. As you read, you will revisit the **Essential Question** and gather your ideas about it in the **Response Log** that appears on page R5. At the end of the unit, you will have the opportunity to write a **short story** related to sports and games. Filling out the Response Log will help you prepare for this writing task.

*You can also go online to access the **Response Log**.*

Notice & Note

READING MODEL

BALL HAWK

For more information on these and other signposts to Notice & Note, visit the **Reading Studio.**

You are about to read the short story "Ball Hawk." In it, you will notice and note signposts that will give you clues about the story's characters and ideas that are expressed from the narrator's point of view. Here are three key signposts to look for as you read this short story and other works of fiction.

When you read or infer questions like these—questions that express a challenge or, sometimes, serious confusion—pause and ask yourself whether you have found a **Tough Questions** signpost:

"What in the world did you think you were doing?"

"Is this really what you want to do?"

"What could I possibly do?"

"How could I ever understand?"

"Why did this happen?"

Tough Questions You may have been there—in an argument with a friend or a relative. You find yourself asking or answering some tough questions about your feelings or maybe about your relationship.

Authors of fiction often present situations in which a character asks **Tough Questions** that reveal inner struggles. The struggles may be within that character, or they may reveal a struggle that another character is facing. When you come across Tough Questions in a story, ask yourself what they make you wonder about. They usually point to some inner conflict that helps reveal an important idea in the story. The paragraphs below illustrate a student's annotation within "Ball Hawk" and a response to a Notice & Note signpost.

43 "I hate this game!"

44 Uncle Tommy shook his head. "Why did you keep playing it so long?"

45 "Because the other guys won't let me quit. No . . . because my mom wants so bad for me to play baseball."

46 "And why is that?"

47 "Because she's got some idea that Indians should play baseball."

48 "Why?"

49 "Because there are teams with Indian names. Right?"

50 I looked over at Uncle Tommy and he shook his head.

Anchor Question When you notice this signpost, ask: What does this make me wonder about?

What tough questions does Uncle Tommy ask Mitchell?	"Why did you keep playing it [baseball] so long?" Why does his mom want him to play baseball? Why does she think Indians should play baseball?
What inner struggle do these questions reveal? Whose struggle is it?	This is Mitchell's struggle. The questions show that he is struggling to understand why he plays a game that his father was very good at but that he himself is not.

Words of the Wiser To whom do you turn for encouragement or advice? Just as in real life, a story character may offer **Words of the Wiser** to the main character. These words of wisdom or advice often help the main character with a problem. Paying attention to these moments in a story can help readers understand the story's theme or life lesson and how it relates to the main character. In the following example, a student underlined and responded to Words of the Wiser.

28 Sometimes Uncle Tommy made it all seem so easy.

29 "Mitchell," he said, "things that are supposed to come easy aren't always that easy to do."

30 Uncle Tommy, the mind-reading Zen master.

Anchor Question
When you notice this signpost, ask: What's the lesson for the character?

What words of wisdom or advice does the older character give?	"Mitchell, ... things that are supposed to come easy aren't always that easy to do."
What is Uncle Tommy referring to? Why might this be helpful advice for Mitchell?	He is referring to baseball. He is encouraging Mitchell to believe that he can improve his game if he works harder at it.

Aha Moment Have you ever worked for what seemed like hours on a homework problem, only to have the answer come to you all at once, as a "surprise"? These **Aha Moments** happen in fiction, too. For example, a character may realize a problem or its solution, or may suddenly reach a broader undertanding about life. Here, a student marked and responded to an Aha Moment.

When you see phrases like these, pause to see if it's an **Aha Moment**:

"All of a sudden . . ."

"for the first time . . ."

"and just like that . . ."

"I realized . . ."

67 "How can this hawk catch a bird in flight at ninety miles an hour?" Uncle Tommy said.

68 "Because he sees it?" I asked.

69 Uncle Tommy shook his head. He wanted me to think.

70 "Because he sees where it's going to be," I said.

Anchor Question
When you notice this signpost, ask: How might this change things?

What word(s) tell you that Mitchell has realized something about baseball?	"Because he sees where it's going to be."
How might this realization help Mitchell with his conflict?	It might help him change his focus, enabling him to hit the ball more accurately.

BALL HAWK

Short Story by **Joseph Bruchac**

? ***ESSENTIAL QUESTION:***

How do sports bring together friends, families, and communities?

QUICK START

Have you ever struggled to do something that you thought would be easy? Discuss how anxiety might affect how you play a sport.

ANALYZE POINT OF VIEW

In a work of fiction, the **narrator** is the voice that tells the story. The author's choice of narrator becomes a story's **point of view.** Authors choose a point of view in order to give readers a certain perspective on the story. The three types of point of view are shown in this chart.

POINT OF VIEW IN NARRATIVES		
First Person	**Third-Person Limited**	**Third-Person Omniscient ("All-Knowing")**
• Narrator is a story character. • Narrator uses first-person pronouns such as *I*, *me*, *mine*, *we*, *us*, and *our*. • Reader sees events and characters through the narrator's eyes.	• Narrator is not a story character and is outside the story. • Narrator uses third-person pronouns such as *he*, *she*, *him*, *her*, and *their*. • Reader sees events and characters through one character's eyes.	• Narrator is not a story character and is outside the story. • Narrator uses third-person pronouns such as *he*, *she*, *him*, *her*, and *their*. • Reader is shown different characters' thoughts and feelings.

As you read "Ball Hawk," consider how the point of view affects the way you understand the story.

GENRE ELEMENTS: SHORT STORY

- includes the basic elements of fiction—setting, characters, plot (including conflict), and theme
- centers on one particular moment or event in life
- can be read in one sitting

SET A PURPOSE

When you **set a purpose** for reading, you choose one or more specific reasons to read a text. For example, in reading a short story, you might set a purpose of following how an author uses **characterization,** the methods that help develop each character. These methods can include presenting (and commenting about) the character's thoughts, words, and actions, and looking at how the setting influences the characters. An author can also develop a character through other characters' thoughts, words, and actions towards that character.

As you read "Ball Hawk," set the purpose of noticing which methods the author uses to develop the character of Mitchell. Consider how Mitchell responds to the story events, to the setting, and to the other characters—and how other characters respond to him.

GET READY

CRITICAL VOCABULARY

clique **consecutive** **mascot** **federal** **talon**

To see how many Critical Vocabulary words you already know, use them to complete the sentences.

1. In school, he was never part of any particular __________.
2. The owl swooped down and snatched up the field mouse in its __________.
3. Union High School's __________ is a roaring tiger.
4. Because of the blizzard, school was canceled for three __________ days.
5. The __________ budget is approved by the U.S. Congress.

LANGUAGE CONVENTIONS

Commonly Confused Words Many words challenge writers because they look similar and sound alike. Because each word of this kind is actually a word, electronic spell-checkers can't tell if the wrong word is being used. Here are some examples of commonly confused words.

accept / except **affect / effect** **than / then** **to / two / too**

As you read "Ball Hawk," note the spellings of words that are similar, such as *its* and *it* in this example from the text:

A very big bird, the circle of <u>its</u> soaring flight carrying <u>it</u> closer to us.

ANNOTATION MODEL

NOTICE & NOTE

As you read, notice and note signposts, including **Tough Questions, Words of the Wiser,** and **Aha Moments.** In the model, you can see one reader's notes about the opening paragraphs of "Ball Hawk."

1 "Indians invented baseball."

2 That's what Uncle Tommy Fox said on the day <u>I was ready to throw in my glove and quit the Long Pond High School team for</u> good. It was one of his typically cryptic remarks and, as usual, it started me thinking.

The narrator is a player on a school baseball team.

Uncle Tommy has helped the narrator's thinking in the past. Maybe he will be a wise voice in this story.

BACKGROUND

Joseph Bruchac *(b. 1942) lives in Greenfield Center, New York, where he grew up. While he was a student at Cornell University, he began to consider a career as a writer. Today, as a professional storyteller and the author of more than 120 books for adults and young people, Bruchac creates works that often are rooted in the traditions of his Abenaki heritage. He also writes poetry and music that reflect his Native American ancestry.*

BALL HAWK

Short Story by Joseph Bruchac

SETTING A PURPOSE

As you read, pay attention to how Mitchell tries to connect to his late father. Note details that help you understand Mitchell's personality, his feelings and motivations, and the conflict he faces.

1 "Indians invented baseball."

2 That's what Uncle Tommy Fox said on the day I was ready to throw in my glove and quit the Long Pond High School team for good. It was one of his typically cryptic remarks and, as usual, it started me thinking.

3 Quite frankly, if Uncle Tommy hadn't come into my life when he did, I probably would have ended up dyeing my hair purple and going goth.[1] (I would, I might add, have been the first to do that in Long Pond High School, which is barely big enough to have **cliques.** My high school's size is one of the reasons why I was still, pathetic as I was with a glove and a bat, a regular member of the varsity nine. There just weren't that many eligible candidates.)

[1] **going goth**: adopting the thinking and appearance of those who are attracted to things that most people find dark, gloomy, and mysterious.

Notice & Note

Use the side margins to notice and note signposts in the text.

ANALYZE POINT OF VIEW

Annotate: In paragraph 3, mark the words that tell you what point of view the author is using in this story.

Identify: What is that point of view, and what does Mitchell reveal about himself in this paragraph?

clique
(klĭk) *n.* If you are part of a *clique*, you belong to a small group of friends that doesn't allow outsiders.

4 Uncle Tommy, though, saved me from turning my back on being a skin. I'd been hanging around Uncle Tommy ever since he moved up here to work in the Indian Village and my mom introduced him to me in her German accent.

5 "Mitchell, it vould be gut for you to meet anudder real Indianishe mann und he vas ein freund of you vater."

SET A PURPOSE

Annotate: Remember the purpose you have set: noting how the author uses characterization. In paragraph 6, mark Mitchell's thoughts about playing baseball.

Infer: How does Mitchell's attitude toward baseball help to characterize him?

6 It wasn't just that Uncle Tommy was, indeed, a real Indian, albeit of a different tribe than my father. Or that this broad-shouldered old Indian guy with long gray braids and a friendly face really did seem to like me and enjoy taking on that role of being an uncle. Or that he knew more about being Indian, really being Indian, than anyone else I'd ever met. He also had a sense of humor and we both needed it when it came to me and baseball. For some reason, everyone thought I should be playing it. True, I'd always been good at other sports like football and wrestling, but baseball had me buffaloed. My mother had gotten it into her head that being an Indian I should of course not just play baseball but excel at it. Even striking out in nineteen **consecutive** at-bats had failed to disabuse her of that certainty.

consecutive

(kən-sĕk´yə-tĭv) *adj.* When things are *consecutive*, they follow one after another without interruption.

7 Why baseball? Well, as little as my mom knew about American sports, she had heard of the Cleveland Indians and the Atlanta Braves. So she figured it was a game that honored Indians and thus I should be part of it. Yeah, I know. But try to explain to an eager German immigrant mother about stereotyping and American Indians being used as **mascots.**

mascot

(măs´kŏt´) *n.* A *mascot* is a person, animal, or object used as the symbol of an organization, such as a sports team.

8 Plus my dad had been a really great baseball player. He'd been playing armed forces ball when Mom met him in Germany.

9 He was the best baseball player in the history of our family. He was even better than his grandfather, who'd played baseball at the Carlisle Indian School and in the summer Carolina semi-pro leagues with Jim Thorpe.[2] On the ball field, my Dad was unstoppable. He could hit almost any pitch. If he'd had the right breaks, and hadn't gotten his right knee ruined when he was in the service, he could have gone pro.

ANALYZE POINT OF VIEW

Annotate: In paragraph 10, mark Mitchell's description of the aftermath of his father's death.

Critique: How does seeing this description through Mitchell's eyes affect the reader?

10 We played pitch and catch together almost every day during the seven years we shared before his truck was hit head-on by a drunk driver, leaving his half-Indian son to be raised in the sticks by the wife he had brought back with him at the end of his tour of duty with the marines, which had concluded in der Vaterland.[3]

[2] **Jim Thorpe:** Native American athlete (1887–1953), most famous as a track-and-field star and All-American football player but also excelling in a variety of other sports.

[3] **der Vaterland:** German for "the Fatherland," or land of one's ancestors. (Mitchell's mother is German.)

11 Anyhow, going back to that day when I was ready to pack it all in, it was a game we were sure to win. But even though we were leading the Hurleytown Hornets by a score of 6–0 and it was the bottom of the seventh inning, I still had to take at least one more turn at bat. When there's only twelve guys on your whole team and you're the center fielder, you can't avoid it.

12 I wiped my hands on my knees, knocked imaginary dirt off my cleats. Nineteen, I thought.

13 The Hurleytown pitcher smiled when he saw me come up to the plate. All the pitchers in the Northern league did that. Then he mouthed the words. Easy out. I hate it when they do that.

14 I looked over toward the stands. My mom was smiling and nodding at me, even though she had both fists clenched around her soda can so hard that it looked like an hourglass. Uncle Tommy, who was next to her, just kept his face blank. I was grateful for that.

15 The pitcher wound up, kicked high just to show off, and let it go. Fastball, high and outside just where I like it. I took a cut that would have knocked down a wall if I'd been holding a sledgehammer. Unfortunately all I had was a bat. WHIFFF!

16 Strike one.

17 I don't have to tell you what happened with the next two pitches. Just the usual. Twenty in a row.

18 Mercifully, we finished the game without my coming around in the batting order again and us winning 7–1. I took my time in the locker room, soaped my long black hair and rinsed it out twice. Half of me hoped everybody would be gone by the time I came out. But the other half of me desperately wanted to not be alone, wanted somebody to be there waiting for me.

SET A PURPOSE

Annotate: In paragraph 18, mark words and phrases that reveal what Mitchell looks like and how he feels after the game. (Remember: these are methods of characterization.)

Infer: Why do you think Mitchell is confused after the game? What does it suggest about his character?

19 That's what I was thinking as I shuffled out of the gym, my duffel bag in one hand and my towel in the other. Then I saw Uncle Tommy still sitting there, all alone in the bleachers. He raised a hand, gesturing for me to join him.

20 It might have been my mom who encouraged Uncle Tommy to stay around and wait for me. But maybe not. After all, Uncle Tommy had been faithfully watching in the stands each time I whiffed out. He came to all my games, not just football in the the fall, where I'd found my groove in my sophomore year at both tight and D-end. Tackling other ballplayers, blocking and snagging the occasional pass were right up my alley. Unlike trying to tag that white little pill with either glove or bat.

WORDS OF THE WISER

Notice & Note: In paragraph 21, underline Uncle Tommy's comment to Mitchell. Then, circle the later paragraph that explains the meaning of that comment.

Analyze: What is Uncle Tommy trying to tell Mitchell? Why does Mitchell need to be reminded of this?

21 "Indians invented baseball," Uncle Tommy said again. We were sitting at the very top of the stands where we had a great view of the high peaks that were beginning to turn red in the setting April sun. I knew he had to get back to his place and check on the hawks before dark, but he wasn't making a move to stand up, so I stayed put. My uniform was in my bag, but I had pulled my glove out and I was punching my left fist into it.

22 I looked up at him, ready to smile if I saw him grinning. But his face was serious.

23 "You know what I mean," he said.

24 Well, I did. I'd heard the whole rap before. There were no team sports in Europe before those early explorers stumbled into the new world and found Indians playing all kinds of team games—from lacrosse to basketball. Rubber balls were invented by Indians.

25 But I didn't say anything. I just pounded my glove a little harder.

26 Uncle Tommy looked up and nodded his head. I followed his gaze. There was a distant speck getting closer. A very big bird, the circle of its soaring flight carrying it closer to us. It wasn't Hawk or any of the other birds that Uncle Tommy was nursing back to health. It was bigger. An eagle. Pretty soon it was right overhead. I wondered how Uncle Tommy could do that. Call a great bird like that to us.

27 Folks around here knew that whenever anyone came across a big bird that had been hurt, maybe tangled with a power line or sideswiped by a truck, a hawk or an owl or even an eagle like the one above us, they could bring it to Uncle Tommy. He didn't have one of those **federal** licenses to care for birds of prey, but whenever game wardens came out to check on him, they never found anything. Uncle Tommy never caged or tied down any of his birds. He let them fly free. If they were too hurt to fly he kept them somewhere safe that the federal people couldn't find.

federal

(fĕd´ər-əl) *adj.* Something that is *federal* relates to the U.S. government in Washington, D.C., and not to state and local governments.

28 Sometimes Uncle Tommy made it all seem so easy.

29 "Mitchell," he said, "things that are supposed to come easy aren't always that easy to do."

30 Uncle Tommy, the mind-reading Zen master.

31 "Meaning what?" I said, like I was supposed to do.

32 "Do you like playing baseball?" Uncle Tommy asked. Of course he was not answering my question.

33 "Baseball is great," I said. "It's just me. I stink."

34 "Hmm," Uncle Tommy said. Not a question, not a comment, but a lot more than both.

35 "Okay, so I'm good at running bases. Better than most, I guess. And when I do finally get the ball I can throw it hard and straight. But half the time I go out to shag a fly ball, I miss it. You ever notice how when I yell 'I've got it,' all the other fielders start praying?"

36 "Hmm," Uncle Tommy said again. He really wasn't going to let go of this, was he?

37 "Well, what about my batting?" I asked. "The only way I could ever get a hit was if the ball was as big as a watermelon and you set it up on a tee."

38 "And painted a bull's-eye on it?" Uncle Tommy said.

39 I couldn't help it. I had to laugh. For a while. Then I stopped, feeling empty inside.

40 "I quit!" I yelled, standing up and throwing my glove out onto the field. "I'm done with it."

41 Uncle Tommy didn't bat an eye at my temper tantrum. He just kept looking out at the mountains. So I stood there, not sure whether I should climb out of the stands and stomp off or go down on the field and pick up my glove.

42 "Why'd you say that?" Uncle Tommy finally asked in a soft voice.

43 "I hate this game!"

44 Uncle Tommy shook his head. "Why did you keep playing it so long?"

45 "Because the other guys won't let me quit. No . . . because my mom wants so bad for me to play baseball."

46 "And why is that?"

47 "Because she's got some idea that Indians should play baseball."

48 "Why?"

49 "Because there are teams with Indian names. Right?"

50 I looked over at Uncle Tommy and he shook his head.

51 "Mitchell," he said, "I knew your dad when he played ball at Haskell Indian School. My playing days were way behind me then, but I was there teaching in the crafts program. He was

NOTICE & NOTE 

TOUGH QUESTIONS

Notice & Note: In paragraphs 33–40, mark the complaints that Mitchell has about the way he plays baseball.

Analyze: What internal conflict or struggle do these lines reveal?

LANGUAGE CONVENTIONS

Annotate: To recognize the correct spelling of a commonly misspelled word, pay attention to its use in texts. Underscore the words in paragraph 49 that are often misspelled.

Compare: Choose one word and write down the other ways to spell the word. Think of a sentence where each word is used correctly.

NOTICE & NOTE

AHA MOMENT

Notice & Note: Mark the two things that Mitchell suddenly realizes in paragraphs 52 and 53.

Predict: What do you think Mitchell will do, now that he knows why he hasn't been playing well?

SET A PURPOSE

Annotate: In paragraph 58, mark Mitchell's response to Uncle Tommy's telling him that they would start training the next day.

Infer: What does this response suggest about Mitchell?

good enough to have pro scouts looking at him until he decided to go with the military instead. But even then he was a star on those armed forces teams."

52 I started crying then. Uncle Tommy was right. My mom wanted me to play baseball because she knew how much Dad loved the game. She'd met him when she came to one of his games on the base in Germany. She fell in love with the way he ran like a deer after hitting the ball over the fence. Then she fell in love with him.

53 But he'd never be here in the bleachers to watch me play the game he loved best of all. I wanted so badly to connect with him that—even though I knew it was impossible—my mind was twisted against itself whenever I went out onto the field.

54 Uncle Tommy's hand was on my shoulder. He stayed silent until I'd cried myself out. Then he climbed down out of the stands with me when I went to pick up my glove—which had landed far out in left field.

55 "Time to check on the hawks," he said.

56 Uncle Tommy never drove. Instead he'd let me take him places in the old beater truck I'd bought with the money I'd earned working summers with him at the Indian Village, teaching the tourists about real Native people. Neither one of us said anything until we were almost at his place.

57 "Mitchell, maybe your mind is getting clear now, but you still need to train your eye," he said as we pulled in the drive. "We'll start tomorrow morning."

58 I came back at dawn. Of course he was already up and waiting for me with his own glove, a beautiful old Louisville Slugger,[4] and a whole box of baseballs. All stuff that he'd stored in that little attic of his, which somehow seemed to have more storage space than a cargo ship. He'd never let me go up there, but he was always producing unexpected things from it. Like that time he brought down two saddles and blankets and all the gear for riding and roping calves. But that's another story.

59 "Batting practice," he said, pointing at the home plate he had set up against the side of his house.

60 Uncle Tommy had been a pitcher when he was in Indian school and it turned out he could still bring it—fastball, slider, even a tricky little curve.

61 "Focus," he'd say. "Don't see anything except that ball getting bigger. Connect." Then he would whiz another one past me. But by Sunday afternoon I started making contact.

62 "Are you slowing the pitches down?" I said.

[4] **Louisville Slugger:** official bat of Major League Baseball, originally designed by "Bud" Hillerich of Louisville, Kentucky.

63 "Nope." Uncle Tommy smiled. "You are." He got ready to throw again. "Relax with power," he said. "Hard and easy."

64 He had another trick up his sleeve. "The way we always used to learn," he said, "was by watching nature. I got another teacher for you here."

65 He wrapped a deerskin around his arm and we walked out back.

66 "Hawk," he called, holding up his arm. Uncle Tommy never gave names to wild animals more than that. A deer was just "Deer," a bear was just "Bear." But when he called out the word "Hawk," the one hawk he was calling to was always the one that would come. This time it was the big red-tail. It dove down out of the tree, braked with its wings, and reached out its big **talons** to grasp his arm.

67 "How can this hawk catch a bird in flight at ninety miles an hour?" Uncle Tommy said.

68 "Because he sees it?" I asked.

69 Uncle Tommy shook his head. He wanted me to think.

70 "Because he sees where it's going to be," I said.

71 "Go ahead," Uncle Tommy said. He lifted his arm and the hawk took flight. It whistled as it rose and then began circling overhead. I cut a piece of meat from the flank of the road-killed doe we'd picked up from the main road that morning. It was a piece about the size of a baseball. I cocked my left arm and heaved it.

72 Before it could hit the ground, that red-tail caught it out of midair with its claws.

73 Our next game was Wednesday afternoon. Instead of the usual heavy feeling of hopeless despair, I was feeling sick to my stomach. I felt like I might even throw up. And that wasn't a bad thing. Whenever I threw up in the locker room before I went out on the mat to wrestle, I usually ended up doing good. In another couple of minutes we'd be heading out on the field. My gut roiled.

NOTICE & NOTE

ANALYZE POINT OF VIEW

Annotate: Mark the words and phrases in paragraph 66 that suggest that Mitchell thinks Uncle Tommy has a special connection with animals.

Analyze: How does reading about Uncle Tommy from Mitchell's perspective shape the way readers feel about the character of Uncle Tommy?

talon
(tăl′ən) *n.* A *talon* is the claw of a bird of prey.

SET A PURPOSE

Annotate: In paragraph 73, mark words and phrases that describe how Mitchell usually feels before a game and how he is feeling before this game.

Infer: How does this change help to characterize Mitchell?

74 "Excuse me, guys," I said, heading for the john.

75 "Hey," Robby Mills, our shortstop said, "Sabattis is about to lose his lunch."

76 "Cool," Zach Branch said. He was on the wrestling team with me.

77 It wasn't that big a game that day for most of us. It was the Carrier Falls Cougars we were playing and we'd beaten them already a few weeks ago by a score of 4–1, despite my striking out three times. But it was big enough for me. It started in the top of the third inning when I called for a fly ball and not only caught it, but threw it back in quick and hard enough to catch the Cougars runner who'd been on base between second and third. My first double play! Robbie almost cracked my ribs when he came running out from shortstop to hug me.

78 Bottom of the third, I was the second batter up. I looked up just before the pitch and thought I saw a bird circling above the field. Then the pitcher reared back and let it fly. It was a curveball. I saw that clearly as it came toward me. I swear I could even see that there was a smudge of green from the turf on the ball's lacing as it rotated toward me. My swing was strong, but relaxed at the same time. Hard and easy. And I connected.

AHA MOMENT

Notice & Note: In paragraph 79, mark Mitchell's accomplishment.

Predict: What do you think this will mean for Mitchell?

79 The ball hit the sweet spot on the bat. It was a sound half crack and half chunk, a sound I had heard before, just plain music. And the ball was rising, heading up and out, and I knew it was going far past any of the fielders, way out beyond the fence. People were yelling at me to run, but I was just standing there, watching it go, flying toward the sun.

80 And that was when the yelling stopped. It stopped as that hawk dove. It caught the ball in its claws, banked, flapped its wings, and floated off toward the distant mountains, taking what should have been my first home run with it.

81 "You got it, Dad," I whispered. Don't ask me why I said that or if it makes any sense. I mean, I knew it was just Uncle Tommy's red-tail.

82 I turned to the umpire, whose mouth was open as he watched the big bird disappear.

83 "Hey," I said in a soft voice, "I think I know what you should call it." Then I told him.

84 A big grin came to his face and he pointed off in the direction the hawk had gone.

85 He yelled it out and everybody in the park went wild.

86 The pitcher was so rattled by what had happened that he threw me an easy one on his next pitch that I stroked over the third baseman's head for a double.

NOTICE & NOTE

87 I ended up that day with two more doubles and a sacrifice bunt to my credit. We won 5–2. And I played out the rest of that season with a batting average of .285 and a reputation as a better than average fielder. I even had a grand slam home run the last game of the season. But the best moment I ever had in baseball came that day against the Cougars. It came to me because of what Uncle Tommy taught me about letting go of anger and putting my heart in the game. It allowed me to have my best hit ever, even if it ended up being a foul ball.

ANALYZE POINT OF VIEW

Annotate: In paragraph 87, mark sentences that reveal that the narrator is reflecting on that day and what he has learned.

Analyze: Why do you think that the narrator tells this story from the perspective of looking back on events, rather than as they actually are happening? What benefit does this perspective have?

CHECK YOUR UNDERSTANDING

Answer these questions before moving on to the **Analyze the Text** section on the following page.

1 According to Mitchell, what is Uncle Tommy's best characteristic?

A The fact that Uncle Tommy knew Mitchell's father

B The fact that Uncle Tommy is a *real Indian*

C His sense of humor about dealing with life

D His spiritual connection with the natural world

2 The author has Mitchell tell about Uncle Tommy's care for injured birds of prey in order to —

F emphasize Uncle Tommy's compassionate nature

G suggest that Uncle Tommy has a hidden past

H compare Uncle Tommy to a fierce predator

J praise Uncle Tommy's knowledge of Indian folklore

3 According to Mitchell, why was the hit that the hawk intercepted his best hit ever?

A The fact that a hawk had taken his hit earned him the respect of his teammates.

B It was the first hit he made because he truly cared and was no longer angry.

C He knew that the hit was powerful enough to produce a home run.

D It was a great hit, which he followed with other good hits in the same game.

RESPOND

ANALYZE THE TEXT

Support your responses with evidence from the text. NOTEBOOK

1. **Analyze** Review paragraphs 3 and 10. What point of view is used in describing the setting in which Mitchell lives? How does this setting affect Mitchell as a character?
2. **Infer** Refer to your "Set a Purpose" notes about Mitchell's characterization. Why do you think that Uncle Tommy twice reminds Mitchell that "Indians invented baseball"? Why are these words an important part of Mitchell's characterization?
3. **Interpret** In the language of baseball, a "ball hawk" is a player who is skilled in catching fly balls. Why is "Ball Hawk" an appropriate title for this story?
4. **Analyze** When a writer provides hints that suggest future events in a story, it's called **foreshadowing.** Identify and explain an example of foreshadowing in "Ball Hawk."
5. **Notice & Note** What does Uncle Tommy do to help Mitchell overcome his anger and work on his baseball skills?

RESEARCH

Like Mitchell's father, many well-known Major League Baseball players were (and are) Native Americans. Research these baseball players. Record details abut their origins, teams, and achievements.

BASEBALL PLAYER	ACHIEVEMENTS
Louis Sockalexis	
Charles Albert Bender	
Zachariah Davis Wheat	

RESEARCH TIP

When you scan search results, look for websites that are more likely to include information that is accurate and current. This includes sites that end in *.gov*, *.org*, and *.edu*. For sites that end in *.com*, use your judgment. Ask yourself who published the information and what the purpose might be. Evaluate whether the information seems credible, well researched, and unbiased.

Extend In the first paragraph of Bruchac's story, Uncle Tommy notes that "Indians invented baseball." In fact, there were other ways that Indians became familiar with the game. Find out how a lot of Native Americans were introduced to baseball in the 1800s and 1900s.

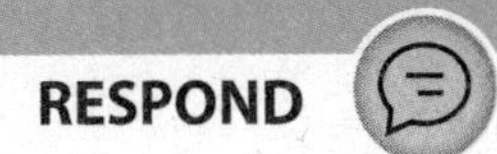

CREATE AND ADAPT

Go to **Writing Narratives** in the **Writing Studio** to help with the epilogue.

Write an Epilogue Write a three- to four-paragraph epilogue or concluding section in which you describe Mitchell's views of baseball a year after the story ends.

- ❑ Brainstorm how you think Mitchell will feel about baseball and about himself in a year.
- ❑ Begin your epilogue by noting where Mitchell is in a year and what he's doing. You may want to continue to write the story from the first-person point of view to help you explore Mitchell's concerns.
- ❑ End the epilogue by explaining how Mitchell feels about baseball and whether he plans to continue playing.

Go to **Participating in Collaborative Discussions** in the **Speaking and Listening Studio** for help.

Create a Baseball Card Using details from the story and your own imagination, create a baseball card for Mitchell.

- ❑ As a group, review the text and note details about Mitchell's appearance, background, and batting average. Find baseball cards online to use as a reference for the card's design and layout.
- ❑ Create your card. Draw a picture of Mitchell on the front. Put biographical information and batting average on the back.
- ❑ Share and compare your card with the cards that a few classmates created. Discuss the differences in how you portrayed Mitchell and what specific details from the story shaped your portrayal.

RESPOND TO THE ESSENTIAL QUESTION

? How do sports bring together friends, families, and communities?

Gather Information Review your annotations and notes on "Ball Hawk." Then, add relevant details to your Response Log. As you determine which information to include, think about:

- how Mitchell changed
- why Uncle Tommy was important
- how seeing events through Mitchell's eyes affected the story

At the end of the unit, use your notes to help you write a short story.

ACADEMIC VOCABULARY

As you write and discuss what you learned from the short story, be sure to use the Academic Vocabulary words. Check off each of the words that you use.

- ❑ **attitude**
- ❑ **consume**
- ❑ **goal**
- ❑ **purchase**
- ❑ **style**

CRITICAL VOCABULARY

WORD BANK
clique
consecutive
mascot
federal
talon

Practice and Apply Mark the letter of the answer to each question.

1. Which of the following is an example of a **federal** employee?
   a. the president of the U.S. **b.** the governor of your state
2. Which of the following would have a **talon**?
   a. an eagle **b.** a sparrow
3. Which of the following would more likely be a team **mascot**?
   a. a ship **b.** a panther
4. Which of the following is three **consecutive** days?
   a. Monday, Wednesday, Friday **b.** Thursday, Friday, Saturday
5. Which of the following would more likely be found in a **clique**?
   a. a popular group of friends **b.** the best athletes in a league

VOCABULARY STRATEGY: Word Origins

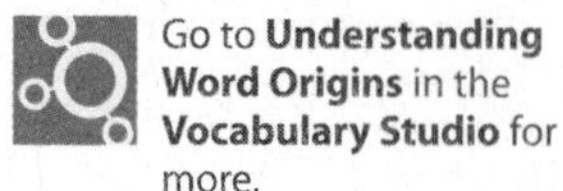
Go to **Understanding Word Origins** in the **Vocabulary Studio** for more.

Etymologies show the origin of a word across time. Being aware of the origin and historical development of an unfamiliar word can help you understand how the current word form evolved. Study this example of the etymology of the Critical Vocabulary word *talon.*

Middle English *taloun* < Old French *talon,* heel < Latin *talus,* ankle

The etymology for *talon* shows that the word is from Middle English but has its root in a Latin word meaning "ankle."

Practice and Apply Use a dictionary to find the etymology of each Critical Vocabulary word in the chart below. Record what you learn.

CRITICAL VOCABULARY WORD	ETYMOLOGY
clique	
mascot	

LANGUAGE CONVENTIONS: Commonly Confused Words

Words that sound alike but have different meanings and different spellings can cause problems for writers. Look at this example from "Ball Hawk."

"Baseball is great," I said. "It's just me. I stink."

In this example, *it's* (meaning "it is") is often confused with *its* (the possessive form of *it*). Some other commonly confused words include *accept/except, past/passed, affect/effect, there/their/they're,* and *to/two/too.*

It is important to review your writing to make sure that you are using commonly confused words correctly. People reading your work may not understand your message if you use words incorrectly. Rereading your writing to correct any errors will help you communicate more effectively. If you are unsure about which spelling to use in a sentence, consult a dictionary and determine which word has the meaning that will fit in your sentence.

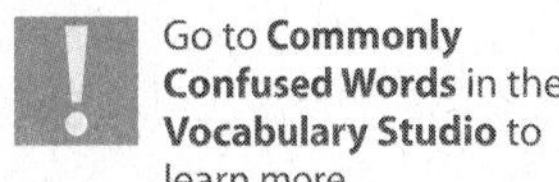
Go to **Commonly Confused Words** in the **Vocabulary Studio** to learn more.

Practice and Apply Mark the word that correctly completes each sentence. Then write the meaning of the word on the line.

1. Janine didn't want the game to (**affect/effect**) her friendship with Laila.

   ____

2. The basketball players wanted (**their/there/they're**) own jerseys.

   ____

3. Mitchell swung the bat (**to/two/too**) soon.

   ____

4. Everyone in the bleachers (**accept/except**) Jake's parents cheered the referee's call.

   ____

5. Uncle Tommy didn't want the (**past/passed**) to upset Mitchell.

   ____

ANALYZE & APPLY

GET IN THE ZONE: THE PSYCHOLOGY OF VIDEO GAME DESIGN

Informational Text by **Aaron Millar**

? ***ESSENTIAL QUESTION:***

How do sports bring together friends, families, and communities?

QUICK START

Describe an experience that you or a character in a film or TV show has had while playing a video game. What was the player's focus? Did anything unexpected happen?

PREDICT

Making predictions as you read nonfiction texts means making an educated guess about what the author will discuss next. As you read on, you may confirm or change that prediction. Identifying clues in elements such as the following can help you make predictions.

- **Text Features:** Subheadings, boldfaced words, and graphics often reveal ideas that you can use to inform your predictions.
- **Structures:** The organization of the text (for example, cause/effect or sequence) helps you predict what the author will explain next.

Use the chart below as you analyze the selection.

PREDICTION	TEXT EVIDENCE THAT CONFIRMS IT

GENRE ELEMENTS: INFORMATIONAL TEXT

- provides factual information and/or explanations
- presents evidence to support key ideas
- often contains text features, such as subheadings
- includes magazine and newspaper articles, legal documents, essays, and speeches

ANALYZE SUBJECTIVE AND OBJECTIVE POINT OF VIEW

Point of view refers to the perspective from which an article is written. A first-person point of view uses pronouns such as *I*, *me*, and *we*. A third-person point of view uses pronouns such as *he*, *she*, *it*, and *they*. Authors of nonfiction write in a subjective or objective point of view.

- When using a **subjective point of view,** an author includes personal thoughts, opinions, and emotions.
- When using an **objective point of view,** an author presents fact-based information in an unbiased way.

The author uses language to develop his or her **voice,** or unique style, and **tone,** or attitude toward a subject. Voice and tone can influence point of view. As you read the selection, consider how the author's use of language shapes voice and tone and develops point of view, and think about the author's purpose in choosing a specific point of view.

GET READY

CRITICAL VOCABULARY

absorb **wholly** **immerse** **irrelevant** **disorient**

To see how many Critical Vocabulary words you already know, use them to complete these sentences.

1. Waking up in the middle of the night can __________ someone.
2. While traveling in Spain, Becca tried to __________ local customs.
3. The committee ignored Raul's objections to the new regulations, calling them __________ to the discussion.
4. Jonathan would__________ himself in his notes to study for tests.
5. She dedicated her time __________ to learning to play guitar.

LANGUAGE CONVENTIONS

Comma Splices and Run-On Sentences A comma splice is a punctuation error. It happens in compound sentences when a comma is used when there is no coordinating conjunction. One way to correct this error is to use a semicolon (;) to separate the independent clauses.

I played the video game for two hours, I finally won.

I played the video game for two hours; I finally won.

A run-on sentence occurs when two or more sentences are written as if they were one sentence. Authors avoid run-ons by separating the sentences or with punctuation and coordinating conjuntions.

ANNOTATION MODEL

NOTICE & NOTE 

As you read, look for places where you might make predictions. You can also mark details that suggest the author's point of view. In the model, you can see one reader's notes about one part of the text.

2 Sound familiar?

3 Frustration is something every gamer knows all too well. But why do some video games completely absorb us in their world while others leave us howling at the screen? The answer has less to do with your ability to press buttons than it does with what's happening in your brain. Good games are designed to get you "in the zone" —a heightened state of concentration, and enjoyment, that psychologists call flow.

The author asks a question. I predict that he'll explain why gaming experiences vary.

Facts are given with no emotion or opinion.

BACKGROUND

There's no question that video games are a popular pastime. From the appearance of the first video-game consoles and arcade video games in the 1970s to today's generation of online 3D and virtual reality games, they have captured the attention of players of all ages. Players have their favorite games—but what makes some games more popular than others? In this selection, author Aaron Millar gives his answer to that question.

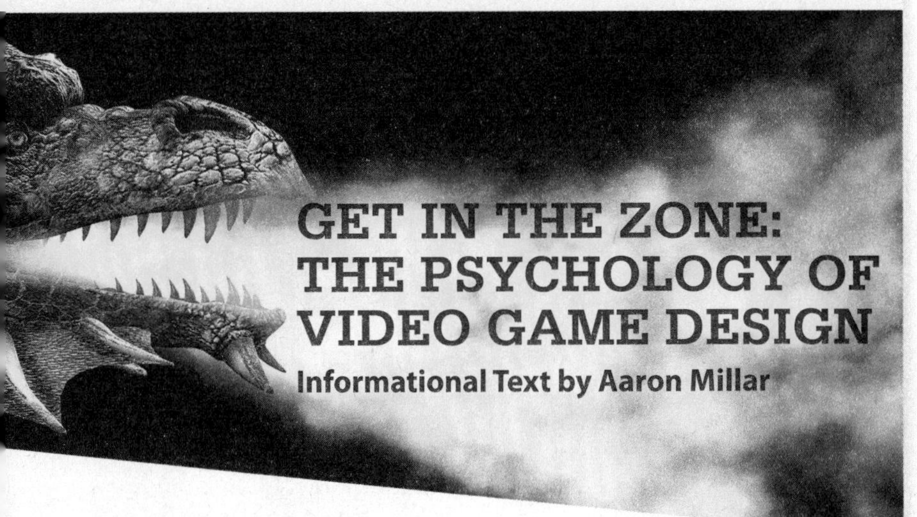

GET IN THE ZONE: THE PSYCHOLOGY OF VIDEO GAME DESIGN

Informational Text by Aaron Millar

SETTING A PURPOSE

As you read, pay attention to clues in the text that help you predict what the author will discuss in each section. Think, too, about whether the author's point of view is largely subjective, largely objective, or a mix of both—and how you can tell.

1 The dragon rises above me, breathing flames into the night air. Stone ramparts crumble in the township; houses burn. Screams echo all around me. I have only one chance. His jaws open. I draw my sword. But before I can react he's snatching me into his talons, throwing me in his mouth, and the hero … dies. In exactly the same place. Again. It's completely unfair. I throw my control pad on the floor, scream at the screen, and walk out of my bedroom in disgust.

2 Sound familiar?

3 Frustration is something every gamer knows all too well. But why do some video games completely **absorb** us in their world while others leave us howling at the screen? The answer has less to do with your ability to press buttons

Notice & Note

Use the side margins to notice and note signposts in the text.

ANALYZE SUBJECTIVE AND OBJECTIVE POINT OF VIEW

Annotate: Mark details in paragraph 1 in which the author is talking about himself.

Critique: Why do you think the author chose this point of view? How does this convey the author's voice?

absorb
(əb-zôrb´) *v.* Things that *absorb* you occupy your time or attention.

NOTICE & NOTE

than it does with what's happening in your brain. Good games are designed to get you "in the zone"—a heightened state of concentration, and enjoyment, that psychologists call flow.

QUOTED WORDS

Notice & Note: Mark the explanation that Jamie Madigan gives in paragraph 4.

Evaluate: What topic is Madigan explaining? Why is he qualified to speak about this topic?

4 In a state of flow even the most difficult tasks feel effortless and easy to complete. Just beat your best lap time by 10 seconds? That's flow. Killed the monster you were stuck on for two weeks? Welcome to the zone. "In a flow state," explains psychologist Jamie Madigan, author of psychologyofvideogames.com, "you don't have to think. Your performance is automatic. The rest of the world falls away and you are **wholly** focused on the screen." Top athletes and rock stars describe this state of mind when they're performing at their best. But gamers have an edge: unlike the real world, video games are designed to get us into this state as quickly as possible—and keep us there. It's why we play: flow is fun. But some games are better than others. And here's why.

wholly
(hō´lē) *adv.* If a speech deals *wholly* with the history of the solar system, that is the only topic the speaker discusses.

NOTICE & NOTE 

Challenge

5 If you kill the dragon the first time, it's boring; don't kill him the hundredth time and it's just plain annoying. Flow happens only when there's a perfect balance between the challenge of the game and the skill level of the player. "It should be difficult," Madigan says, "but just possible."

6 The reason has to do with the amount of information our minds can hold at any one time. Imagine your brain is like a backpack. If it's filled to the top with just the skills required for the game, there's no room left for any distractions. You're completely **immersed** in that imaginary world. But put in too much and your backpack will break—you'll get stressed and fed up with playing; too little, and you'll start thinking about that party next week.

7 It's a delicate balancing act: in order to keep us in the zone, games have to increase their level of difficulty at precisely the same rate at which players improve their level of skill. And

PREDICT
Annotate: Mark the subheading that introduces paragraphs 5–7. Predict what you think will be discussed under that subheading.

Analyze: Review your prediction after you read the section. Did the text reflect your predictions? Explain.

immerse
(ĭ-mûrs´) *v.* If you *immerse* yourself in an activity, that activity is the only thing that you are focused on.

NOTICE & NOTE

everyone's different. "The secret," according to Madigan, "is designing games that have really clear feedback so that you know when you're doing something well or poorly, and why."

Focus

8 Imagine fighting a horde of zombies while being distracted by something out the window. Not easy, right? Flow requires focus. The games we love force us to concentrate at just the right level—but in order to get us in the zone, they must *direct* our concentration in the right way too.

9 That's because focus, our ability to pay attention, is like a flashlight beam—it can only shine on one or two things at a time. Too much information, or **irrelevant** info, on screen and our focus blows a fuse. We become **disoriented,** unmotivated, and unsure of what to do. The zombies win.

irrelevant
(ĭ-rĕl´ə-vənt) *adj.* Something that is *irrelevant* is unrelated to the matter under consideration.

disorient
(dĭs-ôr´ē-ĕnt´) *v.* To *disorient* is to make someone or something lose a sense of direction.

10 Ever been lost in a dungeon, not sure if you're supposed to find a key, move a block, or start again? That's bad flow. The best game designers keep us in the zone by steering our attention, like movie directors, from one challenge to the next—we're simply along for the ride.

Reward

11 Fighting the dragon should be fun, but we need a reason to keep trying too. Goals are built into games to keep us coming back for more. But goals without rewards are like pancakes without maple syrup: hard to swallow and a lot less sweet.

PREDICT
Annotate: In paragraph 11, mark where the author says that goals need to become "sweet."
Predict: What do you predict will be the author's focus in this final section?

12 That's because rewards release a chemical called dopamine in our brain, which feels good. When you get an A+ on your test, that warm feeling inside is the reward center of your brain having a party. And that same chemical is released by virtual rewards too. Just leveled up, or beat your best score? Hello, dopamine.

13 The key, according to Madigan, is designing games with "micro-rewards that are linked to longer term goals." Saving the king is a worthy mission, but should I storm the castle or sneak in undetected? The best games break long-term goals into clear, manageable chunks and reward us for achieving each one: search the store room for a grappling hook; steal the key from the guards; scale the tallest tower. Bingo. The king's free and has just given me my own province to rule.

ANALYZE SUBJECTIVE AND OBJECTIVE POINT OF VIEW
Annotate: Mark one opinion that appears in this section.
Analyze: Does the fact that an opinion is included mean that this whole section has a subjective point of view? Why or why not?

14 Rewards are like fuel for flow. We need to keep filling up if we're going to slay the dragon, build our empire, and make it to the end of the game.

PSYCHOLOGICAL EDGE: TIPS FOR GAMERS

- Games are most fun when the level of difficulty is just above your level of skill. It should be hard, but not impossible. If you're screaming at the screen, it's probably a mismatch. Try manually adjusting the level of challenge instead.
- Increase your gaming flow by removing distractions before you play: turn off the lights, stop texting, and focus all your attention on the screen.
- If the game feels too open-ended, or you're not sure what to do next, try breaking down big goals into more immediate and manageable chunks.

CHECK YOUR UNDERSTANDING

Answer these questions before moving on to the **Analyze the Text** section on the following page.

1 In paragraph 3, the author introduces the idea of "flow" in order to —

A describe a strategy used by successful players of video games

B explain why some video games are better than others

C show how creators of video games work together

D encourage readers to try different kinds of video games

2 According to the section called <u>CHALLENGE</u>, why do players of video games often give up?

F The game requires too much button pressing in complicated patterns.

G The game has been designed to be impossible to win.

H The game contains too much information that is not really important.

J The game requires concentration but does not offer much enjoyment.

3 What is the purpose of the bulleted points in the final section?

A They give readers advice about how to play video games better and enjoy them more.

B They summarize the kinds of rewards that players of video games like best.

C They present the main points regarding "flow."

D They list and rate several popular video games.

ANALYZE THE TEXT

Support your responses with evidence from the text. NOTEBOOK

1. **Summarize** Reread paragraphs 3 and 4. Then summarize in a few sentences what the author means by "flow" in video games.
2. **Analyze** Where in the text does the point of view change, and how does it change? How does the structure of the article help express the author's attitude toward the subject?
3. **Cause/Effect** According to the article, how do micro-rewards affect the player's experience of the game? How are they related to the achievement of long-term goals?
4. **Analyze** What are two different types of evidence the writer offers to support his discussion of the concept of flow? Which type of evidence do you think is more effective? Explain.
5. **Notice & Note** Reread Madigan's quotation in paragraph 7. Based on what you know about him from paragraph 4, how do you think he came to understand feedback in video games?

RESEARCH

RESEARCH TIP
General questions, like the ones in this chart, are a good way to start doing your research. However, be ready to get more specific. As you start to see results, you may want to rephrase your questions, or create new and more precise questions, to search for the best, most interesting information.

In a small group, research a career in video game development. Think about which aspects of video game development you want to know more about. For example, are you interested in coming up with gaming concepts, programming them, or creating visuals? Find out about the skills needed for this career.

QUESTION	ANSWER
Which career in video games interests me the most?	
What kind of training and education do I need for this career?	
What are some of the challenges and rewards of this career?	

Extend Find out about a video gaming convention that takes place each year. Which companies exhibit during these conferences? What are some of the career-related activities that take place?

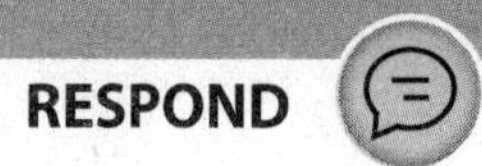

CREATE AND ADAPT

Write an Objective Summary Write a summary of "Get in the Zone: The Psychology of Video Game Design."

- ❑ Review the text, your answers to the guided reading questions, and any other notes you made while reading.
- ❑ Remember that the text is organized into sections. Write a summary for each section; then put section summaries together.
- ❑ Make sure that the summary includes only the most important information. You don't want to include every detail.
- ❑ Use your own words, but stick to the facts. To make the summary objective, leave out your personal feelings and opinions.

Discuss a Video Game Adapt what you learned in "Get in the Zone: The Psychology of Video Game Design" to a discussion about another game. In a small group, give a rating to a video game you have played (or would like to play) in terms of the concept of flow.

- ❑ Choose a specific game. In the discussion, include precise details about the game.
- ❑ Describe your experience (real or imagined) in playing the game. In particular, evaluate its flow—that is, how well it makes you concentrate on and enjoy the action.
- ❑ Offer praise about the game or suggestions for improving it.

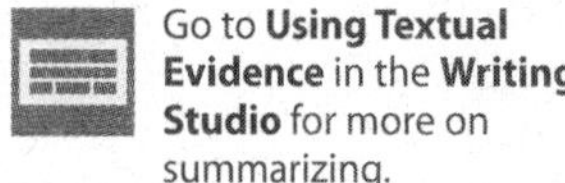
Go to **Using Textual Evidence** in the **Writing Studio** for more on summarizing.

RESPOND TO THE ESSENTIAL QUESTION

? How do sports bring together friends, families, and communities?

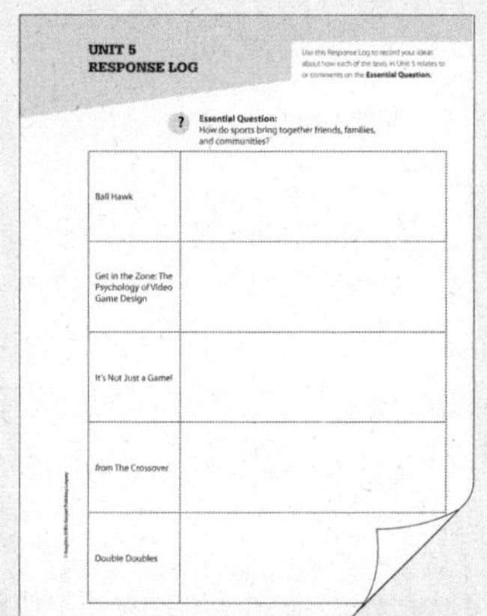

Gather Information Review your notes on "Get in the Zone: The Psychology of Video Game Design." Then, add details to your Response Log. As you determine which information to include, think about:

- your experience with video games
- what makes playing video games enjoyable

At the end of the unit, use your notes to help you write a short story.

ACADEMIC VOCABULARY

As you write about and discuss what you learned from the informational text, be sure to use the Academic Vocabulary words. Check off each of the words that you use.

- ❑ **attitude**
- ❑ **consume**
- ❑ **goal**
- ❑ **purchase**
- ❑ **style**

RESPOND

CRITICAL VOCABULARY

WORD BANK
absorb
wholly
immerse
irrelevant
disorient

Practice and Apply Mark the letter of the word whose meaning is similar to each Critical Vocabulary word. Verify your answers using an online dictionary or thesaurus.

1. absorb:	**a.** bleed	**b.** consume	**c.** sing
2. wholly:	**a.** totally	**b.** partially	**c.** fortunately
3. immense:	**a.** enormous	**b.** intelligent	**c.** miniature
4. irrelevant:	**a.** dreamlike	**b.** appropriate	**c.** unnecessary
5. disorient:	**a.** clarify	**b.** confuse	**c.** doubt

VOCABULARY STRATEGY: Context Clues

Go to **Context Clues** in the **Vocabulary Studio** for more.

When you come across an unfamiliar word in a text, use the following strategy to determine the word's meaning.

Step 1	Step 2	Step 3	Step 4
Determine the likely meaning using **context**, the surrounding words and sentences.	Substitute the likely meaning for the word in the sentence to see if it makes sense.	Look up the word in a print or digital dictionary to verify the likely meaning.	Determine which definition after the entry word best fits with the context.

Look at this example from "Get in the Zone: The Psychology of Video Game Design":

> **We become *disoriented*, unmotivated, and unsure what to do.**

The nearby phrase *unsure what to do* provides a clue: The meaning of *disoriented* has something to do with a feeling of confusion. Try using *confused* instead of *disoriented* in the sentence. Both meanings make sense. A dictionary verifies the meaning by giving this definition for *disoriented*: "mentally confused or losing a sense of direction."

Practice and Apply Find the sentence containing the word *undetected* in paragraph 13 of the selection. Then, use the four steps above to determine the word's meaning. Write it below.

LANGUAGE CONVENTIONS: Comma Splices and Run-on Sentences

The **semicolon** (;) is a punctuation mark that has a variety of uses. For example, when two independent clauses express complete and related ideas, a semicolon can be used to connect them, rather than a comma plus a coordinating conjunction. In this example from "Get in the Zone: The Psychology of Video Game Design," the semicolon takes the place of a comma and the coordinating conjunction *and*.

Stone ramparts crumble in the township; houses burn.

In your own writing, you can use semicolons to avoid **comma splices** (which occur when only a comma is used to connect independent clauses) and **run-on sentences** (which occur when there is no punctuation or conjunction to connect independent clauses). Note these examples.

COMMA SPLICE: This new video game is terrific, in fact, I could play it every day.
REVISION: This new video game is terrific; in fact, I could play it every day.

RUN-ON SENTENCE: I'm going to tell Jalayne about this game she will probably want to play it with me.
REVISION: I'm going to tell Jalayne about this game; she will probably want to play it with me.

Practice and Apply Use semicolons to correct the error in each of the following sentences. Then identify whether the original sentence had a comma splice or was a run-on sentence.

1. Jalayne is an experienced player I'm just a beginner.
2. There are some terrific video games on sale this weekend the store is clearing the shelves to make room for a new shipment.
3. Jalayne has been to a video game conference in San Antonio, Texas, next week she will attend one in Richmond, Virginia.

Now draft your own paragraph about what makes video games captivating. Look for ways to connect related ideas, such as using semicolons. Edit your draft to make sure you avoid comma splices and run-on sentences.

Go to **Run-on Sentences** and **Semicolons** in the **Grammar Studio** to learn more.

IT'S NOT JUST A GAME!

Informational Text by **Lori Calabrese**

? *ESSENTIAL QUESTION:*

How do sports bring together friends, families, and communities?

QUICK START

Do you like to play sports? Watch sports? Discuss with a partner how important you think sports are to people's lives today, and why.

SET A PURPOSE

Before reading an informational text, you'll want to **set a purpose**—that is, make a plan for what you want to get out of your reading. One tool for setting a purpose is a K-W-L Chart. You can use a chart like this one to list what you already know about the topic (in this case, sports) and what you want to know as you read. Then, as you read and afterward, you can record what you learned from the text.

What I **K**now	
What I **W**ant to Know	
What I **L**earned	

This technique can help you monitor your comprehension and decide when you need to reread, ask questions, use what you already know, or make notes to help you understand the text.

GENRE ELEMENTS: INFORMATIONAL TEXT

- provides facts and explanations
- includes details that support a main idea about the topic
- answers *who, what, where, when, why,* and/or *how* questions
- may include text features such as subheadings to help organize information

ANALYZE ORGANIZATIONAL PATTERNS

Effective informational writing almost always follows an **organizational pattern,** or structure. For example, an author may present information in chronological order (the time order in which events happened) or in order of importance (usually with the most important information at the end).

Sometimes, however, an author chooses a **descriptive pattern.** The author presents a variety of kinds of information about the topic—historical background, characteristics, examples, comments from experts, comparisons, and so on. To give structure to the presentation, the author may use subheadings, such as these examples from "It's Not Just a Game!"

Different Sports for Different Folks
Making Sports Work for Us

As you read "It's Not Just a Game!" look for the ways in which the author presents various kinds of information. Consider how each kind of information helps you understand the topic.

GET READY

CRITICAL VOCABULARY

accomplishment **negotiate** **mutual** **isolate** **utilization**

To see how many Critical Vocabulary words you already know, write the word asked for in each question.

1. Which word goes with *separate*? ______________
2. Which word goes with *achievement*? ______________
3. Which word goes with *shared*? ______________
4. Which word goes with *discuss* and *bargain*? ______________
5. Which word goes with *use* and *implementation*? ______________

LANGUAGE CONVENTIONS

Complex Sentences and Subject-Verb Agreement In this text, you will see several **complex sentences**—sentences made from one independent clause and at least one subordinate clause. A complex sentence, therefore, contains at least two examples of a subject and verb working together. In every case, the subject and verb need to **agree** in number. Note these examples:

Whether you run a race, bounce a basketball, or hurl a baseball home, you do it because it's [it is] fun.

That might explain why sports are likely to be as old as humanity.

As you read and write about "It's Not Just a Game!" remember the importance of subject-verb agreement in complex sentences.

ANNOTATION MODEL

NOTICE & NOTE

As you read, mark details you connect to and details you want to learn more about. You can also mark information that the author uses to describe her topic and note how it helps you understand. In the model, you can see one reader's notes about a section of "It's Not Just a Game!"

1 Whether you run a race, bounce a basketball, or hurl a baseball home, you do it because it's fun. Some scientists claim play is a natural instinct—just like sleep. That might explain why [sports are likely to be as old as humanity.]

These are sports I know. I like running and playing hoops.

"as old as humanity" = I hope the author follows up with more historical info about sports.

BACKGROUND

Lori Calabrese *worked as a TV producer for ten years before deciding to become a writer after the birth of her children. Her first book was the well-received picture book* The Bug That Plagued the Entire Third Grade. *She also has written many nonfiction articles for young people, including "It's Not Just a Game!" Calabrese says that she is "forever probing people and places in search of information." "I love research," she admits—"in fact, I can't get enough."*

IT'S NOT JUST A GAME!

Informational Text by Lori Calabrese

SETTING A PURPOSE

As you read, think about what you like and dislike about sports. How does the information the author presents give you more insights into the wide world of sports—and into your own experiences with them?

1 Whether you run a race, bounce a basketball, or hurl a baseball home, you do it because it's fun. Some scientists claim play is a natural instinct—just like sleep. That might explain why sports are likely to be as old as humanity.

2 Some claim sports began as a form of survival. Prehistoric man ran, jumped, and climbed for his life. Hunters separated themselves by skill, and competition flourished. Wall paintings dating from 1850 B.C., that depict wrestling, dancing, and acrobatics, were discovered in an Egyptian tomb at Bani Hasan.[1] The Ancient Greeks

Notice & Note

Use the side margins to notice and note signposts in the text.

ANALYZE ORGANIZATIONAL PATTERNS

Annotate: In paragraph 2, mark references to three groups of people from the past.

Analyze: Review the entire paragraph. How does the author use time order to organize information?

[1] **Bani Hasan** (bän′ē hä-sŏn′): ancient Egyptian burial site, located along the Nile River.

NOTICE & NOTE

revolutionized sports by holding the world's first Olympic games at Olympia in 776 B.C. But it wasn't until the early nineteenth century, that sports as we know them came into play. (Pardon the pun!) Modern sports such as cricket,[2] golf, and horse racing began in England and spread to the United States, Western Europe, and the rest of the world. These sports were the models for the games we play today, including baseball and football.

SET A PURPOSE

Annotate: In paragraph 3, mark the evidence that supports the idea that organized sports are serious play.

Connect: Did you already know this information? Explain.

3 All organized sports, from swimming to ice hockey, are considered serious play. There are rules to obey, skills and positions to learn, and strategies to carry out. But Peter Smith, a psychology professor at Goldsmiths, University of London, and author of *Understanding Children's Worlds: Children and Play* (Wiley, 2009), says, "Sport-like play is usually enjoyable, and done for its own sake."

Different Sports for Different Folks

4 Sports come in many shapes and sizes. Both team and individual sports have advantages and disadvantages, but most people find that from an early age, they are drawn toward one or the other. In a team sport like soccer, you're part of a group, striving to be a winning team. That means putting the team ahead of your own **accomplishments.** You must learn to get along with your teammates and share responsibility. In an individual sport like tennis, you're usually only concerned about your own performance. That can make these sports more challenging.

accomplishment

(ə-kŏm´plĭsh-mənt) *n.* An *accomplishment* is a task that you succeed in doing.

The Ultimate Value of Sports

QUOTED WORDS

Notice & Note: Mark the source of the quotation in paragraph 5.

Evaluate:: Why would this source be a valuable one to quote?

5 Whether it's football or golf, there's little doubt about the value of sports. According to the American Academy of Pediatrics (AAP), "play is essential to the cognitive, physical, social, and emotional well-being of children and youth." Play not only exercises our bodies, it also exercises our minds. Sports teach us about ourselves and our world. We learn how to **negotiate** plans, settle disagreements, and how to monitor our attitude. The skills we learn playing can be applied to school and work. Since organized sports are a hands-on, minds-on learning process, they stimulate our imagination, curiosity, and creativity. The growing science of play is armed with research claims that play, and thus sports, is important to healthy brain development. We use language during play to solve problems, we use thinking when we follow directions to a game, and we

negotiate

(nĭ-gō´shē-āt´) *v.* When you *negotiate*, you work with others to reach an agreement.

[2] **cricket** (krĭk´ĭt): English team sport, played with a bat, ball, and wickets.

use math skills to recognize averages and odds of each sports play.

6 Sports also raise our energy level and act as antidepressants. Activity increases the brain's level of chemicals called *endorphins,* which boost mood. When we start moving and having fun, we feel good about ourselves.

Forgetting the Fun

7 In a perfect world, everyone would have fun playing sports. But that's not always the case. Sports can get aggressive and cause scrapes, bruises, and broken bones. They can also hurt us psychologically. David Elkind, professor emeritus of Child Development at Tufts University and author of *The Power of Play,* says that when young children play self-initiated games such as tag or hide and seek, "misunderstandings and hurt feelings are part of the learning process, and happen in a context of **mutual** respect. Those that arise in organized team sports, don't have the same supportive network, the sense of competition outweighs the sense of cooperation, and can be hurtful to the child's sense of self and self-esteem." Playing sports is usually fun, but sometimes we can get frustrated. It might be because of the pressure to win, parents who yell and scream from the stands, or coaches who treat us unfairly. Sports are supposed to bring people together, but they can also drive people apart. When sports are separated into skill level, gender, or ethnicity, some players feel **isolated,** begin to forget the fun in sports, and even want to quit. Sports may not always be a

NOTICE & NOTE 

LANGUAGE CONVENTIONS

Annotate: The last sentence of paragraph 6 is a complex sentence, made of an independent clause and a subordinate clause. In each clause, mark the subject and its verb.

Identify: How do you know that each verb agrees with its subject?

ANALYZE ORGANIZATIONAL PATTERNS

Annotate: Mark the subheading that introduces paragraph 7.

Analyze: Review the first few sentences of paragraph 7. How does the subheading help readers understand the author's change in focus?

mutual

(myo͞o´cho͞o-əl) *adj.* Something is *mutual* when everyone treats each other the same way or shares the same feeling.

isolate

(ī´sə-lāt´) *v.* When you *isolate* something, you separate it so that it is apart or alone.

NOTICE & NOTE

SET A PURPOSE

Annotate: Mark new information that you learned from reading paragraphs 8 and 9.

Critique: Why do you think this information is valuable for everyone to know?

utilization

(yo͞ot′l-ĭ-zā′shən) *n. Utilization* is when you put something to use in an effective way.

ANALYZE ORGANIZATIONAL PATTERNS

Annotate: In paragraphs 11–13, mark three positive effects of sports when people watch others play them.

Connect: Which effect means the most to you? Why?

positive experience, but even when they're not, they give us a dose of how to face life's challenges.

Making Sports Work for Us

8 Playing sports doesn't mean you have to play on a varsity team. And very few people have what it takes to be a professional athlete. But your school basketball coach or gymnastics teacher has found a way to make play their work. And in doing so, they've found the work best suited to who they are. According to Elkind, "Whenever we combine play with work, as in our hobbies, cooking, gardening, sewing, and carpentry, it is the full **utilization** and integration of all our interests, talents, and abilities. It's an activity that makes us feel whole."

9 Play is so important to our development that the United Nations High Commission for Human Rights has included it as a right of every child.[3] In other words, it's your birthright to play! And there's no better place to play and learn about the world than on a sports field. So regardless of *your* sport—from swimming to soccer—play to have fun and you'll automatically win!

Keep Your Eye on the Ball

10 Are your eyes glued to the TV when a basketball superstar takes the court or a baseball superstar steps to the plate? While fans fill arenas, even more click their TVs on at home to watch athletes slam a puck into a net or hit a ball with a fat stick. Play is not only something to do, it's something to watch others do.

11 Sports are a form of entertainment. The joy you and your teammates get by working together is the same joy your family, friends, and other spectators get when they watch. Fans experience the thrill of victory and the agony of defeat,[4] just like the players on the field. Think of all the applauding, shouting, and yelling that happen at sporting events. It's a way for many of us to live vicariously through the players' actions.

12 Sports are also social events, opportunities for strangers to cheer together and debate outcomes. A Saturday morning game is a great way to spend time with family.

13 Sports involve learning, too. Fans research players, teams, and the sports themselves. How many fans do you know who are walking encyclopedias of sports trivia?

[3] **United Nations High Commission for Human Rights:** In 1989, the United Nations passed the *Convention on the Rights of the Child*, a treaty that protects the human rights of every child.

[4] **the thrill of victory and the agony of defeat:** This common sports phrase was originally part of the introduction to *Wide World of Sports*, a popular TV program that ran from 1961 to 1998.

14 Why do so many of us watch sports and have a favorite team? Studies show that it fills both emotional and psychological needs. We feel self-confident and experience joy when our favorite team wins. Sports fulfill our human need to belong, and many fans, whether their team wins or loses, enjoy the suspense that allows them to release their emotions. Where we live, our family background, peer pressure, and our own sense of self *(identity)* all determine which baseball cap we wear and why we root for *our* team.

15 So the next time you put your Red Sox cap on and tune in to the game, remember it's not just about the amazing pitchers and batters, but about the way you feel when you watch *your team* play.

CHECK YOUR UNDERSTANDING

Answer these questions before moving on to the **Analyze the Text** section on the following page.

1 The author includes information about the Greeks in order to —

A explain how we know which sports ancient peoples played

B prove that "sports" was once a means for survival

C encourage readers to play the games the Greeks once played

D show that an ancient people had a high regard for sports

2 According to paragraph 7, why can a negative experience in sports still have a positive effect?

F It encourages people to work together to solve problems.

G It can make people more compassionate toward their enemies.

H It can help people learn to deal with other difficult experiences.

J It teaches people to think carefully about their priorities.

3 What does the section <u>Keep Your Eye on the Ball</u> contribute to this text?

A It explains why entertainment is the greatest benefit of sports.

B It explains that sports benefit spectators as well as players.

C It quotes experts about the various benefits of sports.

D It outlines the physical benefits that result from playing sports.

RESPOND

ANALYZE THE TEXT

Support your responses with evidence from the text. NOTEBOOK

1. **Interpret** How does the title "It's Not Just a Game!" reflect the main idea of this text?
2. **Cause/Effect** According to the author, why can individual sports be more challenging than team sports?
3. **Summarize** How does the author support the idea that sports can build our brains, not just our bodies?
4. **Evaluate** In paragraph 9, the author tells readers, "[P]lay to have fun and you'll automatically win!" Do you agree with this statement? Why?
5. **Notice & Note** Reread the quotation in paragraph 3. How does it contribute to a greater understanding of sports?

RESEARCH

In "It's Not Just a Game!" the author includes a little information about sports history in general. Now it's time to get specific. Choose a sport that you enjoy or are curious about. Do some research to learn about its history and complete the graphic organizer below.

RESEARCH TIP

Don't believe everything you read online. It's always a good idea to get information from sites you know are reliable—and from more than one site. It's especially smart to check multiple reliable sites if you have any doubts about whether a piece of information is correct.

____________________(NAME OF SPORT)
When and Where It Began
How It Spread and Became Popular
Differences in How It Is Played Today

Connect Compare your findings with those of a classmate who chose a different sport. What can you learn from each other?

CREATE AND ADAPT

Write a Poem Write a poem about your favorite sport.

- ❑ Include characteristics of the sport that make it your favorite. (You may get some ideas by thinking about some of the positive aspects of sports discussed in "It's Not Just a Game!")
- ❑ Focus on the main idea or feeling you want to convey. Then brainstorm for vivid details that will make your ideas clear to readers.
- ❑ Decide whether to use rhyme and rhythm in your poem or to have your poem flow in an unstructured way.

Go to **Writing as a Process** in the **Writing Studio** for help in writing a poem.

Present an Infographic Meet with a partner and use the information from your research to create an infographic poster that shows both the positive and the negative aspects of the sport or sports that you learned about. Then present the graphic to the class.

- ❑ Use information from "It's Not Just a Game!" to discuss ways in which the sport(s) you chose benefits players and fans and the ways in which it is challenging. Make lists of these benefits and challenges.
- ❑ Choose images and decide on text to include—and how to present that text visually (for example, through captions or callout boxes).
- ❑ Sketch out possible designs. Revise to keep text brief and to ensure that the images and text work together. When you have a sketch that you both like, create a final version to present.

Go to **Using Media in a Presentation** in the **Speaking and Listening Studio** to learn more.

RESPOND TO THE ESSENTIAL QUESTION

? How do sports bring together friends, families, and communities?

Gather Information Review your annotations and notes on "It's Not Just a Game!" Then, add relevant details to your Response Log. As you determine which information to include, think about:

- what people can learn by playing sports
- how sports can be used to benefit all students and their schools

At the end of the unit, you can refer to your notes when you write a short story.

ACADEMIC VOCABULARY

As you write and discuss what you learned from the informational text, be sure to use the Academic Vocabulary words. Check off each of the words that you use.

- ❑ **attitude**
- ❑ **consume**
- ❑ **goal**
- ❑ **purchase**
- ❑ **style**

CRITICAL VOCABULARY

WORD BANK
accomplishment
negotiate
mutual
isolate
utilization

Practice and Apply Complete each sentence to show that you understand the meaning of the vocabulary word.

1. The senator's greatest **accomplishment** was when she . . .
2. Because the two sides agreed to **negotiate**, . . .
3. Fans of the same sports team have a **mutual** . . .
4. Doctors decided to **isolate** the patient because . . .
5. Plans for **utilization** of the empty building included . . .

VOCABULARY STRATEGY: Reference Resources

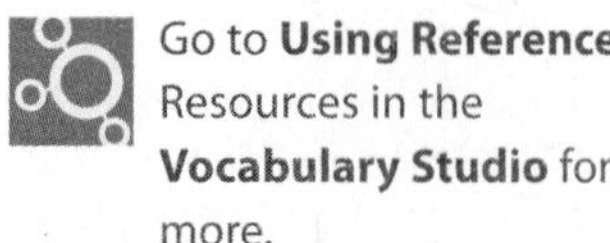
Go to **Using Reference** Resources in the **Vocabulary Studio** for more.

A **thesaurus** is a reference aid that lists synonyms, or words with similar meanings. Writers can use a print or digital thesaurus to help them find the exact word they need. A thesaurus entry usually looks something like this:

isolate *v.* confine, cut off, disconnect, keep apart, remove, quarantine, seclude, segregate, separate, set apart

The fact that a thesaurus shows you several synonyms doesn't mean that all of the synonyms would work equally well in a sentence. Choose the synonym that best captures the meaning you want to convey and reflects your style as a writer.

Practice and Apply Choose four words in paragraph 12 of "It's Not Just a Game!" Use a print or digital thesaurus to find synonyms for those words. Then, rewrite the paragraph, using what you think are appropriate synonyms for the words you chose.

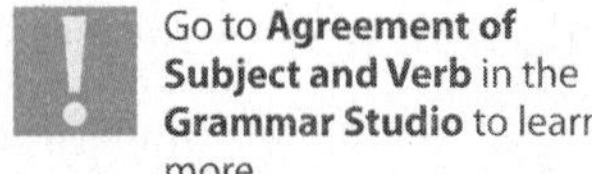

LANGUAGE CONVENTIONS: Complex Sentences and Subject-Verb Agreement

A **complex sentence** is made from one independent clause and at least one subordinate clause. In a complex sentence, it is important for the subject and its verb to **agree** in number. **Subject-verb agreement** means that if the subject is singular, the verb must also be singular; if the subject is plural, the verb must also be plural. Note these examples from "It's Not Just a Game!":

> **Since organized sports are a hands-on, minds-on learning process, they stimulate our imagination, curiosity, and creativity.**
>
> **Play is not only something to do, it's something to watch others do.** (Note that one verb is part of a contraction.)
>
> **We feel self-confident and experience joy when our favorite team wins.** (*Team* is considered a singular noun. Note that the subject in the independent clause, *we,* works with two verbs.)

Go to **Agreement of Subject and Verb** in the **Grammar Studio** to learn more.

Practice and Apply These complex sentences are based on "It's Not Just a Game!" Whenever you see a choice of verbs in parentheses, mark the correct verb and then mark the subject with which it agrees.

1. I (wonder/wonders) if wrestlers (was/were) as popular in ancient Egypt as they (is/are) today.
2. Rules (keeps/keep) games functioning in an orderly way, especially when a player (makes/make) a mistake.
3. Because people (has/have) different interests, (there's/there are) a sport for just about everyone.

Now draft a paragraph about the value of sports. Use your own ideas and refer to the ideas in "It's Not Just a Game." Make sure to include at least two complex sentences in your paragraph. Edit your draft to ensure your sentences have correct subject-verb agreement.

COLLABORATE & COMPARE

NOVEL IN VERSE

from THE CROSSOVER

by **Kwame Alexander**

pages 407–411

COMPARE THEME

From sonnets to haiku, from ballads to epic poems, from odes to elegies, poets are always seeking creative freedom in poetic forms, old and new. Think about how the form of each poem—along with its use of rhythm, sound devices, and figurative language—creates layers of meaning.

ESSENTIAL QUESTION:

How do sports bring together friends, families, and communities?

POEM

DOUBLE DOUBLES

by **J. Patrick Lewis**

pages 417–419

from The Crossover

QUICK START

Have you ever heard a rap with a story that caught your imagination? What happened? What about the rap made it special?

ANALYZE NOVEL IN VERSE

A **narrative poem** tells a story. Some narrative poems are brief, like old ballads that were originally sung. Others are book-length, including ancient works such as the *Odyssey* and *Beowulf.*

Throughout history, new forms of narrative poetry have emerged. For example, the **verse novel** is a novel-length narrative told in poetry instead of prose. As you read "JB and I," "At the End of Warm-Ups, My Brother Tries to Dunk," and "The Sportscaster" by Kwame Alexander, note examples of these characteristics of verse novels:

Organized into **scenes**, each with a setting and a plot
Presents a **speaker** and other characters, often interacting and even conflicting; usually shows the speaker's emotions
May include **graphical elements** (unusual line breaks and line length; unusual punctuation and type styles/sizes)
Expresses a **theme** in each scene, working together for a "life lesson" that relates to the verse novel as a whole

GENRE ELEMENTS: VERSE NOVEL

- has many of the characteristics of a story, including setting, characters, and plot (which may include conflict)
- is structured in groups of lines instead of in paragraphs
- usually uses vivid word choices and figurative language to make the topic easy to visualize
- expresses a theme, or a lesson about life

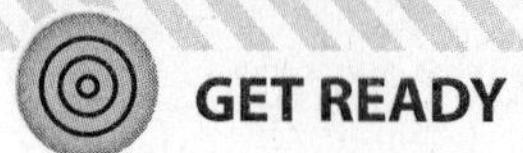

GET READY

ANALYZE METAPHOR AND PERSONIFICATION

Poets often use **figurative language** to express their ideas in imaginative ways. Figurative language is not literally true, but it can be used to emphasize ideas, create mental images, or stir readers' emotions. Two common types of figurative language used in poetry are metaphor and personification.

In a **metaphor**, the poet compares two basically unlike things that have one or more qualities in common. A metaphor makes a direct comparison and does not use the words *like* or *as.*

The basketball court was a swarm of activity.

This metaphor compares the players to a swarm of insects. It helps create a feeling of intense, fast-moving action.

In **personification**, the poet gives human qualities to an animal, object, or idea.

The ball thought about things for a moment and then dropped through the net.

This personification creates the mental image of a basketball that does not fall through the net right away. It adds suspense to the scene.

As you read these three poems by Kwame Alexander, look for examples of figurative language. Think about what the poet wants to say and the kind of mental image or feeling he wants to create.

ANNOTATION MODEL

NOTICE & NOTE 

As you read, think about the elements of verse novels. You can also mark examples of figurative language and other interesting details. In the model, you can see one reader's notes about a scene from *The Crossover.*

. . . I snicker
but it's not funny to him,
especially when I take off from center court,
my hair like wings,
each lock lifting me higher and HIGHER
like a 747 ZOOM ZOOM!

This may be an important moment in the plot.

The figurative language helps me "see" the scene.

The different sizes of types remind me of the sound of a plane taking off.

NOTICE & NOTE 

BACKGROUND

Kwame Alexander *(b. 1968) is an American poet, novelist, and educator. He has written more than two dozen books and has won numerous literary awards. These include the prestigious John Newbery Award, the Coretta Scott King Author Honor Book Award, and the Lee Bennett Hopkins Poetry Award, all in recognition of* The Crossover. *Alexander frequently travels to schools—both in the United States and around the world—where he reads and discusses poetry and leads writing workshops.*

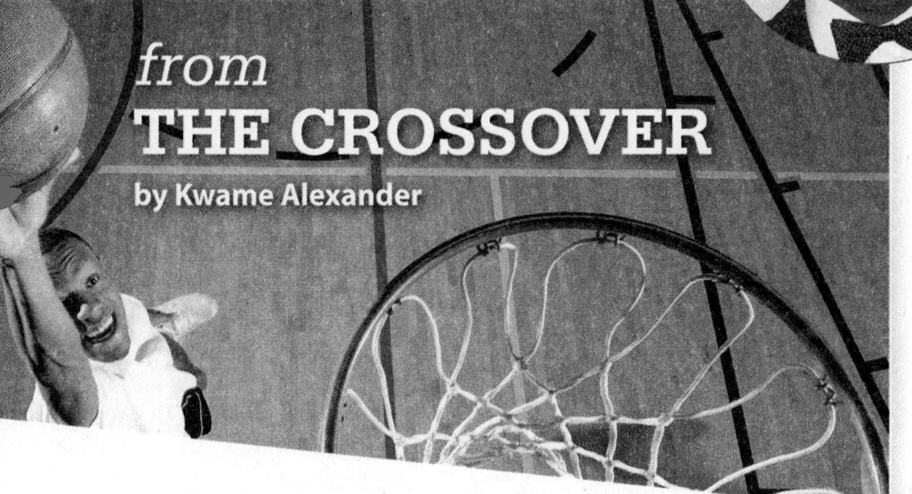

from THE CROSSOVER

by Kwame Alexander

PREPARE TO COMPARE

As you read these three poems, think about the story that they tell and the way that Alexander tells it. Note the ways in which he brings the sport of basketball to life and relates it to personal relationships.

JB and I

are almost thirteen. Twins. Two basketball goals at
opposite ends of the court. Identical.
It's easy to tell us apart though. I'm

an inch taller, with dreads to my neck. He gets
his head shaved once a month. I want to go to Duke,
he flaunts Carolina Blue. If we didn't love each other,

we'd HATE each other. He's a shooting guard.
I play forward. JB's the second
most phenomenal baller on our team.

Notice & Note

Use the side margins to notice and note signposts in the text.

ANALYZE NOVEL IN VERSE

Annotate: In lines 1–9, underline examples of unusual line breaks. Circle an unusual type style.

Analyze: Why do you think the poet used these graphical elements?

NOTICE & NOTE

He has the better jumper, but I'm the better
slasher. And much faster. We both
pass well. Especially to each other.

To get ready for the season, I went
to three summer camps. JB only went to
one. Said he didn't want to miss Bible school.

What does he think, I'm stupid? Ever since
Kim Bazemore kissed him in Sunday school,
he's been acting all religious,

thinking less and less about
basketball, and more and more about
GIRLS.

CONTRASTS AND CONTRADICTIONS

Notice & Note: Mark the way in which the speaker says that JB has changed.

Connect: Imagine a big change in someone close to you. How do you think that change would make you feel?

At the End of Warm-Ups, My Brother Tries to Dunk

Not even close, JB.
What's the matter?
The hoop too high for you? I snicker
but it's not funny to him,
especially when I take off from center court,
my hair like wings,
each lock lifting me higher and HIGHER
like a 747 ZOOM **ZOOM!**
I throw down so hard,
the fiberglass trembles.
BOO YAH, Dad screams
from the top row.
I'm the only kid
on the team
who can do that.

The gym is a loud, crowded circus.
My stomach is a roller coaster.
My head, a carousel.
The air, heavy with the smell
of sweat, popcorn,
and the sweet perfume
of mothers watching sons.

ANALYZE NOVEL IN VERSE

Annotate: In lines 1–8, mark the words that the speaker is either saying to or thinking about JB.

Infer: A narrative's plot usually focuses on a conflict. What conflict do you see in these lines?

ANALYZE METAPHOR AND PERSONIFICATION

Annotate: In lines 9–18, mark an example of a metaphor and an example of personification.

Critique: How does this figurative language contribute to the reader's understanding and enjoyment of the poem?

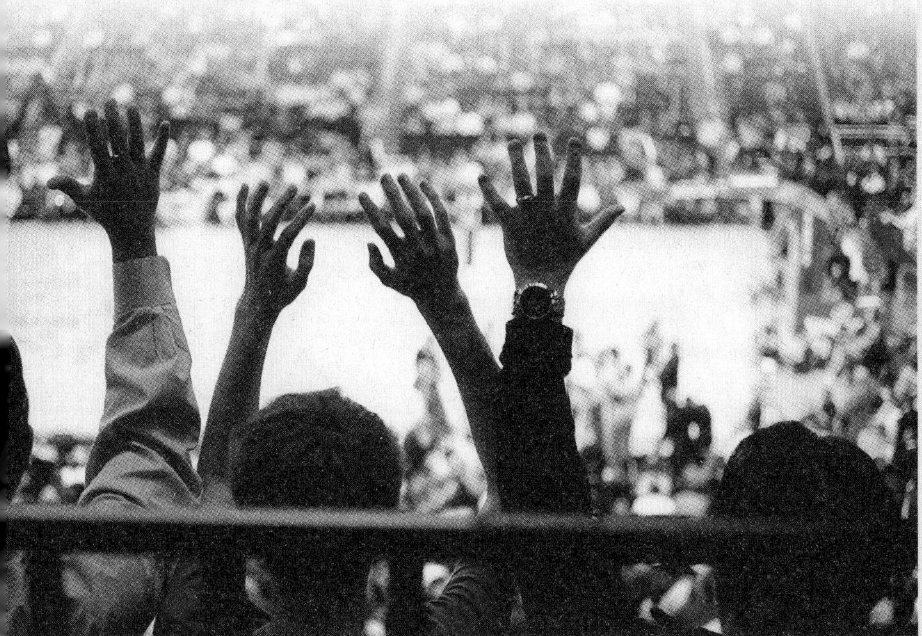

Our mom, a.k.a. Dr. Bell, a.k.a. The Assistant Principal,
is talking to some of the teachers
on the other side of the gym.
I'm feeling better already.
Coach calls us in,
does his Phil Jackson impersonation.
Love ignites the spirit, brings teams together, he says.
JB and I glance at each other,
ready to bust out laughing,
but Vondie, our best friend,
beats us to it.
The whistle goes off.
Players gather at center circle,
dap[1] each other,
pound each other.
Referee tosses the jump ball.
Game on.

[1] **dap** (dăp): to give a congratulatory greeting by tapping a closed fist on top of and on the bottom of the other person's fist.

NOTICE & NOTE 

WORDS OF THE WISER

Notice & Note: Mark the advice that the coach offers to the players.

Interpret: What lesson does the coach want the players to learn?

NOTICE & NOTE

ANALYZE NOVEL IN VERSE

Annotate: Mark examples of unusual punctuation, capitalization, and line length in "The Sportscaster."

Analyze: Why do you think the poet chose these unique graphical elements?

The Sportscaster

JB likes to taunt and
trash talk
during games
like Dad
used to do
when he played.

When I walk onto
the court
I prefer silence
so I can
Watch
React
Surprise.

I talk too,
but mostly
to myself,
like sometimes
when I do
my own
play-by-play
in my head.

CHECK YOUR UNDERSTANDING

Answer these questions before moving on to the **Analyze the Text** section on the following page.

1 According to the speaker in "JB and I," why is JB more interested in being religious than in playing basketball?

A JB had a spiritual experience at camp.

B JB is not as good a slasher as the speaker is.

C JB is interested in a girl at church.

D JB is trying to please his parents.

2 Near the end of "At the End of Warm-Ups, My Brother Tries to Dunk," the brothers probably are tempted to laugh because —

F they already have been trying hard to make the coach's advice work

G their teammate Vondie is making fun of the coach as he talks

H the coach does a terrible job of imitating a famous NBA coach

J the coach's advice is the opposite of their feelings toward each other

3 Which statement best describes the brothers' father as we see him in the second and third scenes?

A He misses the days when he was a basketball player.

B He has a bond with his sons because of basketball.

C He is not as impressed with his two sons as his wife is.

D He attends his sons' games only because he must.

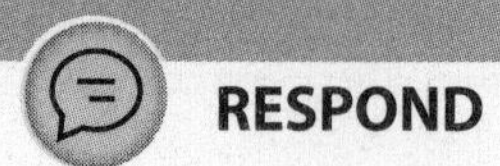

RESPOND

ANALYZE THE TEXT

Support your responses with evidence from the text. NOTEBOOK

1. **Compare** In lines 1–2 of "JB and I," the speaker compares JB and himself to "goals at / opposite ends of the court." According to lines 3–15, how are the speaker and JB different?
2. **Infer** How does the use of capital letters in "JB and I" and "At the End of Warm-Ups, My Brother Tries to Dunk" affect your understanding of the speakers' personality?
3. **Connect** Review lines 16–18 of "At the End of Warm-Ups, My Brother Tries to Dunk." What mental images do these metaphors create and how do they help express what the speaker is feeling?
4. **Synthesize** Think about these three verse novel scenes. What theme do the scenes, taken together, suggest?
5. **Notice & Note** How does the speaker contrast himself with his brother in "The Sportscaster"? To which brother do you think the term *sportscaster* applies better, and why?

RESEARCH

Research the rules of another team sport that you play or that interests you. Use the graphic organizer to analyze some of its key elements.

QUESTION	ANSWER
How many players are on each team?	
What is the role of each type of player?	
How are points scored?	
What are some key rules of the game? What happens if a rule is not followed?	

Connect With a small group, discuss the rules for the game. Which rules do you think make for a better game? Which rules do you think should be changed, and why?

RESEARCH TIP

The rules of a sport can change over time. As you research the rules of the sport you have chosen, check the date for each source and make sure that your information is current.

CREATE AND DISCUSS

Write a Letter Write a letter to the poet requesting information about what inspired him to write *The Crossover*.

- ❑ Write a friendly letter that includes a heading with an address and a date, a greeting, the body of the letter, and a closing (such as Sincerely,) and a signature.
- ❑ Introduce yourself and say something about what you liked about the scenes from *The Crossover* that you read.
- ❑ Ask him questions about why he wrote these poems. (Possible questions: Did you play any sports in your youth? Which character in *The Crossover* do you identify with the most?)
- ❑ Ask him why he chose the form of a verse novel and what was the most difficult part of creating it.
- ❑ Throughout, use a friendly but respectful tone.

Go to **Writing as a Process** in the **Writing Studio** for help.

Create a Podcast Work in a small group to create a podcast in which participants discuss their responses to the excerpt from *The Crossover*.

- ❑ Review your answers and notes that you made while reading. Highlight notes that you would want to share in a discussion.
- ❑ As a group, plan your questions. Be sure to ask how the text makes you curious about the rest of this verse novel. Plan a role for each member of your group, including a moderator.
- ❑ Practice your discussion before you record it. Work with your teacher to record the podcast and possibly post it.

Go to **Participating in Collaborative Discussions** and **Using Media in a Presentation** in the **Speaking and Listening Studio** for guidance.

RESPOND TO THE ESSENTIAL QUESTION

How do sports bring together friends, families, and communities?

Gather Information Review your annotations and notes on these scenes from *The Crossover*. Then, add relevant details to your Response Log. As you determine which information to include, think about:

- how sports affect people's lives
- what makes someone a good player at a sport
- how competition shapes players' attitudes

At the end of the unit, refer to your notes as you write a short story.

ACADEMIC VOCABULARY

As you write and discuss what you learned from the verse novel, be sure to use the Academic Vocabulary words. Check off each of the words that you use.

- ❑ **attitude**
- ❑ **consume**
- ❑ **goal**
- ❑ **purchase**
- ❑ **style**

POEM

DOUBLE DOUBLES

by **J. Patrick Lewis**

pages 417–419

COMPARE THEME

Now that you've read three scenes from the verse novel *The Crossover*, read "Double Doubles," in which siblings who play another sport share their thoughts about their sport—and about each other. As you read, think about the similarities and differences in how each poet presents his speakers. After you are finished, you will collaborate with a small group on a final project that involves an analysis of both poets' work.

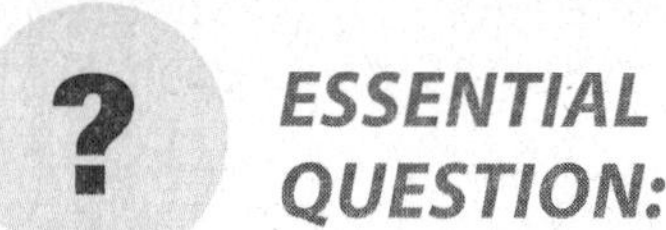

ESSENTIAL QUESTION:

How do sports bring together friends, families, and communities?

NOVEL IN VERSE

from THE CROSSOVER

by **Kwame Alexander**

pages 407–411

Double Doubles

QUICK START

Have you ever heard a duet, a song in which two artists sing—sometimes singing to each other and sometimes singing together? What makes the "conversation" in a duet different from a performance in which only one person sings?

ANALYZE A TWO-VOICE POEM

Most poems have a single voice. It is the voice of the speaker, who tells about personal experiences, feelings, and thoughts. A popular new form of poetry, however, is known as the **two-voice poem.** In this kind of poem, two distinct voices are heard. They may be conversing with each other, or they both may be trying to talk to you at the same time. Reading this kind of poem, or hearing it read aloud, allows you to see two points of view about a topic or theme at the same time. It also encourages you to explore similarities and differences between the poem's speakers.

Note these characteristics of two-voice poems:

- They are meant to be read aloud by two people, each assuming the voice of one of the speakers.
- Graphical elements are very important. Two-voice poems are usually set up in two columns, with each column representing just one speaker's voice. If both speakers are meant to speak the same words at the same time, either the shared words appear in both columns or the poet creates a middle column for those words. (Sometimes, the poet may choose to write in alternating stanzas, with every other stanza spoken by the same speaker.)
- They should be read sequentially, from left to right, line by line and from top to bottom.

Watch for and make notes about these characteristics as you read "Double Doubles."

GENRE ELEMENTS: TWO-VOICE POETRY

- is more about thoughts and feelings than about a story
- expresses ideas about a topic or theme from the perspective of two different speakers
- is structured in a way that makes it clear which lines are spoken by one voice and which are spoken by both voices
- like other kinds of poems, expresses a theme, or a lesson about life

MAKE INFERENCES

Poets rarely state directly every idea they want to express. However, since poets choose their words carefully, you often can find clues in the text that help build understanding. If you combine these clues with what you already know, you will be well on your way to identifying a poem's speaker or speakers and the ideas expressed in the poem.

An **inference** is a logical guess based on text evidence—the "clues" in the text—plus your own knowledge and experience. For an inference to be reasonable, it must be supported by **textual evidence** along with **previous knowledge and personal experience.** Using a diagram like the one below can help you make reasonable inferences.

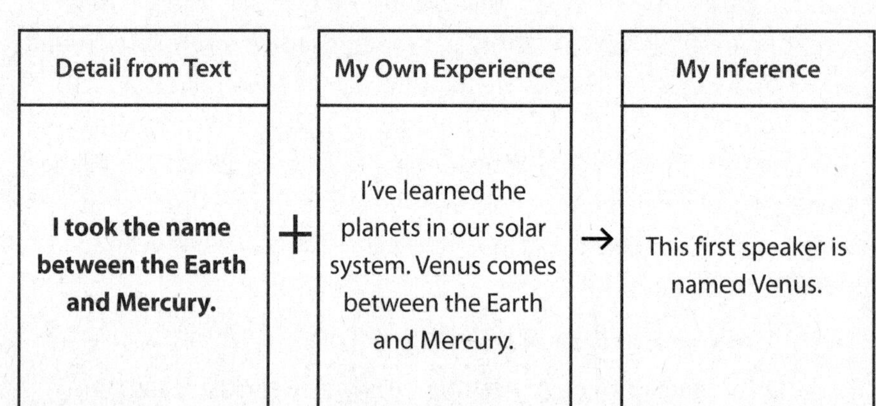

Detail from Text
I took the name between the Earth and Mercury.
+
My Own Experience
I've learned the planets in our solar system. Venus comes between the Earth and Mercury.
→
My Inference
This first speaker is named Venus.

READING SELF-SELECTED TEXTS

Use the chart on the right to make inferences about any text, including those you may have selected on your own.

As you make inferences, be sure to connect what you already know and have experienced with evidence from the text.

ANNOTATION MODEL

NOTICE & NOTE 

As you read, think about the elements of two-voice poems. You can also mark inferences that you make as you read. In the model, you can see one reader's notes about part of "Double Doubles."

Voice 1	Voice 2	Notes
The Williams sisters	The Williams sisters	Each column represents one of the two sisters' voices.
Read each other better		
	than *a* to *z*	I can infer from this detail that the sisters have a close bond.
and everything between.		
Momentum	Momentum	
	takes us to	
the final tie-break.		
Match point is only one	Match point is only one	I wonder why they both speak this line but not the next one?
	quick ace away. . . .	

NOTICE & NOTE 

BACKGROUND

J. Patrick Lewis *(b. 1942) is an American poet who served as the Poetry Foundation's Children's Poet Laureate from 2011 to 2013. He has published numerous books of poetry; indeed, he says, "[W]hat truly transports me is poetry, and so I spend most of my working hours thinking of themes to develop into manuscripts." In addition to his prolific writing and editing career, Lewis regularly visits classrooms to spread appreciation for poetry.*

DOUBLE DOUBLES

by J. Patrick Lewis

PREPARE TO COMPARE

As you read, keep track of who is speaking, and when. Add your knowledge to clues in the text to make inferences about the speakers and their perspective on their sport and their relationship.

I took the name	
between the Earth	
and Mercury.	
We took our game	We took our game
to beaded stars above.	to beaded stars above.
My sister's	My sister's
	lobs and
volleys	
so astonish me,	so astonish me,
the score	
	our score
	is usually
plenty—	plenty—
	love.

Notice & Note

Use the side margins to notice and note signposts in the text.

MAKE INFERENCES

Annotate: In lines 1–14, mark words that you think are sports terms.

Infer: Which sport are these speakers discussing? Who are these speakers? (Skim the rest of the poem to check.)

ANALYZE A TWO-VOICE POEM

Annotate: Mark examples of lines that are spoken by both voices.

Analyze: Why you think the poet chose these lines to be spoken by both voices?

AGAIN AND AGAIN

Notice & Note: In lines 19–32, mark two examples of teamwork.

Cause/Effect: What is the likely result of the teamwork, given this repeated idea?

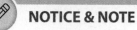

	I play as if I know
where she'll be going.	
We move together	We move together
	like a fine machine.
The Williams sisters	The Williams sisters
read each other better	
	than *a* to *z*
and everything between.	
Momentum	Momentum
	takes us to
the final tie-break.	
Match point is only one	Match point is only one
	quick ace away.
	As soon as I see sister
	Venus rising,
I know why	
double doubles	double doubles
players play.	players play.

CHECK YOUR UNDERSTANDING

Answer these questions before moving on to the **Analyze the Text** section on the following page.

1 The back-and-forth between the two speakers is meant to represent —

A a family argument

B the age difference between the sisters

C the way a tennis match is played

D a cheering crowd

2 Which set of lines indicates that the Williams sisters consider each other an extraordinary tennis player?

F *We took our game / to beaded stars above.* (lines 4–5)

G *My sister's / lobs and / volleys / so astonish me* (lines 6–9)

H *The Williams sisters / read each other better / than a to z.* (lines 19–21)

J *Match point is only one / quick ace away.* (lines 26–27)

3 According to this poem, what advantage do the Williams sisters have over other players?

A The moves of both sisters are always identical.

B They both have been playing tennis for a long time.

C Love for the game of tennis makes both of them great.

D They each know everything about the way the other plays.

RESPOND

ANALYZE THE TEXT

Support your responses with evidence from the text. NOTEBOOK

1. **Make Inferences** How do you think the sisters feel about each other? Which details support your inference?
2. **Interpret** In lines 10–11, how does the sister (Serena) correct what Venus says? Why do you think she makes this correction?
3. **Identify Patterns** Except for the first sentence, every sentence in the poem is "shared," with each speaker taking part. Why do you think the poet chose to include both speakers in almost every sentence?
4. **Synthesize** Lines 1–5 include references to the sky. What other lines make a similar reference? What do these references add to your understanding of the poem?
5. **Notice & Note** Earlier in this lesson, you identified two examples of teamwork in lines 19–32 of "Double Doubles." What is another example, earlier in the poem? What do the examples suggest about a theme for this poem?

RESEARCH

RESEARCH TIP
As you research the careers of living people, consider watching interviews, news clips, commentary, and other video sources that you find at reliable websites.

Research the tennis careers of Serena and Venus Williams. Use the organizer below to gather information and make comparisons.

QUESTION	VENUS	SERENA
When was each sister born?		
Who introduced each sister to tennis?		
As of 2017, what was each sister's highest ranking in singles? In doubles?		
As of 2017, how many Grand Slam singles titles had each sister won?		
As of 2016, how many Olympic gold medals had each sister won?		

Extend With a partner, discuss the reference to "beaded stars" (line 5). How does it seem to apply to the sisters' careers? How does it add to the mental image created in lines 4–5 of the poem?

CREATE AND PRESENT

Write a Two-Voice Poem Write a two-voice poem that expresses two viewpoints about a subject.

- ❑ Choose two speakers (two real or imaginary people, or even two objects) who might have a perspective on the same topic.
- ❑ Draft the poem. Allow each speaker to voice his or her own thoughts and feelings and to respond to the other speaker. Remember that some lines should be voiced by both speakers.
- ❑ Review your draft with a classmate. Revise to make each speaker's views clearer or to point more clearly to a theme.
- ❑ You may wish to work with a partner to present your final version of the poem orally to the class.

Go to **Writing as a Process** in the **Writing Studio** to learn more.

Critique a Poem With a partner, plan and present an oral critique of "Double Doubles." Use the ideas below to guide your discussion.

- ❑ Review your notes about "Double Doubles," and then read the poem aloud with your partner.
- ❑ Consider how successfully the poet created two speakers and structured the poem to show each speaker's thoughts and feelings. Is the poem easy to read or challenging? In addition, discuss the poem's theme. Include text evidence for your views.
- ❑ Together, organize your comments. Practice and work to communicate your ideas, speaking clearly and at a good volume. Use gestures to help your audience understand. Be prepared to respond to questions after you present your critique.

Go to **Participating in a Collaborative Discussion** in the **Speaking and Listening Studio** for more help.

RESPOND TO THE ESSENTIAL QUESTION

? How do sports bring together friends, families, and communities?

UNIT 5
RESPONSE LOG

Ball Hawk

Get in the Zone: The Psychology of Video Game Design

It's Not Just a Game!

from The Crossover

Double Doubles

Gather Information Review your notes on "Double Doubles." Then, add relevant details to your Response Log. As you determine which information to include, think about:

- the admiration that athletes may have for each other
- the nature and advantages of teamwork
- the feeling of being close to winning a game

At the end of the unit, use your notes to help you write a short story.

ACADEMIC VOCABULARY

As you write about and discuss what you learned from the two-voice poem, be sure to use the Academic Vocabulary words. Check off each of the words that you use.

- ❑ **attitude**
- ❑ **consume**
- ❑ **goal**
- ❑ **purchase**
- ❑ **style**

Collaborate & Compare

from THE CROSSOVER
Novel in Verse
by Kwame Alexander

DOUBLE DOUBLES
Two-Voice Poem
by J. Patrick Lewis

COMPARE THEME

The scenes from both *The Crossover* and "Double Doubles" are about siblings who play sports. Because the poems are about the same topic, they share many similarities—but there are differences, too.

A poem's **theme** is a message about life that the poet wishes to convey to the reader. Poets rarely state themes directly. The reader must infer the theme based on details from the text. Work with a group and complete the diagram below to help you analyze and record similarities and differences in the two poets' work. Think about how these details affect your understanding of the poems' themes. One detail has been included.

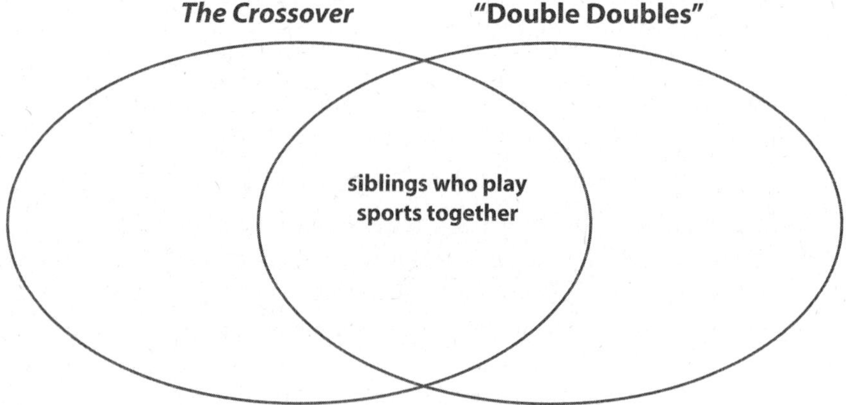

ANALYZE THE TEXTS

Discuss these questions in your group.

1. **Critique** With your group, discuss the organizational structure of each selection. How are the selections' structures different? Is the organization of each selection appropriate to its content? Explain.
2. **Compare** With your group, review details from both selections that express how playing a sport affects the siblings' relationship. Cite text evidence in your discussion.
3. **Analyze** What types of figurative language appear in each poem? How do they help you understand each poem's theme?
4. **Synthesize** What have you learned from these selections about how sports can affect siblings who play together?

COLLABORATE AND PRESENT

Now, your group can continue exploring the ideas in these texts by identifying and comparing their themes. Follow these steps:

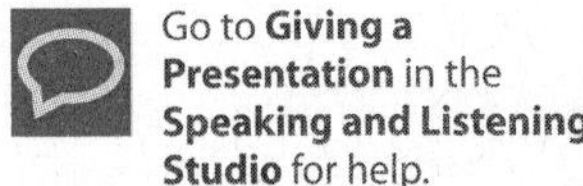
Go to **Giving a Presentation** in the **Speaking and Listening Studio** for help.

1. **Identify Important Details** With your group, review your completed Venn Diagram. Identify the most important details from each poem that you listed. Discuss points of agreement and disagreement about these details and try to come to a consensus. Remember to cite evidence from the texts.

2. **Determine Themes** Work together to infer the theme of each poem based on details. Then, decide on a statement that concisely expresses each theme. Use the graphic organizers below to help organize your thoughts as you work together.

Detail:	Detail:	Detail:	Detail:

Theme:

Detail:	Detail:	Detail:	Detail:

Theme:

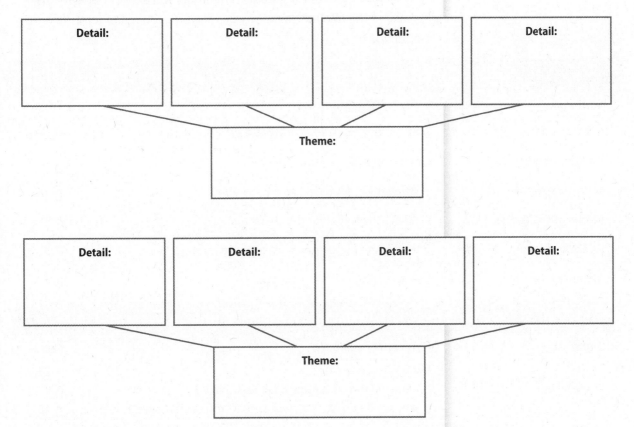

3. **Compare Themes** As a group, decide whether the themes of the selections are similar or different. Use details from your analysis of the poems to support your theme statements.

4. **Make a Class Presentation** In your group, practice making a presentation of your ideas to other students in the class. Be sure to clearly state your position about whether the poems have similar or different themes. Use your graphic organizers or other visuals to make your presentation clear and concise.

INDEPENDENT READING

Reader's Choice

? ESSENTIAL QUESTION:

How do sports bring together friends, families, and communities?

Setting a Purpose Select one or more of these options from your eBook to continue your exploration of the Essential Question.

- Read the descriptions to see which text grabs your interest.
- Think about which genres you enjoy reading.

Notice & Note

In this unit, you practiced noticing and noting three signposts: **Words of the Wiser, Tough Questions,** and **Aha Moment.** As you read independently, these signposts and others will aid your understanding. Below are the anchor questions to ask when you read literature and nonfiction.

Reading Literature: Stories, Poems, and Plays

Signpost	Anchor Question	Lesson
Contrasts and Contradictions	Why did the character act that way?	p. 99
Aha Moment	How might this change things?	p. 3
Tough Questions	What does this make me wonder about?	p. 362
Words of the Wiser	What's the lesson for the character?	p. 363
Again and Again	Why might the author keep bringing this up?	p. 3
Memory Moment	Why is this memory important?	p. 2

Reading Nonfiction: Essays, Articles, and Arguments

Signpost	Anchor Question(s)	Lesson
Big Questions	What surprised me? What did the author think I already knew? What challenged, changed, or confirmed what I already knew?	p. 265 p. 183 p. 437
Contrasts and Contradictions	What is the difference, and why does it matter?	p. 183
Extreme or Absolute Language	Why did the author use this language?	p. 182
Numbers and Stats	Why did the author use these numbers or amounts?	p. 264
Quoted Words	Why was this person quoted or cited, and what did this add?	p. 437
Word Gaps	Do I know this word from someplace else? Does it seem like technical talk for this topic? Do clues in the sentence help me understand the word?	p. 265

INDEPENDENT READING

You can preview these texts in Unit 5 of your eBook.

Then, check off the text or texts that you select to read on your own.

☐ 

SHORT STORY

Batting After Sophie
Sue Macy

Find out how a young softball player learns to respect her coach's decisions and become a true team player.

☐ 

SHORT STORY

Amigo Brothers
Piri Thomas

Learn how Felix and Antonio respond to an opportunity to box that threatens to undermine their friendship.

☐ 

BLOG

Bridging the Generational Divide Between a Football Father and Soccer Son
John McCormick

Can people who are passionate about different sports ever understand each other's point of view?

☐ 

SCIENCE WRITING

Arc of Triumph
Nick D'Alto

How can understanding the science of the parabola, or curve, improve your performance in sports?

Collaborate and Share Work with a partner to discuss what you learned from at least one of your independent readings.

- Give a brief synopsis or summary of the text, describing a time that your personal knowledge or experience helped you make an inference about the text you selected.
- Describe any signposts that you noticed in the text and explain what they revealed to you.
- Describe what you most enjoyed or found most challenging about the text. Give specific examples.
- Decide if you would recommend the text to others. Why or why not?

Go to the **Reading Studio** for more resources on **Notice & Note.**

Write a Short Story

Go to the **Writing Studio** for help writing your short story.

This unit focuses on the ways in which sports and games affect society and individuals. For this writing task, you will write a short story that portrays some aspect of sports or game-playing. For an example of a well-written short story you can use as a mentor text, review the story "Ball Hawk."

As you write your short story, you can use the notes from your Response Log, which you filled out after reading the texts in this unit.

Writing Prompt

Read the information in the box below.

This is the topic or context for your short story.

> **Many people enjoy playing individual and team sports and games, ranging from soccer to chess to video games. Competition can teach us many things about ourselves.**

Think carefully about the following question.

This is the Essential Question for this unit. How would you answer this question based on the texts in this unit?

> **How do sports bring together friends, families, and communities?**

Now mark the words that identify exactly what you are being asked to produce.

Write a short story about a character who is involved in a team or individual sport, or in a game played by one or more people. You may present either a positive view or a critical view of the sport or game.

Be sure to—

Review these points as you write and again when you finish. Make any needed changes.

- ❑ establish, develop, and resolve a conflict
- ❑ introduce and develop characters, events, and setting with dialogue, pacing, and descriptive details
- ❑ include a series of related events that lead to a climax
- ❑ use transitions among paragraphs to show sequence
- ❑ end with a conclusion that reveals a theme

1 Plan

Authors of narratives make many choices as they plan their work. Think about these questions as you begin planning your story.

- **CHARACTERS:** What does the main character look like? How does he or she speak and act? Who are the other characters in the story?
- **POINT OF VIEW:** Who tells the story? If a character narrates the story, using pronouns *I* or *we,* the author is using a first-person point of view. If the narrator is not a story character, the author is using a third-person point of view. A third-person narrator may be limited (describing events as characters see them) or omniscient (revealing characters' thoughts and feelings).
- **SETTING:** The setting of your story is the time and place in which it occurs. Where does the story take place?
- **CONFLICT:** Conflict is the struggle between people or ideas that the main character must overcome. What does he or she want? What obstacles must he or she overcome to achieve that goal?

Short Story Planning Table	
Characters	
Point of View	
Setting	
Conflict	

Background Reading Review the notes you have taken in your Response Log after reading the texts in this unit. These texts provide background reading that may give you some ideas that you can use when planning your short story.

Go to **Writing Narratives: Point of View and Characters** for help in planning your short story.

Notice & Note

From Reading to Writing

As you plan your story, apply what you've learned about signposts to your own writing. Remember that writers use common features, called signposts, to help convey their message to readers.

Think about how you can incorporate evidence of an **Aha Moment** into your story.

Go to the **Reading Studio** for more resources on **Notice & Note**.

Use the notes from your Response Log as you plan your short story.

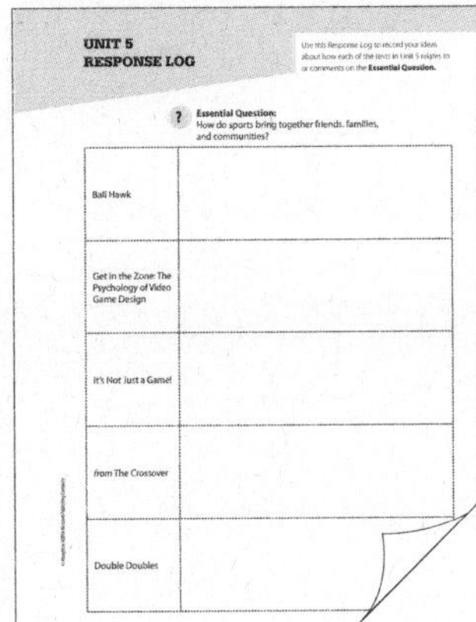

UNIT 5 RESPONSE LOG

Use this Response Log to record your ideas about how each of the texts in Unit 5 relates to or comments on the **Essential Question.**

? Essential Question: How do sports bring together friends, families, and communities?

Ball Hawk	
Get in the Zone: The Psychology of Video Game Design	
It's Not Just a Game!	
from The Crossover	
Double Doubles	

Go to **Writing Narratives: Narrative Structure** for help organizing your short story.

Organize Your Ideas After gathering ideas for your story's characters, point of view, setting, and conflict, you need to determine the plot. The term *plot* refers to the series of events in a story. The major events in the plot of most stories are defined in the story map below. You can use a similar diagram to record ideas for the plot of your own story.

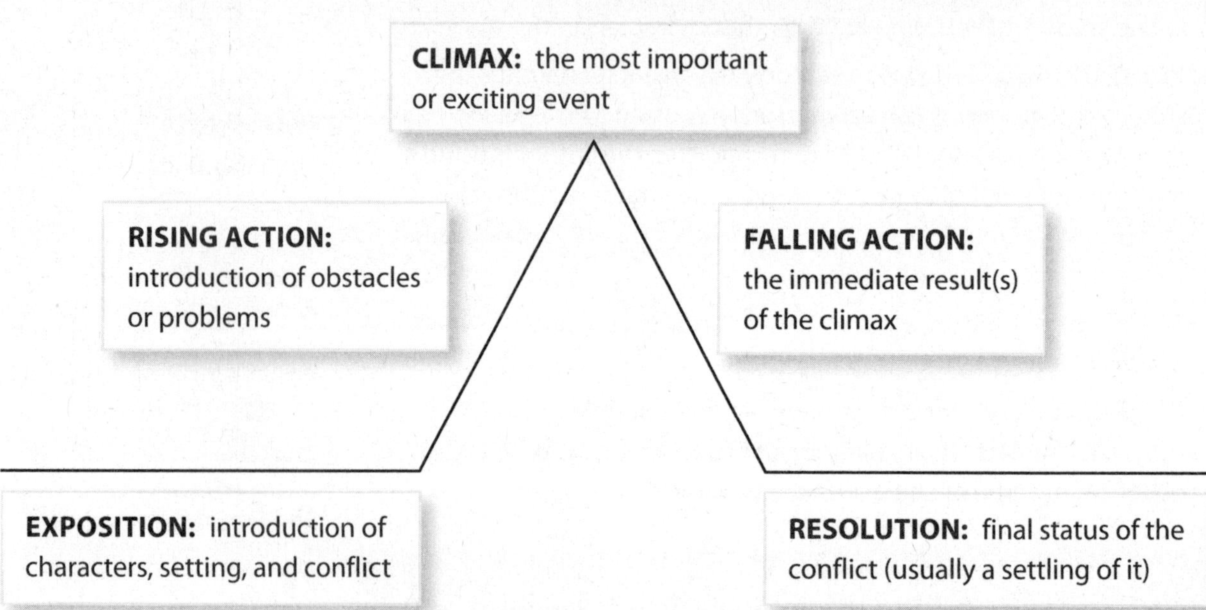
CLIMAX: the most important or exciting event
RISING ACTION: introduction of obstacles or problems
FALLING ACTION: the immediate result(s) of the climax
EXPOSITION: introduction of characters, setting, and conflict
RESOLUTION: final status of the conflict (usually a settling of it)

2 Develop a Draft

You may prefer to draft your short story online.

Once you have completed your planning activities, you will be ready to draft your short story. Refer to your plot diagram and any notes you took as you studied the texts in the unit. These will provide a kind of map for you to follow as you write. Using a word processor or online writing application makes it easier to make changes or move sentences around later when you are ready to revise your first draft.

Use the Mentor Text

BALL HAWK
How do sports bring together friends, families, and communities?

Author's Craft

Your introduction is your first chance to draw readers into your story. Introduce the conflict early to create suspense. Note how the author captures the readers' attention, introduces a conflict, and creates suspense in the opening sentences of "Ball Hawk."

"Indians invented baseball."

That's what Uncle Tommy Fox said on the day I was ready to throw in my glove and quit the Long Pond High School team for good. It was one of his typically cryptic remarks and, as usual, it started me thinking.

Quite frankly, if Uncle Tommy hadn't come into my life when he did, I probably would have ended up dyeing my hair purple and going goth.

The author opens the story with an intriguing quotation that makes readers want to know more. Then he introduces the conflict of the story: The narrator wants to quit the team, but Uncle Tommy doesn't want him to.

Apply What You've Learned To capture your readers' attention, you might open your story with dialogue. Providing clues about characters and the obstacles they have to overcome is another good way to begin.

Genre Characteristics

To develop characters and make them believable, authors may describe how characters look, act, talk, and think. Notice how the author of "Ball Hawk" creates a vivid picture of Uncle Tommy.

Or that this broad-shouldered old Indian guy with long gray braids and a friendly face really did seem to like me and enjoy taking on that role of being an uncle. Or that he knew more about being Indian, really being Indian, than anyone else I'd ever met. He also had a sense of humor and we both needed it when it came to me and baseball.

The author (speaking through the main character, the narrator) shows what the character looks like, tells us what he knows, and tells us that he has a sense of humor.

Apply What You've Learned To help your readers understand and visualize your characters, include vivid, precise words and phrases as well as sensory details in your description.

WRITING TASK

Go to **Writing Narratives: The Language of Narratives** for help revising your short story.

3 Revise

On Your Own Once you have written your draft, go back and look for ways to improve your short story. As you reread and revise, think about whether you have achieved your purpose. The Revision Guide will help you focus on specific elements to make your writing stronger.

Revision Guide		
Ask Yourself	**Tips**	**Revision Techniques**
1. Does my introduction grab readers' attention?	**Highlight** the introduction.	**Introduce** a character. **Add** dialogue and descriptions of setting.
2. Are my characters easy to imagine and believable?	**Underline** examples of characters' authentic words and actions.	**Add** words and actions that seem authentic.
3. How well does the setting affect characters and help shape the plot?	**Highlight** details of setting. **Underline** details that affect characters and help shape the plot.	**Add** sensory details to descriptions of setting.
4. Is the conflict in the story clear? Do events build to a climax?	**Circle** details about the conflict. **Highlight** the climax.	**Mark** the beginning of each event. **Add** a strong climax.
5. Does the pacing keep the action moving, building interest and suspense?	**Underline** events that build interest and suspense.	**Delete** any unnecessary events.
6. Does my conclusion reflect a theme, or message about life?	**Highlight** the conclusion. **Underline** phrases or sentences that reflect the theme.	**Insert** phrases or sentences that give strong hints about and/or state the theme.

ACADEMIC VOCABULARY

As you conduct your **peer review,** be sure to use these words.

- ❑ **attitude**
- ❑ **consume**
- ❑ **goal**
- ❑ **purchase**
- ❑ **style**

With a Partner Once you and your partner have worked through the Revision Guide on your own, exchange papers and evaluate each other's stories in a **peer review.** Provide revision suggestions for at least three of the items in the guide. Explain why you think your partner's draft should be revised and what your suggestions are.

When receiving feedback from your partner, listen attentively and ask questions to make sure you understand the revision suggestions.

4 Edit

Once you have addressed the organization, development, and flow of ideas, improve the finer points of your draft. Edit for the proper use of standard English conventions and correct any misspellings or grammatical errors.

Go to **Quotation Marks** in the **Grammar Studio** to learn more.

Language Conventions

Correct Punctuation of Dialogue Dialogue is what characters say to each other in a story. Errors in the punctuation of dialogue can confuse readers about who is speaking or about when characters stop speaking and action resumes. Here are some rules for punctuating dialogue.

Use quotation marks to enclose a direct quotation—a character's exact words.

- "Time to check on the hawks," he said.

Direct quotations usually begin with an uppercase letter. However, when the speaker interrupts a quoted sentence, the second part of the quotation begins with a lowercase letter.

- "Mitchell," he said, "things that are supposed to come easy aren't always that easy to do."

A period or a comma is always placed inside the closing quotation marks. The same is true of a question mark or an exclamation point unless the entire sentence is a question or an exclamation.

- "I quit!" I yelled, standing up and throwing my glove out onto the field. "I'm done with it."

Begin a new paragraph each time the speaker changes.

- "Why'd you say that?" Uncle Tommy finally asked in a soft voice.
  "I hate this game!"

5 Publish

Finalize your short story and choose a way to share it with your audience. Consider these options:

- Read your short story aloud to the class.
- Post your short story on a classroom or school website.
- Submit your short story to a literary magazine.

WRITING TASK

Use the scoring guide to evaluate your short story.

Writing Task Scoring Guide: Short Story			
	Organization/Progression	**Development of Ideas**	**Use of Language and Conventions**
4	• The event sequence is smooth and clearly structured, creating suspense and building to a strong, satisfying conclusion. • The pacing is effective. • Transition words are successfully used to signal shifts in setting. • The conclusion clearly reflects a theme, or message, about life.	• A conflict is skillfully introduced, developed, and resolved. • A clear setting is effectively used to shape the plot. • Characters are well developed, compelling, and believable. • Dialogue and descriptions are used successfully.	• A consistent point of view is maintained. • Vivid, precise words and phrases, as well as sensory language, are used to describe the setting and the characters. • Spelling, capitalization, and punctuation are correct. • Grammar and usage are correct.
3	• The event sequence is generally well structured and creates some suspense, but it includes some extraneous events. • Pacing is somewhat uneven and confusing. • Transition words are used sporadically. • The conclusion hints at a possible theme or message but does not present it clearly.	• A conflict is introduced, developed, and resolved. • The setting somewhat shapes and affects the characters and the conflict. • Characters are interesting and have some believable traits. • Dialogue and descriptions are not consistently effective.	• The point of view is mostly consistent. • Some descriptive words and phrases are used, but there could be more sensory details. • Spelling, capitalization, and punctuation are correct. • Some grammatical and usage errors are repeated in the story.
2	• Some of the story's events are structured unclearly and distract from the plot. • Pacing is choppy or distracting. • Transition words are used ineffectively, if at all. • The conclusion does not reflect a theme, or message, about life.	• The conflict is introduced but not developed or resolved. • The setting is not clearly established and does not impact the story. • Characters are not adequately developed. • The story lacks sufficient dialogue and descriptions.	• The point of view is inconsistent. • The story lacks precise words and phrases and has little sensory language. • Spelling, capitalization, and punctuation are often incorrect but do not make reading difficult. • There are some grammar and usage errors, but the ideas are often still clear.
1	• The story does not have a clear sequence of events or plot. • There is no evidence of pacing. • Transition words are not used. • The conclusion is inappropriate to the story or is missing.	• The story has no identifiable conflict. • The setting is vague. • Characters are underdeveloped or not believable. • Dialogue and descriptions are missing.	• A clear point of view has not been established. • The story lacks precise language and sensory details. • Many spelling, capitalization, and punctuation errors are present. • Many grammatical and usage errors obscure the meaning of the writer's ideas.

Reflect on the Unit

By completing your short story, you have created a writing product that pulls together and expresses your thoughts about the reading you have done in this unit. Now is a good time to reflect on what you have learned.

Reflect on the Essential Question

- How do sports bring together friends, families, and communities? How has your answer to this question changed since you first considered it when you started this unit?
- What are some examples from the texts you've read that show the kinds of lessons people can learn from sports and how sports can create conflict and/or bring people together?

Reflect on Your Reading

- Which selections were the most interesting or surprising to you?
- From which selection did you learn the most about the value of sports?

Reflect on the Writing Task

- As you were writing your story, where did you get your ideas? Did new ideas send you in a new direction with your plot?
- What difficulties did you encounter while working on your short story? How might you avoid them next time?
- What improvements did you make to your short story as you were revising?

UNIT 5 SELECTIONS

- "Ball Hawk"
- "Get in the Zone: The Psychology of Video Game Design"
- "It's Not Just a Game!"
- from *The Crossover*
- "Double Doubles"

UNIT 6

CHANGE AGENTS

ESSENTIAL QUESTION:

What inspires you to make a difference?

> **Be greedy for social change, and your life will be endlessly enriched.**
>
> Ann Cotton

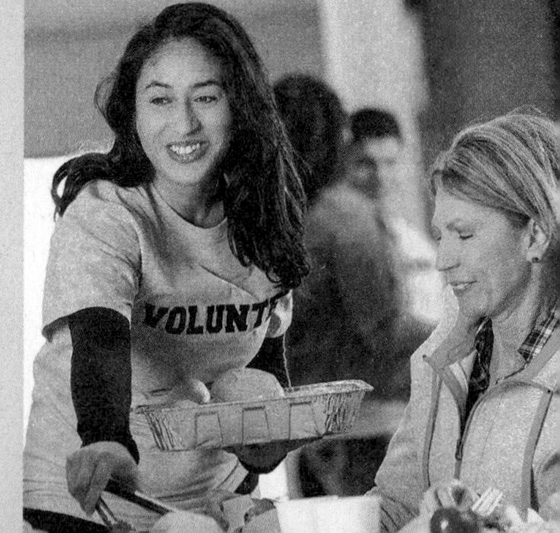

ACADEMIC VOCABULARY

Academic Vocabulary words are words you use when you discuss and write about texts. In this unit you will practice and learn five words.

☑ **contrast** ❑ **despite** ❑ **error** ❑ **inadequate** ❑ **interact**

Study the Word Network to learn more about the word **contrast**.

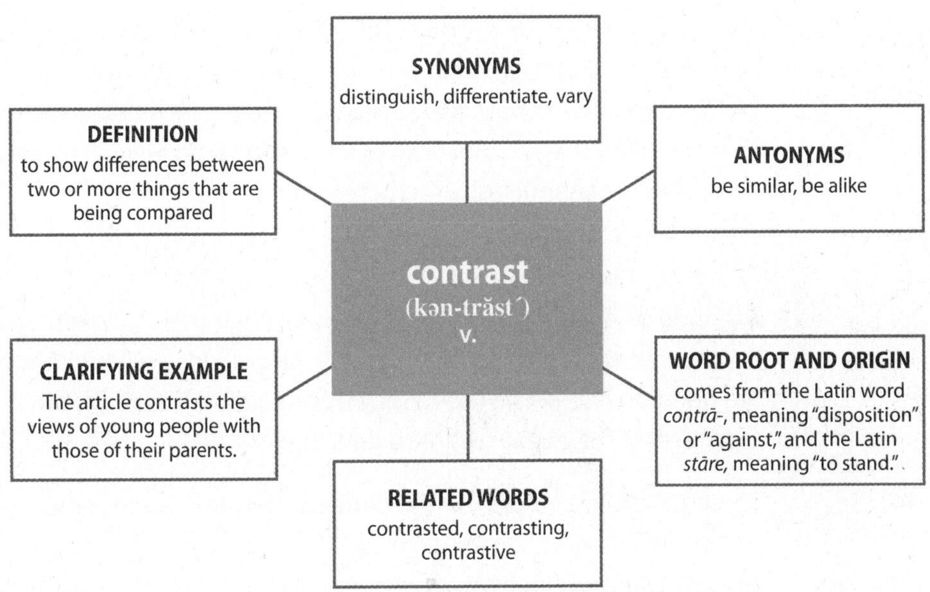

SYNONYMS
distinguish, differentiate, vary
DEFINITION
to show differences between two or more things that are being compared
ANTONYMS
be similar, be alike
contrast
(kən-trăst´)
v.
CLARIFYING EXAMPLE
The article contrasts the views of young people with those of their parents.
WORD ROOT AND ORIGIN
comes from the Latin word *contrā-*, meaning "disposition" or "against," and the Latin *stāre*, meaning "to stand."
RELATED WORDS
contrasted, contrasting, contrastive

Write and Discuss Discuss the completed Word Network with a partner, making sure to talk through all of the boxes until you both understand the word, its synonyms, antonyms, and related forms. Then, fill out Word Networks for the remaining four words. Use a dictionary or online resource to help you complete the activity.

*Go online to access the **Word Networks**.*

RESPOND TO THE ESSENTIAL QUESTION

In this unit, you will explore how and why people work to change societies and the communities in which they live. As you read, you will revisit the **Essential Question** and gather your ideas about it in the **Response Log** that appears on page R6. At the end of the unit, you will have the opportunity to write a **research report.** Filling out the Response Log will help you prepare for this writing task.

*You can also go online to access the **Response Log**.*

UNIT 6
RESPONSE LOG

Essential Question:
What inspires you to make a difference?

Craig Kielburger Reflects on Working Toward Peace	
from It Takes a Child	
Sometimes a Dream Needs a Push	
A Poem for My Librarian, Mrs. Long	
Frances Perkins and the Triangle Factory Fire	
from The Story of the Triangle Factory Fire	

R6 Response Log

Notice & Note

READING MODEL

CRAIG KIELBURGER REFLECTS ON WORKING TOWARD PEACE

For more information on these and other signposts to Notice & Note, visit the **Reading Studio.**

You are about to read the personal essay "Craig Kielburger Reflects on Working Toward Peace." In it, you will notice and note signposts that will give you clues about the author's purpose and message. Here are three key signposts to look for as you read this personal essay and other works of nonfiction.

When you read language like the following, pause and consider whether it might be an **Extreme or Absolute Language** signpost:

terms that indicate certainty or completeness—*all, none, everyone, no one, always, never, totally*

statements that express an uncompromising position—*we must all agree; no one should . . .*

language that is provocative—*spinach should be outlawed*—or that is exaggerated—*nothing in the universe . . .*

Extreme or Absolute Language Suppose that a friend invites you on an amusement park ride. She says it is *the best ride ever* and that you are going to *love it*. The friend may think you'll like the ride, but it may also be that she doesn't want to go alone.

Similarly, when authors use **Extreme or Absolute Language,** they usually have a purpose for doing so. Paying attention to Extreme or Absolute Language signposts can provide clues to the author's purpose and biases, point to the main idea the author wants to convey, and help you draw conclusions about the author's key points.

The paragraph below shows a student's annotation within Kielburger's essay and a response to an Extreme or Absolute Language signpost:

1 When I was very young I dreamed of being Superman, soaring high above the clouds and swooping down to snatch up <u>all of the bad people seeking to destroy our planet</u>. I would spend hours flying across the park, stopping momentarily to kick a soccer ball in my path or to pat my dog, Muffin, who ran faithfully at my heels.

Anchor Question
When you notice this signpost, ask: Why did the author use this language?

What language is provocative or exaggerated?	"all of the bad people seeking to destroy our planet"
Why might the author have used this language?	The author may want to emphasize his commitment to a cause, even at an early age.

Quoted Words If you read that a well-known children's doctor advises, "Exercising every day is essential to good health," what would you think? Does using a quotation make the advice more convincing?

Authors use **Quoted Words** to provide support for a point. Quoted Words might be the thoughts of an expert on the subject, someone who is important to the author, or someone who witnessed an event. When you read quoted words, ask yourself why the author included them and what they help you understand. Here a student marked an example of Quoted Words in Kielburger's essay:

> 14 When I returned home my mother asked me, "Are you certain you aren't gifted?" I realized that I had given the wrong answer. I was gifted, and the more I reflected, the more I concluded that I had never met a person who was not special or talented in some way.

Anchor Question
When you notice this signpost, ask: Why was this person quoted or cited, and what did this add?

What quoted words does the author include?	"Are you certain you aren't gifted?"
Why might the author have included this quotation?	The author shows how important his mother's question was to him and how it changed his thinking.

Big Questions In nonfiction texts, you will find facts that support your understanding of an issue. Sometimes you will also read details that make you rethink how you look at that issue. As you read, ask yourself: What is challenging, changing, or confirming what I already know? Here a student marked up a detail in Kielburger's essay related to a Big Question that prompted rethinking.

When you see details like these, pause and consider the **Big Questions** signpost:

- Identify details that confirm what you already know.
- Note details that prompt you to reexamine what you think, feel, or believe.

> 5 I have met children like eight-year-old Muniannal, in India, with a pretty ribbon in her hair, but no shoes or gloves, who squats on the floor every day separating used syringes gathered from hospitals and the streets for their plastics. When she pricks herself, she dips her hand into a bucket of dirty water. She dreams of being a teacher.

What detail challenged what you thought?	"She dreams of being a teacher."
Why might the author have included this challenging detail?	The author may be asking us to think about how every child has dreams and how those dreams can come true.

ANALYZE & APPLY

CRAIG KIELBURGER REFLECTS ON WORKING TOWARD PEACE

Personal Essay by **Craig Kielburger**

? ESSENTIAL QUESTION:

What inspires you to make a difference?

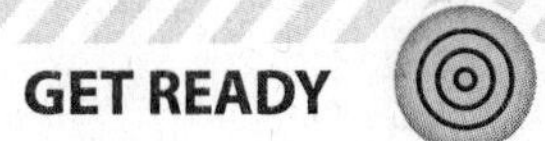

QUICK START

Have you ever seen something on TV or read a story that made you want to take action? With a group, discuss your ideas.

QUESTION

Effective readers **question** what they are reading and look for answers in the text. Asking questions helps you deepen your understanding and gain information. Readers' questions often focus on the following:

- What is the **controlling idea** or thesis of the text? What is the writer's position on the topic or subject of the text?
- What **supporting evidence,** such as examples, does the author provide to support the controlling idea? Why is the author including certain details?
- Does what the author is saying make sense to me? Why or why not?
- What questions arise after reading the piece? What additional information would help me form a response to it?

Taking notes and writing down questions as you read and afterward is an effective strategy for deepening your understanding of the text. Use a chart like the one below.

NOTES	QUESTIONS
Author read about a boy his age forced to work long hours. . . .	Why did this happen? Can it be stopped from happening again?

GENRE ELEMENTS: PERSONAL ESSAY

- short work of nonfiction that deals with a single subject
- written from a first-person point of view
- includes author's opinions, feelings, and/or insights based on personal experience
- often written in casual language to feel like a conversation with readers

ANALYZE AUTHOR'S POINT OF VIEW

The author of a personal essay often writes from a first-person **point of view,** using first-person pronouns, such as *I, me,* and *we*. The author might write from an objective or a subjective point of view, or both. When writing from an **objective point of view,** the writer presents information in an unbiased way. When writing from a **subjective point of view,** the writer includes personal ideas, values, feelings, and beliefs.

As you read the personal essay, think about the author's point of view by noting these features in the text:

- statements of the author's opinions
- details and examples from the author's experiences
- words and descriptions that have emotional impact
- the writer's **tone,** or attitude toward a subject
- the use of language that allows you to hear the writer's **voice,** or unique personality

GET READY

CRITICAL VOCABULARY

syringe **possession** **inquire** **capacity** **exploitation**

To see how many Critical Vocabulary words you already know, use them to complete the sentences.

1. Congress passed a law to prevent the __________ of migrant workers.
2. José decided to __________ about the new bike that he saw for sale on the corner.
3. The nurse drew the liquid medicine into the __________.
4. She saw many promising engineers in her __________ as a science teacher.
5. Dalia packed every __________ into the back of her car and drove across the country.

LANGUAGE CONVENTIONS

Commas In this lesson, you will learn about the effective use of commas. In general, commas are used to separate words, phrases, clauses, and ideas in a sentence. As you read "Craig Kielburger Reflects on Working Toward Peace," note how the author's use of commas clarifies his ideas.

ANNOTATION MODEL

NOTICE & NOTE

As you read, notice and note signposts, including **Extreme or Absolute Language** and **Quoted Words.** Ask yourself this **Big Question:** What changed, challenged, or confirmed what I already knew? Here is an example of how one reader responded to a paragraph in "Craig Kielburger Reflects on Working Toward Peace."

7 Poverty is the biggest killer of children. More than 1.3 billion people—one-quarter of the world's population—live in absolute poverty, struggling to survive on less than one dollar a day. Seventy percent of them are women and children. I dream of a day when people learn how to share, so that children do not have to die.

I didn't know that! Why is this so?

These are dramatic words. I think the author may be trying to convince me of something.

NOTICE & NOTE 

BACKGROUND

In 1995—when **Craig Kielburger** *(b. 1982) was only twelve years old—he and several classmates founded Free the Children, an organization to help young people. Now called WE Charity, the organization raises social awareness in schools and works in developing countries to provide education and healthcare programs. This essay comes from* Architects of Peace: Visions of Hope in Words and Images, *published when Kielburger was a teenager.*

CRAIG KIELBURGER REFLECTS ON WORKING TOWARD PEACE

Personal Essay by Craig Kielburger

SETTING A PURPOSE

In this essay, Kielburger calls for a fairer, more just world. As you read, pay attention to how he describes his experiences as a young activist.

Notice & Note

Use the side margins to notice and note signposts in the text.

1 When I was very young I dreamed of being Superman, soaring high above the clouds and swooping down to snatch up all of the bad people seeking to destroy our planet. I would spend hours flying across the park, stopping momentarily to kick a soccer ball in my path or to pat my dog, Muffin, who ran faithfully at my heels.

2 One day, when I was twelve years old and getting ready for school, I reached for the newspaper comics. On the front page was a picture of another twelve-year-old boy from Pakistan, with a bright red vest and his fist held high. According to the article, he had been sold into bondage[1] as

ANALYZE AUTHOR'S POINT OF VIEW

Annotate: Mark sentences in paragraph 2 that have an emotional impact.

Analyze: How do these sentences affect the reader? How would you describe the author's point of view, or perspective, in this paragraph?

[1] **bondage:** the state of being held as a slave.

NOTICE & NOTE

a weaver and forced to work twelve hours a day tying tiny knots to make carpets. He had lost his freedom to laugh and to play. He had lost his freedom to go to school. Then, when he was twelve years old, the same age as me, he was murdered.

3 I had never heard of child labor and wasn't certain where Pakistan was—but that day changed my life forever. I gathered a group of friends to form an organization called Free the Children.

4 Over the past four years, in my travels for Free the Children, I have had the opportunity to meet many children around the world—children like Jeffrey, who spends his days in a Manila garbage dump, alongside rats and maggots, where he sifts through decaying food and trash, trying to salvage a few valuable items to help his family survive. He dreams of leaving the garbage dump one day.

5 I have met children like eight-year-old Muniannal, in India, with a pretty ribbon in her hair, but no shoes or gloves, who squats on the floor every day separating used **syringes** gathered from hospitals and the streets for their plastics. When she pricks herself, she dips her hand into a bucket of dirty water. She dreams of being a teacher.

syringe
(sə-rĭnj´) *n.* A *syringe* is a medical instrument used to inject fluids into the body.

6 I have met children in the sugarcane fields of Brazil who wield huge machetes close to their small limbs. The cane they cut sweetens the cereal on our kitchen tables each morning. They dream of easing the hunger pains in their stomachs.

7 Poverty is the biggest killer of children. More than 1.3 billion people—one-quarter of the world's population—live in absolute poverty, struggling to survive on less than one dollar a day. Seventy percent of them are women and children. I dream of a day when people learn how to share, so that children do not have to die.

8 Every year, the world spends $800 billion on the military, $400 billion on cigarettes, $160 billion on beer, and $40 billion playing golf. It would only cost an extra $7 billion a year to put every child in school by the year 2010, giving them hope for a better life. This is less money than Americans spend on cosmetics in one year; it is less than Europeans spend on ice cream. People say, "We can't end world poverty; it just can't be done." The 1997 United Nations Development Report carries

QUESTION
Annotate: Underline words, phrases, or sentences that are unclear or confusing to you in paragraph 8.

Connect: What questions could you ask to help clarify any confusion?

NOTICE & NOTE

a clear message that poverty can be ended, if we make it our goal. The document states that the world has the materials and natural resources, the know-how, and the people to make a poverty-free world a reality in less than one generation.

9 Gandhi[2] once said that if there is to be peace in the world it must begin with children. I have learned my best lessons from other children—children like the girls I encountered in India who carried their friend from place to place because she had no legs—and children like José.

10 I met José in the streets of San Salvador, Brazil, where he lived with a group of street children between the ages of eight and fourteen. José and his friends showed me the old abandoned bus shelter where they slept under cardboard boxes. They had to be careful, he said, because the police might beat or shoot them if they found their secret hideout. I spent the day playing soccer on the streets with José and his friends—soccer with an old plastic bottle they had found in the garbage. They were too poor to own a real soccer ball.

11 We had great fun, until one of the children fell on the bottle and broke it into several pieces, thus ending the game. It was getting late and time for me to leave. José knew I was returning to Canada and wanted to give me a gift to remember him by. But he had nothing—no home, no food, no toys, no **possessions.** So he took the shirt off his back and handed it to me. José didn't stop to think that he had no other shirt to wear or that he would be cold that night. He gave me the most precious thing he owned: the jersey of his favorite soccer team. Of course, I told José that I could never accept his shirt, but he insisted. So I removed the plain white T-shirt I was wearing and gave it to him. Although José's shirt was dirty and had a few small holes, it was a colorful soccer shirt and certainly much nicer than mine. José grinned from ear to ear when I put it on.

12 I will never forget José, because he taught me more about sharing that day than anyone I have ever known. He may have been a poor street child, but I saw more goodness in him than all of the world leaders I have ever met. If more people had the heart of a street child, like José, and were willing to share, there would be no more poverty and a lot less suffering in this world. Sometimes young people find life today too depressing. It all seems so hopeless. They would rather escape, go dancing or listen to their favorite music, play video games or hang out with their friends. They dream of true love, a home of their own, or

[2] **Gandhi:** Mohandas Karamchand Gandhi (1869–1948; more commonly called Mahatma Gandhi), a leader of India whose belief in justice inspired many people around the world.

QUOTED WORDS

Notice & Note: Whose idea does the author reference (as an indirect quotation) in paragraph 9?

Analyze: Why do you think the author used this quotation?

BIG QUESTIONS

Notice & Note: What changed, challenged, or confirmed what you already knew in paragraphs 10 and 11?

Analyze: Why might the author have included this information?

possession
(pə-zĕsh´ən) *n.* A *possession* is something you own.

EXTREME OR ABSOLUTE LANGUAGE

Notice & Note: Mark statements in paragraph 12 that seem to exaggerate or overstate a point.

Evaluate: How does this use of extreme language affect how you feel about the author's message?

having a good time at the next party. At sixteen, I also like to dance, have fun, and dream for the future. But I have discovered that it takes more than material things to find real happiness and meaning in life.

13 One day I was the guest on a popular television talk show in Canada. I shared the interview with another young person involved in cancer research. Several times during the program this young man, who was twenty years old, told the host that he was "gifted," as indicated by a test he had taken in third grade. Turning my way, the host **inquired** whether I, too, was gifted. Never having been tested for the gifted program, I answered that I was not.

inquire
(ĭn-kwīr´) *v.* If you *inquire* about something, you ask about it.

14 When I returned home my mother asked me, "Are you certain you aren't gifted?" I realized that I had given the wrong answer. I was gifted, and the more I reflected, the more I concluded that I had never met a person who was not special or talented in some way.

15 Some people are gifted with their hands and can produce marvelous creations in their **capacity** as carpenters, artists, or builders. Others have a kind heart, are compassionate, understanding, or are special peacemakers; others, again, are humorous and bring joy into our lives. We have all met individuals who are gifted in science or sports, have great organizational skills or a healing touch. And, of course, some people are very talented at making money. Indeed, even the most physically or mentally challenged person teaches all of us about the value and worth of human life.

capacity
(kə-păs´ĭ-tē´) *n.* A person's *capacity* is his or her role or position.

16 I think that God, in fact, played a trick on us. He gave each and every person special talents or gifts, but he made no one gifted in all areas.

17 Collectively, we have all it takes to create a just and peaceful world, but we must work together and share our talents. We all need one another to find happiness within ourselves and within the world.

LANGUAGE CONVENTIONS

Annotate: Mark the commas in paragraphs 16 and 17.

Identify: Why is each comma necessary?

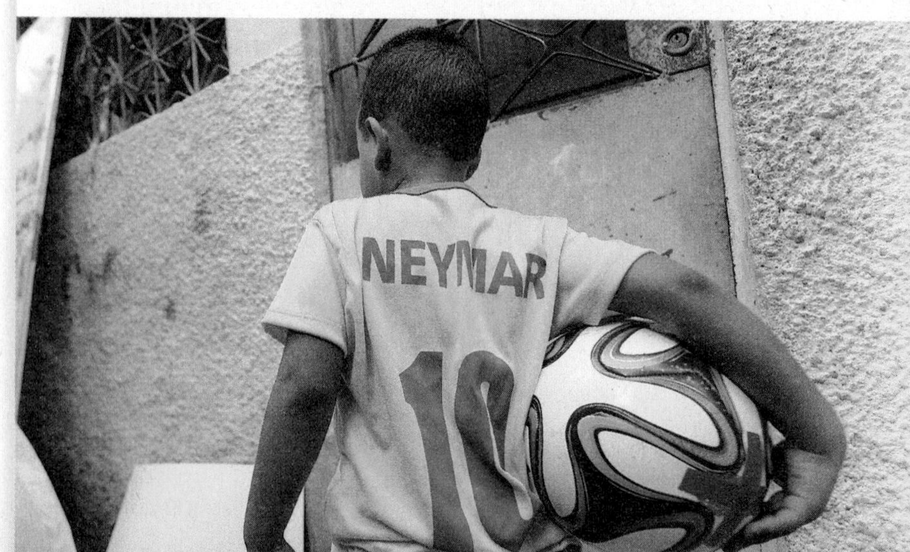

NOTICE & NOTE 

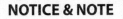

18 I realize, now, that each of us has the power to be Superman and to help rid the world of its worst evils—poverty, loneliness, and **exploitation.** I dream of the day when Jeffrey leaves the garbage dump, when Muniannal no longer has to separate used syringes and can go to school, and when all children, regardless of place of birth or economic circumstance, are free to be children. I dream of the day when we all have José's courage to share.

exploitation
(ĕk´sploi-tā´shən) *n. Exploitation* is the unfair treatment or use of something or someone for selfish reasons.

QUESTION

Annotate: Underline the author's ultimate dream.

Connect: What questions do you have about how sharing could help the children mentioned in this paragraph?

CHECK YOUR UNDERSTANDING

Answer these questions before moving on to the **Analyze the Text** section on the following page.

1 The author refers to <u>dreams</u> at the end of paragraphs 4, 5, 6, and 7 in order to —

A indicate that every child has hope for a better future

B explain what happens to children who live in poverty

C point out how different the children are from each other

D prove that poverty affects children all around the world

2 The author's main purpose in telling the story of José is to —

F describe how some homeless children live

G encourage sharing by showing that everyone has something to offer

H show that children who live in poverty still find time for play

J explain that although childhood poverty seems hopeless, it is not

3 Which statement best expresses the author's controlling idea in this personal essay?

A Child bondage is a problem faced by children around the world.

B Education is the key to ending childhood poverty.

C Everyone has the capacity to help end poverty, but it requires cooperation.

D Every person is gifted, but each person is gifted in his or her own way.

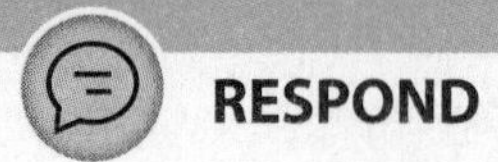

ANALYZE THE TEXT

Support your responses with evidence from the text. NOTEBOOK

1. **Cause/Effect** How does the story about the murdered boy reflect Kielburger's subjective point of view on life and the world?
2. **Critique** Reread paragraphs 6 and 7. Why do you think Kielburger provides this kind of supporting evidence? What effect might he hope this information has on the reader? How effective is this information in supporting his controlling idea?
3. **Draw Conclusions** What is Kielburger's purpose in saying that he is gifted in paragraph 14?
4. **Analyze** How does Kielburger connect the introduction and conclusion of his essay?
5. **Notice & Note** Throughout the essay, Kielburger uses extreme or absolute language—for example, "We have all met individuals who are gifted . . ." and ". . . so that children do not have to die." Explain the effect that such language has on the reader and whether you think it helps the author achieve his purpose.

RESEARCH

RESEARCH TIP
Most charities have a domain name that ends in *.org* or *.net*. A charity's homepage usually features a menu across the top that helps users navigate the site and directs them to the information they seek, including how they can support the organization's mission.

After reading the essay, what questions do you have about how to help children like Jeffrey, Muniannal, and José? Write them in the chart. One has been done for you. Then research to find answers. You can start by looking up WE Charity, which shares many of the goals of Free the Children.

QUESTIONS	ANSWERS
What causes the children's poverty?	

Connect Meet with a small group to share your findings. Does the information you gained affect your response to Kielburger's essay? Discuss why or why not.

CREATE AND DISCUSS

Write a Research Report Write a short (1–2 pages) research report about WE Charity.

- ❑ Review your findings from the Research on the previous page.
- ❑ Organize your findings and ideas by creating an outline. Then write a working thesis statement.
- ❑ Write your report, using your outline as a guide. Include details and other evidence from your research to support your ideas.

Go to **Conducting Research** in the **Writing Studio** to learn more.

Discuss with a Small Group A slogan of the WE movement is "Making doing good, doable." Discuss whether Craig Kielburger was a rare example of a young humanitarian or whether all young people have the capacity to act on their social awareness.

- ❑ As a group, review the essay and discuss the qualities that you think allowed Craig Kielburger to do what he did.
- ❑ Then talk about whether these qualities are rare or if all young people share them. How much help do you think he received from his parents and teachers? How important is this support?
- ❑ Finally, discuss how a person who wants to make a difference might get started.

Go to **Participating in Collaborative Discussions** in the **Speaking and Listening Studio** for help.

RESPOND TO THE ESSENTIAL QUESTION

What inspires you to make a difference?

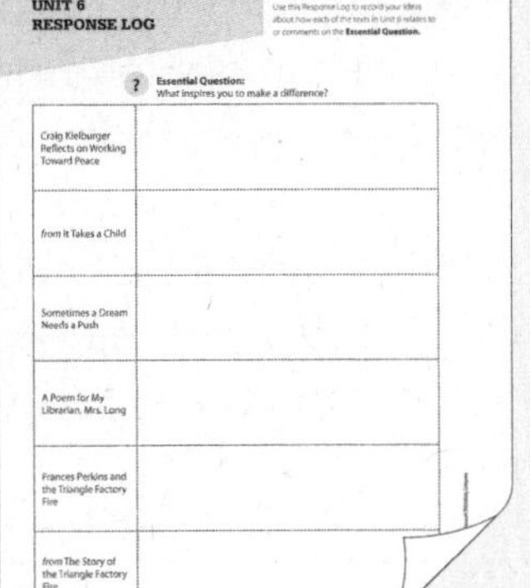

UNIT 6 RESPONSE LOG

Use this Response Log to record your ideas about how each of the texts in Unit 6 relates to or comments on the **Essential Question.**

Essential Question: What inspires you to make a difference?

Craig Kielburger Reflects on Working Toward Peace	
from It Takes a Child	
Sometimes a Dream Needs a Push	
A Poem for My Librarian, Mrs. Long	
Frances Perkins and the Triangle Factory Fire	
from The Story of the Triangle Factory Fire	

R6 Response Log

Gather Information Review your annotations and notes on "Craig Kielburger Reflects on Working Toward Peace." Then, add relevant details to your Response Log. As you determine which information to include, think about:

- what caused Kielburger to start his charity
- what kinds of problems children around the world face
- what solutions Kielburger has identified

At the end of the unit, use your notes to help you write a research report.

ACADEMIC VOCABULARY

As you write about and discuss what you learned from the personal essay, be sure to use the Academic Vocabulary words. Check off each of the words that you use.

- ❑ **contrast**
- ❑ **despite**
- ❑ **error**
- ❑ **inadequate**
- ❑ **interact**

RESPOND

WORD BANK
syringe
possession
inquire
capacity
exploitation

CRITICAL VOCABULARY

Practice and Apply Identify the Critical Vocabulary word that is most closely related to the boldfaced word in each question. Be prepared to explain your choices.

1. Which word goes with **answer**? __________
2. Which word goes with **needle**? __________
3. Which word goes with **underpaid**? __________
4. Which word goes with **ownership**? __________
5. Which word goes with **skill**? __________

VOCABULARY STRATEGY: Word Origin

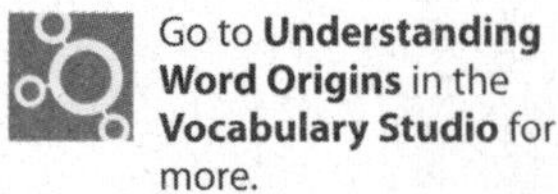

Go to **Understanding Word Origins** in the **Vocabulary Studio** for more.

Word origin, or etymology, tells you which language a word came from and gives you the historical development of the word. For example, if you look in a dictionary, you will see that the word *capacity* comes most recently from Middle English. However, it can be traced back through Old French and finally to the Latin word *capācitās,* from *capāx,* which means "spacious." *Capacity* has several meanings, one of which is "the maximum amount that something can hold."

Practice and Apply Follow these steps to explore the origin of each of this lesson's other Critical Vocabulary words.

- Look up each word in a print or online dictionary. You may want to look at a simpler form of the word as noted in the chart below.
- Find each word's origin or etymology. For help, look at the front or back of a dictionary. There will be a section that explains how the etymology is noted and what the abbreviations used mean.
- Write each word's origin and original meaning in the chart. Is the word's meaning related to the original meaning? How?

VOCABULARY WORD	ORIGIN/MEANING
syringe	
possession (possess)	
inquire	
exploitation (exploit)	

LANGUAGE CONVENTIONS: Commas

Commas have a variety of purposes. Used correctly, they help writers communicate effectively. They show readers which words and phrases go together and indicate which part of a sentence is most important. They can also create pauses, which give readers a moment to think about what they are reading. In "Craig Kielburger Reflects on Working Toward Peace," commas are used for several reasons, including these:

Go to **More Uses of the Comma** in the **Grammar Studio** to learn more uses.

- To set off introductory words or phrases:

  Indeed, even the most physically or mentally challenged person teaches all of us about the value and worth of human life.

- To set off nonessential words, phrases, and clauses:

  If more people had the heart of a street child, like José, and were willing to share, there would be no more poverty and a lot less suffering in this world.

- To separate dependent clauses from independent clauses:

  Although José's shirt was dirty and had a few small holes, it was a colorful soccer shirt and certainly much nicer than mine.

- To separate two independent clauses joined by one of the coordinating conjunctions: *and, but, or, for, nor, so,* or *yet:*

  He may have been a poor street child, but I saw more goodness in him than all of the world leaders I have ever met.

Practice and Apply Write your own sentences with commas using the examples from "Craig Kielburger Reflects on Working Toward Peace" as models. Your sentences can be about Craig Kielburger's work or about a topic related to helping others. When you have finished, share your sentences with a partner and compare your use of commas.

ANALYZE & APPLY

MEDIA

from

IT TAKES A CHILD

Documentary by
Judy Jackson

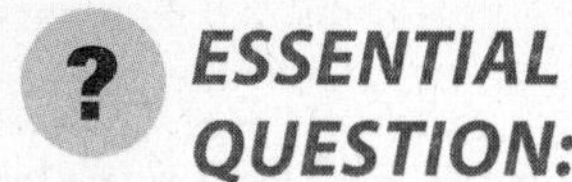

What inspires you to make a difference?

QUICK START

What problem or issue do you feel strongly about? What would you be willing to do to solve that problem? Discuss your ideas with a partner.

ANALYZE A DOCUMENTARY

A **documentary** is a nonfiction film about important people, events, issues, or places. Documentaries include **interviews, film footage, voice-over narration,** and **sound effects** to convey information, mood, and tone, or the author's attitude toward the subject. As you watch the film clip, think about how these features work together.

GENRE ELEMENTS: DOCUMENTARY

- includes interviews filmed specifically for the documentary
- contains filmed material—or footage—that gives information about the topic
- features voice-over narration—the voice of an unseen speaker—to give facts or explain
- includes sound effects used for a variety of purposes

FEATURE	STRATEGIES FOR VIEWING
Interviews feature experts on the subject or someone close to the person or event.	Consider the person being interviewed. Does he or she have special knowledge or present another side of the story?
Footage can include film clips, reports, photos, and interviews about a subject.	Consider why the footage was chosen. Does it reveal the filmmaker's attitude toward the topic? Does it show emotions?
Voice-over narration is scripted to present key facts and explain their importance.	Listen to the voice-over narration. Does it change from speaker to speaker? Does the language contribute to mood or tone?
Sound effects include music and sounds that show mood and signal shifts in the topic.	Follow music cues. Do they signal a change in setting or mood? Listen for sound effects. Do they clarify events?

BACKGROUND

When child activist Craig Kielburger was twelve years old, he became interested in the plight of child laborers. Inspired by the story of twelve-year-old Iqbal, a child labor activist who had been murdered in South Asia, Kielburger realized that a child could make a difference in the world. Kielburger then traveled to South Asia to see child labor first hand. With the help of a film crew, he documented his journey so that the world could see what he had witnessed.

SETTING A PURPOSE

As you view the documentary, think about why Kielburger decided to make this journey and what he wanted to find out. Notice the ways that filmmaking and news reporting come together to help you understand Kielburger's reasons for traveling to South Asia. Write down any questions you have during viewing. NOTEBOOK .

To view the video, log in online and select **"It Takes a Child"** from the unit menu.

As needed, pause the documentary to make notes about what impresses you or about ideas you might want to talk about later. Replay or rewind so that you can clarify anything you do not understand.

ANALYZE MEDIA

Support your responses with evidence from the documentary.

NOTEBOOK

1. **Infer and Summarize** What is the controlling idea, or thesis, of the documentary? Describe the scenes that take place in the film and how those scenes support the key idea.
2. **Analyze** Identify the filmmaker's purpose(s) in making the documentary. What key parts of the film convey the purpose(s)?
3. **Infer** Think about the features the filmmaker uses. Explain how the filmmaker uses interviews, film footage, voice-over, and sound effects to clarify the issues presented in the documentary.
4. **Analyze** How does the opening introduce the setting? What combination of features works together in the opening to create a sense of the place Kielburger is visiting and to help you understand the setting?
5. **Compare and Contrast** The voice-over narration includes two narrators: an unnamed speaker and Craig Kielburger. The unnamed narrator is objective, while Craig Kielburger's narration is subjective. Compare and contrast the language and types of information given by the two narrators. How does each contribute to the mood and tone of the documentary?

RESEARCH

RESEARCH TIP

Because information on the Internet is not regulated for accuracy, ensure accuracy either by using only reputable sources (those ending in *.edu*, *.gov*, and *.org*) or by verifying by using multiple sources.

Many other young activists are currently working to solve problems they care about. With a partner, do some research to find two examples of other young activists and the problems they are working to solve. Record your information in the chart.

ACTIVIST	PROBLEM

Connect How would you present your information in a documentary about one of the young activists you researched? With your partner, sketch out the sound and visual elements you would include to convey this information.

CREATE AND PRESENT

Write a Personal Essay Write a personal essay about an encounter with a social activist or an experience with social action that was inspirational.

- ❑ Jot down ideas about the experience and why it was meaningful.
- ❑ Use your ideas to create an outline. Your outline should show the events in a logical order.
- ❑ Write your essay, using the first-person point of view. Use colorful and specific words to describe exactly what you saw, heard, and felt.
- ❑ In your conclusion, summarize why the event or person was inspirational.

Go to **Writing as a Process** in the **Writing Studio** for more help.

Produce a Podcast With a partner, create an audio recording for a podcast review of the documentary clip from *It Takes a Child.*

- ❑ Make notes about visual and sound elements in the documentary that particularly impressed you, both positively and negatively.
- ❑ Explain how the choice of screen scenes affects the impact of the words spoken in the interviews. Include an assessment of whether viewers should see the entire documentary.
- ❑ Create the recording of your review with a partner, speaking in a conversational tone and enunciating clearly. Share your podcast with a larger group.

Go to **Using Media in a Presentation** in the **Speaking and Listening Studio** to learn more.

RESPOND TO THE ESSENTIAL QUESTION

What inspires you to make a difference?

Gather Information Review your annotations and notes on the film clip from *It Takes a Child.* Then, add relevant details to your Response Log. As you determine which information to include, think about:

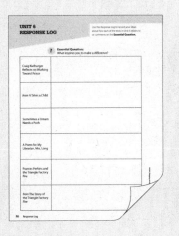

- what motivated Craig Kielburger's journey
- how you think people might react to the documentary

At the end of the unit, use your notes to help you write a research report.

ACADEMIC VOCABULARY

As you write about and discuss what you learned from the documentary, be sure to use the Academic Vocabulary words. Check off each of the words that you use.

- ❑ **contrast**
- ❑ **despite**
- ❑ **error**
- ❑ **inadequate**
- ❑ **interact**

SOMETIMES A DREAM NEEDS A PUSH

Short Story by **Walter Dean Myers**

? ***ESSENTIAL QUESTION:***

What inspires you to make a difference?

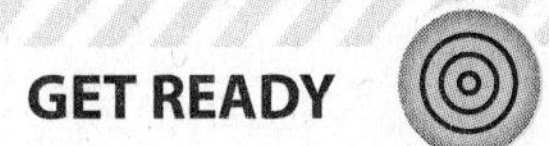

QUICK START

How might guilt, or feelings of regret, affect your relationship with someone? List some ideas and then discuss them with a small group.

ANALYZE REALISTIC FICTION

Realistic fiction is fiction that is set in the real, modern world. The characters, setting, problems, and resolution are all believable.

- The characters behave like real people when faced with modern life's problems and conflicts.
- The dialogue reflects the age and culture of the characters.
- The setting is a real or realistic place (for example, a modern city). The story takes place in the present or recent past.
- The conflicts that the characters face can be internal or external. These conflicts often reflect social issues or problems that real people are likely to face.

As you read "Sometimes a Dream Needs a Push," look for these realistic elements to help you analyze the story.

GENRE ELEMENTS: REALISTIC FICTION

- includes the basic elements of fiction: setting, characters, plot, conflict, and theme
- centers on one particular moment or event in life
- if in the form of a short story, can be read in one sitting

ANALYZE CHARACTER QUALITIES

Character **qualities** may be physical traits (such as athletic ability) or personality traits (such as shyness). Just as in real life, a fictional character's qualities can influence events and relationships. Characters' qualities can affect how they interact and how they resolve both internal and external conflicts in a story. As you read "Sometimes a Dream Needs a Push," make inferences about the qualities of Chris and his father based on their words, thoughts, and actions. Here is one example. You can use a similar chart to record your own ideas.

CHARACTER	WORDS, THOUGHTS, ACTIONS	INFERENCE
Chris	I hadn't told any of the kids about my father coming to practice. I wasn't even sure he was going to show up.	Chris doesn't want to get his hopes up. He has been disappointed before.
Chris's father	"Sometimes I think he blames himself," Mom said. "Whenever he sees you in the wheelchair he wants to put it out of his mind."	Chris's dad feels guilty. He is more quiet and distant because of his guilt.

GET READY

CRITICAL VOCABULARY

concession   collision   congestion   turnover   fundamental

To see how many Critical Vocabulary words you already know, use them to complete the sentences.

1. There was so much __________ in the hallway that students were late getting to their classes.
2. The __________ stand at the theater sells great popcorn.
3. The play resulted in a __________ when the point guard lost possession of the ball.
4. Texting while driving resulted in a deadly __________.
5. She learned the __________ skills of creating a smartphone app.

LANGUAGE CONVENTIONS

Consistent Verb Tense In this lesson, you will learn about using verb tenses, which indicate the times of events, correctly. Consistent verb tenses help show the sequence of events.

Afterward, the team voted, and the Hartsdale Posse all agreed that we wanted to play in the league.

Here, the time frame for the three actions (*voted*, *agreed*, and *wanted*) are the same: the past. Therefore, all three verbs use the past tense. As you read "Sometimes a Dream Needs a Push," pay attention to the author's use of consistent verb tenses.

ANNOTATION MODEL

NOTICE & NOTE 

As you read, look for realistic text details. You can also mark up details that suggest each character's qualities. In the model, you can see one reader's notes about part of "Sometimes a Dream Needs a Push."

1 You might have heard of my dad, Jim Blair. He's six five and played a year of good basketball in the pros before tearing his knee up in his second year. The knee took forever to heal and was never quite the same again. Still, he played pro ball in Europe for five years before giving it up and becoming an executive with a high-tech company.	Chris probably admires his dad. His dad was a good athlete and may be rather competitive. The setting is in the present-day United States.

NOTICE & NOTE 

BACKGROUND

Walter Dean Myers *(1937–2014) was born in West Virginia but grew up in the Harlem community of New York City. He developed a love of reading and writing in school and went on to write at least five pages a day over his lengthy career. He published more than 100 books for young people, often focusing on the experiences of young African Americans. Myers received great recognition, including two Newbery Honor Book Awards and several Coretta Scott King Awards.*

SOMETIMES A DREAM NEEDS A PUSH

Short Story by Walter Dean Myers

SETTING A PURPOSE

As you read, pay attention to how the father and son interact with each other. How do these characters' thoughts, feelings, and actions reveal their individual qualities—and help you understand their relationship?

1 You might have heard of my dad, Jim Blair. He's six five and played a year of good basketball in the pros before tearing his knee up in his second year. The knee took forever to heal and was never quite the same again. Still, he played pro ball in Europe for five years before giving it up and becoming an executive with a high-tech company.

2 Dad loved basketball and hoped that one day I would play the game. He taught me a lot, and I was pretty good until the accident. It was raining and we were on the highway, approaching the turnoff toward our house in Hartsdale, when a truck skidded across the road and hit our rear bumper. Our little car spun off the road, squealing as Dad tried to bring it under control. But he couldn't avoid the light pole. I remember seeing the broken windows, hearing Mom yelling, amazingly bright lights flashing crazily in front of me. Then everything

Notice & Note

Use the side margins to notice and note signposts in the text.

ANALYZE CHARACTER QUALITIES

Annotate: Mark words and phrases in paragraphs 2 and 3 that tell you about Chris and his father.

Analyze: How would you describe each character? How do you think Chris's becoming physically disabled has changed their relationship?

NOTICE & NOTE

was suddenly dark. The next thing I remember is waking up in the hospital. There were surgeries and weeks in the hospital, but the important thing was that I wasn't going to be walking again.

3 I didn't like the idea, but Mom and I learned to live with it. Dad took it hard, real hard. He was never much of a talker, Mom said, but he talked even less since I was hurt.

4 "Sometimes I think he blames himself," Mom said. "Whenever he sees you in the wheelchair he wants to put it out of his mind."

5 I hadn't thought about that when Mr. Evans, an elder in our church, asked me if I wanted to join a wheelchair basketball team he was starting.

6 "We won't have the experience of the other teams in the league," he said. "But it'll be fun."

7 When I told Mom, she was all for it, but Dad just looked at me and mumbled something under his breath. He does that sometimes. Mom said that he's chewing up his words to see how they taste before he lets them out.

ANALYZE REALISTIC FICTION

Annotate: In paragraph 8, circle words and phrases that Chris uses that reflect his age. Underline text details that describe a modern setting for the story.

Critique: How do these details make the story seem realistic? Why are details such as these important to how the reader perceives the story?

8 Our van is equipped with safety harnesses for my chair, and we used it on the drive to see a game between Madison and Rosedale. It was awesome to see guys my age zipping around in their chairs playing ball. I liked the chairs, too. They were specially built with rear stabilizing wheels and side wheels that slanted in. Very cool. I couldn't wait to start practicing. At the game, Mom sat next to me, but Dad went and sat next to the **concession** stand. I saw him reading a newspaper and only looking up at the game once in a while.

concession
(kən-sĕsh´ən) *n.* Sporting and entertainment events often feature *concession* stands where food and drinks are sold.

9 "Jim, have you actually seen wheelchair games before?" Mom asked on the way home.

10 Dad made a little motion with his head and said something that sounded like "Grumpa-grumpa" and then mentioned that he had to get up early in the morning. Mom looked at me, and her mouth tightened just a little.

ANALYZE CHARACTER QUALITIES

Annotate: In paragraph 11, mark Chris's thoughts about his dad's reaction to the game.

Infer: Why do you think Chris's dad reacts this way? What does Chris's desire to play wheelchair basketball tell you about Chris's character?

11 That was okay with me because I didn't want him to talk about the game if he didn't like it. After washing and getting into my pj's I wheeled into my room, transferred to the bed, and tried to make sense of the day. I didn't know what to make of Dad's reaction, but I knew I wanted to play.

12 The next day at school, tall Sarah told me there was a message for me on the bulletin board. Sarah is cool but the nosiest person in school.

13 "What did it say?" I asked.

14 "How would I know?" she answered. "I don't read people's messages."

NOTICE & NOTE 

15 “Probably nothing important,” I said, spinning my chair to head down the hall.

16 “Just something about you guys going to play Madison in a practice game and they haven’t lost all season,” Sarah said. “From Nicky G.”

17 “Oh.”

18 The school has a special bus for wheelchairs and the driver always takes the long way to my house, which is a little irritating when you’ve got a ton of homework that needs to get done, and I had a ton and a half. When I got home, Mom had the entire living room filled with purple lace and flower things she was putting together for a wedding and was lettering nameplates for them. I threw her a quick “Hey” and headed for my room.

19 “Chris, your coach called,” Mom said.

20 “Mr. Evans?”

21 “Yes, he said your father had left a message for him,” Mom answered. She had a big piece of the purple stuff around her neck as she leaned against the doorjamb. “Anything up?”

22 “I don’t know,” I said with a shrug. My heart sank. I went into my room and started on my homework, trying not to think of why Dad would call Mr. Evans.

ANALYZE CHARACTER QUALITIES

Annotate: Mark text details in paragraph 22 that show how Chris feels when his mother tells him about the phone call.

Interpret: Why might Chris feel this way? What does this scene suggest about Chris’s feelings toward his father?

23 With all the wedding stuff in the living room and Mom looking so busy, I was hoping that we’d have pizza again. No such luck. Somewhere in the afternoon she had found time to bake a chicken. Dad didn’t get home until nearly seven-thirty, so we ate late.

24 While we ate Mom was talking about how some woman was trying to convince all of her bridesmaids to put a pink streak in their hair for her wedding. She asked us what we thought of that. Dad grunted under his breath and went back to his chicken. He didn’t see the face that Mom made at him.

25 “By the way”—Mom gave me a quick look—”Mr. Evans called. He said he had missed your call earlier.”

26 “I spoke to him late this afternoon,” Dad said.

27 “Are the computers down at the school?” Mom asked.

28 “No, I was just telling him that I didn’t think that the Madison team was all that good,” Dad said. “I heard the kids saying they were great. They’re okay, but they’re not great. I’m going to talk to him again at practice tomorrow.”

CONTRASTS AND CONTRADICTIONS

Notice & Note: Mark Chris’s dad’s comments in paragraph 28.

Compare: How do these comments differ from his attitude up to this point in the story? What does this new information suggest about Chris’s dad?

29 “Oh,” Mom said. I could see the surprise in her face and felt it in my stomach.

30 The next day zoomed by. It was like the bells to change classes were ringing every two minutes. I hadn’t told any of the kids about my father coming to practice. I wasn’t even sure

NOTICE & NOTE

ANALYZE CHARACTER QUALITIES

Annotate: In paragraph 31, mark text details that show what Chris thinks, feels, and does when his father shows up to practice.

Infer: How does Chris's reaction reflect his internal conflict about his father's presence?

CONTRASTS AND CONTRADICTIONS

Notice & Note: Review paragraphs 37–39. How do Chris's dad's skill and confidence change when he sits in the wheelchair?

Predict: What do you think he will come to realize about wheelchair basketball?

he was going to show up. He had made promises before and then gotten called away to work. This time he had said he was coming to practice, which was at two-thirty, in the middle of his day.

31 He was there. He sat in the stands and watched us go through our drills and a minigame. I was so nervous, I couldn't do anything right. I couldn't catch the ball at all, and the one shot I took was an air ball from just behind the foul line. We finished our regular practice, and Mr. Evans motioned for my father to come down to the court.

32 "Your dad's a giant!" Kwame whispered as Dad came onto the court.

33 "That's how big Chris is going to be," Nicky G said.

34 I couldn't imagine ever being as tall as my father.

35 "I was watching the teams play the other day." Dad had both hands jammed into his pockets. "And I saw that neither of them were running baseline plays and almost all the shots were aimed for the rims. Shots off the backboards are going to go in a lot more than rim shots if you're shooting from the floor."

36 Dad picked up a basketball and threw it casually against the backboard. It rolled around the rim and fell through. He did it again. And again. He didn't miss once.

37 "I happen to know that you played pro ball," Mr. Evans said, "and you're good. But I think shooting from a wheelchair is a bit harder."

38 "You have another chair?" Dad asked.

39 Mr. Evans pointed to his regular chair sitting by the watercooler. Dad took four long steps over to it, sat down, and

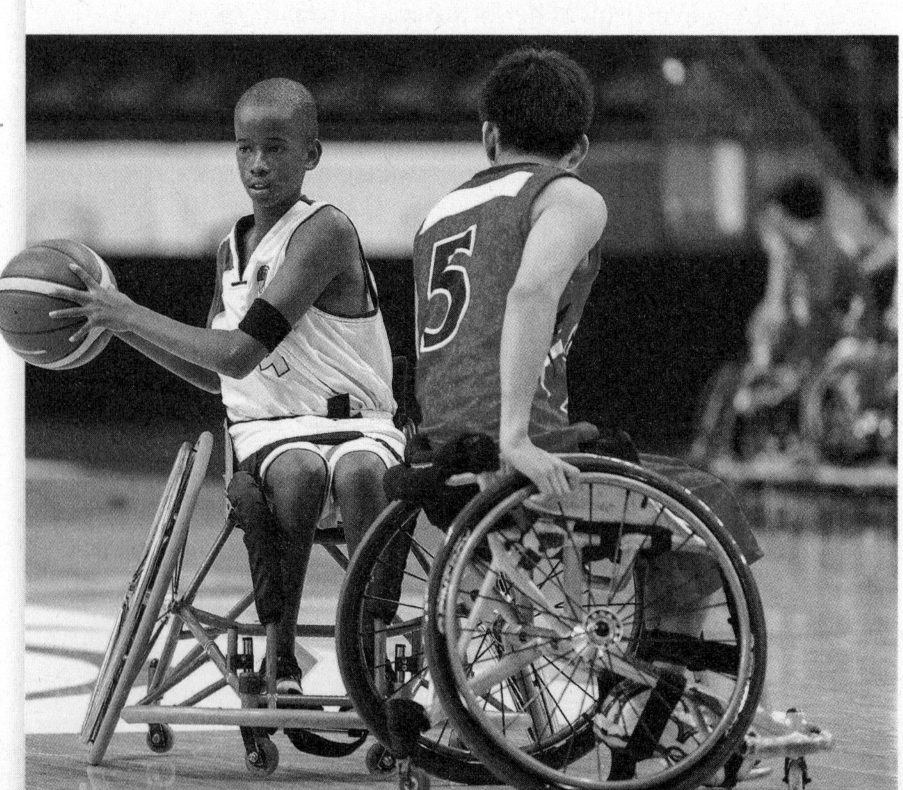

wheeled himself back onto the floor. He put his hands up and looked at me. I realized I was holding a ball and tossed it to him. He tried to turn his chair back toward the basket, and it spun all the way around. For a moment he looked absolutely lost, as if he didn't know what had happened to him. He seemed a little embarrassed as he glanced toward me.

40 "That happens sometimes," I said. "No problem."

41 He nodded, exhaled slowly, then turned and shot a long, lazy arc that hit the backboard and fell through.

42 "The backboard takes the energy out of the ball," he said. "So if it does hit the rim, it won't be so quick to bounce off. Madison made about twenty percent of its shots the other day. That doesn't win basketball games, no matter how good they look making them."

43 There are six baskets in our gym, and we spread out and practiced shooting against the backboards. At first I wasn't good at it. I was hitting the underside of the rim.

44 "That's because you're still thinking about the rim," Dad said when he came over to me. "Start thinking about a spot on the backboard. When you find your spot, really own it, you'll be knocking down your shots on a regular basis."

45 Nicky G got it first, and then Kwame, and then Bobby. I was too nervous to even hit the backboard half the time, but Dad didn't get mad or anything. He didn't even mumble. He just said it would come to me after a while.

46 Baseline plays were even harder. Dad wanted us to get guys wheeling for position under and slightly behind the basket.

47 "There are four feet of space behind the backboard," Dad said. "If you can use those four feet, you have an advantage."

48 We tried wheeling plays along the baseline but just kept getting in each other's way.

49 "That's the point," Dad said. "When you learn to move without running into each other you're going to have a big advantage over a team that's trying to keep up with you."

50 Okay, so most of the guys are pretty good wheeling their chairs up and down the court. But our baseline plays looked more like a **collision** derby. Dad shook his head and Mr. Evans laughed.

51 We practiced all week. Dad came again and said we were improving.

52 "I thought you were terrible at first," he said, smiling. I didn't believe he actually smiled. "Now you're just pretty bad. But I think you can play with that Madison team."

53 Madison had agreed to come to our school to play, and when they arrived they were wearing jackets with their school colors and CLIPPERS across the back.

ANALYZE REALISTIC FICTION

Annotate: Circle words and phrases that Chris's dad uses in paragraphs 44 and 47 that provide realistic details about playing wheelchair basketball.

Evaluate: What do details such as these add to the story?

LANGUAGE CONVENTIONS

Annotate: Mark the verbs in paragraph 50.

Analyze: Why is there a change in verb tense between the first sentence of the paragraph and the last two sentences?

collision
(kə-lĭzh´ən) *n.* When the two things crash into each other, the result is a *collision*.

NOTICE & NOTE

54 We started the game and Madison got the tip-off. The guy I was holding blocked me off so their guard, once he got past Nicky G, had a clear path to the basket. The first score against us came with only ten seconds off the clock.

55 I looked up in the stands to see where Mom was. I found her and saw Dad sitting next to her. I waved and she waved back, and Dad just sat there with his arms folded.

56 Madison stopped us cold on the next play, and when Bobby and Lou bumped their chairs at the top of the key, there was a man open. A quick pass inside and Madison was up by four.

turnover
(tûrn´ō´vər) *n.* In basketball, a *turnover* is a loss of possession of the ball.

57 We settled down a little, but nothing worked that well. We made a lot of wild passes for **turnovers,** and once, when I was actually leading a fast break, I got called for traveling when the ball got ahead of me, and I touched the wheels twice before dribbling. The guys from Madison were having a good time, and we were feeling miserable. At halftime, we rolled into the locker room feeling dejected. When Dad showed up, I felt bad. He was used to winning, not losing.

58 "Our kids looked a little overmatched in the first half," Mr. Evans said.

59 "I think they played okay," Dad said, "just a little nervous. But look at the score. It's twenty-two to fourteen. With all their shooting, Madison is just eight points ahead. We can catch up."

60 I looked at Dad to see if he was kidding. He wasn't. He wasn't kidding, and he had said "we." I liked that.

ANALYZE REALISTIC FICTION

Annotate: In paragraph 60, mark Chris's reaction to his dad's assessment of the team.

Evaluate: What makes Chris's reaction to his father realistic? How realistic is the conflict in their relationship? Why?

61 We came out in the second half all fired up. We ran a few plays along the baseline, but it still seemed more like bumper cars than basketball with all the **congestion.** Madison took twenty-three shots in the second half and made eight of them plus three foul shots for a total score of forty-one points. We took seventeen shots and made eleven of them, all layups off the backboard, and two foul shots for a total of thirty-eight points. We had lost the game, but everyone felt great about how we had played. We lined up our chairs, gave Madison high fives before they left, and waited until we got to the locker room to give ourselves high fives.

congestion
(kən-jĕs´chən) *n. Congestion* is overcrowding, such as when too many vehicles cause a traffic jam.

62 Afterward, the team voted, and the Hartsdale Posse all agreed that we wanted to play in the league. Dad had shown us that we could play, and even though we had lost we knew we would be ready for the next season.

63 Dad only comes to practice once in a while, but he comes to the games when they're on the weekend. At practice he shows us **fundamentals,** stuff like how to line your wrist up for a shot, and how the ball should touch your hand when you're ready to shoot. That made me feel good even if he would never

fundamental
(fŭn´də-mĕn´tl) *n.* A *fundamental* is a basic but essential part of an object or a system.

NOTICE & NOTE 

talk about the games when he wasn't in the gym. I didn't want to push it too much because I liked him coming to practice. I didn't want to push him, but Mom didn't mind at all.

64 "Jim, if you were in a wheelchair," she asked, "do you think you could play as well as Chris?"

65 Dad was on his laptop and looked over the screen at Mom, then looked over at me. Then he looked back down at the screen and grumbled something. I figured he was saying that there was no way he could play as well as me in a chair, but I didn't ask him to repeat it.

ANALYZE CHARACTER QUALITIES

Annotate: In paragraph 65, underline Chris's interpretation of his father's grumbles.

Analyze: What does this interpretation suggest about Chris's confidence? What does it suggest about his relationship with his father?

CHECK YOUR UNDERSTANDING

Answer these questions before moving on to the **Analyze the Text** section on the following page.

1 Which statement best explains why this story is an example of realistic fiction?

A The characters are people whom the author knows.

B The author includes details about an actual sport.

C The conflict in the story is one that happens to everyone.

D The author included only details that really happened.

2 Read this sentence from paragraph 7.

> *Mom said that he's chewing up his words to see how they taste before he lets them out.*

The sensory language in this sentence highlights the father's —

F confusion

G hesitation

H sense of humor

J wish for secrecy

3 Using the first-person point of view allows the author to —

A explain why the father takes an interest in wheelchair basketball

B describe each character's feelings about the accident

C reveal the narrator's relationship with his father

D inform readers about the rules of wheelchair basketball

RESPOND

ANALYZE THE TEXT

Support your responses with evidence from the text. NOTEBOOK

1. **Make Inferences** Consider what you know about Chris's character. What do you think motivates him to join the wheelchair basketball team? Why?
2. **Analyze** In what ways has the relationship between Chris and his dad changed by the end of the story?
3. **Evaluate** Think about the relationship between Chris and his mom and between Chris and his dad. What elements of the story make each relationship seem realistic?
4. **Synthesize** Think about the story's title. Whose dream is the author referring to? What do you think the dream is? Explain the significance of the title.
5. **Notice & Note** How does Chris's dad's opinion of and interest in wheelchair basketball change from the beginning of the story to the end? Why?

RESEARCH

RESEARCH TIP
The best sources for information about the rules of a sport are often organizations dedicated to or related to that sport. These web addresses usually end in *.org*. Also, as you scroll through your search results, scan the brief description under each result to find the sites that are most likely to have the information you seek.

In the short story, Chris joins a wheelchair basketball team. Research wheelchair basketball. Record what you learn in the chart.

QUESTION	ANSWER
What are the key rules of wheelchair basketball?	
How do the wheelchairs used for the game differ from everyday wheelchairs?	

Extend When and why did people first begin playing wheelchair basketball? Find out about the origins of wheelchair basketball.

CREATE AND PRESENT

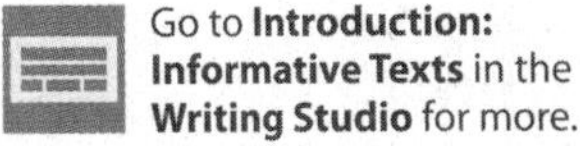

Go to **Introduction: Informative Texts** in the **Writing Studio** for more.

Write an Informational Article Using the research you found on wheelchair basketball, write a one- to two-page informational article about this sport.

- ❑ Review your research. Decide what information you want to include and how you want to organize it.
- ❑ Include the controlling idea or thesis you want to convey in the first paragraph. In each paragraph that follows, include a key idea that connects to the controlling idea or thesis and is supported by evidence from your research.
- ❑ In your final paragraph, summarize your findings and restate the main idea in an engaging way.

Go to **Using Media in a Presentation** in the **Speaking and Listening Studio** for help.

Create a Video Critique In pairs, tape brief critiques, or reviews, of the story. Switch roles as the on-camera reviewer and the recorder.

- ❑ Discuss the story with your partner. Go beyond a discussion of likes and dislikes. For example, what part of the story did you most connect with?
- ❑ Write the outline of a short critique. Include a brief summary and your responses to the story's characters, setting, and plot.
- ❑ Before taping your critiques, practice delivering them. Speak clearly; use appropriate gestures and facial expressions. Consider ways to add interest to your videos, such as using a basketball court as a location and a basketball as a prop.

RESPOND TO THE ESSENTIAL QUESTION

? What inspires you to make a difference?

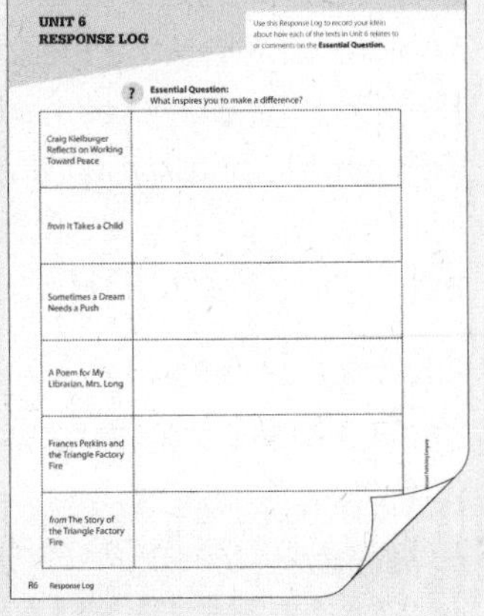

UNIT 6 RESPONSE LOG

Use this Response Log to record your ideas about how each of the texts in Unit 6 relates to or comments on the **Essential Question.**

? **Essential Question:** What inspires you to make a difference?

Craig Kielburger Reflects on Working Toward Peace	
from It Takes a Child	
Sometimes a Dream Needs a Push	
A Poem for My Librarian, Mrs. Long	
Frances Perkins and the Triangle Factory Fire	
from The Story of the Triangle Factory Fire	

R6 Response Log

Gather Information Review your annotations and notes on "Sometimes a Dream Needs a Push." Then, add relevant details to your Response Log. As you determine which information to include, think about:

- the reasons that people become involved in sports
- how athletes train for competition
- the value of teamwork

At the end of the unit, refer to your notes to help you write a research report.

ACADEMIC VOCABULARY

As you write and discuss what you learned from the short story, be sure to use the Academic Vocabulary words. Check off each of the words that you use.

- ❑ **contrast**
- ❑ **despite**
- ❑ **error**
- ❑ **inadequate**
- ❑ **interact**

CRITICAL VOCABULARY

WORD BANK
concession
collision
congestion
turnover
fundamental

Practice and Apply Mark the letter of the answer to each question. Be prepared to explain your response.

1. Where would you be more likely to find a **concession** stand?
   a. a forest **b.** a football stadium
2. Which of the following might be involved in a **collision**?
   a. two buildings **b.** two bicycles
3. Which of the following is more likely to cause highway **congestion**?
   a. a stalled car **b.** mild temperatures
4. Which of the following would more likely lead to a **turnover** during a sports game?
   a. misplaying the ball **b.** taking a timeout
5. Which of the following is a **fundamental** of learning to ride a bike?
   a. exercise **b.** braking

VOCABULARY STRATEGY: Context Clues

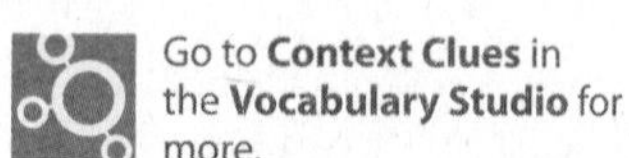

Go to **Context Clues** in the **Vocabulary Studio** for more.

When you encounter an unfamiliar word, **context clues**—hints that appear in surrounding words, sentences, or paragraphs—can help you determine the meaning. Consider this example from the story:

> **We ran a few plays along the baseline, but it still seemed more like bumper cars than basketball with all the congestion.**

Look for clues to the meaning of *congestion* in the surrounding text. Running the plays seemed "more like bumper cars than basketball." This phrase helps you contrast wheelchairs moving on a basketball court with the way that bumper cars move in a limited area. You can infer, then, that *congestion* means "crowded."

Practice and Apply Use context clues to define these words from "Sometimes a Dream Needs a Push."

WORD	CONTEXT CLUES	MY GUESSED DEFINITION	DICTIONARY DEFINITION
equipped	(paragraph 8)		
arc	(paragraph 41)		
dejected	(paragraph 57)		

LANGUAGE CONVENTIONS: Consistent Verb Tense

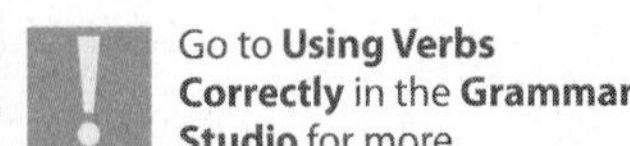

Go to **Using Verbs Correctly** in the **Grammar Studio** for more.

A verb's **tense** shows a particular time that an action occurs.

Present: Chris plays basketball.

Present perfect: Chris has played basketball.

Past: Chris played basketball.

Past perfect: Chris had played basketball.

Future: Chris will play basketball.

Future perfect: Chris will have played basketball.

Shifting tenses within sentences or paragraphs can be confusing unless it is done correctly. Follow these two rules to help you control verb tense shifts in your writing:

- Shift verb tense within a sentence only when there is a shift in the time frame.
- Shift verb tense within a paragraph only when it is necessary to refer to events that occurred in the past or to events that will occur in the future.

The chart shows examples from "Sometimes a Dream Needs a Push."

SENTENCE TYPE	EXAMPLE
Consistent Verb Tense (past tense)	Mom looked at me, and her mouth tightened just a little.
Correct Shift in Verb Tense (from past tense to past perfect tense)	I looked at Dad to see if he was kidding. He wasn't. He wasn't kidding, and he had said "we." I liked that.

Practice and Apply Write your own sentences using consistent verb tenses or correctly shifting verb tenses. Your sentences can be about the story's events or characters. When you have finished, share your sentences with a partner and compare them.

A POEM FOR MY LIBRARIAN, MRS. LONG

(You never know what troubled little girl needs a book)

Poem by **Nikki Giovanni**

? *ESSENTIAL QUESTION:*

What inspires you to make a difference?

QUICK START

The poem you are about to read is about a person who influenced the poet's life. Make some notes about a person who has helped to shape your character, personality, likes, or dislikes.

Description of the Person	How This Person Affected Me

ANALYZE FREE VERSE POETRY

"A Poem for My Librarian, Mrs. Long" is an example of **free verse poetry,** a form with no set patterns of rhythm and rhyme. Instead, the language flows like everyday speech. Although free verse differs from conventional poetry in form, it may include some of the same literary techniques, such as imagery and figurative language. Here are some of the techniques poets use in free verse poetry and an example of each from Nikki Giovanni's poem.

TECHNIQUE	EXAMPLE
Use of punctuation and capitalization in unique ways	And up the hill on vine street / (The main black corridor) sat our carnegie library
Varied length of stanzas and lines to suit stylistic effects	Late at night with my portable (that I was so proud of) / Tucked under my pillow
Use of sensory language to create vivid mental images	Which I visited and inhaled that wonderful odor / Of new books
Use of sound devices, such as repetition and alliteration to create a mood and convey meaning	Hat in hand to ask to borrow so that I might borrow

As you read the poem, note other examples of these techniques and think about the meaning they convey in the poem.

GENRE ELEMENTS: FREE VERSE POETRY

- uses irregular rhythm and line length; may group lines into stanzas
- may use little or no rhyme; often resembles natural speech
- may use unconventional punctuation or capitalization
- may use sound devices and figurative language

ANALYZE THEME

A **theme** is a message about life or human nature that an author shares with the reader. Readers can infer one or more themes by thinking about an author's **tone,** or attitude toward the subject, and by considering what is said and how ideas come together.

In "A Poem for My Librarian, Mrs. Long," the poet is also the speaker, reflecting on her childhood experiences. After describing everyday activities, she turns her attention to her love of books. The poem is dedicated to Mrs. Long, a librarian who likely endured adversity so that the young girl could read the books she wanted.

To determine a theme in a poem, look for ideas that the poet develops over the course of the poem and how they build on one another. This chart shows text evidence for one theme in the poem.

Text evidence:	**Text evidence:**	**Text evidence:**
And up the hill on vine street / (The main black corridor) . . .	Hat in hand to ask to borrow so that I might borrow . . .	Probably they said something humiliating since southern / Whites like to humiliate southern blacks
Theme: Helping someone may mean standing up to prejudice.		

As you read the poem, consider what seems most important about the poet's relationship with Mrs. Long. What theme might that suggest?

ANNOTATION MODEL

NOTICE & NOTE 

As you read, notice the author's descriptions and use of sensory language, and the mood and mental images that they create. You can also mark up unusual line lengths, capitalization, and punctuation. This model shows one reader's notes for the first stanza of "A Poem for My Librarian, Mrs. Long."

At a time when there was no tv before 3:00 P.M.
And on Sunday none until 5:00
We sat on front porches watching
The jfg sign go on and off greeting
The neighbors, discussing the political
Situation congratulating the preacher
On his sermon

lowercase tv and jfg suggest they are not important

line break emphasizes "watching"

image of a close family and neighborhood; warm mood

NOTICE & NOTE 

BACKGROUND

Nikki Giovanni *(b. 1943) has been one of the best known American poets since publishing her first book of poetry in 1968. Giovanni grew up in the racially segregated South. When Giovanni attended college, she became a part of a movement of African American writers who were finding new ways to express pride in their distinct culture. In addition to her poetry collections, Giovanni is also an award-winning children's author.*

A POEM FOR MY LIBRARIAN, MRS. LONG

(You never know what troubled little girl needs a book)

Poem by Nikki Giovanni

SETTING A PURPOSE

In the poem, Nikki Giovanni looks back at her childhood and the people who most influenced her. As you read, think about how Giovanni's childhood experiences shaped her dreams and her writing.

At a time when there was no tv before 3:00 P.M.
And on Sunday none until 5:00
We sat on front porches watching
The jfg[1] sign go on and off greeting
The neighbors, discussing the political
Situation congratulating the preacher
On his sermon

Notice & Note

Use the side margins to notice and note signposts in the text.

MEMORY MOMENT

Notice & Note: According to lines 1–7, what were the main activities for the poet as a child?

Critique: There's no mention of a librarian yet. Why might that be so?

[1] **jfg:** a brand of coffee that was popular in Knoxville, Tennessee; an old electrically lit sign for the coffee is a famous landmark in Knoxville, Tennessee.

ANALYZE FREE VERSE POETRY

Annotate: In lines 17–21, circle words that normally would be capitalized. Underline short lines in the stanza.

Analyze: What effect does the unconventional capitalization have? How do the shorter lines convey meaning?

ANALYZE THEME

Annotate: Mark what Mrs. Long said and did in lines 24–39.

Interpret: How does the poet feel about Mrs. Long? What message is the poet sending about the power of people like Mrs. Long?

There was always radio which brought us
Songs from wlac in nashville and what we would now call
Easy listening or smooth jazz but when I listened
Late at night with my portable (that I was so proud of)
Tucked under my pillow
I heard nat king cole and matt dennis, june christy and
ella fitzgerald
And sometimes sarah vaughan sing black coffee
Which I now drink
It was just called music

There was a bookstore uptown on gay street
Which I visited and inhaled that wonderful odor
Of new books
Even today I read hardcover as a preference paperback only
As a last resort

And up the hill on vine street
(The main black corridor) sat our carnegie library[2]
Mrs. Long always glad to see you
The stereoscope[3] always ready to show you faraway
Places to dream about

Mrs. Long asking what are you looking for today
When I wanted *Leaves of Grass* or alfred north whitehead
She would go to the big library uptown and I now know
Hat in hand to ask to borrow so that I might borrow
Probably they said something humiliating since southern
Whites like to humiliate southern blacks

But she nonetheless brought the books
Back and I held them to my chest
Close to my heart
And happily skipped back to grandmother's house
Where I would sit on the front porch
In a gray glider and dream of a world
Far away

[2] **carnegie library:** a library built with money donated by the businessman Andrew Carnegie.

[3] **stereoscope:** an optical instrument with two eyepieces used to create a three-dimensional effect when looking at two photographs of the same scene.

I love the world where I was
I was safe and warm and grandmother gave me neck kisses
When I was on my way to bed

But there was a world
Somewhere
Out there
And Mrs. Long opened that wardrobe
But no lions or witches[4] scared me
I went through
Knowing there would be
Spring

[4] **wardrobe . . . lions or witches:** refers to *The Lion, the Witch and the Wardrobe,* a fantasy novel by C.S. Lewis; in the story, four children visit a land called Narnia via the wardrobe, or closet, in a spare room.

NOTICE & NOTE 

ANALYZE FREE VERSE POETRY

Annotate: In the final stanza of the poem, mark words that rhyme.

Analyze: What idea does this use of rhyme help to emphasize? How does it contribute to a theme?

CHECK YOUR UNDERSTANDING

Answer these questions before moving on to the **Analyze the Text** section on the following page.

1 The poem's speaker discovers another world through —

A drinking coffee

B reading books

C talking to neighbors

D watching television

2 What does the stanza break between lines 42 and 43 help the poet convey most clearly?

F the contrast between the poet's two worlds

G the distance the poet sometimes traveled

H the respect she has for Mrs. Long and other librarians

J the childhood dreams the poet had for her future

3 Why is the first stanza important to the poem?

A It provides clues about the poem's main theme.

B It conveys the personality of the poet.

C It introduces the poet's childhood world.

D It states a problem the poet had as a child.

ANALYZE THE TEXT

Support your responses with evidence from the text. NOTEBOOK

1. **Infer** The subtitle of the poem is "(You never know what troubled little girl needs a book)." What might that subtitle suggest about a theme of the poem?

2. **Evaluate** Words like *amused, thoughtful, grateful, hopeful,* and *angry* can be used to describe the tone of a poem. In your opinion, which of these words best fits the poem? Explain.

3. **Interpret** An **allusion** is a reference to a well-known person, place, event, or work of literature. The final stanza of this poem makes an allusion to C. S. Lewis's novel *The Lion, the Witch and the Wardrobe,* in which the heroes end a witch's curse of endless winter. Why might the poet have ended the poem with this allusion?

4. **Analyze** How does the poet's use of punctuation and capitalization contribute to the poem's meaning?

5. **Notice & Note** Reread the last stanza of the poem. What words would you use to describe the poet as a child? Think about the mental images that the descriptions of her childhood memories created as you read the poem. Why do your words fit?

RESEARCH

Find out more about Nikki Giovanni and then answer these questions.

QUESTION	ANSWER
Ms. Giovanni refers to her grandmother in the poem. What influence did her grandmother have on her?	
What other kinds of themes does Nikki Giovanni explore in her poetry?	
What other poems about libraries has she written?	

Connect In a small group, discuss how the other poems about libraries that Nikki Giovanni wrote are similar to "A Poem for My Librarian, Mrs. Long."

RESEARCH TIP

Use specific search terms when searching online. For example, you might search "library poems by Nikki Giovanni" to find more poems about libraries. As you scan search results, look for reputable websites, usually those that end in *.org* and *.edu.*

CREATE AND WRITE

Write a Free Verse Poem Pay tribute to a person whom you admire by writing a free verse poem about that person.

- ❑ Include specific examples of qualities or actions that make this person exceptional.
- ❑ Choose sensory words and phrases to describe the person or your feelings about the person.
- ❑ Consider how you will use punctuation, capitalization, and line breaks to emphasize specific ideas and create meaning.

Go to **Writing as a Process** in the **Writing Studio** for more help.

Write a Letter Write a letter to Nikki Giovanni. In it, share your opinion of "A Poem for My Librarian, Mrs. Long" and any other of her poems you have read. Adapt any notes you took while reading her work. Use these guidelines to help you plan and draft your letter.

- ❑ Open with the date and an appropriate greeting (for example, "Dear Ms. Giovanni").
- ❑ State your opinion clearly and politely, using descriptive words and phrases. Support your opinion with specific examples from the poems. Use transitions to move from one point to the next.
- ❑ Provide a concluding thought that sums up your opinion. Remember to end the letter with an appropriate closing (for example, "Sincerely") and your signature.

RESPOND TO THE ESSENTIAL QUESTION

? What inspires you to make a difference?

Gather Information Review your annotations and notes on "A Poem for My Librarian, Mrs. Long." Then, add relevant details to your Response Log. As you determine which information to include, think about:

- the jobs people do that can inspire others
- the importance of books
- how people make a difference to other people

At the end of the unit, refer to your notes as you write a research report.

ACADEMIC VOCABULARY

As you write and discuss what you learned from the poem, be sure to use the Academic Vocabulary words. Check off each of the words that you use.

- ❑ **contrast**
- ❑ **despite**
- ❑ **error**
- ❑ **inadequate**
- ❑ **interact**

COLLABORATE & COMPARE

HISTORY WRITING

FRANCES PERKINS AND THE TRIANGLE FACTORY FIRE

by **David Brooks**

pages 479–485

COMPARE AUTHORS' PURPOSES AND MESSAGES

When authors write about history, their purpose is often to explain what happened. As you read these texts—two texts about the same topic—note what is similar and what is different about their explanations. Think about what main idea, or message, each one expresses. After you read both selections, you will collaborate with a small group on a final project.

ESSENTIAL QUESTION:

What inspires you to make a difference?

HISTORY WRITING

from

THE STORY OF THE TRIANGLE FACTORY FIRE

by **Zachary Kent**

pages 493–495

Frances Perkins and the Triangle Factory Fire

QUICK START

If you and a friend both described the same event, would your accounts be the same? In a small group, discuss why they might differ.

ANALYZE HISTORY WRITING

History writing is a type of literary nonfiction that combines the features of a narrative text (a true story with a setting, characters, and a plot) and an informational text (paragraphs covering key ideas and factual details). Authors write from a unique perspective, or view of topics, which the following clues can help you identify.

CLUE	WHAT CLUE TELLS YOU
Tone	**Tone** is the author's attitude toward the topic. Consider how the author's language expresses emotions that affect your understanding of the topic.
Point of View	A **subjective** point of view means that the author includes personal opinions. An **objective** point of view means that the author focuses only on the facts.
Emphasis	Note which facts the author emphasizes. Why do you think the author highlights those facts?
Portrayals	Does the author include any **primary sources,** such as quotations from people who witnessed or took part in an event? If so, what do the primary sources tell you?

As you read "Frances Perkins and the Triangle Factory Fire," look for clues like the ones in the chart.

GENRE ELEMENTS: INFORMATIONAL TEXT

- focuses on real people and events from the past
- often tells a true story, with factual details acquired through research
- presents the interactions between people and events
- may hint at the author's own view of the topic

DETERMINE KEY IDEAS

Selections that are history writing will have a **controlling idea,** or thesis. The controlling idea is also called a **key idea,** or the most important idea about the topic. It may be stated explicitly in a sentence, or it may be implied. Each paragraph or section also will have a key idea that provides support for the controlling key idea.

Key ideas are supported by **details,** facts, and other information that clarify the key ideas. As you read history writing, think about key ideas and information that answer questions such as *Where and when did the event take place? Who was involved? What were the event's causes and effects? How does this information help me understand the topic?*

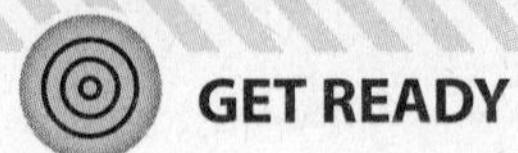

GET READY

CRITICAL VOCABULARY

lobby **fatal** **distinguish** **indifferent**

To preview the Critical Vocabulary words, complete each sentence with a word from the list.

1. Without treatment, that disease could become __________.
2. In the snowstorm, the truck driver could not __________ the road from the ditch beside it.
3. The workers decided to __________ their boss for a raise.
4. No one in the neighborhood was __________ about the need for a new school.

LANGUAGE CONVENTIONS

Pronoun-Antecedent Agreement In this lesson, you will learn about making sure that pronouns agree with their antecedents (the nouns or other pronouns to which they refer) in number, gender, and person. In this example, notice that the singular pronoun *it* agrees with *elevator,* its singular antecedent:

> The people rode to the first floor in an **elevator. It** got stuck on the second floor, and the people had to wait.

As you read, see how pronoun-antecedent agreement helps you understand key ideas and details.

ANNOTATION MODEL

NOTICE & NOTE

As you read, note how the author presents the historical topic. You can also mark up key ideas and the information that supports them. In the model, you can see one reader's notes about part of "Frances Perkins and the Triangle Factory Fire."

1 . . . But back in 1911, there were nice brownstones on the northern side of the park and factories on its eastern and southern sides, drawing young and mostly Jewish and Italian immigrant workers. One of the nice homes was owned by Mrs. Gordon Norrie, a society matron descended from two of the men who signed the Declaration of Independence.

The contrast between the brownstones and the factories may be a key idea.

The author uses "nice" twice, but not to describe the factories.

BACKGROUND

David Brooks *(b. 1961) was born in Canada and grew up in New York City. He started his career as a police reporter in Chicago. Today, Brooks is perhaps best known as a newspaper columnist and television analyst. His commentary and writings often focus on culture and social issues. In his book* The Road to Character, *in which this piece of history writing appears, Brooks explores what inspired individuals such as Frances Perkins to become leaders and help change society for the better.*

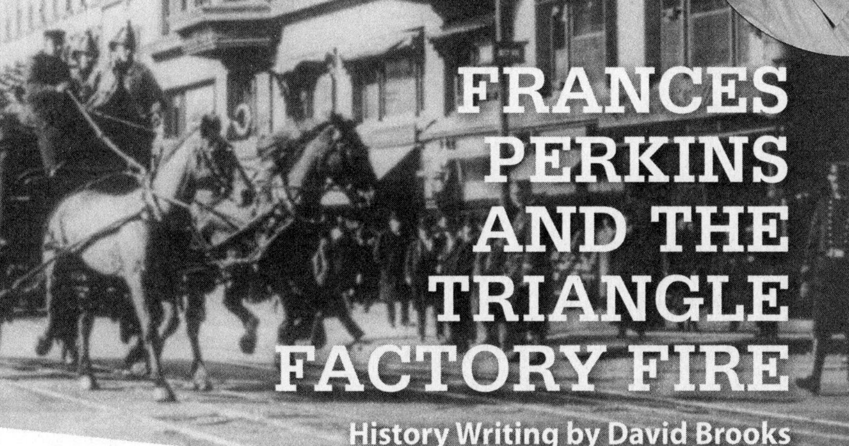

FRANCES PERKINS AND THE TRIANGLE FACTORY FIRE

History Writing by David Brooks

PREPARE TO COMPARE

As you read, consider how the author presents facts and other evidence to explain a tragic but significant historical event and its effects. This information will help you compare Brooks's account of the fire with an account of the same event by Zachary Kent, which follows it.

Notice & Note

Use the side margins to notice and note signposts in the text.

1 Today, the area around Washington Square Park in lower Manhattan is surrounded by New York University, expensive apartments, and upscale stores. But back in 1911, there were nice brownstones on the northern side of the park and factories on its eastern and southern sides, drawing young and mostly Jewish and Italian immigrant workers. One of the nice homes was owned by Mrs. Gordon Norrie, a society matron descended from two of the men who signed the Declaration of Independence.

2 On March 25, Mrs. Norrie was just sitting down to tea with a group of friends when they heard a commotion outside. One of her guests, Frances Perkins, then thirty-one, was from an old but middle-class Maine family, which could also trace its lineage back to the time of the

ANALYZE HISTORY WRITING

Annotate: Mark the facts presented about Frances Perkins in paragraph 2.

Infer: Why do you think the author includes these facts about Perkins? What do they tell you about her?

NOTICE & NOTE

lobby
(lŏb´ē) *v.* To *lobby* is to attempt to influence politicians to support the cause that you represent.

BIG QUESTIONS

Notice & Note: In paragraph 4, circle what people thought they were seeing. Then underline what they actually were seeing.

Connect: Did the truth surprise you, or did it confirm what you already knew? Explain.

DETERMINE KEY IDEAS

Annotate: In paragraph 7, mark details that help explain why some workers decided to jump.

Predict: Do you think that this is a key idea in the text? Why or why not?

Revolution. She had attended Mount Holyoke College and was working at the Consumers' League of New York,[1] **lobbying** to end child labor.

3 A butler rushed in and announced that there was a fire near the square. The ladies ran out. Perkins lifted up her skirts and sprinted toward it. They had stumbled upon the Triangle Shirtwaist Factory, one of the most famous fires in American history. Perkins could see the eighth, ninth, and tenth floors of the building ablaze and dozens of workers crowding around the open windows. She joined the throng of horrified onlookers on the sidewalk below.

4 Some saw what they thought were bundles of fabric falling from the windows. They thought the factory owners were saving their best material. As the bundles continued to fall, the onlookers realized they were not bundles at all. They were people, hurling themselves to their death. "People had just begun to jump as we got there," Perkins would later remember. "They had been holding on until that time, standing in the windowsills, being crowded by others behind them, the fire pressing closer and closer, the smoke closer and closer.

5 "They began to jump. The window was too crowded and they would jump and they hit the sidewalk," she recalled. "Every one of them was killed, everybody who jumped was killed. It was a horrifying spectacle."

6 The firemen held out nets, but the weight of the bodies from that great height either yanked the nets from the firemen's hands or the bodies ripped right through. One woman grandly emptied her purse over the onlookers below and then hurled herself off.

7 Perkins and the others screamed up to them, "Don't jump! Help is coming." It wasn't. The flames were roasting them from behind. Forty-seven people ended up jumping. One young woman gave a speech before diving, gesticulating passionately, but no one could hear her. One young man tenderly helped a young woman onto the windowsill. Then he held her out, away from the building, like a ballet dancer, and let her drop. He did the same for a second and a third. Finally, a fourth girl stood on the windowsill; she embraced him and they shared a long kiss. Then he held her out and dropped her, too. Then he himself was in the air. As he fell, people noticed, as his pants ballooned out, that he wore smart tan shoes. One reporter wrote, "I saw his face before they covered it. You could see in it that he was a real man. He had done his best."

[1] **Consumers' League of New York:** organization founded in 1891 and dedicated to improve working conditions and other social issues.

8 The fire had started at about 4:40 that afternoon, when somebody on the eighth floor threw a cigarette or a match into one of the great scrapheaps of cotton left over from the tailoring process. The pile quickly burst into flames.

9 Somebody alerted the factory manager, Samuel Bernstein, who grabbed some nearby buckets of water and dumped them on the fire. They did little good. The cotton scraps were explosively flammable, more so than paper, and there was roughly a ton of the stuff piled on the eighth floor alone.

10 Bernstein dumped more buckets of water on the growing fire, but by this point they had no effect whatsoever, and the flames were spreading to the tissue paper patterns hanging above the wooden work desks. He ordered workers to drag a fire hose from a nearby stairwell. They opened the valve, but there was no pressure. As a historian of the fire, David Von Drehle, has argued, Bernstein made a **fatal** decision in those first three minutes. He could have spent the time fighting the fire or evacuating the nearly five hundred workers. Instead, he battled the exploding fire, to no effect. If he had spent the time evacuating, it is possible that nobody would have died that day.

11 When Bernstein finally did take his eyes off the wall of fire, he was astonished by what he saw. Many of the women on the eighth floor were taking the time to go to the dressing room to retrieve their coats and belongings. Some were looking for their time cards so they could punch out.

12 Eventually, the two factory owners up on the tenth floor were alerted to the fire, which had already consumed the eighth floor and was spreading quickly to their own. One of them, Isaac Harris, gathered a group of workers and figured it was probably suicidal to try to climb down through the fire. "Girls, let us go up on the roof! Get on the roof!" he bellowed. The other owner, Max Blanck, was paralyzed by fear. He stood frozen with a look of terror on his face, holding his youngest daughter in one arm and his elder daughter's hand with the other. A clerk, who was evacuating with the firm's order book, decided to throw it down and save his boss's life instead.

13 Most of the workers on the eighth floor were able to get out, but the workers on the ninth floor had little warning until the fire was already upon them. They ran like terrified schools of fish from one potential exit to another. There were two elevators, but they were slow and overloaded. There was no sprinkler system. There was a fire escape, but it was rickety and blocked. On normal days the workers were searched as they headed home, to prevent theft. The factory had been designed

LANGUAGE CONVENTIONS

Annotate: Circle the pronouns *them* and *they* in paragraph 9. Then underline the phrase that is the antecedent for both pronouns.

Analyze: How does this example of pronoun-antecedent agreement help you understand the author's explanation of the attempt to control the fire?

fatal

(fāt´l) *adj.* A *fatal* decision is a choice that results in death.

ANALYZE HISTORY WRITING

Annotate: In paragraph 11, mark text details of what was happening on the eighth floor.

Infer: What do you think the author's point of view is about this scene, and why?

DETERMINE KEY IDEAS

Annotate: In paragraph 13, mark words and phrases that describe the conditions of the factory.

Analyze: How did the factory conditions force workers to make "life-and-death decisions"?

NOTICE & NOTE

to force them through a single choke point[2] in order to get out. Some of the doors were locked. As the fire surrounded them, the workers were left to make desperate life-and-death decisions with limited information in a rising atmosphere of fire, smoke, and terror.

ANALYZE HISTORY WRITING

Annotate: In paragraph 14, mark the sentences that describe Katie Weiner's actions.

Interpret: How would you describe the author's tone at this point? Explain.

14 Three friends, Ida Nelson, Katie Weiner, and Fanny Lansner, were in the changing room when the screams of "Fire!" reached them. Nelson decided to sprint for one of the stairwells. Weiner went to the elevators and saw an elevator car descending the shaft. She hurled herself into space, diving onto the roof. Lansner took neither course and didn't make it out.

15 Mary Bucelli later described her own part in the vicious scramble to get out first: "I can't tell you because I gave so many pushes and kicks. I gave and received. I was throwing them down wherever I met them," she said of her co-workers. "I was only looking for my own life. . . . At a moment like that, there is big confusion and you must understand that you cannot see anything. . . . You see a multitude of things, but you can't **distinguish** anything. With the confusion and the fight that you take, you can't distinguish anything."

distinguish
(dĭ-stĭng´gwĭsh) *v.* To *distinguish* one thing from another means perceiving them as being different or distinct.

16 Joseph Brenman was one of the relatively few men in the factory. A crowd of women were pushing between him and the elevators. But they were small, and many of them were faint. He

[2] **choke point** a narrow passage; a point of congestion or blockage.

The *New York World,* a major newspaper of the early 20th century, conveyed the dramatic details of what became known as a major industrial disaster.

The World.

154 KILLED IN SKYSCRAPER FACTORY FIRE; SCORES BURN, OTHERS LEAP TO DEATH.

700 WORKERS, MOSTLY GIRLS, TRAPPED; BODIES OF DEAD HEAP THE STREETS; ONLY ONE FIRE ESCAPE FOR ALL.

shoved them aside and barreled his way onto the elevator and to safety.

17 The fire department arrived quickly but its ladders could not reach the eighth floor. The water from its hoses could barely reach that high, just enough to give the building exterior a light dousing.

Shame

18 The horror of the Triangle Shirtwaist Fire traumatized the city. People were not only furious at the factory owners, but felt some deep responsibility themselves. In 1909 a young Russian immigrant named Rose Schneiderman had led the women who worked at Triangle and other factories on a strike to address the very issues that led to the fire disaster. The picketers were harassed by company guards. The city looked on indifferently, as it did upon the lives of the poor generally. After the fire there was a collective outpouring of rage, fed by collective guilt at the way people had self-centeredly gone about their lives, callously **indifferent** to the conditions and suffering of the people close around them. "I can't begin to tell you how disturbed the people were everywhere," Frances Perkins remembered. "It was as though we had all done something wrong. It shouldn't have been. We were sorry. Mea culpa! Mea culpa!"[3]

[3] **Mea culpa!** (mā´ə kŭl´pə): a cry meaning "I am at fault!"

DETERMINE KEY IDEAS

Annotate: In paragraph 18, mark the descriptive word that appears twice (once as an adverb, once as an adjective) and refers to the general attitude of people toward factory workers before the fire.

Critique: Why is the idea that these words represent a key idea in the text?

indifferent
(ĭn-dĭf´ər-ənt) adj. Someone who is *indifferent* has no feelings one way or another about something.

NOTICE & NOTE

ANALYZE HISTORY WRITING

Annotate: In paragraphs 19–20, mark what Rose Schneiderman says about the idea of "fellowship."

Infer: Why do you think the author included this primary source? What additional information does it provide?

DETERMINE KEY IDEAS

Annotate: In paragraph 21, mark the first sentence that tells you about the change in Frances Perkins after the fire.

Cite Evidence: How does the author support this key idea?

19 A large memorial march was held, and then a large meeting, with all the leading citizens of the city. Perkins was on stage as a representative of the Consumers' League when Rose Schneiderman electrified the crowd: "I would be a traitor to those poor burned bodies if I were to come here to talk good fellowship. We have tried you, good people of the public—and we have found you wanting! . . .

20 "We have tried you, citizens! We are trying you now and you have a couple of dollars for the sorrowing mothers and brothers and sisters by way of a charity gift. But every time the workers come out in the only way they know to protest against conditions which are unbearable, the strong hand of the law is allowed to press down heavily upon us. . . . I can't talk fellowship to you who are gathered here. Too much blood has been spilled!"

21 The fire and its aftershocks left a deep mark on Frances Perkins. Up until that point she had lobbied for worker rights and on behalf of the poor, but she had been on a conventional trajectory, toward a conventional marriage, perhaps, and a life of genteel good works. After the fire, what had been a career turned into a vocation.[4] Moral indignation set her on a different course. Her own desires and her own ego became less central and the cause itself became more central to the structure of her life. The niceties of her class fell away. She became impatient with the way genteel progressives went about serving the poor. She became impatient with their prissiness, their desire

[4] **vocation** (vō-kā´shən): a strong commitment to a certain course of action.

In 1933, Frances Perkins became the first female U.S. Cabinet member as Secretary of Labor.

to stay pure and above the fray. Perkins hardened. She threw herself into the rough and tumble of politics. She was willing to take morally hazardous action[5] if it would prevent another catastrophe like the one that befell the women at the Triangle factory. She was willing to compromise and work with corrupt officials if it would produce results. She pinioned herself to this cause for the rest of her life.

[5] **morally hazardous action:** an action that may result in increased risk to oneself or others and that some may consider to be inappropriate.

CHECK YOUR UNDERSTANDING

Answer these questions before moving on to the **Analyze the Text** section on the following page.

1 What key idea could a reader most likely determine from the details in paragraph 10?

A No one could have prevented the fire.

B Cotton dust and scraps are flammable.

C Poor decisions made the fire much worse.

D A growing fire cannot be stopped.

2 In paragraph 15, the author includes a direct quotation from Mary Bucelli in order to —

F explain the factory workers' actions during the fire

G persuade readers that the fire could have been prevented

H explain why the fire spread so quickly

J describe what happened after the fire

3 Which sentence best explains why Frances Perkins devoted the rest of her life to bringing reform to the lives of workers?

A She always had been interested in helping the poor.

B She was deeply affected by the tragic fire at the factory.

C She was unhappy about the indifference that city leaders showed toward the poor.

D She wanted workers' children to have a better life than their parents had had.

ANALYZE THE TEXT

Support your responses with evidence from the text. NOTEBOOK

1. **Cite Evidence** What does the information in paragraph 13 indicate about working conditions in the factory? Cite details from the text that support your answer.
2. **Analyze** Reread paragraphs 8–10. What are the author's tone and point of view as he describes the start of the fire and the first attempts to extinguish it? How can you tell?
3. **Infer** What can you infer from text details about the quality of firefighting equipment at this time in history?
4. **Critique** In paragraph 7, the author describes several people who jumped to their death. What does this information add to your understanding of the most important key idea about the event?
5. **Notice & Note** Review the details about Frances Perkins's life before and after the fire. How did the fire change Perkins's life? Did this change surprise you? Why or why not?

RESEARCH

Find out more about Frances Perkins. Research the two questions below and one more that you generate on your own. Note what you learn in the chart.

RESEARCH QUESTIONS	DETAILS ABOUT PERKINS'S LIFE
What was Perkins's childhood like?	
Why was Perkins called "the woman behind the New Deal"?	

Extend With a small group, share your questions and discuss what you learned about Perkins's life. After your discussion, do you have more questions about Perkins's life? With your group, list these and discuss how you could research them.

RESEARCH TIP

The best research sources are accurate, credible, and balanced. What should you do, though, if two quality sources provide different information about the same topic, such as different birthdates for a historical figure? It's always helpful to compare multiple sources with one another—and then try to find a few additional quality sources to use for comparison as well. If most of the sources agree, and they're all reliable, then you can feel more confident about the information you present.

CREATE AND DISCUSS

Go to **Writing as a Process** in the **Writing Studio** for help.

Write an Ode Use what has inspired you from reading this piece of history writing to create an ode. (An ode is a short, serious poem in which a speaker expresses personal thoughts and feelings, often as a tribute to a person or event.) Perhaps your ode could honor the factory workers who died or Frances Perkins and her work as a reformer.

- ❑ Choose the specific topic for your ode and the message you will convey.
- ❑ Draft your ode, using any poetic structure you like. Choose details and language that will help readers share your feelings about the topic.
- ❑ Review your draft. Make revisions that will show the speaker's feelings and the overall message of the ode more clearly.

Go to **Participating in Collaborative Discussions** in the **Speaking and Listening Studio** to learn more.

Discuss the Primary Sources With a partner, review what each quotation in the text adds to your understanding of the event.

- ❑ Use clues within the primary source itself to help you discuss its main idea, or message. For example, what is the speaker's point of view of the event? What is the speaker's tone, and why does the tone matter?
- ❑ To build on your partner's ideas, ask clarifying questions. For example, what do you think Rose Schneiderman means to convey by her use of the word *traitor* (paragraph 19)?

RESPOND TO THE ESSENTIAL QUESTION

? What inspires you to make a difference?

Gather Information Review your annotations and notes on "Frances Perkins and the Triangle Factory Fire." Then, add relevant details to your Response Log. As you determine which information to include, think about:

- people's responses to tragic events
- ways to support people affected by a tragic event
- steps that may help prevent a similar event from happening again

At the end of the unit, you can use your notes to help you write a research report.

ACADEMIC VOCABULARY

As you write and discuss what you learned from the piece of history writing, be sure to use the Academic Vocabulary words. Check off each of the words that you use.

- ❑ **contrast**
- ❑ **despite**
- ❑ **error**
- ❑ **inadequate**
- ❑ **interact**

RESPOND

CRITICAL VOCABULARY

WORD BANK
lobby
fatal
distinguish
indifferent

Practice and Apply Identify the Critical Vocabulary word that is most closely related to the boldfaced word in each question. Be prepared to explain your choices.

1. Which vocabulary word goes with **unimportant**?

 ____

2. Which vocabulary word goes with **disastrous**? ______________
3. Which vocabulary word goes with **distinct**? ______________
4. Which vocabulary word goes with **influence**? ______________

VOCABULARY STRATEGY: Latin Roots

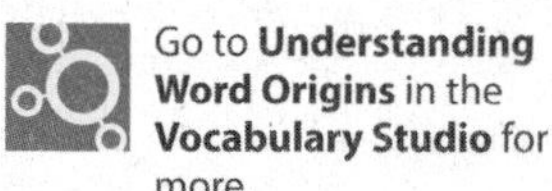

Go to **Understanding Word Origins** in the **Vocabulary Studio** for more.

A **root** is a word part that came into English from an older language. Roots from Latin appear in many English words. Note this comment by Mary Bucelli in "Frances Perkins and the Triangle Factory Fire":

> **You see a multitude of things, but you can't distinguish anything.** (paragraph 15)

The word *distinguish* contains a root, *sting,* from the Latin word *dīstinguere,* which means "to separate." You can see the root meaning in the word *distinguish;* it literally means separating what you perceive, or being able to tell things apart. Recognizing the root *sting* can help you figure out the meanings of other words that include this root.

Practice and Apply In each sentence, identify the word with the Latin root *sting* or its variation *ting*. Write what each word means. Use a print or digital dictionary to check your ideas.

1. There are many kinds of maple trees, but most people think that one maple tree is indistinguishable from another.

 ____

2. Despite the criticism they got, they would not let anyone extinguish their dream.

 ____

3. Although many of her players were undistinguished, the coach led them to win games by inspiring them to work hard as a team.

 ____

4. A fire extinguisher works by removing one or more of the three elements of every fire: oxygen, heat, and fuel.

 ____

LANGUAGE CONVENTIONS:
Pronoun-Antecedent Agreement

To keep your writing clear, make sure that the pronouns that you use agree with their antecedents in number (singular or plural), gender (male, female, or neuter), and person (first, second, or third).

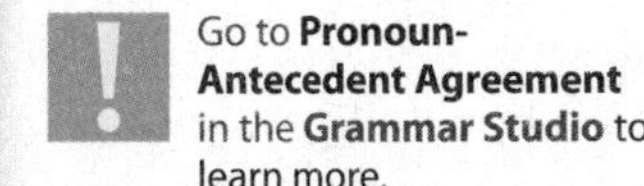

Go to **Pronoun-Antecedent Agreement** in the **Grammar Studio** to learn more.

	SINGULAR PRONOUNS	PLURAL PRONOUNS
First person	I / me / my, mine	we / us / our, ours
Second person	you / you / your, yours	you / you / your, yours
Third person	he, she, it / him, her, it / his, her, hers, its	they / them / their, theirs

Look at these examples from "Frances Perkins and the Triangle Factory Fire" and examine the pronouns and their antecedents.

- Notice how the pronouns *his* and *he* agree with their antecedent, *Bernstein,* in number (singular), gender (male), and person (third):

  When Bernstein finally did take his eyes off the wall of fire, he was astonished by what he saw. (paragraph 11)

- Notice how the pronoun *its* agrees with its antecedent, *fire department,* in number (singular), gender (neuter), and person (third):

  The fire department arrived quickly but its ladders could not reach the eighth floor. (paragraph 17)

- Notice how the pronoun *she* agrees with its antecedent, *Perkins,* in number (singular), gender (female), and person (third):

  Perkins hardened. She threw herself into the rough and tumble of politics. She was willing. . . . (paragraph 21)

Practice and Apply Write 4 or 5 sentences that summarize this piece of history writing. Try to use different pronouns. As you do, check to make sure that the pronouns agree with their antecedents. Use the examples and chart above as guides.

HISTORY WRITING

from

THE STORY OF THE TRIANGLE FACTORY FIRE

by **Zachary Kent**

pages 493–495

COMPARE AUTHORS' PURPOSES AND MESSAGES

Now that you've read "Frances Perkins and the Triangle Factory Fire," read an excerpt from *The Story of the Triangle Factory Fire*. As you read, think about the similarities and differences in how each author presents information about the same event. After you are finished, you will collaborate with a small group on a final project that involves an analysis of both texts.

ESSENTIAL QUESTION:

What inspires you to make a difference?

HISTORY WRITING

FRANCES PERKINS AND THE TRIANGLE FACTORY FIRE

by **David Brooks**

pages 479–485

from The Story of the Triangle Factory Fire

QUICK START

What can a person do after learning of a tragic event such as a fire, flood, or tornado? Brainstorm ideas with a partner or small group.

PARAPHRASE

When you **paraphrase,** you restate information that you read or hear using your own words. Here is one way you might paraphrase a sentence from *The Story of the Triangle Factory Fire.*

ORIGINAL TEXT	PARAPHRASE
They examined workers' filthy living conditions and witnessed the dangers of crippling machinery and long work hours in dusty, dirty firetraps. (paragraph 3)	They inspected where the workers lived and worked. They found unhealthy homes and dangerous working conditions.

Paraphrasing key ideas and important details can help you understand and remember what you read. As you read the selection, write short paraphrases next to important information.

ANALYZE TEXT STRUCTURE

Effective history writing has a **text structure**—a particular way of organizing ideas and information to support multiple topics and categories and subcategories in a text.

- **Chronological order,** or time order, is the arrangement of events in the sequence in which they occur—what happens first, second, and so on. When reading history writing, pay attention to dates, times, and signal words such as *next, then, before, after, later,* and *finally.*

Days after the fire, city officials searched the rubble for clues.

Then the owners were charged with manslaughter.

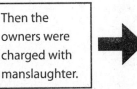

After a three-week trial, a jury found the owners not guilty.

- **Problem-solution** refers to a structure in which a problem is stated and then solutions are proposed and analyzed. Words that may signal a problem include *challenge* and *issue.* Words that may signal a solution include *propose, answer,* and *conclude.*

As you read the selection, look for words and phrases that signal how the information is arranged to help you understand the text.

GENRE ELEMENTS: INFORMATIONAL TEXT

- a blend of narrative and informational writing that deals with people and events from the past
- presents the interactions between people and events to maintain interest
- uses an organizational pattern to present key ideas and supporting details
- may use language that suggests the author's perspective

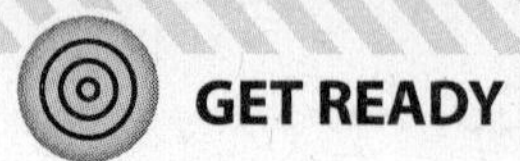

GET READY

CRITICAL VOCABULARY

hideous **corridor** **enact** **reformer**

To preview the Critical Vocabulary words, replace each boldfaced word with a different word or words that have the same meaning.

1. The building once was beautiful, but now it was falling apart and looked (**hideous**) _______________.
2. The (**corridor**) _______________ was crowded with busy people.
3. After a tragic event, people often demand that politicians (**enact**) _______________ laws to prevent a similar event from happening.
4. One (**reformer**) _______________ can make a positive difference in the lives of many people.

LANGUAGE CONVENTIONS

Subject–Verb Agreement and Prepositional Phrases In sentences, verbs must agree with (or match) their subjects in number. If subjects and verbs don't agree, readers may be confused. Look at this sentence:

The workers in the factory are weaving.

Are weaving (the verb) agrees with *workers* (the subject). Notice the prepositional phrase *in the factory* does not change the subject-verb agreement. As you read the excerpt from *The Story of the Triangle Factory Fire,* notice subject–verb agreement.

ANNOTATION MODEL

NOTICE & NOTE 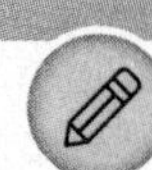

As you read, note the text structure. You can also mark up passages and paraphrase them. In the model, you can see one reader's notes about this text from *The Story of the Triangle Factory Fire.*

3 . . . In October 1911 the city established a Bureau of Fire Prevention to inspect safety standards in other buildings. Five months earlier the New York State legislature created a special Factory Investigating Commission. Through the next four years Commission investigators crawled and pried through the rooms and cellars of factories and tenement houses all across the state.

These phrases tell me that the special commission was created before the Bureau of Fire Prevention was established.

My paraphrase: "Investigators spent four years inspecting factories and run-down apartment buildings."

NOTICE & NOTE

BACKGROUND

Zachary Kent *(b. 1951) is the author of more than fifty books for young readers. He writes primarily about history. A historical event such as the Triangle Factory Fire can be so dramatic and so haunting that it compels generations that follow to dissect its details and trace its impact. In Kent's account, he recounts what happens and examines the fire's long-term effects.*

from THE STORY OF THE TRIANGLE FACTORY FIRE

History Writing by Zachary Kent

PREPARE TO COMPARE

As you read, pay attention to the way in which the author presents information about this deadly fire, especially how he structures or organizes facts and other details. Consider what you learn about the aftermath of the fire and why the author includes this information.

1 In the days following the fire, city officials sifted through the charred rubble at the Asch Building and tried to fix the fault for the tragedy. Fire Chief Croker angrily stated, "There wasn't a fire escape anywhere fronting on the street by which these unfortunate girls could escape." Doors that opened inward instead of outward, overcrowding in work areas, and blocked exits also were to blame. Fire Marshal William Beers stunned New Yorkers by soon declaring, "I can show you 150 loft buildings far worse than this one." Lillian D. Wald of the Joint Board of Sanitary Control also reported on the general situation. "The conditions as they now exist are **hideous**. . . . Our investigators have shown that there are hundreds of buildings which invite disaster just as much as did the Asch structure."

Notice & Note

Use the side margins to notice and note signposts in the text.

PARAPHRASE

Annotate: Mark text details in paragraph 1 that reveal the building's condition when the fire occurred.

Interpret: In your own words, describe the condition of the building when the fire took place.

hideous
(hĭd´ē-əs) *adj.* When something is *hideous,* it is repulsive or revolting.

NOTICE & NOTE

corridor
(kôr′ĭ-dər) *n.* A *corridor* is a narrow hallway or passageway.

QUOTED WORDS

Notice & Note: In paragraph 2, mark the three speakers whom the author quotes.

Infer: Why do you think the author includes three very different quotations in this paragraph?

2 Accused of ignoring their employees' safety, Triangle owners Blanck and Harris were charged with manslaughter. During the three week trial angry citizens packed the courtroom. Outside, in the **corridors,** women screamed, "Murderers! Murderers! Make them suffer for killing our children!" Lawyers argued that Blanck and Harris kept all of the Triangle doors locked during the workday, therefore causing many of the deaths. Weighing the evidence, however, the jury returned a verdict of not guilty. "I cannot see that anyone was responsible for the disaster," explained juror H. Houston Hierst. "It seems to me to have been an act of the Almighty."[1] The New York *Call* viewed the matter differently. "Capital can commit no crime," it angrily declared, "when it is in pursuit of profits."

3 Furious New Yorkers refused to let the issue rest. In October 1911 the city established a Bureau of Fire Prevention to inspect safety standards in other buildings. Five months earlier the New York State legislature created a special Factory Investigating Commission. Through the next four years Commission investigators crawled and pried through the rooms and cellars of factories and tenement houses[2] all across the state. They examined workers' filthy living conditions and witnessed the dangers of crippling machinery and long work hours in dusty, dirty firetraps.

ANALYZE TEXT STRUCTURE

Annotate: In paragraph 4, mark words and phrases that signal chronology, or time order.

Analyze: Remember that the fire happened in 1911. What does this later chronology of events tell the reader about the effects of the fire?

4 As a result of the Commission's shocking findings, New York State quickly passed thirty-three new labor laws by 1914. These laws formed the foundation of New York State's Industrial Code, the finest in the nation. Soon other states followed New York's example and **enacted** protective labor laws.

enact
(ĕn-ăkt′) *v.* If you *enact* something, you make it into a law.

5 One Factory Commission investigator had witnessed the fateful Triangle fire. Frances Perkins said, "We heard the fire engines and rushed . . . to see what was going on. . . . We got there just as they started to jump. I shall never forget the frozen horror which came over us as we stood with our hands on our throats watching that horrible sight, knowing that there was no help."

PARAPHRASE

Annotate: Reread paragraphs 5–6. Mark the quotation by Frances Perkins that you connect with more.

Interpret: In your own words, paraphrase that quotation. Why did you choose it?

[1] **an act of the Almighty:** a term that refers to events or actions that are beyond the control of human beings (and, therefore, that happen through the will of God).

[2] **tenement houses:** very run-down city apartments where the poor and immigrants often live.

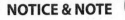

NOTICE & NOTE 

6 In 1933 President Franklin Roosevelt named Frances Perkins secretary of labor. She and other social **reformers** dedicated their lives to insuring worker safety throughout the country. "They did not die in vain and we will never forget them," vowed Perkins. From the ashes of the tragic Triangle factory fire came help for millions of United States laborers today.

reformer
(rĭ-fôrm´) *n.* A *reformer* seeks to improve or correct practices or behaviors that cause harm.

ANALYZE TEXT STRUCTURE
Annotate: In paragraph 6, mark words and phrases that help you determine the chronology, or time order, of this paragraph.

Critique: Do you agree that the workers would not be forgotten, even today? Why or why not?

CHECK YOUR UNDERSTANDING

Answer these questions before moving on to the **Analyze the Text** section on the following page.

1 According to the author, what statement by Fire Marshal William Beers stunned New Yorkers?

A The Triangle Factory building was going to be rebuilt.

B Other factory buildings were in even worse condition.

C The Triangle Factory owners were being charged with crimes.

D There was no more money left to fight other fires.

2 In paragraph 2, how does the juror's viewpoint compare to that of angry citizens?

F Only the citizens felt that the fire could have been prevented.

G Jurors believed that the fire was the fault of the workers.

H Only the jurors believed that the fire was not the owners' fault.

J Jurors and citizens agreed that the fire was no one's fault.

3 Which conclusion is best supported by the information in this piece of history writing?

A The fire resulted in New York City's becoming the safest city in the United States.

B After the fire, American industry saw a decline in the number of women in the workplace.

C Even after the fire, the problem of unsafe working conditions was never addressed.

D The fire resulted in new laws being passed to improve the safety of workers.

ANALYZE THE TEXT

Support your responses with evidence from the text. NOTEBOOK

1. **Cite Evidence** What was true of factories in New York City before the Triangle Factory Fire? Cite details from the text that support your answer.
2. **Summarize** In two or three sentences, summarize the changes that occurred in the aftermath of the tragedy. Be sure to mention the time period over which the changes happened.
3. **Critique** What is the author's main method of organization in this piece of history writing? Why is it useful for the author's purpose?
4. **Evaluate** Review the primary source quotations in the text. How well do they help readers better understand the fire's aftermath?
5. **Notice & Note** Review the statement by Frances Perkins in the final paragraph. Why did the author include Perkins's comment? What does it add to this account of the Triangle Factory Fire?

RESEARCH

Think of something or someone you want to learn more about in connection with the Triangle Factory Fire. For example, do you want to learn more about the working conditions before the fire? More about the laws that were enacted after the fire? More about the historical figures named in the article? Choose a topic that interests you and is related to the fire. Research the topic and record what you learn in the chart. Also use the chart to keep track of the sources you used.

RESEARCH TIP
For many historical topics, consider looking for both primary and secondary sources. Primary sources provide personal, subjective views of the event because they are created by someone who took part or witnessed it. Primary sources include diaries, autobiographies, and photographs. Secondary sources provide an overview of the event and factual details.

TRIANGLE FACTORY FIRE
What or Who: ______________

Explanation/description	**Primary sources**
Significance	**Secondary sources**

Connect In the final paragraph, Frances Perkins is quoted as saying, "They did not die in vain. . . ." With a small group, discuss how what you learned relates to Perkins's statement.

CREATE AND ADAPT

Write Historical Fiction Create a fictional narrative based on information from the selection and your own research. Remember: historical fiction includes real places, people, and events, but writers use their imagination to create scenes, dialogue, and characters.

- ❑ Choose a situation related to the fire. Establish a point of view: a first-person narrator or third-person narrator. Review information from the selection and your research to gather details.
- ❑ List key events in chronological order. Use vivid language to describe feelings and actions. Include a conclusion that follows from the sequence of events.
- ❑ Read your narrative aloud to yourself or to a classmate and make any revisions that you think will make the story more powerful.

Go to **Writing Narratives: Point of View and Characters** in the **Writing Studio** for more help.

Create a Graphic Novel Page Adapt the courtroom scene described in paragraph 2 of *The Story of the Triangle Factory Fire* into a page for a graphic novel.

- ❑ Visualize the scene. Then, identify the key images so that your readers also can visualize it.
- ❑ In a graphic novel, space for words is limited, so decide which dialogue and descriptive words and phrases are most essential for the scene.
- ❑ Share your first draft with a classmate and ask for feedback. Revise the images or words for the greatest impact; then share your final version in a brief presentation.

Go to **Using Media in a Presentation** in the **Speaking and Listening Studio** to learn more.

RESPOND TO THE ESSENTIAL QUESTION

? What inspires you to make a difference?

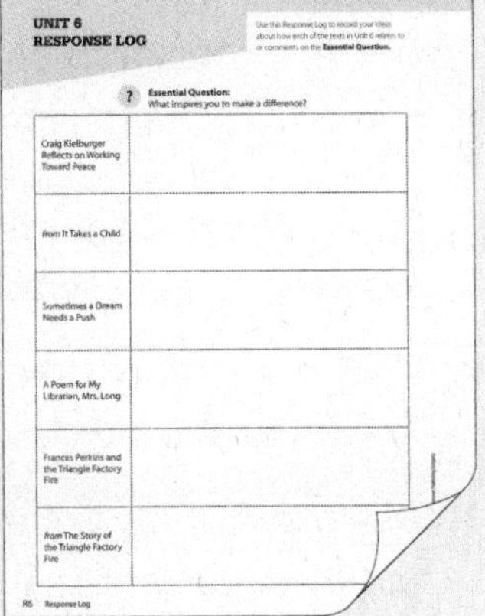

UNIT 6 RESPONSE LOG

Use this Response Log to record your ideas about how each of the texts in Unit 6 relates to or comments on the **Essential Question.**

? **Essential Question:** What inspires you to make a difference?

Craig Kielburger Reflects on Working Toward Peace	
from It Takes a Child	
Sometimes a Dream Needs a Push	
A Poem for My Librarian, Mrs. Long	
Frances Perkins and the Triangle Factory Fire	
from The Story of the Triangle Factory Fire	

R6 Response Log

Gather Information Review your notes on the excerpt from *The Story of the Triangle Factory Fire*. Then, add relevant details to your Response Log. As you determine which information to include, think about:

- the sequence of key events that took place after the fire
- why these events took place when they did

At the end of the unit, use your notes to help you write a research report.

ACADEMIC VOCABULARY

As you write and discuss what you learned from the piece of history writing, be sure to use the Academic Vocabulary words. Check off each of the words that you use.

- ❑ **contrast**
- ❑ **despite**
- ❑ **error**
- ❑ **inadequate**
- ❑ **interact**

RESPOND

CRITICAL VOCABULARY

WORD BANK
hideous
corridor
enact
reformer

Practice and Apply Answer each question by using the Critical Vocabulary word in a complete sentence.

1. Why might people react with shock if they saw something that was **hideous**?
2. Why is it important to keep a **corridor** clear of obstacles?
3. What can people do to persuade local politicians to **enact** a law?
4. How would you describe a **reformer** who helps bring about a positive change in society?

VOCABULARY STRATEGY: Connotations and Denotations

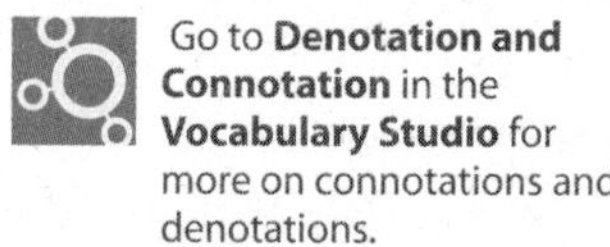

Go to **Denotation and Connotation** in the **Vocabulary Studio** for more on connotations and denotations.

A word's **denotation** is its literal, dictionary meaning. A word's **connotation** comes from the ideas and feelings associated with the word. The author of *The Story of the Triangle Factory Fire* chose some words because of their connotation. He also chose quotations whose speakers likely did the same, as in this comment by Lillian D. Wald:

> **The conditions as they now exist are hideous. . . .**

The choice of *hideous* suggests that the conditions were terrible and revolting. The word suggests an image that would upset most readers.

Some words have positive connotations; other words have negative connotations. To determine a word's connotation, examine the context of the phrase, sentence, or paragraph in which the word appears.

Practice and Apply For each item, mark the word you think better expresses the meaning of the sentence. Use a print or online dictionary to help you. Then explain your choice to a partner.

1. "Furious New Yorkers refused to let the issue rest."
   The people were (**serious, determined**).
2. "They examined workers' filthy living conditions. . . ."
   The workers' living conditions were (**disgusting, messy**).
3. "As a result of the Commission's shocking findings, New York State quickly passed thirty-three new labor laws. . . ."
   The findings were (**surprising, alarming**).
4. "She and other social reformers dedicated their lives to insuring worker safety. . . ."
   These reformers were (**helpful, devoted**).

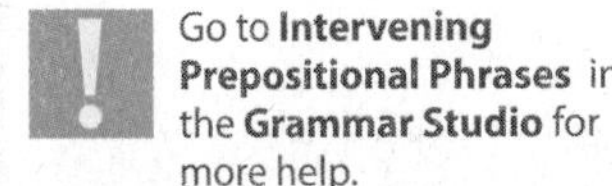

LANGUAGE CONVENTIONS: Subject–Verb Agreement and Prepositional Phrases

Go to **Intervening Prepositional Phrases** in the **Grammar Studio** for more help.

As you know, the subject and verb in a clause must agree in number. **Agreement** means that if the subject is singular, the verb is also singular, and if the subject is plural, the verb is also plural. Most verbs show the difference between singular and plural only in the third person of the present tense. In the present tense, the third-person singular forms ends in *-s*.

Singular	Plural
I work	we work
you work	you work
she, he, it works	they work

However, the verb *be* causes subject-verb agreeement issues because this verb doesn't follow the usual patterns. It is important to pay particular attention to agreement with this verb.

FORMS OF *BE*			
Present Tense		**Past Tense**	
Singular	**Plural**	**Singular**	**Plural**
I am	we are	I was	we were
you are	you are	you were	you were
she, he, it is	they are	she, he, it was	they were

In addition, you need to pay attention to words between a subject and a verb. A verb only agrees with its subject. Therefore, when a prepositional phrase or other words come between a subject and a verb, ignore them and focus on identifying the subject and making sure the verb agrees with it. Notice the prepositional phrase "of the tragic Triangle factory fire" does not change the agreement of *ashes* and *came* in this example from *The Story of the Triangle Factory Fire*:

> **From the ashes of the tragic Triangle factory fire came help for millions of United States laborers today.**

Practice and Apply Choose the verb that agrees with the subject.

1. Today, the victims of the Triangle factory fire (**is** / **are**) remembered.
2. The safety of workers (**wasn't** / **weren't**) as important as today.
3. Citizens in the courtroom (**was** / **were**) furious with the verdict.
4. Investigators in the tenement buildings (**was** / **were**) searching for dangerous conditions.
5. The details of the 1911 fire (**anger** / **angers**) public safety officials.

RESPOND

Collaborate & Compare

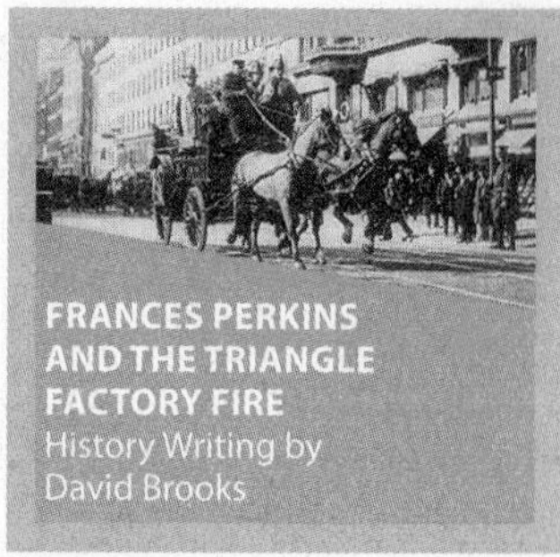

FRANCES PERKINS AND THE TRIANGLE FACTORY FIRE
History Writing by David Brooks

from **THE STORY OF THE TRIANGLE FACTORY FIRE**
History Writing by Zachary Kent

COMPARE AUTHORS' PURPOSES AND MESSAGES

Why compare the **purpose** (reason for writing) and **message** (most important idea) of two authors who wrote about the same historical event? Comparing the texts can give you a greater understanding of the event and new insights into the lives of the people involved.

With a partner, complete the chart and then determine each author's purpose and message. Finally, discuss how the texts are similar and how they differ. Cite text evidence in your discussion.

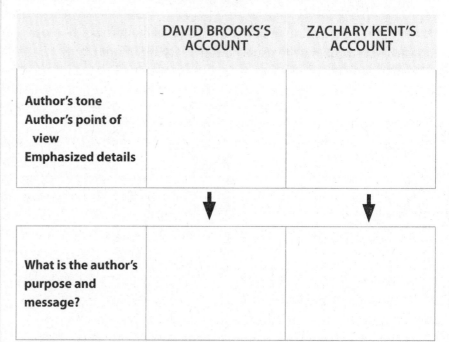

	DAVID BROOKS'S ACCOUNT	ZACHARY KENT'S ACCOUNT
Author's tone **Author's point of view** **Emphasized details**		
	↓	↓
What is the author's purpose and message?		

ANALYZE THE TEXTS

Discuss these questions in your group.

1. **Cause/Effect** Which of the two texts would you use to research the effects of the Triangle Fire? Why?
2. **Compare** Look back at both texts to find mention of Frances Perkins. Why is she an important person to know about?
3. **Infer** What kinds of sources did both authors use in researching this topic?
4. **Connect** What idea presented by both authors is most relevant to us today? Why?

RESEARCH AND SHARE

Now, your group can continue exploring the ideas presented in these texts. As a team, collaborate on research about another significant fire in history and its effects. Then present your findings in an oral presentation. Follow these steps:

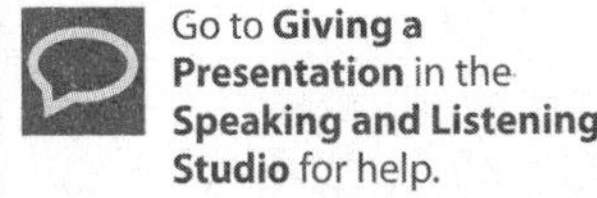

Go to **Giving a Presentation** in the **Speaking and Listening Studio** for help.

1. **Focus Your Research** As a group, decide on a historic fire to research. Begin by searching general terms such as "great fires in history" or specific historic fires such as the Great Fire of London (1666), the Great Fire of Chicago (1871), or the Iroquois Theater Fire (1903). Use your search results to help you choose the fire you all want to explore.
2. **Gather Information** Once you've agreed on the focus of your research, plan how you will each gather information using credible online and print resources. You can use a **web** to guide your research and to record information about the fire. Then use it as a framework for an oral presentation of your findings.

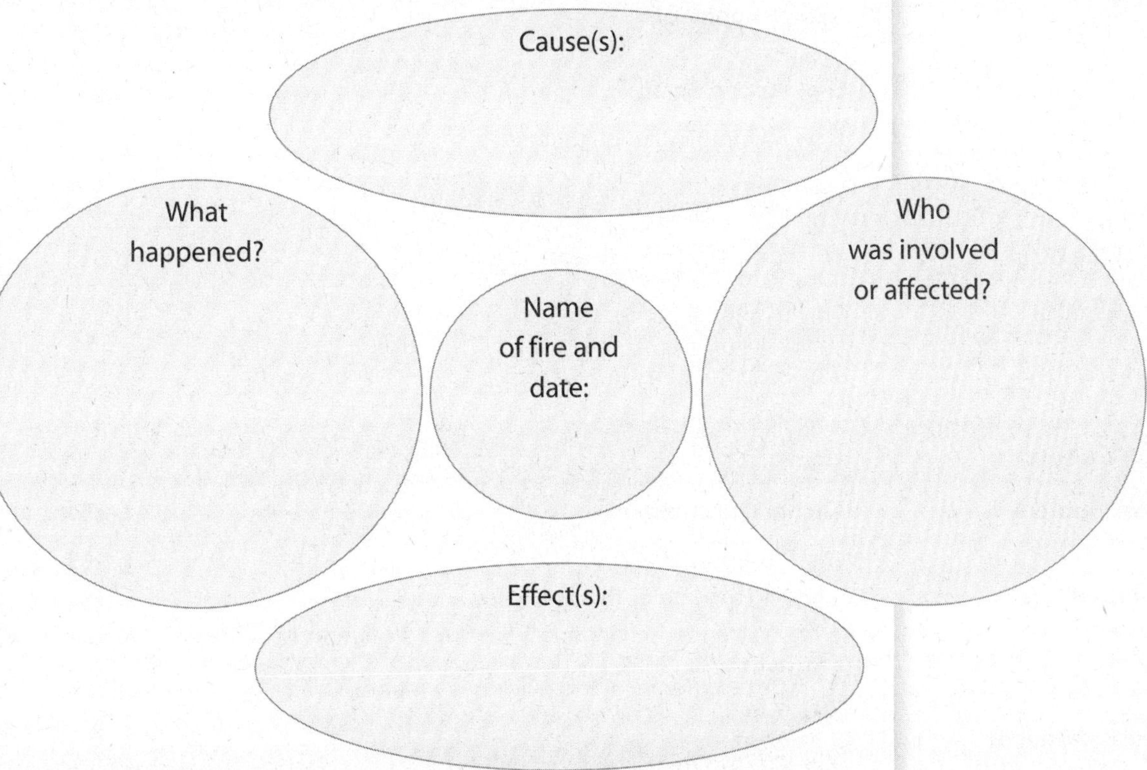

3. **Present What You Learn** Everyone in your group is now an expert on this historic fire and its effects. Discuss which aspects of the fire you each will present and how you will present the information. Consider including a timeline and other images to enhance your presentation. Also prepare for follow-up questions from your audience.

RESEARCH TIP

When incorporating information from the sources you find, be sure to guard against plagiarism—that is, using someone else's words and not giving the person credit for them. If you quote or paraphrase a source, keep information about the source and give credit in your work.

INDEPENDENT READING

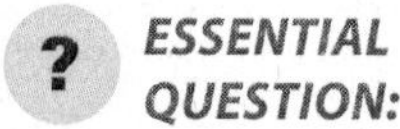

ESSENTIAL QUESTION:

What inspires you to make a difference?

Reader's Choice

Setting a Purpose Select one or more of these options from your eBook to continue your exploration of the Essential Question.

- Read the descriptions to see which text grabs your interest.
- Think about which genres you enjoy reading.

Notice & Note

In this unit, you practiced asking **Big Questions** and noticing and noting two signposts: **Extreme or Absolute Language** and **Quoted Words.** As you read independently, these signposts and others will aid your understanding. Below are the anchor questions to ask when you read literature and nonfiction.

Reading Literature: Stories, Poems, and Plays		
Signpost	**Anchor Question**	**Lesson**
Contrasts and Contradictions	Why did the character act that way?	p. 99
Aha Moment	How might this change things?	p. 3
Tough Questions	What does this make me wonder about?	p. 362
Words of the Wiser	What's the lesson for the character?	p. 363
Again and Again	Why might the author keep bringing this up?	p. 3
Memory Moment	Why is this memory important?	p. 2

Reading Nonfiction: Essays, Articles, and Arguments		
Signpost/Strategy	**Anchor Question(s)**	**Lesson**
Big Questions	What surprised me? What did the author think I already knew? What challenged, changed, or confirmed what I already knew?	p. 265 p. 183 p. 437
Contrasts and Contradictions	What is the difference, and why does it matter?	p. 183
Extreme or Absolute Language	Why did the author use this language?	p. 182
Numbers and Stats	Why did the author use these numbers or amounts?	p. 264
Quoted Words	Why was this person quoted or cited, and what did this add?	p. 437
Word Gaps	Do I know this word from someplace else? Does it seem like technical talk for this topic? Do clues in the sentence help me understand the word?	p. 265

INDEPENDENT READING

You can preview these texts in Unit 6 of your eBook.

Then, check off the text or texts that you select to read on your own.

ARTICLE

Difference Maker: John Bergmann and Popcorn Park
David Karas

Learn how people are making a difference to the condition of wildlife and domesticated animals that are distressed.

AUTOBIOGRAPHY

***from* Walking with the Wind**
John Lewis

Explore how the words of a young preacher inspired a lifetime of political activism.

SHORT STORY

Doris Is Coming
ZZ Packer

What happens when a young girl in the early 1960s refuses to be intimidated by the racist rules of her hometown?

INFORMATIONAL TEXT

Seeing Is Believing
Mary Morton Cowan

Find out how the work of a single photographer helped change the lives of America's poorest children.

Collaborate and Share Get with a partner to discuss what you learned from at least one of your independent readings.

- Give a brief synopsis or summary of the text.
- Describe any signposts that you noticed in the text and explain what they revealed to you.
- Describe what you most enjoyed or found most challenging about the text. Give specific examples.
- Decide if you would recommend the text to others. Why or why not?

Go to the **Reading Studio** for more resources on **Notice & Note.**

WRITING TASK

Write a Research Report

Go to the **Writing Studio** for help writing your research report.

This unit focuses on people working for social change—the many challenges they encounter, as well as their accomplishments. For this writing task, you will research and write a report about a person you read about in the unit whom you admire and would like to know more about. For an example of a well-written report you can use as a mentor text, review the excerpt from *The Story of the Triangle Factory Fire*.

As you write your research report, you can use the notes from your Response Log, which you filled out after reading the texts in this unit.

Writing Prompt

This is the topic or context for your research report.

Read the information in the box below.

> **Some people are willing to do whatever is necessary to make the world a better place—no matter how difficult the task.**

This is the Essential Question for this unit. How would you answer this question, based on the text in this unit?

Think carefully about the following question.

> **What inspires you to make a difference?**

Now mark the words that identify exactly what you are being asked to produce.

Research and write about one of the figures you read about in this unit. In your report, write about the challenges that person faced and the accomplishments he or she ultimately achieved.

Be sure to—

Review these points as you write and again when you finish. Make any needed changes.

- ❑ provide a strong controlling idea or thesis statement and an introduction that catches the reader's attention and states the topic
- ❑ develop the topic using specific facts, definitions, and examples to support the thesis statement
- ❑ clearly organize ideas and concepts to make connections
- ❑ use appropriate transitions to connect ideas and to create coherence within and across paragraphs
- ❑ identify, gather, and document various sources of information
- ❑ provide a conclusion that summarizes main points and refers to the controlling idea or thesis statement

Plan

First you need to look at all the people in the unit and decide which person you would like to research and write about. Are you interested in someone who is doing things now or someone in the past?

Develop Research Questions Once you have decided who you will write about, you can narrow your topic by generating questions. For example, you might ask "What unique background and experiences motivated this person?" or "Who was most affected by his or her actions?" After you have done some preliminary research, you may need to refine your research questions to narrow your focus or find a more interesting angle to write about. Use the table below, or one like it, to assist you in planning your draft.

Research Report Planning Table	
Initial Research Question	What caused Frances Perkins to become interested in worker safety?
Refined Research Question	How did Frances Perkins and other reformers help make workplaces safer?

Preview Sources After you have questions that seem correctly focused, search for a variety of sources to find available information. Skim the sources you find to decide if they are are **relevant**—covering the target aspect of your topic; **accurate**—including information that can be verified by more than one source; and **objective**—presenting multiple, and unbiased, viewpoints on the topic. As you continue to conduct research for your report, you can use these initial previewed sources to decide if other sources are credible, or reliable and trustworthy.

Background Reading Review the notes you have taken in your Response Log after reading the texts in this unit. This background reading will help you choose someone to write about and the aspects of his or her life and work you will focus on.

Go to **Conducting Research: Starting Your Research** for help planning your research report.

Notice & Note

From Reading to Writing

As you plan your research report, apply what you've learned about signposts to your own writing. Remember that writers use common features, called signposts, to help convey their message to readers.

Think about how you can incorporate **Quoted Words** into your report.

Go to the **Reading Studio** for more resources on Notice & Note

Use the notes from your Response Log as you plan your report.

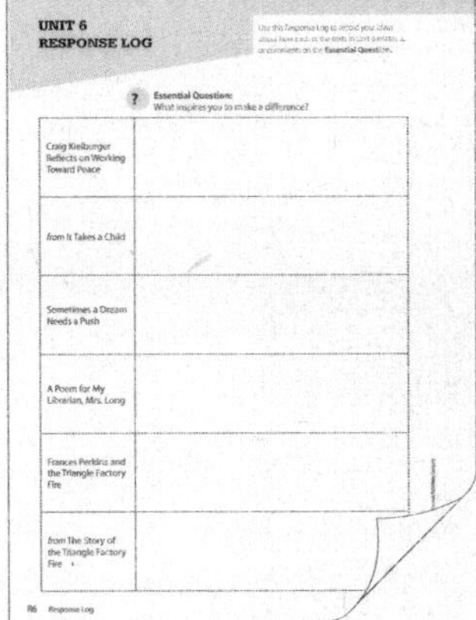

WRITING TASK

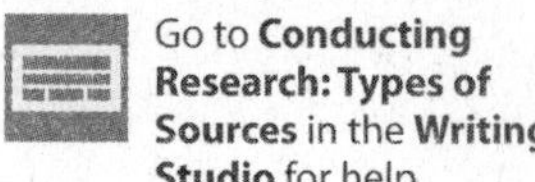

Go to **Conducting Research: Types of Sources** in the **Writing Studio** for help.

Research Your Report The next step in planning your report is to use your list of previewed sources and expand your research to decide on at least three relevant and reliable sources, both online and in print. These might include **primary sources** such as letters or diary entries, as well as **secondary sources** such as encyclopedias.

Organize Your Information You can use the chart below to take notes from your sources. These notes might include direct quotations, summaries, or paraphrases to support your ideas. Be sure to keep accurate records about your sources so that you can create **academic citations** that include the author, title, and publication information for each print and digital source. Ask your teacher about the format that you should use for your citations.

Subject of Research Report: ________		
Background of person	Challenges faced	Accomplishments
Primary Sources Used:		
Secondary Sources Used:		

 Develop a Draft

You may prefer to draft your research report online.

After research and planning, draft your report. Refer to your planning table, the chart, as well as any notes you took as you studied the texts in the unit. Using a word processor or online writing application can make it easier to create and revise your first draft. As you work, keep in mind that you should identify the sources of your information. Recording your sources as you write will make your work accurate and help you avoid **plagiarizing,** or using someone else's words or ideas.

Use the Mentor Text

Author's Craft

Fiction authors and poets are not the only writers to use descriptive language and literary devices. To capture your readers' attention and help them visualize what you describe, use precise words. You might also consider using devices like alliteration and parallel structure to create interest and emphasize certain key ideas.

Through the next four years Commission investigators crawled and pried through the rooms and cellars of factories and tenement houses all across the state. They examined workers' filthy living conditions and witnessed the dangers of crippling machinery and long work hours in dusty, dirty firetraps.

The writer uses strong verbs and adjectives and employs alliteration (dusty, dirty) and parallel structure (crawled and pried through the rooms and cellars of factories and tenement houses).

Apply What You've Learned To maintain your reader's attention, use strong verbs, specific adjectives, and concrete nouns.

Genre Characteristics

Supporting details are words, phrases, sentences, and quotations that tell more about a key idea. Notice how the author of *The Story of the Triangle Factory Fire* uses a quotation by the fire chief to support a key idea about why so many people died in the fire.

In the days following the fire, city officials sifted through the charred rubble at the Asch Building and tried to fix the fault for the tragedy. Fire Chief Croker angrily stated, "There wasn't a fire escape anywhere fronting on the street by which these unfortunate girls could escape."

The author provides evidence, including quotations, to explain why the girls died.

Apply What You've Learned The details you include in your report should be clearly related to ideas about the person you are researching. Quotations might come from the subject of your report, his or her family members, coworkers, and government officials.

3 Revise

Go to **Conducting Research: Refocusing Your Inquiry** for help with revising your report.

On Your Own Once you have written your draft, go back and look for ways to improve your research report. As you reread and revise, think about whether you have achieved your purpose. The Revision Guide will help you focus on specific elements to make your writing stronger.

Revision Guide		
Ask Yourself	**Tips**	**Revision Techniques**
1. Is my topic clear?	**Mark** the thesis statement.	**Add** a thesis statement.
2. Does each paragraph have a topic sentence related to the controlling idea, or thesis statement?	**Highlight** the topic sentence of each paragraph.	**Delete** unrelated ideas or **rearrange** information into separate paragraphs. **Add** a topic sentence.
3. Are there supporting facts and examples for each key idea?	**Underline** facts, examples, and quotations that support your key idea.	**Add** more facts, examples, and quotations from your notes.
4. Are ideas organized logically? Do transitions connect ideas? Is there coherence within and across paragraphs?	**Highlight** transitional words and phrases within and between paragraphs.	**Rearrange** sentences and paragraphs to organize ideas logically. **Add** transitions to connect ideas and create coherence.
5. Is information gathered from a variety of sources, all cited correctly?	**Underline** references to sources.	**Add** more sources for variety. **Cite** all sources correctly.
6. Does the conclusion summarize the key ideas?	**Underline** the summary.	**Review** the topic sentence in each paragraph. **Add** a summary statement.

ACADEMIC VOCABULARY

As you conduct your **peer review,** be sure to use these words.

- ❑ **contrast**
- ❑ **despite**
- ❑ **error**
- ❑ **inadequate**
- ❑ **interact**

With a Partner After working through the Revision Guide on your own, exchange papers with a partner and evaluate each other's drafts in a **peer review**. Take turns reading or listening to each other's reports and offer suggestions based on the Revision Guide to make the reports more effective. When receiving feedback from your partner, listen attentively and ask questions to make sure you fully understand the revision suggestions.

4 Edit

Once you have revised your research report, you can improve the finer points of your draft. Edit for the proper use of standard English conventions, such as correct punctuation, and be sure to correct any misspellings or grammatical errors.

Go to the **Grammar Studio: Punctuation** to learn more.

Paraphrasing to Avoid Plagiarism

Finding sources is an important part of developing a research report. But equally important is paraphrasing those sources correctly to avoid plagiarism and citing all of your sources.

Go to **Using Textual Evidence: Attribution** in the **Writing Studio** for more help with research.

- When you **paraphrase,** you restate information in your own words.
- **Plagiarism** is the unauthorized use of someone else's work. When you plagiarize, you present someone else's work as if it was your own.

Learning to paraphrase correctly can help you avoid plagiarism. The chart below contains an excerpt from *The Story of the Triangle Factory Fire* and two paraphrases. The first paraphrase uses too many of the author's original words. The second paraphrase is done correctly.

Original text	Furious New Yorkers refused to let the issue rest. In October 1911 the city established a Bureau of Fire Prevention to inspect safety standards in other buildings.
Incorrect paraphrase	Angry New Yorkers would not let the issue rest. The city set up a Bureau of Fire Prevention in October 1911 to inspect other buildings' safety standards.
Correct paraphrase	New Yorkers pressed for change, resulting in the establishment of the Bureau of Fire Prevention in 1911. The bureau's job was to ensure that other buildings met safety standards.

5 Publish

Finalize your research report by examining your work for interest, accuracy, and correct citations. Choose a way to share your report with your audience. Consider these options:

- Post your report on a school website.
- Produce a multimodal presentation of your essay.

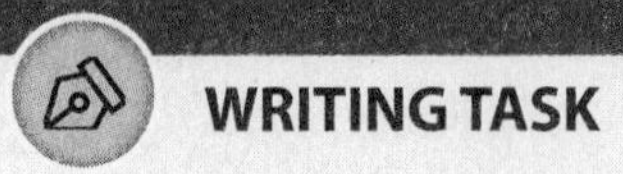

WRITING TASK

Use the scoring guide to evaluate your research report.

Writing Task Scoring Guide: Research Report			
	Organization/Progression	**Development of Ideas**	**Use of Language and Conventions**
4	• The organization is effective and logical throughout the report. • Transitions clearly show the relationship among ideas from one paragraph to another. • There is coherence within and across paragraphs.	• The thesis statement is clear and the introduction is engaging, reflecting depth of thought. • The thesis statement is well developed with relevant facts, concrete details, interesting quotations, and specific examples from reliable sources. • The conclusion effectively summarizes the information presented.	• The writing maintains a formal style throughout. • Language is strong and precise. • There is sentence variety. • Spelling, capitalization, and punctuation are correct. • Grammar and usage are correct. • Research sources are cited and paraphrased correctly.
3	• The organization is confusing in a few places. • A few more transitions are needed to connect related ideas. • There is coherence within and across paragraphs.	• The thesis statement is clear, reflecting some depth of thought, but the introduction could do more to grab readers' attention. • The thesis statement needs more support from relevant facts, details, quotations, and examples from reliable sources. • The conclusion summarizes the information presented.	• The style is inconsistent in a few places. • Language is too general in some places. • There is some sentence variety. • A few spelling, capitalization, and punctuation errors are present. • Some errors in grammar and usage are repeated. • Sources are not cited or punctuated consistently.
2	• The organization is logical in some places but often doesn't follow a pattern. • More transitions are needed throughout to connect ideas. • There is little coherence within and across paragraphs.	• The thesis statement is unclear and does not reflect depth of thought. The introduction could be more engaging. • The development of ideas is minimal. The facts, details, quotations, and examples are not relevant or are ineffectively presented. • The conclusion is only partially effective.	• The style is informal in many places. • Overly general language is used. • Most sentences are structured in the same way. • Spelling, capitalization, and punctuation are often incorrect but do not make reading difficult. • Grammar and usage are often still clear. • Only one or two research sources are cited, using incorrect format and punctuation.
1	• A logical organization is not used; information is presented randomly. • Transitions are not used, making the report difficult to understand. • There is no coherence within and across paragraphs.	• The thesis statement is unclear, or the introduction is missing or confusing. • Facts, details, quotations, and examples come from unreliable sources or are missing. • The conclusion is missing.	• The style is inappropriate for the report. • Language is too general to convey the information. • There is no sentence variety. • Many spelling, capitalization, and punctuation errors are present. • Many grammatical and usage errors appear. • Research sources are not cited.

Participate in a Panel Discussion

In this unit, you read about people who were inspired to solve problems. In this activity, you will draw from the selections you read to participate in a panel discussion about commitment to a cause. Recognize that a successful participant in a panel discussion—

Go to **Participating in Collaborative Discussions** in the **Speaking and Listening Studio** for help developing your panel discussion.

- makes a clear, logical generalization about the topic
- uses quotations and specific examples to illustrate ideas
- responds politely to the moderator and other group members
- evaluates other group members' contributions
- summarizes the discussion by synthesizing ideas

1 Prepare for a Panel Discussion

Work with your classmates to prepare for the discussion.

- Form a group. Choose three selections from this unit, including the excerpt from *The Story of the Triangle Factory Fire*, for the discussion.
- Select one student to be the moderator. The rest of your classmates will be your audience during the panel discussion.
- Create a schedule that shows the order in which panel members will speak and for how long. Develop rules for the appropriate times for the moderator or the audience to ask panel members questions.
- **Gather Evidence** Work individually to analyze what your chosen selections suggest about commitment to a cause. Note specific details, examples, and quotations that support your views. Then consider your experiences. Ask yourself questions as you take notes.

QUESTION	EVIDENCE
What degree of positive change might one person or group hope to accomplish?	
Are good intentions enough? How knowledgeable does a person need to be in order to take on an issue?	
What are the benefits or drawbacks of committing to a cause?	

2 Practice the Panel Discussion

Work individually to outline your ideas and develop a clear controlling idea. Then prepare to "think on your feet" as you present your ideas to your group. The moderator and group members will ask questions about your ideas to prepare you for the real discussion. The moderator should time each panel member's contribution and suggest length adjustments. The moderator should also write notes for opening remarks and concluding remarks. Based on the practice session, make changes to your written response to the texts.

As you work collaboratively, be sure to follow discussion rules:

- ❑ listen closely to each other
- ❑ don't interrupt
- ❑ stay on topic
- ❑ ask only helpful, relevant questions
- ❑ provide only clear, thoughtful, and direct answers

Provide and Consider Advice for Improvement

As a listener, pay close attention. Take notes about ways that presenters can improve their presentations and more effectively use verbal and nonverbal techniques. Paraphrase and summarize each presenter's key ideas to confirm your understanding, and ask questions to clarify any confusing ideas.

As a presenter, listen closely to questions and consider ways to revise your work to make sure your points are clear and logically sequenced.

- Effective **verbal techniques** include clearly enunciating words and speaking at an appropriate rate and volume.
- Effective **nonverbal techniques** include making eye contact, varying facial expressions, and using meaningful gestures.

3 Present the Discussion

Now it's time to present your panel discussion before the rest of the class. Have your outline at hand for reference. Here are some guidelines for the discussion:

- Have the moderator use his or her notes for opening remarks to introduce the topic, panelists, and format for the discussion. The moderator will ask the first question and facilitate discussion.
- Speak directly to the panel and audience. Refer to your notes for your main points, but don't just read from your notes.
- Listen closely so that you can respond appropriately.
- After the panel discussion, have the moderator invite panelists and the audience to ask questions.
- Conclude by having the moderator summarize the discussion and thank the panelists for their participation.

Reflect on the Unit

By completing your research report and engaging in a panel discussion, you have expressed your thoughts about the reading you have done in this unit as well as the information you discovered in your research. Now is a good time to reflect on what you have learned.

Reflect on the Essential Question

- What inspires you to make a difference? How has your answer to this question changed since you first considered it?
- What are some examples you've read of people who are inspired to make a difference—both from the unit and from other sources?

Reflect on Your Reading

- Which selections were the most interesting or surprising to you?
- From which selection did you learn the most about how people become inspired to make the world a better place?

Reflect on the Writing Task

- What difficulties did you encounter while working on your research report? How might you avoid them next time?
- What parts of the report were the easiest and hardest to write? Why?
- What improvements did you make to your report during revision?

Reflect on the Speaking and Listening Task

- Were you able to defend your ideas? Did the discussion cause you to rethink your point of view? If so, why?
- What was your favorite part of participating in the panel discussion?
- In what ways was the panel discussion successful? What might you do differently the next time?

UNIT 6 SELECTIONS

- **"Craig Kielburger Reflects on Working Toward Peace"**
- **from *It Takes a Child***
- **"Sometimes a Dream Needs a Push"**
- **"A Poem for My Librarian, Mrs. Long"**
- **"Frances Perkins and the Triangle Factory Fire"**
- **from *The Story of the Triangle Factory Fire***

RESOURCES

HMH *INTO LITERATURE* STUDIOS

For more instruction and practice, visit the HMH *Into Literature* Studios.

Reading Studio

Writing Studio

Speaking & Listening Studio

Grammar Studio

Vocabulary Studio

UNIT 1 RESPONSE LOG

Use this Response Log to record your ideas about how each of the texts in Unit 1 relates to or comments on the **Essential Question.**

Essential Question:
What helps people rise up to face difficulties?

Rogue Wave	
The Flight of Icarus	
Icarus's Flight	
Women in Aviation	
Thank You, M'am	
A Police Stop Changed This Teenager's Life	

UNIT 2 RESPONSE LOG

Use this Response Log to record your ideas about how each of the texts in Unit 2 relates to or comments on the **Essential Question.**

? **Essential Question:**
What can blur the lines between what's real and what's not?

Heartbeat	
The Camera Does Lie	
Two Legs or One?	
The Song of Wandering Aengus	
Eldorado	
The Governess *from* The Good Doctor	
from The Governess	

UNIT 3 RESPONSE LOG

Use this Response Log to record your ideas about how each of the texts in Unit 3 relates to or comments on the **Essential Question.**

? **Essential Question:**
What does it mean to be in harmony with nature?

Never Retreat *from* Eyes Wide Open	
from Mississippi Solo	
The Drought	
Allied with Green	
Ode to enchanted light	
Sleeping in the Forest	
from Trash Talk	
You're Part of the Solution	

UNIT 4 RESPONSE LOG

Use this Response Log to record your ideas about how each of the texts in Unit 4 relates to or comments on the **Essential Question.**

? **Essential Question:**
Why is the idea of space exploration both inspiring and unnerving?

Martian Metropolis	
Dark They Were, and Golden-Eyed	
Challenges for Space Exploration	
What If We Were Alone?	
Seven Minutes of Terror	
Space Exploration Should Be More Science Than Fiction	
Humans Should Stay Home and Let Robots Take to the Stars	

UNIT 5 RESPONSE LOG

Use this Response Log to record your ideas about how each of the texts in Unit 5 relates to or comments on the **Essential Question.**

? **Essential Question:**
How do sports bring together friends, families, and communities?

Ball Hawk	
Get in the Zone: The Psychology of Video Game Design	
It's Not Just a Game!	
from The Crossover	
Double Doubles	

UNIT 6 RESPONSE LOG

Use this Response Log to record your ideas about how each of the texts in Unit 6 relates to or comments on the **Essential Question.**

? Essential Question:
What inspires you to make a difference?

Craig Kielburger Reflects on Working Toward Peace	
from It Takes a Child	
Sometimes a Dream Needs a Push	
A Poem for My Librarian, Mrs. Long	
Frances Perkins and the Triangle Factory Fire	
from The Story of the Triangle Factory Fire	

Using a Glossary

A glossary is an alphabetical list of vocabulary words. Use a glossary just as you would a dictionary—to determine the meanings, parts of speech, pronunciation, and syllabification of words. (Some technical, foreign, and more obscure words in this book are defined for you in the footnotes that accompany many of the selections.)

Many words in the English language have more than one meaning. This glossary gives the meanings that apply to the words as they are used in the selections in this book.

The following abbreviations are used to identify parts of speech of words:

adj. adjective *adv.* adverb *n.* noun *v.* verb

Each word's pronunciation is given in parentheses. A guide to the pronunciation symbols appears in the Pronunciation Key below. The stress marks in the Pronunciation Key are used to indicate the force given to each syllable in a word. They can also help you determine where words are divided into syllables.

For more information about the words in this glossary or for information about words not listed here, consult a dictionary.

Pronunciation Key

Symbol	Examples
ă	pat
ā	pay
ä	father
âr	care
b	bib
ch	church
d	deed, milled
ĕ	pet
ē	bee
f	fife, phase, rough
g	gag
h	hat
hw	which
ĭ	pit
ī	pie, by
îr	pier
j	judge
k	kick, cat, pique
l	lid, needle* (nēd′l)

Symbol	Examples
m	mum
n	no, sudden* (sud′n)
ng	thing
ŏ	pot
ō	toe
ô	caught, paw
oi	noise
o͝o	took
o͞o	boot
o͝or	lure
ôr	core
ou	out
p	pop
r	roar
s	sauce
sh	ship, dish
t	tight, stopped
th	thin
th	this
ŭ	cut

Symbol	Examples
ûr	urge, term, firm, word, heard
v	valve
w	with
y	yes
z	zebra, xylem
zh	vision, pleasure, garage
ə	about, item, edible, gallop, circus
ər	butter

Sounds in Foreign Words

Symbol	Examples
KH	*German* ich, ach; *Scottish* loch
N	*French*, bon (bôN)
œ	*French* feu, œuf; *German* schön
ü	*French* tu; *German* über

*In English the consonants *l* and *n* often constitute complete syllables by themselves.

Stress Marks

The relevant emphasis with which the syllables of a word or phrase are spoken, called stress, is indicated in three different ways. The strongest, or primary, stress is marked with a bold mark (′). An intermediate, or secondary, level of stress is marked with a similar but lighter mark (′). The weakest stress is unmarked. Words of one syllable show no stress mark.

GLOSSARY OF ACADEMIC VOCABULARY

abnormal (ăb-nôr′məl) *adj.* not typical, usual, or regular; not normal

affect (ə-fĕkt′) *v.* to have an influence on or effect a change in something

aspect (ăs′pĕkt) *n.* a characteristic or feature of something

attitude (ăt′ĭ-to͞od′) *n.* a manner of thinking that reflects a person's feelings; a particular state of mind

complex (kŏm′plĕks′) *adj.* consisting of many interwoven parts that make something difficult to understand

consume (kən-so͞om′) *v.* to buy things for your own use or ownership

contrast (kən-trăst′) *v.* to show differences between two or more things that are being compared

cultural (kul′chər-əl) *adj.* of or relating to culture or cultivation

despite (dĭ-spīt′) *prep.* in spite of; even though

element (ĕl′ə-mənt) *n.* a part or aspect of something

ensure (ĕn-sho͝or′) *v.* to make sure or certain

error (ĕr′ər) *n.* a mistake

evaluate (ĭ-văl′yoo-āt′) *tr.v.* to examine something carefully to judge its value or worth

feature (fē′chər) *n.* a prominent or distinctive part, quality, or characteristic

focus (fō′kəs) *v.* to direct toward a specific point or purpose

goal (gōl) *n.* the object toward which your work and planning is directed; a purpose

inadequate (ĭn-ăd′ĭ-kwĭt) *adj.* not enough or sufficient to fulfill a need or meet a requirement

interact (ĭn′tər-ăkt′) *v.* to act upon each other

participate (pär-tĭs′ə-pāt′) *v.* to be active and involved in something or to share in something

perceive (pər-sēv′) *v.* to become aware of something directly through any of the senses

potential (pə-tĕn′shəl) *adj.* capable of doing or being something; having possibility

purchase (pûr′chĭs) *v.* to buy

rely (rĭ-lī) *v.* to depend on something or someone for support, help, or supply

resource (re′-sors′) *n.* something that can be used for support or help

specify (spĕs′ə-fī′) *v.* to state exactly or in detail what you want or need

stress (strĕs) *v.* to put emphasis on something

style (stīl) *n.* the combination of techniques that a writer uses to make his or her work effective and unique

task (tăsk) *n.* an assignment or work done as part of one's duties

text (tĕkst) *n.* a literary work that is regarded as an object of critical analysis

valid (văl′ĭd) *adj.* convincing or having a sound reason for something

GLOSSARY OF CRITICAL VOCABULARY

absolute (ăb´sə-lo͞ot´) *adj.* Something that is without qualifications or exceptions is ***absolute.***

absorb (əb-zôrb´) *v.* Things that ***absorb*** you occupy your time or attention.

accelerate (ăk-sĕl´ə-rāt´) *v.* When something ***accelerates***, its speed increases.

accomplishment (ə-kŏm´plĭsh-mənt) *n.* An ***accomplishment*** is a task that you succeed in doing.

adaptability (ə-dăp´tə-bĭl´ĭ-tē) *n.* People who have ***adaptability*** can change to survive and fit in with new circumstances.

addiction (ə-dĭk´shən) *n.* An ***addiction*** is a habit upon which a person becomes physically or emotionally dependent.

administration (ăd-mĭn´ĭ-strā´shən) *n.* A president's ***administration*** is his or her term of office.

advancement (ăd-văns´mənt) *n.* Something that is an ***advancement*** is an improvement or step forward.

anxiety (ăng-zī´ĭ-tē) *n.* ***Anxiety*** is an uneasy, worried feeling.

aquifer (ăk´wə-fər) *n.* An ***aquifer*** is an underground layer of rock that contains water.

arboretum (är´bə-rē´təm) *n.* An ***arboretum*** is a place where many trees are grown for educational or viewing purposes.

atmosphere (ăt´mə-sfîr´) *n.* An ***atmosphere*** is the gaseous mass or envelope that surrounds a planet.

avalanche (ăv´ə-lănch´) *n.* An ***avalanche*** is a large mass of snow, ice, dirt, or rocks falling quickly down the side of a mountain.

barren (băr´ən) *adj.* Something that is empty and lacking interest or charm is ***barren***.

beneficial (bĕn´ə-fĭsh´əl) *adj.* When something is ***beneficial,*** it is good or favorable.

bogus (bō´gəs) *adj.* Something that is ***bogus*** is fake or not genuine.

burden (bûr´dn) *v.* If you ***burden*** someone, you create a situation that is difficult or stressful for him or her.

capacity (kə-păs´ĭ-tē) *n.* A person's ***capacity*** is his or her role or position.

clique (klĭk) *n.* If you are part of a ***clique***, you belong to a small group of friends that doesn't allow outsiders.

collision (kə-lĭzh´ən) *n.* When the two things crash into each other, the result is a ***collision***.

colonize (kŏl´ə-nīz´) *v.* When you ***colonize*** a place, you send a group of people to a new place to establish a colony or settlement.

combustion (kəm-bŭs´chən) *n.* ***Combustion*** is the process of burning, which produces heat and light.

commute (kə-myo͞ot´) *n.* A ***commute*** is a person's travel to and from work or school.

concession (kən-sĕsh´ən) *n.* Sporting and entertainment events often feature ***concession*** stands where food and drinks are sold.

congestion (kən-jĕs´chən) *n.* ***Congestion*** is overcrowding, such as when too many vehicles cause a traffic jam.

consecutive (kən-sĕk´yə-tĭv) *adj.* When things are ***consecutive***, they follow one after another without interruption.

continuity (kŏn´tə-no͞o´ĭ-tē) *n.* In the movies, ***continuity*** refers to making sure that things that were filmed at different times or out of sequence look as if they were filmed at the same time or in the intended sequence.

convivial (kən-vĭv´ē-əl) *adj.* A person who is ***convivial*** enjoys the company of others in a sociable manner.

corridor (kôr´ĭ-dər) *n.* A ***corridor*** is a narrow hallway or passageway.

crucial (kro͞o´shəl) *adj.* Something that is ***crucial*** is extremely important or significant.

deck (dĕk) *n.* The ***deck*** is the platform on a ship or boat where people stand.

GLOSSARY OF CRITICAL VOCABULARY

delirious (dĭ-lîr′ē-əs) *adj.* Someone who is ***delirious*** is temporarily confused, often because of fever or shock.

dignified (dĭg′nə-fīd′) *adj.* Someone or something that is ***dignified*** has or shows honor and respect.

discrepancy (dĭ-skrĕp′ən-sē) *n.* When there is a ***discrepancy*** between two things, there is a difference or disagreement.

disorient (dĭs-ôr′ē-ĕnt′) *v.* To ***disorient*** is to make someone or something lose a sense of direction.

distinguish (dĭ-stĭng′gwĭsh) *v.* To ***distinguish*** one thing from another means perceiving them as being different or distinct.

donate (dō′nāt′) *v.* To ***donate*** is to give, or contribute, something to a person, cause, or fund.

dubious (do͞o′bē-əs) *adj.* If something is ***dubious***, it is questionable or not to be relied upon.

elaborate (ĭ-lăb′ər-ĭt) *adj.* Something that is ***elaborate*** has been carefully planned and constructed with great attention to detail.

embarrass (ĕm-băr′əs) *v.* To ***embarrass*** is to cause to feel uncomfortable or self-conscious.

enact (ĕn-ăkt′) *v.* If you ***enact*** something, you make it into a law.

encounter (ĕn-koun′tər) *n.* An ***encounter*** is a short meeting that is unplanned or unexpected.

entail (ĕn-tāl′) *v.* To ***entail*** means to have or require.

erupt (ĭ-rŭpt′) *v.* When something ***erupts***, it develops suddenly.

ethereal (ĭ-thîr′ē-əl) *adj.* If something is ***ethereal***, it is light and airy.

exhibition (ĕk′sə-bĭsh′ən) *n.* An ***exhibition*** is an organized presentation or show.

exploitation (ĕk′sploi-tā′shən) *n.* ***Exploitation*** is the unfair treatment or use of something or someone for selfish reasons.

fatal (fāt′l) *adj.* A ***fatal*** decision is a choice that results in death.

federal (fĕd′ər-əl) *adj.* Something that is ***federal*** relates to the U.S. government in Washington, D.C., and not to state and local governments.

forlorn (fər-lôrn′) *adj.* Something that is ***forlorn*** appears lonely or sad.

frantic (frăn′tĭk) *adj.* If you do something in a ***frantic*** way, you do it quickly and nervously.

fundamental (fŭn′də-mĕn′tl) *n.* A ***fundamental*** is a basic but essential part of an object or a system.

futile (fyo͞ot′l) *adj.* When something is ***futile***, it has no useful or meaningful result.

geothermal (jē′ō-thûr′məl) *adj.* ***Geothermal*** relates to the internal heat of the earth.

habitat (hăb′ĭ-tăt′) *n.* In this instance, a ***habitat*** is a structure that provides a controlled environment for living in very hostile or even deadly locations.

heirloom (âr′lo͞om′) *n.* An ***heirloom*** is a valued possession that was passed down in a family.

hideous (hĭd′ē-əs) *adj.* When something is ***hideous***, it is repulsive or revolting.

hoax (hōks) *n.* A ***hoax*** is something that is meant to trick or fool someone.

idle (id′l) *v.* When you ***idle***, you pass time without doing anything purposeful.

immerse (ĭ-mûrs′) *v.* If you ***immerse*** yourself in an activity, that activity is the only thing that you are focused on.

indifferent (ĭn-dĭf′ər-ənt) *adj.* Someone who is ***indifferent*** has no feelings one way or another about something.

Inferior (ĭn-fîr′ē-ər) *adj.* If something is ***inferior***, it is lower in value and quality.

infinitely (ĭn′fə-nĭt-lē) *adv.* ***Infinitely*** means to a great extent, or with no limits.

inquire (ĭn-kwīr′) *v.* If you ***inquire*** about something, you ask about it.

insulate (ĭn′sə-lāt′) *v.* When you ***insulate*** something, you prevent the passage of heat through it.

interaction (ĭn´tər-ăk´shən) *n.* An *interaction* occurs when people speak or otherwise are in contact with one another.

inundate (ĭn´ŭn-dāt´) *v.* To *inundate* is to overpower with a huge amount of something.

irrelevant (ĭ-rĕl´ə-vənt) *adj.* Something that is *irrelevant* is unrelated to the matter under consideration.

isolate (ī´sə-lāt´) *v.* When you *isolate* something, you separate it so that it is apart or alone.

latch (lăch) *v.* To *latch* means to hold onto or get hold of.

lobby (lŏb´ē) *v.* To *lobby* is to attempt to influence politicians to support the cause that you represent.

madame (mə-dăm´) *n.* *Madame* is a form of polite address for a woman.

mascot (măs´kŏt´) *n.* A *mascot* is a person, animal, or object used as the symbol of an organization, such as a sports team.

median (mē´dē-ən) *n.* A *median* is a dividing area between opposing lanes of traffic on a highway or road.

metabolism (mĭ-tăb´ə-lĭz´əm) *n.* A living thing's *metabolism* is the chemical processes that give it energy and produce growth.

mistrust (mĭs-trŭst´) *v.* To *mistrust* is to be without confidence or trust.

moderate (mŏd´ər-ĭt) *adj.* When something is kept *moderate*, it is kept within a certain limit.

moot (mo͞ot) *adj.* Something that is *moot* is unimportant or irrelevant.

muse (myo͞oz) *v.* When you *muse*, you say something thoughtfully.

mutual (myo͞o´cho͞o-əl) *adj.* Something is *mutual* when everyone treats each other the same way or shares the same feeling.

navigation (năv´ĭ-gā´shən) *n.* The *navigation* of a ship or boat is the act of guiding it along a planned course.

negotiate (nĭ-gō´shē-āt´) *v.* When you *negotiate*, you work with others to reach an agreement.

obituary (ō-bĭch´o͞o-ĕr´ē) *n.* An *obituary* is a public notice of a person's death.

obsess (əb-sĕs´) *v.* If you *obsess* over something, your mind is filled with thinking about a single topic, idea, or feeling.

pendulum (pĕn´jə-ləm) *n.* A *pendulum* is a weight that is hung so that it can swing freely. Sometimes it is used in timing the workings of certain clocks.

plague (plāg) *v.* To *plague* something is to cause hardship or suffering for it.

porthole (pôrt´hōl´) *n.* A *porthole* is a circular window on a boat or ship.

possession (pə-zĕsh´ən) *n.* A *possession* is something you own.

precaution (prĭ-kô´shən) *n.* A *precaution* is an action taken to avoid possible danger.

procession (prə-sĕsh´ən) *n.* In a *procession*, people or things move along in an orderly and serious way.

prominent (prŏm´ə-nənt) *adj.* If something is *prominent*, it stands out.

prowess (prou´ĭs) *n.* *Prowess* is the strength and courage someone has.

radiation (rā´dē-ā´shən) *n.* *Radiation* is energy transmitted in the form of waves or particles.

recede (rĭ-sēd´) *v.* To *recede* means to become fainter or more distant.

reformer (rĭ-fôrm´ər) *n.* A *reformer* seeks to improve or correct practices or behaviors that cause harm.

reliable (rĭ-lī´ə-bəl) *adj.* A person or object that can be trusted, or depended on, is *reliable*.

remorseful (rĭ-môrs´fəl) *adj.* If you are *remorseful*, you feel very sorry about something that you have done.

repulse (rĭ-pŭls´) *v.* Something that *repulses* you makes you want to reject it because you find it disgusting.

restrictive (rĭ-strĭk´tĭv) *adj.* When something is *restrictive*, it is limiting in some way.

ruse (ro͞oz) *n.* A *ruse* is a plan meant to deceive someone.

scarcity (skâr′sĭ-tē) *n.* When you experience a ***scarcity*** of something, you have a shortage or lack of that thing.

scurry (skûr′ē) *v.* To ***scurry*** means to hurry along with light footsteps.

sketchy (skĕch′ē) *adj.* If someone or something seems ***sketchy***, you doubt its authenticity or trustworthiness.

splinter (splĭn′tĕr) *v.* To ***splinter*** means to break up into sharp, thin pieces.

submerge (səb-mûrj′) *v.* To ***submerge*** is to descend beneath the surface of the water.

subtly (sŭt′lē) *adv.* To do something ***subtly*** means to do it in a manner hard to notice or perceive—that is, not obviously.

suede (swād) *n.* ***Suede*** is leather that is treated to be fuzzy and soft.

swell (swĕl) *n.* A ***swell*** is a long, unbroken wave.

syringe (sə-rĭnj′) *n.* A ***syringe*** is a medical instrument used to inject fluids into the body.

talon (tăl′ən) *n.* A ***talon*** is the claw of a bird of prey.

token (tō′kən) *n.* A ***token*** serves as an expression or a sign of something else.

turnover (tûrn′ō′vər) *n.* In basketball, a ***turnover*** is a loss of possession of the ball.

upright (ŭp′rīt′) *adv.* Someone or something that sits or stands ***upright*** is in a strictly vertical position.

utilization (yo͞ot′l-ĭ-zā′shən) *n.* ***Utilization*** is when you put something to use in an effective way.

wholly (hō′lē) *adv.* If a speech deals ***wholly*** with the history of the solar system, that is the only topic the speaker discusses.

INDEX OF SKILLS

D

E

INDEX OF TITLES AND AUTHORS

ACKNOWLEDGMENTS

"Allied with Green" from *There is No Long Distance Now: Very Short Stories* by Naomi Shihab Nye. Text copyright © 2011 by Naomi Shihab Nye. Reprinted by permission of HarperCollins Publishers.

Excerpts from *The American Heritage Dictionary of The English Language, Fifth Edition.* Text copyright © 2016 by Houghton Mifflin Harcourt Publishing Company. Reprinted by permission of Houghton Mifflin Harcourt Publishing Company.

"Ball Hawk" by Joseph Bruchac from *Baseball Crazy* by Nancy Mercado. Text copyright © 2008 by Joseph Bruchac. Reprinted by permission of Barbara Kouts, Literary Agent.

"The Camera Does Lie" by Meg Moss from *Muse,* July/August 2013. Text copyright © 2013 by Carus Publishing Company. Reproduced by permission of Carus Publishing Company. All Cricket Media material is copyrighted by Carus Publishing Company d/b/a Cricket Media, and/or various authors and illustrators. Any commercial use or distribution of material without permission is strictly prohibited. Please visit http://cricketmedia.com/licensing for licensing and http://www.cricketmedia.com for subscriptions.

"Chapter 2: The Summoned Self" from *The Road to Character* by David Brooks. Text copyright © 2015 by David Brooks. Reprinted by permission of Random House, an imprint and division of Penguin Random House LLC and Penguin Books Ltd. All rights reserved. Any third party use of this material, outside of this publication, is prohibited. Interested parties must apply directly to Penguin Random House LLC for permission.

"Craig Kielburger Reflects on Working Toward Peace" (retitled from "Reflections on Working Toward Peace") from *Architects of Peace* by Michael Collopy. Text copyright © 2000 by Michael Collopy. Used by permission of Michael Collopy.

Excerpt from *The Crossover* by Kwame Alexander. Text copyright © 2014 by Kwame Alexander. Reprinted by permission of Houghton Mifflin Harcourt.

"Dark They Were, and Golden-Eyed" by Ray Bradbury. Text copyright © 1949 by Standard Magazines, renewed © 1976 by Ray Bradbury. Reprinted by permission of Don Congdon Associates, Inc. Photocopying, printing and other reproduction rights are strictly prohibited.

"Double Doubles" from *Vherses: A Celebration of Outstanding Women* by J. Patrick Lewis. Text copyright © 2005 by J. Patrick Lewis. Reprinted by permission of the Creative Company.

"The Drought" by Amy Helfrich. Text copyright © by Amy Helfrich. Reprinted by permission of Amy Helfrich.

"Get in the Zone: The Psychology of Video Game Design" by Aaron Millar from *Muse,* May/June 2015. Text copyright © 2015 by Carus Publishing Company. Reprinted by permission of Carus Publishing Company. All Cricket Media material is copyrighted by Carus Publishing Company d/b/a Cricket Media, and/or various authors and illustrators. Any commercial use or distribution of material without permission is strictly prohibited. Please visit http://cricketmedia.com/licensing for licensing and http://www.cricketmedia.com for subscriptions.

"The Governess" from *The Good Doctor* by Neil Simon. Text copyright © 1974 by Neil Simon, renewed 2002. Reprinted by permission of Gary N. DaSilva. Professionals and amateurs are hereby warned that *The Good Doctor* is fully protected under the Berne Convention and the Universal Copyright Convention and is subject to royalty. All rights, including without limitation professional, amateur, motion picture, television, radio, recitation, lecturing, public reading and foreign translation rights, computer media rights and the right of reproduction, and electronic storage or retrieval, in whole or in part and in any form, are strictly reserved and none of these rights can be exercised or used without written permission from the copyright owner. Inquiries for stock and amateur performances should be addressed to Samuel French, Inc., 235 Park Avenue South, Fifth Floor, New York, NY 10003; email: info@samuelfrench.com. All other inquiries should be addressed to Gary N. DaSilva, 111 N. Sepulveda Blvd., Suite 250, Manhattan Beach, CA 90266-6850; mail@garydasilva.com

"Heartbeat" by David Yoo. Text copyright © 2005 by David Yoo. Reprinted by permission of Writers House, LLC, on behalf of David Yoo.

"Icarus's Flight" from Mystery, So Long by Stephen Dobyns. Originally published by Penguin. Text copyright © 2006 by Stephen Dobyns. Reprinted by permission of Harold Ober Associates Incorporated.

"It's Not Just a Game" by Lori Calabrese from *Odyssey,* July 2009. Text copyright © 2009 by Carus Publishing Company. Reprinted by permission of Carus Publishing Company. All Cricket Media material is copyrighted by Carus Publishing Company d/b/a Cricket Media, and/or various authors and illustrators. Any commercial use or distribution of material without permission is strictly prohibited. Please visit http://cricketmedia.com/licensing for licensing and http://www.cricketmedia.com for subscriptions.

"Martian Metropolis" by Meg Thatcher from *Muse,* July/August 2016. Text copyright © 2016 by Carus Publishing Company. Reprinted by permission of Carus Publishing Company. All Cricket Media material is copyrighted by Carus Publishing Company d/b/a Cricket Media, and/or various authors and illustrators. Any commercial use or distribution of material without permission is strictly prohibited. Please visit http://cricketmedia.com/licensing for licensing and http://www.cricketmedia.com for subscriptions.

Excerpt from *Mississippi Solo* by Eddy Harris. Text copyright © 1988 by Eddy L. Harris. Reprinted by permission of Lyons Press.

"Never Retreat" from *Eyes Wide Open* by Paul Fleischman. Text copyright © 2014 by the Brown-Fleischman Family Trust. Reprinted by permission of Candlewick Press.

"Ode to Enchanted Light" from *Odes to Opposites* compiled by Ferris Cook. Originally published in Spanish as "Oda a la luz encantada" from *Tercer Libro de las Odas* by Pablo Neruda, translated by Ken Krabbenhoft. Translation copyright © 1995 by Ken Krabbenhoft. Text copyright © 1995 by Pablo Neruda and Fundación Pablo Neruda. Text compilation copyright © 1995 by Ferris Cook. Reprinted by permission of Bullfinch/Hachette Book

Group USA and Agencia Literaria Carmen Balcells S.A. All rights reserved.

"Poem for My Librarian, Mrs. Long" from *Acolytes* by Nikki Giovanni. Text copyright © 2007 by Nikki Giovanni. Reprinted by permission of HarperCollins Publishers.

Quote by Ann Cotton from "Leading Questions" by Alison Benjamin from The Guardian, March 28, 2007. Text copyright © 2007 by Guardian News & Media Limited. Reprinted courtesy of Guardian News & Media Limited.

Quote by Amelia Earhart. Text copyright © by Amelia Earhart. Reprinted by permission of CMG Worldwide.

Quote by Phiona Mutesi from "Game of her life" by Tim Crothers, originally published in ESPN The Magazine, January 10, 2011. Text copyright © 2011 by ESPN, Inc. Reprinted by permission of ESPN. All rights reserved.

Excerpt from *Red-Tail Angels: The Story of the Tuskegee Airmen of World War II* by Patricia and Fredrick McKissack. Text copyright © 1995 by Patricia and Frederick McKissack. Reprinted by permission of Bloomsbury Publishing Inc.

"Rogue Wave" from *Rogue Wave and Other Red-Blooded Sea Stories* by Theodore Taylor. Text copyright © 1996 by Theodore Taylor. Reprinted by permission of the Theodore Taylor Estate and the Watkins/Loomis Agency.

"Sleeping in the Forest" from *Twelve Moons* by Mary Oliver. Text copyright © 1972, 1973, 1974, 1976, 1977, 1978, 1979 by Mary Oliver. Reprinted by permission of Charlotte Sheedy Literary Agency on behalf of the author and Little, Brown and Company. All rights reserved.

"Sometimes a Dream Needs a Push" from *Flying Lessons* by Walter Dean Myers. Text copyright © 2017 by Walter Dean Meyers. Reprinted by permission of DeFiore and Company. *Flying Lessons* published by Crown Books for Young Readers/Random House Children's Books in partnership with We Need Diverse Books. The story first appeared in *Boys' Life* © 2007.

"The Song of Wandering Aengus" from *The Wind in the Reeds* by William Butler Yeats. Text copyright © 1989 by Anne Yeats. Reprinted by permission of United Agents, LLP, a subsidiary of A.P. Watt, on behalf of Caitríona Yeats.

Excerpt from *Stories of the Gods and Heroes* by Sally Benson. Text copyright 1940 and renewed © 1968 by Sally Benson. Reprinted by permission of Dial Books for Young Readers, an imprint of Penguin Young Readers Group, a division of Penguin Random House LLC. All rights reserved. Any third-party use of this material, outside of this publication, is prohibited. Interested parties must apply directly to Penguin Random House LLC for permission.

Excerpt from *The Story of the Triangle Factory Fire* by Zachary Kent. Text copyright © 1989 by Children's Press, Inc. Reprinted by permission of Children's Press, an imprint of Scholastic Library Publishing, Inc. All rights reserved.

"Thank you M'am" from *Short Stories* by Langston Hughes. Text copyright © 1996 by Ramona Bass and Arnold Rampersad. CAUTION: Users are warned that this work is protected under copyright laws and downloading is strictly prohibited. The right to reproduce or transfer the work via any medium must be secured with Farrar, Straus and Giroux. Reprinted by permission of Hill and Wang, a division of Farrar, Straus & Giroux, Inc. and Harold Ober Associates, Inc.

"This Teenager Was Walking for Hours to and from Work - Until a Police Stop Changed His Life" by Amy B. Wang from *The Washington Post* September 30, 2016. Text copyright © 2016 The Washington Post. Reprinted by PARS International on behalf of the Washington Post. All rights reserved. Protected by the Copyright Laws of the United States. The printing, copying, redistribution, or retransmission of this Content without express written permission is prohibited. www.washingtonpost.com

"The 12 Greatest Challenges for Space Exploration" by Annie Leckie from *Wired* February 16, 2016. Text copyright © 2016 by Condé Nast. Reprinted by permission of Condé Nast.

"Two Legs of One?" from *Forty Folk Stories from Around the World* retold by Josepha Sherman. Text copyright © 1996 by Josepha Sherman. Reprinted by permission of Marian Reiner on behalf of the publisher August House, Inc.

"What If We Were Alone?" from *The Way It Is: New and Selected Poems* by William Stafford. Text copyright © 1987, 1998 by William Stafford and the Estate of William Stafford. Reprinted by permission of The Permissions Company, Inc. on behalf of Graywolf Press, Minneapolis, Minnesota, www.graywolfpress.org and Kim Stafford.